63 563

book is to be returned on or before
the stamped below.

BOURNEMOUTH COLLEGE
OF TECHNOLOGY

COLLEGE LIBRARY

D1423236

THOMAS CARLYLE: THE CRITICAL HERITAGE

THE CRITICAL HERITAGE SERIES

GENERAL EDITOR: B. C. SOUTHAM, M.A., B.LITT. (OXON.)
Formerly Department of English, Westfield College, University of London

---

For list of books in the series see back end paper

THOMAS CARLYLE

THE CRITICAL HERITAGE

Edited by
JULES PAUL SEIGEL

Department of English
University of Rhode Island

YEOVIL COLLEGE
LIBRARY

LONDON: ROUTLEDGE & KEGAN PAUL

First published 1971
by Routledge and Kegan Paul Limited
Broadway House
68–74 Carter Lane
London, EC4V 5EL

© Jules Paul Seigel 1971

No part of this book may be reproduced in
any form without permission from the
publisher, except for the quotation of
brief passages in criticism

ISBN 0 7100 7090 X

BOURNEMOUTH COLLEGE
OF TECHNOLOGY
COLLEGE LIBRARY

WITHDRAWN

563

824.8 Car   SE1

Printed in Great Britain by
W & J Mackay & Co Ltd, Chatham

General Editor's Preface

The reception given to a writer by his contemporaries and near-contemporaries is evidence of considerable value to the student of literature. On one side we learn a great deal about the state of criticism at large and in particular about the development of critical attitudes towards a single writer; at the same time, through private comments in letters, journals or marginalia, we gain an insight upon the tastes and literary thought of individual readers of the period. Evidence of this kind helps us to understand the writer's historical situation, the nature of his immediate reading-public, and his response to these pressures.

The separate volumes in the *Critical Heritage Series* present a record of this early criticism. Clearly, for many of the highly productive and lengthily reviewed nineteenth- and twentieth-century writers, there exists an enormous body of material; and in these cases the volume editors have made a selection of the most important views, significant for their intrinsic critical worth or for their representative quality—perhaps even registering incomprehension!

For earlier writers, notably pre-eighteenth century, the materials are much scarcer and the historical period has been extended, sometimes far beyond the writer's lifetime, in order to show the inception and growth of critical views which were initially slow to appear.

In each volume the documents are headed by an Introduction, discussing the material assembled and relating the early stages of the author's reception to what we have come to identify as the critical tradition. The volumes will make available much material which would otherwise be difficult of access and it is hoped that the modern reader will be thereby helped towards an informed understanding of the ways in which literature has been read and judged.

B.C.S.

To
Cathy
Julia Anne, Sean, and Jessica

Y0056248

Contents

CONTENTS

viii

Obituaries and *Reminiscences* (1881)

Preface

The essays collected here should not be taken as the best of the Victorian legacy. Rather they are meant to be representative of the varied reactions to Carlyle; for whether explicitly or not, it was the man, his whole literary stance, which was generally under review. The nineteenth-century man-of-letters as critic was not intimidated by a formalized methodology of criticism. Furthermore, the purposes of the Victorian review-essay were many: a reviewer under the guise of reviewing a book could lobby for political interests, or lecture on religious heresy, or better yet, he could create a work of art in itself (as Carlyle and Arnold and others often did). But Carlyle's writing almost always fomented political and religious controversy, and his essays invariably precipitated an outpouring of diverse and heated responses. Consequently I have tried to balance polemic with analysis, hostility with admiration. Although no collection of reviews can ever resurrect the forces which were at work during Carlyle's day, it can hope to throw light upon some of the dark areas of the Victorian period.

Acknowledgments

Of the many books on Carlyle, the most valuable for a study of this kind is the indispensable *A Bibliography of Thomas Carlyle's Writings and Ana* (1928) by Isaac W. Dyer, to which I am indebted. For attributions to anonymous and pseudonymous reviews I have turned to the extremely helpful *The Wellesley Index to Victorian Periodicals 1824–1900*, Vol. I (1966), and to its editor Walter E. Houghton. To both Walter and Esther Houghton I owe more than thanks for their friendship and encouragement over the past several years. A word of thanks to my friends and colleagues Professors Ernest Moncada, Stanley Cashdollar, and Richard Neuse, whose knowledge of the classics greatly aided me in preparing the text itself; and to Dave Taylor, Kathleen Schlenker, and Donna Barker of the University of Rhode Island Library for locating much of the material in this volume in other libraries throughout the country. I would also like to express my appreciation to the University of Rhode Island Research Committee for awarding me a most helpful grant-in-aid with which to pursue this study.

Chronological Table

1795   Carlyle born, Ecclefechan, Scotland

1823–4   *Schiller's Life and Writings. London Magazine* (October 1823; January, July–September 1824)

1825   *Life of Friedrich Schiller.* London (Enlarged and revised in book form)

1827   *Jean Paul Friedrich Richter. Edinburgh Review* (June)

1828   *Burns. Edinburgh Review* (December)

1829   *Signs of the Times. Edinburgh Review* (June)

        Voltaire. Foreign Review (April)

1831   *Cruthers and Jonson or the Outskirts of Life. A True Story. Fraser's Magazine* (January)

1832   *Boswell's Life of Johnson. Fraser's Magazine* (May)

        Goethe's Works. Foreign Quarterly Review (August)

1833   *Sartor Resartus. Fraser's Magazine* (November and December)

1834   *Sartor Resartus. Fraser's Magazine* (February–April, June–August)

        Fifty-eight copies printed from the magazine type

1835   *Death of the Rev. Edward Irving. Fraser's Magazine* (January)

1836   *Sartor Resartus.* Boston

1837   *French Revolution.* London

1838   *Sartor Resartus.* London

1839   *Critical and Miscellaneous Essays.* London

1840   *Chartism* (published December 1839). London

1841   *On Heroes, Hero-Worship and the Heroic in History.* London

1843   *Past and Present.* London

1845   *Oliver Cromwell's Letters and Speeches.* London

1848   *Louis Philippe, Repeal of the Union, Legislation for Ireland, Death of Charles Buller (London Examiner); Ireland and the British Chief Governor, Irish Regiments of the New Era (Spectator)*

1849   *Occasional Discourse on the Nigger Question. Fraser's Magazine* (December)

1850   *Latter-Day Pamphlets.* London

1851   *Life of John Sterling.* London

1858–65   *History of Frederick the Great.* 6 vols. London

Note on the Text

The materials contained in this volume follow the original texts. Long quotations from Carlyle have been deleted and replaced with references to the Centenary Edition (New York, 1896–9) of his works. Often book and chapter references as well as volume numbers appear so that a reader with any other text may locate the deleted passage.

Introduction

Few literary figures in the nineteenth century generated as much response in the public press as Thomas Carlyle. By the 1840s he commanded
attention from most of the literary journals of his day. The range of the
responses was great, from eulogy to denunciation. Even within the file
of one review alone, over a period of years, the attitudes often varied
drastically. So complicated and passionate were the reactions of Carlyle's
contemporaries towards him that any generalizations about his critical
reception must be qualified.

Carlyle's raids upon the Benthamites and the new economic and
political bureaucrats; his contempt for hidebound Toryism, rose-water
philanthropy, mammonism, and all forms of cant and sham; his irreverence toward the fruits, often bitter, of a mechanical and industrial
age, and his scorn for the dogmas of democracy brought him face to
face with his critics. A prophet in the true biblical sense, Carlyle spoke
out boldly, passionately through hyperbole, paradoxical truism, direct
exhortation, and any rhetorical device with which he could bludgeon
his readers into agreement and belief. As he saw it, Victorian England
was bent on self-destruction: the aristocracy was interested in protecting
its privileges; the new, wealthy middle class was busy enjoying its
rights; the Utilitarians were intent on building a philosophy on the
physiological-psychological doctrines of pleasure and pain; and Macaulay, spokesman for Whig liberalism, was insisting that an acre in
Middlesex was worth more than a principality in Utopia.

To this vision of his times, Carlyle reacted strongly; we may indeed
agree with George Meredith that he was a 'heaver of rocks and not a
shaper'. As he addressed himself to the cultural upheavals going on
about him, his reviewers in turn responded to his political, social, and
psycho-religious pronouncements, often matching his intensity but
rarely his art. The reverence of his admirers and disciples bordered on
hero-worship; his detractors were hostile, scolding and carping angrily.
The responses to Carlyle crystallized around his well-known and often
repeated ideas of hero-worship, his dynamic style, his religious posture,

and his impracticality (as Arthur Clough put it, he led the Victorians into the wilderness and left them there).

The distinct turning point in Carlyle's reception, from the time of his early contributions to the *London Magazine* and the *Foreign* and *Edinburgh Reviews* in the 1820s to his posthumous *Reminiscences* (1881), came at mid-century with the publication of the *Latter-Day Pamphlets*. The *Pamphlets*, written with unrelenting causticity, were a devastating attack not only upon red-tapism, modern bureaucracy, and so much more that Carlyle considered a sham, but also upon democracy, Parliament, and negroes. Here Carlyle's angle of vision has shifted drastically. He is no longer the prophet of hope as in *Sartor Resartus* (1838), or the sage with a vision of a better England as in *Past and Present* (1843). Instead he is the prophet of doom, contemptuous of the important political and social achievements of the nineteenth century. It must be stressed that, however shrill and strident these *Pamphlets* were, they did not reflect a departure from Carlyle's role as social critic. As early as *On Heroes* (1841) and four years later in *Oliver Cromwell's Letters and Speeches*, Carlyle's ideas regarding absolutism and his doctrines of hero-worship seemed to have been hardening. His style as well as his content began to change as the exploratory techniques of *Sartor Resartus* and *The French Revolution* gradually gave way to the intense and troubled rhetoric of the *Latter-Day Pamphlets*.

Despite these strong responses to Carlyle's most outspoken doctrines, he remained in the eyes of many as the most powerful influence of his day, particularly among the young. Francis Espinasse (using the pseudonym of Lucian Paul) writes in the *Critic* (14 June 1851):

Perhaps the best way to estimate the nature and extent of Carlyle's influence is to consider the strange variety of minds which have been irresistibly drawn into his immediate sphere, and sought his counsel or co-operation. Other thinkers have had their fixed circles of admirers or worshippers, but every circle has sent its quota to Carlyle's. Call over the roll of persons who have been in relations with him, and what contemporary can show the like. A 'world-poet' like Goethe; ecclesiastics like the Bishop of St. David's, Dr. Arnold, of Rugby, Dr. Chalmers, and Professor Maurice; statesmen like Sir Robert Peel and the late Charles Buller; agitations, the Anti-Corn-Law League and the Secular School Association; hard, practical men, like Edwin Chadwick, and Mr. Whitworth, the competitor for the honour of sweeping Manchester streets; revolutionists, Mazzini and Cavaignac; men of letters in every department, and of every conceivable shade of opinion—Southey, Lockhart, Jeffrey, John Sterling, John Stuart Mill, Ebenezer Elliott, Thomas Cooper, the Chartist, Samuel Rogers, Samuel Bamford, the American Emerson, Miss Martineau, Leigh Hunt, Monckton Milnes, and all the young men of talent of the day. And, practically, no useful scheme or measure has been carried out of late years, from the founding of the London Library to the repeal of the Corn-Laws, which does not owe something to him (277–278).

Such a statement may seem to pitch Carlyle too high (to that list, however, a host of others—Dickens, Meredith, Morris, Ruskin, Lawrence, and more—could readily be added), but even George Eliot (No. 35), indeed a more reliable source than Espinasse, can remark in 1855 that

there is hardly a superior or active mind of this generation that has not been modified by Carlyle's writings; there has hardly been an English book written for the last ten or twelve years that would not have been different if Carlyle had not lived. The character of his influence is best seen in the fact that many of the men who have the least agreement with his opinions are those to whom the reading of *Sartor Resartus* was an epoch in the history of their minds. The extent of his influence may be seen in the fact that ideas which were startling novelties when he first wrote them are now become common-places.

His influence, whether for good or ill, was always spoken of in superlatives: 'We know of many greater writers, in every sense, than Mr. Carlyle is; but, perhaps, there is no living English author—if he can properly be called so—who has a stronger and deeper hold on the minds of the English community.'[1]

2

EARLY PUBLICATION

Carlyle's early years as a writer were ones of poverty and struggle lasting until the success of *The French Revolution* (1837) when he was a man of forty-two years. At twenty-four he was still uncertain of a profession. He had rejected the thought of entering the ministry, had grown tired of teaching, and had moved to Edinburgh, where he studied law, science, German literature, and earned a meagre living turning out biographical and historical articles for David Brewster's *Edinburgh Encyclopaedia*. In 1822 the situation eased somewhat when he accepted a position to tutor Judge Charles Buller's two sons for two hundred pounds a year, a handsome sum to the impoverished Carlyle; and, of more importance, the position gave him time to write. Carlyle had met Jane Baillie Welsh in 1821, and had begun his long epistolary courtship, a courtship frustrated as much by Carlyle's social status as by his lack of money.

3

His first literary success, opening the door to a career as a professional writer, came in 1823 and 1824, when he published a series of articles on the life and writings of Schiller in the *London Magazine*, but it was not until the publication of his article on Jean Paul Richter (1827) in the influential *Edinburgh Review* that he became recognized as a member of the community of literary journalists. This success led immediately to other articles, three of which appeared in the *Foreign Review* (1828): 'Goethe', 'Goethe's Helena', and 'The Life and Writings of Werner', for which he received £135. The essays, 'Novalis', 'Burns', 'Life of Heyne', 'German Playwrights', 'Voltaire', 'Signs of the Times', 'Characteristics', and others followed, all written at Craigenputtock, the remote family farm of Jane Welsh.

By 1831 Carlyle had completed *Sartor Resartus*, and with £60 he had borrowed from his friend, Francis Jeffrey (who was editor of the *Edinburgh Review* until 1829), he set out alone for London to find a publisher for what was to be his most famous work. After several discouraging refusals, he sold the work to James Fraser for about £83. *Sartor Resartus* appeared serially in *Fraser's Magazine* from 1833 to 1834, and Fraser complained that the work was meeting with disapproval from many quarters. In the meantime, Emerson was planning an American edition of *Sartor Resartus*, for which he provided an anonymous Preface. Although Emerson had obtained 150 subscriptions before publication, the American edition, unfortunately, yielded Carlyle no profits.

But Carlyle had not been idle. He had meanwhile completed *The French Revolution*, and Fraser published it in three volumes, selling for £1 11s. 6d. Sales began slowly but accelerated. It was Emerson again who watched over the two-volume American edition (selling for $2.50) of 1,000 copies which sold out in thirteen months. For his labours, Carlyle received 74 cents from each copy sold, 50 cents going to the bookseller as commission. A second English edition was not needed for two years; nevertheless, by then, Fraser, pleased with the sales of *The French Revolution*, offered to bring out *Sartor Resartus* in book form, as well as a collection of Carlyle's early essays. But he procrastinated, and in the meantime, Emerson brought out a four-volume edition (1838-9) of Carlyle's miscellaneous essays in Boston. Thus for a second time an American publisher brought out a Carlyle edition first, a testimony both to Carlyle's friendship with Emerson and to the American reading public. By 1840 piracy had become a serious threat to Carlyle and Emerson's business operation and necessitated their developing means to circumvent losses from cheap reprint houses in New York and Philadelphia and from hawkers who were selling pirated English books in the streets for pennies.

After the moderate financial success of *The French Revolution*, it was no longer necessary for Carlyle to eke out a living by contributing regularly to the periodicals, though many of his later important essays— 'Irish Essays' (1848), 'Occasional Discourse on the Nigger Question' (1849) and 'Shooting Niagara: and After?' (1867) to mention a few— did appear first in periodicals.

Now that the tide had turned, Carlyle's works became the object of periodical reviews. James Anthony Froude's assertion that Carlyle paid little attention to the reviewers needs to be qualified: at least through the mid-1840s, Carlyle was vitally interested in the responses to his works (see *Notes* 10, 11, 16). In a conversation (1849) reported by Sir Gavan Duffy, Carlyle attacked contemporary criticism as the 'idlest babble', but indicated that 'Thackeray, John Sterling and John Mill have written of my work in various quarters with appreciation and more than sufficient applause'.[2] But as Carlyle became more eccentric and less flexible, he paid less attention to criticism. He read what his critics wrote, but he was never an inveterate collector of reviews. He certainly was not moved by criticism as were many of his contemporaries. Tennyson's 'silence', for example, followed adverse criticism in 1832 and 1833 and Rossetti suffered from paranoia after attacks by Robert Buchanan. The public outcries over the *Latter-Day Pamphlets* (1850) worried Carlyle but did little to change his mind, at least consciously, as we see in this letter to his brother John (29 April 1850): 'The barking babble of the world continues in regard to these Pamphlets, hardly any wise word at all reaching me in reference to them; but I must say out my say in one shape or another, and will, if Heaven help me, not minding that at all.'[3] Furthermore Froude assures us that the outcry had no adverse effect on the sale of his works, since Carlyle's followers, about three thousand loyal readers, bought all of his works. Carlyle corroborates this in a letter to his mother (29 March 1850): 'The noise about these Pamphlets is very great, and not very *musical*,—but indeed I take care not to hear it, so don't care. Chapman [his publisher] is about printing the fourth thousand of No. One, which he thinks naturally is good work. What he means to give *me*, I do not yet ascertain; but have decided that he shall let me know accurately in black on white within a week,—while I have the hank in my own hand!'[4]

It is indeed ironic that the same *Latter-Day Pamphlets* which brought down upon Carlyle the most hostile criticisms of his career also brought him the assurance that he had finally escaped from the poverty of his early years:

I am not so heavy-laden today . . . as I have been for many a day. I have money enough (no beggarly terrors about finance now at all). I have still some strength, the chance of some years of time. If I be true to myself, how can the whole posterity of Adam, and its united follies and miseries, quite make ship-wreck of me?[5]

REVIEWING IN THE PERIODICAL PRESS

Matthew Arnold's complaint in 'The Function of Criticism at the Present Time' (*National Review*, 1864) that periodical reviews pandered to political and religious biases, that they had no free play of mind, is clearly reflected in their attitudes toward Carlyle. It is not surprising that some writers, while reviewing Carlyle, polemicized unashamedly for their party or Church. Even though the reviewers lobbied for certain political, social, or religious interests—'sects' and 'parties' as Arnold irreverently called them—there were still many perceptive and unbiased reviews of Carlyle; those, for example, by James Martineau (No. 36), John Sterling (No. 10), Richard H. Hutton (No. 43), and others fulfil Arnold's wish that criticism show 'disinterestedness'.

The reaction of the political heavies—such as the *Edinburgh Quarterly*, the *Westminster Review*, *Blackwood's*, and the *Quarterly Review*—were inconsistent, though it may be said that Carlyle was treated more favourably by the Tory *Quarterly* than by the Whig *Edinburgh*, which did not devote a full review to him until Herman Merivale belatedly reviewed *The French Revolution* in 1840 (No. 8). The philosophical radicals of the *Westminster* reacted positively, understandably so, since several of the complimentary early reviews were by close friends: John Stuart Mill puffed *The French Revolution* of 1837 (No. 6) and John Sterling, in a sixty-eight-page review, examined his works in 1839 (No. 10). Although these reviews were by friends, they demonstrate more critical and philosophical perception than the reviews by zealous church-men or politicking men of letters.

In a period marked by spiritual crises and the loss of religious faith by many Victorians, Carlyle's religious convictions and ethical pro-nouncements were taken very seriously. Some reviewers in the religious Press used his doctrines to strengthen their own creeds; others de-nounced him in the name of their own personal dogma. Because of

Carlyle's unorthodox religious stance, his belief in a transcendent reality, his reliance upon intuition instead of reason, and particularly his concept of the hero, the orthodox reviewers took it upon themselves to expose his infidelity.

His championing of strong heroes was condemned by many churchmen who felt that England needed gentle heroes, men of the Christian spirit, and not Mahomets, Cromwells, Napoleons, Luthers, Fredericks —figures Carlyle had set before the public as heroes. In a hostile review of *Oliver Cromwell's Letters and Speeches* in the Catholic *Dublin Review* (September 1846, xxi, 68–9), George Crolly, priest and professor at St. Patrick's College, Maynooth (he titles his review, 'The Great Irish Insurrection'), finds similarities among the characteristics of the Puritans and Carlyle's heroes who are 'bigoted, intolerant, and quote the Old Testament instead of the Gospel'. In fact, Carlyle's heroes are still found 'among evangelical swaddlers, methodists, and covenanters and Mr. Carlyle need not fear that the species shall become extinct so long as hatred of truth, hypocrisy, and avarice reign in the heart of man'.

Reverend George Gilfillan, a Scottish dissenter, in an account of Carlyle's *Life of John Sterling* (*Eclectic Review*, December 1851, civ, 719), voices his strong disapproval that Carlyle has broken with all established religious traditions. 'He sneers at Coleridge's theosophic moonshine— at Sterling's belief in a "personal God"' and the 'unmitigated contempt he pours out on the clergy, and on the Church, and by inference and insinuation, upon the "traditions" and the "incredibilities" of Christianity—all point to the foregone conclusion which he has, we fear, long ago reached'.

Carlyle's religious verdicts often polarized his reviewers. Some were willing to accept him as a prophet of a new organic philosophy, shaping and giving direction to religious thought (No. 17 and No. 36), while others regarded him as a heretic, a dangerous moral influence, particularly on the young. One writer[6] in a lead article in the Congregationalist *British Quarterly Review* (August 1849, x, 34) cautioned his readers that Carlyle was 'by no means a safe author to put into the hands of young men who do not bring some power of independent thinking to what they read'. A reviewer in the High Church *Christian Remembrancer* (March 1842, n.s., vii, 349–50) alerts his readers to the possible dangers of Carlyle's judgments:

What his formal religious opinions are we know not; and must beg, in at present characterising much of his writing as infidel, not for a moment to be understood as calling the author an infidel. It is quite possible for a man who considers himself a believer, to cherish, unknown to himself, an unbelieving temper; and all the more is this the case with one who writes and thinks like Mr. Carlyle in a mystical and reverential tone. This latter circumstance makes it imperatively our duty to put his readers on their guard. He says many things so eloquently religious, that they may fancy all is safe, or at least they may not be alive to the extent of their danger.

3

EARLY ESSAYS

In 1834 when Carlyle settled in London at 5 Cheyne Row, his early essays and reviews contributed to *Fraser's Magazine* and to the *Edinburgh and Foreign Reviews* were already known to many readers in England. In America, as well, he had acquired a reading public even before the publication of *Sartor Resartus* (1836).[7] His many essays—published anonymously[8] in the British periodicals—on Richter, Novalis, Goethe, Voltaire, 'Signs of the Times', and others—were eagerly read by the New England literati; particularly attractive to the emerging transcendentalists in rebellion against Calvinistic Congregationalism were his essays on German literature. In 1838 James Freeman Clarke (*The Western Messenger* [February 1838], v, 418), a chief spokesman for the transcendentalists, speaks of Carlyle's American influence as having long since been achieved:

For ourselves, we hardly know how to describe the feelings with which we first perused his articles in some old numbers of the *Foreign Review* which we happened upon, one day, in the *Boston Athenaeum*. There was a freshness and unworn life in all he said, new and profound views of familiar truths, which seemed to open a vista for endless reflection. It was as if we saw the angels ascending and descending in Jacob's dream. It was, as it sometimes happens when we are introduced to a person with whom we have strong affinities—in ten minutes we are wholly intimate—we seem to have known him all our life. . . .

When he began to write, eight or ten years ago, what did we know of German writers? Wieland's *Oberon*, Klopstock's *Messiah*, Kotzebue's plays, Schiller's *Robbers*, Goethe's *Werther*. . . . But of all this we knew little. Much praise then, to Mr. Carlyle, for having introduced us to this fair circle of gifted minds.

All readers, however, were not equally enamoured of Carlyle's talents. In 1831, Timothy Walker, a Harvard graduate and Cincinnati

8

lawyer, attacked Carlyle's 'Signs of the Times' in the leading American journal, the *North American Review* (July, xxxiii, 130). In denouncing Carlyle's speculative transcendentalism and defending Locke's psychology against Carlyle's charges that it was mechanistic ('Give us Locke's Mechanism, and we will envy no man's Mysticism'), Walker was striking a blow against the pernicious influence of transcendentalism.

In 1833 Carlyle's *Life of Schiller* was brought out by Park Benjamin, a Boston man of letters, and in the next year it was noted briefly in the *New England Magazine* (February, vi) and reviewed favourably in both the *North American Review* (July, xxxix) and the *Christian Examiner* (July, xvi); in the latter by Frederick Henry Hedge, whose early articles helped bring the transcendental movement into existence. Despite the notices of his early essays, Carlyle's broad recognition as a literary figure in America dates from the publication of *Sartor Resartus*.[9]

'Sartor Resartus' and 'The French Revolution'
One of the first reviews (1834) of *Sartor Resartus*, Carlyle's richest and most complex work, was Alexander Everett's clumsy treatment (No. 2) in the *North American Review*. This review was later held up for ridicule as it was reprinted under the heading of 'Testimonies of Authors' and appended to subsequent editions of *Sartor*. Emerson's brother, Charles, remarked that to read 'Carlyle in the N.A. Review is like seeing your brother in jail; & that A. Everett is the sheriff that put him in'.[10] Two years later, after *Sartor* was published in book form in Boston, it was reviewed by N. L. Frothingham in the *Christian Examiner* (No. 3). Frothingham, a staunch Unitarian rationalist and no great friend of the transcendentalists, perceptively prophesied that *Sartor Resartus* would provoke two distinct reactions: on the one hand, there will be those who will defame the mystic book, pronounce it unintelligible, affected, and offering nothing by way of philosophy; on the other, there will be those who will admire its wild extravagancies, find hidden wisdom and systems of philosophy in it. Frothingham's analysis prefigures the polarized nature Carlylian criticism would eventually take.

In England, we should recall, *Sartor* appeared serially (*Fraser's Magazine*, 1833–4) and was not brought out in book form until 1838. In 1835, several months after he met Carlyle, the young John Sterling wrote to him on the subject of *Sartor Resartus* (No. 1). His frank and incisive reactions are some of the earliest and most substantive criticisms of *Sartor Resartus*. Sterling went to the heart of the work, raising critical questions which would be focused on by other reviewers later in the century. While recognizing Carlyle's similarities to Rabelais, Montaigne, Sterne, and Swift, Sterling is, nevertheless, opposed to this strange new style ('A good deal of this is positively barbarous'), the jerking, spasmodic, often violent syntax and the use of inversion. Although he found the style capable of force and emphasis, he labelled it faulty and fatiguing. Moreover, Sterling was bothered because Teufelsdröckh did not believe in a 'Living *Personal* God, essentially good, wise, true, and holy, the Author of all that exists; and a reunion with whom is the only end of all rational beings'. The rest of the discussion of a 'personal God' is edited out of Sterling's letter by Carlyle. Sterling's point is worth noting since Carlyle's rejection of a personal God, a Christ, as ultimate Saviour was finally to turn many of Carlyle's most ardent Christian admirers against him. His refusal to accept a spiritual Christ led indirectly to his worship of flesh and blood heroes, culminating in a reliance on force as a remedy for social injustices. F. D. Maurice writing about *On Heroes* (No. 14) shares Sterling's concern.

Carlyle admired Sterling's views but replied 'expressing the solemnest *denial*', and assured Sterling he was

neither Pagan nor Turk, nor circumcised Jew, but an unfortunate Christian individual resident at Chelsea in *this* year of Grace; neither Pantheist nor Pottheist, nor any Theist or *ist* whatsoever, having the most decided contempt for all manner of Systembuilders and Sect founders—so far as contempt may be compatible with so mild a nature; feeling well beforehand (taught by experience) that all such are and even must be *wrong*. By God's blessing, one has got two eyes to look with; and also a mind capable of knowing, of believing: that is all the creed I will at this time insist on. And now may I beg one thing: that whenever in my thoughts or your own you fall on any dogma that tends to estrange you from me, pray believe *that* to be *false*;—false as Beelzebub till you get clearer evidence.[11]

It was not, however, Sterling's 'letter' nor the talk about *Sartor* among London intellectuals, but the reviews of *The French Revolution* (1837) that caused Jane, Carlyle's wife, to remark that Carlyle was now famous. The first work to carry his name on the title page, *The French Revolution* brought him the fame he enjoyed for the next forty years.

In writing this history, Carlyle departed radically from the classical histories of the eighteenth century and played out his role of Prophet, warning the new wealthy classes and the English aristocracy that theirs, too, could be the fate of the Girondists and the French aristocracy. Carlyle's was a history of men and heroes, dramatic in movement. His style was unique: the explosive rhetoric, the use of the persona ('the dramatization of discussions' as John Holloway[12] has aptly put it), the rich metaphoric and expressive style replacing the traditional narrative; the humour, the imperative voice, the irony—all this caught the Victorian reviewer off guard.

The history prompted inept and facile remarks, such as those by Lady Morgan in the middle-brow *Athenaeum* (No. 5), who dismissed a new history of the French revolution as superfluous ('What need have we of a new History of the French Revolution? We have the contemporary history of that gigantic event in superabundance; and the time is not yet arrived for christening ourselves Posterity'), and who censured the style as crude, extravagant—neologisms, coxcombry carried through three long volumes. Similar attacks upon Carlyle's style were to continue throughout the century, particularly by those who upheld the neo-classical principles of decorum.[13]

A corrective to Lady Morgan's dismissal was Thackeray's favourable notice in the London *Times* (No. 7). Despite some reservations about Carlyle's departures from simple Addisonian English (but one 'speedily learns to admire and sympathize with it'), Thackeray immediately recognized the intrinsic social and political meaning: 'We need scarcely recommend this book and its timely appearance, now that some of the questions solved in it seem almost likely to be battled over again.' Alick and James, Carlyle's brothers, were with him when he received this review and they made him sit down in the shade of some beech trees and 'read it over to them'.[14] It was not long before Carlyle was noticed by all the major journals.

John Stuart Mill's account (No. 6) remains the classic review of *The French Revolution*, its opening sentence memorable: 'This is not so much a history as an epic poem.' Mill—who had gathered many of the reference books for Carlyle, and who was his companion on Sunday walks during its composition—praises his originality, sincerity, creativeness, and his ability to make the abstract facts of the past become realities of the present, alongside his painstaking and accurate investigation of the historical facts.

A later review (1840) of *The French Revolution* by Herman Merivale (No. 8), written from a Whig economic and political bias, provoked Carlyle to several angry letters. It was more than Merivale's sanctioning of *laissez-faire* that troubled Carlyle; it was his assertion that the

every day utility of free institutions is, not that they guarantee the toiler against hunger—would that it were otherwise!—but that they create a vast and powerful class interested in the maintenance of order; and infuse into that class a spirit and intelligence which render it adequate to the task. They cannot ensure the labourer against want; but they give scope to his energy, if he has any; they cannot heal the evils of competition, but they secure to the competitors fair play.

After reading the review, Carlyle wrote to John Sterling (19 September 1840):

My Reviewer of whom you spoke, is not Macaulay, as was at first told me, but one Merivale whom I think you know about. He is a slightly impertinent man, with good Furnival's Inn Faculty, with several Dictionaries and other succedanea about him,—small *knowledge* of God's Universe as yet, and small hope of getting much. Those things struck me somewhat: first, the man's notion of Dumouriez's Campaign,—*platitude absolute*: second, the idea that Robespierre had a *religion* in that Etre Supreme of his,—O Heaven, what then is Cant?—third, that the end of liberal government was not to remedy 'Hunger' but to keep down the complaint of it; pigs *must* die, but their squealing shall be suppressed! *Aus dem wird nichts* [Out of him comes nothing]. There is no *heart* of understanding in an intellect that can believe such things; a heart paralytic, dead as a pound of logwood! I was heartily glad to hear this heart was *not* Macaulay's; of whom I have still considerable hopes.[15]

Merivale's review surely annoyed Carlyle a good deal since he repeated his charges about pigs dying without squealing in two other letters, to his brother John (24 July 1840) and to his brother Alick (20 [23] July 1840).[16]

WORKS

The growing attention that Carlyle was beginning to command is evident from the early reviews of his 'works', although they were not *actually* collected until 1857. However, Carlyle was to be reckoned with, and the leading periodicals took it upon themselves to assess this new and dynamic writer for their readers. A case in point is T. Chisholm Anstey's review of Carlyle's 'Works' in the *Dublin Review*, 1838 (No. 9), which is actually a criticism of *The French Revolution*, *Sartor Resartus*, and the *Lectures on the History of Literature* which Anstey heard Carlyle deliver in the spring of 1838. This account in the *Dublin* (the Catholic answer to the rival *Edinburgh* and *Quarterly Reviews*) is particularly significant in that it appeared two years before either the *Edinburgh* or *Quarterly* devoted a full review to Carlyle. Anstey's enthusiasm and admiration are indicative of Carlyle's widespread appeal among the young in the late 1830s and 1840s.[17] Very decidedly influenced by

Carlyle, yet fresh from his own conversion to Roman Catholicism, Anstey is able to find much of his own creed in Carlyle's works, but he rejects those Carlylian dogmas which do not square with his Roman Catholicism. He objects to Carlyle's strictures that Catholicism is a dead formula:

His earnestness of belief, his sincerity of heart, are beautiful and soul possessing. His learning is immense, his industry untiring; his shrewdness, his power of detecting the truth amid masses of error quite extraordinary. Yet he imagines the Church a dead thing, in so far as its influence now-a-days is concerned! How is this?

Anstey's purpose, however, is to urge Catholics to read Carlyle, a true religious spirit—wayward perhaps—but honest, a deep-sighted and independent man, one who deals with the heart as well as the head.

A fifty-seven-page account of Carlyle's 'Works' by Reverend William Sewell (No. 11) in the *Quarterly* may well be taken as representative of how conservative churchmen and Tories reacted to Carlyle in 1840. On several points Sewell is in agreement with Carlyle: his conviction that the times are fast approaching spiritual disaster, that faith is necessary for all men, and that the universe represents the mysteries of God. But Sewell challenges the core of Carlyle's philosophy, namely his belief in the primacy of individual intuition over reason and the institutionalized Church. Sewell reluctantly concedes that German philosophy (brought to England by Coleridge and Carlyle) has been effective in awakening the country to the dangers of the eighteenth-century philosophies of mechanism and sensationism, but Sewell insists that faith can be restored only through the Church. Individual and national salvation is dependent upon the continuity of divine revelation preserved from the weakness of human corruption, in the sanctity of the Church. 'Even when the heart and head go wrong, the Church is still commanded to proclaim her creed, to celebrate her worship, to warn, exhort, and to teach, at least by words and actions; and these words and actions are true in the highest sense of truth. They correspond with the only reality, and only foundation for a true belief in the nature of God.' Furthermore, in criticizing Carlyle's Germanisms, Sewell associates the purity of an English style with national virtue and morality, and German with dangerous and speculative theories of religion and theology: 'Learn to talk in German, and as Germans talk, and you will soon learn to think in German, and thinking in German, you will cease to think as an Englishman.' Five years later in the *Dublin Review* (see

p. 227), Sir Peter LePage Renouf, pointing to Sewell's remarks, indicates the foolishness of such insular nationalism.

Carlyle read Sewell's review and in a letter to Thomas Ballantyne (8 October 1843) 'wondered, as he [Sewell] reciprocally does, to find how lovingly in many directions he and I went along together, always till we arrived at the conclusion, and how *there* we whirled around to the right and to the left about, and walked off like incompatibles, mutually destructives, like fire walking off from water'.[18] Sewell was by no means enamoured of Carlyle and was reported by F. D. Maurice to have been denouncing him at Oxford in his lectures. In hesitating to do an article on Carlyle (No. 14), Maurice wrote (5 April 1840) to Edward Strachey:

As to Carlyle, I do not know—I will think it over again; but I fear I must not go out of my way to pay him compliments. There is no need of it, for his fame is most rampant, and men are beginning to talk and cant after him in all directions. Sewell, I hear, denounces him in his lectures, and Whewell is very indignant, and believes he is doing greatest mischief. Hare has much the same opinion. So that I shall grieve friends, and perhaps only encourage what has need to be repressed, except by sympathy and by the fullest acknowledgement of Carlyle's great merits. Therefore I object to Sewell, Whewell, and Hare. But I believe there is no need to bring him into notice; that he attracts as much as is good for him or the world; and that the best for both is, when he comes naturally in one's way, to say kindly and honestly what one thinks of him.[19]

'On Heroes', 'Hero-Worship'
On Heroes was originally a series of lectures given by Carlyle in May 1840. The concept of the hero had been advanced earlier by Carlyle in *Sartor Resartus, The French Revolution,* and in his early lectures and periodical essays.

His idea of the hero was a combination of the *Vates*, the prophet who sees into the Divine Idea of the World, and of Fichte's idea that the true poet is a priest teaching men that this world is only a garment covering the Divine Idea. Hero-worship, as Walter Houghton has pointed out, cuts directly through Victorian culture; during a period of radical change, the demand for moral inspiration, for political and social leadership increases.[20] The publication of Carlyle's lectures brought before a wide reading audience a work which carried one of Carlyle's central dogmas on its title page, a doctrine with great appeal to Victorian readers; and because his heroes ranged so widely across history, from Odin to Napoleon, from Dante to Luther, almost any reviewer could find something to praise or to blame. Indeed, modern interpretations of Carlyle's heroes follow a similar pattern.

Three articles in the *Christian Remembrancer*, an organ of the Established Church, represent something of the critical range regarding *On Heroes*. The reviewer (March 1842, n.s., iii) recognizes that hero-worship is a principle congenial to the temper of his age, that it is a generous and purifying feeling to admire such men as Dante, Shakespeare, Bacon, Newton, and Burke. But he insists that one must experience this feeling with 'continual self-mistrust', always aware that the 'greatness' being admired and worshipped is God's work. Carlyle unfortunately imposes no such limitations. His only fear is 'lest great men be not exalted enough. Idolatry would seem in his eyes to be no sin' (348–9).

Although the reviewer acknowledges that there is much that is true and divine in paganism and Mohammedanism, he contends that Carlyle's 'notions of Odin and Scandinavian mythology are . . . vitiated by a fallacy that runs throughout—we mean the assumption that man has to start from imperfect and false religions, and gradually to rise to nobler and true ones. But holy Scripture tells us of an original revelation made to the sons of men, and, consequently, views idolatry as apostasy, and condemns it "without excuse"' (350).

The fear that Carlyle is guilty of idolatry and of advocating dangerous religious doctrines is seen more clearly in the same journal a year later when William Thomson, later the Archbishop of York, ruthlessly attacks a second edition of *On Heroes* (No. 13).[21] Thomson acknowledges that the aim of his paper is to show that the 'whole philosophy of this writer is defective and unsatisfactory', and he concludes that the principle common to all of Carlyle's heroes is 'radical pugnacity' and that 'true heroism, it seems, is a nearer relation to chartism, and corn-law leaguerism, than most persons suspect'.

Carlyle's heroes are summarily dismissed by Thomson: Mahomet, an impostor, was perhaps guided more by 'dyspeptic visions' than by communings with the 'real and credible'; Luther, when in the tower, was beset by 'apparitions and devilries', rather than strengthened by firm faith; Burns, a writer of 'blasphemous and impure verses', a man of the 'lowest animal appetites', was never humble enough to apologize and was addicted to whisky as well as to fathering a 'quarter dozen illegitimate children'. In short, concludes Thomson: '*It is not a Christian Book.*'

This parochial account prompted a sharp answer from F. D. Maurice (No. 14) who defended some of Carlyle's heroic principles, namely that his heroes believed in a spiritual reality and refused to accept semblances in place of it.[22] Maurice, in advocating the integrity of the individual conscience, was presenting a view more compatible with the twentieth-century Church than the nineteenth. In his support of Carlyle, Maurice was certainly not courting any favours from him (he thought that Carlyle would not thank him for his advocacy).[23] He was however deeply concerned with the inflexibility of the Church and with its inability to recognize its own complacency and dogmatism. Maurice maintains that he is grateful to such an author who is able to shock men out of 'stupefaction of customary convictions' and to show them they 'must learn to mean what they say and, must strive to act as they mean'.

'Past and Present'

Past and Present (1843) was part of Carlyle's answer to the 'Condition of England Question' and despite its satirical thrusts at almost every level of English society, from its new breed of capitalists to its do-nothing aristocracy, its Plugsons of Undershot and Jabesh Windbags, it nevertheless maintains a sanity of artistic balance. It is in many ways Carlyle's most representative work. Writing to Emerson (29 August 1842), Carlyle complained of the increasing difficulties he was experiencing trying to finish a work he had begun sometime earlier on Cromwell.[24] He was, moreover, deeply distressed over the poverty he had recently seen in Scotland and with the social unrest among the workers in Manchester. Also, while doing research on Cromwell, he had visited the poorhouse at St Ives where he saw strong and able paupers willing to work but unable to find employment. It was his deep concern over these conditions, coupled with his reading of the *Chronicle of Jocelin of Brakelond*—a narrative depicting life in the twelfth-century Abbey of St Edmunds under Abbot Samson—that led him to put aside his work on Cromwell and turn to *Past and Present*. It was finished in March and published in April.

The book, a series of dramatic and ironic contrasts, illuminates the social and political ills of the 1840s as they appear in the light of the feudal society of the middle ages. *Past and Present* sold fast and 'created at once admiration and a storm of anger',[25] and was noticed in over a dozen periodicals. *Tait's Edinburgh Magazine* (June 1843, x) and Leigh Hunt's *Examiner* (29 April 1843) reviewed the work positively, the latter pronouncing it 'wilder, more lawless, more outrageous than ever' but enriched with passages of 'rugged energy, strong original feeling, exquisite gentleness, surpassing beauty and tenderness'; the reviewer wishes Carlyle success and joins him in a 'hearty prayer for the speedy substitution of a *Past* Abbot Samson Government in place of our *Present* Government of Quack' (260). *Tait's* praises its evangelical tone, and sees it as a sermon on the text that money is the root of all evil and that work is often the best kind of prayer. The reviewer finally pronounces it a 'very good book'.

Once more Lady Morgan took up her pen to review Carlyle, making known her impatience with his inability to set forth practical measures for reform, calling the book a failure (*Athenaeum*, 13 May 1843). She confirmed her opinion in a second notice of the work the following week, insisting, moreover, that Carlyle's comparison of the past with the present was puerile ('Any school-boy would muster fact enough to show the infinite superiority of modern times in every particular, both moral and physical' (453–4)).

In *Blackwood's Magazine*, William H. Smith (No. 15) echoes Lady Morgan's charges that Carlyle does not give practical solutions to practical problems, but praises the strong moral tone in which he feels Carlyle examines his generation. A believer in progress, Smith's sharpest criticism relates to Carlyle's unhealthy estimate of the present time, pronouncing the parallel which Carlyle draws between the past and present as whimsically false. And *The Times* (6 October 1843), too, chides Carlyle for being impractical, contending that politics are practical, and philosophy is 'but a lamp, which, however useful, and necessary itself, will never supply a man with either hands or materials to work with'. Recognizing Carlyle as a genius but not 'creative', the reviewer virtually dismisses *Past and Present* as a work containing 'the same characters', as in his works of the past, but now with some 'sundry new personages'.

Sir Peter LePage Renouf's review (No. 17) in the *Dublin* is unquestionably important because of his agreement with Carlyle's diagnosis of the condition of England. Renouf, too, sees the presence not only of individual sin, but also of national sin: 'Yes! there is *such* a thing as national sin:—not only individuals but nations may forget God, and leaving out all considerations of the just and the unjust betake themselves to the Godless question of expediency.' The Catholic *Dublin Review* was consistently a stronger ally of Carlyle's than were the other major quarterlies in his assaults upon religious malaise.

As we can see from the documents collected here, the criticisms of Carlyle remained without synthesis: with *Past and Present*, the secular journals attack him for not providing precise remedies for the ills he so elaborately diagnoses; the conservatives still attack his neologisms, Germanisms, rude and unorthodox style; the liberals distrust his courting of strong heroes and his flirting with autocracy and his other growing anti-democratic sentiments. Carlyle's most representative work received such mixed reactions because it was interpreted primarily as literature of reality, rather than that of the imagination.

'Latter-Day Pamphlets'

If any one work succeeded in calling down upon Carlyle the wrath even of his friends, it was the *Latter-Day Pamphlets* (1850). This series of eight pamphlets was hastily and painfully written in a period from December through July. It received more attention from the press than any single work, and, with very few exceptions—American pro-slavers such as George Fitzhugh (No. 30) and the Southern periodicals—it was reviewed negatively.

Carlyle's strident and sarcastic attacks upon prisoners, vagrants, blacks and indiscriminate philanthropy—his ruthless championing of arbitrary authority; his belief in the beneficent whip—turned his most ardent followers against him, widening the breach between himself and his reading public, and earned the hostility of the Press. *Punch* (No. 26) ineffectually denounced him, and even his close friend, David Masson, was forced to admit that Carlyle was at the time 'unpopular with at least one half of the Kingdom' (No. 28). Strong praise for his fiery denunciations of officialdom and parliamentary cant—perhaps the fiercest attack on bureaucracy in the nineteenth century—came from the *Examiner* (29 June 1850), but the *Leader* (4 May 1850) was more restrained: 'As we said a great truth lies underneath the vehement outburst of *The Stump Orator*; and people will feel it, when they overcome their astonishment at its exaggerations. But if they accept the denunciations of this pamphlet literally they will pronounce the writer a mere juggler throwing about paradoxes. This pamphlet is the event of the week' (133).

The criticism followed the general pattern: Carlyle offers nothing new, he lacks practical wisdom (No. 27), his style is atrocious (No. 26). But now the criticism intensified as Carlyle presented his doctrines with a harsh and offensive rhetoric. His lack of artistic balance and wit, his need to chastise and scold openly, caustically, and categorically alienated him from the majority of his critics. Carlyle was aware of the response to the *Pamphlets* as he referred to the 'howl of execration' (D. A. Wilson, IV, 250).

Actually the howl began earlier when Carlyle published a series of essays on the Irish Question in the *Spectator* and *Examiner* during the spring of 1848, followed by 'Occasional Discourse on the Nigger Question', in *Fraser's Magazine* (December 1849), two months before the first *Pamphlet* appeared (Nos. 24 and 25). His Messianism in the Irish essays aroused little public comment, but it did annoy such a good friend as John Stuart Mill (No. 23) and signalled the beginning of the break between Carlyle and many of his young liberal followers.

In America the Northerners were both disappointed and outraged with the *Pamphlets*. The shock was most severe to those who did not expect him to turn so savagely upon revered institutions of nineteenth-century liberalism, in particular, universal suffrage. Elizur Wright devoted a forty-eight-page pamphlet ('Perforations in the "Latter-Day Pamphlets", By one of the Eighteen Million Bores' [Boston, 1850]) to answering Carlyle's charges. America was in no mood for kings; concludes Wright:

The truth we claim to be, that we are beginning to have sense enough to dispense with kings and born rulers, and do our own governing in a quiet and inexpensive way, and with this faculty we will take in good part the broad hint to make our calls shorter and less frequent at Cheyne Row, and console ourselves as well as we can for the absence among our progeny of any such wise, noble and admirable souls, as he who compliments negro slavery from that smug domicile (48).

The disenchantment with Carlyle is further recorded by Oliver Wendell Holmes:

There were Americans enough ready to swear by Carlyle until he broke his staff meddling with our anti-slavery conflict, and buried it so many fathoms deep that it could never be fished out again (*Our Hundred Days in Europe*, Boston, n.d. 139–40).

'The Life of John Sterling'
The *Life of John Sterling* (1851), a beautiful and sympathetic biography of Carlyle's young friend, created a lull in the storm generated by the *Latter-Day Pamphlets*. The tone is temperate, the arguments are muted, and the attitude toward the subject is warm. Despite this radical change of pace, which many critics heartily welcomed (No. 32), Carlyle further alienated himself from many readers with his attacks in the biography against Coleridge and the Church of England (No. 33). George Gilfillan (*Eclectic Review*, December 1851, n.s., ii, 721) is greatly alarmed

over Carlyle's blows against the essential truths of Christianity, seeing here a crisis of faith. Carlyle 'shook Sterling's attachment to Coleridge, and thus to Christianity; stripping him of that garment of "moonshine", he left him naked. Shattering the creed Sterling had attained, he supplied him with no other.' A notice in the *Spectator* (25 October 1851, xxiv, 1023-4) concurs:

For good or evil, Mr. Carlyle is a power in the country; and those who watch eagerly the signs of the times have their eyes fixed upon him. What he would have us leave is plain enough, and that too with all haste, such as a sinking ship that will carry us—state, church, and sacred property—down along with it. But whither would he have us fly? Is there firm land, be it ever so distant? Or is the wild waste of waters, seething, warring round as far as eye can reach, our only hope?—the pilot-stars, shining fitfully through the parting of the storm clouds, our only guidance? There are hearts in this land almost broken, whose old traditional beliefs, serving them at least as moral supports, Mr. Carlyle and teachers like him have undermined . . . Mr. Carlyle has no right, no man has any right, to weaken or destroy a faith which he cannot or will not replace with a loftier.

However, such reviewers as George Eliot (No. 31) and F. W. Newman (No. 32) who could divorce themselves from the passionate controversy which was carried on in the periodicals (No. 34) found much to praise in this biography, perhaps one of the most underrated and neglected biographies of the century.

'Frederick the Great'
It was almost eight years later before the first two volumes of Carlyle's six-volume *Frederick the Great* (1858-65) were to appear, and by now Carlyle was seventy. Although *Frederick* was widely reviewed, it was regarded in much the same way that his more recent works had been. The litany was familiar: his style is inscrutable; he is impractical; yet he is earnest, honest, and a man to be reckoned with. An interesting two-part review by Sir E. B. Hamley appeared in *Blackwood's Magazine* (February 1859, lxxxv and July 1865, xcviii). The title speaks for itself, 'Mirage Philosophy'. In the 1859 essay, Hamley defended progress and the 'fair, broad, honest face of England' against Carlyle who, he felt, had exaggerated blots into fatal cankers (138-42). Hamley, a soldier, writer, and member of what was referred to as the Military Staff of *Blackwood's*, wrote a more favourable second notice in 1865. An exception to the usual objections was Herman Merivale's review (No. 38) in the *Quarterly*. This is indeed more congratulatory than his earlier

review of *The French Revolution* in the *Edinburgh* (No. 8). The review
is sympathetic, even warm in as much as Merivale is pleased that the
'Master of Paradoxes' has finished his herculean labours which 'will
remain in truth a great work, and a substantial contribution at once to
accurate history and to high literature'.

Obituaries and 'Reminiscences'

When Carlyle died in 1881, the leading writers of the day took up their
pens to write his obituary and to assess his stormy literary career. It is
the obituaries and the reviews of *Reminiscences*—written in sorrow immediately following the shock of Jane's death in 1866, but not published
until a month after Carlyle's death—that give us our final view of
Carlyle as seen by his contemporaries. The responses were mixed,
closely following the pattern we have seen throughout these documents.
But by 1881 many new periodicals had come into existence—the
Nineteenth Century, Macmillan's, Cornhill, the *Academy*—replacing the
old heavies. There is more objectivity, less parochialism, less polemiciz-
ing. The emphasis now is more psychological as Carlyle's religious
'heresies' are passed over. He is no longer an infidel, as the orthodox
once saw him, but a man who illustrated the rigidity of Calvinism, now
much out of fashion.

Many Victorian readers were offended by Carlyle's self-recrimina-
tions and feelings of guilt in the *Reminiscences* over his unkindnesses to
Jane—recollections now quite understandable as necessary outlets for
grief. And Carlyle's caustic sketches of De Quincey, Lamb, and
Coleridge precipitated a whole series of sharp reactions. Andrew Lang
(No. 44) objected to the contemptuous 'blows and kicks' against
Carlyle's contemporaries, despite his high estimate of Carlyle as one of
the 'greatest of literary forces'. George Bentley (*Temple Bar*, May 1881,
lxii, 23) complains that 'probably in English literature there is nowhere
to be found written by a man so eminent and so religiously minded, a
more unkind, splenetic book'. J. C. Morison (*Fortnightly Review*, April
1881, xxxv, 461), an early disciple of Carlyle's at Oxford, sadly admits
that here he sees Carlyle sneering behind people's backs. He is curt and
unseemly, 'inwardly bankrupt of hope, faith, and charity, looking on
the world with moody anger and querulous unsatisfied egotism'. In
August, Grant Allen (*Temple Bar*, lxii, 517) summed up at least one side
of the reaction to the *Reminiscences*:

The hymns of praise sank into a quaver of consternation. Carlyle's eldest friends
were his violent assailants. Worshippers became scorners. There never was

such a change of opinion. When the veiled prophet exhibited his expressive countenance to his friends there was considerable disappointment; the *Reminiscences* . . . led to a frantic stampede of enthusiasts.

However, perceptive and sympathetic essays by Richard H. Hutton (No. 43) and Leslie Stephen (No. 42) reflect a balanced attempt to assess Carlyle's long career; and Edward Dowden (No. 41) explains the paradoxical nature of his sensibility. An anonymous reviewer refers to Carlyle in the *Saturday Review* (No. 40) as 'the greatest living writer of his time' and goes on to defend Carlyle's concept of heroes, explaining that if Carlyle insisted on the right of the hero to compel 'the obedience of ordinary men', it was always on the condition that he was a hero and 'not a vulgar despot'. For him Carlyle's influence was all-pervasive: 'He has inspired and modified a mode of thought rather than the opinions of one or two generations.' Yet there was no more unanimity towards Carlyle at his death than there had been during his life. None the less this new generation of critics, demonstrating a quality of understanding, recognized that the career of a most amazing man had come to an end. Perhaps Leslie Stephen's comment that Carlyle was the 'noblest man of letters of his generation' was the truly fitting epitaph.

4

AFTER 1881

The years immediately following his death saw Carlyle's reputation decline rapidly. The reaction to the *Reminiscences* in some circles was so violent that one might agree with Carlyle's excellent bibliographer, Isaac W. Dyer, that it emanated as much from a dislike of Carlyle himself as from objections to his characterizations of his contemporaries. Moreover, petty gossip regarding Carlyle's supposed impotence, reported by Froude—then later repeated by Frank Harris—led to tiresome and petty allegations and counter-allegations.

But it was more than a prurient interest in Carlyle's domestic life which precipitated his literary decline. As nineteenth- and twentieth-century democracy advanced, his hold over the public diminished. The First World War and the years that followed were also disastrous, not only for Carlyle, but for all things Victorian. Norwood Young (*Carlyle: His Rise and Fall*, New York [1927]), for instance, unconvincingly accuses Carlyle of proclaiming ideas which led directly to the First World War. He argues:

There would have been no eagerness for war in Germany but for the military prestige of Prussia; which was based principally upon the Frederick legend which Carlyle helped to disseminate. . . . It was the fable of Frederick, surrounded by enemies, beating off their huge forces, defying the world, that gave Prussianized Germany the conviction that its army was unconquerable, that victory was certain (331).

One group of twentieth-century writers—H. J. C. Grierson, Pieter Geyl, and J. Salwyn Schapiro—condemn Carlyle's worship of intuition, emotionalism, and force, and see him as a forerunner of fascism and racism.[26] Perhaps the high-water mark of such criticism was Eric Bentley's brilliant but eccentric *A Century of Hero Worship* (Philadelphia, 1944). A year after the publication of this work, Bentley announced in *The American Scholar* (Winter, 1945–6) that Carlyle was dead:

To observe that he is still read in the graduate schools may, unhappily, be but a confirmation of this fact. When a writer is read only by those who are professionally obliged to read him it can scarcely be said that he is a living force. However thorough and reverent an embalming may be, it seldom results in resurrection.

But this fallen star seems to be rising, and no student of the nineteenth century can hope to come to terms with the spirit of that age by either ignoring or patronizing Carlyle.

Other twentieth-century studies of great value view Carlyle in a highly positive way. Basil Willey and Ernst Cassirer commend his devotion to the search for social reform and religious truth.[27] The many very recent studies of Carlyle, those by G. B. Tennyson, Albert J. LaValley, and George Levine, are impressive for their close critical analyses of Carlyle's art and ideas in relation to his struggle with the perplexing and frustrating forces of emerging modern life.[28]

Carlyle was, as Richard Hutton said, a 'spiritual volcano', and the thrust of his influence was personal as well as literary, the essence of which has unfortunately been lost in the smoke of history. For all his irascibility, imperiousness of will, human weaknesses and mistakes, he was a man of great integrity and sincerity—qualities which even his most hostile critics recognized. It was precisely this directness, his personal head-on battle with the complexities of life as we know it today, his refusal to compromise in an age in which compromise was a way of life, that makes him such an amazing figure. Despite themselves, the Victorians recognized this. And because of his earnestness, Carlyle was able to provoke his contemporaries into taking a stand.

23

Although the responses to Carlyle were often sharply polarized between his idolators and his maligners, they were more often—and understandably so—ambivalent, illuminating the intellectual and emotional conflicts of the reviewers themselves as well as the character of the age.

NOTES

1 James Moncreiff reviewing *Oliver Cromwell's Letters and Speeches* in the *North British Review* (February 1846), iv, 506.

2 *Conversations with Carlyle* (London, 1892), 91.

3 Quoted in James A. Froude, *Thomas Carlyle, A History of His Life in London* (London, 1884), ii, 36.

4 *New Letters of Thomas Carlyle*, ed. Alexander Carlyle (London, 1904), ii, 92.

5 See Froude, *Thomas Carlyle, Life in London*, ii, 38. The passage is probably from Carlyle's *Journal* but it is not so indicated by Froude.

6 Herodotus Smith (Francis Espinasse) attributes this essay to George H. Lewes. See the *Critic* (1851), x, 427–8 and Espinasse's *Literary Recollections* (London, 1893), esp. 366–89.

7 See William Silas Vance, 'Carlyle in America Before *Sartor Resartus*', *American Literature* (May 1936), vii, 363–75.

8 About 90 per cent of all articles were anonymous before 1870, and well over 90 per cent for the whole century (Walter E. Houghton, 'Reflections on Indexing Victorian Periodicals', *Victorian Studies* (December 1963), vii, 194.)

9 Frank Luther Mott, 'Carlyle's American Public', *Philological Quarterly* (July 1925), iv, 245–64.

10 *The Journals and Miscellaneous Notebooks of Ralph Waldo Emerson*, ed. Martin M. Sealts, Jr. (Cambridge, USA, 1965), v, 95.

11 *Letters of Thomas Carlyle to John Stuart Mill, John Sterling and Robert Browning*, ed. Alexander Carlyle (London, 1923), pp. 193–4.

12 *The Victorian Sage* (New York, 1953), p. 27 and pp. 1–85.

13 Almost ten years later, James Moncreiff was continuing the attack on Carlyle's style, charging him with debasing the purity of language, calling his writing the 'incoherent ramblings of a lunatic' (509). It aggravates Moncreiff's 'bile to such a degree' that he can 'hardly command sufficient coolness to consider the substance of the book as it deserves' (524).

14 D. A. Wilson, *Carlyle on Cromwell and Others* (London, 1925), iii, 14.

15 *New Letters*, i, 213.

16 See James A. Froude, i, 164–5, and *The Letters of Thomas Carlyle to His Brother Alexander With Related Family Letters*, ed. Edwin W. Marrs, Jr. (Cambridge, USA, 1968), p. 500.

17 See Merivale, p. 76 and compare with a comment by Francis Jacox (writing under the pseudonym of 'Monkshood') in his 'Thomas Carlyle', *Bentley's*

Miscellany (1856), xl, 550: 'The distaste for Carlylism, rife in so large and natural a measure, has been vastly sped in its growth and intensity by the author's mimic satellites, who spaniel him at heels, and, incompetent to imitate what is inimitable in his manner, gravely caricature and soberly travesty and seriously burlesque what is very easily affected in his mannerisms. What is perhaps an extravagance in him, becomes an extravaganza in them.'

18 *New Letters*, i, 215.

19 *The Life of Frederick Denison Maurice* (New York, 1884), i, 280.

20 *The Victorian Frame of Mind* (New Haven, 1957).

21 It is possible that William Thomson also wrote the earlier review of *On Heroes* (March 1842), although the first essay is much less critical than the later one. Thomson's opening sentence of the August 1843 review begins: 'Having noticed this work when it first appeared, we are only drawn to it again by the early demand for a second edition, followed as closely by a new work of the same prolific author.'

22 In a letter to Daniel Macmillan (31 August 1843), Maurice wrote: 'I cannot find that Carlyle leads us directly to a centre; but I do find that he makes us despair for want of one, and that he expresses the indistinct wailings of men in search of it better than all the other writers of our day. I have been writing a defence of him for the *Christian Remembrancer* (where he has been stupidly attacked), mainly on the ground that he is perfectly indispensable to clergymen as showing them their own ignorance, and sin, and the deep wants of the age with which they profess to deal', *The Life of Frederick D. Maurice*, i, 348–9.

23 Maurice was wrong. In his *Journal*, Carlyle wrote: 'A word from F. Maurice in defence of me from some Church of England reviewer is also gratifying', Froude, *Thomas Carlyle, Life in London*, i, 297.

24 *The Correspondence of Emerson and Carlyle*, ed. Joseph Slater (New York, 1964), p. 328.

25 Froude, *Thomas Carlyle, Life in London*, i, 244.

26 *Carlyle and Hitler* (1933), *Debates With Historians* (1956), 'Thomas Carlyle, Prophet of Fascism', *Journal of Modern History* (June 1945), xvii.

27 *Nineteenth Century Studies* (1949), *The Myth of the State* (1946).

28 *Sartor Called Resartus* (1965), *Carlyle and the Idea of the Modern* (1968), *The Boundaries of Fiction* (1968).

SARTOR RESARTUS

1834–6

1. John Sterling, letter to Carlyle

Letter to Thomas Carlyle on *Sartor Resartus*, 29 May 1835, quoted in Carlyle's *Life of John Sterling* (1851), xi, 108–17.

John Sterling (1806–44), young radical and idealist, friend of Carlyle, Emerson, and other notables, showed much promise when at Trinity College, Cambridge; yet he left without taking a degree. In 1828, he, Frederick Denison Maurice, and other young 'Apostles' took over the *Athenaeum*. This was a short-lived endeavour, and Sterling turned to other idealistic ventures such as the Anti-Indian Charter Society and the passionately pursued venture to assist the exiled Spanish patriot, Torrijos. However well intentioned, the expedition ended in disaster. In 1834, he was ordained deacon at Cambridge and took a curacy at Herstmonceux under Julius Hare, his friend and later biographer. Sterling resigned, however, after eight months because of renewed threats of tuberculosis. Years of religious struggle were to follow for Sterling, a struggle which became the subject of a bitter controversy, especially after the publication of Carlyle's *Life of John Sterling* (1851), a book quite different from Hare's portrayal of Sterling as a saintly young man. See Introduction, p. 9.

Herstmonceux near Battle, 29th May 1835.

My dear Carlyle,—I have now read twice, with care, the wondrous account of Teufelsdröckh and his Opinions; and I need not say that it has given me much to think of. It falls-in with the feelings and tastes which were, for years, the ruling ones of my life; but which you will

26

not be angry with me when I say that I am infinitely and hourly thankful for having escaped from. Not that I think of this state of mind as one with which I have no longer any concern. The sense of a oneness of life and power in all existence; and of a boundless exuberance of beauty around us, to which most men are well-nigh dead, is a possession which no one that has ever enjoyed it would wish to lose. When to this we add the deep feeling of the difference between the actual and the ideal in Nature, and still more in Man; and bring in, to explain this, the principle of duty, as that which connects us with a possible Higher State, and sets us in progress towards it,—we have a cycle of thoughts which was the whole spiritual empire of the wisest Pagans, and which might well supply food for the wide speculations and richly creative fancy of Teufelsdröckh, or his prototype Jean Paul.

How then comes it, we cannot but ask, that these ideas, displayed assuredly with no want of eloquence, vivacity or earnestness, have found, unless I am much mistaken, so little acceptance among the best and most energetic minds in this country? In a country where millions read the Bible, and thousands Shakspeare; where Wordsworth circulates through book-clubs and drawing-rooms; where there are innumerable admirers of your favourite Burns; and where Coleridge, by sending from his solitude the voice of earnest spiritual instruction, came to be beloved, studied and mourned for, by no small or careless school of disciples?—To answer this question would, of course, require more thought and knowledge than I can pretend to bring to it. But there are some points on which I will venture to say a few words.

In the first place, as to the form of composition,—which may be called, I think, the Rhapsodico-Reflective. In this the *Sartor Resartus* resembles some of the master-works of human invention, which have been acknowledged as such by many generations; and especially the works of Rabelais, Montaigne, Sterne and Swift. There is nothing I know of in Antiquity like it. That which comes nearest is perhaps the Platonic Dialogue. But of this, although there is something of the playful and fanciful on the surface, there is in reality neither in the language (which is austerely determined to its end), nor in the method and progression of the work, any of that headlong self-asserting capriciousness, which, if not discernible in the plan of Teufelsdröckh's *Memoirs*, is yet plainly to be seen in the structure of the sentences, the lawless oddity, and strange heterogeneous combination and allusion. The principle of this difference, observable often elsewhere in modern literature (for the same thing is to be found, more or less, in many of our most genial

27

works of imagination,—*Don Quixote*, for instance, and the writings of Jeremy Taylor), seems to be that well-known one of the predominant objectivity of the Pagan mind; while among us the subjective has risen into superiority, and brought with it in each individual a multitude of peculiar associations and relations. These, as not explicable from any one *external* principle assumed as a premiss by the ancient philosopher, were rejected from the sphere of his æsthetic creation: but to us they all have a value and meaning; being connected by the bond of our own personality, and all alike existing in that infinity which is its arena.

But however this may be, and comparing the Teufelsdröckhean Epopee only with those other modern works,—it is noticeable that Rabelais, Montaigne and Sterne have trusted for the currency of their writings, in a great degree, to the use of obscene and sensual stimulants. Rabelais, besides, was full of contemporary and personal satire; and seems to have been a champion in the great cause of his time,—as was Montaigne also,—that of the right of thought in all competent minds, unrestrained by any outward authority. Montaigne, moreover, contains more pleasant and lively gossip, and more distinct good-humoured painting of his own character and daily habits, than any other writer I know. Sterne is never obscure, and never moral; and the costume of his subjects is drawn from the familiar experience of his own time and country: and Swift, again, has the same merit of the clearest perspicuity, joined to that of the most homely, unaffected, forcible English. These points of difference seem to me the chief ones which bear against the success of the *Sartor*. On the other hand, there is in Teufelsdröckh a depth and fervour of feeling, and a power of serious eloquence, far beyond that of any of these four writers; and to which indeed there is nothing at all comparable in any of them, except perhaps now and then, and very imperfectly, in Montaigne.

Of the other points of comparison there are two which I would chiefly dwell on: and first as to the language. A good deal of this is positively barbarous. 'Environment,' 'vestural,' 'stertorous,' 'visualised,' 'complected,' and others to be found I think in the first twenty pages,—are words, so far as I know, without any authority; some of them contrary to analogy; and none repaying by their value the disadvantage of novelty. To these must be added new and erroneous locutions; 'whole other tissues' for *all the other*, and similar uses of the word *whole*; 'orients' for *pearls*; 'lucid' and 'lucent' employed as if they were different in meaning; 'hulls' perpetually for *coverings*, it being a word hardly used, and then only for the husk of a nut; 'to insure a man of mis-apprehension'; 'talented,' a mere newspaper and hustings word, in-vented, I believe, by O'Connell.

I must also mention the constant recurrence of some words in a quaint and queer connection, which gives a grotesque and somewhat repulsive mannerism to many sentences. Of these the commonest offender is 'quite'; which appears in almost every page, and gives at first a droll kind of emphasis; but soon becomes wearisome. 'Nay,' 'manifold,' 'cunning enough significance,' 'faculty' (meaning a man's rational or moral *power*), 'special,' 'not without,' haunt the reader as if in some uneasy dream which does not rise to the dignity of nightmare. Some of these strange mannerisms fall under the general head of a singularity peculiar, so far as I know, to Teufelsdröckh. For instance, that of the incessant use of a sort of odd superfluous qualification of his assertions; which seems to give the character of deliberateness and caution to the style, but in time sounds like mere trick or involuntary habit. 'Almost' does more than yeoman's, *almost* slave's service in this way. Something similar may be remarked of the use of the double negative by way of affirmation.

Under this head, of language, may be mentioned, though not with strict grammatical accuracy, two standing characteristics of the Pro-fessor's style,—at least as rendered into English: *First*, the composition of words, such as 'snow-and-rosebloom maiden': an attractive damsel doubtless in Germany, but, with all her charms, somewhat uncouth here. 'Life-vision' is another example; and many more might be found. To say nothing of the innumerable cases in which the words are only intelligible as a compound term, though not distinguished by hyphens. Of course the composition of words is sometimes allowable even in English: but the habit of dealing with German seems to have produced, in the pages before us, a prodigious superabundance of this form of expression; which gives harshness and strangeness, where the matter would at all events have been surprising enough. *Secondly*, I object, with the same qualification, to the frequent use of *inversion*; which generally appears as a transposition of the two members of a clause, in a way which would not have been practised in conversation. It certainly gives emphasis and force, and often serves to point the meaning. But a style may be fatiguing and faulty precisely by being too emphatic, forcible and pointed; and so straining the attention to find its meaning, or the admiration to appreciate its beauty.

Another class of considerations connects itself with the heightened and plethoric fulness of the style: its accumulation and contrast of imagery; its occasional jerking and almost spasmodic violence;—and above all, the painful subjective excitement, which seems the element and groundwork even of every description of Nature; often taking the shape of sarcasm or broad jest, but never subsiding into calm. There is also a point which I should think worth attending to, were I planning any similar book: I mean the importance, in a work of imagination, of not too much disturbing in the reader's mind the balance of the New and Old. The former addresses itself to his active, the latter to his passive faculty; and these are mutually dependent, and most co-exist in certain proportion, if you wish to combine his sympathy and progressive exertion with willingness and ease of attention. This should be taken into account in forming a style; for of course it cannot be consciously thought of in composing each sentence.

But chiefly it seems important in determining the plan of a work. If the tone of feeling, the line of speculation are out of the common way, and sure to present some difficulty to the average reader, then it would probably be desirable to select, for the circumstances, drapery and accessories of all kinds, those most familiar, or at least most attractive. A fable of the homeliest purport, and commonest every-day application, derives an interest and charm from its turning on the characters and acts of gods and genii, lions and foxes, Arabs and Affghauns. On the contrary, for philosophic inquiry and truths of awful preciousness, I would select as my personages and interlocutors beings with whose language and 'whereabouts' my readers would be familiar. Thus did Plato in his *Dialogues*, Christ in his Parables. Therefore it seems doubtful whether it was judicious to make a German Professor the hero of *Sartor*. Berkeley began his *Siris* with tar-water; but what can English readers be expected to make of *Gukguk* by way of prelibation to your nectar and tokay? The circumstances and details do not flash with living reality on the minds of your readers, but, on the contrary, themselves require some of that attention and minute speculation, the whole original stock of which, in the minds of most of them, would not be too much to enable them to follow your views of Man and Nature. In short, there is not a sufficient basis of the common to justify the amount of peculiarity in the work. In a book of science, these considerations would of course be inapplicable; but then the whole shape and colouring of the book must be altered to make it such; and a man who wishes merely to get at the philosophical result, or summary of the whole, will regard the details and illustrations as so much unprofitable surplusage.

The sense of strangeness is also awakened by the marvellous combinations, in which the work abounds to a degree that the common
reader must find perfectly bewildering. This can hardly, however, be
treated as a consequence of the *style*; for the style in this respect coheres
with, and springs from, the whole turn and tendency of thought. The
noblest images are objects of a humorous smile, in a mind which sees
itself above all Nature and throned in the arms of an Almighty
Necessity; while the meanest have a dignity, inasmuch as they are
trivial symbols of the same one life to which the great whole belongs.
And hence, as I divine, the startling whirl of incongruous juxtaposition,
which of a truth must to many readers seem as amazing as if the Pythia
on the tripod should have struck-up a drinking-song, or Thersites had
caught the prophetic strain of Cassandra.

All this, of course, appears to me true and relevant; but I cannot help
feeling that it is, after all, but a poor piece of quackery to comment on a
multitude of phenomena without adverting to the principle which lies
at the root, and gives the true meaning to them all. Now this principle
I seem to myself to find in the state of mind which is attributed to
Teufelsdröckh; in his state of mind, I say, not in his opinions, though
these are, in him as in all men, most important,—being one of the best
indices to his state of mind. Now what distinguishes him, not merely
from the greatest and best men who have been on earth for eighteen
hundred years, but from the whole body of those who have been working forwards towards the good, and have been the salt and light of the
world, is this: That he does not believe in a God. Do not be indignant,
I am blaming no one;—but if I write my thoughts, I must write them
honestly.

Teufelsdröckh does not belong to the herd of sensual and thoughtless men; because he does perceive in all Existence a unity of power;
because he does believe that this is a real power external to him and
dominant to a certain extent over him, and does not think that he is
himself a shadow in a world of shadows. He has a deep feeling of the
beautiful, the good and the true; and a faith in their final victory.

At the same time, how evident is the strong inward unrest, the
Titanic heaving of mountain on mountain; the storm-like rushing over
land and sea in search of peace. He writhes and roars under his consciousness of the difference in himself between the possible and the
actual, the hoped-for and the existent. He feels that duty is the highest
law of his own being; and knowing how it bids the waves be stilled into

an icy fixedness and grandeur, he trusts (but with a boundless inward misgiving) that there is a principle of order which will reduce all confusion to shape and clearness. But wanting peace himself, his fierce dissatisfaction fixes on all that is weak, corrupt and imperfect around him; and instead of a calm and steady coöperation with all those who are endeavouring to apply the highest ideas as remedies for the worst evils, he holds himself aloof in savage isolation; and cherishes (though he dare not own) a stern joy at the prospect of that Catastrophe which is to turn loose again the elements of man's social life, and give for a time the victory to evil;—in hopes that each new convulsion of the world must bring us nearer to the ultimate restoration of all things; fancying that each may be the last. Wanting the calm and cheerful reliance, which would be the spring of active exertion, he flatters his own distemper by persuading himself that his own age and generation are peculiarly feeble and decayed; and would even perhaps be willing to exchange the restless immaturity of our self-consciousness, and the promise of its long throe-pangs, for the unawakened undoubting simplicity of the world's childhood; of the times in which there was all the evil and horror of our day, only with the difference that conscience had not arisen to try and condemn it. In these longings, if they are Teufelsdröckh's, he seems to forget that, could we go back five thousand years, we should only have the prospect of travelling them again, and arriving at last at the same point at which we stand now.

Something of this state of mind I may say that I understand; for I have myself experienced it. And the root of the matter appears to me: A want of sympathy with the great body of those who are now endeavouring to guide and help onward their fellow-men. And in what is this alienation grounded? It is, as I believe, simply in the difference on that point: viz. the clear, deep, habitual recognition of a one Living *Personal* God, essentially good, wise, true and holy, the Author of all that exists; and a reunion with whom is the only end of all rational beings. This belief ＊ ＊ ＊ [*There follow now several pages on 'Personal God,' and other abstruse or indeed properly unspeakable matters; these, and a general Postscript of qualifying purport, I will suppress; extracting only the following fractions, as luminous or slightly significant to us:*]

Now see the difference of Teufelsdröckh's feelings. At the end of book iii. chap. 8, I find these words: 'But whence? O Heaven, whither? Sense knows not; Faith knows not; only that it is through mystery to mystery, from God to God.

32

> "We *are such stuff*
> As dreams are made of, and our little life
> Is rounded with a sleep." '

And this tallies with the whole strain of his character. What we find everywhere, with an abundant use of the name of God, is the conception of a formless Infinite whether in time or space; of a high inscrutable Necessity, which it is the chief wisdom and virtue to submit to, which is the mysterious impersonal base of all Existence,—shows itself in the laws of every separate being's nature; and for man in the shape of duty. On the other hand, I affirm, we do know whence we come and whither we go!—

* * * And in this state of mind, as there is no true sympathy with others, just as little is there any true peace for ourselves. There is indeed possible the unsympathising factitious calm of Art, which we find in Goethe. But at what expense is it bought? Simply, by abandoning altogether the idea of duty, which is the great witness of our personality. And he attains his inhuman ghastly calmness by reducing the Universe to a heap of material for the idea of beauty to work on.—

* * * The sum of all I have been writing as to the connection of our faith in God with our feeling towards men and our mode of action, may of course be quite erroneous: but granting its truth, it would supply the one principle which I have been seeking for, in order to explain the peculiarities of style in your account of Teufelsdröckh and his writings. * * * The life and works of Luther are the best comment I know of on this doctrine of mine.

Reading over what I have written, I find I have not nearly done justice to my own sense of the genius and moral energy of the book; but this is what you will best excuse.—Believe me most sincerely and faithfully yours. . .

2. Alexander Hill Everett, from an unsigned review, *North American Review*

October 1835, xli, 454–82

Alexander Hill Everett (1790–1847), editor and diplomat, was born in Boston and educated at Harvard. As private secretary to John Quincy Adams, he travelled to Russia and later served as *chargé d'affaires* at The Hague. His diplomatic experience helped to produce two works, *Europe* (1822) and *America* (1827). In 1830, he became the editor of the *North American Review* to which he also contributed articles. This extract begins after a brief account of the 'Editorial Difficulties', Bk. I, ch. ii, in *Sartor Resartus*. See Introduction, p. 9.

Such is the account, given by the 'present editor,' of the origin of this little work. Though professing in general a good deal of respect for his author, he at times deals pretty freely with him:—'Thou foolish Teufelsdroeckh!' and even 'Thou rogue!' are among the titles which are occasionally bestowed on him. For ourselves, we incline to the opinion, that the only rogue in the company is the 'present editor.' We have said that the volume came before the public under rather suspicious circumstances, and, after a careful survey of the whole ground, our belief is, that no such persons as Professor Teufelsdroeckh or Counsellor Heuschrecke ever existed; that the six paper bags, with their China-ink inscriptions and multifarious contents, are a mere figment of the brain; that the 'present editor' is the only person who has ever written upon the Philosophy of Clothes; and that the *Sartor Resartus* is the only treatise that has yet appeared upon that subject;—in short, that the whole account of the origin of the work before us, which the supposed editor relates with so much gravity, and of which we have given a brief abstract, is in plain English, a *hum*.

Without troubling our readers at any great length with our reasons for entertaining these suspicions, we may remark, that the absence of all other information on the subject, excepting what is contained in the work, is itself a fact of a most significant character. The whole German press, as well as the particular one where the work purports to have been printed, seems to be under the control of *Stillschweigen und Co.*—Silence and Company. If the Clothes-Philosophy and its author are making so great a sensation throughout Germany as is pretended, how happens it that the only notice we have of the fact is contained in a few numbers of a monthly magazine, published at London? How happens it that no intelligence about the matter has come out directly to this country? We pique ourselves, here in New England, upon knowing at least as much of what is going on in the literary way in the old Dutch mother-land, as our brethren of the fast-anchored isle; but thus far we have no tidings whatever of the 'extensive, close-printed, close-meditated volume,' which forms the subject of this pretended commentary. Again, we would respectfully inquire of the 'present editor,' upon what part of the map of Germany we are to look for the city of *Weissnichtwo*—'Know-not-where,' at which place the work is supposed to have been printed and the author to have resided. It has been our fortune to visit several portions of the German territory, and to examine pretty carefully, at different times and for various purposes, maps of the whole, but we have no recollection of any such place. We suspect that the city of *Know-not-where* might be called, with at least as much propriety, *Nobody-knows-where*, and is to be found in the kingdom of *Nowhere*. Again, the village of *Entepfuhl*,—'Duck-pond,'—where the supposed author of the work is said to have passed his youth, and that of *Hinterschlag*, where he had his education, are equally foreign to our geography. Duck-ponds enough there undoubtedly are in almost every village in Germany, as the traveller in that country knows too well to his cost, but any particular village, denominated Duck-pond, is to us altogether *terra incognita*. The names of the personages are not less singular than those of the places. Who can refrain from a smile, at the yoking together of such a pair of appellatives as Diogenes Teufels-droeckh? The supposed bearer of this strange title is represented as admitting, in his pretended autobiography, that 'he had searched to no purpose through all the Herald's books in and without the German Empire, and through all manner of Subscribers-Lists, Militia-Rolls, and other Name-Catalogues; but had nowhere been able to find the name Teufelsdroeckh, except as appended to his own person.' We can readily believe this, and we doubt very much whether any Christian parent would think of condemning a son to carry through life the burden of so unpleasant a title. That of Counsellor *Heuschrecke*,—Grasshopper,—

though not offensive, looks much more like a piece of fancy work than a 'fair business transaction.' The same may be said of *Blumine*—Flower-Goddess,—the heroine of the fable, and so of the rest.

In short, our private opinion is, as we have remarked, that the whole story of a correspondence with Germany, a university of Nobody-knows-where, a Professor of Things in General, a Counsellor Grasshopper, a Flower-Goddess Blumine, and so forth, has about as much foundation in truth, as the late entertaining account of Sir John Herschel's discoveries in the moon. Fictions of this kind are, however, not uncommon, and ought not, perhaps, to be condemned with too much severity; but we are not sure that we can exercise the same indulgence in regard to the attempt, which seems to be made to mislead the public as to the substance of the work before us, and its pretended German original. Both purport, as we have seen, to be upon the subject of Clothes, or Dress. *Clothes, their Origin and Influence*, is the title of the supposed German treatise of Professor Teufelsdroeckh, and the rather odd name of *Sartor Resartus*,—the Tailor Patched,—which the present editor has affixed to his pretended commentary, seems to look the same way. But though there is a good deal of remark throughout the work in a half-serious, half-comic style upon dress, it seems to be in reality a treatise upon the great science of Things in General, which Teufelsdroeckh is supposed to have professed at the university of Nobody-knows-where. Now, without intending to adopt a too rigid standard of morals, we own that we doubt a little the propriety of offering to the public a teatise on Things in General, under the name and in the form of an Essay on Dress. For ourselves, advanced as we unfortunately are in the journey of life, far beyond the period when dress is practically a matter of interest, we have no hesitation in saying, that the real subject of the work is to us more attractive than the ostensible one. But this is probably not the case with the mass of readers. To the younger portion of the community, which constitutes every where the very great majority, the subject of dress is one of intense and paramount importance. An author who treats it appeals, like the poet, to the young men and maidens,—*virginibus puerisque*,—and calls upon them by all the motives which habitually operate most strongly upon their feelings, to buy his book. When, after opening their purses for this purpose, they have carried home the work in triumph, expecting to find in it some particular instruction in regard to the tying of their neckcloths, or the cut of their corsets, and meet with nothing better than a dissertation on Things in General, they will,—to use the mildest terms,—not be in very good humor. If the last improvements in legislation, which we have made in this country, should have found their way to England, the author, we think, would stand some chance of being *Lynched*. Whether his object in this piece of *supercherie* be merely pecuniary profit, or whether he takes a malicious pleasure in quizzing the dandies, we shall not undertake to say. In the latter part of the work, he devotes a separate chapter to this class of persons, from the tenor of which we should be disposed to conclude, that he would consider any mode of divesting them of their property very much in the nature of a spoiling of the Egyptians.

The only thing about the work, tending to prove that it is what it purports to be, a commentary on a real German treatise, is the style, which is a sort of Babylonish dialect, not destitute, it is true, of richness, vigor, and at times a sort of singular felicity of expression, but very strongly tinged throughout with the peculiar idiom of the German language. This quality in the style, however, may be a mere result of a great familiarity with German literature, and we cannot, therefore, look upon it as in itself decisive, still less as outweighing so much evidence of an opposite character.

From what has been said, our readers will gather, with sufficient assurance, that the work before us is a sort of philosophical romance, in which the author undertakes to give, in the form of a review of a German treatise on dress, and a notice of the life of the writer, his own opinions upon Matters and Things in General. The hero, Professor Teufelsdroeckh, seems to be intended for a portrait of human nature as affected by the moral influences to which, in the present state of society, a cultivated mind is naturally exposed. Teufelsdroeckh is a foundling, brought up by poor but respectable parents, and educated for the legal profession. He is called to the bar, or, as the phrase is in Germany, admitted as a listener (*auscultator*), and having little business and no property, finds himself rather at a loss for the means of subsistence. While lingering in this uncertain state, he forms an acquaintance with an English traveller, named Towgood, and is patronized to a certain extent by Count Zahdarm, a nobleman whose lady occasionally invites him to a sort of entertainment, which would be called here a blue-stocking party, or *Blue Congress*, but which is dignified in Germany by the more classical title of an *æsthetic tea*. At one of these 'æsthetic teas,' he falls in love with the Flower-Goddess Blumine, alluded to above, who seems to be a sort of *demoiselle de compagnie* to the Countess, and who, after lending for a time an apparently favorable ear to his suit, all

37

at once changes her mind, and marries his English friend Towgood. This result increases the uneasiness under which Teufelsdroeckh was previously laboring, and he finally quits his profession and place of residence, and sets forth upon his travels, which appear to have been extensive, and are described with sufficient exactness, though in general terms. The worst thing about his case is, that in addition to want, idleness, and disappointment in love and friendship, he fell into a kind of scepticism, or rather absolute unbelief. From this, however, he is gradually restored by a series of changes in his intellectual and moral character, amounting altogether to a sort of philosophical conversion. These changes are described in successive chapters under the titles of the 'Everlasting No', the 'Centre of Indifference', and the 'Everlasting Yea', which may be said to constitute the kernel of the work. Being now in a comfortable frame of mind, the wanderer appeals to his pen as a means of obtaining subsistence, and by a diligent use of it obtains pretty soon the professorship of Things in General at the University of Nobody-knows-where. Here he flourishes in tranquil contentment, and publishes the remarkable, close-printed, close-meditated volume, which forms the subject of the present editor's learned commentary.

Such is the general outline of the story. As a specimen of the style, we extract the following account of the first appearance in the world of the learned professor of *Allerley-Wissenschaft*.

[Twenty-two pages of extracts from the following chapters—'Genesis', 'Romance', 'The Everlasting No', 'The Centre of Indifference', and 'The Everlasting Yea'—follow. The review ends with this comment:]

We must here close our extracts from this little volume, which, as our readers, we trust, are by this time aware, contains, under a quaint and singular form, a great deal of deep thought, sound principle, and fine writing. It is, we believe, no secret in England or here, that it is the work of a person to whom the public is indebted for a number of articles in the late British Reviews, which have attracted great attention by the singularity of their style, and the richness and depth of their matter. Among these may be mentioned particularly those on *Characteristics* and the *Life of Burns* in the Edinburgh Review, and on *Goethe* in the Foreign Quarterly. We have been partly led to take this notice of the work before us by the wish, which the author expresses, that a knowledge of his labors might penetrate into the Far West. We take pleasure in introducing to the American public a writer, whose name is yet in a great measure unknown among us, but who is destined, we think, to occupy a large space in the literary world. We have heard it intimated, that Mr. Carlyle has it in contemplation to visit this country, and we can venture to assure him, that, should he carry this intention into effect, he will meet with a cordial welcome. If his conversation should prove as agreeable as his writings, and he should feel a disposition to take up his abode in the 'Far West,' we have little doubt that he may find in some one of the hundred universities of our country, a *Weissnichtwo*, at which he may profess his favorite science of Things-in-General with even more satisfaction and advantage, than in the Edinburgh Review or Fraser's Magazine.

3. Nathaniel L. Frothingham, from an initialled review, *Christian Examiner*

September 1836, xxi, 74–84

Nathaniel L. Frothingham (1793–1870) graduated from Harvard in 1811 and was later summoned to the First Church of Boston. A dignified and scholarly man, he was a staunch opponent of the transcendental movement. In fact, so out of sympathy with the New England transcendentalists, Frothingham practically disowned his son. Octavius Brooks, when he learned that he had been enticed into the embraces of Theodore Parker. See Introduction, p. 9.

In giving our readers some account of this singular production, we will begin by reversing the usual method of our vocation, and instead of a review utter a prophecy. Indeed the book is so very odd, that some departure from the common course seems the most appropriate to any notice of it. We predict, then, that it will not be read through by a great many persons, nor be liked by all its readers. Some will pronounce it unintelligible, or boldly deny that it has any good sound meaning. Some will be deterred by its Latin porch and German decorations from having any thing to do with what seems not intended for their accommodation; while perhaps their neighbour, attracted by the quaintness of the title, *Sartor Resartus,—The Tailor Sewed Over,—*and thinking only of being amused in a passive way, will soon find his mistake, and declare himself imposed upon. The taste of some will be offended by what they will call its affectation and mannerism, and you shall not easily dispossess them of the notion, that the style is a jargon and the philosophy stark nought.

These are they that will rise up to defame and vilipend the elaborate and mystic book of *The Philosophy of Clothes,* by Dr. Diogenes Teufelsdröckh (Asafœtida), Professor Things in General at the University of Weissnichtwo (Know-not-where), and living in the attic floor of the highest house in its Wahngasse (Whimsey Street). Even his choice phrases and profoundest speculations shall be as unsavoury to them as the drug, from which he has rather unaccountably,—to say the least of it,—taken his name. But then we plainly foresee that there will be others, who will make very different account of our Professor's lucubrations. They will admire his wildest extravagances, and discover in his most playful disportings a hidden wisdom; even as the worshippers of Goethe found, and find still, a perfect system of philosophy and a whole canon of Scripture in the wondrous *diablerie* of the *Faust.* They will admit nothing in him to be obscure, nothing tedious. They will talk rather mystically about him at times, and as if they would form round him a special school of the initiated. Every novelty of the least pretension being now-a-days 'a new revelation of man to himself,' they will adjudge this 'philosophy of clothes' to be among the leading phenomena of modern thought. Its style will be copied by young aspirants for literary fame. It will be quoted from the pulpit. It will be read aloud to enthusiastic circles of most intelligent persons.

For our own part, we shall not be much surprised either at the neglect and aversion that it will experience in some quarters, or the unqualified admiration that it will excite in others. We think that they may both be explained equally well, without impeaching the critical acuteness of either of the parties; though we by no means profess ourselves to stand indifferent, or as a middle term, between them. We retain the lease of a small tenement in the *Wahngasse* ourselves, and frankly own that this book has great charms for us. It is written with an earnest and full spirit, though under a freakish form. It is the work of a contemplative, fervent, accomplished mind. It abounds with just and original thoughts, mixed up with the most diverting fancies, and expressed in a style which, though rather grotesque, is of extraordinary copiousness, beauty, and power. The peculiarity, indeed, of the style is just that which will be most objected to and most relished, according to the tastes of different readers. We see nothing to forgive in it, though it is one of the last to be proposed for imitation. It certainly could not be changed without destroying the whole harmony of the performance. It is not only the appropriate dress, but a part of the very substance, of the work. If any will persist in calling it affected, we can only say that it seems to fall very naturally from the pen that employs it, and that such affectations are not often to be met with. If any should wonder how it came to be adopted by the author of *The Life of Schiller*, we think that, if they will but turn to the same author's masterly translation of John Paul's (Richter's) *Life of Quintus Fixlein*, the mystery will be found solved at once. It seems to have been caught from familiarity with that strange genius, and suits perfectly the assumed character which he here undertakes to sustain.

Mr. Carlyle, who is well understood to be the only Professor Teufelsdröckh we are to think of, has published nothing as yet under his own name. His translations from the German novelists did not tell the English public to whom it was indebted for them. *The Life of Schiller* was anonymous. His chief reputation, both here and at home, arose from several remarkable articles in the British Reviews, of which the parentage would never have been known, if they had not excited the general curiosity. *Sartor Resartus* first appeared in several successive numbers of *Fraser's Magazine*. He collected it into a volume for the gratification of his friends; and of that volume this is an exact reprint, with the exception of a preface by the American editors, which is short and neat and just what it should be. The last literary announcement of his is a work on the French Revolution. We are looking for it among the pleasant things that are to come, and should have been favored with it perhaps before now, but for one of those disasters which Sir Isaac Newton has been famed for enduring so patiently. One of the volumes was confided in manuscript to a friend, and was burnt up,—by what ravenous chance we never learned. The contents had to be reproduced. It remains to be seen what the result will be of that most heart-sinking of all toil. We are happy, however, to have his own assurance that 'the burnt ashes have again grown leaves, after a sort'; though almost two volumes were still to be gone through with, at mid-summer of the past year. The last rumor we heard of his more personal projects was, that he was thinking of making a voyage before the next winter to the United States.

Sartor Resartus, according to its *form*, is a dissertation on clothes, or rather, selections from such a dissertation, composed by the German sage whose name we do not desire again to repeat, and interspersed with extracts from his autobiography. It is fragmentary of course. Its desultory starts and unlooked-for combinations remind us sometimes of Sterne, though it does not imitate, nor is it indebted to him. It is more easy and serious than he. It is never on the strain after mere singularity. It carries a deeper significance in its vagaries. We need hardly say, that it is every way above him in elevation of sentiment and reach of thought, in heart and conscience, as well as in invention and imagery and wealth of expression. That unscrupulous humorist has the impudence to say, in a preface to his 'Sermon on Conscience,' that the sermon had 'already appeared in the body of a *moral* work, more read than understood.' Our author's work is indeed a moral one. It is never loose and indecent in its sportiveness; and if you now and then meet with what is less refined than you can desire, it will have at least a sober intent, and probably the coarseness will be somewhat wrapped up, as it is in the Latin of Count Zähdarm's epitaph.

It loves to bring together the low and the lofty, the learned and vulgar, the strange and familiar, the tragic and comic, into rather violent contrasts. We cannot say that it is always clear and sprightly. The words are often unusual, the digressions bewildering, the objects in view not very manifest. But it will seldom fail to repay a careful attention. The device of making a book by pretending to edit the papers of another person may appear to be rather a stale one, and has certainly been of late pressed quite unconscionably into the service. But in the present instance it was absolutely essential to the management of the author's plan, and has been so ingeniously availed of as quite to reconcile us to it. . . .

Whether congenial or not with our tastes and intellectual habits, it is certainly one of the most extraordinary works of our day. It is wrought with great learning and ingenuity, though without the appearance of effort. It throws out the noblest conceptions as if at play, and its sparkling expressions seem kindled by the irrepressible fervor of a brilliant mind. It has imagination enough to give a poet renown; more sound religion and ethics than slumber in the folios of many a body of divinity; more periods that one would copy down in his note-book, to read and read again, than are to be found in all the writings together of many a one who has made himself famous everywhere for having written well. It is not equally sustained in every part; how should it be?—but we can scarcely look where we shall not find something of tenderness or sublimity or wit or wisdom;—something that makes us feel, and makes us reflect too, as deeply as some more pretending 'Aids to Reflections.'

What we chiefly prize in it is its philosophic, spiritual, humane cast of thought. It is in thorough opposition to the materialism and mechanisms of our grooved and iron-bound times. It resists the despotism of opinion seeking to rule by crowds and suffrages and machinists' devices. It soars away far beyond the theories of Utilitarian calculators. It spurns every thing shallow. It expands and lifts itself above every thing contracted. It places us at a free distance from the turmoil of vulgar and selfish life. It exposes many an abuse and illusion of the passing ages. It is spirit. Warm with kind affections, and almost wild with generous aspirations after the broadest truth and the highest good, it is elevating when it most amuses us. It even perplexes us to some wholesome intent. It rebukes the hard dogmatism of conceited disputers, till it makes it look as poor and as ridgy as it really is. Here are true 'Materials for Thinking,' while much that circulates with that label is but an insisting that men shall think perversely. . . .

We started with the acknowledgment that this book would be distasteful to many. But we fearlessly commend it to another many, who will find their hearts greatly in unison with it. It is not a work to be glanced at here and there. It should not be read through in a breath. It must be conned carefully, and not too much at a time. We do not say that it never put our very selves out of patience; but we declare in all sincerity, that we believe few books of its compass will reward the exercise of patience better.

4. Unsigned notice, *Tait's Edinburgh Magazine*

September 1838, v, 611–12

By what fatality was it that the most *radically* Radical speculation upon men and things, which has appeared for many years, should have first come abroad in a violent Tory periodical? This work, which was, but cannot always be, neglected in England, has been reprinted in America, in which land we have the authority of the late traveller Miss Martineau for saying, that the prophet has found the honour and acceptance not at first awarded in his own country. A collected edition of the papers, which went through several numbers of *Fraser's Magazine*, has, however, at length appeared in London; and we are farther promised Mr Carlyle's Miscellaneous Works, which, we presume, must include his editorial labours also, or *The Life and Opinions of Herr Teufelsdröckh*, that true philosopher of the Radical school, and original expounder of '*the Philosophy of Clothes.*' He is a somewhat mysterious personage this said Professor Teufelsdröckh—'a Voice publishing tidings of the Philosophy of Clothes; undoubtedly a spirit addressing spirits.' His English editor cannot promise the *Discloser* 'a paramount popularity in England.' Apart from the choice of the subject, the manner of treating it 'betokens rusticity and academic seclusion, unblamable, indeed inevitable in a German, but fatal to success with our public.'

[quotes 'He speaks out' to 'this of Teufelsdröckh', Bk. I, iv, 23–5]

We must, however, leave the reader to discover how these singular characteristics of the Professor are unfolded in the course of his lucubrations on the Philosophy of Clothes. These lucubrations have puzzled both the Old and the New World. Editors and *Booksellers' Tasters* have been at a loss what to make of them, or even to determine whether the affair presented as a translation from the German, was not what the English call a *hoax*, and the Yankees a *hum*. The *North American* Reviewer had been nearly fairly bitten, though his rare sagacity finally discovered that Professor Teufelsdröckh is about as real a personage as Tristram Shandy's father, Captain Gulliver, or Don Quixote. We can,

44

no more than the English translator, promise the Professor's discursive, light, profound, quaint, and humorous disquisitions, a permanent popularity in England; but this we promise: those who can *taste* him, will not easily forget his race.

5. Lady Sydney Morgan, an unsigned review, *Athenaeum*

20 May 1837, 353–5

Lady Sydney Morgan (1783?–1859), popular sentimental novelist and mover in fashionable London society, often wrote on Irish patriotic subjects, producing such novels as *The Wild Irish Girl* (1806), *O'Donnel, A National Tale* (1814), *Florence M'Carthy* (1816) and others, some of which went through many editions. She contributed a series of articles to the *New Monthly Magazine* on Absenteeism. See Introduction, p. 11.

Originality of thought is unquestionably the best excuse for writing a book; originality of style is a rare and a refreshing merit; but it is paying rather dear for one's whistle, to qualify for obtaining it in the university of Bedlam. Originality, without justness of thought, is but novelty of error; and originality of style, without sound taste and discretion, is sheer affectation. Thus, as ever, the *corruptio optimi* turns out to be *pessima;* the abortive attempt to be more than nature has made us, and to add a cubit to our stature, ends by placing us below what we might be, if contented with being simply and unaffectedly ourselves. There is not, perhaps, a more decided mark of the decadence of literature, than the frequency of such extravagance; especially, if it eventually becomes popular. The youth of literature is distinguished by a progressive approach to simplicity and to good taste; but the culminating point once attained, the good and the beautiful, as the Italian poet sings, become commonplace and tiresome,—'caviare to the general'; and the sound canons of criticism and of logic are capriciously deserted, to produce no matter what, provided it be new. Let it not, however, be thought that we advocate the theory of a permanent Augustan age, and 'giving our days and nights to Addison.' Language is a natural fluent; and to arrest its course is as undesirable as it is difficult. Style, to be good, must bear a certain relation to the mind from which it emanates; and when new ideas and new sciences change the national character, the modes of national expression must change also. Our received ideas, therefore, of classical styles are narrow and unphilosophic; and are derived from the fact, that as far as regards the dead languages, the classical era was followed, not by an increasing, but a decreasing civilization; and that the silver and brazen ages of the Greek and Latin tongues were produced by a deterioration of mind as well as of language. When, however, great changes arrive suddenly and unprepared, they produce, not reforms merely, but revolutions; and in revolutions, literary as well as political, there occurs between the overthrow of the old and the creation of the new, an epoch of transition in which all monstrous and misshapen things are produced in the unguided search of an unknown and unimagined beauty. In such an epoch of transition we believe a large portion of the literature of Germany still to exist; in such an epoch is the literature of *la jeune France;* but when an English writer is found to adopt the crudities and extravagancies of these nascent schools of thought, and to copy their mannerisms without rhyme, reason, taste, or selection, we can only set it down to an imperfection of intellect, to an incapacity for feeling, truth, and beauty, or to a hopeless determination to be singular, at any cost or sacrifice.

The applicability of these remarks to the *History of the French Revolution* now before us, will be understood by such of our readers as are familiar with Mr. Carlyle's contributions to our periodical literature. But it is one thing to put forth a few pages of quaintness, neologism and a whimsical coxcombry; and another, to carry such questionable qualities through three long volumes of misplaced persiflage and flippant pseudo-philosophy. To such a pitch of extravagance and absurdity are these peculiarities exalted in the volumes before us, that we should pass them over in silence, as altogether unworthy of criticism, if we did not know that the rage for German literature may bring such writing into fashion with the ardent and unreflecting; at least, in cases where the faults we deprecate are not pushed, as in the present instance, to a transcendental excess. Under that impression, however, we must take occasion to protest against all and sundry attempts to engraft the idiom of Germany into the king's English, or to transfuse the vague verbiage and affected sentimentality of a sect of Germans into our simple and intelligible philosophy. As yet, the barriers which separate prose from verse, in our language, are firm and unbroken; as yet, our morals and metaphysics are not quite Pindaric; and our narrative may be understood by any plain man who has learned to read. We are not habitually in the clouds, rapt and inspired; and we can read the great majority of our native authors without thinking of a strait waistcoat.

With respect to language, in particular, every nation must be permitted to 'speak for itself;' and the pedantry of engrafting on any language foreign modes of expression, is unmitigated folly. Words may successfully be naturalized when they express new ideas; but foreign grammatical idioms are ever ill-assorted patches, which disfigure, and cannot adorn, the cloth to which they are appended. The German compound substantive, for instance, will always appear ludicrous in our simple monosyllabic tongue; and when introduced into prose, is worse than ludicrous,—it is mischievous. It is often sufficiently difficult to detect a confusion of idea, even when that idea is expressed at full, in a sentence of many words; but a compound substantive is merely the sign of such a sentence, the sign of a sign; and its full and precise meaning can only be obtained by intense and laborious study. Such words are misleading and dangerous; and the proper raw material for the construction of *galimatias*. By their use, an author may fancy himself sublime, when he is only ridiculous; he may conceit himself original, when he is only uttering a commonplace truism in a new way.

This last remark brings us at once to the matter of the book. What need have we of a new *History of the French Revolution*? We have the contemporary history of that gigantic event in superabundance; and the time is not yet arrived for christening ourselves Posterity. We have looked carefully through these volumes; and, their peculiarity of style and the looseness of their reasoning apart, we have not found a fact in them that is not better told in Mignet, and twenty other unpretending historians. There is, moreover, in them the deadly *crambe repetita*[1] of referring the faults and the failures of the Revolution to the speculative opinions, or 'philosophism,' as the author calls it, of the eighteenth century. 'Faith,' he says, 'is gone out; scepticism is come in. Evil abounds and accumulates; no one has faith to withstand it, to amend it, to begin by amending himself.' Now, faith and scepticism had nothing directly to do with the affair; it was want, and misery, and oppression in the lower classes, utter corruption and incapacity in the higher, that

[1] Stale repetitions.

made the revolt. Or if the faith in a state religion must be admitted to be necessary to ensure a tame submission to wrong, the leaders in that infidelity were the Church dignitaries, who polluted their own altars. Society has subsisted under all modifications of popular belief; but the faith necessary to its prosperity, is a faith in truth, in honour, honesty, patriotism, and public virtue; and this had, in revolutionary France, been choked in the highest classes by the precepts and the examples of the hierarchy, while it lived and flamed in the confiding masses that trusted too implicitly to any knave who affected the garb of patriotism. Had the people possessed a little less faith in the virtues of the Church and State authorities, they would have prevented the revolution, by nipping its causes in the bud. Louis XIV., the Regent, and Louis XV., would never have existed such as they were; and events would have taken another direction.

The faults which we have been compelled thus to denounce, are the more provoking, as they are not unmingled with many finely conceived passages, and many just and vigorous reflections. The author's mind is so little accustomed to weigh carefully its own philosophy, and is so thoroughly inconsistent with itself, that the grossest absurdity in speculation does not prevent his perceiving and adopting truths in the closest relation of opposition to it. Thus, while he attributes evils innumerable to infidelity and philosophism, and openly preaches passive obedience, religious and political, he does not the less wisely sum up the material causes of the revolt, and put forth many just views of men and things, and of the multiplied errors committed both 'within and without the walls of Troy.' So, too, as to style, amidst an all-pervading absurdity of mannerism, there are passages of great power, and occasionally of splendid, though impure eloquence. Had the author been bred in another school, we should say that he might have written well and usefully; if we did not think that his admiration of that school must be in some way connected with defects in the native constitution of his mind. Having, however, expressed our unfavourable opinion thus freely, it becomes a duty to back our assertions by proof, and to give extracts as well of excellencies as of defects. In the following passage we have inconsistency of thought, vagueness of expression, and quaintness of style, all mixed together:—

Meanwhile it is singular how long the rotten will hold together, provided you do not handle it roughly. For whole generations it continues standing, 'with a ghastly affectation of life,' after all life and truth has fled out of it: so loath are men to quit their old ways; and, conquering indolence and inertia, venture on new. Great truly is the Actual; is the Thing that has rescued itself from bottom-less deeps of theory and possibility, and stands there as a definite indisputable Fact, whereby men do work and live, or once did so. Wisely shall men cleave to that, while it will endure; and quit it with regret, when it gives way under them. Rash enthusiast of Change, beware! Hast thou well considered all that Habit does in this life of ours; how all Knowledge and all Practice hang wondrous over infinite abysses of the Unknown, Impracticable; and our whole being is, an infinite abyss, *overarched* by Habit, as by a thin Earth-rind, laboriously built together?

If things naturally hold together when they are rotten, the inference is in favour and not against a voluntary effect of change, and then, what are 'realities rescued from the bottomless depths of theory,' but down-right jargon and no-meaning?

Next, look, we pray thee, reader, at the following on the siege of Gibraltar

Neither, while the War yet lasts, will Gibraltar surrender. Not, though Crillon, Nassau-Siegen, with the ablest projectors extant, are there; and Prince Condé and Prince d'Artois have hastened to hell. Wondrous leather-roofed Floating-batteries, set afloat by French-Spanish *Pacte de Famille*, give gallant summons: to which, nevertheless, Gibraltar answers Plutonically, with mere torrents of red-hot iron,—as if stone Calpe had become a throat of the Pit; and utters such a Doom's-blast of a *No*, as all men must credit.

There is an historical style with a vengeance! Pistol's 'he hears with ears' is plain English to it. The author's estimate of Necker is not high:—

[quotes 'We saw Turgot' to 'in Thelusson's Bank!' Vol. I, Bk. II, ch. v, 46–8]

The following sketch, with all its mannerisms, its affected present tense, and its absurdities, is lively and pregnant:—

[quotes 'For at present' to 'not such laughter' Vol. I, Bk. II, ch. vi, 48–50]

In the author's remarks on the Girondins there is much truth buried in mere jargon:—

[quotes 'In fact' to 'continually flow' Vol. III, Bk. III, ch. iv, 137–8]

Such then is the *History of the French Revolution*, as seen and declared by Mr. Carlyle; for in similar strains he jogs on till he arrives at Bonaparte's war on the Sections of Paris, with which he concludes;

summing up in the following vague, unsatisfactory, childish, 'most lame and impotent conclusion'—

[quotes 'The ship is' to 'not yet shot' Vol. III, Bk. VII, ch. vii & viii, 320–2]

Readers, have we made out our case?

6. John Stuart Mill, from an unsigned review, *London and Westminster Review*

July 1837, xxvii, 17–53

John Stuart Mill's (1806–73) review of *The French Revolution* is probably best known because of the familiar yet almost unbelievable account of the burned draft of the first volume and Mill's desire to make retribution. The story has often been told how Mill had taken the manuscript of the first volume home to read and had, in fact, suggested some criticisms, namely a plainer style. But accidentally the maid threw the manuscript into the fireplace. In part this review is a result of Mill's desire to make some amends since Carlyle had—in a very sensitive and incredibly understanding letter—rejected Mill's offer of £200 for compensation, as being too great a sum. Significant is the fact that Mill received an advance copy of *The French Revolution* in order, as he later explained to Robert Barclay Fox (16 April 1840), to accelerate the success of Carlyle's work—'a book so strange & incomprehensible to the greater part of the public, that whether it should succeed or fail seemed to depend upon the turn of a die —but I got the first work, blew the trumpet before it at its first coming out & by claiming for it the honour of the highest genius frightened the small fry of critics from pronouncing a hasty condemnation, got fair play for it & then its success was sure' (*The Earlier Letters of John Stuart Mill, 1812–48*, ed. Francis E. Mineka [Toronto, 1963], XIII, 427). See Introduction, p. 11.

For the earlier letter to Carlyle, recommending changes in style, see *The Letters of John Stuart Mill*, ed. Hugh S. R. Elliot (London, 1910), I, 100.

This is not so much a history, as an epic poem; and notwithstanding, or even in consequence of this, the truest of histories. It is the history of the French Revolution, and the poetry of it, both in one; and on the whole no work of greater genius, either historical or poetical, has been produced in this country for many years.

It is a book on which opinion will be for some time divided; nay, what talk there is about it, while it is still fresh, will probably be oftenest of a disparaging sort; as indeed is usually the case, both with men's works and with men themselves, of distinguished originality. For a thing which is unaccustomed, must be a very small thing indeed, if mankind can at once see into it and be sure that it is good: when, therefore, a considerable thing, which is also an unaccustomed one, appears, those who will hereafter approve, sit silent for a time, making up their minds; and those only to whom the mere novelty is a sufficient reason for disapproval, speak out. We need not fear to prophesy that the suffrages of a large class of the very best qualified judges will be given, even enthusiastically, in favor of the volumes before us; but we will not affect to deny that the sentiment of another large class of readers (among whom are many entitled to the most respectful attention on other subjects) will be far different; a class comprehending all who are repelled by quaintness of manner. For a style more peculiar than that of Mr. Carlyle, more unlike the jog-trot characterless uniformity which distinguishes the English style of this age of Periodicals, does not exist. Nor indeed can this style be wholly defended even by its admirers. Some of its peculiarities are mere mannerisms, arising from some casual association of ideas, or some habit accidentally picked up; and what is worse, many sterling thoughts are so disguised in phraseology borrowed from the spiritualist school of German poets and metaphysicians, as not only to obscure the meaning, but to raise, in the minds of most English readers, a not unnatural nor inexcusable presumption of there being no meaning at all. Nevertheless, the presumption fails in this instance (as in many other instances); there is not only a meaning, but generally a true, and even a profound meaning; and, although a few dicta about the 'mystery' and the 'infinitude' which are in the universe and in man, and such like topics, are repeated in varied phrases greatly too often for our taste, this must be borne with, proceeding, as one cannot but see, from feelings the most solemn, and the most deeply rooted which can lie in the heart of a human being. These transcendentalisms, and the accidental mannerisms excepted, we pronounce the style of this book to be not only good, but of surpassing excellence; excelled, in its kind, only by the great masters of epic poetry; and a most suitable and glorious vesture of a work which is itself, as we have said, an epic poem.

To any one who is perfectly satisfied with the best of the existing histories, it will be difficult to explain wherein the merit of Mr. Carlyle's

book consists. If there be a person who, in reading the histories of
Hume, Robertson, and Gibbon (works of extraordinary talent, and the
works of great writers) has never felt that this, after all, is not history—
and that the lives and deeds of his fellow-creatures must be placed
before him in quite another manner, if he is to know them, or feel
them to be real beings, who once were alive, beings of his own flesh
and blood, not mere shadows and dim abstractions; such a person, for
whom plausible talk *about* a thing does as well as an image of the thing
itself, feels no need of a book like Mr. Carlyle's; the want, which it is
peculiarly fitted to supply, does not yet consciously exist in his mind.
That such a want, however, is generally felt, may be inferred from the
vast number of historical plays and historical romances, which have
been written for no other purpose than to satisfy it. Mr. Carlyle has
been the first to show that all which is done for history by the best
historical play, by Schiller's *Wallenstein*, for example, or Vitet's
admirable trilogy,* may be done in a strictly true narrative, in which
every incident rests on irrefragable authority; may be done, by means
merely of an apt selection and a judicious grouping of authentic facts.

It has been noted as a point which distinguishes Shakspeare from
ordinary dramatists, that *their* characters are logical abstractions, his are
human beings: that their kings are nothing but kings, their lovers
nothing but lovers, their patriots, courtiers, villains, cowards, bullies,
are each of them that, and that alone; while his are real men and women,
who have these qualities, but have them in addition to their full share
of all other qualities (not incompatible), which are incident to human
nature. In Shakspeare, consequently, we feel we are in the world of
realities; we are among such beings as really could exist, as do exist, or
have existed, and as we can sympathise with; the faces we see around
us are human faces, and not mere rudiments of such, or exaggerations
of single features. This quality, so often pointed out as distinctive of
Shakspeare's plays, distinguishes Mr. Carlyle's history. Never before
did we take up a book calling itself by that name, a book treating of
past times, and professing to be true, and find ourselves actually among
human beings. We at once felt, that what had hitherto been to us mere
abstractions, had become realities; the 'forms of things unknown,'

* *Les Barricades*; *Les Etats de Blois*; and *La Mort de Henri III*, three prose plays or rather
series of dramatic scenes, illustrative of the League and the period of the religious wars in
France. A work scarcely heard of in this country, but which well deserves to be so. The
author, like so many of the rising literary notabilities of France (from M. Guizot downwards), is now unhappily withdrawn from literature, by place-hunting, and *doctrinaire*
politics.

which we fancied we knew, but knew their names merely, were, for the first time, with most startling effect, 'bodied forth' and 'turned into shape.' Other historians talk to us indeed of human beings; but what do they place before us? Not even stuffed figures of such, but rather their algebraical symbols; a few phrases, which present no image to the fancy, but by adding up the dictionary meanings of which, we may hunt out a few qualities, not enough to form even the merest outline of what the men *were*, or possibly *could* have been; furnishing little but a canvas, which, if we ourselves can paint, we may fill with almost any picture, and if we cannot, it will remain for ever blank.

Take, for example, Hume's history; certainly, in its own way, one of the most skilful specimens of narrative in modern literature, and with some pretensions also to philosophy. Does Hume throw his own mind into the mind of an Anglo-Saxon, or an Anglo-Norman? Does any reader feel, after having read Hume's history, that he can now picture to himself what human life was, among the Anglo-Saxons? how an Anglo-Saxon would have acted in any supposable case? what were his joys, his sorrows, his hopes and fears, his ideas and opinions on any of the great and small matters of human interest? Would not the sight, if it could be had, of a single table or pair of shoes made by an Anglo-Saxon, tell us, directly and by inference, more of his whole way of life, more of how men thought and acted among the Anglo-Saxons, than Hume, with all his narrative skill, has contrived to tell us from all his materials?

Or descending from the history of civilization, which in Hume's case may have been a subordinate object, to the history of political events: did any one ever gain from Hume's history anything like a picture of what may actually have been passing, in the minds, say, of Cavaliers or of Roundheads during the civil wars? Does any one feel that Hume has made him figure to himself with any precision what manner of men these were; how far they were like ourselves, how far different; what things they loved and hated, and what sort of conception they had formed of the things they loved and hated? And what kind of a notion can be framed of a period of history, unless we begin with that as a preliminary? Hampden, and Strafford, and Vane, and Cromwell;—do these, in Hume's pages, appear to us like beings who actually trod this earth, and spoke with a human voice, and stretched out human hands in fellowship with other human beings; or like the figures in a phantasmagoria, colorless, impalpable, gigantic, and in all varieties of attitude, but all resembling one another in being shadows? And suppose he had done his best to assist us in forming a conception of these leading characters: what would it have availed, unless he had placed us also in the atmosphere which they breathed? What wiser are we for looking out upon the world through Hampden's eyes, unless it be the same world which Hampden looked upon? and what help has Hume afforded us for this? Has he depicted to us, or to himself, what all the multitude of people were about, who surrounded Hampden; what the whole English nation were feeling, thinking, or doing? Does he show us what impressions from without were coming to Hampden—what materials and what instruments were given him to work with? If not, we are well qualified, truly, from Hume's information, to erect ourselves into judges of any part of Hampden's conduct!

Another very celebrated historian, we mean Gibbon—not a man of mere science and analysis, like Hume, but with some (though not the truest or profoundest) artistic feeling of the picturesque, and from whom, therefore, rather more might have been expected—has with much pains succeeded in producing a tolerably graphic picture of here and there a battle, a tumult, or an insurrection; his book is full of movement and costume, and would make a series of very pretty ballets at the Opera-house, and the ballets would give us fully as distinct an idea of the Roman empire, and how it declined and fell, as the book does. If we want that, we must look for it anywhere but in Gibbon. One touch of M. Guizot removes a portion of the veil which hid from us the recesses of private life under the Roman empire, lets in a ray of light which penetrates as far even as the domestic hearth of a subject of Rome, and shows us the government at work making that desolate; but no similar gleam of light from Gibbon's mind ever reaches the subject; *human life*, in the times he wrote about, is not what he concerned himself with.

On the other hand, there are probably many among our readers who are acquainted (though it is not included in Coleridge's admirable translation) with that extraordinary piece of dramatic writing, termed *Wallenstein's Camp*. One of the greatest of dramatists, the historian of the Thirty Years' War, aspired to do, in a dramatic fiction, what even *his* genius had not enabled him to do in his history—to delineate the great characters, and, above all, to embody the general spirit of that period. This is done with such life and reality through ten acts, that the reader feels when it is over as if all the prominent personages in the play were people whom he had known from his childhood; but the author did not trust to this alone: he prefixed to the ten acts, one introductory act, intended to exhibit, not the characters, but the element they moved in. It is there, in this preliminary piece, that Schiller really depicts the Thirty Years' War; without that, even the other ten acts, splendid as they are, would not have sufficiently realized it to our conception, nor would the Wallensteins and Piccolominis and Terzskys of that glorious tragedy have been themselves, comparatively speaking, intelligible.

What Schiller must have done, in his own mind, with respect to the age of Wallenstein, to enable him to frame that fictitious delineation of it, Mr. Carlyle, with a mind which looks still more penetratingly into the deeper meaning of things than Schiller's, has done with respect to the French Revolution. And he has communicated his picture of it with equal vividness; but he has done it by means of real, not fictitious incidents. And therefore is his book, as we said, at once the authentic History and the Poetry of the French Revolution.

It is indeed a favorite doctrine of Mr. Carlyle, and one which he has enforced with great strength of reason and eloquence in other places, that all poetry suitable to the present age must be of this kind: that poetry has not naturally anything to do with fiction, nor is fiction in these days even the most appropriate vehicle and vesture of it; that it should, and will, employ itself more and more, not in inventing un-realities, but in bringing out into even greater distinctness and im-pressiveness the poetic aspect of realities. For what is it, in the fictitious subjects which poets usually treat, that makes those subjects poetical? Surely not the dry, mechanical *facts* which compose the story; but the *feelings*—the high and solemn, the tender or mournful, even the gay and mirthful contemplations, which the story, or the manner of relating it, awakens in our minds. But would not all these thoughts and feelings be far more vividly aroused if the facts were *believed;* if the men, and all that is ascribed to them, had actually *been;* if the whole were no play of the imagination, but a truth? In every real fact, in which any of the great interests of human beings are implicated, there lie the materials of all poetry; there is, as Mr. Carlyle has said, the fifth act of a tragedy in every peasant's death-bed; the life of every heroic character is a heroic poem, were but the man of genius found, who could *so* write it! Not falsification of the reality is wanted, not the representation of it as being any thing that it is not; only a deeper understanding of what it is; the power to conceive, and to represent, not the mere outside surface and costume of the thing, nor yet the mere logical definition, and *caput mortuum* of it—but an image of the thing itself in the concrete, with all that is loveable, or hateable, or admirable, or pitiable, or sad, or solemn, or pathetic, in it, and in the things which are implied in it.

That is, the thing must be presented as it can exist only in the mind of a great poet: of one gifted with the two essential elements of the poetic character—creative imagination, which, from a chaos of scattered hints and confused testimonies, can summon up the Thing to appear before it as a completed whole: and that depth and breadth of feeling which makes all the images that are called up appear arrayed in whatever, of all that belongs to them, is naturally most affecting and impressive to the human soul.

We do not envy the person who can read Mr. Carlyle's three volumes, and not recognize in him both of these endowments in a most rare and remarkable degree. What is equally important to be said—he possesses in no less perfection that among the qualities necessary for his task, seemingly the most opposite to these, and in which the man of poetic imagination might be thought likeliest to be deficient; the quality of the historical day-drudge. A more pains-taking or accurate investigator of facts, and sifter of testimonies, never wielded the historical pen. We do not say this at random, but from a most extensive acquaintance with his materials, with his subjects, and with the mode in which it has been treated by others.

Thus endowed, and having a theme the most replete with every kind of human interest, epic, tragic, elegiac, even comic and farcical, which history affords, and so near to us withal, that the authentic details of it are still attainable; need it be said, that he has produced a work which deserves to be memorable? a work which, whatever may be its immediate reception, 'will not willingly be let die;' whose reputation will be a growing reputation, its influence rapidly felt, for it will be read by the writers; and perhaps every historical work of any note, which shall hereafter be written in this country, will be different from what it would have been if this book were not.

The book commences with the last illness of Louis XV which is introduced as follows:—

[quotes the first two paragraphs of Bk. I]

The loathsome deathbed of the royal debauchee becomes, under Mr. Carlyle's pencil, the central figure in an historical picture, including all France; bringing before us, as it were visibly, all the spiritual and physical elements which there existed, and made up the sum of what might be termed the influences of the age. In this picture, and in that of the 'Era of Hope' (as Mr. Carlyle calls the first years of Louis XVI) there is much that we would gladly quote. But on the whole we think these introductory chapters the least interesting part of the book; less distinguished by their intrinsic merit, and more so by all the peculiarities of manner which either are really defects, or appear so. These chapters will only have justice done them on a second reading: once familiarized with the author's characteristic turn of thought and expression, we find many passages full of meaning, which, to unprepared minds would convey a very small portion, if any, of the sense which they are not only intended, but are in themselves admirably calculated to express: for the finest expression is not always that which is the most readily apprehended. The real character of the book, however, begins only to display itself when the properly narrative portion commences. This, however, is more or less the case with all histories, though seldom to so conspicuous an extent.

The stream of the narrative acquires its full speed about the hundred and sixty-fifth page, and the beginning of the fourth book. The introductory rapid sketch of what may be called the coming-on of the Revolution, is then ended, and we are arrived at the calling together of the States General. The fourth book, first chapter, opens as follows:—

[quotes most of Vol. I, Bk. IV, ch. i, 115–20 and 'Up, then' to 'animated enough' ch. ii, 121–2]

Has the reader often seen the state of an agitated nation made thus present, thus palpable? How the thing paints itself in all its greatness— the men in all their littleness! and this is not done by reasoning about them, but by showing them. The deep pathos of the last paragraph, grand as it is, is but an average specimen; as, indeed, is the whole passage. In the remaining two volumes and a half there are scarcely five consecutive pages of inferior merit to those we have quoted. The few extracts we can venture to make, will be selected, not for peculiarity of merit, but either as forming wholes in themselves, or as depicting events or situations, with which the reader, it may be hoped, is familiar.* For the more he previously knew of the mere outline of the facts, the more

* It may be hoped; scarcely, we fear, expected. For considering the extraordinary dramatic interest of the story of the Revolution, however imperfectly told, it is really surprising how little, to English readers, even the outline of the facts is known. Mr. Carlyle's book is less fitted for those who know nothing about the subject, than for those who already know a little. We rejoice to see that a translation of Thiers is announced. As a mere piece of narrative, we know nothing in modern historical writing so nearly resembling the ancient models as Thiers' *History*: we hope he has met with a translator who can do him justice. Whoever has read Thiers first, will be the better fitted both to enjoy and to understand Carlyle.

he will admire the writer, whose pictorial and truly poetical genius enables him for the first time to fill up the outline.

Our last extract was an abridged sketch of the State of a Nation: the next shall be a copious narrative of a single event: the farfamed Siege of the Bastille. How much every such passage must suffer by being torn from the context, needs scarcely be said; and nothing that could be said, could, in this case, make it adequately felt. The history of the two previous days occupies twenty-two pages, rising from page to page in interest. We begin at noon on the fourteenth of July:—

[quotes 'All morning' to '*La Bastille est prise!*' Vol. I, Bk. V, ch. vi; large sections of Bk. VI, ch. iii, 226–9; all of Bk. VII, ch. iv; almost all of Bk. VII, ch. v; Bk. VII, ch. vi, 260–1; Bk. VII, ch. ix, 276; Bk. VII, ch. x, 277–81]

And what (it may be asked) are Mr. Carlyle's *opinions?*

If this means whether is he Tory, Whig, or Democrat; is he for things as they are, or for things *nearly* as they are; or is he one who thinks that subverting things as they are, and setting up Democracy is the main thing needful? we answer, he is none of all these. We should say that he has appropriated and made part of his own frame of thought, nearly all that is good in all these several modes of thinking. But it may be asked, what opinion has Mr. Carlyle formed of the French Revolution, as an event in universal history; and this question is entitled to an answer. It should be, however, premised, that in a history upon the plan of Mr. Carlyle's, the opinions of the writer are a matter of secondary importance. In reading an ordinary historian, we want to know his opinions, because it is mainly his *opinions* of things, and not the things themselves, that he sets before us; or if any features of the things themselves, those chiefly, which his *opinions* lead him to consider as of importance. Our readers have seen sufficient in the extracts we have made for them, to be satisfied that this is not Mr. Carlyle's method. Mr. Carlyle brings the thing before us in the *concrete*—clothed, not indeed in *all* its properties and circumstances, since these are infinite, but in as many of them as can be authentically ascertained and imaginatively realized: not prejudging that some of those properties and circumstances will prove instructive and others not, a prejudgment which is the fertile source of misrepresentation and one-sided historical delineation without end. Everyone knows, who has attended (for instance) to the sifting of a complicated case by a court of justice, that as long as our image of the fact remains in the slightest degree vague and hazy and undefined, we cannot tell but that what we do *not* yet distinctly see may be precisely that on which all turns. Mr. Carlyle, therefore, brings us *acquainted* with persons, things, and events, before he suggests to us what to think of them: nay, we see that this is the very process by which he arrives at his own thoughts; he paints the thing to himself—he constructs a picture of it in his own mind, and does not, till afterwards, make any logical propositions about it at all. This done, his logical propositions concerning the thing may be true, or may be false; the thing is there, and any reader may find a totally different set of propositions in it if he can; as he might in the reality, if *that* had been before him.

We, for our part, do not always agree in Mr. Carlyle's opinions either on things or on men. But we hold it to be impossible that any person should set before himself a perfectly true picture of a great historical event, as it actually happened, and yet that his judgment of it should be radically wrong. Differing partially from some of Mr. Carlyle's detached views, we hold his theory, or theorem, of the Revolution, to be the true theory; true as far as it goes, and wanting little of being as complete as any theory of so vast and complicated a phenomena can be. Nay, we do not think that any rational creature, now that the thing can be looked at calmly, now that we have nothing to hope or to fear from it, can form any second theory on the matter.

Mr. Carlyle's view of the Revolution is briefly this: That it was the breaking down of a great Imposture: which had not always been an Imposture, but had been becoming such for several centuries.

Two bodies—the King and Feudal Nobility, and the Clergy—held their exalted stations, and received the obedience and allegiance which were paid to them, by virtue solely of their affording *guidance* to the people: the one, directing and keeping order among them in their conjunct operations towards the pursuit of their most important temporal interests; the other, ministering to their spiritual teaching and culture. These are the grounds on which alone any government either claims obedience or finds it: for the obedience of twenty-five millions to a few hundred thousand never yet was yielded to avowed tyranny.

Now, this guidance, the original ground of all obedience, the privileged classes *did* for centuries give. The King and the Nobles led the people in war, and protected and judged them in peace, being the fittest persons to do so who then existed; and the Clergy did teach the best doctrine, did inculcate and impress upon the people the best rule of life then known, and did believe in the doctrine and in the rule of life which they taught, and manifested their belief by their actions and believed that, in teaching it, they were doing the highest thing appointed to mortals. So far as they did this, both spiritual and temporal rulers deserved and obtained reverence, and wil ing loyal obedience. But for centuries before the French Revolution, the sincerity which once was in this scheme of society was gradually dying out. The King and the Nobles afforded less and less of any real guidance, of any real protection to the people; and even ceased more and more to fancy that they afforded any. All the important business of society went on without them, nay, mostly in spite of their hindrance. The appointed spiritual teachers ceased to do their duty as teachers, ceased to practise what they taught, ceased to believe it, but alas, not to cant about it, or to receive wages as teachers of it. Thus the whole scheme of society and government in France became one great Lie: the places of honor and power being all occupied by persons whose sole claim to occupy them was the pretence of being what they were not, of doing what they did not, nor even for a single moment attempted to do. All other vileness and profligacy in the rulers of a country were but the inevitable consequences of this inherent vice in the condition of their existence. And, this continuing for centuries, the government growing ever more and more consciously a Lie, the people ever more and more perceiving it to be such, the day of reckoning, which comes for all impostures, came for this: the Good would no longer obey such rulers, the Bad ceased to be in awe of them, and both together rose up and hurled them into chaos.

Such is Mr. Carlyle's idea of what the Revolution was. And now, as to the melancholy turn it took, the horrors which accompanied it, the iron despotism by which it was forced to wind itself up, and the smallness of its positive results, compared with those which were hoped for by the sanguine in its commencement.

Mr. Carlyle's theory of these things is also a simple one: That the men, most of them good, and many of them among the most instructed of their generation, who attempted at that period to regenerate France, failed in what it was impossible that any one should succeed in: namely in attempting to found a government, to create a new order of society, a new set of institutions and habits, among a people having no convictions to base such order of things upon. That the existing government, habits, state of society, were bad, this the people were thoroughly convinced of, and rose up as one man, to declare, in every language of deed and word, that they would no more endure it. What was, was bad; but what was good, nobody had determined; no *opinion* on that subject had rooted itself in the people's minds; nor was there even any person, or any body of persons, deference for whom was rooted in their minds and whose word they were willing to take for all the rest. Suppose, then, that the twelve hundred members of the Constituent Assembly had even been gifted with perfect knowledge what arrangement of society was best:—how were they to get time to establish it? Or how were they to hold the people in obedience to it when established? A people with no preconceived reverence, either for it or for them; a people like slaves broke from their fetters—with all man's boundless desires let loose in indefinite expectation, and all the influences of habit and imagination which keep mankind patient under the denial of what they crave for, annihilated for the time, never to be restored but in some quite different shape?

Faith, doubtless, in representative institutions, there was, and of the firmest kind; but unhappily this was not enough: for all that representative institutions themselves can do, is to give practical effect to the faith of the people in something else. What is a representative constitution? Simply a set of contrivances for ascertaining the convictions of the people; for enabling them to declare what men they have faith in; or, failing such, what things the majority of them will insist upon having done to them—by what *rule* they are willing to be governed. But what if the majority have not faith in any men, nor know even in the smallest degree what things they wish to have done, in what manner they would be governed? This was the condition of the French people. To have made it otherwise was possible, but required time; and time, unhappily, in a Revolution, is not given. A great man, indeed, may do it, by inspiring at least faith in himself, which may last till the tree he has planted has taken root, and can stand alone; such apparently was Solon,★ and such perhaps, had he lived, might have been Mirabeau: nay, in the absence of other greatness, even a great quack may temporarily do it; as Napoleon, himself a mixture of great man and great quack, did in some measure exemplify. Revolutions sweep much away, but if any Revolution since the beginning of the world ever founded anything, towards which the minds of the people had not been growing for generations previous, it has been founded by some individual man.

Much more must be added to what has now been said, to make the statement of Mr. Carlyle's opinions on the French Revolution anything

★ A more definite, as well as, we think, a juster idea of this great man, than we have met with elsewhere, may be found in Mr. Bulwer's *Athens*; a book which, if it be completed as it has been begun, will, by its effect in correcting prejudices which have been most sedulously fostered, and diffusing true notions on one of the most interesting of all parts of the world's history, entitle its author to no humble meed of praise.

like complete; nor shall we any further set forth, either such of those opinions as we agree in, or those, far less numerous, from which we disagree. Nevertheless, we will not leave the subject without pointing out what appears to us to be the most prominent defect in our author's general mode of thinking. His own method being that of the artist, not of the man of science—working as he does by figuring things to himself as wholes, not dissecting them into their parts—he appears, though perhaps it is but appearance, to entertain something like a contempt for the opposite method; and to go as much too far in his distrust of analysis and generalization, as others (the Constitutional party, for instance, in the French Revolution) went too far in their reliance upon it.

Doubtless, in the infinite complexities of human affairs, any general theorem which a wise man will form concerning them, must be regarded as a mere approximation to truth; an approximation obtained by striking an average of many cases, and consequently not exactly fitting any one case. No wise man, therefore, will stand upon his theorem only—neglecting to look into the specialities of the case in hand, and see what features *that* may present which may take it out of any theorem, or bring it within the compass of more theorems than one. But the far greater number of people—when they have got a formula by rote, when they can bring the matter in hand within some maxim 'in that case made and provided' by the traditions of the vulgar, by the doctrines of their sect or school, or by some generalization of their own—do not think it necessary to let their mind's eye rest upon the thing itself at all; but deliberate and act, not upon knowledge of the thing, but upon a hearsay of it; being (to use a frequent illustration of our author) provided with spectacles, they fancy it not needful to use their eyes. It should be understood that general principles are not intended to dispense with thinking and examining, but to help us to think and examine. When the object itself is out of our reach, and we cannot examine into it, we must follow general principles, because, by doing so, we are not so likely to go wrong, and almost certain not to go far wrong, as if we floated on the boundless ocean of mere conjecture; but when we are not driven to guess, when we have means and appliances for observing, general principles are nothing more or other than helps towards a better use of those means and appliances.

Thus far we and Mr. Carlyle travel harmoniously together; but here we apparently diverge. For, having admitted that general principles (or *formulæ*, as our author calls them, after old Mirabeau, the crabbed *ami des hommes*) are helps to observation, not substitutes for it, we must add, that they are *necessary* helps, and that without general principles no one ever observed a particular case to any purpose. For, except by general principles, how do we bring the light of past experience to bear upon the new case? The essence of past experience lies embodied in those logical, abstract propositions, which our author makes so light of:—there, and no where else. From them we learn what has ordinarily been found true, or even recall what we ourselves have found true, in innumerable unnamed and unremembered cases, more or less resembling the present. We are hence taught, at the least, what we shall *probably* find true in the present case; and although this, which is only a probability, may be lazily acquiesced in and acted upon without further inquiry as a certainty, the risk even so is infinitely less than if we began without a theory, or even a probable hypothesis. Granting that all the facts of the particular instance are within the reach of observation, how difficult is the work of observing, how almost impossible that of disentangling a complicated case, if, when we begin, no one view of it appears to us more probable than another. Without a hypothesis to commence with, we do not even know what end to begin at, what points to inquire into. Nearly every thing that has ever been ascertained by scientific observers, was brought to light in the attempt to test and verify some theory. To start from some theory, but not to see the object through the theory; to bring light with us, but also to receive other light from whencesoever it comes; such is the part of the philosopher, of the true practical *seer* or person of insight.

Connected with the tendency which we fancy we perceive in our author, to undervalue general principles, is another tendency which we think is perceptible in him, to set too low a value on what constitutions and forms of governments can do. Be it admitted once for all, that no form of government will enable you, as our author has elsewhere said, 'given a world of rogues, to produce an honesty by their united action;' nor when a people are wholly without faith either in man or creed, has any representative constitution a charm to render them governable well, or even governable at all. On the other hand, Mr. Carlyle must no less admit, that when a nation *has* faith in any man, or any set of principles, representative institutions furnish the only regular and peaceable mode in which that faith can quietly declare itself, and those men, or those principles, obtain the predominance. It is surely no trifling matter to have a legalized means whereby the guidance will always be in the hands of the Acknowledged Wisest, who, if not always the really wisest, are at least those whose wisdom, such as it may be, is the most available for the purpose. Doubtless it is the natural law of representative governments that the power is shared, in varying proportions, between the really skilfullest and the skilfullest quacks; with a tendency, in easy times, towards the preponderance of the quacks, in the 'times which try men's souls,' towards that of the true men. Improvements enough may be expected as mankind improve, but that the best and wisest shall always be accounted such, *that* we need not expect; because the quack can always steal, and vend for his own profit, as much of the good ware as is marketable. But is not all this to the full as likely to happen in every other kind of government as in a representative one? with these differences in favor of representative government, which will be found perhaps to be its only real and universal pre-eminence: That it alone is government by consent—government by mutual compromise and compact; while all others are, in one form or another, governments by constraint: That it alone proceeds by quiet muster of opposing strengths, when that which is really weakest sees itself to be such, and peaceably gives away; a benefit never yet realized but in countries inured to a representative government; elsewhere nothing but actual blows can show who is strongest, and every great dissension of opinion must break out into a civil war.

We have thus briefly touched upon the two principal points on which we take exception, not so much to any opinion of the author, as to the tone of sentiment which runs through the book; a tone of sentiment which otherwise, for justness and nobleness, stands almost unrivalled in the writings of our time. A deep catholic sympathy with human nature, with all natural human feelings, looks out from every page of these volumes; justice administered in love, to all kind of human beings, bad and good; the most earnest exalted feeling of moral distinctions, with the most generous allowances for whatever partial confounding of these distinctions, either natural weakness or perverse circumstances can excuse. No greatness, no strength, no goodness or lovingness, passes unrecognized or unhonored by him. All the sublimity of 'the simultaneous death-defiance of twenty-five millions' speaks itself forth in his pages—not the less impressively, because the unspeakable folly and incoherency, which always in real life are not one step from, but actually pervade, the sublimities of so large a body (and did so most notably in this instance) are no less perceptible to his keen sense of the ludicrous. We presume it is this which has caused the book to be accused, even in print, of 'flippancy,' a term which appears to us singularly misapplied. For is not this mixture and confused entanglement of the great and the contemptible, precisely what we meet with in nature? and would not a history, which did not make us not only see this, but feel it, be deceptive; and give an impression which would be the more false, the greater the general vivacity and vigor of the delineation? And indeed the capacity to see and feel what is loveable, admirable, in a thing, and what is laughable in it, at the same time, constitutes humor; the quality to which we owe a Falstaff, a Parson Adams, an Uncle Toby, and Mause Headriggs and Barons of Bradwardine without end. You meet in this book with passages of grave drollery (drollery unsought for, arising from the simple statement of facts, and a true natural feeling of them) not inferior to the best in Mr. Peacock's novels; and immediately or soon after comes a soft note as of dirge music, or solemn choral song of old Greek tragedy, which makes the heart too full for endurance, and forces you to close the book and rest for a while.

Again, there are aphorisms which deserve to live for ever; characters drawn with a few touches, and indicating a very remarkable insight into many of the obscurest regions of human nature; much genuine philosophy, disguised though it often be in a poetico-metaphysical vesture of a most questionable kind; and, in short, new and singular but not therefore absurd or unpractical views taken of many important things. A most original book; original not least in its complete sincerity, its disregard of the merely conventional: every idea and sentiment is given out exactly as it is thought and felt, fresh from the soul of the writer, and in such language (conformable to precedent or not) as is most capable of representing it in the form in which it exists there. And hence the critics have begun to call the style 'affected;' a term which conventional people, whether in literature or society, invariably bestow upon the unreservedly natural.*

In truth, every book which is eminently original, either in matter or

---

* A curious instance of this occurred lately. Mr. D'Israeli, a writer of considerable literary daring, tried in his novel, *Henrietta Temple*, one of the boldest experiments he had yet ventured upon, that of making his lovers and his other characters speak naturally the language of real talk, not dressed up talk; such language as all persons talk who are not in the presence of an audience. A questionable experiment—allowable as an experiment, but scarcely otherwise; for the reader does not want pure nature, but nature idealised; nobody wants the verbiage, the repetitions and slovenlinesses, of real conversation, but only the substance of what is interesting in such conversation, divested of these. There was much which might have been said by critics against Mr. D'Israeli's experiment; but what did they say? 'Affectation!'—that was their cry. Natural conversation in print looked so unnatural to men of artificiality; it was so unlike all their experience—of books!

style, has a hard battle to fight before it can obtain even pardon for its originality, much less applause. Well, therefore, may this be the case when a book is original, not in matter only or in style only, but in both; and, moreover, written in prose, with a fervor and exaltation of feeling which is only tolerated in verse, if even there. And when we consider that Wordsworth, Coleridge, and others of their time, whose deviation from the beaten track was but a stone's throw compared with Mr. Carlyle, were ignominiously hooted out of court by the wise tribunals which in those days dispensed justice in such matters, and had to wait for a second generation before the sentence could be reversed, and their names placed among the great names of our literature, we might well imagine that the same or a worse fate awaits Mr. Carlyle; did we not believe that those very writers, aided by circumstances, have made straight the way for Mr. Carlyle and for much else. This very pheno-menon, of the different estimation of Wordsworth and Coleridge, now, and thirty years ago, is among the indications of one of the most conspicuous new elements which have sprung up in the European mind during those years; an insatiable demand for realities, come of conven-tionalities and formalities what may; of which desire the literary phasis is, a large tolerance for every feeling which is natural and not got-up, for every picture taken from the life and not from other pictures, however it may clash with traditionary notions of elegance or congruity. The book before us needs to be read with this catholic spirit; if we read it captiously, we shall never have done finding fault. But no true poet, writing sincerely and following the promptings of his own genius, can fail to be contemptible to any who desire to find him so; and if even Milton's 'Areopagitica,' of which now, it would seem, no one dares speak with only moderate praise, were now first to issue from the press, it would be turned from with contempt by every one who will think or speak disparagingly of this work of Mr. Carlyle. . . .

7. William Makepeace Thackeray, an unsigned review, *The Times*

3 August 1837, 6

William Makepeace Thackeray (1811–63), Carlyle's friend throughout the years, pleased him greatly with this review. When Thackeray died suddenly on 12 December 1863, Carlyle wrote to Richard Monckton Milnes: 'He had many fine qualities, no guile or malice against any mortal; a big mass of soul, but not strong in proportion; a beautiful vein of genius lay struggling in him. Nobody in our day wrote, I should say, with such perfection of style. Poor Thackeray!—adieu! adieu!' (Quoted in D. A. Wilson, *Carlyle*, V, 532.) See Introduction, p. 11.

Since the appearance of this work, within the last two months, it has raised among the critics and the reading public a strange storm of applause and discontent. To hear one party you would fancy that the author was but a dull madman, indulging in wild vagaries of language and dispensing with common sense and reason, while, according to another, his opinions are little short of inspiration, and his eloquence unbounded as his genius. We confess, that in reading the first few pages we were not a little inclined to adopt the former opinion, and yet, after perusing the whole of this extraordinary work, we can allow, almost to their fullest extent, the high qualities with which Mr. Carlyle's idolators endow him.

But never did a book sin so grievously from outward appearance, or a man's style so mar his subject and dim his genius. It is stiff, short, and rugged, it abounds with Germanisms and Latinisms, strange epithets, and choking double words, astonishing to the admirers of simple Addisonian English, to those who love history as it gracefully runs in Hume, or struts pompously in Gibbon—no such style is Mr. Carlyle's. A man, at the first onset, must take breath at the end of a sentence, or, worse still, go to sleep in the midst of it. But those hardships become lighter as the traveller grows accustomed to the road, and he speedily learns to admire and sympathize; just as he would admire a Gothic cathedral in spite of the quaint carvings and hideous images on door and buttress.

There are, however, a happy few of Mr. Carlyle's critics and readers to whom these very obscurities and mysticisms of style are welcome and almost intelligible; the initiated in metaphysics, the sages who have passed the veil of Kantian philosophy, and discovered that the 'critique of pure reason' is really that which it purports to be, and not the critique of pure nonsense, as it seems to worldly men: to these the present book has charms unknown to us, who can merely receive it as a history of a stirring time, and a skilful record of men's worldly thoughts and doings. Even through these dim spectacles a man may read and profit much from Mr. Carlyle's volumes.

He is not a party historian like Scott, who could not, in his benevolent respect for rank and royalty, see duly the faults of either: he is as impartial as Thiers, but with a far loftier and nobler impartiality.

No man can have read the admirable history of the French ex-minister who has not been struck with this equal justice which he bestows on all the parties and heroes of his book. He has completely mastered the active part of the history: he has no more partiality for court than for regicide—scarcely a movement of intriguing kind or republican which is unknown to him or undescribed. He sees with equal eyes Madame Rolan or Marie Antoinette—bullying Brunswick on the frontier, or Marat at his butcher's work or in his cellar—he metes to each of them justice, and no more, finding good even in butcher Marat or bullying Brunswick, and recording what he finds. What a pity that one gains such a contempt for the author of all this cleverness! Only a rogue could be so impartial, for Thiers but views this awful series of circumstances in their very meanest and basest light, like a petty, clever statesman as he is, watching with wonderful accuracy all the moves of the great game, but looking for no more, never drawing a single moral from it, or seeking to tell aught beyond it.

Mr. Carlyle, as we have said, is as impartial as the illustrious Academician and Minister; but with what different eyes he looks upon the men and the doings of this strange time! To the one the whole story is but a bustling for places—a list of battles and intrigues—of kings and governments rising and falling; to the other, the little actors of this great drama are striving but towards a great end and moral. It is better to view it loftily from afar, like our mystic poetic Mr. Carlyle, than too nearly with sharp-sighted and prosaic Thiers. Thiers is the *valet de chambre* of this history, he is too familiar with its dishabille and off-scouring: it can never be a hero to him.

It is difficult to convey to the reader a fair notion of Mr. Carlyle's powers or his philosophy, for the reader has not grown familiar with the strange style of this book, and may laugh perhaps at the grotesque-ness of his teacher: in this some honest critics of the present day have preceded him, who have formed their awful judgments after scanning half a dozen lines, and damned poor Mr. Carlyle's because they chanced to be lazy. Here, at hazard, however, we fall upon the story of the Bastille capture; the people are thundering at the gates, but Delaunay will receive no terms, raises his drawbridge, and gives fire. Now, cries Mr. Carlyle with an uncouth Orson-like shout:

[quotes 'Bursts forth Insurrection' to 'Bastille is still to take' Vol. I, Bk. V, ch. vi, 190–1]

Did 'Savage Rosa' ever 'dash' a more spirited battle sketch? The two principal figures of the pieces, placed in skilful relief, the raging multitude and sombre fortress admirably laid down! In the midst of this writing and wrestling 'the line too labours (Mr. Carlyle's line labours perhaps too often), and the words move slow.' The whole story of the fall of the fortress and its defenders is told in a style similarly picturesque and real.

[quotes 'The poor Invalides' to *'La Bastille est prise!'* Vol. I, Bk. V, ch. vi, 195]

This is prose run mad—no doubt of it—according to our notions of the sober gait and avocations of homely prose; but is there not method in it, and could sober prose have described the incident in briefer words, more emphatically, or more sensibly? And this passage, which succeeds the picture of storm and slaughter, opens (grotesque though it be), not in prose, but in noble poetry, the author describes the rest of France during the acting of this Paris tragedy—and by this peaceful image admirably heightens the gloom and storm of his first description:—

O, evening sun of July, now at this hour, thy beams fall slant on reapers amid peaceful woody fields; on old women spinning in cottages; on ships far out in the silent main; on balls at the Orangerie of Versailles, where high-rouged Dames are even now dancing with double-jacketted Hussar-officers, and also on this roaring bell-porch of a Hôtel-de-Ville! Babel Tower, with the confusion of tongues, were not Bedlam added with the conflagration of thoughts, was no type of it. One forest of distracted steel bristles in front of an electoral committee, points itself in horrid radii against this and the otheraccused breast. It was the Titans warring with Olympus, and they, scarcely crediting it, have conquered!

The reader will smile at the double-jackets and rouge, which never would be allowed entrance into a polite modern epic, but, familiar though they be, they complete the picture, and give it reality, that gloomy rough Rembrandt-kind of reality which is Mr. Carlyle's style of historic painting.

In this same style Mr. Carlyle dashes off the portraits of his various characters as they rise in the course of the history. Take, for instance, this grotesque portrait of vapouring Tonneau Mirabeau, his life and death; it follows a solemn, almost awful picture of the demise of his great brother:—

[quotes 'Here, then' to 'so die the Mirabeaus' Vol. II, Bk. III, ch. vii, 147]

Mr. Carlyle gives this passage to 'a biographer,' but he himself must be the author of this History of a Tub; the grim humour and style belong only to him. In a graver strain he speaks of Gabriel:—

[quotes 'New Mirabeaus' to 'far from help' Vol. II, Bk. III, ch. vii, 147–8]

. . . The reader, we think, will not fail to observe the real beauty which lurks among all these odd words and twisted sentences, living, as it were, in spite of the weeds; but we repeat, that no mere extracts can do justice to the book; it requires time and study. A first acquaintance with it is very unprepossessing, only familiarity knows its great merits, and values it accordingly.

We would gladly extract a complete chapter or episode from the work—the flight to Varennes, for instance, the huge coach bearing away the sleepy, dawdling, milk-sop royalty of France; fiery Bouillé spreading abroad his scouts and Hussars, 'his electric thunder-chain of military out-posts,' as Mr. Carlyle calls them with one of his great similes. Paris in tremendous commotion, the country up and armed, to prevent the King's egress, the chance of escape glimmering bright until the last moment, and only extinguished by bewildered Louis himself, too pious and too out-of-breath, too hungry and sleepy, to make one charge at the head of those gallant dragoons—one single blow to win crown and kingdom and liberty again! We never read this hundred-times told tale with such a breathless interest as Mr. Carlyle has managed to instil into it. The whole of the sad story is equally touching and vivid, from the mean ignominious return down to the fatal 10th of August, when the sections beleaguered the King's palace, and King Louis, with arms, artillery, and 2,000 true and gallant men, flung open the Tuileries gates and said 'Marchons! marchons!' whither? Not with vive le Roi, and roaring guns, and bright bayonets, sheer through the rabble who barred the gate, swift through the broad Champs Elysées, and the near barrier,—not to conquer or fall like a King and gentleman, but to the reporters' box in the National Assembly, to be cooped and fattened until killing time; to die trussed and tranquil like a fat capon. What a son for St. Louis! What a husband for brave Antoinette!

Let us, however, follow Mr. Carlyle to the last volume, and passing over the time, when, in Danton's awful image, 'coalized Kings made war upon France, and France, as a gage of battle, flung the head of a King at their feet,' quote two of the last scenes of that awful tragedy, the deaths of bold Danton and 'seagreen' Robespierre, as Carlyle delights to call him.

[quotes 'On the night' to 'and to us' and 'Danton carried' to 'memory of men' Vol. III, Bk. VI, ch. ii, 255–8 and 259–60]

This noble passage requires no comment, nor does that in which the poor wretched Robespierre shrieks his last shriek, and dies his pitiful and cowardly death. Tallien has drawn his theatrical dagger, and made his speech, trembling Robespierre has fled to the Hôtel-de-Ville, and Henriot, of the National Guard, clatters through the city, summoning the sections to the aid of the people's friend.

[quotes 'About three in the morning' to 'and to us' Vol. III, Bk. VI, ch. vii, 283–6]

The reader will see in the above extracts most of the faults and a few of the merits, of this book. He need not be told that it is written in an eccentric prose, here and there disfigured by grotesque conceits and images; but for all this, it betrays most extraordinary powers—learning, observation, and humour. Above all, it has no CANT. It teems with sound, hearty, philosophy (besides certain transcendentalisms which we do not pretend to understand), it possesses genius, if any book ever did. It wanted no more for keen critics to crie fie upon it! Clever critics who have such an eye for genius, that when Mr. Bulwer published his forgotten book concerning Athens, they discovered that no historian was like to him; that he, on his Athenian hobby, had quite out-trotted stately Mr. Gibbon; and with the same creditable unanimity they cried down Mr. Carlyle's history, opening upon it a hundred little piddling sluices of small wit, destined to wash the book sheer away; and lo! the book remains, it is only the poor wit which has run dry.

We need scarcely recommend this book and its timely appearance, now that some of the questions solved in it seem almost likely to be battled over again. The hottest Radical in England may learn by it that there is something more necessary for him even than his mad liberty—the authority, namely, by which he retains his head on his shoulders and his money in his pocket, which privileges that by-word 'liberty' if often unable to secure for him. It teaches (by as strong examples as ever taught anything) to rulers and to ruled alike moderation, and yet there are many who would react the same dire tragedy, and repeat the experiment tried in France so fatally. 'No Peers—no Bishops—no property qualification—no restriction of suffrage.' Mr. Leader bellows it out at Westminster, and Mr. Roebuck croaks it at Bath. Pert quacks at public meetings joke about hereditary legislators, journalists gibe at them, and moody starving labourers, who do not know how to jest, but can hate lustily, are told to curse crowns and coronets as the origin of their woes and their poverty, and so did the clever French spouters and journalists gibe at royalty until royalty fell poisoned under their satire; and so did the screaming hungry French mob curse royalty until they over-threw it: and to what end? To bring tyranny and leave starvation, battering down bastilles to erect guillotines, and murdering kings to set up emperors in their stead.

We do not say that in our own country similar excesses are to be expected or feared; the cause of complaint has never been so great, the wrong has never been so crying on the part of the rulers, as to bring down such fearful retaliation from the governed. Mr. Roebuck is not Robespierre, and Mr. Attwood, with his threatened legion of fiery Marseillois, is at best but a Brummagem Barbaroux. But men alter with circumstances; six months before the kingly *déchéance* the bitter and bilious advocate of Arras spake with tears in his eyes about good King Louis, and the sweets and merits of constitutional monarchy and hereditary representation: and so he spoke, until his own turn came, and his own delectable guillotining system had its hour. God forbid that we should pursue the simile with regard to Mr. Roebuck so far as this; God forbid, too, that he ever should have the trial.

True; but we have no right, it is said, to compare the Republicanism of England with that of France, no right to suppose that such crimes would be perpetrated in a country so enlightened as ours. Why is there peace and liberty and a republic in America? No guillotining, no ruthless Yankee tribunes retaliating for bygone tyranny by double oppression? Surely the reason is obvious—because there was no hunger in America; because there were easier ways of livelihood than those offered by ambition. Banish Queen, and Bishops, and Lords, seize the lands, open the ports, or shut them, (according to the fancy of your trades' unions and democratic clubs, who have each their freaks and hobbies,) and are you a whit richer in a month, are your poor Spitalfields men vending their silks, or your poor Irishmen reaping their harvests at home? Strong interest keeps Americans quiet, not Government; here there is always a party which is interested in rebellion. People America like England, and the poor weak rickety republic is jostled to death in the crowd. Give us this republic to-morrow, and it would share no better fate; have not all of us the power, and many of us the interest, to destroy it?

8. Herman Merivale, from an unsigned review, *Edinburgh Review*

July 1840, lxxi, 411–45

Herman Merivale (1806–74) was elected to a professorship of political economy at Oxford and delivered several important lectures which led to his appointment as Under-Secretary of State for the Colonies. Later he took the permanent position as Under-Secretary for India under Sir James Stephen. A writer of great energies, Merivale contributed over sixty articles to such leading periodicals as the *Edinburgh Review*, the *Foreign Quarterly Review*, and the *Quarterly Review*. See No. 38 and Introduction, p. 11.

Few writers of the present time have risen more rapidly into popularity than Mr. Carlyle, after labouring through so long a period of comparative neglect. Whatever judgment critics may be pleased to pass on him, it is certain that his works have attracted of late no common share of attention. His little school of sectaries has expanded into a tolerably wide circle of admirers. His eccentricity of style has become the parent of still greater eccentricities in others, with less genius to recommend them; and his mannerism has already infected, to a certain extent, the fugitive literature of the day. Clever young writers delight in affecting his tone of quaint irony, and indulgent superiority; and many a scribe, whose thoughts have about as much originality as the almanac for the year, fancies that he gives them an air of novelty and impressiveness by clothing them in a barbarous garb, for the fashion of which their prototype must hold himself to a certain extent responsible.

It must be said, in justice to Mr. Carlyle, that this unusual success has been bravely achieved by dint of personal energy and merit, and against a host of difficulties. Self-educated, we believe, and nurtured on the very quintessence of German transcendentalism, with little of the ordinary British discipline to counteract it, he could only clothe his own thoughts in the same uncouth foreign livery in which the parent thoughts had been clothed when first his mind received and appropriated them. He seemed a solitary or rare example of one who, in his native country, had unlearned his native language; and was as much a stranger among us as Jean Paul or Ludwig Tieck might have been, if suddenly transferred from their own metaphysical cloud-land to our matter-of-fact atmosphere. His difficulty of expressing his meaning otherwise was palpable and natural; that he was altogether free from affectation, we cannot, in conscience, believe: but the manner had grown very closely to the substance. Accordingly, there were numbers of readers to whom, for a long time, neither wit, nor sense, nor philosophy, could make his lucubrations even tolerable—who were forced to throw them aside almost unattempted, with a pettish *si non vis intelligi*.[1] That many have greatly altered both their estimate of, and feeling toward him, we attribute partly to the gradual change in himself; for extended French and English reading have made a different writer of him; and though still dark and rugged enough at times, he is 'daylight and champaign' compared with his former self. But the principal cause is, that he has forced himself, style and all, on public attention. His peculiar vein of philosophy, his mode of judging of things and men with an earnest irony, his tone of thought, sometimes original and always independent, have compelled even those whom his oddities of manner most repulsed to tolerate him; while, to many, they have made the oddities themselves palatable: so that, at the present day, we doubt whether it is the matter or the manner which tells most on his followers and admirers. For our own part, our dislike to his bastard English is unconquered and unconquerable; and this, together with the endless scraps of Schiller, and Goethe, and Richter, which are interwoven (without the trouble of any thing deserving the name of a translation) in his composition—the constant repetition of the same figures and the same jokes—the constant harping upon the same monotonous strain of thought—have made the task of going honestly through these three volumes rather a heavy one;—notwithstanding all the interest of detached scenes, and the vigour of thought and barbarian eloquence of language which often characterise the accompanying reflections. Indeed, we suspect that his firmest adherents are apt rather to dip into him than peruse him; he writes for the desultory readers and thinkers of the day; and has served his apprenticeship, and acquired his peculiarities, in the school of journal and essay writing. And this is one among several reasons which cause us to prefer, as a matter of taste, the biographical sketches which are scattered

[1] If you do not wish to be understood.

through his recently published *Miscellanies*, to these continuous volumes. But though they are written rather in a fragmentary style, and made up of detached scenes and *points*, after the fashion into which writers so educated naturally fall; yet there is a sort of dramatic unity of purpose running through the whole, and so peculiar as amply to repay investigation.

There is one mode of discussing the French Revolution which is very satisfactory from its simplicity, and from the little trouble of thought and discrimination which it gives to the historian adopting it. It is by applying to the consideration of it the ordinary rules of morality, as they are inculcated in national schools, and declared in assize sermons, and judicial charges. Resistance to established authority is a crime—interfering with our neighbour's property a crime—taking his life a crime. Consequently, the whole French Revolution was a great crime; all who engaged in it were criminals—some more, undoubtedly, and some less; and according as the individual writer is more or less atrabilious in his temperament, he will be more profuse in excuses for the weaker sinner, or in denunciations of the stronger. But that which points the moral of his narrative, and gives at the same time zest to his labours, is the tracing out the action of the presiding Nemesis of that great drama;—the retribution, national and private, which visited each separate sin on the people at large, and which followed each individual actor into the very recesses of his own home or heart. This is what may be called the orthodox method of writing the history of the French Revolution; it was once exclusively popular in England, and is still not without followers; but, notwithstanding its obvious completeness and rotundity, it does not seem altogether to satisfy the present generation of inquirers.

Another theory, which has also met with no small success, was that which dealt wholly in abstractions—arranged royalty, feudalism, democracy, and so forth, in wellbalanced antitheses—and elevated the nature and importance of the final cause of those events, until the moral character of separate acts and actors sank into insignificance. That final cause, in the view of such writers, was the regeneration of France. All who co-operated in that work must answer to their judge, if there be a judge, for their personal thoughts and deeds: in the eyes of the historian, who can look to results only, they stand justified. Given the proposition, that it was necessary the Revolution should succeed—and given also, that a September massacre, and a regicide, and a reign of terror, were necessary to its success; then a Danton, a Robespierre, and a Fouquier-

Tinville were necessary parts of the machinery—like the wheels and cylinders of a cotton-mill, by which the raw material must be crushed, and pulled, and divided, before the finished fabric can be produced. To quarrel with them as moral agents is therefore simply a loss of time—unphilosophical, absurd, and pedantic. This theory was also very much in favour a few years back: it is that on which the popular histories of Mignet and Thiers are mainly constructed; and its peculiar language might be traced, during the years of the Restoration, among many English writers also.

But its fashion has passed away. It is out of favour, because the democrats of France having, by their own energy, a second time revolutionized the state, and found France almost as far from regeneration as ever, are less satisfied than heretofore with the all-sufficiency of their theories. But there is another and a more general cause for this. Men have become within these few years more searching in their inquiries; their views are not so much bounded by mere politics as heretofore, (which regard men in masses only;) they are more accustomed to penetrate below the surface of those conventional ethics on which most social systems are very insecurely founded. It is the struggle of these new speculations for utterance, still confusedly mingled with the relics of the abstract political systems of which we have not yet got rid, which at once produces such writers as Mr. Carlyle, and prepares the triumph which he has achieved over prejudice, distrust, and misunderstanding. His is the philosophy of transition, of doubt, and of sanguine expectation; it rejects old 'formulas' as barren; but instead of resting content in scepticism, it endeavours to lead the mind back to certain elementary principles, and to direct it in anticipation to future discoveries, as yet barely descried or dimly imagined; visionary lands of promise perhaps, but attractive as the fabled Eldorado to youthful enterprise. To him, the mainspring of all speculation concerning the French Revolution, lies in the thought of the five-and-twenty millions of ignorant and poverty-stricken serfs who lay in bondage at its commencement, whom it will need many revolutions, or changes as great as revolutions, wholly to emancipate.

[quotes 'Masses, indeed' to 'for a time' Vol. I, Bk. II, ch. ii, pp. 33–34]

This is the great hoard of volcanic matter, whose eruptions, when the time for them is arrived, shake, and will continue to shake the states of the world. The French Revolution was but one expression of the inarticulate and confused cry of these millions struggling—not for paper rights of men, not for constitutions *à la Sieyes*, or worship of the Supreme Being *à la Robespierre*; but for what they knew not how to define, except in the expression of universal craving and need of physical comfort—of rank as fellow-men and fellow-citizens with the privileged—of religion, consolation, instruction. While these masses exist, and their wants exist, so long are all institutions and 'formulas' in danger; if not precisely from a new inundation of 'Sans Culottism,' certainly from some outbreaking or other of similar tendencies. Woe be to those who withhold from them their due: woe, most of all, to those parties, churches, sects, and individuals, whose scruples and wranglings, dignified with the name of religious objections, continue to obstruct the supply of that which sums up all others—the want of education!

To those who habitually see the French Revolution in this light, special causes sink into insignificance. 'Philosophedom,' spread of infidelity, disordered finances, contagion of English and American ideas—all these become merely circumstances which contributed to modify the course of the great eruption; but the thing itself was inevitable and predestined. If so, the men who took part in it were less agents than patients;—men who may have conceived that they were forwarding or impeding it, but in reality the very sport of the impulses they thought to control. . . .

We have preferred to let Mr. Carlyle's views speak for themselves, so far as our prosaic analysis may serve to represent what he has developed in scattered passages, full of fire and eloquence, but with his own characteristic vagueness, diffuseness, and repetition. We feel this to be more for our reader's purpose than to exercise our ingenuity in criticising or combating them. In detail, the temptation to do so would be endless. The great merit of Mr. Carlyle as a writer, and the great pleasure which his writings give, arise from their *suggestive* character. He is always furnishing hints for thought; a slight sentence, a passing observation, often seem to open long vistas of reflection; but he rarely thinks out a subject for his reader: he never weighs, and reasons, and arrives at balanced conclusions. His brief outlines first arrest the attention, and then provoke objection: we feel tempted to debate and argue every point with him, proposition by proposition; but it is wonderful on how much more cordial terms we part with a companion of this description—angered though we may have felt at times by mutual contradiction—than with one of those formal and useful guides who fall under the general denomination of historian—to which, in plain truth, Mr. Carlyle has no title whatever.

On one point, however, we cannot refrain from a few words of protest. We mean the theory implied throughout his pages, which makes hunger the one great mover of revolution, *de facto*, and *de jure*—the conclusive test of misgovernment—the black spot in the heart of all states. This is a question which it is in some respects painful to confront; but it is necessary to speak plainly on it.

That hunger has existed and does exist in old communities, under every variety of government, must at least be conceded as a fact. Its wan and menacing face scowls on us every where from the background—in history and in actual observation. That political systems may have much influence in increasing or diminishing its intensity, we do not wish to deny; but there is a law of human nature at the bottom, far more powerful than these, of which the terrible strength is tacitly admitted even by those who have inveighed most loudly against its expounders. Take the state of society immediately before the French Revolution, for instance: how absurd it is to hold up to public ignominy (as Mr. Carlyle, somewhat inconsistently, has done) the vices and follies of a worn-out dynasty and aristocracy, when it is evident, that if hunger causes and justifies revolution, their guilt is comparatively small? Had Louis the Well-beloved been as pious as Louis the Saint, as popular as the Good, as chaste as the Thirteenth of his name, and as powerful as the Fourteenth, would the condition of the rye-bread and chestnut consuming multitudes of central France have been much better? Somewhat improved it doubtless is at present; but is there not still hunger enough to justify blowing both Chambers, and the citizen-King along with them, into the air? Or, let Mr. Carlyle examine the state of the people in some of the densely peopled Swiss Cantons, where almost every male citizen has a share in the government. He will find sufficient distress to account on his own principles for any revolution, and yet nothing whatever (except a little property) for revolution to fasten upon.

It is impossible to say how extensively the prevalent dread of the multitude, stimulated by doctrines such as these, tends to produce a selfish political adherence, and hopelessness of amelioration. It is with little heart, if at all, that men are induced to take a share in practical reforms—in curtailing this or that excrescence and in suppressing this or that abuse—whose minds are overpowered by a sense of that fundamental deficiency under which they conceive all society to labour. Mr. Carlyle's own conclusions from his theories may be very different; but these are the more ordinary and natural. He seems to believe in the power of government to raise the poorer class altogether out of its present position by legislation. When asked, what are the remedies which he proposes—he answers, very much in the tone of a man forced to say *something*—emigration—and education. The first, in the sense of a general measure, the merest of all delusions. The second, doubtless in its ultimate effects, a lightener of many of the evils which afflict humanity; but even were it attainable, which our wretched jealousies place out of the question, still of very indirect and distant influence upon this particular disorder;—especially in a country of which the population gains at the rate of half a million a-year, and depends for subsistence mainly on the power of underselling foreigners by a fraction per cent. To say that the evil is imminent and enormous, and to point out these as the only means of averting it, is to bid society despair. The logic of Fear is different. The timid and selfish are apt to conclude, that as the lower classes have been kept down hitherto, so they may be kept down a little longer. It may last our time. But in order that it should, it is absolutely necessary to lay aside small political differences, and unite against the common enemy. This is no time for framing constitutions with nice checks and jealous contrivances: in such a crisis, the best government is the simplest and strongest. We appeal confidently to our readers, whether this is not, in the present day, the most popular argument in favour of despotism, and whether such views as Mr. Carlyle's do not inevitably tend to strengthen it.

It would be a worthier task for the historian to disabuse the public mind of those gloomy speculations and unmanly alarms. The every day utility of free institutions is, not that they guarantee the toiler against hunger—would that it were otherwise!—but that they create a vast and powerful class interested in the maintenance of order; and infuse into that class a spirit and intelligence which render it adequate to the task. They cannot ensure the labourer against want; but they give scope to his energy, if he has any; they cannot heal the evils of competition, but they secure to the competitors fair play. We say nothing here of their civilizing and ennobling effects upon the nature of man, although these, too, indirectly contribute to the spread of physical welfare. If along with these advantages they *had* also the inconvenience attributed to them of encouraging discontent and turbulence, and rendering poverty dangerous, these mischiefs would be abundantly compensated. But the French Revolution, whatever else it may prove, proves the contrary of this: it shows that tyranny produces a more desperate population than the most licentious freedom.

With views such as these, and with a genius altogether averse from the ordinary pragmatical method of history, we shall not be surprised at finding that this work turns out rather to resemble a set of lectures, very loosely collected, on striking personages and striking events, just as these may happen to seize the writer's fancy. The *men* of the Revolution are the prominent objects in his portraiture. And in this respect his subject is an unfortunate one; partly because Mr. Carlyle, with all his reading, has acquired no clearer conception of the French character than philosophers of thorough Teutonic breed usually do: (and for this reason, among others, we long to see him engaged in the more congenial occupation of delineating the sterling characters of our own civil wars;) partly because the 'men of the Revolution' are, after all, so extremely uninteresting a race, and it is so impossible to make heroes of them whether for purposes of history or romance. Surely never was so great a drama transacted by personages so utterly destitute, in his own language, 'of what one can call originality, invention, natural stuff, and character.' It seemed as if it was a part of the original purpose of its management, that the intellectual growth of France should be dwarfed for a season, in order that the work might develope itself without the agency of superior talent to forward or counteract it; for if we compare the leaders of parties during the struggle not only with the great men of former days, but even with the *élite* of the generation which has succeeded, their extreme inferiority seems manifest at once. Mr. Carlyle, therefore, assuredly deserves some honour as an artist, if not as a faithful interpreter of the past, for having contrived to make something of such unpromising materials: by grouping his figures well, and by clothing them all in the livery of his own speculative destiny, he has contrived to throw a sort of lustre even over the shallow Girondins and worthless Jacobins, with whom his history chiefly deals.

And what personage is there, in fact, who may not be invested with some interest, when he is brought before us, not as a dry name which is to occur occasionally through a certain number of pages, but as a human being, a creature of like passions with ourselves, an agent with ourselves in the great work of Providence or Fate; whom we are commanded to take by the hand, to address as a brother, to see him act what he was destined to perform, to hear him account in his own way for his actions, and explain the obscure purpose and meaning of his short historical existence. . . .

It would, perhaps, not be very difficult to show how this mode of viewing historical reality, as to individual men, is connected with that sort of indulgent fatalism which we have mentioned as the characteristic of the moral views of Mr. Carlyle. Men are treated as agents who had a part to perform—a work to do—until we almost cease for a time to regard them as any thing else. There is no such thing as accident in Mr. Carlyle's phraseology, any more than in Duke Wallenstein's. . . .

Merely reading of the sayings and deeds of Marat, we shrink from him as something loathsome and polluting. But call him up, with our author, and address him as a brother man—a man who eat, drank, slept, loved, feared, and hated like other mortals, but vexed all the time with a 'fixed idea,' (a phrase borrowed from Mignet)—apostrophize him as 'remarkable horse-leech' or 'dog-leech,'—'Cassandra Marat,'—'hapless, squalid, Marat,'—and the monster vanishes by degrees; and we have before us instead, only one among the most remarkable of the many bewildered creatures who were playing at cross-purposes through the strange and crowded show called the French Revolution.

But Mr. Carlyle is a hero-worshipper, and energy is with him the indispensable, nay the exclusive, quality of heroism. In a world of formulas, to use his own favourite expression, his delight is to fix on men or women in whom there was *reality*, whether for good or for ill. Mirabeau and Danton, Madame Roland and Charlotte Corday, are almost the only four, of all the personages of his history, to whom this eminence is assigned. 'He had many sins,' he says of the second, 'but one sin he had not: that of cant. No hollow formalist, deceptive and self-deceptive, ghastly to the natural sense, was this: but a very man: with all his dross he was a man: fiery-real, from the great fire-bosom of nature herself.' But Mirabeau is his especial favourite. There is something in the 'grandiosity' of the man, affected though it often was, still more. perhaps in his contemptuous hostility to the forms and laws of a world with which he had been at war from his youth upwards. in which his spirit particularly rejoices. The philosopher's imagination is captivated by the figure of the adventurous demagogue just as a quiet citizen. of a romantic turn of mind. sometimes is by those of the ferocious and sarcastic brigands who figure in Turpin novels and Jack Sheppard dramas. Thus he has been seduced, we think, into ascribing to him even more importance than he really possessed as an actor; and far more of sincerity and depth than existed in his character. . . .

The next characteristic of Mr. Carlyle's historical style, and that which after all proves its greatest attraction to the majority of readers, is its picturesqueness. Detached scenes are often admirably drawn, and always with spirit and vivacity, rather to the prejudice of the connecting parts. It is this which renders it so agreeable a book to read in fragments, and so difficult to read through. Truth, that is, accuracy of detail, is hardly to be looked for in them. Verisimilitude his recitals frequently have; and it is surprising to perceive the life-like reality which is communicated to stories so familiar as those of the chief events of the Revolution, by the mere art of the word-painter. The insurrection of the 5th October, 1789, the flight to Varennes, the mutiny at Nancy, are admirable specimens of almost epic energy. Others, and among the most elaborate of these pictures, please us less—probably from the sense of exaggeration which they convey.

Mr. Carlyle has attained his success in this particular (his own peculiar genius apart,) in some measure through his method of taking his colours and perspectives invariably from contemporary narratives analysed by himself, and never at secondhand. The advantage which such a process gives, in point of fire and force, may easily be conjectured: whether it is equally advantageous for the purposes of truth, admits of some doubt. Contemporary relations of occurrences so strange and so rapidly following each other as the principal events of the Revolution, are useful in one respect; they give us the immediate view of them, before the partisans of opposite leaders and opposite principles have made up their mind in what way to manufacture them for their own several purposes. As corrections of received stories, therefore, no historian will deny their importance; but they will seldom afford sufficiently solid footing for independent narratives; not even when we have the advantage of comparing the impressions made on several observers by the very same incident. Each sees rarely more than a part; and each combines the impressions of the little he has actually seen with the vague notions he has collected at second-hand; or from preconceived opinions only, as to the greater portion which he did not see. The result is a confused grouping of objects, which it requires a clear head and, if we may use the expression, something of a military eye to disentangle; and these are no qualities of Mr. Carlyle. His account of the Bastile affair, for example, abstracted as it is from the pages of Besenval, Dussaulx, Fauchet, and we know not how many pamphleteers and newswriters more, is full of warlike clamour and riotous hubbub, just about as like the real event as the sieges in *Ivanhoe* and *Old Mortality*. After reading it through, the student would be quite as much puzzled as at the beginning, to know who took the Bastile, and why it surrendered; for the eloquent narrator has all but missed the one military point of the story, namely, that after several hours of ineffectual shouting and musket-firing on the part of the mob, the arrival of a piece or two of cannon belonging to the *Gardes Françaises* decided the event. And what unparalleled bathos, when, after page upon page of 'fire-deluge,' 'fire-Maelstrom,' and fustian enough to furnish out a German ode on the battle of Leipzig or Borodino, the list of casualties is summed up at least at eighty-three besiegers, and *one* of the besieged!

The simplest reader, who has not quite attained to Mr. Carlyle's pitch of sincerity and chivalrous credulity, must be startled at some of the phenomena which this campaign [September 1792] presents. Dumouriez's famous boast about Thermopylæ seems to have passed current for want of reflection upon the simple fact—that his Thermopylæ was never attacked, and *was* turned. His pass of the Argonne was left fairly in the rear of the Prussians. So far is plain; but the common notion is, that this success was attained at an enormous sacrifice, owing to Dumouriez's admirable strategic dispositions: for instance,

Through the woods, volleying War reverberates, like huge gong-music, or Moloch's kettle-drum, borne by the echoes; swoln torrents boil angrily round the foot of rocks, floating pale carcasses of men. In vain! Islettes village, with its church steeple, rises intact in the mountain-pass, between the embosoming heights: your forced marchings and climbings have become forced slidings, and tumblings back. From the hill-tops thou seest nothing but dumb crags, and endless wet moaning woods. . . . Four days! days of a rain as of Noah, without fire, without food.—Vol. iii. 63.

Alas! that picturesque history should be brought to the vulgar tests of geography and meteorology! The 'mountains' and 'torrents' of the Argonne are altogether as fabulous as the Noachian deluge with which he has vexed the invaders. The Prussian retreat had not even the excuse of bad weather. All historians, without exception, and Dumouriez himself among the number, speak of the inclemency of the season; and yet M. Michaud, in his recent memoir of that general, proves the contrary.* Such is the value of loose assertion. September, 1792, was what it usually is in that part of Europe—one of the finest portions of the year. No rain fell (except on one day, the 8th,) from the first to the 20th, the date of the affair at Valmy. Then there were three or four showery days; and again, fine weather to the end of the month. The equinoctial rains did not set in until the beginning of the next, when the invaders were already in full retreat. The Prussians turned the Argonne, not in discouragement and disorder, but in full force and good disposition. On

* *Biographie Universelle*, Supplement.

the 20th they had cut off the French from the road to Paris, and con-
fronted Kellermann at Valmy, with 50,000 to 25,000—the latter in a
position utterly indefensible. Dumouriez, effectually separated from
his lieutenant, was watched by a superior force in his insulated camp at
St. Ménéhould—a still worse position; so bad, that Napoleon, who had
examined the field of these operations with peculiar attention, said that
nothing whatever could have induced *him* to remain in it in Dumouriez's
place, '*unless there were some secret negotiations, of which we know nothing.*'
A few days before, ten thousand of his men had run from fifteen hundred Prussian hussars. Such was the army *behind* Brunswick; Paris was
before him;—*Gironde* and *Mountain* holding each other by the throat
in the expiring Assembly; the Convention not yet met, and the vast
city one scene of terror and disorder. In this state of things, Dumouriez
writes to the Assembly in the well-known and enigmatical words, '*Tout
est réparé et je réponds de tout;*' and with reason. After a few hours' ineffectual cannonading, leaving some two or three hundred men *hors de
combat* on both sides, Brunswick retires in perfect order; commences
a retrograde movement to the frontier; and thereby decides the fate of
France, of her king, kingdom, and many millions of men, the victims
of three-and-twenty years of bloodshed. And we are to content ourselves for this strange solution of the greatest crisis in the history of
modern Europe by the notion that Brunswick was frightened by the
bravery of the Sans-Culotte invincibles;—in Mr. Carlyle's harmonious
language, by 'rock-ranks,' and shouts of *Vive la Patrie!* . . .

9. Thomas Chisholm Anstey, from an unsigned review, *Dublin Review*

October 1838, v, 349–76

Thomas Chisholm Anstey (1816–73) was one of the earliest converts to come out of the Oxford Movement. As lawyer, later member of the House of Commons, he supported many liberal causes and became notorious for his attacks against Lord Palmerston's government. In 1854, he was nominated to attorney-general in Hong Kong, where his radical reforms led to his suspension in 1858. He then turned to a private law practice in Bombay, where he eagerly gave legal assistance to the native population. Anstey, a young disciple of Carlyle, is remembered for copying in shorthand Carlyle's unpublished *Lectures on the History of Literature* as he heard them delivered in Portman Square. The *Lectures* were published in 1892.

Jane Carlyle, who once chatted with Anstey for more than an hour, reported to her husband that Anstey was all 'agog' about *Sartor Resartus*, that he rhapsodized about Carlyle, and that the Jesuits were 'enchanted with all they find in you. Your "opinions about sacrifice", &c., &c., are entirely conformable to theirs!' (*Letters and Memorials of Jane Welsh Carlyle* [London, 1883], I, 107.)

Anstey begins his review of Carlyle with a discussion of the dangers of the progressive characteristics of pantheism. Yet, however dangerous, the pantheist's love of the positive could lead undisciplined wanderers to the bosom of the Church. It is at this point in the review that the extract begins. See Introduction, p. 12.

Meanwhile, they love the positive,—abhor negations,—and hold the Christian faith on a pantheistic basis. This is the case with Mr. Carlyle; obviously so to his readers; in all probability unknown to Mr. Carlyle himself.

But while we say this, once more let us carefully guard against misconstruction. We cannot, do not mean, that Mr. Carlyle is not a Christian. A fervent, sincere Christian is he, though not of the Catholic order. More than that,—we find him more and more departing from the ranks which produced him, more and more diverging from dissent, gradually approximating to the truth. When we look to what his countrymen, Hume and Robertson, were, and then to what he is, shall we not bless the change? The worst that Mr. Carlyle can find it in his honest heart to say of us, is, that our time is past, that *we* now exist no longer; that, while Catholicity lasted, it did not amiss, but well; that it now does well no more, only because it can exist no more! An immense progress this! Though the homage be not as yet ample enough, it is still much,—much especially for one nursed in the lap of a rigid Presbyterianism. For Mr. Carlyle is a Scot, in birth, in feeling: a warmer admirer of Knox we never knew;—Luther and Knox divide the mental empire over him. And this reminds us that Mr. Carlyle, in spite, if not in consequence, of the laws of 'infinite progress' and 'finite creeds,' is not without his inconsistencies. We have him now praising Hildebrand—now lauding Martin Luther: now testifying of the beauty of Catholic repentance, and attributing to its inspiration the golden numbers of Dante—now denying that, till Luther, that doctrine was any other than a secret known to one or two of the more pious monks: now anathematising the inroads of logic on the demesne of faith—now censuring the Papal anathema pronounced upon those inroads. We have him by turns contented to put quietly up with any dogma, however erroneous and absurd, provided it be heartily believed in, and productive of practical results of an useful sort,—and again railing at the *errors, per se,* of the Romish Church: by turns deploring the rationalism, argumentation, encyclopædism, of the last three centuries, or exulting over their suicidal end impending upon the present century: and again commending Luther and his myrmidons for their supposed recognition of the pure light of *reason,*—and dealing forth his convictions that, though 'the venerable Hildebrand' may well be supposed a believer in Popery, the modern increment of learning and knowledge precludes the belief that any Catholic, 'except a highly *irrational* one,' can possibly be sincere! For our parts, we demand only of Mr. Carlyle for

ourselves and our fellows, no greater favour than he lends to the construction and appreciation of our faithful forefathers: let him, if he
really thinks that they did well, that they believed sincerely, that their
history—the history of the middle age—is but a record of what Göthe
calls 'the triumph of belief over unbelief—those two antagonist principles in man:' if, we say, it is thus he thinks of them, we entreat him
to add us to their number, and judge of us in the same category as of
them; for then we are willing to abide the inference he may draw from
it, ready to confess ourselves of the unenlightened. Or rather, if he
condemns us merely because he thinks that the Catholics of this day
have but preserved the dead forms of doctrine and discipline bequeathed by their ancestors, but that the spirit of life which then animated them has fled for ever, let him study us once again: there are
those among us whose word and work shall give him cause to review
his hasty censure, and abandon an accusation certainly novel at this
day and in this country. It is hard that the defamers of the middle age
should seek to fix on us their groundless calumnies of the past; and that,
on the other hand, when one of sincere mind appears and vindicates that
glorious era, we should be told, through his lips, that we have no part
in its glories, no sympathy, no affinity with its heroes. But we perceive
here at work a peculiar species of enthusiasm, a fanaticism against long-
established formulas, excellent within limits, reprehensible only when
carried to a too great extent. It is this aversion to mere formulas which
so eminently characterises our author; this hatred of form for the form's
sake, in an age wherein, for the most part, form and symbol are everything, genuineness and intrinsic worth nothing. The prevailing errors
of our day are many: among the most sickly and nauseous of these, is
that eternal setting of the sign above the thing signified,—that perpetual
identification of the means with the end. By 'paper constitutions' shall,
in these times, the Peninsula be civilized? by 'venerable constitutions,'
shall a starving people be restrained from violence, and filled as with
food? By State-Church endowments, shall our England be recognized
for a prime model of a Christian commonwealth? But we anticipate.
For Mr. Carlyle these helps are only valuable in themselves, in proportion to the extent to which good shall be realised by them; otherwise,
in his ears, the phraseologies within which *form* demands that we contain our speech,—as, for example, the terms, 'Enlightened Age,' 'Glorious Constitution,' 'Church and State,' 'Greatest happiness of the greatest
number,' 'Public Decorum,' and the like,—are perfectly lost and thrown
away. He values all this precisely, as he emphatically says, 'according

to the *meaning* there is in it,' and that meaning, one denoted by facts and actions, not simply by a spoken synonym. All the rest is to him 'a Quackery,' 'a Formula,' 'a Sham.' And heartily do we concur in this. But Mr. Carlyle, we beg leave to tell him, has reason to beware of a contrary error. There is a fanaticism against formulas, as there is one in their favour. True it is that an '*unmeaning* formula' sickens and disgusts one: let us, however, take heed lest we pronounce too soon and immaturely on the want of meaning in any given formula. On what evidence does he rely to support his sweeping conclusion that all Catholicism is now nothing but a dead formula, and that so it must ever be with a creed laying claim to eternal duration? If he lays this doctrine down *à priori*, let him, in his turn, beware of a *formulism* which is the more dangerous, as its sphere is more comprehensive. We, too, *à priori*, demonstrate the eternity of our creed, and we next maintain it by the secondary aid which an appeal to its long annals and to our interior consciousness will bestow. Till Mr. Carlyle shall have done as much, or either part, it will not be for him to treat our holy religion as one of the dead formulas of human imagining. Nor are we satisfied with his definition of a religious creed, which we have in more than one passage of his works, viz. 'a system of the universe;' nor with his application of the rules of mutation existing in ordinary or worldly things, to this sublime, this divine transcendent thing. Let Mr. Carlyle receive our expostulations in a good spirit, for they are framed out of a deep regard for his sincerity and good faith: let him be assured that, if his appreciation of modern events be faulty or imperfect, it is in this solitary but momentous particular,—the influence of the sound and healthy belief of Catholics over their outward actions and way of life; and that, if he would render his portraiture of Modern History altogether life-like, he must, once for all, give recognition to that great fact. It was thus that he was enabled to understand the middle age, a phenomenon that has baffled his predecessors, who judged it with Protestant eyes. The moral influence of the Church over the minds of men, was weaker perhaps in the troubled times at the beginning of this century, certainly more embarrassed and circumscribed of operation, than it is now; and with Napoleon, of all others, that influence must have been of small personal consideration: yet, the memorable charge which that great conqueror and scorner of the ancient things gave to his envoy at the Papal court, shows that he knew too well the vitality of the Catholic faith to set at nought its influence, as Mr. Carlyle would seem to do. His words were, 'Be careful to treat the Pope as you would one who has five hundred thousand men at his back.' Let Mr. Carlyle ponder well these words, and lay them deeply to heart, if he would appreciate rightly the present condition of the Christian world, and the influences that are at work within it. We know that he sometimes gives vent to the outpourings of his thankfulness, that the German writers have delivered him from the bondage of the prejudices of his childhood, and that he anticipates for the future as much improvement in the present state of his opinions, as that is itself an improvement on those he yesterday held. Hence his aversion to a *premature* profession of his peculiar religious dogmas: herein our promised apology for the use of that word, *premature!* If it be his wish that those opinions shall continue to grow on, and resolve themselves into new matter, and germinate anew, though in other forms, let him neglect no ailment of growth or reproduction. His earnestness of belief, his sincerity of heart, are beautiful and soul-possessing. His learning is immense; his industry untiring; his shrewdness, his power of detecting the truth amid masses of error, quite extraordinary. Yet he imagines the Church a dead thing, in so far as its influence now-a-days is concerned! How is this? Because we repeat, he has never studied her modern history with the attention he has given to her past annals,—to the annals, ancient and modern, of every other department of thought and feeling. He begins by assuming her to be dead: no wonder, then, that he considers any study on his part of her present condition to be utterly valueless, and as time thrown away. Let him, we entreat, discard this *prejudgment*, which is peculiarly his own, as he has manfully discarded the *prejudices* of his education, which were not his own, but instilled into him by those he loved and reverenced, and let him sit calmly down to this important investigation. We promise him that he shall discover, to his abundant satisfaction, that the religion of Saint Gregory the Seventh and of the Crusades is still 'a reality,'— no hollow formula 'or sham,'*—making its voice heard, and its powers felt, in every part of the civilized globe; working out its destinies here below in every phasis of outward manifestation,—in Poland martyred —in Ireland, militant—in Belgium, triumphant!

And now having, as we believe, sufficiently pointed out in what respects our bounden duty as Catholics compels our disapprobation of Mr. Carlyle and his writings, let us yield ourselves to a far more grateful duty, and one for which he happily affords abundant occasion,— that of commendation. And who that, with us, has turned away palled

---

* Mr. Carlyle loves Germany: so do we. We recommend to his notice that highly able work, Ranke's *History of the Popes*, reviewed in our last Number.

and heart-sick with the strained conceits and conventionalisms of the last two or three ages—ages of quacks and deluders of all kinds—but will hail with us the appearance of a genuine man on the vacant stage of our national literature. We cannot do too much homage to our author's leading, pervading quality,—the steadiness in aiming at the truth, guided by a singular developement within him of the Scottish calmness and shrewdness of view, and lit up and vivified with an impassioned enthusiasm in that pursuit,—a holy, pure enthusiasm, that must some day have its good results for the single-minded being who has yielded to its sweet influence. To this source are to be traced his deep research, and his honest independance in judgment: for a mind like his, it is but a poor reason in favour of any given conclusion, that this or that distinguished writer held it before him. In short, he is not a man of the last century; nor were such as himself in the contemplation of Sterne or Tristram Shandy, when the latter, tracing out in epitome the great results of modern British *historisms* and *philosophisms*, cried aloud: 'Tell me, ye learned, shall we for ever be adding so much to the *bulk*, so little to the *stock*? Shall we for ever make new books, as apothecaries make new mixtures, by pouring only out of one vessel into another?' Mr. Carlyle is an 'imitator' of no one, and, therefore, no portion in the mock-heroic denunciations which follow the above passage, would, in Sterne's view, have fallen on him. He adds little to the 'bulk' in adding so much to the 'stock' of knowledge; prizing rather, among literary virtues, the golden one of *silence*. When he prevails on himself to utter his thoughts, it is evidently because he holds himself bound to utter them by a sort of mission to that end, unintelligible to littérateurs of bibliopolist views. Hence we have had frequent reason to lament that Mr. Carlyle has said too little, but never, were it to the amount of a single word, that he has said too much. It is with him a common phrase,★ 'When speech has done its best, silence has still to supply all that is unsaid, more than has been said! The word I am now uttering is of time, of to-day: Eternity is silent! all great things are silent!' Surely this man is not likely to 'darken his wisdom by words without knowledge;' to encumber his pages with phrases idle and undigested. Hence, therefore, it is, that his chiefest and mightiest work on that stirring, momentous subject of all others, the French Revolution,—a work that has almost exhausted all that can well be said by man on its causes, events, and actors,—containing more real matter of reflection than any one of the voluminous treatises on the same phenomenon which have been written

★ Vide his Lectures and Miscellaneous Works, passim.

here and abroad, is offered to the public in the short compass of three octavo volumes! A trashy novelist of the day would not have been satisfied with less space for the developement of his *blasé* conceits, than enables the far-seeing intelligence of Mr. Carlyle to lay bare the secret influences which rule the destinies of empires. And not only beyond the writers who have gone before him has he greatly succeeded in understanding and delineating that great political phenomenon; but, we venture to say, almost unqualifiedly, that he alone has understood and delineated it, establishing for himself most fully and undoubtedly an exclusive title to the name,—Historian of the French Revolution! Nor can we doubt that in every honest, generous heart, his views, in greater part, will find an echo. For to the heart as to the head he addresses himself. Deep-sightedness has taught him to abjure the foolish and wicked casuistry which seeks to sever public from the side of private virtue, or can see utility apart from the moral law. 'There can be,' he somewhere says, 'no seeing eye without a seeing heart.' To him, self-sacrifice, —courage in man to do the good that is in him amid scorn and suffering, —are all in all. Yet never have we met with any writer who exacts less of humanity, who is more disposed to set off in relief to the blackness he pourtrays, moral features of a fairer kind. Robespierre seems to be the only one of his historical characters in whom he despairs of exhibiting one solitary redeeming characteristic. It is, too, a great satisfaction, of a melancholy kind, that such an exception is so rare: bad, indeed, is the portion of him in whose person it is offered! Yet not false pity, but rather a rigorous sentiment of justice, has dictated to our author his course in this regard: he feels it his duty to investigate, without prejudice or affection, the chronicled career of his actors, for the purpose of drawing thence, for our appreciation, only those incidents which were their own, the forthcomings of their own hearts, the realities which live for ever to the weal or woe of the doers, and their posterity. Doubtless the task is difficult,—a sore trial to an author's sincerity and good judgment; and if, in general, historians have, at the outset, proposed it to themselves, we can only say that we hardly know one that has kept himself faithful to it to the end. But their neglect or failure are not required to make illustrious the complete success of Mr. Carlyle in bringing to a conclusion the duty he had the courage to undertake. Unlike the generality of the writers, who are called historians, throughout his work he has not a hero in view; blaming and commending, ridiculing and admiring the same man, and the same opinions too, as the former oscillate in well-doing, or the latter change their aspect in the altering positions of events. Robespierre, we repeat, is the only wretched object of whom he speaks in an unvarying strain of horror and disgust. For his cause, it is the common one of justice and mercy: men and systems are judged of by relation only to that standard.

There are two blanks in Mr. Carlyle's history, which can only be supplied by a Catholic pen; the first origin of the French Revolution, and the present means of arresting its march in the onward path of destruction. With respect to the first, we consider the seeds to have been originally sown in that spring-time of European calamity, the Protestant Reformation. The Catholic Church, for Mr. Carlyle 'a dead thing,' affords the solution of the second question.

The principles of negation, or Protestantism, which, about the time of that ally of Islam, Francis the First, (for Reformation is fortunate in her princes!) had insinuated themselves into the ductile French mind, continued thenceforth more and more to develope themselves in a thousand different channels, ramifying from the same source, till, in the eighteenth century, under the unhappy regency of the Duke of Orleans, and the reign of Louis XV, they had become absorbed in that general abandonment, by the upper classes, of religious profession, if not of belief, to which the way had been already paved by a co-extensive corruption of morality. It was found easier, not to say more spirited, to maintain and justify, upon principle, the want of all principle, than at the same time to condemn and exhibit it. Such, indeed, had been the way with the vicious of former times; a modern enlightenment went farther. Vice and Virtue were ascertained to be mere conventionalisms: according to the school of Hume, they were but the hallowed names of Utility and Inutility, through the medium of which, in darker times, the science of politics had been considerably explained to the vulgar by the learned and adept. It was therefore taught publicly, that, with a new era of human affairs, ethics must undergo a change: it was well for the superstition of their forefathers to teach that what is moral is useful; but it was for themselves to reverse this order, by explaining that what is virtuous is only so because it is useful; that all else is of imposture and fabrication. An opinion once seriously entertained influences action. The rulers embraced with ardour the new suggestion—adopted it—made it their standard and rule of government. Religion had too long shielded the poor; an *imperium in imperio* was intolerable; the Gallican liberties (or slaveries) were doubtless much, but not every thing, in the progress of material domination, and the subjugation of the spiritual authority. Destroy it,—and a fair field would open itself to king-craft and state-craft: thenceforth woe to him who should gainsay either! At whatever cost, religious opinion must be driven back, even as public opinion had long since been; then would administration prosper in irresponsibility. For themselves, the great men of the state (and here Mr. Carlyle catches up the clue to that eventful history) had already adopted into practice the golden rule of scepticism, which consists simply of the denial of all creed or law, excepting such as are comprised in the three pithy and facile positions,—'Belief in one's own existence,—belief that money will buy money's worth,—belief that pleasure is pleasant.' Propositions that are simple enough, and absurd withal; yet, in practice, fatal to the actor, insupportable to the acted on! 'Poor fellow!' said an infidel surgeon once, within our hearing, who seemed deeply shocked at hearing of the sudden death of a favourite comic actor,—'poor fellow! Well! life is short and uncertain. There is only one way, you know—*to enjoy ourselves while we are here!*' The grandees of France did so, with impunity, while faith subsisted among the masses. Decorum, that blessed shadow, covering more sins than ever charity did, appearing, in general, not till the substance has fled far away,—decorum was still preserved in high places and the streets; just so much of it, at least, as would suffice for an engine of strong government, without lending thereby too much of support to the supersensual, or of consideration to its ministers. For the time was not yet come when it was completely to be laid aside. The Jesuits having gone, the monastic orders were to be suppressed, and their lands forfeited to the state; tithes were to follow, and then the secular endowments, when it should be practicable: but the privileged nobility, not the lower classes, should thereby be advantaged. In the mean time, peace and order were to be kept up: the governed were to continue in the ways of religion, and in that name to bow to the powers of darkness and of sensualism that filled the high stations of authority. And for a time it was so; but an example had been set, too brilliant to be long concealed from the gaze of the depressed myriads, and finally it was followed. The multitude, like the few, became infidel, or believed itself to be so. The results were obvious.

[quotes 'French philosophism' to 'new in history' Vol. I, Bk. I, ch. ii, p. 14]

Scepticism and profligacy, hand-in-hand, made their ominous journey through France,—Versailles being the starting-point. The one aimed at the heart through the head, the other acted on the head through the heart; by opposite means attaining to one end. It became clear to every enlightened Frenchman that this world of ours was but a hypothesis, a thing of chance, owning no God but force, no laws but those of matter. To physics every thing was reducible: morality, duty, faith, were words of vague import, and discarded accordingly: or if admitted, their significations were altered to square with the fundamental laws of gravitation and repulsion, or others of the visible order. Thus the least materialist of the sophists at that time defined morality to be the palate, by whose smack we judge of the utility or inutility of actions! Nothing was received that was not of the visible, or reducible to it: all things else had no existence for the enlightened. The moral of all this was, that the spirit of sacrifice, the soul of all things desirable here below, made way for that of egotism and covetousness. . . .

And when Mr. Carlyle, taking, for the clergy in general, that model of unworthy primates, Loménie de Brienne, charges the whole body of the faithful, clergy and laity, with the same aping reverence of formula, the same indifference to its spirit and significance, which characterises the rest of France at that period; when he reduces to a sordid love of tithe and benefice, the zeal of the generality of priests, and the fervour of the rest, to a dramatic and unmeaning swagger after martyrdom, which the good-humoured populace would not indulge,— we would ask him to explain to us the phenomenon, as it must doubtless seem to him, of the thousands of exiled priests,

Who undeprived, their benefice forsook,—

when the constitutional hierarchy was tendered for their adhesion, by subscribing a schismatic oath. This country alone received and sheltered many thousands of these virtuous sufferers for conscience sake.* How, too, does he reconcile with the absence of healthy belief, the deadness of Catholicity within the heart, the paralysis of soul, that too real martyrdom of the faithful, as of one man, of which the traces left us in the massacre at the Carmes, in the noyades, in the fusillades, in the deportations, are assuredly too clear not to be discoverable by one of his sincerity? And if the famous revolt of the brave Vendeans has not been perfectly understood by our author, and if the object for which that gallant band strove mightily, to the well-nigh undoing of the revolution itself, has seemed so unaccountable to his intelligence, as to justify the

* It has been said that at one time there were as many as 20,000 of these exiles in this kingdom alone.

expression of a sort of pity for their bewilderment, it is because Mr. Carlyle has refused to recognise this one fact, has shut his eyes to this truth which lay before him,—that Catholicity is the mother of action; a vital, undying, imperishable principle; not a name, a formula,—but a substantial essence, pervading all, ruling all; and not to be disregarded among this world's influences by him who seeks to know the past, or to forewarn the future! It was said by an enemy, who knew us better than Mr. Carlyle, 'As for the Papist, he can as soon not be, as not be active!'* And the return of peace and moral health to the bosom of distracted France, which we have witnessed, and, in still increasing development, are daily witnessing, is not referrible to any human source—Code Napoléon, Restoration, or Dynasty of August—but, under God, to the struggles, and prayers, and tears of those chosen ones, of whom it may well be said, that, 'for their sakes those days were shortened.'

As to the archbishop-elect of Paris himself, we will only record of him what has been left to us by his contemporary, the Abbé Barruel, a man to whose pages we direct Mr. Carlyle, if he seeks a true estimation of the majority among the French clergy that had not bowed the knee to Baal or Ashtaroth,—state-craft or libertinism. It will be seen that he, at least, was not disposed to abide by the standard of Brienne, as the measure of his own moral dignity.

The man who best seconded in this, (the suppression of religious orders,) was one who had succeeded in making his very colleagues believe, that he had some fitness for government, and who ended by gaining for himself a place in the number of ministers whom ambition has rendered imbecile. This man was Brienne, Archbishop of Toulouse, afterwards Archbishop of Sens, then prime-minister, then public apostate, and now dead, amid contempt and execration. . . . Brienne, all degraded, all abhorred, as he is, is not as yet at the point of infamy he merits. It is not known that he was the friend, the confidant of D'Alembert; and that he was in the Church, just what D'Alembert might have been as Archbishop in an assembly of commissioners charged with the reform of the religious bodies.†

And much more to the same purport. We shall dismiss this subject by an earnest protest, as against Mr. Carlyle's views thereupon in general, so especially against his strictures on the celebrated Abbé Maury, afterwards cardinal, as wholly unjustifiable, and, indeed, unsupported by Mr. Carlyle himself with any tangible statement of facts.

* Fuller's Worthies.
† Barruel, *Hist. du Jacobinisme*, vol. i. p. 121.

The more remarkable parts of our author's work, if we can particularize any portions where all is so remarkable, are those wherein are sketched the personal characters of the great actors in the drama. This he has done with great judgment, proportionate, as it seems to us, to the rarity of character. For, as he well remarks in another place,★ 'a greater work was never done in the world's history by men so small.' He enumerates but three, Mirabeau, Danton, and Napoleon: we question whether the latter ought to have been included among the men of the *Revolution*; but, with that reserve, we cordially agree with him. There is a melancholy interest, as his readers have experienced, in tracing with our author the tumultuous course of thoughts and things, both good and evil, issuing from hearts like those of the two first-named, big, indeed, with greatness, and original and genuine nature, but unrayed upon by the faintest glimmer of faith, unwarmed by the least scintillation from the high altar of heaven. In them we see of what nature are man's resources when left to himself by divine abandonment; how grand, terrific, and, withal, how ineffectual. In Mirabeau there is the indomitable energy of man, alike displayed in sorrow as in guilty joy, in labours Herculean, as in the prison-gloom; whether directed to the elevation of the people, as far as mere man could elevate such a people, or, as in his latter days, to the repression of the popular excitement, in favour of that monarchy, on which it had now somewhat too extensively encroached. There was in him the strong and self-possessing consciousness, that within himself lay the strength of purpose and the vigour of fulfilment which should achieve the end he had in view, were all the world his adversary. Light lay the dust upon his head! Among the sceptics of his day, he was the best; a man of much nature, and, as such, a vicious being not wholly without virtues, and great virtues! Not among the least of these do we set his hatred of the hypocrisy and formulism which surrounded him on every side; his clear appreciation of the moment at which any given political implement had ceased to be of use, and commenced to be an incumbrance. . . .

So Danton, 'the Mirabeau of the sansculottes,' as Mr. Carlyle calls him, all-fearful, all-hateful as he is, as any one must be, of fiery energy, of far-reaching foresight, who, having abjured God, and being of God forsaken, lives in a time of moral earthquake, social overthrow, bloody vengeance, in short, of French Revolution,—despite all this, Danton, of himself, or, at any rate, ranked among his fellows of the clubs, deserves more of sympathy, say even pitying admiration, than his brother man

★ *London and Westminster Review*, vol. iv. p. 385.

YEOVIL COLLEGE
LIBRARY

seems inclined to award to him. Again, we must bear in mind, that in him we witness the workings of a God-abandoned nature. At least we may say this of him, that if, in his blind fury against *all* form, he discriminated not between the temporal and eternal,—the creed and the charter; yet that neither did he, with the Robespierres and the Sièyes, attempt to set up anything instead of the ancient things he had destroyed, awaiting rather the ebb of the public feeling before he should direct his solicitude to the choice of a suitable channel. His cruelty, too, was rather one of a supposed necessity, than of choice: nay more, that necessity was real and not supposed, if the universe were such and so regulated as Danton would believe it! When *motive* was lost,—swallowed up in the blind gulphs of sensualism,—*dissuasives* became most essential; but with belief in judgment, justice, and a world to come, religious dissuasives, too, had perished: what was left him, then, but those of the secular, sensual order,—those elements which, summing up themselves, resulted in the reign of terror? Hence, and not otherwise, terror became the order of the day, at least as far as it depended upon Danton. Thus, too, he at any rate accomplished one great thing,—he rescued his country from the fangs of Brunswick, a thing which, without him, had not been done.

[quotes 'Brawny Danton' to 'in these days' Vol. III, Bk. I, ch. vi, 46–47]

Such was Danton, 'a truth—clad in hell-fire—but still a truth.' Yet this extraordinary man was doomed to expiate his crimes against God in the hands of that most loathsome of created formulists, Robespierre; of him who *decreed* 'the existence of the Supreme Being;' solemnly, *i.e.* 'in sky-blue coat, and black breeches,' inaugurating the new worship, by burning atheism in effigy of 'pasteboard steeped in turpentine!' Yet this would-be prophet, this 'Mahomet Robespierre,' as our author happily calls him, was the mean instrument whereby Danton was stricken down; which being done, he, too, the baser criminal, rendered to the guillotine the inadequate forfeit of his own enormities. Such is man, and such the strength of his counsel! . . .

The work before us terminates, rightly enough, with the armed interference of Buonaparte, and the restoration of order, better known as the 13th Vendémiaire. To carry out the revolution is at present impossible; we cannot predicate that it has even now ended; 'like a bas-relief sculpture, it does not conclude, but merely ceases.' In the meantime, let our utilitarian readers derive a moral from their experience of that event hitherward to the present time. Belief is the one thing needful! Without it, in vain are the governed weak, the rulers strong, property fenced and warranted by acts of Parliament, power, law, and influence, invested in its possessors; the whole is hollow and baseless; duty wants its motive, and action is healthfulness; the husk and shell of the constitution are there, but its soul and significance are forgotten. To what purpose, then, shall we preach utility, pleasure of virtue, and other *names*, being not agreed even as to what is pleasure, what utility? Why do we addict ourselves to the rights of man, and not extend our inquiries to his duties,—to the doctrine of the cross,—to the spirit of self-sacrifice,—without which his rights become identical and co-extensive with the might that is within him? Let them credit us, unless we do so, the best formula that human wit can fabricate for the world's guidance is to us a dead thing,—nay, more, a lie in action, working nought but delusions and wretchedness. . . .

10. John Sterling, from an unsigned review, *London and Westminster Review*

October 1839, xxxiii, 1–68

John Sterling, the author of this review, had in 1835 written directly to Carlyle criticizing *Sartor Resartus*. See No. 1.

All countries at all times require, and England perhaps at present not less than others, men having a faith at once distinct and large, the expression of what is best in their time, and having also the courage to proclaim it, and take their stand upon it. Many a one there is among us, prompted by the blind fire of feeling and the blast of conscience, who adopts fervently, even fiercely, some mode or fragment of an old creed, pushes it to all extremes, presses it on all hearers, and exhibits all the vehemence and self-reliance of a prophet, but one to whom clear vision is wanting. For where the general insight and elevation necessary in our day for an adequate view of man, exist, there must the difficulties be most keenly

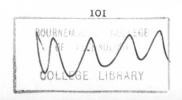
BOURNEMOUTH COLLEGE
OF ART AND
COLLEGE LIBRARY

felt which lie in the way of any recognized tradition, or render it at least insufficient. Knowledge, without belief, and belief without knowledge, divide in the main the English world between them. The apparent exceptions are generally cases of compromise, when men are content to half-believe one thing and half say another; for a whole belief would demand its own complete expression. And in the repeating by rote, for the sake of quiet, of popular creeds and formulas, the sense of discontent and doubt which lurks in the heart asserts itself by stammering and reluctant sighs or sneers. Semi-sincere persuasions, and semi-candid declarations, make up our limbo of public opinion. There is often, perhaps most often, heart in the words; but often too—how often who dare ask? within the heart a lie.

It is not to be denied that we have also in literature and society many a man who proposes his scheme of human life and of the universe. But they almost all labour under the evil that these schemes are fatally partial or superficial. Some one breaks off a corner of our nature—calls it suggestion, or association, or self-interest, or sympathy, or pleasure and pain, or profit and loss, or the nervous system; and lifting up the fragment, says 'Behold! this is the essence of man.' He builds a hut with a few stones of Thebes or Babylon in the corner of some immeasurable ruin, and exclaims, 'Lo! the hundred-gated town restored—See here rebuilt the city of the great King.'

As these theories, which have all their plausibility, their use, and their vestige of truth in them, take in but some small grains, some faint shadows of what man is, therefore the living soul of man, with its longings and capacities of faith, refuses to acknowledge them. They sprung from no unfathomable depth of craving for reality, glow with no full stream of life; and accordingly they have no hold on any but the cold and recluse spinner of inferences; or the empty self-seeker of this world, who considers knowledge as ornamental, and looks at himself in the mirror, whether of glass or of human eyes, with more complacency when he can say, 'I, too, am a philosopher.'

Of all such pale and shrivelled theories it is the common characteristic that they belong to minds skilled more or less in dialectics and the management of terms, but poorly furnished with the large and solid stuff of human nature which should furnish the premises of their schemes. The senses indeed may be acute, and the appetites voracious, as well as the understanding quick and patient; but the breast is comparatively empty of love, of hope, of awe; the will distains to bow under aught higher than itself; and the dead artificial parasol of self-conceit, which can be raised or lowered, opened or folded, painted and tricked out at pleasure, is substituted for the infinite concave of Heaven, beneath whose vault man walks at once humbled and inspired.

Of such speculators it is the inevitable and deadly lot that the over-powering consciousness of what is lowest and most chaotic in us, rather than of the higher and brighter—the spirit-man—supplies the materials which the intellect works on, from which it draws its thin unbroken clue of speculation. And having only this to start from and to shape with, the finer and truer the power of syllogizing, the more coherently worth-less is the whole result. Of far nobler and more fruitful promise than such a man is the poor bewildered visionary, perhaps fanatic, who feels a surge of dim forces in his soul, which he cannot explain, or can only explain into something as unsubstantial as a dream. On his great world of life, now confused and dark, peace will assuredly one day descend and morning open. He will find that Paradise was preparing for him while it seemed to him that all was hell.

But in our day such visionaries are less and less possible. The spread of shallow but clear knowledge, like the cold snow-water issuing from the glaciers, daily chills and disenchants the hearts of millions once credulous. Daily, therefore, does it become more probable that mil-lions will follow in the track of those who are called their betters. Thus will they find in the world nothing but an epicurean style, to be man-aged, with less dirt and better food, by patent steam-machinery; but still a place for swine, though now the swine may be washed, and their vic-tuals more equally divided.

Is it not then strange that in such a world, in such a country, and among those light-hearted Edinburgh Reviewers, a man should rise and proclaim a creed; not a new and more ingenious form of words, but a truth to be embraced with the whole heart, and in which the heart shall find, as his has found, strength for all combats, and consolation, though stern not festal, under all sorrows? Amid the masses of English printing sent forth every day, part designed for the most trivial entertainment, part black with the narrowest and most lifeless sectarian dogmatism, part, and perhaps the best, exhibiting only facts and theories in physical science, and part filled with the vulgarest economical projects and details, which would turn all life into a process of cookery, culinary, political, or sentimental—how few writings are there that contain like these a distinct doctrine as to the position and calling of man, capable of affording nourishment to the heart and support to the will, and in har-mony at the same time with the social state of the world, and with the most enlarged and brightened insight which human wisdom has yet attained to?

We have been so little prepared to look for such an appearance that it is difficult for us to realize the conception of a genuine coherent view of life thus presented to us in a book of our day, which shall be neither a slight compendium of a few moral truisms, flavoured with a few immoral refinements and paradoxes, such as constitute the floating ethics and religion of the time; nor a fierce and gloomy distortion of some eternal idea torn from its pure sphere of celestial light to be raved about by the ignorant whom it has half-enlightened and half made frantic. But here, in our judgment—that is, in the judgment of one man who speaks considerately what he fixedly believes—we have the thought of a wide, and above all, of a deep soul, which has expressed, in fitting words, the fruits of patient reflection, of piercing observation, of knowledge many-sided and conscientious, of devoutest awe, and faithfullest love. To expound his faith in our language will seem not unpresumptuous, while his own is at hand and may be read by all. But as a hint and foretaste of what is written in his works, it may be said that Mr. Carlyle thus teaches:—

I.

The Universe, including Man as its Chief Object, is all a region of Wonder and mysterious Truth, demanding, before all other feelings, Reverence as the Condition of Insight.

2.

For he who rejects from his Thoughts all that he cannot perfectly analyze and comprehend, all that claims veneration, never will meditate on the primary fact of Existence. Yet what is so necessary to the Being of a Thing, so certainly the deepest secret in it, as Being itself? All else in an object—all qualities and properties viewed without reverence to this, which is their root and life, cannot, rightly speaking, be understood, though they may be counted, measured, and handled.

3.

Religion therefore is the highest bond between Man and the Universe. The world rises out of unknown sacred depths before the soul, which it ever draws into contemplation of it. It repels the man into entire ignorance only when he fails to acknowledge the unfathomable Depth which he and it belong to.

4.

But at best we are immensely ignorant. Around us is a fullness of life, now vocal in a tone, now visible in a gleam, but of which we never can measure the whole compass, or number and explore its endless forces.

5.

Yet, to him that looks aright, the divine substance of all is to be seen kindling at moments in the smallest, no less than in the grandest thing that is—for Existence is itself divine, and awakens in him who contemplates, a sense of divinity such as men of old were fain to call prophetic.

6.

This sense of the Divine, penetrating and brightening a man's whole nature, attuning his utterance, and unfolding into images that blaze out of the darkness of custom and practice, and shape themselves into a completeness of their own—this is Poetry—the highest Form of the Godlike in Man's being, the freest recognition of the God-like in All.

7.

As there is a Poetic Light dormant in all Things, to which the Music of our Feelings gives the signal of awakening—so especially is this true of man, in whom dwells the Knowledge of Existence as well as the Fact.

8.

Thus the seer finds in his brethren, of every age and land, the most perplexing, indeed, startling, woeful, but also the highest, fairest, amplest, all-suggestive figures of his life-long vision.

9.

But to know and understand even Man is not for man the foremost task. We are made, by the craft of Nature—of Him whom Nature clothes, veils, and manifests—chiefly to be ourselves makers. To work, to do, is our calling—that for which we were called forth to be.

10.

Knowledge and Strength in their highest and most harmonious energy, are the reward only of the noblest effort. But all who toil in any work, when the work is not a mere winnowing of chaff, are doing humanly, worthily.

11.

Therefore, to trace men and their ways through the dusky mazes of the Past, and among all the confusions of our own time,—to see what they are doing, and how, and why—is itself a work fit for a thoughtful and affectionate mind, and will not be without fruit either for them or him.

12.

But in the survey of all things round us, and in the experience of ourselves, which we shall certainly gain if we attempt such devout and
sympathetic observation, Evil, Grief, Horror, Shame, Follies, Errors,
Frailties of all kinds, will needs press upon the eye and heart. And thus
the habitual temper of the best will rather be strenuous and severe than
light and joyous.

13.

A cutting sorrow, a weary indignation, will not be far from him who
duly weighs the world. But in unswerving labour for high ends, in
valour, and simplicity in truth with himself and with all men, there
shall still be a sustaining power. So shall he have faith in a good ever
present, but bleeding and in mourners' garments among the sons of men.
And by perseverance to the end, life may be completed bravely and
worthily, though with no bacchanalian triumph. . . .

[There follows a discussion of Carlyle's indebtedness to the Germans
—Kant, Goethe, Schiller and especially Jean Paul Richter.]

Further, it must be said, that true as is his devotion to the truth, so
flaming and cordial is his hatred of the false, in whatever shapes and
names delusions may show themselves. Affectations, quackeries, tricks,
frauds, swindlings commercial or literary, baseless speculations, loud
ear-catching rhetoric, melodramatic sentiment, moral drawlings and
hyperboles, religious cant, clever political shifts, and conscious or half-
conscious fallacies, all in his view, come under the same hangman's
rubric,—proceed from the same offal heart. However plausible, popular and successful, however dignified by golden and purple names, they
are lies against ourselves, against whatever in us is not altogether rep-
robate and infernal. His great argument, theme of his song, spirit of his
language, lies in this, that there is a work for man worth doing, which
is not to be done with the whole of his heart, not the half or any other
fraction. Therefore, if any reserve be made, any corner kept for something unconnected with this true work and sincere purpose, the whole
is thereby vitiated and accurst. So far as his arm reaches he is undoing
whatever in nature is holy; ruining whatever is the real creation of the
great worker of all. This truth of purpose is to the soul what life is to the
body of man; that which unites and organizes the mass, keeping all the
parts in due proportion and concord and restraining them from sudden
corruption into worthless dust.

From this turn of mind and ground-plan of conviction it follows, that to Mr. Carlyle the objects of chief interest are memorable persons—men who have fought strongly the good fight. And more especially, though not exclusively, does he revere and study those living nearest to our own time and circumstances, in whom we may find monumental examples of the mode in which our difficulties are to be conquered. These men he rejoices, and eminently succeeds, in delineating; in enabling us to see what is essential and physiognomical in each, and how the facts of nature and society favoured and opposed the formation of his life into a large completeness. The hindrances such a man had to overcome, the energies by which he vanquished them, and the work, whatever it may have been, which he thus accomplished for mankind, appear in these pictures with lucid clearness, marked with a force and decision of hand and style worthy of the greatest masters.

Thus having taken anxious measure of the perplexities and dangers of human life in its higher progresses, he has learnt also to pity, with a mother's tenderness, the failings and confusions of those against whom these hostile forces have prevailed. His proudest and most heroic odes in honour of the conquerors are mingled with or followed by some strain of pity for those who have fallen and been swallowed up in the conflict. The dusky millions of human shapes that flit around us, and in history stream away, fill him with an almost passionate sorrow. Their hunger and nakedness, their mistakes, terrors, pangs, and ignorances, press upon his soul like personal calamities. Of him, more than of all other English writers, perhaps writers of any country, it is true, that not in words and fits of rhetorical sentiment, but in the foundation of his being, man, however distant and rude a shadow, is to him affecting, venerable, full of a divine strength, which, for the most part, is rather cramped and tortured than ripened to freedom in this fleshly life and world. This kind of feeling must be felt as truly distinguishing him by all who read his works. For though similar expressions to some of his have been used by many, from no one, at least in our language, have they proceeded with so resolute and grand a force of radiant clearness and adamantine conviction.

Only when the sufferers are in the foreground and his main objects, does he seem to forget that their oppressors or despisers, the tyrannous, luxurious, frivolous, empty-hearted, are also themselves victims, playing the part of destroyers: that circumstances had done wrong to them, no less than to those whom they harass and degrade: and that to be slowly poisoned with sweet baits in the flush and abundance of life, and so to sink away in sottish dreams, is not at all less horrible than to be gradually starved and worn to death, while courage, or at least dumb endurance, confronts the inevitable blow, and hope whispers in the sharpened ear, that a better destiny lies beyond. But when these base and selfish souls of lower earth—the men of pleasure, who, to all beneath them, are men of pain—come themselves before him, he well comprehends what they perhaps could least understand, that they too are to be pitied as well as blamed; although the tragedy of their lives is not that to which it is most important to call a world of spectators.

Thus loving the ideal realised in things and persons, not expounded in systematic thought; zealous as a missionary for the concrete, and towards the abstract severe as an inquisitor; this writer very naturally holds in detestation all attempts to give dialectics any important place in human life. He admits, indeed, that reflection inevitably produces thoughts which find no sufficient symbols in any single objects, but are the ideal roots of whole classes of existence, and finally pass into one great principle of life originating and organizing all that is. But the attempt to define this in any precise form of words, though it has been the aim, as he admits, of many of the greatest among men, meets with small sympathy from him. Above all does he scorn, rend, explode, and excommunicate while he despises, the endeavour to trace out the various lines and steps by which this first principle is logically arrived at, and then again from it are deduced the conceptions corresponding to the facts of the universe.

Now although in Mr. Carlyle's view of this matter there be, as we believe, some, perhaps much prejudice, his judgment is mainly determined by an indubitable truth which he sees with clearest eyes; and only, as we think, regards it too exclusively. It is certain that men with whom this enterprise of logical construction and deduction has been the great task of life, have seldom been open to a sufficient course of outward and inward experience not to undervalue all but the scanty set of facts on which they base their scheme. Nay, more, inasmuch as these facts have not been looked at by the light of analogies from many others, there are sides even of them which the theory takes no account of. Thus it never can exhaust, that is, adequately interpret, even the things which it counts worthy of notice. The man, fancying his brain the sunny mirror of the universe, lives in fact in a small sham world, where there is at best a spark of light amid thick shadows that wear hardly a semblance of realities.

Further still, as he who has devoted himself exclusively or chiefly to the formation and arrangement of definitions is likely to have been led thereto by a preponderance of the merely ratiocinative faculty, and a deficiency of the nobler and more substantial powers, these, and their correlatives in objects, are not what he is apt to seek for or to acknowledge anywhere. His theory is likely to leave out whatever is deepest and most essential in the universe. Now all things being linked together and interfused, in the lowest things there must be some power or capacity corresponding to something above it, and by which it is ultimately related to the highest of all. But this is precisely what the too narrow and mechanical inquirer cannot comprehend. Therefore even the lowest and most lifeless forms of things, which correspond best to his own stiff and angular faculty of reasoning, are as to their true meaning and most important relations, altogether beyond his ken.

As the merely logical thinker is apt to be thus defective in his views, so also in his practice is he sure to be detected as artificial and abortive. By a judicious use of the phraseology of the day, and the exercise of conjuring ingenuity in rather a higher than the manual mode, he may easily pass, while he deals only with words, for a wise, almost an all-wise, Doctor. But when he comes to deal with things as a practical worker, his ignorance of that which is essential in them necessarily baffles him, as often as he quits the vulgar empirical rules which rest merely on unsystematic experience. Success in his own department—of definition and refutation—and blindness to all beyond it, fill him with hopeless conceit and self-assurance, and failing in all that he attempts practically, he will most often be led to throw the blame upon the poor unconscious World, which, having its own affairs to attend to, obstinately and spitefully will not be what he has so demonstratively proved it is. . . .

We have said that this writer's great power is in historic delineation of men and events, to which he gives extraordinary vividness and boldness; and this, not by knack or system, or a draughtsman's eye for the outwardly picturesque, but by intense feeling of the effectual and expressive every where, and of the relation in which all objects stand to the natural hearts of men. But there is another series of facts for which his mind is far less generously open, than for the characters and deeds of persons. These are the beliefs which each age and individual has framed for himself, or accepted. To these he does not give much heed; of course not denying, or mistaking, the certainty that all beliefs have followed each other in the history of the world according to a fixed law, and are connected by the same with all the circumstances of each generation; and that, in obedience to this law, they emerge, unfold themselves, pass away, or are transmuted into other modes of faith. But he dwells on little else than the importance of the spirit with which the creed is held, the degree of seriousness and devotion in the believer's mind, rather than the quality and amount of truth which his belief embodies.

Now it is no unfruitful and minute, but a spacious and teeming field of thought, which spreads before us when we begin to inquire, not so much what manner of man was Heraclitus or Plato, Athanasius, or Luther, or Leibnitz—as what was the doctrine that each of them taught; what view did it unfold of Nature, Man, and God; how was it linked with what had gone before, and what followed it; and how did the truth of the one mind become moulded by the thoughts of generations before it passed into the reason of the following sage; and how changed by him did it again go forth to create and burn within the bosoms of its next inheritors?

Assuredly Mr. Carlyle would not deny this to be worth considering. But it is not a study with which, so far as we can see, he concerns himself peculiarly. And in consequence of this indifference of his, one is sometimes tempted, in reading him, to fancy that in his view, it is only a delusion, however unavoidable, by which importance is attached to the beliefs and denials of mankind; the honesty and zeal with which we believe being very slightly dependent on the object of our faith. No doubt the stupid arrogance of multitudes does lean with ridiculous weight on many theories or phrases which for them in their state of feeling might really be shuffled, and interchanged, and redistributed among the contending parties by mere chance, without any but the slightest effect upon their state of soul. And remarkable it sometimes is, when an ordinary mortal, who unwillingly pays his yearly taxes, and willingly reads his daily newspaper, professes, with full belief that he believes, some scheme of faith such as might suit a disguised archangel, such as ought to encircle the adoring head with a halo of mythological glories, and raise the feet in sovereign loftiness above the cares and perturbations of mortality, while the man shall all the while be crawling in the mire, and thinking only of his prospective mess of pottage. Yet there is some relation, most definite and certain, however indirect, between his creed and him. The fetish religion of Africa as clearly bears the marks of negro-barbarism, as the epicurism of Lucretius, and the stoicism of Marcus Aurelius, express the refinement of Rome. The philosophy of Aristotle is not accidentally, but by the necessity of the man's constitution and circumstances, distinct from the lore of Plato; the theology of Augustine from that of Fenelon; and again, the speculations of the Brahmins from those of the Rabbins. It must be worth while to understand what these distinctions are, whence they arise, and to what they tend; for the expressed belief is a standard, though not an infallible one, whereby to ascertain that real belief which is as genuine a fact of man's life as any other. No belief is ever professed by any one, which has not been at some time the real conviction of somebody. And the thoughts that a man thinks are, when we can really ascertain them, as significant of what he is as any action of his life. . . .

It must also be considered that, having looked piercingly and bravely into the doings of the world, and found much thereof false, and much more only half true, he is constantly led to speak of things either held in esteem or blandly tolerated, and to convey his knowledge of their worthlessness in a tone of quiet, deliberate scorn, which couples itself in friendly dissonance with his fervid worship of many a ragged, outcast heroism;—as the answer of an Arab Sheik to the messenger of a Pasha requiring the free son of the desert to pay tribute, compared with his welcome to his tents of the naked, wandering stranger.

Add to this, that Mr. Carlyle's resolution to convey his meaning at all hazards, makes him seize the most effectual and sudden words in spite of usage and fashionable taste: and that, therefore, when he can get a brighter tint, a more expressive form, by means of some strange— we must call it—Carlylism; English, Scotch, German, Greek, Latin, French, Technical, Slang, American, or Lunar, or altogether superlunar, transcendental, and drawn from the eternal Nowhere,—he uses it with a courage which might blast an academy of lexicographers into a Hades, void even of vocables.

We should infer from Mr. Carlyle's style that he is not naturally fluent, or at least had not been led in very early life, when alone, perhaps, it can be done, to use with smooth dexterity a conventional mechanism of discourse on all the topics known in civilized life. Where this, which may be called the rain-spot or parish-pump faculty, has been much developed, it is very difficult, if not impossible, to gain that short, sharp, instantaneous mode of expression which says what the speaker feels to be the right thing, and no more, and so leaves it. But if, from circumstances of any kind, whether of personal seclusion, or of silent and severe habits in those about us in childhood, this knack or gift has not been carried to any very awful perfection, such as one finds in barristers, preachers, literary journeymen, leaders of the House of Commons, auctioneers, and the like—and if, nevertheless, there is real matter crowding and glowing for utterance—a man's speech is likely to have a pith and directness otherwise extremely hard of attainment, and which recalls the reason given by old Gaunt, in *Richard II*, for the hope that his own dying counsels may influence the young king:—

> Where words are scarce, they are seldom spent in vain;
> For they breathe truth that breathe their words in pain.

Furthermore, it may be observed, on the choice of words shown in this author's writings, that his clear and irresistible eye for the substantial and significant in all objects, and his carelessness of the merely abstract, show themselves in an immediateness and prominence of expression, to which we see nothing in its kind equal in modern English books. His style is not so much a figured as an embossed one. The shapes which it exhibits have not only neatness and strength, which those of a clever rhetorician often have; but a truth and life, which show them to be prompted by the writer's feeling and experience of things, and not arranged from a calculation of what will be the effect on others.

Having said so much of what strikes us as most remarkable in Mr. Carlyle, it is time for us—more than time—to speak particularly of the contents of the books now before us. The bulkier of these is a collection of Essays, which have appeared in different English periodical works during the last ten or twelve years. We regard them as the most important series of papers that any one man has contributed to the present race of Reviews and Magazines—nay, as incomparably the most so. About two-thirds of the whole relate to German literature, and of these the greater number to authors who, though all now departed, have been living in our own day.

Of these portraits none is so remarkable for its subject as that of Goethe, communicated in two articles, which contain various translated specimens from his works, but chiefly consist of descriptions of his character and life. It is not too much to say, that to these and other labours of the same hand is due almost all the just appreciation of Goethe now existing in England. A few, twenty years ago a very few, there doubtless were in this country who understood that he was on the whole the most remarkable person of modern times. But for the widened and fast widening knowledge of this truth among all who occupy themselves with literature, so that it is no longer a mere secret doctrine, but courts the sunshine and challenges opponents, the chief immediate cause must be found in the zeal with which it has been made known by Mr. Carlyle.

Surely the sight thus presented to us is a sufficiently surprising one. Imagine a man of the mould and aspect of Luther standing forth to proclaim the greatness and immortal beauty of a poet such as Shakspeare. So dramatic, so symbolic is the contrast between the eulogised and the eulogist. They resemble each other, indeed, as two truly great men, of self-coherent thoughts and lives must needs be like. And both of these rise far above the common stature of man. The one how large of bone, how sturdy, and with a look of combat, and of high crusader-enthusiasm. Yet this he readily exchanges for a broad, disdainful scorn of vermin that come nigh him, whom he treads down and brushes into inane abysses with a tyrannous gust of ridicule. This again in turn passes swiftly into bitter natural tears for the misery of those on whose behalf he has armed himself to battle. A man of thews and courage such as seldom have been clothed in knightly mail; resembling, perhaps, a great Christianized giant of romance, a legendary Christopher,—so solid does he stand, so simple, blunt, and inartificial in his stride and bearing. One who in generous courtesy and trustful kindliness is of no less large a frame than in mere strength and exuberance of life. Then look at the man on whom he bends such reverential eyes; tall, indeed, and full, and fixed, and so catching the eye, but far more detaining it by a refined dignity and the perfect look of sculptured gracefulness, and yielding softer and higher music than ever was shed from the image of the divine Memnon over the Egyptian desert. In a word, with much in common, the distinguishing characteristic of the one is indomitable strength, that of the other unblemished symmetry.

The points in Goethe on which Mr. Carlyle emphatically dwells are his conscientious laboriousness; his unbounded tolerance, arising from his universal comprehensiveness; and, lastly, his reverence, not formal but vital, for the truth and love on which the universe is based, and which are the highest manifestations of the life that pervades it. . . .

The glory however remains, and must always remain, for Mr. Carlyle, of having been the first to inform that half of the civilized world whose speech is English, that Goethe is the man to whom, for fulness joined to fineness of nature, at once for capacity and accomplishment, no other of our age can be compared. Nay, the best among them, whom the others must ultimately, however unwillingly, obey, have through him been so informed of, or rather by, the truth, that it rests for them in the main on its just and inalterable grounds. All the knowledge of Goethe which may be added, must cohere with that which he has given, and depend upon it like the bartizans, bridges, court-yards, turrets, and encircling walls, with the immovable gothic* keep, which is the ancestral stronghold of the great castle. Others in England before him, undoubtedly knew the truth on this subject, and some had published it: but no one in such a way as to force it on the attention of all who read miscellaneous literature, and to induce multitudes, especially of younger men, to acquaint themselves with the writings of the one greatest man of our time.

When it is said that Goethe was this, how much is in the words implied! No less than that it is he who has seen widest and deepest into the wants and powers of his age, and has best shown what may be done in it, by those who must, in the end, be the teachers of the others. That he was a much greater man than had been in Europe for several generations, may or may not arise simply from the fact that the age itself was generally a far more complex and more energetic one than those which had immediately preceded. Of his place in it there is likely to be less and less of doubt. Whatever else may be written about him in English, which will hardly surpass in interest what we have before us, these are at least the first at all ample notices, which, when Goethe had been for about half a century established by his works as the first mind in Europe, made Englishmen aware of the fact. Grasshoppers had before chirped for and against the rumoured foreign singer; and these are often pleasant verdant animals. But now it was no grasshopper; the creature is of a different race. *Bos locutus est.* It was the roaring of a bull,† which the mountains needs must hear and reply to. The Divine Monster, renewing the European tale, carried on his back as he rode the waters, the unreluctant muse of Germany.

It need, perhaps, hardly be said, that neither on the subject of Goethe, nor on almost any other, do we profess, or inwardly yield, unconditional assent to Mr. Carlyle. In many things he seems to us hyperbolical and inordinate. In many, negligent of counter considerations. Seeing clearly which scale descends, so zealous is he to recognize the fact for himself, and enforce it on others, that he overlooks the existence of any weight at all, and often there is a heavy one, on the other side of the balance. With reference to Goethe, there is a droll example of what we may venture to call partisanship, which is amusingly unlike the writer's general and most religious accuracy of statement. . . .

The other dissertations on German literature are all of high value,

---

* *Qy.* Gōthic?
† *Roaring bulls* he would him make to tame.
Spenser.

and show an amount of care and sincerity which may be regarded as quite exemplary for such papers. Those on Schiller, Jean Paul, and Novalis are portraits at full length, and living as if done by Rubens. But of these productions we cannot now speak in detail. There are two essays on Frenchmen of the 18th century—Voltaire and Diderot—which are, also, masterpieces of free, strong, and just delineation.

The account of Voltaire especially may, both for the importance of the hero (of the narrative) and for the vigour and solidity of the composition, be considered as a work in this kind which will outlast the Plymouth breakwater and the New Houses of Parliament. It is a singular illustration of the writer's character. . . .

In this essay on Voltaire, as we have referred to it at all, it may be worth while to notice that we find a favourite doctrine of Mr. Carlyle's put forward in these words:—'The thinking and the moral nature, distinguished by the necessities of speech, have no such distinction in themselves; but, rightly examined, exhibit in every case the strictest sympathy and correspondence, are, indeed, but different phases of the same indissoluble unity—a living mind.'

Now in this and all similar statements of the author, it has always seemed to us that he neither does justice to himself nor to his readers. He is haunted, apparently, by some ghost of a theory, which fills him with just antipathy—that the faculties of a man are lifeless, separable things, put together like differently coloured bits of wood in a joiner's inlaid work, so that the chess-player is constructed by a higher effort of the same kind of skill employed in constructing his chess-table: which, could man do nothing better than play chess, might have a show of some meaning. But, to love and make love while playing chess, like Ferdinand and Miranda, or to philosophize over his game, like Nathan the Wise,—this passes the craft of any timber-and toy-work ever imagined before or since the days of Hiram of Tyre.—This notion that juxta-position of dead parts, not conspiration of living powers, is the secret of our being, which is taught by several thinkers, or, omitting the aspirate, tinkers, in psychology, Mr. Carlyle opposes, often with victorious decision and divine feeling, but often, also, as it seems, by all manner of random and amorphous assertions, which, like bursting cannon and reverting congreve-rockets, injure his own cause at least as much as that which he combats. As if a wise man could find no other way of putting aside a fool's wooden buckler but by running full tilt against it with his own head, in which concussion the philosophic skull is not the implement that of the two will be the least damaged.

In this passage, let us ask, what is the value of the assertion that there is *no distinction in themselves between the thinking and the moral nature*? Mr. Carlyle has shown abundantly well that Voltaire was not the greatest of men as a practical, that is, a moral being. Therefore, he says, neither can he have been the greatest of thinkers. The reasoning is perfectly just, because as no one doubts, the same thinking faculty will think better when combined with a good moral nature than with a bad one. Therefore, any man who has been as acute and intellectually susceptible as Voltaire, and has also had a stronger and more religious conscience, must have been a wiser and farther-seeing man than he. And as there is no ground, even independently of experience, for doubting the possibility of this better example of manhood, it is of course likely that Voltaire was not the best of thinkers. It is matter of fact that there have been both better intellects and nobler hearts than his, sometimes separate and sometimes united, forming in the last case the highest class of human beings we know—Socrates, for instance, and Shakspeare.

But after the statement that, because Voltaire was not the best, therefore he was not the wisest of men—a sacred truth—what is the reason given for it? Because *the thinking and the moral nature are but different phases of the same indissoluble unity—a living mind.* But we suppose it must equally be allowed that memory and fancy are also but *different phases,* &c.; therefore all the persons of well-nigh miraculous memory, who could repeat the Bible by rote, and so forth, have been also the most brilliant speakers and writers. So sympathetic sensibility and the talent for number and geometry are but *different phases of the same indissoluble unity.* Therefore Howard and Wilberforce were mathematicians equal to Lagrange and Laplace; and Newton, again, was demonstrably a man of the warmest and liveliest affections.

Mr. Carlyle's mode of stating his opinion must, therefore, as it seems, be abandoned. But to refute him is far less important than to understand him; to know what his essential meaning is, and what is its value. . . .

There is but one other of these biographical representations which we propose to speak of. It is that of Samuel Johnson. Of few men named in English literature has more been said and written than of him. His works are known more or less to all Englishmen who read, and there is still a more substantial record of him in Boswell's Life than in his own writings. On these materials innumerable artists have been at work. For fifty years he has been a perpetual theme of journalists. He is still a sort of venerable name, as of something bigger and more sonorous than other authors of the eighteenth century, not without a shadow of romance—a something between the parish schoolmaster and the Great Mogul. For a considerable time after his death he passed, even among cultivated men, for a profound thinker, a teacher of the principles of human life, and the best of authorities in literary criticism; while, as to his rhetorical ability, the only question seemed to be whether he was great—almost incomparably great—by dint of, or in spite of, his style. Of late years the tide has turned. The habit has grown up of looking wider and deeper in literature than was usual in his day. Men require freedom, energy, picturesqueness, subtlety, even at the cost of a certain neatness and full-dress modishness, then thought indispensable. We have come nearer to reality in all ways, and find, therefore, that we must widen our circle of mental activity as the horizon of nature spreads endlessly around us. Thus the common estimate of Johnson has changed, and younger, fresher gods have drawn off men's attention from the Jove whose shake of his un-ambrosial wig once ruled the world. A prejudiced, emphatic pedant, is probably the sort of description which would most nearly hit the prevalent opinion about him during the last twenty years. Nor has the teaching of men of high talent been wanting recently to enforce this view of his pretensions. But listen to Mr. Carlyle's voice: the scene changes with a flash, and Johnson stands before us, revealed in gigantic size, an object for all ages of reverential love.

By what magic is this done? Nay, it is not by magic, but by that art of which magic, were there such a secret in existence, would be a subordinate handicraft department. With an eye, one of the rarest ever given to man, and sharpened by steadfast use, he sees the essential, the intrinsic in other men, and while he sees it, reads it aloud in a tone which all must hear.

What he tells us of in Johnson is not the theories, the prejudices, the style of the man. It is the man himself. What he had the capacity to be, above all, what he willed to be, and how resolutely. Thus we see the rough, sorrowful, over-violent, voracious, unrefined man, start out as a hero, a worn, unwearied wrestler for conscience sake, whose life was the grand work to which all his written works are but an appendix, and *pièces justificatives*. It is not that he says this, as it is here said, or as any one might say it, in abstract terms, which convey the meaning only as a black profile represents the face—hardly so well, for in it the outline is the fac-simile of a part of the original, but abstract terms express only a general notion, which belongs equally to ten thousand originals, and can therefore accurately image no one of them specially. But Mr. Carlyle so says the thing as to startle the eye with it and stamp it on the heart. For him who has read his account of Johnson, the old, grey, scarred, passionate, but purely good man, is for ever a living being, one whom we have heard with profit, gazed at with veneration; nay, whom we have known as those did not know him at whose tables he sat, and to whose questions he replied. We know him both by faith and insight, inwardly and in his structure, and as a toiling mortal man in this painful land of the Immortal.

Thus, in that flat and meagre English eighteenth century which produced the houses, the furniture, the thoughts, the people, that we are most accustomed to consider decayed and out of date, human life comes before us in one great, awkward image, still a sacred beaming reality. There is no well-known biography of any man written by one who knew him intimately, which sets him so livingly before us in all his breadth and strength, in what was peculiar to him, and not his accidental fringes and appendages, and with all that was truly shaping and influencing in his age and circumstances, as this delineation of Johnson by a man who never saw him in the body,—knew him not till he had been removed from the stage and stage-lamps of the present, to live before the spiritual eye among the starry depths of heaven.

In this singular essay it may be remarked, and well deserves to be thought of, that Mr. Carlyle never appears to have been forcibly struck by the sad unrest, the entire absence of peace in Johnson's whole life. As fixed by his moral strength as the hardest material framework of the earth, and freely standing fast against all temptation, supported also by an unwavering belief in a Divine friend of man ruling the universe, yet was he always anxious and spectre-haunted. Though too stout of heart for legions of fiends to drag him into their pit of darkness, yet he always fancied that He, against whom all fiends are in revolt, would thrust him from his presence over the brink of destruction.

Nor did this arise directly from a thoroughly diseased physical frame infecting the healthy mind, which would perhaps be the commonest solution. For Johnson's view of all beyond the mechanical and palpable had in itself the seeds of all the moral misery which he suffered. The mere moral element, the conscience, was in him nobly but also fearfully predominate. By earnest longing to fulfil the moral law did no man, from Adam to the Baptist, from Paul to Luther, ever yet find peace on earth. Those incapable of self-devouring emotion and brooding melancholy may easily find, in rules of duty, a safeguard against any such wrong-doing as would produce consequences very painful to them; but a fervid and meditative spirit carries conscience with it as a divine curse, if this be not transfigured and glorified into the revelation of a good higher than all laws of duty.

The philosopher has his insight into an ideal self-subsistent first principle, the source and end of all things. The regenerate religious believer enjoys communion with an unseen, ever-present Deity. The poet and poetic artist cultivates his general consciousness of an eternal harmony and beauty pervading all objects, and lending them whatever they enjoy of worth. These are realities of life, in subordination to which the agonizing conscience is reconciled with the universe; and so lights up the soul without consuming it to the ashes of sorrow.

Now in Johnson this higher consciousness never took complete effect. It worked, indeed, negatively and destructively towards the overthrow of all joy, rather than genially towards the realization of a sacred and mysterious peace. Not refreshings were his, but witherings from the face of God. For him the grave was an ultimate den of horrors; not a crypt through which we rise into the bright, eternal temple. In all beyond the material and prudential, his theoretic insight was most dim and weak— a purblind dream of insight. And thus he endeavoured to find a home for his reason in that region of the traditional and authoritative, which is even at best a road to travel on; a mine to work in; but can for no mortal be a place of final rest.

That Mr. Carlyle does not notice in Johnson this absence of serene joy—now different from the vain self-satisfaction of the world!—is an evidence of that characteristic tendency to sympathize with every struggle, and turn away from the fruits of every victory. His applause is never for him that putteth off his armour, but always for him that putteth it on. And the most resolute and mighty preacher in our day, of a Truth to be believed and enjoyed by all, is he who seems least capable of valuing the repose of spirit, the quieting of inward tumults and terrors, which the courage to fight as he fights, has earned for so many weaker men. . . .

The second paper of which we spoke is entitled 'Characteristics.' Of this it is far more difficult to say any reasonable word. In the details and colouring it is full of Mr. Carlyle's spirit. But as a whole, and in its purport, it seems to us (that is, to one living man) obscure, self-contradictory, strained, like the long far-glimmering dream of some wise vision that has been in other ages, or shall in new ages be. This is not said dogmatically, but with full consciousness that the fault may be in the reader, not the writer. For to no reflecting man can it be unknown that the not-understood will often, most often, present itself as the unintelligible, by no defect of light in the object, but by defect of eye in the beholder. It is a droll yet a compassionable fancy of many, that what is called ordinary education, that is to say, a small smattering of Latin, and a large smattering of English, vocables, enables every one, or all but every one, to know at a glance what significance and worth there is in all the uttered speculations of the wisest heads. It is therefore indubitable that Mr. Carlyle may have an idea which, if it could be imparted to the perplexed mind, would enable it to see, in this dissertation, a complete and consistent view of the high matters which are there dealt with. As the case now stands it appears confused, and dark, not with excess of light. Yet the obscure looks nowise inscrutable, but having its explanation in some fallacies most natural and seductive to a man like him with whose works we are now occupied. Would you have a pine forest teeming and arcadian as an orchard? An idle question! Or the inside of a pyramid light and sunny as a green-house? How vain an expectation! Leave we such fancies; and make the best of what we have.

The main argument of the whole exposition is the evil of consciousness; which indeed is with Mr. Carlyle the root of all evil. It is not that in his view, as in that of all wise men, consciousness is liable to its excesses and derangements, but that the fact is itself a mischief and misery to man, and our only wholesome state that in which we work instinctively and spontaneously, not voluntarily and reflectively. . . .

Accordingly, the fact appears to be that—except in rude primitive ages, when greatness could only be spontaneous, not voluntary, instinctive, not reflective—every great man knows what he is; knows it so well and habitually that he never needs to spend his time in affected sentimental speculations on himself. A few flashing looks into his own story, and the meditated experience of life, give to such a man a consciousness which he cannot lose if he would, and would not if he could, of all that he is as an individual time-bubble. But far differently is this knowledge won and employed from the ignorant self-admiration of the fop wasting his life in the worship of an idol, which, like an altar-piece ruined by the smoke of the tapers, becomes the more worthless the longer and more fervently it is honoured.

The reasons by which Mr. Carlyle maintains his view are chiefly these:—

1. In health we are insensible of our bodily functions, and the fact of our having a body at all is recalled to us only by pain, which is the

result of disturbance or sickness: therefore, judging by analogy, the same is true of the mind.

But the fact asserted is only partly real. We are conscious of our bodies by means of their pleasures as well as of their pains. And moreover, the statement is nothing to the purpose. The bodily sensations are totally unlike in kind to the reflective self-consciousness. The true analogy to this, drawn from the body, is the knowledge of his organs and functions which a physiologist acquires by self-observation, and which, so far as it is possible, is by no means incompatible with health. Doubtless, when the body becomes as it were the centre of the man's consciousness, when pain compels the energies of the soul to spend themselves on the sense of misery in the physical frame, this is a consequence of disease, and that in a violent degree. But the evil here is, that the supremacy of the mind is thus suspended by the intrusion of sensations, which, in the sane and normal state of man, are the servants, not the masters, of his reasonable will.

Mr. Carlyle's doctrine is clenched by the assertion that, *Had Adam remained in Paradise there had been no anatomy and no metaphysics.* Now certainly it has not been one of the results of eating the fruit of knowledge to teach us what would or what could not have been our state if we had not tasted of it. Doubtless, as Bonaparte used to say, when he was met by a foul wind, or an unexpected frost—But for this the destinies of the world would have been different!—a proposition not likely to be contested against the master of so many legions, but which we may now venture to smile at. If we can at all conceive a paradisiacal state for so anti-paradisiacal a being as man, it would be one enriched with all our blessings and liable to none of our calamities. But as we conceive the knowledge of anatomy and of metaphysics to be among our most unquestionable, if not our most unmixed, advantages, we, for our parts, should consider Paradise as decidedly improved by the admission of these, and, indeed, of all kinds of science as well as of art. Had Adam remained in a state of childish weakness as well as simplicity, which seems shadowed out in the brief Biblical narrative, he would probably have remained ignorant of many things which even Mr. Carlyle thinks worth knowing. But had he begun to reflect, his thoughts, for aught that we can guess, must have followed the same laws, and been directed to the same objects, as those of his descendants.

2. Life, we are told, exists for purposes *external* to itself, therefore, the turning away our thoughts from these to the processes of life is a practical error.

But surely no. If by these external purposes be meant the handling of material things, life has far wider, higher aims. We may learn and teach truth for the holiness of truth, and not that by her means we may eat, drink, and be clothed. Man, it is admitted, can attain to a knowledge, to some genuine vision, or imagination, of sacred laws to which he is subjected, and a wondrous, boundless system which he belongs to. Is it ideally possible, or is it consistent with fact, that he can do this, and yet not, by an inevitable and no less rightful step onward, begin to sunder what is eternal and divine in those laws from what is spurious and accidental; to widen by experience and reflection the first small arbitrary limits of that system; to consider how, by what bonds of affection and necessity he is connected with the All around him; and to examine where and when he may and must, in order to free and healthful action, cut the temporary ties of custom and opinion by which his range has been confined and his limbs fettered? If he does this, how can the process be distinguished from that of philosophic reflection—inspired intuition, going before, but ever followed by, and alternating with, distinct self-consciousness? For of this self-consciousness, the rise and final maturity are prophetically implied in the mere fact that man can reflect, and cannot live within the circle of his instincts.

3. Much grows in us, and much is given to us, of which we cannot discern the source or trace the law. It is an intuition, an inspiration.— Yea, verily. But so far is denied by no one with whom there need here be argument. And, further, it is manifest that he who would close his mind against all suggestions of the true and beautiful which he cannot pre-define and lay down in program, makes the speculative machinery which ought to be but a tool in his hands a torturing framework to confine them. Therefore, says Mr. Carlyle, to seek to know what can be known without exclusion or self-limitation, is but a diseased craving. Therefore it is a licentious daring and slow self-destruction to reflect at all on ourselves in relation to the Universe and to its Author. And therefore, not only must all higher and ideal truths be taken for granted where they cannot be seen; but even where they can, we must close our eyes, and feel for them groping. Depart then, ye profane! who fancy that life and light are not only organized and methodized in our structure according to a plan which we may partly decipher, but that they enable us to apprehend and meditate the limits which divide this conscious being of ours from the ocean of divine exist-ence surrounding and sustaining it. Yet is it not rather certain that only by such meditation, and the actions which it both prompts and

purifies, can our humanity be preserved at once integral and progressive, neither closing itself against the radiance of the objective universe, nor letting itself lazily dissolve and be lost in those currents from which, not by chance nor vainly, was it distinguished and impersonated into a man?

4. *Genius is ever a secret to itself.*—In the sense of inability to trace the channels and influxes by which what is best comes to it—this has indubitably its share of truth. How far it is true even in this sense may afterwards be considered. But let it first be noticed that the consciousness which has been hitherto spoken of and justified, is the inward contemplation, not of what is peculiar in the individual, but of what is universal in the race—of what characterizes, not a man, but Man. That the man of genius does not know himself to be a man of genius might be altogether true, and yet this very man might study with unwearied scrutiny the workings of his own soul, not as his, but as God's! and as his nearest, and brightest, and by far his faithfullest, and his only perfectly open, summary of God's whole creation.

But even in the other sense, namely, that a man of genius does not know himself to be such, the assertion is to be admired for a certain felicity of courage rather than for any ascertainable precision. There would be far more of truth in the opinion, that there never yet was a man of genius who did not know his own powers. But this it is not necessary to affirm. It is sufficient to maintain that there is no man memorable in literature for the highest talents, who cannot be shown to have well known that he possessed them.

In fact, there is only one person whom Mr. Carlyle ever alleges, and he is a stock example, in proof of his doctrine—this one, of course, is Shakspeare. As here, for instance, he says, '*The Shakspeare takes no airs for writing* Hamlet *and the* Tempest, *understands not that it is anything surprising.*' Probably, indeed, he took no airs, though even this we do not know. He had better work to do than taking airs for *Hamlet*, namely, taking pains for *Othello*. And he was doubtless too thoroughly aware of his own greatness to be vain of it. In his plays he says nothing on himself and his own character and history which can now be recognized to have that meaning. But in dramatic writing how could he speak of himself by name or obvious allusion? And finer and indirect references to his individual feelings and circumstances may, for aught we know, be found in every page; but that our ignorance of the minuter facts of his life entirely conceals them from us. However this may be, we have the evidence of his sonnets to prove that where occasion offered he had no hesitation in speaking of his own genius as of a matter which he was perfectly acquainted with. The XVIIIth, for instance, concludes thus:—

> But thy eternal summer shall not fade,
>   Nor lose possession of that fair thou owest,
> Nor shall death brag thou wanderest in his shade,
>   When in eternal lines to time thou growest:
> So long as men can breathe or eyes can see,
> So long lives this, and this gives life to thee.

The two last lines of XIX are:—

> Yet do thy worst, Old Time: despite thy wrong,
> My love shall in my verse ever live young.

And the two first lines of LV:—

> Not marble nor the gilded monuments
> Of princes, shall outlive this powerful rhyme.

Or look at the end of LXI:—

> Your monument shall be my gentle verse,
>   Which eyes not yet created shall o'er read;
> And tongues to be your being shall rehearse
>   When all the breathers of this world are dead;
> You still shall live (such virtue hath my pen)
> Where breath most breathes,—even in the mouths of men.

And in CVII it is thus written:—

> And thou in this shalt find thy monument
> When tyrant's crests and tombs of brass are spent.

The whole basis of the notion, which these passages superabundantly refute, lies in the apparent indifference with which he treated his plays in not publishing a complete edition of them. But for this there may very possibly have been external reasons which we are not aware of. He did print the larger number of his works, which is sufficient to prove that he aimed at something more than theatrical success. The language of his first editors sounds as if he had intended to publish the whole collection himself, but was prevented by death.

It is also well worth considering, that however high Shakspeare's estimate of his own powers might have been, he had no facts before him from which it was possible to imagine the importance that English books were to obtain in the annals of mankind. The only books then thought of with veneration were in Greek, Latin, or Italian. That an author writing English could thereby become one of the capital figures in human history, was concealed, possibly by nature's kindness, certainly by inevitable circumstances, from him who was best to realize the truth. Spenser, indeed, knew otherwise; but Spenser read Italian, and was a professed imitator of Italian poets, who had done in their language what he wished to do in his. But literature, except as learning, and that chiefly theological, was held in small esteem, and gave no social importance. It is evident that Shakspeare's plays ranked high in general repute among the dramatic productions of his day. As much is plainly stated, as well as elsewhere, also in the preface of his first editors, Heminge and Condell, '*to the great variety of readers.*' Now these same editors prefixed to the volume a dedication as well as a preface. This is addressed to the two brothers, the Earls of Pembroke and of Montgomery. And hear how these friends and comrades of Shakspeare write of his works, even after his death, which might have been expected to raise prodigiously their tone in speaking of him.

Right Honourable, Whilst we studie to be thankful in our particular for the many favors we have received from your L. L., we are faine upon the ill fortune to mingle two the most diverse things that can be, feare and rashness: rashness in the enterprise, and fear of the successe. For, when we value the places your H. H. sustaine, we cannot but know the dignity greater than to descend to the reading of these trifles, and while we name them trifles, we have deprived ourselves of the defence of our dedication. . . . We cannot goe beyond our owne powers. Country hands reach forth milke, creame, fruits, or what they have, and many nations (we have heard) that had not gummes and incense, obtained their requests with a leavened cake. It was no fault to approach their gods by what means they could; and the most, though meanest, of things are made more precious when they are dedicated to temples.

This was the language of the chosen friends whom Shakspeare had commemorated in his will: and among the many proofs of the low estimation in those days of all literature which did not come under the head of learning, it would be hard to discover any to us more striking. An Earl of Pembroke was of too great dignity to descend to the reading of poems, which we now know will be read and treasured by millions when the House of Peers itself shall have sunk into the grave where lie those wondrous Earls; nay, will be the wonder and delight of perhaps new continents sprung from the deep, when England, with her chalky cliffs, shall have melted again into her limitary seas. We know that if in the wreck of Britain, and all she has produced, one creation of her spirit could be saved by an interposing genius to be the endowment of a new world, it would probably be the volume of which the author's friends, after his death, thought it too insignificant to be read by two courtiers of King James I. And because we know this, we fancy it wonderful that they and Shakspeare did not know it, as if the sudden vogue of pamphlets and ballads for a few previous years could have suggested to them any such result. As well might one imagine that Shakspeare ought to have anticipated the discoveries of Newton and the inventions of Watt.

But from this ignorance of his as to the future historical importance of his works, how strange does it seem to infer that he had not discovered his own creative and intellectual superiority to all about him; though of course he had better things to do than habitually to repeat to himself, 'How much sweeter and nobler a singer am I than my elder, Marlowe; how much freer, and fresher, and more bland a spirit than my younger, Jonson; how much more thoughtful, fiery, deep, and substantial than the moonlight soul of Spenser.' Yet that he did not know himself to be all this, we can find neither proof nor probability.

And how far more astonishing is it to suppose, that because he did not foresee the destiny of his works to be the best inheritance of his countrymen through all time, therefore he had not looked into his own mind, and found there—there, where alone it could be found—the interpretation of the dream of human life which floated round him; that he had not discerned in the feelings and thoughts which he was conscious of, the hint and explanation of those which he moulds now into an Imogene, now an Othello, now a Hotspur, now a Falstaff. This must be proved by stronger evidence than even an assertion of Mr. Carlyle's. Nay, properly, no evidence could prove it; for the thing must be seen as true and eternal in itself, or is incapable of being known at all.

As to all the other men most memorable in Christian literature the case is clear. No one can overlook the proud, even fierce, self-consciousness of Dante; the distinct praises which he fearlessly bestows on his own labours; the inward, melancholy scrutiny, which is the theme of the 'Vita Nuova' and the 'Convito'; and the whole plan and tone of the great poem, which may not inaptly be described as a journey through the kingdoms of self consciousness exhibited in images of the outer world, such as the eyes and as the fancy see it.

No less plain is the self-gratulation of Cervantes, and his avowed preference of his own writings to those of his contemporaries; and all who value *Don Quixote* as anything better than a farce, have ever seen that the poet drew the substance of his work, though perhaps undesignedly, from the depths of his own character, its visionary aspirations towards impossible good, and the incongruous failures to which time and circumstance exposed his longings.

That Milton's grandest as well as his most trivial writings are undisguised fragments and glimpses of Milton's individual self, all will admit, and no one more readily than Mr. Carlyle. His moral reason, exalted into the region of pure intelligence, and invested with crystalline glory, constitutes, not suggests, the highest beings of his Heaven. His austere, concentrated, often baffled human affections, are the originals of his earthly personages. And his passionate and gloomy self-will, like his shadow thrown by a flash of lightning upon the snow-wall of an Alpine ridge, supplies the shapes and the demoniac stature of his nether spirits.

Of Goethe it need here only be said, that a graceful and easy, but most assured sense of his own worth, circulates through every fibre of his creations, and is uttered loudly enough on suitable occasions. No writer ever existed in whom one finds more of direct self-observation. Much even in his works which is not in the form of psychological remarks, yet in substance is nothing else, though endued with the most beautiful and cunningest of mythical and fabulous imagery. If Mr. Carlyle persuades himself that Goethe's example lends any support to his theory, the pensive reader cannot fail to be reminded of certain zealous divines, who discover the most peculiar of the Christian mysteries in the legends of Pagan poets, and in rites on which the Christian church made implacable war.

5. We have next an attack on Logic. Here Mr. Carlyle is of the opinion of so many metaphysicians, that a knowledge of the process of drawing inferences from principles is not an important help towards drawing them correctly. Very possibly this is true. This process, however, though the study of it may not be of much importance in the practical art of thinking, is yet one portion of the truth of our nature which does lie completely within our ken, and which it can injure no one to understand. The syllogistic scheme, though as certain as the Rule of Three, is no more than this any substitute for the higher logic by which we decide on the premises we are to reason from. This great and primal science is, precisely on account of its depth and compass, far more difficult to bring within any systematic limits. The knowledge of it is the aim of the highest speculation. The noblest moral effort strives to realize it in the being, and not merely to embrace it in the intelligence. Its realities are the vital germs within all true poetic images.

And these primitive verities are as much more wonderful and beautiful than the logical forms by which we connect them with our experience, as the starry Heavens are sublime in comparison with the brazen tubes and glass lenses of the astronomer.

But this view of the dignity and sanctity of those seminal principles of things and of knowledge, which the technical, drudging logician is apt to overlook, seems no way inconsistent with a belief in the use of logic as a clear exposition of the rules by which mankind instinctively and universally reason from their experience, whatever that experience may be. The inadequacy of such subordinate and instrumental logic to make a man wise, cannot be too clearly seen; but hardly less important is it to understand, that it has no such evil consequences as Mr. Carlyle attributes to it. It is well worth considering, for instance, that the school-men, instead of being, as he seems to imagine, the least wise, were the most wise of all men living in their times, doing many of them the best practical work, and often with hearts awake to all excellence and beauty which the world had then disclosed before the eyes of European men.

When we find a Luther, a Napoleon, a Goethe, cited as intuitive in contrast to dialectic men, is it not plain that they had simply a larger amount of inward and outward facts, and a clearer insight into the master idea of the business in hand than others; and that from these primordial truths they reasoned not with less, but with more logical swiftness and force than others, and the two Germans with a full and sharp consciousness of the process and method of their thoughts?

6. Virtue is next subjected to the same iron yoke and caudine infamy as logic. And here, above all, do we seem to find the inanity, or at least extreme imperfection, of the view propounded to us. Be it admitted—be it enforced by word, deed, and life, that man, to be worthy, must live in a sphere of pure, voluntary impulses to good, the flow of which has become habitual, and is the result of many moral victories. But when men have learnt to reflect on all other things, how is it possible that this alone should not be to them a problem for reflection? Where the will in all its aims is generous and grand, and therefore necessarily, in smaller and more conventional phrase, right, is it not certain that the insight gained by such reflection will in turn corroborate and renew, not debase and infect, the strength of the better promptings? How weak, unstable, vacillating from right to wrong, from truth to falsehood, and certain to be driven from precipitate appetite into dreariest doubt of all things—how dreamy and half sincere is that virtue sure to be, which, unreasoned of, misunderstood, taking itself for granted,

dwells in a mind awakened to the meditative knowledge of other principles, but only not of moral ones!

How sad an image of the chaos and ruin of our age is shown us to mourn over, when a wise and brave man, if such there be on earth, is driven, in the recoil from empirical corruption and mechanic theories of the essentially hyper-mechanical, into hymning the praises of blind ignorance, and well nigh envying the condition of Homer's warriors, or of the peasants who in England, in the nineteenth century after Christ, are left almost as dark as they!

O no! True it cannot be that, *to the popular judgment, he who talks much about virtue in the abstract begins to be suspicious.* . . . *that ages of heroism are not ages of moral philosophy; that virtue, when it can be philosophized of, has become aware of itself, is sickly and beginning to decline.* The great Athenian teacher of virtue was not less, but far more virtuous, than any of those who scoffed at him; far more heroic as a citizen, as a soldier, as a man, than those who would have returned to the old unthinking days of merely manual heroism. Cicero was hardly a worse man than Clodius or Catiline, who wrote no books De Officiis. Seneca was not the most earnest of seekers after truth, but it would have been well for Rome and for the world had he, not Nero, ruled the empire. It was Marcus Aurelius, and not Commodus, who wrote the Meditations which have supplied the motto to *The History of the French Revolution.* In the midst of that dark Syrian corruption, he, who realized in his life a higher good than Plato or Antoninus taught in writing, was also the great preacher and doctor of the truth which he practically revealed; and his works are known as widely as his name; and by himself was it declared that they, too, *are spirit and are life.* Or will it be said that Paul was no ethical expositor, and that Luther never unfolded in many a volume the reason of the law which he obeyed, while he lived in freedom above it?

7. Of Mr. Carlyle's anathema on sentimental morality little need be said. It is most true, and, in our age, most necessary to be spoken; but it makes nothing for his purpose. Not by silence, not by unconsciousness, but by high, earnest teaching, like his own, of what man's true greatness is, may the foul and nauseous imitations, the corpses painted beyond the tint of life, and festering and rotting within, be shown for the dead and shameful things they are.

8. The subsequent passages on the evils of a self-conscious state of society, are in some respects most brilliant, and even suggestive of truth. Yet there can be few readers who will not feel that the author wants the

full and clear command of the idea, which, not being manifest to him, confuses him with hints of its presence, such as only serve to make darkness visible. It is impossible to controvert the proposition, that some one period in history is unhealthy as compared with another; for what measure have we of the moral unhealthiness of a period? To some it might seem that the tenth century, when there was hardly any but theological reflection, and no diffused and public thought at all, was a less healthy age of England than the sixteenth, when there was so much, or than the seventeenth, when there was more of manly, majestic character than in any other time of our annals, and when also there was endless speculation on all the great questions that have ever excited the human mind.

Let us here episodically note, that, in the essay on the *Signs of the Times*, it is somewhat marvellously said of the English nation in Elizabeth's day; 'They had their Shakspeare and Philip Sidney, where we have our Sheridan Knowles and Beau Brummel.' In the strength and richness of human nature, abundant, stately, saturated with life, like tropical vegetation, the days of Elizabeth had at least an apparent superiority to ours. But the point would, perhaps, have been less grotesquely maintained by a reference to Walter Scott and Wellington, rather than to Knowles and Brummel; for in those times also there were to be found in London poets of less than the highest genius, and fops of quite the highest absurdity. But, as to Sidney, it is better worth remarking, that he, like all gentlemen of his age—Mr. Carlyle's peculiarly favoured period—was trained in the scholastic logic; that his own writings are full of ethical dissertations and high-flown speculative rhapsodies on moral excellence; that he patronized not only Spenser but Giordano Bruno—the most abstract intellect among all the metaphysicians of that age; and that his chosen friend was the Lord Brooke, whose writings are still in our hands, and furnish one of the most remarkable memorials of a sleepless, brooding self-consciousness to be found in all English literature.

This in passing. The question of the good and evil arising from, or implied in, the awakened consciousness of a nation, might lead us much further than we can now travel. It can here be only suggested, that the greatest period—incomparably—in the history of the world in this respect, was that of the Reformation. Then the stone effigies and armour, the velvet suits and mantles, of the baronage of all northern Europe—then the gaberdines, and cloaks, and formal decorums of the guilds and arts—then the dust, and bones, and rags, and hunger, and servile rudeness of the labourer—all started and crashed up in new portentous life, with thought working in every head, faith mounting from all hearts through all far-glancing eyes, and the eloquence of true inspiration pouring from millions of long-frozen tongues. When was there ever national self-consciousness, if not now? And who will say that this was not the most accepted of all times—the most brightly illumined page in all the stained and worn, but still legible chronicles of human history?

It may be added, that the noblest day of Germany for greatness of character and public spirit since that of the Reformation, was during the resistance to Napoleon, which followed, and manifestly in a great degree arose from, the manlier culture furnished by the high philosophy and philosophic poetry of the preceding fifty years.

What is more peculiarly and emphatically called a self-conscious state of society, appears to mean only that state in which so much knowledge is spread abroad among the people, that topics necessarily interesting to human beings, but which have hitherto been the property of retired students, or small classes, and distinct professions of men, are now generally discussed, thereby of necessity exciting the stronger feelings natural to larger masses of people, and stirring up men whose incomplete culture makes them more liable than are the learned to head-long impulses, and beliefs at once passionate and visionary. But in these facts what wise man can see a predominance of evil? Where the new conflux of ignorance and knowledge produces, instead of the old torpor, active and hot delusion, there is but the one remedy of giving more knowledge, and so expelling the ignorance which is the poison-element in the fermentation; and when the uproar of the popular mind directs itself against institutions, knowledge will teach them—for blind experience having failed only true knowledge can do it—what is really good in these. Woe to those who attempt the maintenance of what is bad.

Leaving all further notice of the arguments and illustrations in the essay, it may be observed, that of the men who have arisen to public view as thinkers in England during the last twenty years, the one of the most fervid, sincere, far-reaching genius, is also the one of the keenest and deepest self-consciousness. We will not do him the injustice of pointing him out to Mr. Carlyle's abhorrence.

Finally, if we are not to return to some jejune fiction of a state of nature,—that is, to barbarous, to savage, and ultimately to brutal existence,—the consciousness of mankind must be more and more widely awakened, and their minds be thus redeemed from gross animal torpor, and from the hardly less melancholy state of merely mechanical speculation. In the finer and loftier spirits, this consciousness organized and fixed in systematic thought, in images of reality, and in free, self-commanding life and action, must form the substance of all philosophy, all poetry, and all heroism. Its corruption into idle vanity and diseased sentiment is, doubtless, also inevitable. But what good thing is there, what best thing, what love to man, what faith in God, which human frailty does not thus twist and crush into evil? If we are to wait for a good which cannot be abused, will Mr. Carlyle tell us how such is possible for a finite being, capable of infinite advancement, and therefore dissatisfied with what he already possesses, and uncertain of what lies before him? For what is our present life but the dusk and wavering image of the Future and Final seen amidst the smoke of the Past, which slowly and for ever burns around us?

This long examination of a single essay of our author, is an evidence of respect for him, which he, at least, will understand as it is meant. It is natural and unavoidable to speak more concisely when there is only applause to utter. May our readers feel that the admiration we express is no less sincere than the dissent.

Among the works of Mr. Carlyle there is one fiction—*Sartor Resartus—The Life and Opinions of Herr Teufelsdröckh.* This consists of two intertwisted threads, though both spun off the same distaff, and of the same crimson wool. There is a fragmentary, though, when closely examined, a complete biography of a supposed German professor, and along with it, portions of a supposed treatise of his on the philosophy of clothes. Of the three books, the first is preparatory, and gives a portrait of the hero and his circumstances. The second is the biographical account of him. The third, under the rubric of extracts from his work, presents us with his picture of human life in the nineteenth century.

How so unexampled a topic as the philosophy of clothes can be made the vehicle for a philosophy of man, those will see who read the book. But they must read with the faith that, in spite of all appearances to the contrary, it is the jest which is a pretence, and that the real purport of the whole is serious, yea, serious as any religion that ever was preached, far more serious than most battles that have ever been fought since Agamemnon declared war against Priam.

One general consideration may enable the more speculative to understand how things can be united so remote and discrepant as are the visible clothes of men, and the invisible causes of All. Our doings all bear the stamp of some portion of our being. Now, every portion of our being is inseparably linked with all the rest, and therefore each primary art, and every hereditary contrivance of human life, may be used as an emblem leading up to the conception of our whole constitution, and all its relations. Clothes, then, are of this universal indispensable nature, and so have a ground of perennial reality. Further—they, like every thing that all men use, are made more or less symbolical, bear the image of time, country, character, and station, and so are true necessary hieroglyphics in which all the history of mankind is to be found, expressed or understood.

In this book that strange style appears again before us in its highest oddity. Thunder peals, flute-music, the laugh of Pan and the nymphs, the clear disdainful whisper of cold stoicism, and the hurly-burly of a country fair, succeed and melt into each other. Again the clamour sinks into quiet, and we hear at last the grave, mild hymn of devotion, sounding from a far sanctuary, though only in faint and dying vibrations. So from high to low, from the sublime to the most merely trivial, fluctuates the feeling of the poet. Now in a Vulcan's cave of rock, with its smoke and iron tools, and gold rubies; now in dismal mines and dens, and now in fairy bowers, shifting to the vulgarest alleys of stifling cities; yet do we always feel that there is a mystic influence around us, bringing out into sharp homely clearness what is noblest in the remote and infinite, exalting into wonder what is commonest in the dust and toil of every day. In this enchanted island, Prospero, the man of serene art, rules indeed supreme, and has his bidding lightly done, but oftener by a band of shaggy Calibans than by a choir of melodious Ariels. And it is most bewildering of all—for is not the common that which, by disclosing its strangeness, has ever the greatest power to amaze us?—that the Prospero is a man of our age, in our familiar garb, with no magic instruments but the words we all use. Even the Calibans and Ariels of the vision are the dull, customary tribe—peasant, artisan, gentleman, and lady, whom we know by rote as the obvious alphabet of our lives.

'Tis weird work all. If Jean Paul presents to us milk and wine, here, instead of wine, is alcohol and something more, and the milk what one might fancy not of a cow, but a she-mammoth.

Hopeless is the contrast, the contradiction which the book at first presents to all our common world, its laws, and usages, and familiar insignificance. Nothing beautiful is here; nothing calmly, manifestly wise. We look at it not for its worth, but its oddity. Gradually the eye learns to find some dawning coherence and stability, as if it were not merely mist. Then one entanglement untwists itself after another; joint and lineament, plan and structure, appear, intricate indeed, but palpable. At last we cross ourselves, and know not whether to laugh or weep when we find that we were puzzled, not by the want of aught real and substantial in the object, but by the presence of so many more forms of truth and nature than we commonly discern in life: and which yet, although we knew them not, were ever there. These shadows, too, now no longer illusive, are all compacted by their own vital unity, which excludes the unmeaning and alien, and brings the expressive and lasting elements of our time and being, however seemingly discordant, into smooth, indissoluble conjunction. In what seemed a fair-booth, half smoke, half canvass, full of puppets, toys, dolls, refuse trinkets, peering vaguely through thick confusion, there is discovered to be implied nothing less than a model, and that a living one, of the world itself, such as God in his eternity, and man in his six thousand years, have made it. The image is not indeed complete, but broad, full, bright, and most genuine, created and imparted by an earnest soul, to which nothing that lives and grows, and is not a mere idle falsehood, comes as worthless. It is, in fine, a system of highest philosophy in figures of liveliest truth, and wanting only—though this is not a small want—the soft musical roundness and honeyed flow of song, to be a poem such as these latter days of English song have not produced.

Much there is that at the tenth, no less than at the first perusal, must seem affected, arbitrary, and little more than mere burlesque. But the law which unites the capacity for all that is highest and most beautiful with the tendency to see meaning in the commonest, even sordid things —and the experience of all strongest hearts that they must often needs escape, if they would not break upon the spot, from the fierce immensity of feeling into the homely fire-side circle of the ludicrously vulgar,— these (which to no one knowing what is in man, and not merely what comes out of him, can be unknown truths) explain so many seeming anomalies and discords, that all the rest may well be believed equally fitting, or if not, yet but pardonably wrong.

There are, indeed, persons of high faculties and excellent cultivation, to whom a limited, conventional rather than convictional, standard, will make the whole distasteful. But, blessed be that endless dawning which for ever discloses more and more of the eternal within the narrow bounds of time, this temper is ceasing to be that of our age. Those who read the book for the worth that is in it, will assuredly not miss their reward. Yet read without bitter pain it cannot be. The heaps of misery which lie about us intermingled with joys and hopes, are here sundered, and looked at by themselves. The root of sorrow and evil is laid bare, and frightens the sunshine with its blackness. Nay, so intently and right onward does the author pursue his task of denudation, that it seems at last as if something physically dreadful were a-doing, and something half-demoniac were at work; the secret of which impression seems to be, that in this book the mind is not brought into agreement with that great movement of nature of which our universe and life are but the momentary result and manifestation. Science in one way, in another purely imaginative poetry, creating what is quite distinct from the poet's individuality, and in a third mode the calm completeness of active morality—these differently, but all truly, reproduce in a human form the mild, profound unity of the whole system of being. In each of these aspects of things we see how fire and storm, strife and death, pain and evil, are but superficial disturbances of the great concord, which, could we so stand apart from them as to unriddle their meaning, would always be beheld but as necessary to the existence which they seemingly threaten, and elements of that music with which we fancy them, and as practical beings must assume them, to jar. But here in this volume, the orgasm of shaping thought and desolating emotion bursts with ruin through the steadfast bounds of science, of art, and of conscientious activity. The author brings together creation and destruction to work precipitately and face to face in open conflict, not with their true and everlasting though unacknowledged alliance. His own heart reads the purport of their operation, and eagerly feels the greatness of their tasks, but shares none of that sublime tranquillity in which the twain repose, nursed at either breast of their mighty mother.

That in these world-encircling speculations and symbolic designs, which alternate from the small sharpness of Hogarth to the measure-lessness of Michael Angelo, there is much omitted, much distorted and overdrawn, cannot be surprising. He who the most sincerely believes in and admires the excellence of the man and his works, will be able to see no little that he must think altogether mistaken. But be it ever remembered, that there is more of profitable truth in the errors of the wise than in the just conclusions of thoughtless men; and even where there does not appear to be any high principle—perverted into an equally grave delusion, but still there, and to be recognised, though disguised and contorted—yet there is always some great and pure feeling, working, however questionably, and forcing us to reflect on the depth of its source and the grandeur of its objects.

Teufelsdröckh represents it as a mere delirium, that the village of Dumdrudge, having no private Dumdrudgian quarrel with any French village whatever, should send out thirty of her working sons to kill and be killed by thirty French wearers of *sabots*, in some corner of the south of Spain, merely because the rulers of the two countries have fallen out. Yet it needs not a philosopher or poet to see that the village of Dumdrudge had far better do this than wait to have pillage, and massacre, and worse, brought to the parish green and into every cottage by the injured innocents who ravaged Spain rather than England, only because England would not let them visit her first.

Independently of this particular instance, there is a vapid, commonplace view of the whole matter, such as Teufelsdröckh would probably think one had better die than hint at, much less utter, but which is not the less true. For Dumdrudge gains considerably by belonging to a country having a government of some kind. A government must have power to decide on many things, and among these on war and peace, for all its subjects, Dumdrudge included. Being fallible, it may very possibly decide wrong, and nevertheless be better than no government at all. Moreover, with or without rulers, men, being pugnacious, will fight and kill each other; any one man who chooses to go to war for a wife, a wigwam, or a copy of *Sartor Resartus*, having, in a state of nature—that is, a savage state—the power to compel any other man to do battle to the death for these possessions. For constables are decidedly a product of government, and not, like their staves, of vegetation. Finally, few things can be more certain than that fighting is reduced by political society, from every man's most necessary occupation, to be the trade of a comparatively few, even if every Dumdrudge sends her thirty every year to be drilled and shot at.

This view is not fitted, like Teufelsdröckh's, to amuse and elevate the universe; but that with our limited faculties it should appear to us truer than his, is, we must submit, our misfortune rather than our fault. Nor, indeed, when Herr Teufelsdröckh condescends to disguise himself, and to discourse on governments and society like any mouthing quack philanthropist and friend of humanity, is the simple-minded reader to be solely blamed, if for a moment he fancies that the professor is no other than what he pretends to be. When the philosopher seems to consider Botany Bay as the true Atlantis, Utopia, and isle of heroes; the convict-hulk as the ark in which the faithful few are divinely set apart;

and all gaols and treadmills as the sacred retreats and mystic grottoes of
the only modern saints and sages,—whether even a Teufelsdröckh can
pass without suspicion, while teaching a doctrine so subversive of the
Old Bailey and the New Police, let remote posterity decide.

This statement is, in fact, only a very temperate caricature of opinions
which frequently appear in these works. It may be hoped that there are
few readers who will not see them to be errors generated by the corruption of serious truths. They suggest a point of view so neglected and
so unpopular, and at the same time so important as a corrective of the
opposite and reigning onesidedness, that they will probably be of far
more use to mankind than the reiteration of the axiomatic principles
which we have repeated and taken for granted till we have nearly ceased
to understand them.

The book is the most extraordinary mixture we know of the purest
and rarest truth with much truth in itself of equal depth, but here
exaggerated into not merely hyperbolical phrases—of which, indeed,
there is little, if anything—but hyperbolical opinions; opinions, that is,
which have fallen over the battlements they were placed to defend, and
been dashed into separate pieces or confused lumps. Any man who,
although thus erring, at the same time utters much and original wisdom
and poetry, is of course a person of strong abilities, and, if all is done
with unaffected earnestness, must be of strong character also. Here
purpose and faculty, will and talents, are combined and exist in friendly
union, and all in the highest vigour; and it is not the least charm of the
book that it supplies some seminal hints on the mode in which a mind
so marked and so capacious has been formed and ripened. Nay, a
zealous student will often be inclined to suspect that, in Teufelsdröckh,
a British biography looks through the widely different and much exaggerated mask of a German one. It is impossible not to connect the
characteristics which run through all these volumes with such passages
as the following:—

[quotes 'To look through' to 'and a stronghold' Bk. II, x, 164]

In the doctrine of Teufelsdröckh also, as in that of Mr. Carlyle, belief
in Goethe holds a chief place. Yet here, too, it must be said as before,
that those who look in the Professor for any exceeding conformity of
opinion or character with the poet, will be much disappointed. Among
innumerable other differences there is this most marked, that the sympathies of the Privy Councillor are chiefly with the wealthy and cultivated
classes; those of the writer on clothes rather with the poor, the vulgar—

in a word, the cultivating. Goethe respects all established things merely as such, and troubles himself but little to inquire how this or that has grown into authority. Teufelsdröckh's instinct is to embitter himself against all that is, so far as it is the work of man. The reason of the difference, perhaps, is partly this, that Goethe could do all he cared to do, namely, be a poet and thinker of the highest order, in the midst of his actual circumstances; and therefore any disturbance of these was a mere hindrance to him, forcing him to adjust himself to a new state of things. Teufelsdröckh, on the other hand, though perhaps he knows it not, is pre-eminently a moral and political man, in soul if not in act a reformer, and one of Titanic bulk and force. Finding in the present no field and facts adequate to his longings, and unable to rest, like Goethe, in mere imaginations, he finds himself crippled and wounded at every step, and thinks it is his time which is out of joint. Not that, judged even by *his* total standard, the present age is at all inferior to any past one, but that it is his, and therefore partly responsible for his dissatisfaction. For among the many and precious truths which the Professor not only talks of, but knows at heart, this is not one,—that he who has not peace within himself to-day would not have it, whatever he may fancy, were to-day changed into a yesterday or a tomorrow ever so distant, and in its remoteness ever so alluring. Teufelsdröckh discerns, and can point out, a path traversing the far past and the far future; but—as is so often known of a faint track upon a moor—around him, where he is actually walking, he can hardly discover a vestige of it. There all seems confusion; and although he walks forward, as a wise man will, towards the line of path before him, using what marks there are to guide him, yet he journeys in tribulation and horror, inwardly cursing the day that he was born, while he recounts aloud the grounds which he unquestionably has of contentment—nay, of rejoicing. Goethe concerned himself little about the past, except for the use he could make of it, and not at all about the future, because from it he could derive no profit. But he stept cheerfully and bravely on in the midst of the present, where he felt that his work lay, and did his work with joy. With joy Teufelsdröckh works not, but with all the stronger courage, for he toils on, wanting all the poet's cordial impulses of happiness. He finds wisdom and imple-ments, and a niggard but sufficient support, everywhere around him; here a Mentor, there a ship—always bread and water—and, when need-ful, an entrance to the prophetic land of spirits; only nowhere a mild and musical tranquillity of heart, which for many a meaner mortal has stood, as well it might, in lieu of all outward help.

There may perhaps be found some rude analogy between the men, him of Weimar and him of Weissnichtwo, both of the Universe—and the hot spring of Iceland, boiling among snows and blasted rocks, compared with a sunny river flowing from its distant hills by groves and meadows, and beautiful hamlets and kings' porticoes. But the image is far from doing justice to the harsher and less halcyon soul. . . .

[Sterling's comments on *The French Revolution* and Carlyle's similarities with Luther are omitted.]

Here must end our remarks on the admirable writings of a great man. Could it be hoped, that by what has been said, any readers, and especially any thinkers, will be led to give them the attention they require, but also deserve, in this there would be ample repayment, even were there not at all events a higher reward, for the labour, which is not a slight one, of forming and asserting distinct opinions on a matter so singular and so complex. For few bonds that unite human beings are purer or happier than a common understanding and reverence of what is truly wise and beautiful. This also is religion. Standing at the threshold of these works, we may imitate the saying of the old philosopher to the friends who visited him on their return from the temples—Let us enter, for here too are gods.*

Note

Emerson called Sterling's review a 'noble critique'; Carlyle was delighted with it and confided to Mill that this review was a 'splendid Article' in spite of its 'enormous extravagance'; to Sterling, Carlyle was warm—part of the letter dated 29 September 1839 is printed below:

---

* [In giving our readers the benefit of this attempt by one of our most valued contributors (we believe the first attempt yet made) at a calm and comprehensive estimate of a man for whom our admiration has already been unreservedly expressed, and whose genius and worth have shed some rays of their brightness on our own pages; the occasion peculiarly calls upon us to declare what is already implied in the avowed plan of this Review—that its conductors are in no respect identified with the opinions delivered in the present criticism, either when the writer concurs with, or when he differs from those of Mr. Carlyle.

While we hope never to relax in maintaining that systematic consistency in our own opinions, without which there can be no clear and firmly-grounded judgment and therefore no hearty appreciation of the merits of others; we open our pages without restriction to those who, though differing from us on some fundamental points of philosophy, stand within a certain circle of relationship to the general spirit of our practical views, and in whom we recognize that title to a free stage for the promulgation of what they deem true and useful, which belongs to all who unite noble feelings with great and fruitful thoughts.][1]

---

[1] The editorial comments are by John Stuart Mill.

A brave thing, nay a rash and headlong; full of generosity, passionate insight, lightning, extravagance, and Sterlingism: such an 'article' as we have not read for some time past! It will be talked of, it will be admired, condemned, and create astonishment and give offence far and near. My friend, what a notion you have got of *me*. . . . I do not thank you; for I know not whether such things are good, nay whether they are not bad and a poison to one: but I will say there has not man in these Islands been so reviewed in my time; it is the most magnanimous eulogy I ever knew one man utter of another man who he knew face to face, and saw go grumbling about there, in coat and breeches, as a poor concrete reality—very offensive now and then. (See *Letters of Thomas Carlyle to John Stuart Mill, John Sterling and Robert Browning*, ed. Alexander Carlyle [London, 1923], 223–4.)

11. William Sewell, from an unsigned article, *Quarterly Review*

September 1840, lxvi, 446–503

William Sewell (1804–74), divine, friend of John Henry Newman, John Keble, and Edward B. Pusey, was one of the earliest
members of the Tractarian Movement but was alienated from it
when it seemed to be heading toward Rome. For many years a
prominent figure at Oxford, writing and lecturing, Sewell spoke
out on all issues. His judgments, however, were often called into
question. He is reported to have labelled James A. Froude's *The
Nemesis of Faith* a wicked book and then to have thrown a
student's copy into the hall fire, an action which gave rise to the
apocryphal story that the book was burned publicly at Oxford.
See Introduction, p. 13.

These remarkable volumes contain many grave errors: they exhibit
vagueness, and misconception, and apparently total ignorance in points
of the utmost importance. They profess to be on subjects of ethics,
philosophy, and religion, and yet, notwithstanding a plausible phraseology scattered here and there, they make no profession of a definite
Christianity; and if it were fair to put hints and general sentiments
together, and to charge the writer with the conclusions to which they
probably will bring his readers, we should be compelled to describe
them as a new profession of Pantheism. Yet there is so much truth in
them, and so many evidences, not only of an inquiring and deep-
thinking mind, but of a humble, trustful, and affectionate heart, that
we have not the slightest inclination to speak of them otherwise than
kindly. We are very willing to believe that what is false and bad belongs
to the evil circumstances of the day—what is good and true to the
author himself; and to hope that more light and knowledge will bring
him right at last, since already he has advanced so far in defiance of the
difficulties around him.

In one point of view, Mr. Carlyle's writings, and the partial popularity which they have obtained, are a striking symptom of the state of the times. No author of any school confesses more distinctly that for more than a century the English mind has been incapable of originating or appreciating any deep philosophy. Its whole vision, he avows, seems to have been obscured, and perverted to a singular obliquity. The only works professing a graver philosophy, which we can now put into the hands of young students, who wish to know what their immediate ancestors have thought on the weightiest questions respecting man, are those to which the really powerful intellects of Germany and France have pointed, the better with contempt, and the worse with triumph, as the source of most of the follies which subsequently inundated those countries. From these a man may learn that he is made of five senses, and little more; that he is to think for himself, without listening to others; that he is not responsible to man, and consequently not to God, for his opinions, nor, therefore, for his actions; that his whole intellectual power is merely a machine for grinding logic; that it is his right and duty to govern himself, and not to be governed by others; that societies are joint-stock companies for taking care of man's body, leaving his soul to take care of itself; that whatever he thinks and feels is right; that whatever he deems profitable is also good; that his mind may be anatomised and studied as a skeleton in a glass-case, and all its faculties and organs injected and laid out—and that with this, and this alone, we may thoroughly understand it; that it is every man's business to take care of himself; that it is our duty to see the whole of everything; that whatever we cannot see, and force into a syllogism, is false; that mystery is another word for falsehood; that religion is little more than priest-craft; that men can find, and did find it out, at the beginning, by the light of their own understanding; that if religion is to be maintained it should be excluded at least from the ordinary pursuits and speculations of life, and placed in quarantine, as if its very breath would infect the independence and value of truth; that prudent practice has no connexion with profound theory; and that in a world of railroads and steam-boats, printing-presses, and spinning-jennies, deep thinking is quite out of place.

In this country the faint beginning of better things may be traced first in the works of Coleridge and Wordsworth. The former, a vigorous, self-formed, irregular, but penetrative mind, incapable of acquiescing in the meagre fare set before it by the popular literature, was compelled to seek for something more substantial in the new world of

German metaphysics. How largely he was indebted to these for the views, and even words, which he promulgated in England, we need not now inquire. But whatever he may have borrowed, he was a man of true native genius; and Coleridge has undoubtedly given considerable impulse to thought in this country, and dissipated the ennui which the more energetic minds felt in travelling over the smooth uninteresting Macadamised road of modern English literature, where every mile brought back the same prospect, and the end was constantly in view, and not a turn or a chasm, or a rut was permitted to disturb the dulness of its logical perspicuity and case. He put before them statements which they could not understand; hinted at mysteries; indulged in a strange uncouth phraseology, which awakened attention, as a new language; and first taught young minds their own weakness, and then encouraged them to undertake exercises which would create strength. We are very far from thinking Coleridge a safe or sound writer; but he has done good: he opened one eye of the sleeping intellect of this country—and the whole body is now beginning to show signs of animation.

To Mr. Wordsworth the country owes a still greater debt of gratitude. Even he has only made a step to the restoration of better philosophy among us: but it is a great step, in a safer direction, and its influence will be felt far more extensively. It is singular to observe in how many great revolutions, which have altered the course of human opinions and affairs, the impulse and direction have been given, not by one but by two minds, co-operating together, one representing the higher power of the intellect, and the other more of feeling. Plato and Aristotle, Luther and Melancthon, Jerome and Augustine, Cranmer and Ridley, were yoke-fellows of this kind: so Wordsworth, the kind, gentle, affectionate Wordsworth, seems to have been almost paired with the acute, restless, deep-thinking Coleridge. And if God has a work to be done in this land, it is not strange that he should employ instruments to address both the head and the heart. It is in this latter work that Wordsworth has been most efficient. We can scarcely overrate the blessing to this country of recovering a school of poetry quiet, pure, and sober, and yet not superficial—which, even if it be at times, as it certainly is, artificial and affected, is affected in imitation of the better and simpler parts of nature—to supersede the exaggerated phantasmagoria of one school, and the effeminate sensualities of another. Mr. Wordsworth, in the face of ridicule, has attempted this, and, after a long and patient endurance of many slights, he has lived to see his own success.*

* About a year since the University of Oxford conferred on him an honorary degree.

One great, perhaps the greatest, truth of philosophy, and the best foundation for all philosophy, has been brought home and familiarised to ordinary readers by Wordsworth's poetry; and this truth gives the chief value to Mr. Carlyle's speculations: *it is the value of little things.* Perhaps, after all, the whole of human philosophy is nothing more than construing signs, translating one language into another, reading individual facts in general principles, and general principles in individual facts. As philosophy, in the more restricted sense of the word, is the translation of matter into spirit, the tracing of the infinite and invisible, and universal, and spiritual, in the little, palpable, partial hints of the material world; so art in its widest extent, including the whole range of man's creative powers, may be only the same process reversed: it may be the embodying of the same great truths, which philosophy evolves from material forms, in material forms again; the rendering them visible and sensible to common eyes, not capable of discerning or retaining them in their disembodied abstract existence. If this be so, we may understand how philosophy is inseparably connected with art, and especially with poetry; and how much it owes to a poet, who has taught men to look at nature in its minutest forms, in its leaves and insects, and petty movements, and humblest shadows—even in its most degraded creatures—as a deep and awful mystery, before which there is no place for arrogance or conceit; where he who sees nothing but the exterior is little better than an idiot, and he who pierces most deeply, sees the darkest depths beyond. Once make the human being feel that there is more in things around him than he can understand or penetrate, and he will acknowledge a mystery. With mystery will come the sense of his own weakness, humility, and self-distrust, and the still better consciousness of the presence of a greater power. Then follows necessarily *faith*—for in the midst of doubt and darkness man cannot live without faith. If he has no ground for it, as the Christian has, he will invent and imagine a ground for it, as Mr. Carlyle does; he will

---

Persons who were present have asserted, that no enthusiasm in the same assembly, except that with which they received their own illustrious Chancellor, equalled the applause with which the good old man,—'the poet,' as he was then entitled by them, 'of the poor,'—was greeted by a body mostly of young men, who a few years back would have been sighing and looking desperate over the sorrows of Lara or Manfred, and laughing with scorn at Peter Bell and Betty Foy—as if Peter Bell and Betty Foy were the whole of Wordsworth; or a man could not be a poet whose hero was not guilty of incest or murder, a hater and hated of mankind. To have produced such a change, and led insensibly to the formation of an entire new school in poetry—a poetry of deep thought, as well as pure and warm feeling—is a recollection which he may well cherish in the decline of his life as an inexhaustible comfort.

persist in cherishing it, though he can give no reason for it: and thus, though far from the truth, he has yet escaped from the regions farthest opposed to it, from scepticism, cold-heartedness, self-sufficiency—the logical restless cavilling of an intellect which sees nothing beyond itself —and the final dreariness of despair, which comes on as night draws round us, when the understanding can no longer work, and the heart can no more be deluded by its own vain dreams, but must awake and face the frightful realities of a world without a God, because without a creed; and without a creed, because without a Church.

This stirring of English philosophy in two poets has been followed by still more decisive and practical movements in other quarters. A new school of thought and feeling is undoubtedly forming itself: and what is more satisfactory, it does not appear to be gathering itself round any one individual as a nucleus; but one and the same spirit seems to be breaking forth and struggling into life from the most independent sources.

Even in France, where, if in any country, the human heart and mind would seem wholly and irrecoverably dead, or so poisoned by vices of all kinds, that no hope could be cherished of anything pure or elevated emanating from it, there is a school now forming, and acting insensibly on public opinion, which is very little known, but to which we cannot look without much interest, though mingled with no little distrust. Mr. Carlyle has given us a brief and rather contemptuous notice of one voluminous and important work, which has emanated from this school, the *Parliamentary History of the French Revolution*. He himself has been largely indebted to its collection of original documents, in his own strange magic-lantern scenes relating to the Revolution: perhaps he might have acknowledged his obligations more explicitly. . . .

To [his] peculiarity of style we attribute not a little of the interest which Mr. Carlyle's writings have excited. Readers are sick of the weak, vapid slops with which the press is now inundated, when every one who can spell and write, and couple verbs with nominative cases, thinks it his duty to publish. The general correctness of style at present is a remarkable fact. At the time when Aristotle and Plato *thought*, very few of their countrymen could *write* grammatically: and Aristotle himself lays no little stress on correct syntax as a necessary but rare excellence in an orator. At present, when *no one thinks, every one writes* and speaks correctly. In fact, we have been so busy with writing and speaking that we have had no time to think. But Mr. Carlyle has disdained the easy-beaten track, and struck out a new taste in writing, combining, we had almost said, all possible faults, and yet not unlikely to become popular. We have no intention of relapsing into the superficial criticisms of a by-gone day, and regarding style as the most important part of composition. But Mr. Carlyle himself knows, and has taken pains to illustrate a great truth, that between the internal spirit of thought and the external form into which it is cast, there is a vital connexion, as between soul and body. If the spirit is clear, simple, unaffected, unambitious, equable, earnest, and conscious of truth and sincerity, the words which it utters, even though unpolished and illiterate, will present a similar perspicuity, simplicity, and natural eloquence. There will be few of what are called quaintnesses—no flippancies—no strange, abrupt transitions from high to low, from the solemn to the ludicrous—little that is grotesque. Such a man will not deal with words as with counters, which he may toss about and huddle together at random, merely to express his own chance conceptions;—he will use them with caution and reverence as living things, which cannot be emptied of their own power, or be thrown to the world to be the passive symbols of him who uses them, but have their own significancy, and do their own work, and enter into the minds of others to turn and bend them in a mysterious way, so that he who deals with words is dealing with things, and not only with things, but persons. His very language will be to him as a living being, as a minister of God, with which he dares not trifle; but must act towards it reverently, and send it out on its mission with a chastened and quiet heart. . . .

We dwell upon this subject of style because it is not improbable that young persons, captivated by the novelty, and force, and frequent picturesqueness of Mr. Carlyle's ideas, may be also captivated with his language, and think it a necessary appendage to profound thinking, just as wearing no neckcloth was once thought by Cockney apprentices the best preparation for writing poetry like Lord Byron. And as young writers generally commence with words rather than with thoughts, and are more intent on rhetoric than on argument, Mr. Carlyle's faults are the first things likely to attract imitation with his admirers. Now it is objectionable enough for young men to *imitate any* style for it turns their attention more to words than things, and places their mind when writing in a forced and affected position. Let them be taught rules of grammar, and general principles of composition, which may secure them from committing faults; but never propose to them to write like another, instead of like themselves. They may read as many good authors as they like, and their language as well as their sentiments will be insensibly coloured, and moulded by the practice without art or effort: but this is very different from studied imitation. But of all imitations let them avoid Mr. Carlyle's. We are not warning them merely against the violation of classical rules of style, though even this we should lament to see prevail, as we should lament a false taste in architecture, or a fanciful perversion of natural laws in any work of art. But these classical rules are founded on deeper principles than any which Blair has touched on. They are founded on laws of the human mind. And you can no more indulge in playing tricks with language, without distorting the mind, than you can stand before a glass and twist your features into grimaces without disturbing the tone of your feelings. Or rather, if you will play these tricks, your mind is already distorted. It is lamentable to see that Mr. Carlyle's early writings, in which there is far the most truth and genuine good sense, are the most free from his faults. They appear to have gathered on him as he advances. Is it that he is permitting himself to dress up his style like a mountebank to attract popular wonderment, which we have too good an opinion of him to believe? Or is it that his mind itself, as we fear, is becoming embarrassed and perplexed with the speculations into which he is falling, and in which he evidently is struggling about like a man sinking in the water, and just beginning to suspect that he is out of his depth? Some of his early writings* are very pleasing in their language as in their sentiments. In his last works, the *Sartor Resartus*, and *Chartism*, he runs wild in distortions and extravagancies.

It is needless to speculate on the sources of all his affectations. His Essays have been originally, for the most part, drawn up for our periodical publications; and we need not say how much of this literature is written solely to amuse, and to amuse the most worthless class of readers—those who are incapable of regular study, and can or will read nothing but what is trifling and short, and intelligible at first sight. But to please a reader a writer must write as his readers feel; and such readers are beginning to be wearied with the monotonous mechanism of an easy style, and require something to startle and perplex, and to interest their reason with strange combinations and abrupt transitions; just as on the stage genteel comedy is giving way to German sorceries and French atrocities, and as in novels, the most esteemed purveyors cannot write works to sell, unless they select their heroes from Newgate, and

* See, for example, his paper on Boswell . . . but his *Life of Schiller*, which was we believe the first of his publications, appears to us in point of style by far the best of them all.

enlist the sympathies of their readers in the interesting misfortunes of noble-minded murderers, and warm-hearted, affectionate adulterers.

But perhaps Mr. Carlyle's faults are most of all attributable to an intemperate and indiscriminate fondness for German literature—faults, we mean, of style as well as of sentiment. Without entering at present into the subject of opinions, the introduction of a German style into this country would be an evil seriously to be deprecated. It would be worse than a revival of Euphuism. And the many translations of German works which have lately appeared, all of them naturally partaking of the idiomatic character of the originals, may give some cause for apprehension. It must be deprecated in the first place, because it is the very point in which Germans fail most. They think, theorise, examine, compile, and compose with far more energy, patient industry, and at present, we may add, with a far keener sense of the deeper mysteries of Nature, than the English. But, with hardly an exception worth noticing, they cannot write. Something seems to interpose between the conception and the expression of their thoughts—and when these thoughts do force their way, they come forth confused, and distorted, and enigmatic.

Much of this may be attributed to the very causes to which they owe their higher excellencies—to the retired, scholastic, independent habits of most of their thinkers and writers. Excluded from politics; treating religion and theology as a subject for speculation; unaccustomed in their universities to catechetical instruction; valuing truth and knowledge more for their own sake than for popular applause; and comparatively little exposed to those temptations of general society, which too often make literature in England and France to be followed merely as a passport to a temporary reputation, the Germans plod on their way perseveringly and manfully; and throw out their theories and inventions with far less attention than we do to the wants and weaknesses of their readers.

The attempt to analyse and revive the principles of Grecian art, which has been so generally made by Goëthe, Schleiermacher, the Schlegels, and many other of their best writers, is an indication that this defect in beauty of form is felt by those who are most capable of supplying it. But we doubt if it will ever be amended. Not that the Germans want critical powers to analyse and taste to appreciate this beauty, but that a power of creating it such as developed itself in the masters of Grecian art, and the Christian perfecters of Gothic architecture, is a totally distinct faculty, which seems to require for its growth both a more sensitive national genius, and greater habits of intercourse with man, and practical necessities for employing it, than the present state of German society seems to promise. To import therefore from Germany the very production in which they themselves lament their own inferiority, will argue a strange hallucination.

But it should be deprecated also because it is un-English.

We are not speaking now of the study of German literature in general, but simply of the introduction of a foreign style, of which lately many symptoms have appeared. Our novels are crowded with French phrases—our very conversation has become a polyglot—and if our graver literature is infected with German, what will become of our 'pure well of English undefiled?' For the same reason that the choice of a style has a deep moral significancy and moral influence over the individual, the alteration of a national language is not unconnected with deeper changes of national principle. We would not part with our national songs, or national anthem, or introduce a tricolor into the national flag, or substitute some new-fangled attire for our national costume, though many might be found as convenient, and some more becoming. But nationality—and an exclusive, partial nationality, not inconsistent with general benevolence—is a great element in the virtue of a nation; and it is shown in our adherence to these external symbols, but especially in the use of language. Learn to talk in German, and as Germans talk, and you will soon learn to think in German, and thinking in German, you will cease to think as an Englishman. . . .

We would willingly quote more of these just and profound observations. The whole essay on the 'Signs of the Times' is full of similar wisdom; expressed with the same earnestness and truth, and not, we are rejoiced to add, in a morbidly querulous tone. The times, we think with Mr. Carlyle, 'are sick and out of joint;' but it is not for any one to despair, or to condemn without endeavouring to amend. Mr. Carlyle may be too sanguine in his hopes of improvement; but we like him the better for the cheerful steady heart, with which he can venture to face the evils which he sees so clearly. He may have rested his hopes on wholly deceitful ground—on the notion of a continual progress in society, than which few doctrines are more contrary to experience, or more closely connected with mischievous fallacies. He may have no clear insight into the only means by which the diseased frame of society can be healed, and its vigour renovated. He may offer little more advice than to sit still and see what the course of nature will bring forth. But on the supposition on which we are compelled to write, that he has enjoyed few or no opportunities of understanding the true powers and privileges of the Christian Church, in counteracting the very evils which he deplores—that he is ignorant of them because for so many years the Church herself has permitted him, and others around him, to remain in ignorance—this at least must be received as a symptom of a good and elevated nature, and one which would encourage a hope of his finally perceiving truth in all things, that he has neither given way to scepticism, nor plunged into any very wild theories of reformation. Fatalism is the form in which we should fear that his errors will terminate, unless corrected in time;—and in his later works there are too many symptoms of its approach. But we shall hope that better things are in store for one to whom Providence has already vouchsafed much good in the midst of much evil. . . .

[Several pages of Sewell's review regarding Carlyle's correct diagnosis of the problems of the age and his inability to prescribe a cure have been omitted.]

And until once more the principle of faith be restored, we do agree with Mr. Carlyle that there is no hope for this country or this age. Until the child once more looks up to its parent, and its parent to the State, and the State to the Church, and the Church to God, and still as the eye ascends through all these stages, it beholds in each a shadow and a symbol, and a presence of that Power, from which all other power flows—Society cannot exist. It does not exist at present. Society is union; the union of many in one. If there be no union, there is no society; no more than there is union in a heap of sand. Like atoms of sand, men are now tost together; huddled in houses by the chance of birth; thrown up as in heaps into large towns, by a thousand separate eddies—by avarice, or want, or caprice; not bound together, but only not falling apart, in so-called kingdoms, because walls of dead matter hold them in—as mountains, rivers, or seas—or a foreign force, or the mere absence of a dissolving power; and saved from splitting off into innumerable fragments of religious dissent, not because the Church is the centre of their affections and duty, but because their interest, or conceit, or ignorance, or indolence, keeps them each in their place. Society therefore is gone. It is now lying like a long buried corpse, which the air has not yet reached, and its lineaments seem perfect, and the body sound: but if it should please God in his anger by some shock to lay it bare, it will crumble to dust. Let the State withhold its artificial support from the Church, and, with the exception of that large portion which is beginning to be impregnated and held together by a true revivifying spirit, the body which calls itself the Church will fall to pieces. Let a foreign invader attack the State, and we almost doubt if there is a single standard round which the whole nation would rally. Hold out the promise of cheap bread to the starving thousands of Birmingham and Manchester, and you see at once the rent and gap, which is widening between the two arms of our social strength, agriculture and manufacture. Let any social or political movement give the signal, and the young are ready to rise against the old, children against parents, tenant against landlord, pupil against teacher, subject against king. We ask if this be false—if union, where even it seems to exist, is not based both by theorists and in practice upon self-interest—if such an union is union at all—if it be likely to continue, when an external convulsion shall occur to give to each particle a separate bias? And who will venture to say that such a convulsion may not shake us to the centre to-morrow. . . .

Faith, therefore, must be restored; but how? And here it is that we begin to discern that, with all the truth and warm-heartedness, and sound practical observations, which appear in so many parts of Mr. Carlyle's speculations, there is somewhere or another something hollow and unsound, which cannot be trusted. He is a specimen of a naturally good and gifted man, thrown up from the bottom of a corrupted society, almost by a caprice of nature, and struggling by his own efforts to support himself, but struggling in vain. He requires, as all good and wise men must require, the spirit of *faith*; of a child-like, obedient, affectionate, docile reverence to man, as to the minister of God. He requires it both for himself and for Society. He is searching around in the world for objects on which this feeling may fasten. He has never heard, or never listened to the only voice which can give him what he wants; to those nobler strains of Christian wisdom which once were the common voice of Christendom, and in England, even during the worst of times, were never wholly silenced. . . .

But where has Mr. Carlyle found refuge? and what is his prescription against the madness which his own voice prophesies for men like himself?

It is hard to trace and put together his theory, scattered as it is in strange, odd fragments through his several writings; but it is the result of importations from Germany; and it well deserves attention, from its close analogy to the Pantheistic system, which was raised up under similar circumstances, for a similar purpose, in the first centuries of Christianity, and under which, for a time at least—a very short time—

many gifted heathens attempted to shelter themselves, instead of taking refuge in the Church.

Mr. Carlyle does not deny a God; far from it. His whole system is religious. Without a Power infinite in goodness and wisdom, the first want of his nature would be unsupplied. In this he is right; and he is right in laying the foundations of belief not in evidences and logic, but in an inspiration of the heart. Evidence and logic may prove, but can never teach the existence of a God, much less his attributes. They ought, perhaps, to teach it, if men were made of intellect, and intellect alone. But man has a heart as well as a head; and his heart is made to move, and his head to check and control him; and when men appeal to the head to make him move, their blunder is the same as if, when the carriage is to start, they should carefully take off the horses and put on the drag.

Mr. Carlyle has reached a still farther step in the road to truth. Every man, even in this day, save the fool, believes in a God; and believing in a God, he must at least profess to worship him. But the real struggle of wilfulness still remains; and even religion strives to emancipate itself from restraint by denying the inter-position of man as a divinely-constituted authority between his fellow-beings and God. Governments and priesthoods are held to be human contrivances, and human only. As human, they may be changed at will, suspended, or cashiered; and the individual is thus left alone with his Maker; and as his Maker is not visible, nor acts with miraculous interpositions, the individual feels no restraint, and may indulge himself as he chooses. What says Mr. Carlyle?—

[quotes 'True it is' to 'may stand secure' *Sartor Resartus*, Bk. III, ch. vii, 199–200]

So all good and wise men have felt and spoken. Man must have men to reverence as well as God. But where are they to be found? As men—as mere mortal, fleshly creatures—men cannot be reverenced; if anything higher be found in them, it must come from God—and therefore it is only as divine, as connected with or partaking in the Deity, that man can be worshipped. Homer's heroes, therefore, and Eastern Priesthoods, and Alexandrian philosophers, and Roman emperors, and Christian saints, and Christian monarchs, and heathen poets, all bore the name of the deity stamped in some form upon them. They were 'godlike,' or the 'sons of gods,' or 'divine,' or 'deified,' or 'inspired,' or armed with power by the 'grace of God.' But here again man's wilfulness struggles to escape from the law of obedience. How shall he discern the Divine? All that is divine must be revered, must be obeyed; but what is divine? And it is here that Mr. Carlyle, like the multitude, has gone wrong. All talent we know, all goodness, all truths, all warmth of heart, strength of self-denial, energy of purpose, power of art and of science, come from God. Those men then, it is supposed, are to be our guides and our rulers in whom these gifts are found.

The only title wherein I, with confidence, trace eternity is that of King. Konig (King), anciently *Konning*, means Kenning (Cunning), or what is the same thing, Can-ning. Ever must the Sovereign of Mankind be fitly entitled King. Well also was it written by theologians—a king rules by divine right. He carries in him an authority from God, or man will never give it him. Can I choose my own King? I can choose my own King Popinjay, and play what farce or tragedy I may with him; but he who is to be my Ruler, whose will is to be higher than my will, was chosen for me in Heaven. Neither except in such obedience to the Heaven-chosen is Freedom so much as conceivable.

Most true and most catholic! It is the very language which the Church uses—the very principle on which her claims must rest for belief and obedience. But Mr. Carlyle has made no acknowledgement of *her* commission. He has his saints, and martyrs, his religion and priests, his worship, and his temples, but they are chosen by himself; and whom has he chosen? Goethe—Richter—Shakspeare—Burns!!! Goethe above all! These are his heroes and saints! whom he would hold up as models and guides—in whom he recognises the divine—out of whom he would construct a new world, and purify the old. The Romanist leaves our Lord, and chooses his tutelary saint; and his tutelary saint becomes at last a stock, or stone, a morsel of rag, or bit of bone. The Puritan leaves his parish priest and Catholic Church, and follows his own chosen preacher; and in a short time tinkers and cobblers, madmen and fools, seize on the pulpit, and still they are followed and obeyed. Mr. Carlyle too, has chosen his idols; and of all the objects of worship to which a great and good man might be inclined, he has probably chosen the strangest. . . .

[There follows a long impassioned argument against Carlyle's Pantheism and his insistence on faith over reason.]

But Mr. Carlyle's error lies still deeper. If 'the real, the actual, the true', be indeed the object of his worship, and the law of his activity; if it be the only true wisdom and goodness to throw aside all 'lies and quackery' (and surely so it is), let him tell us *what is the true*—where are we to find his *realities*? He is struggling, struggling manfully, against the Sophistry of the day, which denies all truths: but what is *his* Truth? Is he not, after all, a Sophist in disguise?

One kind of *truth*, indeed, he does recognise, namely, the correspondence of man's words, and acts, and symbols with his inward thoughts. Of one kind of *lie* he speaks most strongly, namely, a discordance between these same things. But are these the only truth, and only lie? If a bad man had honesty enough to lay bare all his thoughts; if the profligate threw aside his shame; if the moment we ceased to act up to the principles we profess, and lost the spirit from which the forms we use first emanated, and which they were intended to preserve, that moment we threw those forms away, and every pulse and fibre of the human heart were stripped of its disguise,—would this be *the truth* for which Mr. Carlyle sighs? Alas, he knows little of human nature, who could dream of living in a world such as would then surround us! God himself has hidden the soul beneath a covering of flesh, that we may not behold it naked in the deformity of its imperfect nature, and be shocked by it, or tempted to imitate it, or be hardened in our own evil by the universality of evil around us. And be assured all is not hypocrisy, in which actions do not correspond with *words*. How many miserable men are there who believe—believe most deeply, most earnestly—who would and do pray to be made the means of conveying truth and goodness to others,—who in sincerity and honesty of heart would try at least so far to do the will of God,—and who can command their lips and outward members, though as yet they cannot command their hearts,—and who are to be pitied, chastised, even condemned, but not condemned as wholly liars, like those whose hypocrisy is selfish. If no men could speak of truth or honour, virtue or holiness, externally, but those who are holy within, where should we find human beings to stand on every hill, in every church, day and night, through the world, throwing up the beacon-light of truth, and passing it on from generation to generation? Let us distinguish between the messenger and the message, and guard and keep the message, even where the messenger is not worthy to transmit it. For there is another kind of truth—the only real truth—which Mr. Carlyle himself must acknowledge. If truth be the conformity of acts and words to a certain standard, there is a standard, not only in the mind of man, but in a world external to man. There *are* realities wholly independent of our fancies and opinions. The laws of nature are truths, whatever be our conceptions of them; the laws of morals are immutable, however corrupt may be our conscience: the eternal attributes of God continue the same, though our rationalising theology vacillates and wanders. Ascertain these, and you have the foundation, the only foundation, for truth: bring your thoughts, and words, and actions to correspond with these, and you have obtained *reality*, and cast away 'shams and lies.' Thus physical science would test our conceptions of the phenomena of matter by the experience of general laws: thus ethical science would lay deep the distinctions of right and wrong, not in the varying emotions of our own moral senti-ments, but in an outward objective standard of God's moral nature: thus the Catholic Church would establish a criterion of revealed truth, not in the fallible judgment of human interpretation, but in the positive, external, historical declaration of men who have heard and seen the facts of a revelation.

But how are we to obtain a knowledge of this standard? Mr. Car-lyle will be the first to acknowledge that the whole universe around us, physical, intellectual, and moral, is the creation of one Creator. He goes still farther: he calls it the 'form,' 'the symbol,' 'the vestment,' 'the outward exhibition,' to fleshly eyes, of that invisible Spirit; and he is right: and without forms and outward vestments that Spirit cannot be made known to us. And those forms are in themselves valueless; they are 'shams and lies,' except so far as they represent faithfully the internal attributes of Him from whom all creation flowed, and to whom it must return. And the question between the Pantheist and the Christian, setting aside the fact of a revelation, is simply this: *how* are we to read the knowledge of God; *how* are we to learn his real nature, his true will, from which creation proceeded, according to which it was shaped, and to which we must conform our thoughts, and words, and works, and actions, if we would attain truth, and goodness, and happiness?—It must be, says the Pantheist, from outward forms—from the volume of Nature:—

[quotes 'and truly a volume' to 'avail in practice' *Sartor Resartus*, Bk. III, ch. vii, 205–206]

Mr. Carlyle is right. The book of nature *is* a volume of 'thick-crowded, inextricably intertwisted hieroglyphic writing;' and all the efforts of science *have* done, and *can* do, little more than pick out a few of its commonest and most obvious meanings. But, if these are the only forms supplied us by the Creator of the world, through which to learn His nature—that nature, without a knowledge of which there can be no truth and no goodness—what is to become of man? It is not so with that human spirit, of which directly we see as little as we see of God himself, the knowledge of which is as essential to our moral duties and affections as the knowledge of God is to our religion, and the nature of which we alike learn through forms and symbols. Man's spirit has not only the form or vestment of a body, through which to make itself visible—as the material creation renders visible to us the Deity—but it has also recorded acts, writings, and deeds; and the acts of a man are a still clearer intimation of his character than his physiognomy. But more than this: it has words; and words not only orally delivered, but preserved, and fixed, and capable of transmission in writing; and it is from these mainly that we derive the knowledge of the minds of our fellow-men; from their words more than from their works, and from their works more than from their features. What should we say to a man who should persist in interpreting character by phrenology or physiognomy, without reference to a long course of authenticated actions, and express verbal declarations of sentiment and will? What should we think if our Creator had condemned us to such a mode of ascertaining the movements of the mind in our fellow-creatures? What ought to be our judgment of those who would think it sufficient, and would reject the help of any other information, even though promised and held out? And yet such is the proceeding of the Pantheist in relation to God. He sees nature, the physiognomy of God, spread before him in its beautiful and glorious garb. He is told also of a history of God's dealings, preserved to him in the Bible by the same kind of testimony which he admits and subscribes to in all other histories; and he hears also a boast (let us suppose that it is only a boast) that certain persons are in possession of words spoken by God himself, and declaring His nature and attributes; yet both the last he sets aside, and refuses to consult them, as if they did not exist.

Nature indeed, or rather the God of nature, does speak to us through the eye, as we speak to children through pictures; but without a susceptible heart, without attention, reasoning, a cultivated mind, and a large induction, what are the pictures of nature but the idle luxury of a dumb show? And He speaks to us also through his acts, through his general laws, and the operations of his hands. But who can evolve these rightly from the multitude of shifting phenomena, but the philosopher? And has even the philosopher done this better than Mr. Carlyle suggests? Words, therefore, are still wanting. It is through the ear that we convey to man the past, the future, the deductions of the understanding, abstract principles, general laws, all which lies deeper than the sight. Without words, a revelation from God must be a broken, imperfect hint. But still something else is wanting. Words, without examples by which to interpret them, are cold and often unintelligible symbols. We want symbols of a moral being; and the most perfect of all symbols will be a moral being like ourselves—a form of the Divine Creator embodied in the form of a man. This also God has been pleased to give us. But this personal *form* as well as the *words* of revelation must be preserved through all generations—fixed before us in every spot, the same among every people, meeting us in all our paths, and ready to influence every action. This also God has provided for us in the institution of a Catholic Church, in which not only every minister, but every branch of the body, and every individual member, ought to consider himself the symbol, and more than symbol, the representative and embodying form of its Divine Head. And as this cannot be universally secured in the midst of human corruption, and the soul of man will lapse and fall perpetually from this high standard, therefore it is provided that at least so much of the symbol shall be preserved, as human laws and power can secure by their command over the outward man. Even when the heart and head go wrong, the Church is still commanded to proclaim her creed, to celebrate her worship, to warn, exhort, and teach, at least by words and actions; and these words and actions are true in the highest sense of truth. They correspond with the only reality, and only foundation for a true belief in the nature of God. They are not affected by the errors, or unbelief, or caprice, or hypocrisy of those who exhibit them, any more than the reality of a message is affected by the incredulity or inconsistencies of the messenger. They are not, as Mr. Carlyle would call them, 'shams and lies,' though the men who bear them may indeed be hypocrites and liars; and to the truths our reverence is due, not to a man as man; and it is the highest exercise of that faith and that obedience, on which the Pantheist himself makes the whole world depend, to maintain them steadily and humbly even against temptation, and to see the Divine image in prophecies and types, even when they are clouded and perplexed by the fallibility and corruption of the prophets. . . .

[Sewell's comments which follow are directed to a very moving passage in *Chartism* regarding the 'Condition of England Question'. He quotes 'It is in Glasgow' to 'be cured or kill' Vol. xxix, 143–4.]

And how is it to be cured? By two grand specifics. Our readers are all attention. And what are they? Reading and emigration! reading and emigration!! reading and emigration!!! Is Mr. Carlyle aware that he is required to explain his meaning more at large—that he is generally misunderstood? We can assure him, from our own knowledge, that many of his readers doubt if he is serious. They have a great respect for his powers of mind, for his deep thought, and just sentiments. They conceive that he has thought it desirable to point out strongly and vividly, by a grave juxta-position, the absurdity of our modern theories of reformation, when contrasted with the enormity of the evils to be remedied. He probably is speaking ironically. It is the view which we are inclined to take ourselves. He is not a Pythagorean. With all his veneration for symbols, he does not seem to trust in any *magical* power of words and letters. He must know that both his remedies have been working for a considerable time—that National Schools, even in England, have done much to disseminate the alphabet for many past years—that America is groaning beneath the discharge of the drains which we have opened on her coast—that Australia!—but we must not touch on such a subject—and that all the while the curse and the blight have been spreading more rapidly and more fearfully through every district of our population. Reading and emigration!

Consider for one moment. How has this curse been propagated? How have the wretched thousands of Birmingham and Manchester been engendered and huddled up in those abodes of misery and vice? *By a reading, instructed, enlightened, scientific body of manufacturers?* How have those unhappy slaves to the avarice of their masters been enabled to do their will? By their own quickened intelligence and acuteness? Go into the factories, and ask how few are unable to read and write—how few at least among the parents, though these reading parents may have sold their children to a drudgery which precludes them from attending schools? What are your Mechanics' Institutes, your Penny Magazines, your Penny Satirists, your loathsome sheets of popular blasphemy and profligacy, well written, clever, intelligent, often even scientific, which meet you in the street at every turn, but a proclamation of the triumph of the alphabet? And what is Botany Bay and the Report on the state of Australia, but the triumph of emigration—such an emigration as Mr. Carlyle would carry on—the only one which any Statesman of these days has ever dreamt of. . . .

The real problem still remains,—how to make men religious. Religious teachers we have had already. One religious *man*, a *Divine man*, truly and not figuratively divine, we all acknowledge as our Head;—

Mr. Carlyle himself would not venture openly to repudiate the name; and for a time He did hold together the floating atoms of society: for centuries after centuries, by the strength of that one name, and in the professed unity of His truth, and His law, the world did live in faith; or if faithlessness did creep in, it lurked, sculking and cowardlike, denying itself, and ashamed to be seen. All crimes, even by popular sentiment, were then summed up in infidelity. To be a pagan or an unbeliever was in those days to be, as it were, a murderer or adulterer. Faith was a summary of the decalogue. And in this spirit barbarians were tamed, and invaders rooted quietly in a new soil, and turbulent chieftains were subordinated to kings, and provinces cemented into monarchies, and monarchies consecrated and confirmed by the ministers of God. Civil and social laws were evolved from the germ of the Mosaic code. The hand of peace was laid upon the ferocity of warriors; truces were interposed, sanctuaries of refuge opened, and all the benevolences of religion were brought in to soothe the sternness of an age of war—until a chivalry was formed; and it is no idle sentimentality to mourn with the greatest of modern political philosophers that 'the age of chivalry is gone,' and the age of sophists, economists, and calculators, has succeeded. In the same spirit, arts and sciences, and literature, and a deep philosophy, grew up beneath the shelter of the Church. If wealth was accumulated, it was expanded again in hospitality, in charities, in noble institutions, which are at this day our chief resource for education, and relief of the miseries of life. If civil wars broke out, they were waged to defend king against king, not to overthrow monarchy and dissolve law. Crimes, and ignorance, and deceit, and treachery existed then, as they exist now, as they always must exist, where man is man; but if there was more of ferocity, there was less of selfishness. They were the crimes of untutored men rather than those of a corrupted, sophisticated, depraved, and effete generation. But the age of faith is past, and the age which Mr. Carlyle has described now stands in its place. The same creeds, the same ministry, are ostensibly with us as with our ancestors, even purified and reformed. And true religion, it was thought, would shine out more clearly, and win hearts to it more efficiently by such a reformation. The end has been exactly the reverse; and the reason is twofold. We have gradually lost sight of two great facts, necessary conditions in the inculcation of religion: *first*, that man has a body as well as a soul, and that ignorant, unlettered minds must be addressed through their senses before they can be moulded in their minds: *secondly*, that all the power and wisdom of man can be of no avail in making man religious, without a power communicated from God himself through channels which He has appointed. Until these two facts are once more brought out forcibly, and universally, true religion can make no progress. There must be a fecundation of the heart before the seed sown will take root. The germ of faith and religion must be fed with fresh and continual supplies, day by day, or it will die. This is no theory or mystical pietism, but the plain declaration of Him who is the source and giver of it. The plan of modern religionists has been to starve the mind, to withdraw its appointed nutriment, and then to propose strengthening it by more frequent exercise, and by awakening a keener sense of hunger. This is not the place to do more than hint at the real cause, why in this day it is so hard to 'kindle soul by soul,' and re-inspire mankind with the spirit of faith. But it would be well for those who are concerned in the government of man, whether infant or adult—and it would cut at once the Gordian knot of 'national education'—to think deeply on the problem, and to ask themselves, steadily and calmly, what is the meaning of a system of education carried on without a thought of the *sacraments of the Church*?

It is strange that a philosophical mind like Mr. Carlyle's should know so little of the nature of the very instrument with which *he* purposes to commence his great moral change. Letters are good in their proper place—to some minds they are absolutely essential; and when rightly employed are an invaluable aid to good principles and wise culture. But Plato, who was, indeed, a wiser man than Mr. Carlyle, long before printing was known, anticipated what it would produce. When he, like Mr. Carlyle, attacked an age of Sophists, he did not think that the *first* thing was to teach men to read, and the *second* to instil truth into them by the presence and guidance of their teachers. He reversed the order. He made books subservient to teachers not teachers subservient to books. To obtain religious men was his first object: without them, religious books, he knew, were a dead letter, and with them they would spring up in abundance. But mere reading, according to Plato, instead of strengthening the mind, and assisting the memory, will only weaken it, by removing the necessity of exercise. It will make men, he says, conceited, by constituting them judges and critics instead of learners. It will leave them in their study of truth without a guide, or check, or interpreter; and as human reason at the very highest estimate must be in ignorance and error, so long at least as knowledge is still to be sought, the process of seeking it by ourselves can only end in multiplying mistakes; as every fresh arithmetical calculation, when one false item has been admitted, only increases the perplexity; and as the slightest divergence from a straight line carries us farther from it, the farther we advance. It will distract them, added Plato, into a multitude of different sects; every one being his own judge, and having his own peculiar bias of error, will have an error of his own for a conclusion. With the discovery of new means for circulating thought more thoughts will be circulated; and as the majority of thoughts are bad, the whole atmosphere will become impregnated with evil. There will be nothing to overcome indolence; no power to compel study when the book becomes tedious, or to insist on inquiry when the language is doubtful; and yet every one will have a smattering of knowledge; and thus you will rear up a generation of sickly, effeminate, unbelieving, superficial, capricious, contemptuous minds, between whom all truth will be lost; and you will become (what Mr. Carlyle has described) a *people of sophists*.* Use books in their proper place (precisely where Mr. Carlyle has *not* placed them); make them means of checking the teacher; of guarding truth against corruption; of preserving some record of it through successive generations; of supplying the deficiencies of oral and memorial transmission:—employ them to occupy leisure hours; to exercise independent thought; to supply new food for meditation; to prove, illustrate, enforce the lessons of the lips; to be with us in our closets, on sick-beds, in desert spots, in dying hours: let them be the voice with which we speak to a whole nation at once, even to the most distant lands, and a condensation of collected knowledge, always at hand to be consulted when there is no other tribunal of appeal,—do this, and the alphabet is indeed a gigantic power. And Mr. Carlyle will do well to enforce its communication and adoption, as one out of many means of curing our deep disease.

But here, too, the age has repeated the error, which has more than once been pointed out. They have mistaken the servant for the master; the check and drag on the machine for the propelling power. They think to educate by books, and not by man; and the inevitable result will be, that instead of diminishing the evil, they will only increase it. We are groaning under the effects of conceit, self-will, dissension, and disobedience; and we endeavour to remove them by a process which can engender nothing but more conceit and more self-will.

Nor do we think that Mr. Carlyle's second prescription will be more successful. It is a part, indeed, and an important part, of that grand

* See all this towards the end of the *Phædrus*.

scheme of real reform, which must be concerted and undertaken ere long by some gigantic mind, if the British empire is to retain its position among nations; but which cannot be faced, much less executed, without some deep change in the principles of our readers, and in the feelings of the people. But the disease, both in England and Ireland, is as complicated as it is inveterate; and the proposition of a simple remedy for such a state of things at once betrays the incompetency of the physician.

Before emigration is tried, let us endeavour to occupy our own waste lands. Millions of acres are still unreclaimed, both in Great Britain and Ireland. Stop the gambling speculation of our manufactures, and drain off the surplus population from our towns into the country. Let landlords plant colonies on their commons, and bogs, and mountains; plant them under their own eye, upon right principles of colonization, in organic bodies, with powers of self-government; with social privileges; with the germs of village institutions, especially with that first principle of social life and organization, an efficient ecclesiastical establishment in the centre. Restore something of the feudal spirit into our tenure of land. Raze, if you like, to the ground half an overgrown metropolis, and all the idle, gossipping, gaping water-places, where those men who ought to be each in their own parishes, ruling their estates as the representatives of the great Estate, the Monarchy of the realm, are frittering away time, and money, and dignity, and intellect, in frivolous dissipations. If we are so fond of ruling—and ruling is, indeed, one of our noblest duties—let us rule each in our own appointed sphere. The passion which is now so common, of governing the country, while we neglect our tenants, is at least suspicious. Let each man take care of his own part, and the whole will take care of itself. But without a landlord in every part of the empire, exercising faithfully, and earnestly, and affectionately, the duties of a little monarch, and so carrying into the minutest details, from day to day, the principles of a paternal government, the best laws and wisest legislators, sitting as abstractions in the senate, will only be a mockery. Then give to every landlord the best of coadjutors, appointed for him by God, a good religious clergyman; and let the church draw out her own organization and machinery to meet the wants of the crisis, and rouse herself to fight her battles with firmness, and zeal, and depth of thought, and of learning, without either compromise or intolerance—let all this be done, as it may be done, if each man will do his duty, in his own family and his own heart, and we may yet live. These are the only cures for our evils, the only answer to Mr. Carlyle's question on the condition of England. . . .

Note

Carlyle read the review and reacted to it in several letters. Part of a letter [7 October 1840] to John Stuart Mill is printed below.

My friend Sewell of the *Quarterly* is what the Germans call *ein sonder-barer Christ*; his 'thirty-nine glasses' lift him above comparison with Men or Formulas. In all History, I think, Puseyism seeks its fellow! The poor old Shovel-hat beginning, at this hour of the day, to assert from the house-tops: 'I either came out of Heaven and am a godlike miracle and mystery, or *else* an unfortunate old felt, demanding to be flung to the beggars!' It is the fatallest alternative I ever heard of for the Church of England. (*Letters of Thomas Carlyle to John Stuart Mill, John Sterling and Robert Browning*, ed. Alexander Carlyle (London, 1923), p. 173.)

CHARTISM

1840

12. Unsigned review,
Tait's Edinburgh Magazine

February 1840, n.s. vii, 115–20

Tait's (1832–64), a magazine less expensive than some—selling for a shilling—was an organ of Radical politics, much like its southern ally, the *Westminster Review*. John Stuart Mill and Richard Cobden were numbered among its contributors.

This is, in many respects, a very remarkable Essay, and one which, by leading men to think, must do good.

At present, it is a doubt with many, whether the insecurity and peril which, at this dark crisis, threaten the stability of social order in England, arise from real misery, or chiefly from speculative and imaginary causes. Mr Carlyle appears a believer in the real existence of those social ills, whose origin and presence he intimates by signs and figures, fables and emblems, as if proclaiming—'He that hath an ear to hear let him hear.'

It seems his philanthropic purpose to suspend a few filaments of truth over the fermenting chaotic mass, around which its weltering elements may take form, order, and lucidity; but although the presence of these slender filaments cannot altogether miss the intended effect, they are not always immediately perceptible to ordinary optics.

Lest the truths which he displays be too dazzling, the expositor deems it necessary to interpose a certain hazy atmosphere; or to supply the spectators with smoked glasses, to spare or aid weak vision in the season of the eclipse. Mr Carlyle's dogmas and opinions, when translated, out of his peculiar and often beautiful phraseology, into the humble vernacular, seem those of a philosophic Ultra-Radical of a new type; one, moreover, who, for the sake of a more marked individuality, cultivates a few innocent crotchets; as one man ties his cravat in a certain way, and another sets his hat at a particular angle, in order to be distinguished, in the crowd, from the herd of vulgar men. With these peculiarities, which belong more to manner than to substance, there are, in Mr Carlyle's doctrines, much to admire and to study. They have been and are those of many good and enlightened men. If he occasionally enunciates them with what may seem 'affectations, look ye, and pribble prabble,' even this may have a use; as, to resume our figure, the very high or low, or broad or narrow brim of the hat, or the odd cut of the coat, may attract attention to the wearer, and thence to the sage and the teacher.

If the philosophical-Radical be the general and tolerably correct designation of Mr Carlyle's body of notions in this pamphlet, he also comes forth in the novel, more ephemeral, character of a Tory-Radical; which is the approved name, with a certain party, for every man of large views and liberal sentiments, who does not place implicit faith for social salvation, only through the Bed-Chamber Whigs. It was formerly known that Mr Carlyle was anti-Malthusian, anti-New-Poor-Law, and anti-*Laissez-faire*; which last principle he seems to misapprehend; but never before that he was anti-Whig. Though we have popularly described Mr Carlyle as a philosophical Radical, his actual faith, as revealed through mists and clouds, approximates as nearly to Toryism of a new type—to a kind of Utopian Toryism; nor yet, as he might say, 'altogether new.' It is a kind of heroic Toryism, or intellectual and philosophic Feudalism established in the social body, and derived directly from the gods; a system in which Heaven, the universal bestower, is the alone superior; and the men of genius and goodness, the philosophers and the gifted, are the chiefs and chieftains, the leaders and ministers. All we docile vassals are, of course, under the beatific regimen, to be well taught, well fed, well clothed, and fitly prepared, by a discipline of virtue, for a happy eternity. Although we had no doubts about this alleged hierarchy of Nature's direct ordination, we are certain that very many centuries must elapse before the stamp, the badge of the captains and leaders of the race, can be readily or safely recognised; and are, therefore, disposed to take matters, in the meantime, as, they are, and to make the best of them.

As men of the heroic type, as the guides and philosophers of their kind, Mr Carlyle appears to consider our present rulers, administrators, and legislators, stark naught. He is, as we have hinted, a Tory-Radical.

After the oppression and injustice of many centuries, they have, he alleges, invited the starving and malecontent people to a Barmecide Reform-Feast, which turns out an insulting mockery; and to which, besides, we may add, there is not, as in its prototype, any prospect of a merry and substantial ending.

Mr Carlyle, among other topics of censure, laughs, as every man of common sense must, at the boast of Chartism being put down by the Reform Ministry, and 'in the most effectual and felicitous manner.' His intimations of popular grievances, old as the annals of the world, and now existing, rampant, 'deep-rooted, far-extending,' though wrapt up in fable, parable, and emblem, are sufficiently intelligible; but the statement of these grievances, though sometimes hazy, is unfortunately much clearer than the character of the remedies; about which we are left much in the dark. *Laissez-faire* is proscribed as a doctrine of fools;— but what are rulers to do? They are to make the people happy and contented;—but how?

We are not quite correct in describing Mr Carlyle as a Radical; he is, at best, on some points, scarce a half Radical. He seems to repudiate self-government; and he proposes none other, save what is conveyed in those dark hints about the human demigods, who, in the coming golden age, are to direct all earthly affairs, and who even now might educate, plant colonies, and direct the energies of the masses. Popular election, representative government, he appears to consider comparatively worthless, as remedies for the social and moral ills that afflict the country; in short, we do not at all times quite understand Mr Carlyle, and we are far from being satisfied that he perfectly understands himself. So, when he mutters like an oracle, and gesticulates like a conjuror, drawing his airy or earthy circles, and waving his magical wand, we just wink, and let it pass. But there are better things in his revelations; subtle truths, and quaint devices to give them poignancy; and by these we are attracted.

Justly, for example, does he regard the most virulent of the varied forms which popular discontent is assuming, as symptoms merely of the festering distemper gnawing at the core of the body politic; as boils breaking out on the surface, which indicate the vitiated state of the humours; 'ways of announcing that the disease continues there, and that it would fain not continue there.' He remarks—

Delirious Chartism will not have raged entirely to no purpose, as indeed no earthly thing does so, if it have forced all thinking men of the community to think of this vital matter, too apt to be overlooked otherwise. Is the condition of the English working people wrong; so wrong that rational working men can-not, will not, *and even should not rest quiet under it?* A most grave case, complex beyond all others in the world; a case wherein Botany Bay, constabulary rural police, and such like, will avail but little.

According to Mr Carlyle, when he speaks the plainest,—as a thoughtful wise man, and not as an utterer of dark sayings,—the wisdom of the British Parliament directs itself to every question save that mighty one, more pressing than all the rest put together—'*The Condition-of-England question.*'

[quotes 'We have heard' to 'their duty' XXIX, 120–1 and 'Why are' to 'some light' 123–4]

We have already regretted that Mr Carlyle should imagine that the truths which, as a High Priest, he reveals, are so overpoweringly dazzling that they cannot be presented to vulgar visual organs without the accompaniment of his German smoked glasses. These instruments, in mere matters of taste, may give factitious gorgeousness of colouring; intricacy and even grandeur of form; breadth, and the hazy vagueness which borders on the sublime: but, in affairs of profound interest, as in matters of business and detail, and especially in the development of those systems by which the world is to be regenerated, they sadly impede that quick, clear, apprehensive vision which ought to distinguish philosophers and legislators who aspire to instruct their fellow-men. In the meantime, we take the essay *Chartism*, or the Signs of the Times, as they are expounded by Mr Carlyle, as we find it; recondite, subtle, and, in the pure sense of our ancestors, *witty*, though not always very intelligible or practical. There is a chance that a good many hand-loom weavers may understand these dark utterances, or fancy they do: but if many members of Parliament pretend to do so, our charity will not stretch so far as to cover their ignorance with its mantle.

Mr Carlyle has no faith in statistics. He is right, if he only means the reports of Parliamentary Commissions; yet statistics are as sure as figures, which, again, may be made to prove anything, though never that two and two are less or more than four. Mr Carlyle means that he has no faith in those fallacious statistical reports of national prosperity, and of the people's well-being, which are, from time to time, promul-gated by Whig or by Tory governments, in order that persons of substance, with bowels, may eat their beef and drink their wine in security and comfort, untroubled by the fear or grief of thinking that their neighbours have neither bread nor beer; or by the fear that working men, industrious, skilful men, who have none of these good things of their own, may think of (Chartist-wise) appropriating a portion of those of their neighbours, and affirming that they have good right to it. This has hitherto been one great use of statistics. It is failing: but statistics remain an exact and potent science, not to be despised by the philosophic statesman.

Mr Carlyle likes the harsh, ill-considered New Poor-Law Bill as ill as he does soothing and delusive Parliamentary statistics. He is right again. Had it been possible to give society a fair new start, wise men might have repudiated a Poor Law in any shape. As it was, a better and more gradual measure might have been devised, and a fairer field chosen, in which to make trial of it. It was barely possible to set in operation a worse-timed scheme, independently of its inherent defects.

We are frequently taunted with being blind idolaters of Lord Brougham; assimilating, in this particular instance, to Mr Carlyle's hero-worshippers. When any one can point out to us a public character more worthy of trust and honour, we shall at once transfer our highest homage to his shrine: but, in the meantime, among the blemishes of our heroic man, there was, as we ventured to think, his hasty approval of the New Poor Law; warmly supported, by the way, by those who now the most pertinaciously misrepresent and calumniate him. 'Time enough to hollo when you are out of the wood,' was our remark when Lord Brougham, with benevolent exultation, boasted of the incalculable blessing which this harsh measure was speedily to confer upon the labouring classes. This was six years since. Health and purification may yet come from this harsh cure of an acknowledged distemper; but the foretaste has been irritating and bitter, without being at all sanative. Of the New Poor Law, Mr Carlyle is hopeful; and yet he appears to think worse of it than we did at its worst, and when the Bishop of Exeter displayed deeper insight into human feelings, and the actual condition of the people, than the most Liberal statesmen who took the other side. We have not forgotten that the New Poor Law was, to the full, as much a Tory as a Whig measure; as strenuously supported by the Duke of Wellington and Sir Robert Peel as by Lord Brougham* and Earl

---

* We have heard one of the idolaters of Lord Brougham broach the strange hypothesis, that in supporting the rash, if not stringent and tyrannical Poor Law, his Lordship must have had an after-thought, a concealed purpose, of instigating the people; pricking them forward, by famine and torture, to right themselves, and settle society on a fair basis.— Would Brougham otherwise have supported such a measure, with the Corn Laws in existence; a most unequal pressure of taxation; and all the restrictions on industry in full

Grey. Mr Carlyle hopes that the New Poor Law may be preliminary to some great change; when the benevolent and enlightened rich will take charge of the ignorant and misled poor. We indulge the higher hope that it may be the means of making the industrious classes take charge of themselves, and of banishing the causes of extreme poverty altogether. Until these classes do so, they will assuredly never be properly cared for.

To shew that Mr Carlyle is in the black catalogue of Tory-Radicals, we cite the following passage:—

[quotes 'How Parliamentary Radicalism' to 'the miracle' XXIX, 188–90 and 'That this Poor-Law' to 'for itself' 130–1 and 'The time' to 'as impossible' 139–40]

[The rest of the review is composed of long extracts from *Chartism* and ends with a familiar criticism of Carlyle.]

This chapter ['Not *Laissez-Faire*'] is somewhat wordy and inconclusive; and, as we have said, though Mr Carlyle is clear that a great deal might be both done and undone, he never commits himself to details. It would have been something to have indicated one safe preliminary step, were it but one; and we are left in doubt whether he does not consider even extension of the suffrage a wild illusion, from the manner in which it is alluded to in an extract given above. In education, about which he quibbles, he appears to have some faith, and, like others, little present hope: but, on this head, as on others, when *things* come to be grappled with, Mr Carlyle rather seeks to evade handgrips and a throw, and quaintly gives us to perceive that much may be said on both sides. We leave our intelligent readers to unriddle the following passage for themselves, acknowledging ourselves somewhat at a loss:—

We can conceive, in fine, such is the vigour of our imagination, that there might be found in England, at a dead-lift, strength enough to perform this miracle, and produce it henceforth as a miracle done; the teaching of England to read! Harder things, we do know, have been performed by nations before now, not abler looking than England. Ah me! if by some beneficent chance, there should be an official man found in England who could and would, with deliberate courage, after ripe counsel, with candid insight, with patience, practical sense, knowing realities to be real, knowing clamours to be clamorous and to seem real, propose this thing, and the innumerable things springing from it: wo to any Churchism or any Dissenterism that cast itself athwart the path of that man!

---

force? Had Lord Brougham seen the question in this light, we are sure he would not; yet we strongly doubt our friend's inference deduced from the part which Lord Brougham actually took.

Avaunt, ye gainsayers! is darkness and ignorance of the alphabet necessary for you? Reconcile yourselves to the alphabet, or depart elsewhither! Would not all that has genuineness in England gradually rally round such a man; all that has strength in England?

Now, we are condemned to the sad belief that, if an angel from heaven 'proposed the thing,' he would be opposed for a longer period than we care to reckon. A practical scheme of education, which, if not the best, would be infinitely better than none, might be founded on the simple principle by which small communities co-operate under the authority of an Act of Parliament, to clean, light, and watch their villages and towns. Take, for example, the Police Bill of Edinburgh, and apply its provisions to popular education. Every householder who pays a £5 rent, and upwards, is rated, and pays in proportion to his rent. Every householder, female as well as male, has a vote in annually electing the Police Commissioners of their Ward, and, through these, the business of watching, lighting, &c., &c., is smoothly and easily managed, as that of infant and elementary instruction might be, could those who long lay by, content to see the people perishing in ignorance, only be persuaded still to act upon the principle of *Laissez-faire*. But this, their selfish fears and the love of domination, for the sake of its advantages, will not permit.

Emigration is another and the only other tangible remedy for existing evils that Mr Carlyle indicates in his own quaint manner; and he leaves off with a piece of characteristic anti-Malthusianism, and an account of the atrocious and absurd book he names *Marcus'* pamphlet, which we had, till now, fancied a joke, like Swift's plan for keeping down the population by feeding the people of England with the children of Ireland. After the severe castigation which Christopher North, Esq., bestowed upon Mr Loudon, the dictionary-maker, for his delicate warnings to working men, about the sin or folly of marrying and having children, or more than two, after they had gotten rich, we had fancied that no sane man would again have ventured on this slippery ground. Of *Marcus*, who is a real hard substance, not a grinning phantom, Mr Carlyle reports:—

[quotes 'A shade more' to 'the world's woes' XXIX, 201–2]

Is it surprising that there should be Chartism, and Swinging, and every sort of destructive agent, tearing the society in pieces in which such topics can be gravely discussed, as the only remedies for those evils by which it is devoured?

ON HEROES, HERO-WORSHIP

1841

---

13. William Thomson, from an unsigned review, *Christian Remembrancer*

August 1843, vi, 121–43

William Thomson (1809–90) studied at Queen's College, Oxford. In 1843 he took orders and had several curacies, one under Samuel Wilberforce, then Bishop of Oxford. In 1855 he was made Provost of Queen's College. Although he was sympathetic with some of Benjamin Jowett's liberalizing tendencies at Oxford, he later broke with him after the publication of *Essays and Reviews* (1860), answering it with his *Aids to Faith* (1861). In 1862, he was made Archbishop of York, a position he held for twenty-eight years. See Introduction, p. 15.

Having noticed this work when it first appeared, we are only drawn to it again by the early demand for a second edition, followed so closely by a new work of the same prolific author. If our readers are of opinion that we give an undue importance to the subject, in thus departing from our usage, we can but plead our settled conviction that, in this age of loose and shallow thinking, the works of Thomas Carlyle are eminently calculated to influence the veering opinions of young and old; and that, therefore, it is impossible to overrate their importance. They are rapidly circulated—they are widely read, and greedily—they are on the tables and shelves of Catholic and Sectarian—of scholar and smatterer. Churchmen cling fondly to the hope, that even yet the voice of this new warrior may swell the battle-cry of the Christian ranks; and Dissenters, ever ready to make common cause with the enemies of the Church, find in him a present powerful ally, without inquiring too curiously into the precise nature of his religious tenets. So that, with the forbearance of one, and the gaping admiration of another, Carlyle is fast gaining an influence which, be it good or evil, will be long felt in every joint and muscle of English society. And doubtless, if earnestness and eloquence, working with the stores of a miscellaneous and unusual erudition, can alone entitle to influence, we cannot dispute his claim to eminence. But it shall be the aim of this paper to show that, in matters of more weighty moment, the whole philosophy of this writer is defective and unsatisfactory; that it would unsettle old things without settling new; that it will not brook the test of cool examination; and that when the quiet rays of reason have evaporated the froth of trope and metaphor, there is left to the student a worthless *caput mortuum*, of no use to soul or body. With this hope we shall try to place ourselves in the position of firm, immovable critics, who are determined to try this book 'on Heroes,' on its scientific pretensions, not on its poetic; and to ask what practical gain or loss will accrue to our minds from adopting its views.

The first mistake we notice (not the worst) is that of believing Hero-worship to be unbroken ground. 'How happy,' quoth the author, 'could I but in any measure, in such times as these, make manifest to you the meanings of Heroism, the divine relation (for I may well call it such) which in all times unites a great man to other men; and thus, as it were, not exhaust my subject, but so much as break ground upon it.' [V, 2.] Hero-worship is, in truth, no new subject on which a thinker can break ground in these days. From Plato's *Apology of Socrates*, or earlier, to Lockhart's *Life of Scott*, or later, admiration of heroes has been a recognised element of human character. What are Lives of eminent Statesmen, Lives of the Poets, Pursuit of Knowledge under Difficulties, Books of Martyrs even, and Histories of the Church, or of Nations, but so many recognitions of, and appeals to, it? Nor can the honour of first exhibiting its developments in a scientific form be claimed so late as our times; for every ethical treatise is, or should be, an essay on the admirable or heroic in human character. Besides, the work before us, whatever its merits, does not number among them the systematic exactness which this claim would presuppose, as we hope to make appear in the sequel.

The principle of admiration of the great in others is, in truth, an inseparable part of every mind, and greatest in the greatest. Wherever there appears a young intellect apparently active, but wholly destitute of this one thing, we may safely say it will never be great. Where, on the other hand, strong admiration of what is good and worthy develops itself in attempts at imitation, no matter how lame and awkward at first, there is much hope yet: the chief element of greatness is there, and the rest may follow. May not imitation of the great be, indeed, the God-sent provision for perpetuating truths that should live and actions that should be forgotten? May it not be as much a distinct affection as pride or sexual love, and fitted to its distinct function as much as these? For when men perish and leave their work to others, it might reasonably be expected that the conclusions and cognitions they have wrought out and come at with toilsome watchings and sore trouble, would perish too; because they only, the inventors, had that love for them, that intense overbearing sense of their truth, which led them to push them forward, and to protect them from contempt, as occasion might arise. The next generation, it would seem, will only know them with a calm, scholarly, speculative knowledge, and acquiesce in whatever views about them are least troublesome: they must needs perish. But here begins the function of admiring imitation. Some young disciple, or faithful friend, when all men else would play the stepfather to the bequeathed charge, prefers the strong claim of admiring affection to be its champion and protector. Though the labour that produced the work was never felt by him, and he lacks, therefore, that endearment to it, still the labour-pains of the first, are not more infrangible chains of love than the adoptive admiration of the second, parent. And in this way the discoveries of the testator have often been to the faithful legatee the foundation of farther discoveries and as lasting reputation. Often the most faithful imitator at the outset has ended in being the least imitative and the boldest in original conception; because in him alone the seed sank deep enough to grow: he alone had the digestion for such food as should be equal to the nourishment of a hero. The Plato that has given the world food for thought and study through two thousand years and more, began the world as an admirer and imitator of Socrates; and the future poet of 'Childe Harold' (if Plato will forgive us for naming him here) lay hid in the author of a little volume of imitations of favourite verses, the *Hours of Idleness*, scorned of reviewers and neglected by the world. Nor is this law limited to intellectual prowess; if there had been no brave men before Agamemnon, there had been no Agamemnon neither; and in the highest matter of all, the religion of mankind, good men have, in all ages, begotten a progeny of good men, through this emulative admiration; and the martyr tied to the stake has been a picture preserved and cherished in many hearts, until it brought more martyrs thither.

Moreover, as the principle is universal and indestructible, it must either be directed by competent hands, or it will misdirect itself. 'Nature is not governed but by obeying her;' and contempt of one of her infallible laws will bring its own punishment. If religion, as taught, is barren of examples, is stripped to a scientific nudity, and left unrelieved by the clothing of historic legends—then she has lost her hold on the people in great measure—she is no more popular. The appetite by which the soul takes hold upon her, (if one may speak so,) which the Bible is so benignly provided to supply, is ungratified; and it is not hard to see the end. From that time there begins to grow up quite another system in the heart of the people,—with men for its saints and heroes— with the works of men for its imitable models,—with the falls of men for its warning beacons. But what kind of men the chosen may be, none can calculate. When the clerisy of a nation have desisted from their labour, or fallen into a wrong method of doing it, what usurping teachers shall rise instead none can prophecy. Superstitious belief or lawless scepticism, the creed of Mahomet or of Thomas Paine; ascetic severity or unbounded indulgence; Pythagoreanism or Hedonism, the code of St. Anthony or of Thomas More, may have the best of it, according as there may be in those times men able to advocate the one or the other invitingly, and to kindle that glow of life upon it, the want of which has caused the shrines of a better wisdom to be deserted. The minds of men between twenty and thirty, it has been wisely said, determine what the mind of the age shall be—what it shall look like to a long hereafter, in the page of history. But that period of life is also the season when the quest of models and good examples is most active; when the fancy is flying hither and thither through time and space, to find something on which she may fix herself, and by which she may live. Hence the real responsibility rests on those who are able to determine the fancy of the young to this or that model; who have power to say persuasively, 'rest here and not elsewhere; here is strength, love, and hope, all that can be worth your admiration; turn hither and dwell for ever.' Too often those to whom this influence is given, are unworthy to wield it. But the *power* is theirs, for good or bad: the young men are the hands of the age, doing its imperishable works; and those who move the hands—who teach the young what to prize and admire, are the head. *Nil admirari*[1] may be good enough apathetic philosophy, but *quid admiratur?*[2] is the key to political prophecy.

1 Wonder at nothing, Horace, *Epistles*, I, vi, 1.
2 What does he wonder at?

It is almost superfluous to say, that though there will be everywhere a life-guiding admiration, we are utterly without security for its direction towards things worthy. In proportion as the evil in unaided hearts of men predominates over the good, so are the chances that their heroes will be painted idols—things of putty and fucus—greater than those that they will only reverence what is worth the homage. A small number will value the valuable; the mass of mankind, told by myriads, and outnumbering the sands of the sea, will ever be deluded by the semblance of value. The few will look up only to the good among them; or, should the beggarly age furnish none such, to the good whose shadows are cast on them from other times: the many will buzz and flutter round some predominant foolish person, who has managed, in the churnings of this whirlpool of life, to rise out from surrounding scum, and float at top, himself the lightest. There is in man, in good and bad, the appetite for bowing down, and it will sate itself. Nothing is too mean for idolatry. Look at facts. A querulous Byron is followed by his hosts of imitators, with depressed collars, and foreheads high-shaven, declaring themselves (truly, if they knew all) miserable creatures. Mountebank sophists, in Greece and elsewhere, in senate and pulpit, lecture-room and platform, have had their little day of admiration. Unsexed singers have regaled their noses from jewelled boxes, the gifts of royalty; and dancing girls skilled to walk upon their toes, have gloried in autocratic diamonds. Admiration there must ever be where there is one spark of mere intellectual activity; and this fact of our nature it was not left for Mr. Carlyle to discover. We even question whether he has invented a new name for it.

The highest wisdom of all—the wisdom that made our nature first—has not left this universal appetite without its proper end and object. We turn to the Bible, with its priests and prophets, and apostles and martyrs, but, above all, with that great High Priest, like us in all things except sin; and there we see that if our constitution has made us worshippers and admirers, we are not left without objects worthy to claim, and fitted to attract, our best admiration and worship. 'Follow His steps!' This is the duty laid on us: not without a clear discernment of what our whole being yearns after; namely, an example whereto we may fashion our life, with full confidence of a blessing on the effort. And it would be easy to point out how the errors into which the Church has fallen, from time to time, have their root in a neglect of that one precept; in beginning to imitate other models instead of Him whom it enjoins we should follow. We cannot go into this now; but are content to recommend our readers to examine closely whether all heresy, all division, all neglect of the doctrines, all deviations from the practices of our religion, are not readily traceable to that one cause—the substitution of Hero-worship for God-worship—the adoption of human models in the place of our great Example, human and divine.

Hero-worship (to adopt Mr. Carlyle's nomenclature) is not, however, forbidden to the Christian. He, as well as Mr. Carlyle, looks with fond admiration on his 'hero as prophet;' 'hero as priest;' 'hero as poet;' 'hero as man of letters,' 'hero as king.' But with how mighty a difference! His love and honour for them is bounded by *their* love and honour for their common Head and Example, even the Son of God; and thus he does but honour Christ in their persons. He admires their fidelity to the true faith: that is his mark of a hero. How did they serve our heavenly King, and push the confines of his kingdom upon earth to places before shut out from it? This is what he wishes to know. And when he arrays his heroes by the side of Mr. Carlyle's, he will not blush for them. Elisha, Cyprian, George Herbert, Robert Nelson, Charles I. on one side: and Mahomet, Luther, Shakspere, Rousseau, Cromwell, on the other. Who will weigh the list of the Syncretist with the list of the Churchman? No reader of ours, even for a moment. We repeat, that the Christian too indulges the sentiment of hero-worship, when he commemorates a saint or martyr; when he blesses God's name 'for all His servants departed this life in His faith and fear;' and that to speak of 'breaking ground' on the subject now, is mere idle talk.

We have said that scientific exactness is not the characteristic of the work under notice. Nor is it. Among the author's merits—and he has great ones—we cannot number logical power. A glowing imagination, exulting in the curious grouping of its thoughts, and too proud of its strength to borrow any former style as their vehicle, sympathising warmly with energy in thought and action, yet not impartially with all energy, and pouring forth its sympathy in every form of praise and apology, lights up every page with a hue to which this generation is quite a stranger. Perhaps in no author does the same childlike abandonment of heart to the admiration of the hour, move hand in hand with the same manly power of communicating the emotion to others. With such elements of poetry, the wonder is, that this book has taken the guise of prose lectures, instead of that of an Orphic song. Had we been to criticise the latter, we might have dispensed with a somewhat rude question, which now it is our duty to put; to wit, What does it mean? What does it tell us? What do we carry off from the perusal, besides a beating pulse and reddened cheek? From a poet, who claims the immunities of the divine *afflatus* at the hands of all well-mannered critics, we should not have sought an answer: but of a philosopher, clad in the sober russet garb of prose, we ask the question—and get no answer. In truth, there is much more of Pythian madness than of *Novum Organum*[3] about the whole production; so, perhaps, it is unfair to push the matter.

Be it enough to say, then, that if this book be meant for a prose treatise, if it be not perhaps a translation of a German poem, done into prose after the manner of Macpherson's Ossian, we complain of the suspension of the author's logical faculty, and consequent defect of those scientific conclusions, which, resting on solid durable grounds, might survive the glow of passing emotion, and swell the sum total of our permanent knowledge. It is unfair to wind men up by eloquence to the action-point, without then telling them what to do. All this fine talk, and nothing to come of it! They are drawn on to admire characters they had before contemned, or at best not admired; and this on no ground of reason, but in faith of Mr. Carlyle's infallible insight: they find beauties where was barrenness—greatness, where all seemed small. But what next? They are not told what a hero is; nor how to know one if they meet him; nor how they are to become heroes; nor how to admire the heroic in others. In short, they have heard much eloquent eulogy of certain men, mostly of doubtful reputation, tending to no practical result, at variance with all they have been accustomed to hold, and settling nothing of what it has unsettled. Are they the better? Not much: when the illusion shall have faded from their eyes by time, and they reflect on it in the darkness and solitude of their inmost heart, this mode of treatment will be confessed unsatisfactory, and they will admit by degrees the conviction, that sober reason should have been there, to control the tricksy sprite that has pleased them with idols and things unreal, under the emphatic and often-repeated title of realities.

The list of heroes selected for especial celebration is, indeed, puzzling. What one common mark can be assigned to them all? Real and mythic persons, sane and crazy, moral and immoral, honoured and execrated, self-restraining and wildly self-indulgent, in what common term, which shall be the note of heroism, do they coincide? Such a menagerie! Can any naturalist reduce them into one common genus? First, there is Norse Odin, a Scandinavian god, demi-god, or hero, *if ever he was anything*, which is just the point on which some preliminary scepticism

[3] Francis Bacon, *Novum Organum* (1620). In this work dealing with methods and philosophy of science, Bacon presents a criticism of the past as well as a plan for the future.

might be looked for! Before we admire him as hero, let us know whether he be not a poor shadow of a man, the Hercules of Norse fancies, the Jack Giant-Queller of some Scandinavian story-book maker. 'Grimm,' admits Mr. Carlyle, 'Grimm, the German antiquary, goes so far as to deny that any man Odin ever existed.' Not unreasonable of Grimm; but the author cannot lightly relinquish the fruitful theme. Grimm makes out that Odin is *Wuotan*, Movement; and conjectures that the title Odin was but an attribute of the highest God. Carlyle is ready.

[quotes from 'The Hero as Divinity', 'We must' to 'etymologies like that' V, 24]

But if Grimm were to retort—we cannot *make* a man with etymologies like that! surely the burden of proof would rest on our author, where the disputed point is a piece of fabulous tradition. The retort, however, is not suggested; and Odin, among all his friends and enemies, thus proved 'a reality,' and no 'hearsay,' is passionately chanted of, through five-and-twenty pages of poetry shaken into prose. Yet, after all, Odin *is* a pitiful hearsay; perhaps there was no such man; perhaps, as is more probable, there were a dozen such. The case of Odin, *Movement*, is parallel to that of Zoroaster, *Son of stars*. Goropius Becanus, a Carlylean hero-worshipper, for aught we know, recognised but one of that name, but found no followers; the other *literati*, according to Clericus, varying from two to five Zoroasters. Similar difficulties attend the name of Hercules: and the discussion in both cases tends to the conclusion, that no one has anything better than conjecture to offer us. How privileged must be the intellect that can invest these obscure shadows of one or many with local habitation and corporal unity, and even go out from itself and dwell with them under their cloud! But then so few will care to follow.

The name of Mahomet follows that of Odin—overclouded, too, with no less obscurity of another kind. To the end of time this trisyllable is a riddle, a very symbol of the interrogative attitude of mind. An imposter or a fanatic, which, or how much of each? In the eyes of Mr. Carlyle, neither the one nor the other: by a subtle argument he is proved a true prophet, and no less. Mankind is brought to the poll for it.

The word this man spoke has been the life-guidance now of one hundred and eighty millions of men these twelve hundred years. These hundred and eighty millions were made by God as well as we. A greater number of God's creatures believe in Mahomet's word at this hour than in any other word whatever. Are we to suppose that it was a miserable piece of spiritual legerdemain, this which so many creatures have lived and died by? I, for my part, cannot form any such supposition. I will believe most things sooner than that. One would be entirely at a loss what to think of this world at all, if quackery so grew and were sanctioned here.

Of this precious passage, we first challenge the statistics. Taking the given *computus* of the Mahometans as correct, we flatly deny that they outnumber the professors of other creeds. Those who call themselves Christians are far more. There are about two hundred millions of souls in Europe, of whom, it is mournful truth, many are not Christians: but, to supply the place of these, there are believers in North and South America, in the West Indian islands, in the East Indies, in Syria, in Africa, in Australia, in New Zealand. We think, therefore, that more Christians are in the world than the whole population of Europe, and therefore than the numbers of the Mahometans, as given by Mr. Carlyle. But as such speculations are not really to the purpose, we give them at no more than their worth. We would beg Mr. Carlyle, however, to prove that, of the four great creeds, Christianity, Hinduism, Buddhism, and Mahometanism, the last is not the *least* extensive instead of the most. He will not find it so easy, unless he is content with his own insight and bare assertion, even for statistics.

But now look at the philosophy of the argument. Might not one moment of calm thought have shown him that quackery *does* grow here? that far more than his astounding Mahometan hosts have lived and died in a faith which, practically, takes a little yellow gold for its deity, and avarice for its sole worship? How many millions thought the earth flat, and the sun eternally careering round it? How many, that the globe of earth coursed round the sun? One of these is 'quackery.' How many have lived and died thinking slavery right, and consonant with Divine laws as with human? There is no outrage of nature, no horrible crime, no foolish vision, no pretended religion, but what has found advocates among men. Are we to think that, because these things were done, they were therefore right? But even suppose that: still, contradictory tenets cannot be true together,—there must be quackery somewhere, and we are driven on the old problem at last,—Where is objective truth to be found? 'A false man found a religion!' exclaims Carlyle, 'why, a false man cannot build a brick house.' True enough: he must know the laws and properties of his bricks and mortar, and build his house obedient thereto. So did Mahomet: he knew the men for whom he wrote Alcoran, conversed with angels, went to heaven. He wrought with his materials like a cunning craftsman, no

179

doubt; it was never denied. Yet our bricklayer may be a godless, drunken, ignorant, wife-beating bricklayer, for all his skill, and Mahomet an impostor for all his millions of dupes. Settle for us first, then, not by trumpery metaphors, but by some argument that may satisfy students of ordinary fancy and tolerable keenness in appraising evidence, the question—What was Mahomet? or we go no step farther with you. Were his preternatural communings real and credible, or were they dyspeptic visions, of the same race as the apparitions and devilries that beset Luther in his tower: or were they *mendacia salubria*, wholesome lies, used, as Plato says lies may lawfully be, by way of medicine, to make firm the feeble tottering faith of invalid adherents? It will be time enough after that to bespatter his suspended coffin with golden stars of rhetoric,—to call him 'a messenger from the Infinite Unknown —sent to kindle the world—man of truth and fidelity—pertinent, wise, sincere, altogether solid, brotherly, genuine, full of wild worth, all uncultured—deep-hearted son of the wilderness—open, social, deep soul—alone with his own soul and the reality of things—earnest as death and life,' &c. &c. At present, these eulogies are simply ridiculous. Reality of things, indeed! There never was a phrase more shamelessly abused. . . .

The name of Burns may likewise reasonably arrest us for awhile. It is not ours to *condemn* any of Adam's children; nor even to blame what, unknown their strugglings and temptations, are, in the abstract, deep sins. There must be much in a mind so dangerously gifted to us inexplicable; and we cannot say but that wild, unhappy, fiery-hearted man had more given him to combat with than his strength was able for. Perhaps he struggled hard and christianly, in later days and unseen occasions, with temptations of the strength of devils, and could not cast them out. Poverty, fervent passions, intense faculties, ill-chosen employment, all these things at war one with another, and the unhappy heart of one poor man their battle-field! Presumptuous it were in any, even in one who had known the same trials, to attempt to strike the balance for or against this singular being. Let him rest in peace! lie the earth light upon him, and judgment lighter. . . .

Without condemning Burns as a man, we oppose his exaltation into a hero. And if it be urged that true charity would not only refrain from judging, but also from mentioning matters whereon others will judge, we reply, that immunity of censure can only be justly *claimed* where the friends of the claimant maintain his immunity of praise; and that, though charity may enjoin silence as to the errors of another, a higher charity, even love for all men and for truth, has its claims too, which in this case cannot be satisfied by silence. Admitting, then, that Burns *may* have struggled heroically against temptations, we ask for proof positive that he did so. For blasphemous and impure verses,—for acts of slavish obedience to the lowest animal appetites, where is the atonement, what the apology? Here stand we in the place of the Romish *avvocato del diavolo*, showing cause against Burns's enrolment in the heroic canon. We ask for *some* proof that he was more than a mere blind servant of bad impulses. Mr. Carlyle cannot think that overt acts of defiance to moral law are heroic, else why exclude Jonathan Wild the Great, and the energetic Richard Turpin? 'Jewelled duchesses' and 'waiters and ostlers of Scotch inns' shall not judge for us: too much is involved for that. Be the former 'carried off their feet,' and the latter 'brought out of bed' with the poet's conversation—the matter is not yet settled. The same effect would have followed the exertions of a fiddler. 'Once more a giant original man!' but in what respect a giant? 'A wise, faithful, unconquerable man!' nay, rather, if facts are to speak, and they only, a man foolish in the best wisdom, unfaithful to any aim, and, in the struggle with life, bowed down, prostrated, ground into dust, and utterly conquered even to the very grave. More is the pity! but we cannot, like Mr. Carlyle, read facts backward, nor, like him, apply epithets at random, just as if written on cards, and pulled blindfold out of a bag. Does he forget the poet's addiction to whiskey, and his quarter-dozen illegitimate children? Does he know that Burns was only rescued from a disgraceful difficulty by the death of one of two women to whom he had been paying cotemporaneous addresses? 'Burns, too,' quoth our author, 'could have governed, debated in national assemblies, politicised as few could.'—[V, 192] But how know we that? Might not the intoxications of power have changed the rustic rake and thirsty excise-man into a Nero or Caligula? Mr. Carlyle is not inspired, and his intuitions, without some arguments that may stand as their grounds to our less promptly judging minds, are unsatisfactory. Let him tell us, then, why Burns, mismanaging a few things, is to be made ruler over many things; and what *hero* means, if the Ayrshire bard be one.

Let us now examine the portrait of the 'Hero as Priest.' If words are to retain old meanings, the heroic man is he who exhibits all manly qualities in a larger degree than the multitude. And again, the heroic priest—'the Hero as Priest' is he whose qualifications for the priest's office are higher and better employed than those of others. 'Do your thing, and we shall know you,' is, we fancy, an exclamation of Mr.

Carlyle's, somewhere or other: do your priest's work in the best way, and you are a hero-priest; in a worse way, and you are something else. But the priest must do his own work, if he would avoid sad jumble and confusion, inevitable consequences of intruding into another's province. An example may make our meaning plainer. When a gang of rascals attacked Lambeth Palace to destroy Archbishop Laud, he might have justifiably resisted them, by arming his retainers, sallying forth, and driving the rabble home. This supposed act might have been heroic in another man, but not *for him*; because it would have been an oblivion of the episcopal character for that time—a forgetfulness of its humility, charity, and submissiveness to personal wrong. In estimating any action, we must consider the person and position of the agent, among the other influencing circumstances. Now, in the case of Luther, as treated by Mr. Carlyle, we complain of this very sophism: we are invited to regard him as a 'hero-priest,' (of course we do not approve this title, though we use it for this turn) for actions in themselves, perhaps, heroic, but not for a priest to perform. It might be, he had no choice, no alternative, but (as far as man could see) the utter perdition of the Church on earth, swallowed up by tyranny and unbelief. It was Luther's misfortune (may be pleaded) to light on times when stout resistance to ecclesiastical superiors was the one course pointed to by the finger of conscience, enjoined by the word of God, enforced by circumstance. But this is not pleading to the purpose: a plain *ignoratio elenchi*.[4] We do not make a man a hero for his misfortunes. What we want proved is, that this resistance, in the principle of it, and the way he carried it through, make him a hero-priest, *i.e.* demonstrate him a better priest than others. And if not, what does he here, in defiance of common sense and *Novum Organum*?

Not the least notable of Luther's adventures was his marriage. We are afraid that, being a Romish priest and friar, he must have broken some solemn vows by it; and that his wife, being a nun, showed her first obedience to marital authority by following his example. It would have been more worthy a priest to have performed his vows, 'though it were to his own hindrance.' But, then, it may be urged, St. Paul commends matrimony to all who are tempted by that appetite which it remedies; and Luther, weighing the matter, chose the less offence. But no: he himself says, 'I was not very sorely tempted therewith;' and it is pretty clear, from his own statements,* that the Frau Luther owed her

* Luther's Table Talk, ch. 50.

4 Ignorance of the refutation.

matronly dignity chiefly to the good Martin's hatred for popedom. It might, or might not, be an expedient step: but it was surely a misfortune for a priest, that neither he nor his bride could come at the marriage-bed, except by breaking the chain of an oath.

The pope and Luther were not the best friends; the latter felt himself imperatively commissioned to make war upon the former—sent on earth for no other purpose. His was not the temper to err on the side of charitable silence, in pursuit of such an object. Dr. Johnson would have hugged him for an incomparable hater. 'Popedom,' saith our hero-priest, 'hath been ruled always by the wicked wretches correspondent to their doctrine. . . . None should be made pope but an offscummed incomparable knave and villain.' In another place—'Next after Satan, the pope is a right devil, as well on this Pope Clement may be proved; for he is evil, in that he is an Italian; worse being a Florentine; worst of all in being the son of a——;* is there anything worse? so add the same thereto.' Page after page of the *Colloquia Mensalia*,† (the only work of his we can lay our hand on just now) reeks with these fenny blossoms of rhetoric, to the prejudice of Popes Paul, Alexander, Leo, &c. with their kinswomen; so that, perhaps, for straightforward abuse, this volume would afford the best extant models. Yet, in one place he observes, with wonderful simplicity,—'There are many that complain and think I am too fierce and swift against popedom; on the contrarie, I complain in that I am, alas! too, too mild: I would wish that I could breathe out thunder-claps against pope and popedom, and that every word were a thunderbolt.' That wish accomplished might have shortened the Reformation: yet is it a sinful wish, nevertheless. If this be Lutheran mildness, Lutheran rancour must be something sublime. But (for the present question) it does seem that horrible slander and detraction are unbefitting the mouth of a priest, a bearer of a commission from Him who, 'when he was reviled, reviled not again,'[5] who set an example of combating wickedness in high places by mildness and abstinence from insult, and left no warrant for the contrary course, under any trials, however hard to bear. No doubt much may be said in extenuation of Luther's

---

* This modest omission is *not* the mild Martin's.

† There are circumstances in the literary history of this volume that cast a doubt on the genuineness of portions of it. We quote it without scruple after this caution, because Mr. C. admits the value of its evidence in the following words: 'In Luther's Table Talk, a posthumous book of anecdotes and sayings, collected by his friends, the most interesting now of all the books proceeding from him, *we have many beautiful unconscious displays of the man, and what sort of nature he had.*'

---

[5] 1 Peter ii, 23.

foulness of language; but, once more, this is not the point. Do such parts of his career permit us to rank him with those who have filled the priest's office most worthily? We must think not. The heroism of his character is unquestionable; but it is of a brawling, unloving kind. Call him a hero, but not a hero-priest. How coarse and vulgar—and, therefore, unchristian—his demeanour shows, with that of St. Cyprian, under circumstances not wholly unlike, though far less trying, we grant. . . .

The concluding Lecture, on the 'Hero as King,' though less distasteful, is open to many objections. One only remark we have space to make. In defending Cromwell, great stress is laid on the mature age at which he first launched on the turbulent sea of politics; an argument used before, in pleading the cause of Mahomet. It seems an axiom with our author, that to be orderly until forty is security for man's future soberness and honesty. Is it not, however, more near the truth, that ambition and fanaticism are not the vices of the young, but of the mature? Bravery and the pride of hot blood may carry a young man along the path of ambition; but real ambition, that calm fixedness of eye which singles out from the shadows of the future the object whereto it shall press, and from that time shapes its course thither through good and evil, prosperity and adversity, belongs, we think, to the season of life when 'the hey-day of the blood grows cool and waits upon the judgment.' Assuredly no plea for Mahomet and Cromwell will stand on that ground alone. They say the tiger may be reared a sort of quiet, prodigious, tom-cat, till he tastes blood; but after that, he becomes a changed nature.* Something of the same kind may be true of Cromwell: when he first tasted what he might do, he bethought him how to do it. And for Napoleon, it is perhaps possible to understand him without the hypothesis of his being a hero at all. Plato has laid down the formula of creating such heroes—given an atmosphere of general lawlessness, a tyrant will not fail to spring up there. Born under another aspect, in a well-governed country, the 'little corporal' might have risen to be a respectable colonel and member of the clubs.

But let us now attempt to pierce deeper into the philosophy of the work under notice—to ascertain Mr. Carlyle's esoteric conception of a hero. From what has been brought forward, it appears that of each class he has produced, for the most part, either irrelevant instances, or not

---

* χρονισθεὶς δ' ἀπέδειξεν
ἔθος τὸ πρὺς τοκέων.—κ.τ.λ.[6]

[6] Having grown up, he showed forth his character in accordance with that of his parent *Agamemnon*, 727 ff.

the best. What, then, is the inner principle on which the selection has been made? We have been able to discover one mark only, common to all the examples adduced, which we beg permission to name, but not disrespectfully, *radical pugnacity*. True heroism, it seems, is a nearer relation to chartism, and corn-law-leaguerism, than most persons suspect. It is not enough to be fearless of men, as was Laud; nor to work out with the vigorous hand the plannings of the sagacious head, as did Strafford; nor to 'stand by the dangerous-true at every turn,' as many have done. Mr. Carlyle insists farther, that these qualities shall be exercised on a certain subject matter. What is courage in Luther is flat 'pedantry' in Laud, because the former resisted his lawful rulers, the latter only resisted the resisters. Cromwell claims a blazoned banner in this cemetery of the great; and Strafford goes without memorial into the arms of austere oblivion; and reason good! the former was essentially a radical, the latter the faithful representative of a lawful king. It is so through the whole work, which is no more, after all, than the poetry of radicalism. Radicalism, made conceivable to most minds, either in the shape of the figures of Hume, the poetry of Wakley, the sordid vulgarities of Corn-law Leaguers, or the torch-light meetings and broad pikeheads of Frost and O'Connor, needed embellishment sorely; even Elliott, the inspired smith, a true bard on some ground, droops to a mere rhymester here, nor can coax a single well-tuned chord from his harp when this is the theme. It remained for Thomas Carlyle to fit radicalism with the cestus of beauty, and cleverly he has achieved it. The name Odin, he tells us, is *Wuotan*, Movement, i.e. *agitation*, the very watchword of a true radical; and it seems to stir the ground of our author's heart to find that in the Norse mythology the very gods have a fighting time of it. We are told how Thor belaboured Skrymir with a hammer; and wrestled with an old woman. Mahomet led a life of warfare; and, probably, had he borne the olive-branch instead of the sword, would have found no hymn from this bard. Of Dante* we learn—

[quotes from 'The Hero as Poet', 'His property' to '*nunquam revertar*' V, 88]

---

* We need hardly say, that among the heroes of this volume there are many we value as highly as Mr. Carlyle can. He does not so invariably take us to contemplate false heroes, as he puts them in a false light; he is like an artist, who, being to paint noble mansions invariably draws them from behind, so as to bring into his foreground, stables, kennels, a dung-heap, a wall with scarecrows nailed cruciform. He calls our notice to the very points of character which detract from real heroism.

The greatness of Shakspere, it seems, may all be traced to a piece of law-breaking. 'Had the Warwickshire squire not prosecuted him for deer-stealing, we had, perhaps, never heard of him as a poet!' Luther's claims to notice as a radical have been discussed. How Carlyle must love him for saying, 'if I had business at Leipzig, I would go, though it rained Duke Georges for nine days running!' Knox finds a glowing vindication for speaking strongly to Queen Mary. Johnson forgot the respect due to Bishop Percy, and set the law of assault at defiance by thumping a bookseller: claims that cannot be denied. For Rousseau— 'the French revolution found its evangelist (!) in Rousseau:' sufficient credential of heroism. The 'rugged downrightness' of Burns is doubtless not prized the less, that it took, to use his own words, a 'priest-skelping turn.' Cromwell killed a king; and Napoleon was but a huge wave on the wild sea of French radicalism. So ends Mr. Carlyle's catalogue, down which we have passed without one single omission. It is at least a curious coincidence, that his heroes all offend against magistrate, priest, or law; and agree in no other respect. Is not, as we said, a degree of radical pugnacity the leading feature in his conception of heroism? He seems never sure of his man till he sees him fighting, and the kind of battle he prefers is that waged against things having an *à priori* claim to be held sacred.

Against this little theory of ours may be brought our author's own words:—

[quotes from 'The Hero as King', 'May we' to 'doubly tragical' V, 203–4]

Having cited this fine passage, it contents us to refer it, with the evidences of a contrary way of thinking, just cited, to those who can reconcile the inconsistencies of genius.

But it is idle to insist on minor errors, when one predominant error poisons the whole book. *It is not a Christian book.*

Mr. Carlyle will probably not object to this statement as explained by his own words; but some of 'the accomplished and distinguished, the beautiful, the wise,' who, he says, made up the audience in his lecture-room, will be surprised that the eloquence to which they listened with rapt attention through six days, can by no tolerable stretch of courtesy, be styled other than unchristian. They will, perhaps, wonder, as we do, that he who so highly valued the outspoken earnestness of a Dante or a Johnson, should be so far from imitating what he admires as to manage to leave an auditory in some doubt of the prime fact about him, his religion, from first to last. Reserve on this head seems quite at variance with the whole philosophy (?) of the volume; and it is in truth one great cause of the difficulty of getting at the author's real meaning. Here and there drops out a reverential mention of Christianity; and the expressions of a contrary kind, though there is no mistaking them when considered, are so quietly edged in as to escape consideration, amid the wealth of eloquence that goes before and after. Thus he writes—

Of a man or of a nation we inquire, therefore, first of all, what religion *they* (*sic*) had? Was it heathenism, plurality of gods, more sensuous representation of this mystery of life, and for chief recognised element therein physical force? Was it Christianism; faith in an Invisible, not as real only, but as the only reality; Time, through every meanest moment of it, resting on Eternity; Pagan empire of force displaced by a nobler supremacy, that of Holiness? Was it Scepticism, uncertainty, and inquiry whether there was an unseen world, any mystery of life except a mad one;—doubt as to all this, or perhaps unbelief and flat denial?

Here we do not stop to quarrel with the unaccustomed name* for Christianity, nor with its position between Heathenism and Scepticism, like an honest man tyrannically chained between two hardened gaol-birds; but we do protest against such a definition of the faith by which we strive to live, in which we hope to die. Christianity is not merely 'faith in an Invisible,' it is not mere Platonism or Mahometanism; but faith in *the* Invisible, whose attributes and dealings with men are recorded in the Bible. We protest against the despicable reservation which, by the equivocal syllable *an*, seeks to confound Christians with Turks and Heathens, yet at the same time to deprive them of cause of complaint. We should not know that by *an* Invisible he means *any*, not *one*, Invisible, except by comparing other passages; as this—

[quotes from 'The Hero as Prophet', 'Mahomet's creed' to 'empty and dead!' V, 62–3]

Vain janglings, indeed! How can this man appraise the worth of the efforts made to exclude heresy from the fold of Christ? How, whilst with eyes fast closed against the true peculiarities of our religion, the once-offered Sacrifice, the one Baptism, the communion with Christ, and through Him with all Saints, he persists in assigning to the true faith a definition which may as well stand for Platonism, Gnosticism, Mahometanism, or Mormonism, how can he be taught to feel with those who struggled for the word and letter of the faith committed to

* *Christianismus* is as old a word as Tertullian's time; and, did we not suspect that *Christianism* only stands in the text for the sake of matching better with *Heathenism* and *Scepticism*, we might, perhaps, allow it to be as good a designation of our faith as *Christianity*.

them, resolved to part with neither jot nor tittle! In his detestable system of compromise, that pretends to see truth in all creeds, he evacuates every creed of its truth: and the habit of viewing all the race of men as deluded by shadows, awed by spectres, has ended very congruously in a contempt for the efforts made by the Church in defence of what he thinks her one form of delusion.

It is the natural weapon of an infidelity that dares not speak out, to endeavour to pervert words from old uses, and thus, by confounding the boundaries of right and wrong thinking, to prepare an easy way for the latter. No wonder that we are asked, 'May we not call Shakspere the still more melodious priest of a *true* Catholicism, the "Universal Church" of the Future and of all times?' [V, 111] And again; 'Is not every true reformer, by the nature of him, a *priest* first of all?' [V, 116] No wonder we are told, 'Johnson was a prophet to his people; preached a gospel to them, as all like him always do;' and 'the French Revolution found its evangelist in Rousseau.' 'I many a time say,' we read, 'the writers of newspapers, pamphlets, poems, books, these *are* the real working effective Church of a modern country.' [V, 162] The editors of the *Satirist* and *Weekly Dispatch* have been called many names, but surely they are now first called Churchmen! With like contempt of dictionary, Mr. Carlyle speaks elsewhere of finding in Byron, Rousseau, Shakspere, Goethe, Milton, Burns, 'fragments of a real Church liturgy and body of Homilies.' [V, 163] Those who are *less* charitable, may give this writer credit for enough Latin and Greek to know the meaning of the words he so sedulously mistakes: for our own part, having seen him assigning to *Aristotle* Plato's well-known 'Myth of the Cave,' and to Phalaris the 'Brazen Bull' of poor Perillus, we will give him what credit we can for ignorance. But such ignorance! Ye who fancied that 'Catholic Church' denoted the assemblage of faithful men, wherever on earth the pure word was preached, and the sacraments duly administered, know now that it stands for the holders of a poetical pantheism, painted in play-books and approved by Carlyle! Ye who understand from the word *Priest*, an ordained Presbyter of the Catholic Church, learn that it means 'a worshipper, *in one way or the other*, of the divine truth of things,' [Italics Thomson's, V, 116] whatever that may be! Ye who would confine the sense of the word 'Gospel,' to certain specified revelations of God's will, preserved in your Bibles, know now, that any Samuel Johnson—teacher of 'Moral Prudence,' thumper of book-sellers, talker for victory—may preach a gospel too! Learn, moreover, that the miserable, cracked, and worthless harbinger of anarchy and bloodshed may claim the name Evangelist, as well as the sainted Four! Or at least, if not, say with us that the author of Hero-Worship is an enemy, not over courageous, to the true religion of the Cross. Give us an avowed opponent, and we know how to meet him: but what shall we say to one who uses our watchwords to enter and fire our temples; who comes among us to preach the word of devils, arrayed in the cope and stole?

After this grave accusation, to descend to minor faults will be scarcely tolerated. Yet we cannot finally dismiss our subject without a remark or two that may help to throw light on the author's habits of thought. The trouble might have been spared, if only he had spoken out, told us what his creed was, and what he meant by what he said. As he has left us the riddle, we must be at the pains to solve it. Here is a passage that has been more than once quoted for admiration: let us see how much meaning the words cover. It speaks of Johnson.

[quotes from 'The Hero as Man of Letters', 'Yet a giant' to 'manfulness withal' V, 179]

A giant, invincible soul! a true man's! so we think Johnson's was. But why, pray? Because he would not case his feet in unsought charitable leather! We grant that the great man sitting down to try on these impostor-shoes were a hateful picture; or rather an inconceivable one. But on this very ground we cannot wonder that he *did* not; nor find heroism in a sort of honourable pride, the commonest form of independence in man, which often survives station and wealth, and illuminates wrecked and ruined morals. The quivering drunkard, the pale gamester, would throw such intruding shoes out of window too; but we will not call them 'giant, invincible souls,' who are mere wrecks of honest men. Besides, even to prove this very common virtue or weakness predicable of Johnson, the experiment was not fairly tried. The shoes were worse than an alms, they were a hoax; and no man relishes a hoax, least of all one reminding him of his poverty. Then *such* a hoax! It never succeeded, that we know, except in the fabulous case of Dominie Sampson. New shoes are not so like old: and Johnson probably, thought as much of the insult to his wits as to his poverty. The fact was, he had holes in his shoes, and could not well pay a St. Aldate's shoemaker to cobble them. Fondly imagining, as people do in like cases, that the rents so conspicuous to him, were unseen by others, he continued to make them serve; until, by rude surprise, he found his poverty known, and mocked with gifts. The shoes met their fate: and so ended a piece of clumsy kindness, if kindness it were at all. But the thing needed no notes of admiration, no 'giant, invincible souls.' And with what hidden meaning an *old* pair of shoes is called, just after, a *reality and substance*, and the new ones a *semblance* [V, 179] we cannot pretend to say. *Bad* shoes should be the semblance, if words have a meaning.

This is one among many evidences of Mr. Carlyle's enormous 'organ of wonder.' Mahomet in tears, and Cromwell asking an old comrade to shake hands, are equally miraculous. Nothing about his heroes is unheroic, their tears are crystallized into diamonds, their smallest motions noted in a book. Their lightest act is precious as the nail-paring of the Grand Llama.

Contrast with this exaggeration of trifles his magnanimous indifference to what other men feel in their hearts to be incalculably great and precious; and you have an outline of his philosophy, dim and shadowy enough, but all that he will vouchsafe to show you, or we can gather from him. The most trifling vagaries of his heroes have a worth in his eyes, which belongs not to the religious hopes and feelings of other men. A great intellectual system, of which Christianity and Mahometanism are alike but component portions: a world hastening on to unblemished perfection, to a halcyon time, when she shall be peopled with heroes, believers in one great creed, of which we can discover no more than that it will widely differ from all now held: a consequent belief, that the insight of no man is final; that is, that what a man believes is only true for him, and others may without shame or wrong reject it; these are the chief points of Mr. Carlyle's philosophy, as we read it. If wrongly, the fault is partly his, in not having shown his colours more bravely to all comers. The following passage, with our comment, will point out whither this wretched syncretism tends; and shall conclude our notice.

[quotes from 'The Hero as Priest', 'and on the' to 'incredible hypothesis' V, 119–20]

If Mr. Carlyle aims this at Christianity, we must tell him that its misrepresentation of the fact is of a piece with the philosophic courage which prescribed its guarded reserve of names. The Christian does *not* hold a truth confined to one country or time, to one 'section of a generation.' There has been a witness, more or less outspoken, to his religion, ever since the days of Eve; and for eighteen centuries, fifty-four generations, it has been received truth, not in one country, as is insinuated, but in great nations differing in language, in habits, in previous belief. For much of that time the wide-seeing sun itself could not take in all Christendom at one glance; and the believer in our day is bound in the girdle of a common brotherhood with men whose way of life history will not describe for him,—of whom scarce a mouldering bone or funeral urn, withstanding the wreck of ages, gives token.

And now for the metaphor of Schweidnitz fort. It will be found, like the rest of its tribe, but sorry logic. If it have an application at all, it applies to Mr. Carlyle only. Men enough have fallen into the ditch of error, and there hopelessly perished; but as for their filling up the chasm and making it passable, who expects it? In science, the greatest labourers have been readiest to confess that *their* labour was not final, that they had only been picking up, as it were, stones and shells on the confines of an ocean of truth, that the only lesson of wisdom they had learnt certainly, was 'graciously to know they were no better'. They never fancied they were marching over dead bodies to assured success: the inferior souls who did, we give up to the hero-worshipper's mercy. But in religion the simile fails more signally. What marching over dead bodies there? The Christian moves on over a secure bridge of his own, even over the bow of God's promises, whose top is in the clouds; the only passage for him, unsafe as it may seem to others: whilst the latter are leaping blindly into the ditch, led by lusts and fancies, neither help nor hindrance to the former. In plainer English, there is no progression, no advance of science, no march of intellect, in Christian truth. That revelation came forth complete; and the humble inquirer might be as clearly informed upon it in the days of Nero or Constantine, as of Victoria. So this 'incredible hypothesis,' aimed at the Christian, glances harmlessly from his shield.

If it can touch any, it is the thinker who, receiving the milk of the wisdom of ages on a sour, arrogant stomach, has found in the history of mankind—that tells how they sorely struggled after truth,—how they failed to find it from lack of eyes—how, when it was propounded to them, they had not ears to hear it;—only a ground for the sceptical conclusion that truth *is not*, that the belief in an objective, unalterable standard of truth, which men have battled for as for a necessary of their spiritual life, is a mere delusion, for that the sincere belief of a man is true as far as human things can be, but, *because* all men's contradictory tenets are equally well-grounded, there can be no truth external to men, and at the same time possible for them. Such a thinker, under the pretext of universal tolerance, is universally intolerant: any other mind sides with somebody—he with nobody; the race are all on one common footing;—good, honest, earnest men, but, forsooth, 'thinking their own insight final,' and therefore sadly mistaken. Does Mr. Carlyle suppose that any sect of mèn, blindest idolaters, or Cyprian of Carthage, would have accepted his comprehensive system, and borne with his tolerance? Absurd! they would have said—'Do not tell us that we are in earnest; we know *that*: even maniacs are in earnest. Either confess that we have fast hold on an *outward* truth—that we are doing and speaking in conformity to it, or we have no part nor lot with you.' To tell a Christian that what he maintains is a 'devout imagination,' but 'not final,' will hardly be made palatable to him by the assurance that his earnestness is a sort of truth. It is not which truth that he contends for. The man whose supercilious scepticism thus makes the differences of his fellows the *ground* of his theory, is the true despiser of his race. He is walking over their dead bodies, if any ever so stepped; and it is our sole comfort that he has but a soft, slippery gangway, and will not reach the fort of truth by that road.

14. Frederick Denison Maurice, letter, *Christian Remembrancer*

October 1843, vi, 451–61

This signed letter by Frederick Denison Maurice, 'On the Tendency, of Mr. Carlyle's Writings', was a direct answer to William Thomson's attack on Carlyle's *On Heroes* (see No. 13).

Maurice (1805–72), liberal reformer, theologian, was, like his friend John Sterling, an 'Apostle'—one of that 'gallant band of Platonico-Wordsworthian-Coleridgean anti-Utilitarians'. He was ordained in the Church of England in 1834. However, in 1837 his collected 'Letters to a Quaker' published under the title, *The Kingdom of Christ*, precipitated a number of attacks from the conservative religious press. The attacks continued throughout the rest of his career. His liberal theological views finally cost him his professorships of history and English literature and of divinity at King's College when his *Theological Essays* appeared in 1853. Both Gladstone and Tennyson (in a poem 'To the Rev. F. D. Maurice') defended him. Most important however was Maurice's concern with the working-class movement and its corollary, 'Christian Socialism', of which he was the spiritual leader. See Introduction, p. 15.

My dear sir—The Reviewer of Mr. Carlyle's Hero Worship, in your number for August, complains that the author whom he denounces is read by many Churchmen, because they hope that his voice will, in some way or other, 'swell the battle-cry of the Church.' This hope he tells us is fallacious: Mr. Carlyle's shout is the shout of an enemy; as such it is hailed by dissenters and liberals. Surely we ought to silence it, if we can; not to listen to it, or be pleased by it.

Sir, I am a reader of Mr. Carlyle's works, and I think that I am under very deep obligations to them; I hope, also, that I am a Churchman; but I quite agree with your contributor, that if I, or any man, have studied these books from a notion that they would swell the battle-cry of the Church, our motive has been a very indifferent one, and our reward will be disappointment. I am aware that Mr. Carlyle's works afford some temptation to the feelings which the reviewer attributes to us and our opponents. He indulges in many bitter censures upon Churchmen—these may be read with infinite delight by liberals; he indulges in many bitter censures upon liberals—these may be read with infinite delight by Churchmen. He has written a number of passages which seem to indicate that he regards ecclesiastical institutions with as much respect as his countryman, Mr. Joseph Hume; he has written others, from which it might be gathered that he entertains an affection for them like that of Mr. Newman, or Mr. Kenelm Digby. One party has only to term the latter the unaccountable inconsistencies of an ingenious thinker, the other to welcome them as glorious concessions from one who was led by his education to curse, and had been forced by his honesty to bless: and Mr. Carlyle has a class of admirers from each. What is either party the better for its admiration? I grant you, nothing whatever. It only gets another vote in favour of resolutions which it had carried by acclamation already; it only acquires a new stock of self-complacency and dislike to its opponents, with both of which articles the market was already glutted.

I do not know how it may be with liberals, but it seems to me, sir, that a Churchman may act upon a principle very different from this; nay, as nearly as possible the opposite of it. Judging from his professions, one would not suppose that he would be always on the search for that which is pleasing or flattering to himself; for that which would make him easy, or comfortable and contented. One would fancy that he would have learnt to regard that which is painful and mortifying as exceedingly profitable, and, with his better mind, to welcome it. Sharp reproofs must be prized, one would think, by him, if they are by no one else; he may often say, 'I do not like this, it frets me and torments me;' but he would not dare to say, 'Therefore, as a Churchman, I feel it my duty to reject it, and turn away from it;' rather he would say, 'There is a presumption in its favour, *cæteris paribus*,[1] this is the thing I ought to choose.[1]' If it be asked why we do not, upon this principle, love all the attacks which are made upon us in radical or dissenting journals, my answer is, The main reason for not loving them is, that they are not really attacks upon us, but rather excuses and apologies for us. Most of them say, in terms, 'We do not attack these poor, innocent, and well-meaning clergymen, we only abuse the principles which they

1 Other things being equal.

are supporting, the body to which they belong; apart from these they are well-behaved, even useful, members of society.' These are evidently apologies; circumstances have made us the poor creatures we are—the worst of these circumstances is, the Church itself. I hope we do all honestly, and from our hearts, hate the men who use such language as this, because they utter what we know to be lies; because they treat that which is innocent as guilty, and that which is guilty as innocent. But such feelings do not the least bind us to hate those who abuse us in a real, manly way; those who abuse us, not for suffering our high virtues to be dwarfed by connecting them with that which is in itself vile and contemptible, but who tell us that the Church was good and glorious till we had to do with it, and that we have made it ignominious. This is, at all events, plain, straightforward language; there is no shuffling in it; there is no doubt whether it is directed against some abstract notion, or against persons. If our consciences say 'Not guilty' to it, well and good; then they must be glad that they were put upon their trial; if they confess their sin, they must be glad, too, for what can be worse than keeping it within us unconfessed?

Now it seems to me, sir, that Mr. Carlyle's attacks upon us are of this character: he likes the Church in the middle ages dearly; he has not the slightest respect for the Church in his own day. Yet he does not prefer the one because it was unreformed, or dislike the other because it is Protestant; he looks upon Knox and Luther as heroes and deliverers; he has an intense hatred, hereditary and personal, to Romanism. The reason is, then, that he thinks our forefathers were better and truer men than we are, even under circumstances on the whole less advantageous. I am aware that he sometimes seems to use different language from this; that he talks of the thing which they believed, in being sound and true in their day, and being worn out in ours. I know, also, that he often imputes virtues to Churchmen and statesmen of the middle ages, which they did not possess, and conceals the evidence that they had the same class of vices as ourselves, even when that evidence is contained in the documents to which he appeals.* But, if we look a little closer, we shall find that these very facts only show that Mr. Carlyle does mean something, and something very true, against us. Our own selves granted that the middle ages did not realize the Church ideal as he would pretend

---

* For instance, he has unaccountably passed over an awkward story respecting a certain fish-pool belonging to Abbot Samson, (the middle-age hero of his late fools,) which fish-pool the abbot permitted to deluge the meadows of neighbouring farmers, in spite of their repeated remonstrances, much as any preservers in our day might have done.

they did, but they acknowledged the ideal; they felt it; and it is from our not feeling it, not showing it forth in our lives, but rather merely talking and debating about it, that he concludes the thing has ceased to be, and that what remains is only a sham and counterfeit. Do I think so? God forbid; I believe that the forms which he declares to be dead are witnesses that there is a mind of God which is permanent and ever-lasting, amidst all the varieties and inconsistencies of human faith and feeling; not dead, but witnesses against our death; witnesses alike against those who say that everything is true only as man makes it true, and against those whose own lives are untrue, even while they acknowledge these testimonies, and profess to receive these helps. But Mr. Carlyle's words only tell the more bitterly upon me because I have these convictions; for we have caused that an earnest man—one who really loves the idea of the Church—should believe that what we feel and know to be everlasting belonged only to an age which has passed away. What greater offence could we have committed? what more salutary, though more painful, than to have our offence brought home to us?

It seems to me that he has done us an equally good service, by warn-ing us that we shall not recover what we admire in past times, by repro-ducing the costume and habit of past times; I say, a good service, because I fear we are many of us inclined to fall into this notion, and because I cannot conceive one more at variance with the truth which we profess, or more in accordance with that which is false in Mr. Carlyle. He thinks the Church was alive in the middle ages, and is not alive now. We say it is a kingdom which shall have no end; but do we not practically admit its limitation to one, when we acknowledge that only the circumstances of one age can agree with it, and that we must fetch back those circumstances in order to keep it in health, or to restore its suspended animation? What, sir, did our Lord establish his Church, its sacraments, and its ministry, with no foresight of the changes which should take place in the world of which he is the author and ruler? Did he mean that they should be fit only for dainty times and a regulated atmosphere? Did he not mean that they should dwell in all times and create their own atmosphere? And are we to stand wailing and puling because a middle class has grown up among us; because the age of chivalry has departed; because the days of working men have begun? Are we to repine against Providence for these arrangements in the same breath with which we boast of our piety and reverence, and talk about the permanence of the Church? Are we to sigh and cry because opinion and conventions will soon be no protection to ecclesiastical ordinances;

nay, very soon will be no protection to domestic life, to marriage, to any one moral principle or practice? No; if God wills that these should depart, let us not wish that we could preserve them. Let us rejoice, though with trembling, for ourselves and for others, that the time is come when we cannot rest on these weak defences—when all human life and human institutions, all morality, must ground themselves upon an eternal truth and mystery, or must be left to perish; when the question will be between faith in a Living Being, or universal selfishness and anarchy.

He who shows us that this is the issue to which things are tending may be called an enemy of the Church; he may even fancy himself an enemy of it; he may lead some to become enemies who were ready to be so before; but he is, in the truest sense, our friend, and I maintain that Churchmen have a right to make use of his friendship. Now, no writer of the day, in this sense, has been so truly our friend as Mr. Carlyle; no one has given us so much help, if we will use it, in understanding what kind of battle we have to fight, what manner of time we have fallen upon, what are its wants and cries, what abysses lie beneath our feet. That his *History of the French Revolution*, his *Chartism*, and his *Past and Present*, make out a very bad case for Churchmen, as to their actual doings, I admit; they can raise no battle-cry of favour on that ground; but if there be any books in English literature which prove that unless there be a Divine order—a heavenly society—in the world, it must become an anarchy and a devilish society, they are these. Your reviewer may say that he knew that before: perhaps he did, and perhaps he may not need to have the fact impressed more deeply upon him by the evidence of history, and of those who have studied it in an earnest and impartial spirit; but there are some of us who feel that they want the help which he can dispense with; some of us who are conscious of a continual tendency to be trifling, in the midst of the most tremendous realities, and who do not find that clever Church novels, or clever newspaper articles, are at all sufficient to check this tendency. Such unfortunates, of whom I acknowledge myself to be one, are deeply grateful to any author, who does not merely echo back to them their own notions and opinions, who forces them to listen rather to the awful echoes of the Divine voice in the actual events of the world, and the doings of men; who frightens them out of the lethargy and stupefaction of customary convictions, and shows them that they must learn to mean what they say, and must strive to act as they mean.

But your reviewer will tell me, that there is in Mr. Carlyle a positive leaven of Pantheism. Sir, I believe there is in all of us, in your contributor, and in me, a great leaven of Pantheism, which often hides itself under decorous church-sounding phrases. If he will show me where it lurks in me, and how I may rid myself of it, I shall be grateful to him; and if he will help me to deepen in myself that conviction which is the antagonist one to Pantheism, and the corrector of it—the belief in a personal God, in an actual Living Judge, in a Being who is not one with the world, but its author—my obligations to him will be infinite. To Mr. Carlyle I owe much for driving this last thought home to me, often by strange, always by stern and effectual, methods. That evil must bring forth evil; that there is an eternal difference between right and wrong; that the world was not made by an evil spirit, but by one in whom might and right are eternally and necessarily coincident; that all evil is the counterfeit of something good; these are truths which are continually repeated in his pages, and which only make themselves the more felt from the struggle which they are maintaining with other notions seemingly more universal—really, I believe, far narrower; seemingly more dear to the writer—actually, I believe, only floating on the surface of his mind. That it is easy to adopt these notions, as if they were especially and characteristically Mr. Carlyle's, I acknowledge: it is always easier to take off the scum of a book, than to enter into its spirit; always easier to observe that which either harmonizes with our own theories, or contradicts them, than to receive those practical lessons which might serve for our help and our correction. I doubt not that some may have suffered a certain amount of moral loss from the passages in his works which embody these notions; that is to say, they may have been led by them entirely to abandon certain loose, fragile sentiments, or rather sensations, which were the relics of truths they had learned in their nursery, and which habitual worldliness and insincerity had already reduced to mere shadows. I doubt not, again, that some honest persons have been frightened from reading him by such passages; but I believe that if they had read humbly and honestly they would have found the antidote in himself; the more they appreciated his manliness and truthfulness, the less they would have been affected by his vagueness and bluster; the more they learnt from him to hate all affectation, and cant, and incoherency of every kind, the less harm they would have received from his own.

Your reviewer's remarks on Mr. Carlyle generally are derived from his book on Hero-worship. I willingly grant, that, if his object was to make out a case against the writer whom he undertook to criticise, he has chosen his example well. That which is objectionable in this book lies on the surface. Ordinary readers do not trouble themselves to inquire whether there is anything beneath which is sound and healthy. I do not, indeed, suppose that your reviewer's complaints of the principle of the book, as not new, and the book itself not logical, can much affect even the most inconsiderate. It professes to illustrate one of the oldest and most acknowledged principles in human nature. It is Mr. Carlyle's boast, and his greatest honour, that he dares to bring out the life and meaning of common-place, instead of for ever seeking, like diners-out and journalists, some new thing. And, somehow, one is affected by sundry influences which one does not well know how to divide into categoricals and hypotheticals, by bright sunsets and church-yards, and the faces of children. It may be very wrong to be overcome by anything but a syllogism. Various persons have put in their protest against the weakness, in other days, and in our own; but it has continued, and will continue till the present race of human beings is superseded by one manufactured according to the maxims of Mr. Bentham. But there are other indications in the work which apparently afford a much more just ground of complaint. A writer who speaks of Mahomet, Cromwell, and Rousseau, as heroes, seems, *prima facie,* guilty of a rude insult to the feelings and judgment of his readers. Your reviewer thinks that the evidence of his guilt is increased, not diminished, by the fact that he has joined with these other names, such as that of Dante, with which it is proper and catholic to have sympathy; for he argues, that the quality in the good men which calls forth Mr. Carlyle's admiration must be one which they have in common with the evil men—must be, therefore, itself evil, something which detracts from the worth and completeness of their characters: and, by an ingenious analytical process, he arrives at the conclusion, that the essentially-heroical element, according to Mr. Carlyle, is a radical contempt and defiance of authority. How very satisfactory this conclusion will appear to those who read the review, and who do not read the book reviewed, I can well understand. What can be so satisfactory as an elaborate analysis, leading to a definite, tangible, and, what is still more delightful, a documentary result? Those who do read the book will be tempted to ask themselves whether the reviewer's determination as to what Mr. Carlyle's opinion of the heroical *must be,* or his own declaration of what it is, has most claim to attention and belief; for it so happens that the two statements entirely disagree. Mr. Carlyle says that, in his judgment, (I quote from memory, not having the book at hand), a hero is one who *looks straight into the face of things, is not content with second-hand reports of them, and does not submit to receive semblance for realities.* This quality, not radical defiance of authority, he discovers, in different measure, in all the men of whom he speaks; to this he attributes the power which they exercised and the reverence which they commanded. Now, sir, I believe it will not be denied that Mahomet, Cromwell, and Rousseau did, in their respective ages, exercise a considerable influence; so considerable that the name of the first is inseparably associated with a system of religion which has lasted 1200 years; of the second, with a civil war which has affected the political and religious life of England ever since; of the third, with a revolution which forms the most memorable of all the epochs in European history. Granted, that there was in them a radical defiance of authority; granted, that there was in them a leaven of imposture, of hypocrisy, of sentimental libertinism, of any other evil quality you please, does this explain the secret of their power? I believe it explains the secret of their weakness; I believe that there is a weakness in the results of their proceedings requiring to be accounted for, and that in one of these ways, or in some similar way, it may be accounted for. But the strength requires to be accounted for, too; and I do maintain that the indignation which Mr. Carlyle expresses against those who refer this to an evil, and not to a good, origin, is a just, a moral, a godly indignation. I do not think that there is anything which has so perplexed history, which has been so much at once the fruit and the cause of infidelity, as the opposite notion; or one which it is so much the duty of every christian man who seeks to read history, under the teaching of the Divine Spirit, manfully, and in every form, to encounter. The doctrine of Mr. Carlyle, that good brings forth good, that from evil comes nothing but evil, is, I think, one of the very most precious ever enunciated; one which we should never have lost sight of if we had believed the Bible; one which is itself the real cure for those pantheistic notions respecting the faith and morality of different ages which the work on Hero-Worship, and others of the same kind, seem occasionally to encourage.

If, then, we do want to know why Mahomet, Cromwell, and Rousseau, exercised a power which no mere imposters or charlatans, no mere defiers of authority, ever could exercise, the question remains, whether Mr. Carlyle has rightly expressed the cause and the nature of this power in the words to which I have referred. My own strong conviction is that he has. I conceive Mahomet was able to do what he did, because he felt the will of God to be a reality; because he had ascertained it to be so, not by tradition, but by inward conflicts; and because he was willing to act upon the strength of this conviction. I believe that Cromwell was able to do what he did, because he felt spiritual life to be a reality, and was ready to stake his own existence and reputation, and to destroy whatever stood in his way, for the sake of that conviction. Once more: I believe Rousseau was able to do what he did, because, in a day when conventions alone were worshipped, he discovered, from his own miserable experience, that there is a deep ground of fact below all these, and that they must perish if they set themselves against it. Here is Mr. Carlyle's explanation: I ask, is it not one which throws a brilliant light upon the records of these men's lives, and of the time in which they lived? I ask, again, does it not throw a brilliant light upon our own lives and upon our own times? Do we seriously believe that any man will ever assert a great truth in our day, or bring back one which has been lost; that he will ever work any great reformation in the state of society; that he will ever be anything himself,—if he merely speaks that which he has got by hearsay—if what he speaks is not that which he has wrestled for in his chamber; that which he has a thousand times lost, and which has a thousand times been given him again; that which he continually stammers out in the most ignorant way, which he can seldom utter to others, or even to himself, but which haunts him, and pursues him, and will not let him go; which he knows that the devil is ever plotting to take from him; which he trusts in God shall not be taken from him? Sir, if we mean by standing up for the Church and for tradition, anything which is inconsistent with this, I am sure we shall be knocked down. If any tradition is precious to us, it must be precious because it links itself with our own eternal being; if the Church is precious to us, it must be because it reveals itself to us as that which alone can satisfy the wants of that being. We may fight for it well enough upon other terms, when half the world is on our side to hold fast to it, when no party is cheering us on. When without are fightings and within are fears, when there is a scoffing spirit in the heart repeating the scoffs of wise, and wily, and religious men. This is another work altogether, for which I tremble, lest we should be found very ill prepared when the day comes that demands it of us.

I have admitted that there is one-half of the problem respecting the men treated of in Mr. Carlyle's book which he has not worked out. He has told us, I believe, truly, wherein the strength of Mahomet, of Cromwell, and of Rousseau, lay; he has not told us the cause of their weakness. I am as little inclined to overlook one portion of the facts as

BOURNEMOUTH COLLEGE
OF TECHNOLOGY

COLLEGE LIBRARY

the other. But it seems to me that the person who sets us right about one-half of the case when we were going very wrong, puts us in a better road for finding out the other half than we could possibly be in before. When I have fully acknowledged the might of Mahomet's truth, I am able to account for the vigour, the heart, the magnanimity of the early Mussulmans, for the love of truth and the many noble qualities which are in them still. Reverence for an absolute Being, a belief in His will, as the law of human action and of the world's, are enough to interpret all that was ever great in them—the decay of this belief interprets all the loss they have sustained. But why did these qualities never secure to them freedom, sympathy with men as men— all the qualities which belong to humanity simply as such, and that self-respect which keeps men from the most beastly crimes? To answer this question in Mr. Carlyle's spirit, we should look at what Mahomet denied, as before we looked at what he asserted. We shall find he denied that there ever had been a man in the world who could say, 'I am one with the absolute Being: he that hath seen me hath seen Him.' I say, admit Mr. Carlyle's doctrine as to the secret of what Mahomet was, and what he could do, and you have cleared the road to the discovery of that which he was not—that which he could not do. It is nothing to me whether Mr. Carlyle admits the second position or not— nothing to me whether he would utterly repudiate it, and call me a quack or a sham for proclaiming it: I care nothing for that. He may not be the least obliged to me, but I may be deeply obliged to him for delivering me from an error which I had before, and for enabling me to see a truth, which I had before, more clearly. So, again, in respect to Cromwell: I believe the right acknowledgment of his power is the clue to understand the cause of his impotence. 'He could not execute the christian religion,' says Mr. Carlyle, in his last book, 'and therefore his body swung at Tyburn.' Just so, the thought that the spiritual life in man was everything; that everything which was not this, was not the christian religion; that everything that was not this, was to be taken away. And he found that he could not execute this idea, for it was not the idea of Him who promised to send the Spirit to guide men into all truth, and who said that the Spirit would not testify of itself, but of Him. He never set the spiritual life in man above that fixed and eternal truth of which the man who had the life becomes a partaker. He had appointed fixed and permanent ordinances, to be the witnesses of this truth. The man who would have the life without these, could not 'execute' his religion. The phrase may be strange, but it is a happy and significant one. So, lastly, is it with Rousseau. He did exercise a mighty influence over the minds of men; but we have Mr. Carlyle's testimony, that the constitutions which were based upon the Social Contract 'could not march.' He has shown us—no one so well—what kind of thing that nature proved itself to be, which Rousseau would have made the law-giver of the universe. These facts, too, have need to be accounted for; and having learnt Rousseau's strength consisted in asserting that there is something which is above artifice or convention, we are driven to conclude that this something must be a higher order, a higher life; this higher order, this truer life, being that which is indeed intended for man, and proper to man, but which ceases to be his when he becomes a worshipper of nature, instead of a worshipper of God—when he sets up himself, instead of crucifying himself.

Sir, these conclusions seem to me not at all less valuable because they evolve themselves quietly and naturally out of facts not produced for the purpose of establishing them—out of principles apparently remote from them; and I believe, in like manner, that no statement which the reviewer, or which I could make, of our conviction that the different sides and forms of faith are all contained in the one faith which the Church embodies or the Bible sets forth; that the different Heroes of the world demand a central Hero, who shall be an actual historical Person, who shall concentrate the scattered rays of goodness and power, who shall be one with Humanity and above it; could equal, in moral force, the evidence which a book like Mr. Carlyle's affords, of the necessity of some truth in which all truths shall find their meeting-point and reconciliation; of that truth being not an abstraction, but one which has been embodied in a person; not a congeries of notions, but the foundation of the bond of human life and human society. Not only in those words which indicate the continual feeling after such a centre, but quite as much in those which seem to deny the existence of it, or to substitute some vague, unreal centre for it, does this necessity make itself apparent. And this, I conceive, may be the *Præparatio Evangelica* of our day. To one who has passed through it, we may present our Gospels as they stand, and say, Here is He in whom we believe; here is One who actually lived and suffered; here is strength perfected in weakness; this is He that should come—we need not look for another.

It seems to me, sir, a very serious question, whether it is a safe or light thing to check, by any influence of ours, this kind of evidence from finding its way into the minds of our countrymen. Other kinds of evidence, it is quite clear, have worn themselves out; they are not only ineffective, they actually destroy the effect of that which they profess to recommend to us, and force upon us. And yet I do not think that mere Church authority—the mere saying 'So it is,' can be felt by any one to be a substitute for this evidence. The question always recurs, *What* is? Not, surely, these words which you utter, but that which these words speak of: and how to get men to feel this, to know this, is the difficulty. What a difficulty! Oh! if by any process of doubt or despair it might be overcome; if we might be goaded into realities, compelled to grapple with them, by feeling this solid earth, and the goodly canopy of heaven, nothing but a congregation of vapours! This will be worth our while; but it is better, surely, to meet with one who does not lead us into mere scepticism, who is always looking for something solid; always promising himself, and encouraging others, to believe that it does exist, and may at length be found. What if he does not say confidently that it has been found—if he sometimes insinuates the contrary? The state of mind into which he brings us—it is at least charitable and comfortable to suppose the state of mind in which he is himself—is not one which will quarrel with the source whence the light came, provided it be the light he needs; not one which could say the light must be a delusion, because it looks out from the stars or the sun, not from a glass mirror or a gas lamp. And it is a sad thought to many of us, that, being confident we do know of a light shining from the heavens, which is just what the pilgrim over the earth needs, we have not made it manifest to him, by walking in it, rejoicing in it, proclaiming it; but have led him to think it was no better than some flickering farthing rush candle kindled by ourselves.

Sir, I know well the ready answer to this statement: 'It is all very fine to talk of discovering these truths, or helps to truths, in Mr. Carlyle's writings; but does one in six readers discover them? and are not reviews written for the five in six, not for the one in six? And have not these five need to be warned of a teacher who will assuredly deceive them, whatever benefits he may be fancied to confer on the lucky transcendental individual?'

There is one point in this argument of a delicate nature, which I would rather pass over; but, as I have committed myself so far, I will speak my mind upon it—I mean the office of christian reviewers. What the office of the worldly reviewer is we all know; to detect all the faults which he can in a book or a man; to show how little good can be said of him—especially, if he be a man of thought, or genius, or moral influence, to show how much evil is in him. I should have ventured to

think that the christian critic was not merely to apply these same principles to a different class of writings or persons, but to act upon entirely
different principles. I should have thought that he was especially bound
to use the loving powers with which he is endowed, for the purpose of
bringing to light that which is good in every work or person who is able
to exert any influence over his countrymen, for the very purpose of
making that influence beneficial—of confounding and discomfiting anything that is evil in it. I should have thought (and here I do not wholly
speak from guess; I am not simply casting stones at others less guilty
than myself,) that any one who had failed in doing this, who had been
tempted to write or speak upon any other maxim, would find cause
for frequent and repeated self-reproach and repentance; would feel that
he had wronged his own mind, and not only the minds of others, because perchance he had few or no listeners. But, waiving these points,
upon which I have been over bold in touching, I should like to inquire
who those five in six readers are, for whose especial benefit Churchmen
think it needful to adopt the practice of the world. Are they, in this
particular case, persons who are already readers and admirers of Mr.
Carlyle? The probable effect of such criticism will be to convince them
that Churchmen have no sympathy with that which they have felt to
be true and useful to themselves; whatever, then, they have heard
which is disadvantageous to the Church and its ministers, will be
strengthened and deepened in their mind. To this part of their author's
creed they will cling: what qualifies it they most likely reject. Or are
they persons already disposed to be afraid of this author, with a very
sufficient and reasonable horror of him; these are the very men to whom
he could not do mischief—to whom he might do much good; men
who, if they are to be worth anything as Churchmen, require to be
sifted and winnowed, lest haply, in the day when a mightier winnower
appears, they shall be found chaff and not wheat. So that this kind of
reviewing, which is studiously contrived for the majority, and not for
the minority, has the merit of discountenancing the best, encouraging
the worst in every class of that majority.

As far as my own experience has gone, the warmest admirers of Mr.
Carlyle are to be found among very simple people, women especially,
who love their Bible above all other books, and would hate any which
did not lead them to love it more. Such persons, with that faculty of
love which so far excels the merely judicial faculty in subtlety and
discrimination, have detected something at the heart of his writings
which reached into their deepest faith and convictions, and have thrown

aside, as wholly extraneous, or at all events as unintelligible, what seemed to contradict them. You may tell such readers that they have been all wrong—that you know better; but you will not easily convince them. Not pride, not self-will, but genuine humility, self-distrust, affectionate charity to that which has imparted wisdom, are enlisted against you. Your arguments, and criticisms, and sneers, will not seem to them the least in accordance with the spirit of the Bible or the Church; they will still obstinately declare that Mr. Carlyle has done more to give them a delight in what is living and true, and, therefore, into the Bible and the Church, than you have. Might it not be well to enter into such prejudices a little; to inquire the meaning of them; to see whether they are wholly monstrous.

But I must conclude this long letter. I hold no brief from Mr. Carlyle; he would not thank me for my advocacy. I am jealous, not for his honour, but for that of the body to which I belong; I am sure that it is the body in the world which ought to acknowledge and love truth wherever it manifests itself; the one body which, if it understand its own rights and persons, could afford to do so. How long will its members treat it as a sect, while they boast of it as a Church? How long will they hold that its power is shown in rejecting and denying, not in embracing and harmonizing?

I am, my dear Sir, your obedient servant,

F. Maurice.

[The remarks below followed directly after Maurice's letter.]

[Every thing from Mr. Maurice's pen is sure to be both interesting and important; and therefore we rely on our readers at once justifying us for such a departure from our rules, as is involved in admitting into our pages anything like discussion upon our articles, and acquiescing in the declaration which we now make, that the proceeding is not to be regarded as a precedent. It appears to us, we own, that Mr. Maurice over-rates the difference between his and our estimate of Mr. Carlyle. In most of what he has said we cordially coincide; and he admits that there are elements in Mr. C.'s mind and speculations, which he will not deny to be very dangerous ones. If so, are we not to point out the dangers? Do none of the admiring readers of *The History of the French Revolution, Chartism, Hero-Worship,* &c. with whom he comes in contact, require to have it pointed out to them that fine religious sentiment is not Faith; and that while we are indulging in the one, we are under a very peculiar danger of forgetting the other? Are there no hero-worshippers in whose eyes Genius is all but infallible, and who must be made to see that there is but one Law for man, whether richly or poorly endowed; that the richest gifts of Genius are turned into curses by those who use them as means of separation from their brethren, and that the differences between man and man are as nothing as compared with the links which ought to unite them? Is it safe to allow hero-worship to be turned in the direction of a Rousseau, without one word of protest?

We entirely agree with Mr. Maurice, that it is the office of a christian reviewer rather to seek for and draw out the good there may be in a writer, than to show up all the evil: but he has probably not seen our former article on the *Hero-Worship*, in which we endeavoured, how-ever unsuccessfully, to discharge this duty. He, however, has done it far better than we have, and, cordially thanking him for his interesting and valuable observations, we leave them to take the place of our former article, and, instead of that, to be combined by our readers with our latter one on Carlyle, which we will think to have been much called for; as we do not believe the number of persons who have 'a very sufficient and reasonable horror' of this author, to be nearly so great as Mr. Maurice imagines.]

PAST AND PRESENT

1843

15. William Henry Smith, from an unsigned review, *Blackwood's Edinburgh Magazine*

July 1843, liv, 121–38

William Henry Smith (1808–72) was associated with Mill, Sterling, and Maurice and the founding of the *Athenaeum*, to which, in 1828, he contributed a series of essays for the opening numbers. From 1839 to 1871, he was a regular contributor to *Blackwood's*, writing over 125 essays for that periodical. Though fond of *Sartor Resartus* (the work was his 'constant companion'), his treatment here of *Past and Present* and, four years later, of *Oliver Cromwell's Letters and Speeches*, in this same magazine (April 1847, lxi), is somewhat hostile. This review was the first major notice that Carlyle received in *Blackwood's*. See Introduction, p. 17.

Mr. Carlyle—an astute and trenchant critic might with show of justice, remark—assumes to be the reformer and castigator of his age—a reformer in philosophy, in politics, in religion—denouncing its *mechanical* method of thinking, deploring its utter want of *faith*, and threatening political society, obstinately deaf to the voice of wisdom with the retributive horrors of repeated revolutions; and yet neither in philosophy, in religion, nor in politics, has Mr. Carlyle any distinct dogma, creed, or constitution to promulgate. The age is irreligious, he exclaims, and the vague feeling of the impenetrable mystery which encompasses us, is all the theology we can gather from him; civil society, with its laws and government, is in a false and perilous position, and for all relief and reformation, he launches forth an indisputable morality— precepts of charity, and self-denial, and strenuous effort—precepts most excellent, and only *too* applicable: applicable, unfortunately, after an *à priori* fashion—for if men would but obey them, there had been need of few laws, and of no remedial measures.

This man of faith—our critic might continue—has but one everlast- ing note; and it is really the most sceptical and melancholy that has ever been heard, or heard with toleration, in our literature. He repeats it from his favourite apostle Goethe; 'all doubt is to be cured only—by action.' Certainly, if *forgetting* the doubt, and the subject of doubt, be the sole cure for it. But that other advice which Mr. Carlyle tells us was given, and in vain, to George Fox, the Quaker, at a time when he was agitated by doubts and perplexities, namely, 'to drink beer and dance with the girls,' was of the very same stamp, and would have operated in the very same manner, to the removing of the pious Quaker's doubts. Faith! ye lack faith! cries this prophet in our streets; and when reproved and distressed scepticism inquires where truth is to be found, he bids it back to the loom or the forge, to its tools and its workshop, of whatever kind these may be—there to forget the inquiry.

The religion, or, if he pleases, the formula of religion, which helps to keep men sober and orderly, Mr. Carlyle despises, ridicules; 'old clothes!' he cries, empty and ragged. It is not till a man has risen into frenzy, or some hot fanaticism, that he deserves his respect. An Irving, when his noble spirit, kindled to fever heat, is seized with delirium, becomes worthy of some admiration. A Cromwell is pronounced emphatically to have believed in a God, and *therefore* to have been 'by far the remarkablest governor we have had here for the last five cen- turies or so.' Meanwhile, is it the faith of an Irving, or the God of a Cromwell, that our subtle-minded author would have us adopt, or would adopt himself? If he scorn the easy, methodical citizen, who plods along the beaten tracks of life, looking occasionally, in his demure, self-satisfied manner, upwards to the heavens, but with no other result than to plod more perseveringly along his very earthy track, it follows not that there is any one order of fanatic spirits with whom he would associate, to whose theology he would yield assent. Verily no. He demands faith—he gives no creed. What is it *you* teach? A plain- speaking man would exclaim; where is your church? have you also your thirty-nine articles? have you nine? have you *one* stout article of creed that will bear the rubs of fortune—bear the temptations of prosperity or a dietary system—stand both sunshine and the wind—which will keep virtue steady when disposed to reel, and drive back crime to her penal caverns of remorse? What would you answer, O philosopher! if a simple body should ask you, quite in confidence, where wicked people go to?

Were it not better for those to whom philosophy has brought the sad necessity of doubt, to endure this also patiently and silently, as one of the inevitable conditions of human existence? Were not this better than to rail incessantly against the world, for a want of that sentiment which *they* have no means to excite or to authorize?

The same inconsequence in politics. We have *Chartism* preached by one not a Chartist—by one who has no more his *five points* of Radicalism than his five points of Calvinistic divinity—who has no trust in democracy, who swears by no theory of representative government—who will never believe that a multitude of men, foolish and selfish, will elect the disinterested and the wise. Your constitution, your laws, your 'horse-haired justice' that sits in Westminster Hall, he likes them not; but he propounds himself no scheme of polity. Reform yourselves, one and all, ye individual men! and the nation will be reformed; practice justice, charity, self-denial, and then all mortals may work and eat. This is the most distinct advice he bestows. Alas! it is advice such as this that the Christian preacher, century after century, utters from his pulpit, which he makes the staple of his eloquence, and which he and his listeners are contented to applaud; and the more contented probably to applaud, as, on all hands, it is tacitly understood to be far *too good* to be practised.

In fine, turn which way you will, to philosophy, to politics, to religion, you find Mr. Carlyle objecting, denouncing, scoffing, rending all to pieces in his bold, reckless, ironical, manner—but *teaching* nothing. The most docile pupil, when he opens his tablets to put down the precious sum of wisdom he has learned, pauses—finds his pencil motionless, and leaves his tablet still a blank.

Now all this, and more of the same kind which our astute and trenchant critic might urge, may be true, or very like the truth, but it is not the whole truth.

To speak a little pedantically, [says our author himself in a paper called *Signs of the Times*] there is a science of *Dynamics* in man's fortune and nature, as well as of *Mechanics*. There is a science which treats of, and practically addresses, the primary unmodified forces and energies of man, the mysterious springs of love, and fear, and wonder, of enthusiasm, poetry—religion, all which have a truly vital and *infinite* character; as well as a science which practically addresses the finite, modified developments of these, when they take the shape of immediate 'motives,' as hope of reward, or as fear of punishment. Now it is certain that in former times the wise men, the enlightened lovers of their kind, who appeared generally as moralists, poets, or priests, did, without neglecting the mechanical province, deal chiefly with the dynamical; applying themselves chiefly to regulate, increase, and purify, the inward primary powers of man; and fancying that herein lay the main difficulty, and the best service they could undertake.

In such *Dynamics* it is that Mr. Carlyle deals. To speak in our own plain common-place diction, it is to the elements of all religious feeling, to the broad unalterable principles of morality, that he addresses himself; stirring up in the minds of his readers those sentiments of reverence to the Highest, and of justice to all, even to the lowest, which can never utterly die out in any man, but which slumber in the greater number of us. It is by no means necessary to teach any peculiar or positive doctrine in order to exert an influence on society. After all, there is a moral heart beating at the very centre of this world. Touch *it*, and there is a responsive movement through the whole system of the world. Undoubtedly external circumstances rule in their turn over this same central pulsation: alter, arrange, and modify, these external circumstances as best you can, but he who, by the *word* he speaks or writes, can reach this central pulse immediately—is he idle, is he profitless?

Or put it thus: there is a justice between man and man—older and more stable, and more lofty in its requisitions, than that which sits in ermine, or, if our author pleases, in 'horse-hair,' at Westminster Hall; there is a morality recognized by the intellect and the heart of all reflective men, higher and purer than what the present forms of society exact or render feasible—or rather say, a morality of more exalted character than that which has hitherto determined those forms of society. No man who believes that the teaching of Christ was authorized of heaven —no man who believes this only, that his doctrine has obtained and preserved its heavenly character from the successful, unanswerable, appeal which it makes to the human heart—can dispute this fact. Is he an idler, then, or a dreamer in the land, who comes forth, and on the high-road of our popular literature, insists on it that men should assume their full *moral strength*, and declares that herein lies the salvation of the world? But what can he do if the external circumstances of life are against him?—if they crush this moral energy?—if they discountenance this elevation of character? Alone—perhaps nothing. He with both hands is raising one end of the beam; go you with your tackle, with rope and pulley, and all mechanical appliances, to the other end, and who knows but something may be effected?

It is not by teaching this or that dogma, political, philosophical, or religious, that Mr. Carlyle is doing his *work*, and exerting an influence, by no means despicable, on his generation. It is by producing a certain moral tone of thought, of a stern, manly, energetic, self-denying character, that his best influence consists. Accordingly we are accustomed to view his works, even when they especially regarded communities of men, and take the name of histories, as, in effect, appeals to the individual heart, and to the moral will of the reader. His mind is not legislative; his mode of thinking is not systematic; a state economy he has not the skill, perhaps not the pretension, to devise. When he treats of nations, and governments, and revolutions of states, he views them all as a wondrous picture, which he, the observer, standing apart, watches and apostrophizes; still revealing *himself* in his reflections upon them. The picture *to the eye*, he gives with marvellous vividness; and he puts forth, with equal power, that sort of world-wide reflection which a thinking being might be supposed to make on his first visit to our planet; but the space between—those intermediate generalizations which make the pride of the philosophical historian—he neglects, has no taste for. Such a writer as Montesquieu he holds in manifest antipathy. His *History of the French Revolution*, like his *Chartism*, like the work now before us, his *Past and Present*, is still an appeal to the consciousness of each man, and to the high and eternal laws of justice and of charity—lo, ye are brethren!

And although it be true, as our critic has suggested, that to enlarge upon the misery which lies low and wide over the whole-ground-plot of civilized society, without at the same time devising an effectual remedy, is a most unsatisfactory business; nevertheless, this also must be added, that to forget the existence of this misery would not be to cure it—would, on the contrary, be a certain method of perpetuating and aggravating it; that to *try* to forget it, is as little wise as it is humane, and that indeed such act of oblivion is altogether impossible. If crowds of artizans, coming forth from homes where there is neither food nor work, shall say, in the words that our author puts into their mouths, 'Behold us here—we ask if you mean to lead us towards work; to try to lead us? Or if you declare that you cannot lead us? And expect that we are to remain quietly unled, and in a composed manner perish of starvation? What is it that you expect of us? What is it that you mean to do with us?'—if, we say, such a question is asked, we may not be able to answer, but we cannot stifle it. Surely it is well that every class in the community should know how indissolubly its interest is connected with the well-being of other classes. However remote the man of wealth may sit from scenes like this—however reluctant he may be to hear of them —nothing can be more true than that this distress is *his calamity*, and that *on him* also lies the inevitable alternative to remedy or to suffer.

It accords with the view we have here taken of the writings of Mr. Carlyle, that of all his works that which pleased us most was the one most completely *personal* in its character, which most constantly kept the reader in a state of self-reflection. In spite of all its oddities and vagaries, and the chaotic shape into which its materials have been thrown, the *Sartor Resartus* is a prime favourite of ours—a sort of volcanic work; and the reader stands by, with folded arms, resolved at all events to secure peace within his own bosom. But no sluggard's peace; his arms are folded, not for idleness, only to repress certain vain tremors and vainer sighs. He feels the calm of self-renunciation, but united with no monkish indolence. Here is a fragment of it. How it rebukes the spirit of strife and contention!

To me, in this our life, [says the Professor] which is an internecine warfare with the time-spirit, other warfare seems questionable. Has thou in any way a contention with thy brother, I advise thee, think well what the meaning thereof is. If thou gauge it to the bottom, it is simply this—'Fellow, see! thou art taking more than thy share of happiness in the world, something from *my* share; which, by the heavens, thou shalt not: nay, I will fight thee rather.' Alas! and the whole lot to be divided is such a beggarly matter, truly a 'feast of shells,' for the substance has been spilled out: not enough to quench one appetite; and the collective human species clutching at them! Can we not, in all such cases, rather say— 'Take it, thou too ravenous individual; take that pitiful additional fraction of a share, which I reckoned mine, but which thou so wanted; take it with a blessing: would to heaven I had enough for thee!'

Truisms! Preachments repeated from Solomon downwards! some quick, impatient reader, all animal irritability, will exclaim—Good, but it is the very prerogative of genius, in every age, to revive truisms such as these, and make them burn in our hearts. Many a man in his hour of depression, when resolution is sicklied over by the pale cast of thought, will find, in the writings of Carlyle, a freshening stimulant, better than the wine-cup, or even the laughter of a friend, can give. In some of his biographical sketches, with what force has he brought out the moral resolution which animated, or ought to have animated, the man of whom he is writing! We shall have occasion, by and by, to notice what, to our mind, appears a mere perversion of thought and a mischievous exaggeration in our author, who, in his love of a certain *energy* of character, has often made this energy (apart from a moral purpose) the test and rule of his admiration. But at present turn to his admirable estimation of Dr. Samuel Johnson, and the noble regret which he throws over the memory of Burns. A portion of the first we cannot resist extracting. What a keen mountain air, bracing to the nerves, mortal to languor and complaint, blows over us from passages such as these:

[quotes loosely not indicating the passages he has deleted, 'The Courage' to 'for these' *Boswell's Life of Johnson*, XXVIII, 123–6. A somewhat positive analysis of *The French Revolution* is omitted]

It is time, indeed, that we ourselves turned to this work, the perusal of which has led us to these remarks upon Mr. Carlyle. We were desirous, however, of forming something like a general estimate of his merits and demerits before we entered upon any account of his last production. What space we have remaining shall be devoted to this work.

Past and Present, if it does not enhance, ought not, we think, to diminish from the reputation of its author; but as a *mannerism* becomes increasingly disagreeable by repetition, we suspect that, without having less merit, this work will have less popularity than its predecessors. The style is the same 'motley wear,' and has the same jerking movement— seems at times a thing of shreds and patches hung on wires—and is so full of brief allusions to his own previous writings, that to a reader unacquainted with these it would be scarce intelligible. With all this it has the same vigour, and produces the same vivid impression that always attends upon his writings. Here, as elsewhere, he pursues his authorcraft with a right noble and independent spirit, striking manifestly for truth, and for no other cause; and here also, as elsewhere, he leaves his side unguarded, open to unavoidable attack, so that the most blundering critic cannot fail to hit right, and the most friendly cannot spare.

The *past* is represented by a certain Abbot Samson, and his abbey of St. Edmunds, whose life and conversation are drawn from the chronicle already alluded to, and which has been lately published by the Camden Society.* Our author will look, he tells us, face to face on this remote period, 'in hope of perhaps illustrating our own poor century thereby.' Very good. To get a station in the past, and therefrom view the present,

---

* Chronica *Jocelini De Brakelonda*, de rebus gestis Samsonis Abbatis Monasterii Sancti Edmundi: nunc primum typis mandata, curante Johanne Goge Rokewood. (Camden Society, London, 1840.)

is no ill-devised scheme. But Abbot Samson and his monks form a very limited, almost a domestic picture, which supplies but few points of contrast or similitude with our 'own poor century,' which, at all events, is very rich in point of view. When, therefore, he proceeds to discuss the world-wide topics of our own times, we soon lose all memory of the Abbot and his monastery, who seems indeed to have as little connexion with the difficulties of our position, as the statues of Gog and Magog in Guildhall with the decision of some election contest which is made to take place in their venerable presence. On one point only can any palpable contrast be exhibited, namely, between the religious spirit of his times and our own.

Now, here, as on every topic where a comparison is attempted what, must strike every one is, the manifest partiality Mr. Carlyle shows to the past, and the unfair preference he gives it over the present. Nothing but respect and indulgence when he revisits the monastery of St. Edmunds; nothing but censure and suspicion when he enters, say, for instance, the precincts of Exeter Hall. Well do we know, that if Mr. Carlyle could meet such a monk alive, as he here treats with so much deference, encounter him face to face, talk to him, and hear him talk; he and the monk would be intolerable to each other. Fortunately for him, the monks are dead and buried whom he lauds so much when contrasted with our modern pietists. Could these tenants of the stately monastery preach to him about their purgatory and their prayers—lecture him, as assuredly they would, with that same earnest, uncomfortable, too anxious exhortation, which all saints must address to sinners—he would close his ears hermetically—he would fly for it—he would escape with as desperate haste as from the saddest whine that ever issued from some lath-and-plaster conventicle.

Mr. Carlyle censures our poor century for its lack of faith; yet the kind of faith it possesses, which has grown up in it, which is *here* at this present, he has no respect for, treats with no manner of tenderness. What *other* would we have? He deals out to it no measure of philosophical justice. He accepts the faith of every age but his own. He will accept, as the best thing possible, the trustful and hopeful spirit of dark and superstitious periods; but if the more enlightened piety of his own age be at variance even with the most subtle and difficult tenets of his own philosophy, he will make no compromise with it, he casts it away for contemptuous infidelity to trample on as it pleases. When visiting the past, how indulgent, kind, and considerate he is! When Abbot Samson (as the greatest event of his life) resolves to see and to touch the remains of

St. Edmund, and 'taking the head between his hands, speaks groaning,' and prays to the 'Glorious Martyr that it may not be turned to his perdition that he, miserable and sinful, has dared to touch his sacred person,' and thereupon proceeds to touch the eyes and the nose, and the breast and the toes, which last he religiously counts; our complacent author sees here, 'a noble awe surrounding the memory of the dead saint symbol, and promoter of many other right noble things.' And when he has occasion to call to mind the preaching of Peter the Hermit, who threw the fanaticism of the west on the fanaticism of the east, and in order that there should be no disparity between them in the sanguinary conflict, assimilated the faith of Christ to that of Mahommed, and taught that the baptized believer who fell by the Saracen would die in the arms of angels, and at the very gates of heaven; here, too, he bestows a hearty respect on the enthusiastic missionary, and all his fellow-crusaders: it seems that he also would willingly have gone with such an army of the faithful. But when he turns from the past to the present, all this charity and indulgence are at an end. He finds in his own mechanico-philosophical age a faith in accordance with its prevailing modes of thought—a faith lying at the foundation of whatever else of doctrinal theology it possesses—a faith diffused over all society, and taught not only in churches and chapels to pious auditories, but in every lecture-room, and by scientific as well as theological instructors—a faith in God, as creator of the universe, as the demonstrated author, architect, origina-tor, of this wondrous world; and lo! this same philosopher who looked with encouraging complacency on Abbot Samson bending in adoration over the exhumed remains of a fellow-mortal, and who listens without a protest to the cries of sanguinary enthusiasm, rising from a throng of embattled Christians, steps disdainfully aside from this faith of a peaceful and scientific age; he has some subtle, metaphysical speculations that will not countenance it; he demands that a faith in God should be put on some other foundation, which foundation, unhappily, his country-men, as yet unskilled in transcendental metaphysics, cannot apprehend; he withdraws his sympathy from the so trite and sober-minded belief of an industrious, experimental, ratiocinating generation, and cares not if they have a God at all, if they can only make his existence evident to themselves from some commonplace notion of design and prearrange-ment visible in the world. . . .

Mr. Carlyle not being *en rapport* with the religious spirit of his age, finds therein no religious spirit whatever; on the other hand, he has a great deal of religion of his own, not very clear to any but himself; and thus, between these two, we have pages, very many, of such raving as the following:—

[quotes 'It is even so' to 'familiar to us' Bk. III, ch. 1, 136–7]

What is to be said of writing such as this! For ourselves, we hurry on with a sort of incredulity, scarce believing that it is set down there for our steady perusal. . . .

The whole parallel which he runs between past and present is false—whimsically false. At one time we hear it uttered as an impeachment against our age, that everything is done by committees and companies, shares and joint effort, and that no one man, or hero, can any longer move the world as in the blessed days of Peter the Hermit. Were we disposed to treat Mr. Carlyle as members of Parliament, by the help of their *Hansard*, controvert each other, we should have no difficulty in finding amongst his works some passage—whether eloquent or not, or how far intelligible, would be just a mere chance—in which he would tell us that this capacity for joint effort, this habit of co-operation, was the greatest boast our times could make, and gave the fairest promise for the future. In Ireland, by the way, *one man* can still effect something, and work after the fashion, if not with so pure a fanaticism, as Peter the Hermit. The spectacle does not appear very edifying. Pray—the question just occurs to us—pray has Mr. O'Connell got an *eye*? Would Mr. Carlyle acknowledge that this man has *swallowed all formulas*? Having been bred a lawyer, we are afraid, or, in common Christian speech, we hope, that he has not.

But we are not about to proceed through a volume such as this in a carping spirit, though food enough for such a spirit may be found; there is too much genuine merit, too much genuine humour, in the work. What, indeed, is the use of selecting from an author who *will* indulge in all manner of vagaries, whether of thought or expression, passages to prove that he can be whimsical and absurd, can deal abundantly in obscurities and contradictions, and can withal write the most motley, confused English of any man living? Better take, with thanks, from so irregular a genius, what seems to us good, or affords us gratification, and leave the rest alone.

We will not enter into the account of Abbot Samson; it is a little historical sketch, perfect in its kind, in which no part is redundant, and which, being gathered itself from very scanty sources, will not bear further mutilation, We turn, therefore, from the *Past*, although in a literary point of view, a very attractive portion of the work, and will draw our extracts (they cannot now be numerous) from his lucubrations upon the *Present*. . . .

[The rest of the review is composed mainly of extracts from *Past and Present*. Smith concludes with the following remarks:]

We have already said, that we regard the chief *value* of Mr. Carlyle's writings to consist in the *tone of mind* which the individual reader acquires from their perusal;—manly, energetic, enduring, with high resolves and self-forgetting effort; and we here again, at the close of our paper, revert to this remark: *Past and Present*, has not, and could not have, the same wild power which *Sartor Resartus* possessed, in our opinion, over the feelings of the reader; but it contains passages which look the same way, and breathe the same spirit. . . .

16. Ralph Waldo Emerson, an unsigned review, *Dial*

July 1843, iv, 96–102

Ralph Waldo Emerson (1803–82) and Carlyle began a magnificent transatlantic correspondence when Emerson first read *Sartor Resartus* in *Fraser's Magazine* in 1834. Although Emerson initiated the correspondence, Carlyle was to gain much from this friendship in the next decade as Emerson was to perform many services for the Scotsman, writing the Preface to the first edition of *Sartor Resartus* (Boston, 1836), seeing *The French Revolution* (Boston, 1838) through the press, performing much bibliopoly for Carlyle in the next few years. Taking charge of legal and financial arrangements, Emerson saw that Carlyle gained profits, not only fame. On the other side of the Atlantic, Carlyle returned the favour ('There man! Tit for tat.') by writing a Preface for Emerson's *Essays* which were printed by Fraser. When *Past and Present* arrived in Concord, Emerson once more took charge of the publishing and financial details, though by the time that Little and Brown had come out with an authorized version, a cheap pirated edition had captured the market. Though the edition paid for itself—and Emerson wrote a glorious review of it—this venture was to mark the end of their 'chivalrous international doings' as Carlyle put it. See Introduction, p. 16.

Here is Carlyle's new poem, his Iliad of English woes, to follow his poem on France, entitled *The History of the French Revolution*. In its first aspect it is a political tract, and since Burke, since Milton, we have had nothing to compare with it. It grapples honestly with the facts lying before all men, groups and disposes them with a master's mind,— and with a heart full of manly tenderness, offers his best counsel to his brothers. Obviously it is the book of a powerful and accomplished thinker, who has looked with naked eyes at the dreadful political signs in England for the last few years, has conversed much on these topics with such wise men of all ranks and parties as are drawn to a scholar's house, until such daily and nightly meditation has grown into a great connexion, if not a system of thoughts, and the topic of English politics becomes the best vehicle for the expression of his recent thinking, recommended to him by the desire to give some timely counsels, and to strip the worst mischiefs of their plausibility. It is a brave and just book, and not a semblance. 'No new truth,' say the critics on all sides. Is it so? truth is very old; but the merit of seers is not to invent, but to dispose objects in their right places, and he is the commander who is always in the mount, whose eye not only sees details, but throws crowds of details into their right arrangement and a larger and juster totality than any other. The book makes great approaches to true contemporary history, a very rare success, and firmly holds up to daylight the absurdities still tolerated in the English and European system. It is such an appeal to the conscience and honour of England as cannot be forgotten, or be feigned to be forgotten. It has the merit which belongs to every honest book, that it was self-examining before it was eloquent, and so hits all other men, and, as the country people say of good preaching, 'comes bounce down into every pew.' Every reader shall carry away something. The scholar shall read and write, the farmer and mechanic shall toil with new resolution, nor forget the book when they resume their labor.

Though no theocrat, and more than most philosophers a believer in political systems, Mr. Carlyle very fairly finds the calamity of the times not in bad bills of Parliament, nor the remedy in good bills, but the vice in false and superficial aims of the people, and the remedy in honesty and insight. Like every work of genius, its great value is in telling such simple truths. As we recall the topics, we are struck with the force given to the plain truths; the picture of the English nation all sitting enchanted, the poor enchanted so they cannot work, the rich enchanted so that they cannot enjoy, and are rich in vain; the exposure of the progress of fraud into all arts and social activities; the proposition, that the laborer must have a greater share in his earnings; that the principle of permanence shall be admitted into all contracts of mutual service; that the state shall provide at least school-master's education for all the citizens; the exhortation to the workman, that he shall respect the work and not the wages; to the scholar, that he shall be there for light; to the idle, that no man shall sit idle; the picture of Abbot Samson, the true governor, who 'is not there to expect reason and nobleness of others, he is there to give them of his own reason and nobleness;' and the assumption throughout the book, that a new chivalry and nobility, namely the dynasty of labor is replacing the old nobilities. These things strike us with a force, which reminds us of the morals of the Oriental or early Greek masters, and of no modern book. Truly in these things there is great reward. It is not by sitting still at a grand distance, and calling the human race *larvæ*, that men are to be helped, nor by helping the depraved after their own foolish fashion, but by doing unweariedly the particular work we were born to do. Let no man think himself absolved because he does a generous action and befriends the poor, but let him see whether he so holds his property that a benefit goes from it to all. A man's diet should be what is simplest and readiest to be had, because it is so private a good. His house should be better, because that is for the use of hundreds, perhaps of thousands, and is the property of the traveler. But his speech is a perpetual and public instrument; let that always side with the race, and yield neither a lie nor a sneer. His manners,—let them be hospitable and civilizing, so that no Phidias or Raphael shall have taught anything better in canvass or stone; and his acts should be representative of the human race, as one who makes them rich in his having and poor in his want.

It requires great courage in a man of letters to handle the contemporary practical questions; not because he then has all men for his rivals, but because of the infinite entanglements of the problem, and the waste of strength in gathering unripe fruits. The task is superhuman; and the poet knows well, that a little time will do more than the most puissant genius. Time stills the loud noise of opinions, sinks the small, raises the great, so that the true emerges without effort and in perfect harmony to all eyes; but the truth of the present hour, except in particulars and single relations, is unattainable. Each man can very well know his own part of duty, if he will; but to bring out the truth for beauty and as literature, surmounts the powers of art. The most elaborate history of to-day will have the oddest dislocated look in the next generation. The historian of to-day is yet three ages off. The poet cannot descend into the turbid present without injury to his rarest gifts. Hence that necessity of isolation which genius has always felt. He must stand on his glass tripod, if he would keep his electricity.

But when the political aspects are so calamitous, that the sympathies of the man overpower the habits of the poet, a higher than literary inspiration may succor him. It is a costly proof of character, that the most renowned scholar of England should take his reputation in his hand, and should descend into the ring, and he has added to his love whatever honor his opinions may forfeit. To atone for this departure from the vows of the scholar and his eternal duties, to this secular charity, we have at least this gain, that here is a message which those to whom it was addressed cannot choose but hear. Though they die, they must listen. It is plain that whether by hope or by fear, or were it only by delight in this panorama of brilliant images, all the great classes of English society must read, even those whose existence it proscribes. Poor Queen Victoria,—poor Sir Robert Peel,—poor Primate and Bishops,—poor Dukes and Lords! there is no help in place or pride, or in looking another way; a grain of wit is more penetrating than the lightning of the night-storm, which no curtains or shutters will keep out. Here is a book which will be read, no thanks to anybody but itself. What pains, what hopes, what vows, shall come of the reading! Here is a book as full of treason as an egg is full of meat, and every lordship and worship and high form and ceremony of English conservatism tossed like a football into the air, and kept in the air with merciless kicks and rebounds, and yet not a word is punishable by statute. The wit has eluded all official zeal; and yet these dire jokes, these cunning thrusts, this flaming sword of Cherubim waved high in air illuminates the whole horizon, and shows to the eyes of the universe every wound it inflicts. Worst of all for the party attacked, it bereaves them before-hand of all sympathy, by anticipating the plea of poetic and humane conservatism, and impressing the reader with the conviction, that the satirist himself has the truest love for everything old and excellent in English land and institutions, and a genuine respect for the basis of truth in those whom he exposes.

We are at some loss how to state what strikes us as the fault of this remarkable book, for the variety and excellence of the talent displayed in it is pretty sure to leave all special criticism in the wrong. And we may easily fail in expressing the general objection which we feel. It appears to us as a certain disproportion in the picture, caused by the obtrusion of the whims of the painter. In this work, as in his former labors, Mr. Carlyle reminds us of a sick giant. His humors, are expressed with so much force of constitution, that his fancies are more attractive and more credible than the sanity of duller men. But the habitual exaggeration of the tone wearies whilst it stimulates. It is felt to be so much deduction from the universality of the picture. It is not serene sunshine, but every-thing is seen in lurid stormlights. Every object attitudinizes, to the very mountains and stars almost, under the refractions of this wonderful humorist, and instead of the common earth and sky, we have a Martin's Creation or Judgment Day. A crisis has always arrived which requires

a *deus ex machinê*. One can hardly credit, whilst under the spell of this
magician, that the world always had the same bankrupt look, to foregoing ages as to us,—as of a failed world just recollecting its old with-
ered forces to begin again and try and do a little business. It was perhaps
inseparable from the attempt to write a book of wit and imagination
on English politics that a certain local emphasis and of effect, such as is
the vice of preaching, should appear, producing on the reader a feeling
of forlornness by the excess of value attributed to circumstances. But
the splendor of wit cannot outdazzle the calm daylight, which always
shows every individual man in balance with his age, and able to work
out his own salvation from all the follies of that, and no such glaring
contrasts or severalties in that or this. Each age has its own follies, as
its majority is made up of foolish young people; its superstitions appear
no superstitions to itself; and if you should ask the contemporary, he
would tell you with pride or with regret (according as he was practical
or poetic) that it had none. But after a short time, down go its follies
and weakness, and the memory of them; its virtues alone remain, and
its limitation assumes the poetic form of a beautiful superstition, as the
dimness of our sight clothes the objects in the horizon with mist and
color. The revelation of Reason is this of the unchangeableness of the
fact of humanity under all its subjective aspects, that to the cowering
it always cowers, to the daring it opens great avenues. The ancients are
only venerable to us, because distance has destroyed what was trivial;
as the sun and stars affect us only grandly, because we cannot reach to
their smoke and surfaces, and say, Is that all?

And yet the gravity of the times, the manifold and increasing dangers
of the English state, may easily excuse some over-coloring of the picture, and we at this distance are not so far removed from any of the
specific evils, and are deeply participant in too many, not to share the
gloom, and thank the love and the courage of the counsellor. This book
is full of humanity, and nothing is more excellent in this, as in all Mr.
Carlyle's works, than the attitude of the writer. He has the dignity of a
man of letters who knows what belongs to him, and never deviates
from his sphere; a continuer of the great line of scholars, and sustains
their office in the highest credit and honor. If the good heaven have any
word to impart to this unworthy generation, here is one scribe qualified
and clothed for its occasion. One excellence he has in an age of Mammon
and of criticism, that he never suffers the eye of his wonder to close. Let
who will be the dupe of trifles, he cannot keep his eye off from that
gracious Infinite which embosoms us. As a literary artist, he has great

merits, beginning with the main one, that he never wrote one dull line. How well read, how adroit, what thousand arts in his one art of writing; with his expedient for expressing those unproven opinions, which he entertains but will not endorse, by summoning one of his men of straw from the cell, and the respectable Sauerteig, or Teufelsdrock, or Dryasdust, or Picturesque Traveller says what is put into his mouth and disappears. That morbid temperament has given his rhetoric a somewhat bloated character, a luxury to many imaginative and learned persons, like a showery south wind with its sunbursts and rapid chasing of lights and glooms over the landscape, and yet its offensiveness to multitudes of reluctant lovers makes us often wish some concession were possible on the part of the humorist. Yet it must not be forgotten that in all his fun of castanets, or playing of tunes with a whiplash like some renowned charioteers,—in all this glad and needful vending of his redundant spirits,—he does yet ever and anon, as if catching the glance of one wise man in the crowd, quit his tempestuous key, and lance at him in clear level tone the very word, and then with new glee returns to his game. He is like a lover or an outlaw who wraps up his message in a serenade, which is nonsense to the sentinel, but salvation to the ear for which it is meant. He does not dodge the question, but gives sincerity where it is due.

One word more respecting this remarkable style. We have in literature few specimens of magnificence. Plato is the purple ancient, and Bacon and Milton the moderns of the richest strains. Burke sometimes reaches to that exuberant fulness, though deficient in depth. Carlyle in his strange half mad way, has entered the Field of the Cloth of Gold, and shown a vigor and wealth of resource, which has no rival in the tourney play of these times;—the indubitable champion of England. Carlyle is the first domestication of the modern system with its infinity of details into style. We have been civilizing very fast, building London and Paris, and now planting New England and India, New Holland and Oregon,—and it has not appeared in literature,—there has been no analogous expansion and recomposition in books. Carlyle's style is the first emergence of all this wealth and labor, with which the world has gone with child so long. London and Europe tunnelled, graded, cornlawed, with trade-nobility, and east and west Indies for dependencies, and America, with the Rocky Hills in the horizon, have never before been conquered in literature. This is the first invasion and conquest. How like an air-balloon or bird of Jove does he seem to float over the continent, and stooping here and there pounce on a fact as a symbol which was never a symbol before. This is the first experiment; and something of rudeness and haste must be pardoned to so great an achievement. It will be done again and again, sharper, simpler, but fortunate is he who did it first, though never so giant-like and fabulous. This grandiose character pervades his wit and his imagination. We have never had anything in literature so like earthquakes, as the laughter of Carlyle. He 'shakes with his mountain mirth.' It is like the laughter of the genii in the horizon. These jokes shake down Parliament-house and Windsor Castle, Temple, and Tower, and the future shall echo the dangerous peals. The other particular of magnificence is in his rhymes. Carlyle is a poet who is altogether too burly in his frame and habit to submit to the limits of metre. Yet he is full of rhythm not only in the perpetual melody of his periods, but in the burdens, refrains, and grand returns of his sense and music. Whatever thought or motto has once appeared to him fraught with meaning, becomes an omen to him henceforward, and is sure to return with deeper tones and weightier import, now as promise, now as threat, now as confirmation, in gigantic reverberation, as if the hills, the horizon, and the next ages returned the sound.

Note Part of a letter dated 31 October 1843, indicating Carlyle's pleasure with Emerson's above review, is recorded here:

In this last Number of the *Dial*, which by the bye your Bookseller never forwarded to me, I found one little Essay, a criticism on myself,— which, if it should do me mischief, may the gods forgive you for! It is considerably the most dangerous thing I have read for some years. A decided likeness of myself recognisable in it, as in the celestial mirror of a friend's heart; but so enlarged, exaggerated, all *transfigured*,—the most delicious, the most dangerous thing! Well, I suppose I must try to assimilate it also, to turn it also to good, if I be able. Eulogies, dyslogies, in which one finds no features of one's own natural face, are easily dealt with; easily left unread, as stuff for lighting fires, such is the insipidity, the wearisome *non*entity of pabulum like that: but here is another sort of matter! 'The beautifullest piece of criticism I have read for many a day,' says every one that speaks of it. May the gods forgive you.—I have purchased a copy for three shillings, and sent it to my Mother: one of the *indubitablest* benefits I could think of in regard to it. (For this letter and the complete correspondence, see Joseph Slater's excellent introduction to and edition of *The Correspondence of Emerson and Carlyle* [New York, 1964], esp. pp. 349–50.)

17. Peter LePage Renouf, from an unsigned review, *Dublin Review*

August 1843, xv, 182–200

Peter LePage Renouf (1822–97), Egyptologist, fell under Newman's influence at Oxford and preceded him into the Church. In 1855, he was appointed Professor of Oriental Languages at Catholic University, Dublin, and in 1885, he was made Keeper of the Egyptian and Assyrian Antiquities at the British Museum. His studies in hieroglyphics brought him fame; his celebrated translation of the *Book of the Dead* was most notable. He contributed to the esoteric Catholic journal, *Atlantis*. See Introduction, p. 17.

For the context of Sewell's remarks quoted by Renouf in the early part of this review, see Sewell's essay included here (No. 11, p. 149).

We have read this last production of Mr. Carlyle with feelings of no ordinary interest. Its author, indeed, has far stronger claims upon our attention than the infinite majority of the popular writers of this country. He is not only the most eloquent and energetic writers of the day, but one of the most profound and independent thinkers. And although his mind is one of the most original now exerting its influence on the literature of this country, he comes before us, professedly, in the character of an adept in all the mysteries of the modern German literature and philosophy. Our readers hardly require to be told that it is chiefly to him that we are indebted for what we know of such writers as Novalis, Jean Paul Richter, and Goethe. And Goethe has said* of him, that he is almost more at home in German literature than the Germans themselves. Now, when a person of this character comes

* Eckermann's *Conversations with Goethe*, p. 259 (American translation). This is not by any means Goethe's only testimony to Mr. Carlyle's great powers. At p. 230, he says, 'We are weakest in the æsthetic department, and may look long before we meet such a man as Carlyle.' . . . 'Carlyle has written a life of Schiller, and judged him throughout as it would be difficult for a German to judge.'

forward and offers his opinion in the boldest and most uncompromising manner upon those very subjects which are agitating the public mind, we should hardly be fulfilling our duties as reviewers, if we neglected to direct the attention of our readers to a work, in the matter of which so many of them must feel deeply interested.

To many persons, indeed, Mr. Carlyle's German studies and avowed German leanings are a matter of great annoyance, not so much because they are certain, *à priori*, that Germans must, necessarily, be wrong, as because their national feeling will not allow them to tolerate foreign importations of any kind. 'Learn to talk in German,' says Mr. Sewell, 'and as Germans talk, and you will soon learn to think in German, and thinking in German, *you will cease to think as an Englishman.*' In which sapient observation our readers will please to observe that the great grievance complained of is not 'incorrect thinking,' but the 'not thinking as an Englishman.'

We have already spoken of Mr. Carlyle as one of the most eloquent writers of the day. The work before us reminds us more than almost any other we ever read, of Coleridge's remark, that 'wherever you find a sentence musically worded, of true rhythm and melody in the words, there is something deep and good in the meaning too.' Our readers will, we are sure, on perusing *Past and Present*, agree with us in applying this remark to it.

It is, indeed, a wonderful book throughout; so full of thought in every sentence, and so perfectly connected in all its parts, that it is with great diffidence that we venture to point out, in a very imperfect manner, a few of its most striking features. In most cases it will be best to let Mr. Carlyle speak for himself.

The object-matter of the whole book may be learnt from the opening sentence of the Proem.

The condition of England, on which many pamphlets are now in the course of publication, and many thoughts unpublished are going on in every reflective head, is justly regarded as one of the most ominous, and withal one of the strangest, ever seen in this world. England is full of wealth, of multifarious produce, supply for want in every kind; yet England is dying of inanition.

Few people now-a-days could be found to deny this fearful truth,— it is acknowledged on all hands, but how few can strictly be said to *believe* it. Most people are content with acknowledging it in the same way as they do the fact that two sides of a triangle are greater than the third, and there is an end of it. That all and each of us are as much personally interested in this truth as if our own house were burning over our heads, is what seems to strike nobody. The more honour then to Mr. Carlyle, who sees it more clearly than most persons are disposed to do, and who, though altogether unconnected with a certain set of political alarmists, draws a most vivid and frightful picture of the present state of things in England,—the more frightful because it is undeniably a true one.

The fact, however, being admitted, two questions naturally arise from it:—to what causes are we to attribute the evils under which we labour? and, by what means can we remedy these evils?—the solution of the latter question evidently depending upon that of the former. Here every person has a different theory, all more or less founded on some one truth, which put forth to the exclusion of other truths equally undeniable, sounds to all but partisans very like falsehood. One person thinks the repeal of the corn laws will set all things right; his neighbour thinks the suppression of the Anti-corn Law League would quiet all disturbances; a third person has set his heart upon the ballot; and a fourth sees the root of all evil in the game laws; another is quite positive that the spread of democratic feeling is the one mischief; while the majority are equally positive that the contrary is the case. In short, 'Conservatives' propose 'conservative' measures as the cure for all evils; 'Liberals' 'liberal' measures.

Differing widely from all parties, and yet absolutely from none, Mr. Carlyle takes a much deeper view both of the extent and the cause of our political evils. He would, no doubt, say that both parties were right to a certain extent, and only wrong from taking a partial view of the truth. The 'liberals' of course consider Mr. Carlyle as fighting on their side, and are very fond of quoting all the severe things he says against the powers that be, against the corn laws, their supporters, &c. &c. But there cannot be a greater mistake than to imagine that he is one of the party;—his political opinions coincide much with those of his favorite Goethe:

> No apostle of liberty much to my heart ever found I,
> Licence each for himself, this was at bottom their want.
> Liberator of many! first dare to be servant of many:
> What a business is that: wouldst thou know it, go try!

Accordingly, in his *Chartism* and elsewhere, he spoke very freely indeed about parliamentary radicalism; and that his opinion is not changed is visible from the work before us.

[quotes 'Bull is a born conservative' to 'not inquiring further' Bk. III, ch. v, 162–3]

All this, however, is a very different thing from saying that he perfectly approves of all the proceedings of Sir Robert Peel's government.

There is a noble conservatism as well as an ignoble. Would to heaven, for the sake of conservatism itself, the noble alone were left, and the ignoble, by some kind, severe hand, were ruthlessly lopped away, forbidden evermore to shew itself! For it is the right and noble alone that will have victory in this struggle; the rest is wholly an obstruction, a postponement, and fearful imperilment of the victory.

Among the annoyances of ignoble conservatism, he reckons the corn laws; 'defended,' he says, 'by arguments which would make the angels, and almost the very jackasses, weep.' And were he the conservative party of England, 'he would not for an hundred thousand pounds an hour allow the corn laws to continue.' At the same time he is very far from thinking that the repeal of the corn laws is the one thing necessary. 'By no reform bill, ballot box, five point charter, by no boxes or bills, or charters,' is this to be obtained.

The abrogation of the corn laws might, he thinks, afford life to the nation for twenty years, like the shadow on King Hezekiah's dial; but, by this time they would have relapsed into their old course, in spite of free trades and abrogations.

Nor will more universal representation secure the desideratum, and sending members to parliament by bribery, though an infamous solecism (and he has a whole chapter about it), is not the only thing to be cured, for, 'what can the incorruptiblest *Bobuses* elect, if it be not some *Bobissimus*, should they find such.'

'Unworking aristocracies' are a great evil, and carry with them the seeds of their own dissolution; they are 'like a tree planted on precipices; from the roots of which all the earth has been crumbling.' But it is not by abolishing aristocracies that we shall gain our end.

If the convulsive struggles of the last half century have taught poor struggling convulsed Europe any truth, it may perhaps be this, as the essence of innumerable others: that Europe requires a real aristocracy, a real priesthood, or it cannot continue to exist. Huge French revolutions, Napoleonisms, then Bourbonisms, with their corollary of Three Days, finishing in very unfinal Louis-Philippisms: all this ought to be didactic! All this may have taught us, that false aristocracies are insupportable; that no aristocracies, liberty, and equalities, are impossible; that true aristocracies are at once indispensable, and not easily obtained.

But all these matters, however important in themselves, are but the surface of things; we must look far deeper, if we really wish to know the source of all the thousand evils which threaten us on every side. Mr. Carlyle has pointed it out in his previous works, but never so energetically as in this.

[quotes 'There is no longer any God' to 'desperateness next hour' Bk. III, ch. i, 136–7]

This awful truth is now acknowledged by minds* of the most opposite character; would to God that we only knew how to act in accordance with our convictions. If we only did our part, each man according to his capabilities, much might be hoped for. But alas! we have only to look around us, nay,—too often into our own bosoms,— to be convinced of the justice with which Mr. Carlyle inveighs against the unreality which prevails everywhere:—

From this the highest apex of things downwards, through all strata and breadths, how many fully-awakened realities have we fallen in with? alas, on the contrary, what troops and populations of phantasies, not God-veracities, but Devil-falsities, down to the very lowest stratum. You will walk in no public thorough-fare, or remotest byeway of English existence, but you will meet a man, an interest of men, that has given up hope in the everlasting, true, and placed its hope in the temporary, half, or wholly false.

Many of Mr. Carlyle's readers are annoyed beyond measure at, what *they* consider, his tedious repetition of protests against the shams, the formulas, the unveracities, the quackeries, the doggeries, &c., &c., of the flunkey species. This only betrays how utterly they fall short of his real meaning, and to how little purpose even words of fire are addressed to those who *will* not understand. They can have little in common with a writer who is terribly alive to the fact that—

Human affairs now circulate everywhere, not healthy life-blood in them, but as it were a detestable copperas banker's ink; and all is grown acrid, divisive,— threatening dissolution; and the huge tumultuous life of society is galvanic, devil-ridden, too truly possessed by a devil! For, in short, Mammon *is* not a god at all; but a devil, and even a very despicable devil. Follow the devil faithfully, you are sure enough to go to the devil: whither else *can* you go?

* See Mr. Bosanquet's 'Principia, or, the Principles of Evil manifesting themselves in these last times, in Religion, Philosophy, and Politics.'—*Burns.*

Mammon indeed is no sham, it is truly the only veracity we have left; and this brute-god has usurped the place of the Most High.

Oh it is frightful when a whole nation, as our fathers used to say, has 'forgotten God;' has remembered only Mammon, and what Mammon leads to! . . . Not one false man but does unaccountable mischief; how much, in a generation or two, will twenty-seven millions, mostly false, manage to accumulate? The sum of it, visible in every street, market-place, senate-house, circulating library, cathedral, cotton mill, and union workhouse, fills one *not* with a comic feeling.

The most distressing thing too is, that this accursed gospel of Mammonism is not preached in those places alone which would naturally be dedicated to its worship, as the mart or market-place,—but from the very chairs of moral philosophy, by those whose especial duty it should be to resist its claims. And if they do these things in a green tree, what shall be done in the dry?

The haggard despair of cotton-factory, coal-mine operatives, Chandos-farmer labourers, in these day, is painful to behold; but not so painful, hideous, to the inner sense, as that brutish god-forgetting profit and loss philosophy, and life theory, which we hear jingled on all hands of us, in senate-houses, sporting clubs, leading articles, pulpits and platforms, everywhere as the ultimate gospel and candid plain-English of man's life, from the throats and pens and thoughts of all but all men!

Look at our universities. At Cambridge, as far as we are aware, no moral philosophy of any kind is professed. Oxford and London, however, have text books of their own. And what is the doctrine taught by these books as to the final cause of human action?

'Actions are to be estimated by their tendency. Whatever is expedient is right. It is the utility of any moral rule alone, which constitutes the obligation of it.'

Such is the doctrine taught in Paley's *Moral Philosophy*, the text-book of the London University. We are not writing in ignorance of the defence set up by the partisans of Paley, which is certainly valid to the extent of vindicating Paley himself from the charge of *practically* advocating anything morally wrong. But the principle itself, however neutralized by Paley's other doctrines, is essentially and radically immoral. . . . Honour to him [Carlyle] and all others, who, in this faithless, mechanical God-denying, devil-fearing generation, lift up their voices, and use all their energies against the soul-destroying gospel of mammonism, in all its developments, forms, and modifications. Till this devil's gospel cease to be preached in every corner of our streets, and to be acted upon in every imaginable department of social life, all the proposed panaceas, reform bills, ballot-boxes, corn-law abrogations, &c. &c. are but so many Morrison's pills, so many efforts of flunkeyism, terminating in puffery. No! as long as we are satisfied with looking at the mere outward appearances, and neglect the inner-facts, the everlasting substance of things, our finest-spun theory must remain a 'formula,'—our most promising remedy a 'sham.'

We have forgotten God, we have no more faith; till *this* be remedied, all remains as before. Remedy it, and all other evils will remedy themselves.

My friend, if thou ever do come to believe in God, thou wilt find all Chartism, Manchester riot, Parliamentary incompetence, ministries of windbag, and the wildest social dissolutions, and the burning up of this entire planet, a most small matter in comparison.

Awake, O nightmare sleepers! awake, arise, or be forever fallen! This is not play-house poetry; it is sober fact. Our England—our world cannot live as it is. It will connect itself with a God again, or go down with nameless throes and fire consummation to the devils.

Now some excellent persons will be tempted to sneer at a writer who puts forward these views. 'We *do* believe in God, and so do most persons now-a-days. There are sad errors abroad, it is true,—very sad errors, but nobody goes to the length of Atheism.' Not so, good people; you do not understand Mr. Carlyle:—you do *not* believe in God as he wishes you to do; otherwise *you* would see that want of faith is the one ruling evil of the day. He does not ask you to believe in God, in the same way as you believe there are mountains in the moon, but even as a man in danger of drowning believes that he must sink or swim. It is because we do not *thus* believe in God that calamities hitherto unheard of have now fallen upon us. Yes! there *is* such a thing as national sin;— not only individuals, but nations, may forget God, and, leaving out all considerations of the just and the unjust, betake themselves to the godless question of expediency. And 'windbag ministries,' who do this, 'strong only in the faith that paragraphs and plausibilities bring votes; that force of public opinion is the primal necessity of things, and highest God we have;' however they may *seem* to prosper for a time, although newspapers may consecrate their leading articles to their service, and quarterly reviews pronounce their policy to be irreproachable, they must roll on—to their own perdition. Justice may be delayed, but come it must and will, even in this world.

[quotes several non-continuous passages from Bk. I, ch. i, 9–11]

We require, then, a government which does 'believe in God,' government of heroes, which will not fear to rule according to the un-deviating principles of justice. But is *this* the first step towards the political regeneration of the country? By no means.

The government cannot do, by all its signalling and commanding, what the society is radically indisposed to do. In the long run, every government is the exact symbol of its people, with their wisdom and unwisdom; we have to say, 'Like people, like government.'

[quotes 'A whole world of heroes' to 'and not evil' Bk. I, ch. vi, 35]

In all this, whatever Bobuses and the Morrison's-Pill Political Economists may think about the matter, there is deep, very deep political wisdom. The only mischief is, that people will not listen to Mr. Carlyle; but he himself is so earnest and so hopeful, that we cannot but join with him, and hope too. Besides this, he is none of your paradoxical writers,—none of your Mr. Palmers and Mr. Sewells, who sit in their chambers, spinning theories for the good of their neighbours, and at the same time shutting their eyes to every thing that goes on in the world: far from it. He sees clearly enough how difficult it will be to change a nation of flunkeys into a nation of genuine men; but, as he truly says, 'no noble task was ever easy.' He is hopeful, nay, almost sanguine: and for this we love and honour him. In his predictions of the future, however, there is none of that arrogant confidence which disgusts us so much in the every-day declamations of political prophets. . . .

Two predictions, nevertheless, he thinks himself warranted in making, as being already possible.

First, 'That a "Splendour of God," in one form or other, will have to unfold itself from the heart of these our industrial ages too, or they will never get themselves organized:' and, secondly, 'That there will again *be* a king in Israel—a system of order and government; and every man shall, in some measure, see himself constrained to do that which is right in the king's eyes. This, too, we may call a sure element of the future; for this, too, is of the eternal; this, too, is of the present, though hidden from most; and without it no fibre of the past ever was.'

We fear much of this must be altogether unintelligible to many of our readers. If so, we beg to assure them that they can hardly do better than purchase Mr. Carlyle's book, and study it attentively. In these days it would be difficult to find more instructive and profitable reading.

We have now given a sketch—a very poor and inadequate one, we fear—of three parts of *Past and Present*. The remaining one, book the second, is intended to illustrate the present and the future by means of the past. This, Mr. Carlyle has done by reviewing, as it were, the *Chronicle of Jocelin of Brakelonda*, published two or three years ago by the Camden society. In doing this, he has given as strong a proof of his depth and power of thought as it is possible to give. . . . Catholicism has its formulæ no doubt, some of them eternal, some only accidental; the latter may perish, the former never. Three hundred years ago, Luther, one of Mr. Carlyle's heroes, loudly protested against the whole Catholic system. Powerful sovereigns, and still more powerful human passions, lent their aid in advancing his Reformation, and every possible advantage that could be desired in establishing a religion was granted him. And now scarcely a soul professes this religion, whilst the Catholic Church remains as vigorous as if Luther had never been born. The world, the flesh, and the devil, have unceasingly waged war against her, but in vain. All their combined efforts have not removed one pebble stone from her battlements; the gibbet, the axe, and the scaffold, have but added to her glories, and furnished her white-robed army with new saints and martyrs. Now, as in other times, is the hand of God with His Church; no weapon that is formed against her prospers, and every tongue that riseth against her in judgment doth she condemn. When an earnest man like Mr. Carlyle has thoroughly studied and mastered a system, his authority against it must be of great weight, to say the very least. But we have no reason, from anything we have read, to think that Mr. Carlyle has come to a *deliberate* opinion as to the merits of Catholicism at this day. He has, no doubt, treated it as an exploded absurdity, as most Protestants do, and as we are ourselves daily in the habit of doing with reference to Mahometanism, and a thousand other religious sects. But, surely, there are reasons enough to induce him to look deeper into the matter than he has done. . . .

The little that Mr. Carlyle says of modern Catholicism in the present volume, betrays the little trouble he gives himself about it. He allows that 'the popish religion is the most vivacious looking religion to be met with at present,' and that the pope is 'the remarkablest pontiff that has darkened God's daylight, or painted himself in the human retina, for these several thousand years.' And 'his poor Jesuits, in the late Indian cholera, were, with a few German doctors, the only creatures whom dastard terror had not driven mad: they descended fearlessly into all gulfs and bedlams, watched over the pillow of the dying, with help, with counsel, and hope; shone as luminous fixed stars, when all else had gone out in chaotic night.' Notwithstanding all this, our author runs off upon a ridiculous story, which a writer in *Fraser's Magazine*,—a very decided flunkey by the way,—pronounces to be 'delectable.' He also seizes upon a bon-mot, attributed some time ago to M. Jouffroy (we believe the report was officially contradicted), to the effect that Catholicism had just about three hundred years to run before its final overthrow. It is really melancholy to see an earnest and truth-loving writer like Mr. Carlyle forced upon expedients like these. In flunkey reviewers for *Fraser's Magazine* the thing is tolerable, in *him* it is wholly unpardonable. When he says that the pope 'discerns that all worship of God is a scenic phantasmagory of wax-candles, organ-blasts, Gregorian chants, &c.' he deserts his own principles, and is satisfied with looking no farther than at 'the transient outer appearances,' instead of penetrating to the 'eternal inner facts.' The papacy of the present day may well be an object of alarm and hatred to thinking men ranged amongst his enemies—none but a fool can despise it. . . .

Whatever Mr. Carlyle may think, and however others may sneer, it is our humble but firm conviction that the papacy is destined not only to outlast all present governments, however strong and secure, but to fulfil a destiny far higher than we have yet seen or read of. We, too, believe in the 'Progress of the Species,' and have no doubt that the whole human race will hereafter bow down in worship before the throne of Christ's vicar upon earth. The Church of God has ere now enjoyed full many triumphs over the world, but far greater glories are yet in store for it. . . .

18. Elizabeth Barrett Browning and Richard H. Horne, unsigned essay, *A New Spirit of the Age*

New York, 1844, pp. 333–48

Elizabeth Barrett Browning (1806–61) wrote a good part of this essay but precisely which part is difficult to determine. Supposedly the then Miss Barrett sent Horne a ten-page manuscript with instructions for him to edit and interpolate freely. Both Isaac W. Dyer (*A Bibliography of Thomas Carlyle's Writing and Ana* [Portland, Maine, 1928]) and Carlisle Moore ('Thomas Carlyle', in *The English Romantic Poets and Essayists*, eds. Carolyn and Lawrence H. Houtchens [New York, 1966]) credit Mrs Browning with most of this essay. What, however, is of importance is the attention paid to Carlyle's artistry rather than the usual concern with his social and political ideas. The concern with 'poetics' ('his use of analogy and subtle association') rather than 'logic' anticipates the approach of John Holloway's illuminating *The Victorian Sage* (New York, 1953).

Always there stood before him, night and day,
Of wayward vary-colored circumstance
The imperishable presences serene,
Colossal, without form, or sense, or sound;
Dim shadows but unwaning presences
Four-faced to four corners of the sky:
And yet again, three shadows, fronting one,
One forward, one respectant, three but one;
And yet again, again and evermore,
For the two first were not, but only seemed,
One shadow in the midst of a great light,

One reflex from eternity on time,
One mighty countenance of perfect calm,
Awful with most invariable eyes.
                                    TENNYSON. *The Mystic.*

Beware when the great God lets loose a thinker on this planet. Then all things
are at risk. There is not a piece of science, but its flank may be turned to-morrow,
there is not any literary reputation, nor the so-called eternal names of fame, that
may not be revised and condemned. . . . He claps wings to the sides of all the
solid old lumber of the world.
                                    EMERSON. *Essay on circles.*

According to the view of the *microcosmus*, what is said of the world
itself, may be said of every individual in it; and what is said of the
individual, may be predicated of the world. Now the individual mind
has been compared to a prisoner in a dark room, or in a room which
would be dark but for the windows of the same, meaning the senses, in
a figure; nothing being in the mind without the mediation of the
senses, as Locke held,—'except,' as Leibnitz acutely added in modification, 'the mind itself.' Thus is it with the individual, and thus with the
general humanity. Were it not for the Something from without, and
the Something within, which are both Revelations, we should sit on
the floor of our dark dungeon, between its close stifling walls, gnawing
vainly with the teeth of the mind, at the chains we wear. But conclusions which genius has leapt successfully, and science proved, have
come to aid us. It is well to talk of the progress of the public mind. The
public mind,—that is, the average intelligence of the many,—never
does make progress, except by imbibing great principles from great
men, which, after long and frequent reiteration, become part of the
moral sense of a people. The educators are the true and only movers.
Progress implies the most active of energies, such as genius is, such as
science is; and general progress implies, and indeed essentially consists
of, individual progresses, men of genius, and other good teachers, working. A Ulysses must pass with the first goat,—call him Nobody, or by
his right name. And to return to our first figure,—what the senses are
to the individual mind, men of genius are to the general mind. Scantily
assigned by Providence for necessary ends, one original thinker strikes
a window out here, and another there; wielding the mallet sharply, and
leaving it to others to fashion grooves and frames, and complete
advantage into convenience.
    That Mr. Carlyle is one of the men of genius thus referred to, and
that he has knocked out his window from the blind wall of his century,

we may add without any fear of contradiction. We may say, too, that it is a window to the east; and that some men complain of a certain bleakness in the wind which enters at it, when they should rather congratulate themselves and him on the aspect of the new sun beheld through it, the orient hope of which he has so discovered to their eyes. And let us take occasion to observe here, and to bear in memory through every subsequent remark we may be called upon to make, that it has not been his object to discover to us any specific prospect—not the mountain to the right, nor the oak-wood to the left, nor the river which runs down between,—but the SUN, which renders all these visible.

When 'the most thinking people' had, at the sound of all sorts of steam-engines, sufficiently worshipped that idol of utilitarianism which Jeremy Bentham, the king, had set up, and which Thomas Carlyle, the transcendentalist, and many others, who never read a page of Bentham's works, have resolved to narrow to their own misconceptions of this philosopher,—the voice of a prophet was heard praying three times a day, with magnanimous reiteration, towards Jerusalem,—towards old Jerusalem, be it observed; and also towards the place of sun-rising for ultimate generations. And the voice spoke a strange language,—nearly as strange as Bentham's own, and as susceptible of translation into English. Not English by any means, the critics said it spoke; nor even German, nor Greek; although partaking considerably more of the two last than of English; but more of Saxon than either, we humbly beg to add. Yet if the grammarians and public teachers could not measure it out to pass as classic English, after the measure of Swift or Addison, or even of Bacon and Milton,—if new words sprang gauntly in it from savage derivatives, and rushed together in outlandish combinations,—if the collocation was distortion, wandering wildly up and down,—if the comments were everywhere in a heap, like the 'pots and pans' of Bassano, classic or not, English or not; it was certainly a true language —a language 'μερόπων ἀνθρώπων;[1] the significant articulation of a living soul: God's breath was in the vowels of it. And the clashing of these harsh compounds at last drew the bees into assembly, each murmuring his honey-dream. And the hearers who stood longest to listen, became sensible of a still grave music issuing like smoke from the clefts of the rock. If it was not 'style' and 'classicism,' it was something better; it was soul-language. There was a divinity at the shaping of these rough-hewn periods.

We dwell the longer upon the construction of Mr. Carlyle's

[1] Of articulate people.

sentences, because of him it is pre-eminently true, that the speech is the man. All powerful writers will leave, more or less, the pressure of their individuality on the medium of their communication with the public. Even the idiomatic writers, who trust their thoughts to a customary or conventional phraseology, and thus attain to a recognized level perfection in the medium, at the expense of being less instantly incisive and expressive (according to an obvious social analogy) have each an individual aspect. But the individuality of this writer is strongly pronounced. It is graven—like the Queen's arrow on the poker and tongs of her national prisons—upon the meanest word of his utterance. He uses no moulds in his modelling, as you may see by the impression of his thumb-nail upon the clay. He throws his truth with so much vehemence, that the print of the palm of his hand is left on it. Let on man scoff at the language of Carlyle—or if it forms part of his idiosyncracy, his idiosyncracy forms part of his truth;—and let no man say that we recommend Carlylisms—for it is obvious, from our very argument, that, in the mouth of an imitator, they would unlearn their uses, and be conventional as Addison, or a mere chaos of capitals, and compounds, and *broken* language.

We have named Carlyle in connection with Bentham, and we believe that you will find in 'your philosophy,' no better antithesis for one, than is the other. There is as much resemblance between them as is necessary for antithetic unlikeness. Each headed a great movement among thinking men; and each made a language for himself to speak with; and neither of them originated what they taught. Bentham's work was done by systematizing; Carlyle's, by reviving and reiterating. And as from the beginning of the world, the two great principles of matter and spirit have combated,—whether in man's personality, between the flesh and the soul; or in his speculativeness, between the practical and the ideal; or in his mental expression, between science and poetry,—Bentham and Carlyle assumed to lead the double van on opposite sides. Bentham gave an impulse to the material energies of his age, of the stuff of which he was himself made,—while Carlyle threw himself before the crushing chariots, not in sacrifice, but deprecation; 'Go aside—*there is a spirit even in the wheels!*' In brief, and to take up that classification of virtues made by Proclus and the later Platonists,—Bentham headed such as were πολιτικαί,[2] Carlyle exalts that which is τελεστική,[3] venerant and religious virtue.

2 Political.
3 Mystical.

Every reader may not be acquainted, as every thinker should, with the *Essays* of R. W. Emerson, of Concord, Massachusetts. He is a follower of Mr. Carlyle, and in the true spirit; that is, no imitator, but a worker out of his own thoughts. To one of the English editions of this volume, Mr. Carlyle has written a short Preface, in which the following gaunt and ghastly, grotesque and graphic passage occurs, and which, moreover, is characteristic and to our immediate point.

In a word, while so many Benthamisms, Socialisms, Fourrierisms, *professing* to have no soul, go staggering and lowing like monstrous mooncalves, the product of a heavy-laden moon struck age; and in this same baleful 'twelfth hour of the night' even galvanic Puseyisms, as we say, are visible, and dancings of the sheeted dead,—shall not any voice of a living man be welcome to us, even because it is alive?

That the disciples of Bentham, and Robert Owen and Fourrier, should be accused of professing to have no soul, because their main object has been to ameliorate the bodily condition of mankind; or that an indifference to poetry and the fine arts, except as light amusements, to be taken alternately with gymnastics and foot-ball, should be construed into a denial of the existence of such things, we do not consider fair dealing. True, they all think of first providing for the body; and, looking around at the enormous amount of human suffering from physical causes, it is no great wonder that they chiefly devote their efforts to that amelioration. A man who is starving, is not in a fit state for poetry, nor even for prayer. Neither is a man fit for prayer, who is diseased, or ragged, or unclean—except the *one* prayer for that very amelioration which the abused philosophers of the body seek to obtain for him. With respect, however, to the disciples of Bentham, Owen, and Fourrier, it is no wonder that he should be at utter variance. No great amount of love 'is lost between them.' Not that Carlyle reads or knows much of their systems; and not that they read or know anything of his writings. In these natural antipathies all philosophers are in an equal state of unreasonableness. Or shall we rather call it wisdom, to follow the strong instincts of nature, without any prevaricating reasonings upon the in-felt fact. Carlyle could make little good out of their systems, if he read them; and they could make nothing at all of his writings. The opposite parties might force themselves to meet gravely, with hard lines of the efforts of understanding in their faces, and all manner of professions of dispassionate investigation and mutual love of truth—and they would clash foreheads at the first step, and part in fury!

'The Body is the first thing to be helped!' cry the Benthamites, Owenites, Fourrierites,—loudly echoed by Lord Ellenborough and the Bishop of London—'Get more Soul!' cries Carlyle, 'and help yourselves!'

But the wants of the body will win the day—the movements of the present age show that plainly. The immortal soul can well afford to wait till its case is repaired. The death-groans of humanity must first be humanely silenced. More Soul, do we crave for the world? The world has long had a sphere full of unused Soul in it, before Christ, and since. If Plato, and Socrates, and Michael Angelo and Raphael, and Shakspere and Milton, and Handel and Haydn, and all the great poets, philosophers, and music-magicians, that have left their Souls among us, have still rendered us no protection against starvation, or the disease and damage of the senses and brain by reason of want of food, in God's name let us now think a little of the Body—the mortal case and medium of his Image. What should we think of a philosopher who went to one of our manufacturing towns where the operatives work from sixteen to eighteen hours a-day, and are nevertheless badly clothed, dirty, and without sufficient food,—and to whom the philosopher, as a remedial measure, suggested that they should get more soul. Many at this hour are slowly, or rapidly, dying from want. Can we tell them to think of their souls? No—give the fire some more fuel, and *then* expect more light, and the warmth of an aspiring flame. That these two extremes of body and soul philosophy, may, as Emerson declares, involve one and the same principle, viz., the welfare and progress of mankind, may be true; but at present the poor principle is 'between two stools'—or between the horns of a dilemma not inaptly represented by Mr. Carlyle's misapplied figure of the staggering moon-calf.

We have observed that Carlyle is not an originator; and although he is a man of genius and original mind, and although he has knocked out his window in the wall of his century—and we know it,—we must repeat that, in a strict sense, he is not an originator. Perhaps our figure of the window might have been more correctly stated as the re-opening of an old window, long bricked up or encrusted over,—and probably this man of a strong mallet, and sufficient right hand, thought the recovery of the old window, a better and more glorious achievement, than the making of many new windows. His office certainly is not to 'exchange new lamps for old ones.' His quality of a 'gold-reviver' is the nearest to a novel acquirement. He tells us what we knew, but had forgotten, or refused to remember; and his reiterations startle and astonish us like informations. We 'have souls,' he tells us. Who doubted it in the nineteenth century; yet who thought of it in the roar of the steam-engine? He tells us that work is every man's duty. Who doubted *that* among the factory masters?—or among the charity children, when spelling from the catechism of the national church, that they will 'do their duty in the state of life to which it shall please God to call them?' Yet how deep and like a new sound, do the words 'soul,' 'work,' 'duty,' strike down upon the flashing anvils, of the age, till the whole age vibrates! And again he tells us, 'Have faith.' Why, did we not know that we must have 'faith?' Is there a religious teacher in the land who does not repeat from God's revelation, year by year, day by day—Have faith? or is there a quack in the land who does not call to his assistance the energy of 'faith?' And again—'Truth is a good thing.' Is *that* new? Is it not written in the theories of the moralist, and of the child?—yes, and in the moral code of Parliament men, and other honourable gentlemen, side by side with bribery and corruption, and the 'melancholy necessity' of the duellist's pistol and twelve paces? Yet we thrill at the words, as if some new thunder of divine instruction ruffled the starry air,—as if an angel's foot sounded down it, step by step, coming with a message.

Thus it is obvious that Mr. Carlyle is not an originator, but a renewer, although his medium is highly original; and it remains to us to recognise that he is none the less important teacher on that account, and that there was none the less necessity for his teaching. 'The great fire-heart,' as he calls it, of human nature may burn too long without stirring; burn inwardly, cake outwardly, and sink deeply into its own ashes: and to emancipate the flame clearly and brightly, it is necessary to stir it up strongly from the lowest bar. To do this, by whatever form of creation and illustration, is the aim and end of all poetry of a high order,—this,— to resume human nature from its beginning, and return to first principles of thought and first elements of feeling; this,—to dissolve from eye and ear the film of habit and convention, and open a free passage for beauty and truth, to gush in upon unencrusted perceptive faculties: for poetry like religion should make a man a child again in purity and unadulterated perceptivity.

No poet yearns more earnestly to make the inner life shine out, than does Carlyle. No poet regrets more sorrowfully, with a look across the crowded and crushing intellects of the world,—that the dust rising up from men's energies, should have blinded them to the brightness of their instincts,—and that understanding (according to the German view) should take precedence of a yet more spiritualized faculty. He is reproached with not being practical. 'Mr. Carlyle,' they say, 'is not practical.' But he is practical for many intents of the inner life, and teaches well the Doing of Being. 'What would he make of us?' say the complainers. 'He reproaches us with the necessities of the age, he taunts us with the very progress of time, his requirements are so impossible that they make us despair of the republic.' And this is true. If we were to give him a sceptre, and cry 'Rule over us,' nothing could exceed the dumb, motionless, confounded figure he would stand: his first words on recovering himself, would be, 'Ye have souls! work—believe.' He would not know what else to think, or say for us, and not at all what to do with us. He would pluck, absently, at the sceptre, for the wool of the fillet to which his hands were accustomed; for he is no king, except in his own peculiar sense of a prophet and priest-king,—and a vague prophet, be it understood. His recurrence to first principles and elements of action, is in fact, so constant and passionate, that his attention is not free for the development of actions. The hand is the gnomon by which he judges of the soul; and little cares he for the hand otherwise than as a spirit-index. He will not wash your hands for you, be sure, however he may moralise on their blackness. Whether he writes history, or philosophy, or criticism, his perpetual appeal is to those common elements of humanity which it is his object to cast into relief and light. His work on the French Revolution is a great poem with this same object;—a return upon the life of humanity, and an eliciting of the pure material and initial element of life, out of the fire and torment of it. The work has fitly been called graphical and picturesque; but it is so *by force of being* philosophical and poetical. For instance, where the writer says that 'Marat was in a cradle like the rest of us,' it is no touch of rhetoric, though it may seem so, but a resumption of the philosophy of the whole work. Life suggests to him the cradle, the grave, and eternity, with scarce a step between. In that brief interval he sometimes exhorts that you should work; and sometimes it would appear as if he exhorted you not to work at all, but to sit still and think. He is dazzled by the continual contemplation of a soul beating its tiny wings amidst the pale vapours of Infinity. Why, such a man (not speaking it irreverently) is not fit to live. He is only fit to be where his soul most aims at. He sinks our corporal condition, with all its wants, and says, 'Be a man!' A dead-man with a promoted spirit seems our only chance in this philosophy.

Carlyle has a great power of re-production, and can bring back his man from the grave of years, not like a ghost, but with all his vital flesh as well as his thoughts about him. The reproduced man thinks, feels, and acts like himself at his most characteristic climax—and the next instant the Magician pitches him into Eternity, saying, 'It all comes to that.' But his power over the man, while he lasts, is entire, and the individual is almost always dealt with as in time-present. His scenes of by-gone years, are all acted now, before your eyes. By contrast Carlyle often displays truth; from the assimilations in the world, he wrings the product of the differences; and by that masterly method of individualising persons, which is remarkable in his historical writing, the reader sometimes attains what Carlyle himself seems to abhor, viz., a broad generalization of principles. His great forte and chief practice is individualization. And when he casts his living heart into an old monk's diary, and, with the full warm gradual throbs of genius and power, throws out the cowled head into a glory; the reason is not, as some disquieted readers have hinted, that Mr. Carlyle regrets the cloistral ages and defunct superstitions,—the reason is not, that Mr. Carlyle is *too* poetical to be philosophical, but that he is *so* poetical as to be philosophical in essence when treating of things. The reason is, that Mr. Carlyle recognizes, in a manner that no mere historian ever does, but as the true poet always will do,—the same human nature through every cycle of individual and social existence. He is a poet also, by his insight into the activity of moral causes working through the intellectual agencies of the mind. He is also a poet in the mode. He conducts his argument with no philosophical arrangements and marshalling of 'for and against;' his paragraphs come and go as they please. He proceeds, like a poet, rather by analogy and subtle association than by uses of logic. His illustrations not only illustrate, but bear a part in the reasoning;—the images standing out, like grand and beautiful caryatides, to sustain the heights of the argument. Of his language we have spoken. Somewhat too slow, broken up, and involved for eloquence, and too individual to be classical, it is yet the language of a gifted painter and poet, the colour of whose soul eats itself into the words. And magnificent are the splendours they display, even as the glooms. Equally apt are they for the sad liveries of pain and distress, and certainly for the rich motleys of the humorous grotesque. His pictures and conjurings-up of this latter kind—chiefly from his original faculty, and method of producing the thing alive and before you, but also by contrast with his usual thoughtful, ardent, and exacting style—are inexpressibly ludicrous. His Latin epitaph on Count Zähdarm, in *Sartor Resartus*, and his account of the courtier whose lower habiliments were stuffed with bran, to look broad and fashionable, but who unfortunately sat down upon a nail, are exquisite. These things are often additionally ludicrous from his giving the actors a dry, historical shape, while the scene itself is utterly absurd and extravagant, but amidst which the narrator seldom appears to move a muscle of his face. It is by reason of this humorous dryness that we sometimes do not know if he would really have us laugh at the thing.

Moreover, it must be stated, that the Prophet of the Circle hath displayed a cloven tongue!—and peradventure the sincerity of his mode of expression in several works may at times have been questionable. The most orthodox dogmatists have often applauded his sayings about a Church, when it has been plain to the initiated readers of his books that he meant no such temple as that, but some untithed field, with a soul in it. In like manner, in his remarks on tolerance in his *Hero-Worship*, he seems to guard himself strongly against imputations of latitudinarianism; whereby the highly orthodox commend him as very proper, and the latitudinarians laugh in their sleeves—he does it so well. It is the same in politics. Radicalism is scoffed at; and the next page lets loose a sweeping radical principle, involving perhaps no small destructiveness for its attainment. On the other side, Tories are gratified by his declarations of reverence for old things, though they may be placed, in order to be the better seen, upon the top of Vesuvius; and the more assimilative and shapely Conservative smiles to hear him speak aloud for the conservation of all things which are good and excellent. The book on *Past and Present*, however, settles most of these doubts. It is all over with him among the high church party; and he laughs as he thinks. But have any of the other parties got him? Not so: he was born to be an independent Thinker; it is his true mission; it is the best thing he can do, and we have no doubt but it is just the thing he *will* do.

We think *Sartor Resartus* the finest of Mr. Carlyle's works in conception, and as a whole. In execution he is always great; and for graphic vigour and quantity of suggestive thought, matchless: but the idea, in this book, of uncovering the world—taking off all the *clothes*—the cloaks and outsides—is admirable. His finest work, as matter of political philosophy, is undoubtedly his *Past and Present*. In this work he is no longer the philosopher of the circle. He allows the world a chance.

The incentive to progression in the great family of mankind, is usually considered to be the desire for happiness, or the prospect of bettering our condition by struggling onward to a given point: but the necessity of progression, as well as the incentive, are perhaps equally attributable to another cause. It may be that Dissatisfaction is the great mover; and that this feeling is implanted as a restless agent to act for ever upon us, so as to urge us onward for ever in our ascending cycles of being. This we should conceive to be Mr. Carlyle's impression. He does not say so, we believe; nor perhaps does he decidedly think so; nevertheless we should say the Philosophy of Dissatisfaction formed a principal element in his many-sided unsystematic view of the struggles of mortality.

The book intitled *Chartism* was a recognition of this principle of dissatisfaction, as manifested by the violent mental and physical forces of a number of enraged sufferers. But we pass through the book as through a journey of many ways and many objects, brilliantly illuminated and pictured in every direction, but without arriving at any clear conclusion, and without gathering any fresh information on the main subject, during the progress. By his not very clear argument about 'might' and 'right,' he has enabled any despot to show some sort of reasoning for any violent act.

His grand remedial proposals for all the evils of the country, by 'Universal Education' and '*General* Emigration,' are rather an evasion of Chartism and its causes; for the Chartists say, 'We have enough education to see the injustice of people being starved in a land of plenty; and as for emigration, we do not choose to go. Go yourselves.'

Past and Present evidences a perception of greater wants than these Education and Emigration plans.

[quotes 'True, all turns' to 'longer with *it*' Bk. III, ch. v, 163–4]

The *History of the French Revolution*, is considered by most people to be Mr. Carlyle's greatest work; not as a history, we presume, nor because it is in three volumes, but chiefly because it is thought to contain a more abundant and varied display of his powers than any of his other works. We can offer no remarks about it so good as those we shall extract from an article written by Joseph Mazzini, which we consider to be one of the most profound, masterly, and earnest-minded critical essays that was ever written. We should also add, that it is full of that admiration and respect which are due to a writer of Mr. Carlyle's genius and character.

[quotes various passages from Mazzini's review 'The French Revolution', *Monthly Chronicle*, V (January 1840), 71–84]

This unfair method of dealing with humanity, this continual disposition to place man at a disadvantage of the most extreme kind, *viz*., by comparison with space and time, and the miraculous round of things, constitutes a prominent feature in the philosophy of dissatisfaction. It is always sure of its blow, and its humiliating superiority; for who can stand before it? We might quote to Mr. Carlyle the words addressed to Mephistopheles—'Seems nothing ever right to you on earth?' One cannot imagine anything done by human hands which would be likely to give Mr. Carlyle much satisfaction. He would be pretty sure to say, at best, 'Work on, and we shall see what else will come of it!' Or, more probably, to quote again from *Faust*, he would remind us that 'Man must err, till he has ceased to struggle.' Hence he would have us sit quietly and be silent. He applauds inactivity and silence; but he also applauds work: he says man must work, and exhorts every one to do his utmost. These contradictions, however, have a central meaning, which we shall attempt to explain. The dissatisfaction, the unhopefulness, and the melancholy that pervades his works are attributable to the same causes.

For the practical dissatisfaction exhibited in Mr. Carlyle's works, we would offer the following elucidation. We think that he so continually negatives the value of work, denies the use and good of doing things, and smiles bitterly or laughs outright at human endeavour, because he considers that so long as the Competitive system—the much applauded 'fair competition'—be the rule of social working life, instead of Co-operation, there can be made no actual step in advance to a better condition of things. So long as one class, whether in trade, politics, art, or literature, is always striving to oppose, pull back, counteract, or plunder the other, no permanent good can supervene. The greatest remedial measure which is sure to let in an overflowing stream of good, he laughs at,—because, after all the long labours of the contest for it, he sees in imagination a number of side-trenches cut to let it off before it reaches the assumed destination, or means taken to let it off after its arrival, by other channels. By the terms 'hero' and 'heroic,' he means true wisdom and moral strength; and the only hope he sees for this world, is that one man should rule over each country, eminent for his heroic worth, because chosen by a people who have at length become themselves not un-heroic, and therefore capable of knowing true greatness, and of choosing their greatest man.

So much for his practical and political dissatisfaction. For his contradictory tone concerning all work, as unavailing and yet a necessity, let him answer for himself:

Thus, like a God-created, fire breathing, spirit-host, we emerge from the Inane; haste stormfully across the astonished earth; then plunge again into the Inane. Earth's mountains are levelled, and her seas filled up, in our passage: can the earth, which is but dead and a vision, resist spirits which have reality and are alive? On the hardest adamant, some foot-print of us is stamped in; the last Rear of the host will read traces of the earliest Van. But whence? O, heaven, whither? Sense knows not; Faith knows not; only that it is through Mystery to Mystery, from God to God.

> 'We *are such stuff*
> As dreams are made of, and our little Life
> Is rounded with a sleep.'[4]

A familiar illustration sometimes helps a philosophical difficulty. The following story, which is highly characteristic of the parties, and is nevertheless of a kind that may be told without violating the trustfulness of private intercourse, will very well answer our present purpose. Leigh Hunt and Carlyle were once present among a small party of equally well-known men. It chanced that the conversation rested with these two—both first-rate talkers, and the others sat well pleased to listen. Leigh Hunt had said something about the Islands of the Blest, or El Dorado, or the Millennium, and was flowing on in his bright and hopeful way, when Carlyle dropt some heavy tree-trunk across Hunt's pleasant stream, and banked it up with philosophical doubts and objections at every interval of the speaker's joyous progress. But the unmitigated Hunt never ceased his overflowing anticipations, nor the saturnine Carlyle his infinite demurs to those finite flourishings. The listeners laughed and applauded by turns; and had now fairly pitted them against each other, as the philosopher of Hopefulness and of the Unhopeful. The contest continued with all that ready wit and philosophy, that mixture of pleasantry and profundity, that extensive knowledge of books and character, with their ready application in argument or illustration, and that perfect ease and good nature, which distinguish each of these men. The opponents were so well matched that it was quite clear the contest would never come to an end. But the night was far advanced, and the party broke up. They all sallied forth; and leaving the close room, the candles and the arguments behind them, suddenly found themselves in presence of a most brilliant star-light night. They all looked up. 'Now,' thought Hunt, 'Carlyle's done for!—he can have no answer to that!' 'There!' shouted Hunt, 'look up there! look at that glorious harmony, that sings with infinite voices an eternal song of

---

[4] *Sartor Resartus,* Bk. III, ch. viii, 212.

hope in the soul of man.' Carlyle looked up. They all remained silent to hear what he would say. They began to think he was silenced at last—he was a mortal man. But out of that silence came a few low-toned words, in a broad Scotch accent. And who, on earth, could have anticipated what the voice said? 'Eh! it's a *sad* sight!'—Hunt sat down on a stone step. They all laughed—then looked very thoughtful. Had the finite measured itself with infinity, instead of surrendering itself up to the influence? Again they laughed—then bade each other good night, and betook themselves homeward with slow and serious pace. There might be some reason for sadness, too. That brilliant firmament probably contained infinite worlds, each full of struggling and suffering beings—of beings who had to die—for life in the stars implies that those bright worlds should also be full of graves; but all that life, like ours, knowing not whence it came, nor whither it goeth, and the brilliant Universe in its great Movement having, perhaps, no more certain knowledge of itself, nor of its ultimate destination, than hath one of the suffering specks that compose this small spot we inherit.

19. Joseph Mazzini, from an unsigned article, *British and Foreign Quarterly Review*

January 1844, xvi, 262–93

Extract from an unsigned article, 'On the Genius and Tendency of the Writings of Thomas Carlyle'.

Joseph Mazzini (1805–72), the liberal Italian patriot and leader of the Young Italy Movement, after years of struggle and voluntary exile in Switzerland and France, finally made his way to England in 1837, where he supported himself by writing reviews in such journals as the *Westminster* and the *Monthly Chronicle*. Mazzini's visits to 5 Cheyne Row were numerous, and he and the Carlyles became warm friends. Indeed, when Mazzini's mail was secretly being read by the Foreign Secretary, Sir James Graham—which led directly to the execution of two young Bandieras brothers, officers in the Austrian navy—Carlyle openly and without being solicited defended Mazzini in the London *Times* (6 June 1844) as a man of 'genius and virtue, a man of sterling veracity, humanity, and nobleness of mind; one of those rare men, numerable, unfortunately, but as units in this world, who are worthy to be called martyr souls; who, in silence, piously in their daily life, understand and practice what is meant by that' (quoted in D. A. Wilson, *Carlyle*, III, 264).

. . . The writer with whom we have now to deal, by the nature of his labours and the direction of his genius, authorizes the examination we propose to make. He is melancholy and grave: he early felt the evil which is now preying upon the world, and from the outset of his career he proclaimed it loudly and courageously.

Call ye that a society [he exclaims in one of his first publications] where there is no longer any social idea extant, not so much as the idea of a common home, but only of a common over-crowded lodging-house? where each, isolated, regardless of his neighbour, turned against his neighbour, clutches what he can get, and cries '*Mine!*' and calls it Peace, because in the cut-purse and cut-throat scramble, no steel knives, but only a far cunninger sort can be employed—where friendship, communion, has become an incredible tradition, and your holiest sacramental supper is a smoking tavern dinner, with cook for evangelist? where your priest has no tongue but for plate-licking, and your high guides and governors cannot guide; but on all hands hear it passionately proclaimed, *Laissez-faire!* Leave us alone of your guidance—such light is darker than darkness—eat your wages, and sleep*.

Mr. Carlyle, in writing these lines, was conscious that he engaged himself to seek a remedy for the evil, nor has he shrunk from the task. All that he has since written bears more and more evidently the stamp of a high purpose. In his *Chartism* he attempted to grapple with the social question; in all his writings, whatever be their subject, he has touched upon it in some one of its aspects. Art is to him but as a means. In his vocation as a writer he fills the tribune of an apostle, and it is here that we must judge him.

There is a multitude around him; and this is the first fact to establish, for it speaks both in favour of the writer and of the public whom he has won over. Since the day when, alone and uncomprehended, he penned the words which we have quoted, Teufelsdröck has made proselytes. The 'mad hopes,' expressed, with an allowable consciousness of the power which stirred within him, in the last chapter of *Sartor Resartus*, have been largely realized. The philosophy of clothes—thanks to the good and bad conduct of the two Dandiacal and Drudge sects—has made some progress. Signs have appeared; they multiply daily on the horizon. The diameter of the two 'bottomless, boiling whirlpools†,' has widened and widened, as they approach each other in a threatening manner; and many readers who commenced with a smile of pity, or scorn of the unintelligible and tiresome jargon, the insinuations, half-ironical half-wild, of the dark dreamer, now look into his pages, with the perseverance of the monks of Mount Athos, to see whether they cannot there discover the 'great thought,' of which they themselves begin to feel the want. They now admire as much as they once scorned, —they admire even when they cannot understand.

Be it so, for this too is good: it is good to see that the great social question, which not long ago was ridiculed, begins to exercise a kind of fascination upon the public mind; to find that even those whose own powers are not adequate to the task, acknowledge the necessity of some

---

* *Sartor Resartus*, Book iii. chap. 6.
† *Sartor Resartus*, Book iii. chap. 10.

solution of the sphinx-like enigma which the times present. It is good to see, by a new example, that neither ignorant levity nor materialist indifference can long suppress the divine rights of intellect.

There are differences between Mr. Carlyle's manner of viewing things and ours, which we have to premise; but we will not do this without first avowing his incontestable merits,—merits which at the present day are as important as they are rare, which in him are so elevated as to command the respect and admiration even of those who rank under another standard, and the sympathy and gratitude of those who, like ourselves, are in the main upon the same side, and who differ only respecting the choice of means and the road to pursue.

Above all, we would note the sincerity of the writer. What he writes, he not only thinks, but feels. He may deceive himself,—he cannot deceive us; for what he says, even when it is not the truth, is yet *true*,—*his* individuality, *his* errors, *his* incomplete views of things,— realities, and not nonentities,—the truth limited, we might say, for error springing from sincerity in a high intellect is no other than such. He seeks good with conscientious zeal, not from a love of fame, not even from the gratification of the discovery; his motive is the love of his fellow-men, a deep and active feeling of duty, for he believes this to be the mission of man upon earth. He writes a book, as he would do a good action. Yet more, not only does he feel all that he writes, but he writes nearly all that he feels. Whatever is in his thoughts and has not yet been put on paper, we may be sure will sooner or later appear. He may preach the merit of 'holding one's tongue;' to those, in truth, who do not agree with him, are such words addressed; but the 'talent of silence' is not his: if sometimes he pretend to reverence it, it is as we may say platonically,—to prevent others speaking ill. But in minds constituted as his, compression of thought is impossible; it must expand, and every prolonged effort made to restrain it will only render the explosion the more violent. Mr. Carlyle is no homœopathist; he never administers remedies for evil in infinitesimal doses; he never pollutes the sacredness of thought by outward concessions or compromise with error. Like Luther, he hurls his inkstand at the head of the devil, under whatever form he shows himself, without looking to the consequences; but he does it with such sincerity, such *naïveté* and good-will, that the devil himself could not be displeased at it, were the moment not critical, and every blow of the inkstand a serious thing to him. We know no English writer who has during the last ten years so vigorously attacked the half-gothic, half-pagan edifice which still imprisons the free flight of the spirit —no one who has thrown among a public much addicted to routine and formalism, so many bold negations, so many religious and social views, novel and contrary to all existing ones, —yet no one who excites less of hostility and animadversion. There is generally so much calmness and impartiality in his attacks, so much conviction in his thoughts, so entire an absence of egotism, that we are compelled to listen to what, if uttered by any other man with anger or contempt, would excite a storm of opposition. There is never anger in the language of Mr. Carlyle; disdain he has, but without bitterness, and when it gleams across his pages, it speedily disappears under a smile of sorrow and of pity, the rainbow after a storm. He condemns, because there are things which neither heaven nor earth can justify; but his reader always feels that it is a painful duty he fulfils. When he says to a creed or to an institution, 'you are rotten —begone!' he has always some good word upon what it has achieved in the past, upon its utility, sometimes even upon its inutility. He never buries without an epitaph, —'*Valeat quantum valere potest.*'[1] Take as an instance, above all, his *History of the French Revolution.*

We place in the second rank his tendencies toward the ideal,—that which we shall call, for want of a better word, his spiritualism. He is the most ardent and powerful combatant of our day in that re-action, which is slowly working against the strong materialism that for a century and a half has maintained a progressive usurpation, one while in the writings of Locke, Bolingbroke or Pope, at another in those of Smith and Bentham, and has tended, by the doctrines of self-interest and material well-being, to the enthronement of selfishness in men's hearts. All the movement of industrial civilization, which has overflooded intellectual and moral civilization, has not deafened him. Amidst the noise of machinery, wheels and steam-engines, he has been able to distinguish the stifled plaint of the prisoned spirit, the sigh of millions, in whose hearts the voice of God whispers at times '*Be men!*' and the voice of society too often cries, 'In the name of Production, be brutes!' and he is come, with a small number of chosen spirits, to be their interpreter. He declares that all the bustle of matter and of industry in movement does not weigh against the calm, gentle and divine whisper that speaks from the depths of a virtuous soul, even when found in the lowest grade of mere machine-tenders; that the producer, not the production, should form the chief object of social institutions; that the human soul, not the body should be the starting-point of all our labours; since the body

[1] Let it be worth as much as it is worth.

without the soul is but a carcase; whilst the soul, wherever it is found free and holy, is sure to mould for itself such a body as its wants and vocation require. In all his writings, in *Sartor Resartus*, in his *Lectures*, in his *Essays* especially, (some of which appear to us to be among the best of Mr. Carlyle's writings,) the standard of the ideal and divine is boldly unfurled. . . .

He penetrates the symbol to arrive at the idea: he seeks God through visible forms, the soul through the external manifestations of its activity. We feel that wherever he found the first suppressed, the second extinguished, nothing would be left for him but idolatry, falsehood, things to despise, or to destroy. For him, as for all who have loved, suffered, and have not lost, in the selfish pursuit of material gratifications, the divine sense which makes us men—it is a profound truth that 'we live, we walk, and we are in God.' Hence his reverence for nature,—hence the universality of his sympathies, prompt to seize the poetical side in all things,—hence, above all, his notion of human life devoted to the pursuit of duty, and not to that of happiness,—'the worship of sorrow and renunciation,' such as he has given it in his chapter 'The Everlasting Yea' of *Sartor Resartus*, and such as comes out in all his works. . . .

We place in the third rank our author's cosmopolitan tendencies,—*humanitarian* we would say, if the word were in use; for cosmopolitism has at the present day come to indicate rather the indifference than the universality of sympathies. He well knows that there is a holy land, in which, under whatever latitude they may be born, men are brethren. He seeks among his equals in intelligence, not the Englishman, the Italian, the German, but *man*: he adores, not the god of one sect, of one period, or of one people, but God; and, as the reflex of God upon earth, the beautiful, the noble, the great, wherever he finds it: knowing well, that whencesoever it beams, it is, or will be, sooner or later for all. His points of view are always elevated; his horizon always extends beyond the limits of country; his criticism is never stamped with that spirit of nationalism (we will not say of nationality, a thing sacred with us all), which is only too much at work amongst us, and which retards the progress of our intellectual life by isolating it from the universal life, derived from the millions of our brethren abroad. He has attached himself earnestly to the widest literature endued with this assimilating power, and has revealed it to us. His Essays on Schiller, on Goethe, on Jean Paul, on Werner, his excellent translations from the German, will remain a testimony of the naturalization which he has given to German literature amongst us; as the beautiful pages in his 'Lectures on Dante,' and some of those which he has devoted to French writers, testify the universality of that tendency which we distinguish here as forming the third characteristic of his mind.

To descend to qualities purely literary, Mr. Carlyle is moreover a powerful artist. Since the appearance of his work on the French Revolution, no one can any longer dispute his claim to this title. The brilliant faculties which were revealed in flashes in his previous writings burst out in this work, and one must have a very limited view of the actual duties of the historian to be able to judge it coldly and to remark its defects. He carries his reader along, he fascinates him. Powerful in imagination, which is apt to discover the sympathetic side of things and to seize its salient point,—expressing himself in an original style, which, though it often appear whimsical, is yet the true expression of the man, and perfectly conveys his thought,—Mr. Carlyle rarely fails of his effect. Gifted with that objectivity, of which Goethe has in recent times given us the highest model, he so identifies himself with the things, events or men which he exhibits, that in his portraits and his descriptions he attains a rare lucidness of outline, force of colouring and graphic precision: they are not imitations, but reproductions. And yet he never loses, in the detail, the *characteristic*, the unity of the object, being, or idea which he wishes to exhibit. He works in the manner of a master, indicating by certain features, firm, deep and decisive, the general physiognomy of the object, concentrating the effort of his labour and the richness of his light upon the central point, or that which he deems such, and placing this so well in relief that we cannot forget it. *Humour*, or the faculty of setting off small things, after the manner of Jean Paul, abounds in his writings. Beside the principal idea, secondary ideas meet us at every step, often new and important in themselves, particles of gold scattered upon the shore by the broad wave of the writer's thought. His epithets, although numerous, are seldom without force: they mark a progression in the development of the idea or the qualities of the object. His diction may have faults; of these we shall not treat here, but we may remark that the charge of obscurity so commonly brought against all thinkers endowed with originality, is, generally speaking, only a declaration of incompetence to comprehend or to judge of their ideas. Moreover his style is, as we have said, the spontaneous expression of the genius of Mr. Carlyle, the aptest form to symbolize his thought, the body shaped by the soul. We would not that it were otherwise; what we require in all things is, *man as he was meant to be.* . . .

That which rules the period, which is now commencing, in all its manifestations,—that which makes every one in the present day complain, and seek good as well as bad remedies,—that which everywhere tends to substitute, in politics, democracy for governments founded upon privilege,—in social economy, association for unlimited competition,—in religion, the spirit of universal tradition for the solitary inspiration of the conscience,—is the work of an *idea*, which not only distances the object, but misplaces the starting-point of human activity; it is the collective thought seeking to supplant, as the point of view in the social organism, the individual thought; the spirit of humanity *visibly* surpassing (for it has been always silently and unperceived at work) the spirit of man. . . . We have begun to suspect, not only that there is upon the earth something greater, more holy, more divine than the individual,—collective Humanity,—an existence always living, learning, advancing toward God of which we are but the instruments, —but that it is alone from the summit of this collective idea, from the conception of the Universal Mind, 'of which,' as Emerson says, 'each individual man is one more incarnation,' that we can derive our function, the rule of our life, the ideal of our societies. We labour at this at the present day. It signifies little that our first essays are strange aberrations: it signifies little, that falling upon their weak side, the doctrines of St. Simon, of Owen, of Fourier and others, who have arisen or shall arise, may be condemned to ridicule. That which is important is the idea common to all these doctrines, and the breath of which has rendered them fruitful; it is the object which they all instinctively propose, the starting-point they take. . . . We thirst for unity: we seek it in a new and larger expression of the mutual responsibility of all men towards each other,—the indissoluble *copartnery* of all generations and all individuals in the human race. We begin to comprehend those beautiful words of St. Paul (Romans 12: 5), 'we being many are one body in Christ, and every one members one of another.' We resolve the incertitude and caprices of individuals into a universality: we seek the intelligence and harmonizing of persons in the collective mass. Such is the tendency of the present times, and whosoever does not labour in accordance with it, necessarily remains behind.

Mr. Carlyle comprehends only the *individual*; the true sense of the human race escapes him. He sympathizes with all men, but it is with the life of each one, and not with their collective life. He readily looks at every man as the representative, the incarnation in a manner, of an idea: he does not believe in a 'supreme idea,' represented progressively by the development of mankind taken as a whole. He feels forcibly (rather indeed by the instinct of his heart, which revolts at actual evil, than by a clear conception of that which constitutes *life*) the want of a bond between the men who are around him: he does not feel sufficiently the existence of the bond between the generations past, present and future. The great religious thought, *the continued development of Humanity by a collective labour, according to an educational plan assigned by Providence*, fore-felt from age to age by a few rare intellects, and proclaimed in the last fifty years by the greatest European thinkers, finds but a feeble echo, or rather no echo at all, in his soul. Progressive from an impulse of feeling, he shrinks back from the idea as soon as he sees it stated explicitly and systematically; and such expressions as 'the progress of the species' and 'perfectibility' never drop from his pen unaccompanied by a taint of irony, which we confess is to us inexplicable. He seems to regard the human race rather as an aggregate of similar individuals, distinct powers in juxtaposition, than as an association of labourers, distributed in groups, and impelled on different paths toward one single object. . . .

We protest, in the name of the democratic spirit of the age, against such ideas. History is not the biography of great men; the history of mankind is the history of the progressive religion of mankind, and of the translation by symbols, or external actions, of that religion. . . .

It is evident that, of the two criteria of certainty, individual conscience and universal tradition, between which mankind has hitherto perpetually fluctuated, and the reconcilement of which appears to us to constitute the only means we possess of recognizing truth, Mr. Carlyle adopts one alone—the first. He rejects, or at least wholly neglects, the other. From this point, in his view, all follows in a natural connexion: individuality being everything, the doctrine of *unconsciousness* follows. The voice of God is heard in the intuition, in the instincts of the soul: to separate the individuality from every human external agency, and to offer it in native purity to the breath of inspiration from above,—this is to prepare a temple to God: God and the individual man—Mr. Carlyle sees no other object in the world. . . . But if we place ourselves in the point of view of the collective existence, Mankind, and regard social life as the continued development of an idea by the life of all its individuals,—if we regard history as the relation of this development in time and space through the works of individuals; if we believe in the *copartnery* and mutual responsibility of generations, never losing sight of the fact that the life of the individual is his development, in a medium fashioned by the labours of all the individuals who have preceded him, and that the powers of the individual are *his* powers grafted upon those of all foregoing humanity,—all our ideas will change. Philosophy will appear to us as the science of the law of life, as 'the soul' (Mr. Carlyle himself once uses this expression in contradiction to the general spirit of his works), 'of which religion, worship is the body;' and the complaint of the intellect, so often looked upon as idle, from Byron down to George Sand, will be to us, what it is in truth, the registered, efficacious protest of the spirit, tormented by presentiments of the future, against a present corrupted and destroyed; and we shall feel that it is not only our right, but our duty, to incarnate our thought in action. For it matters little that *our* individual powers be of the smallest amount in relation to the object to be attained; it matters little that the result of *our* action be lost in a distance which is beyond our calculation: we know that the powers of millions of men, our brethren, will succeed to the work after us, in the same track,—we know that the object attained, be it when it may, will be the result of *all* our efforts combined. . . . Mr. Carlyle seems to us almost always to forget this. Being thus without a sound criterion whereby to estimate individual acts, he is compelled to value them rather by the power which has been expended upon them, by the energy and perseverance which they betray, than by the nature of the object toward which they are directed, and their relation to that object. Hence arises that kind of indifference which makes him, we will not say esteem, but love, equally men whose whole life has been spent in pursuing contrary objects,—Johnson and Cromwell, for example. Hence proceeds that spirit of fatalism (to call things by their right names) which remotely pervades his work on the French Revolution; which makes him sympathize so much with bold deeds, admire ability, under whatever form displayed, and so often hail, at the risk of becoming an advocate of despotism, might as the token of right. He desires undoubtedly *the good* everywhere and always; but he desires it, from whatever quarter it may come—from above or from below,— imposed by power, or proclaimed by the free and spontaneous impulse of the multitude; and he forgets that the *good* is above all a moral question; that there is no good apart from the consciousness of good; that it exists only where it is made, not obtained, by man: he forgets that we are not machines for production, from which as much work as possible is to be extracted, but free agents, called to stand or fall by our works. His theory of *unconsciousness*, the germ of which appears in the *Life of Schiller*, and is clearly defined in his essay 'Characteristics,' although at first view it may indeed appear to acknowledge human spontaneity, yet does emphatically involve its oblivion, and sacrifices, in its application, the social object to an individual point of view.

Genius is not, generally speaking, unconscious of what it experiences or of what it is capable. It is not the suspended harp which sounds (as the statue of Memnon in the desert sounds in the sun) at the changing unforeseen breath of wind that sweeps across its strings: it is the conscious power of the soul of a man, rising from amidst his fellow-men, believing and calling himself a son of God, an apostle of eternal truth and beauty upon the earth, the privileged worshipper of an ideal as yet concealed from the majority: he is almost always sufficiently tormented by his contemporaries, to need a compensation—that of feeling his life in the generations to come. Cæsar, Christopher Columbus, were not unconscious: Dante, when, at the opening of the twenty-fifth chapter of the *Paradiso*, he hurled at his enemies that sublime menace, which commentators without heart and without head have mistaken for a cry of supplication,—Kepler, when he wrote, 'My book will await its reader: has not God waited six thousand years before he created a man to contemplate his works?'*—Shakspeare himself, when he wrote,

> And nothing stands   ★   ★   ★   ★
> And yet, to times in hope, my verse shall stand†

—these men were not unconscious: but even had they been so, even were genius always unconscious, the question lies not there. It is not the consciousness of genius that is important to a man, but of that which he proposes to do: it is the consciousness of the object, and not that of the means, which we assert to be indispensable, whenever man has any great thing to accomplish. This consciousness pervaded all the great men who have embodied their thought,—the artists of the middle ages themselves, who have transferred to stone the aspiration of their souls towards heaven, and have bequeathed to us Christian cathedrals, without even graving their names on a corner-stone. . . . Human thought is disquieted; it questions itself, listens to itself, studies itself: this is evidently not its normal state. Be it so; but what is to be done? must we abolish thought,—deny the intellect the right, the duty of studying itself, when it is sick? This is indeed the result of the essay on 'Characteristics,' one of Mr. Carlyle's most remarkable works. The first part is truly admirable: the evil is there perfectly charactered and the principal symptoms described; but the conclusion is most lame and impotent. It

* *Harmonices Mundi*: libri quinque.
† Sonnets, 60. See also Sonnets 17, 18, 55, 63, 81, etc.

ends by suppressing (*how*, is not indicated) the disquietude, or what he terms the 'self-sentience,' the 'self-survey,' the consciousness. Would it not be better to endeavour to suppress the malady which produces it. . . .

We repeat, that Mr. Carlyle has instinctively all the presentiments of the period; but not understanding, not admitting throughout, where he labours with the intellect rather than with the heart, the collective life, it is absolutely impossible for him to find the means of realization. A perpetual antagonism prevails throughout all that he does; his instincts drive him to action, his theory to contemplation. Faith and discouragement alternate in his works, as they must in his soul. He weaves and unweaves his web, like Penelope: he preaches by turns life and nothingness: he destroys the powers of his readers, by continually carrying them from heaven to hell, from hell to heaven. Ardent, and almost menacing, upon the ground of idea, he becomes timid and sceptical as soon as he is engaged on that of its application. We may agree with him with respect to the aim—we cannot respecting the means; he rejects them all, but he proposes no others. He desires progress, but dislikes progressives: he foresees, he announces as inevitable, great changes or revolutions in the religious, social, political order; but it is on condition that the revolutionists take no part in them: he has written many admirable pages on Knox and Cromwell; but the chances are that he would have written as admirably, although less truly, against them, had he lived at the commencement of their struggles. . . .

There is, in our opinion, something very incomplete, very narrow, in this kind of contempt which Mr. Carlyle exhibits, whenever he meets in his path with anything that men have agreed to call political reform. The forms of government appear to him almost without meaning: such objects as the extension of suffrage, the guarantee of any kind of political right, are evidently in his eyes pitiful things, materialism more or less disguised. What he requires is, that men should grow better, that the number of just men should increase: one wise man more in the world would be to him a fact of more importance than ten political revolutions. It would be so to us also, were we able to create him, as Wagner does his Homunculus by blowing on the furnaces,—if the changes in the political order of things did not precisely constitute those very manifestations which appear to us indispensable to the life of the just and wise man. When a creed is the professed object, we must not capriciously destroy the instruments which may enable us fully to attain it. . . .

Mr. Carlyle's expression of duty is naturally different. Thinking only of individuality, calculating only the powers of the individual, he would rather restrict than enlarge its sphere. The rule which he adopts is that laid down by Goethe,—'Do the duty which lies nearest thee.' And this rule is good, inasfar as it is, like all other moral rules, susceptible of a wide interpretation,—bad, so far as, taken literally, and falling into the hands of men whose tendencies to self-sacrifice are feeble, it may lead to the revival of selfishness, and cause that which at bottom should only be regarded as the wages of duty to be mistaken for duty itself. It is well known what use Goethe, the high-priest of the doctrine, made of this maxim, shrouding himself in what he called 'Art'; and amidst a world in misery, putting away the question of Religion and politics,—'a troubled element for Art,' though a vital one for *man*,—and giving himself up to the contemplation of forms and the adoration of self. There are at the present day but too many who imagine they have perfectly done their duty, because they are kind toward their friends, affectionate in their families, inoffensive toward the rest of the world. The maxim of Goethe and of Mr. Carlyle will always suit and serve such men, by transforming into duties the individual, domestic or other affections,— in other words, the consolations of life. Mr. Carlyle probably does not carry out his maxim in practice; but his principle leads to this result, and cannot theoretically have any other. 'Here on earth we are as soldiers,' he says:—true, but 'we understand nothing, nor do we require to understand anything, of the plan of the campaign.' What law, what sure object can we then have for action, excepting those to which our individual instincts lead us? Religion is the first of our wants, he will go on to say: but whilst to us religion is a belief and a worship in common, an ideal, the realization of which mankind collectively must seek, a heaven, the visible symbol of which the earth must be rendered by our efforts,—to him it is only a simple relation of the individual to God. It ought therefore, according to our view, to preside over the development of collective life; according to his view, its only office is to pacify the troubled soul. . . . Tell us no longer that 'life itself is a disease,— knowledge, the symptom of derangement;' talk no more of a 'first state of freedom and paradisiacal unconsciousness*.' There is more Byron*ism* in these few words than in the whole of Byron. Freedom and paradise are not behind, but before us. Not life itself, but the deviation from life, is disease: life is sacred; life is our aspiration toward the ideal, —our affections, engagements, which will one day be fulfilled, our

* *Essays*—'Characteristics.'

virtues, advanced toward greater. It is blasphemy to pronounce a word of disrespect against it.

The evil at the present day is, not that men assign too much value to life, but the reverse. Life has fallen in estimation, because, as at all periods of crisis and disorganization, the chain is broken which in all forms of belief attaches it through humanity to heaven. It has fallen, because the consciousness of mutual human responsibility, which alone constitutes its dignity and strength, being lost together with the community of belief, its sphere of activity has become restricted, and it has been compelled to fall back upon material interests, little objects, minor passions. It has fallen, because it has been too much individualized; and the remedy lies in re-attaching life to heaven,—in raising it again, in restoring to it the consciousness of its power and sanctity. . . .

The function which Mr. Carlyle at present fulfils in England appears to us therefore important, but incomplete. Its level is perhaps not high enough for the demands of the age; nevertheless it is noble, and nearer to the object which we have pointed out than that perhaps of any other living writer. All that he combats is indeed really false, and has never been combated more energetically: that which he teaches is not always true. His longings belong to the future—the temper and habits of his intelligence attach him to the past. Our sympathies may claim the one half of the man,—the other half escapes us. All that we regard as important, he considers so also; all that we foresee, he foresees likewise. We only differ respecting the road to follow, the means to be adopted: we serve the same God, we separate only in the worship. Whilst we dive into the midst of present things, in order to draw inspiration from them, while we mingle with men in order to draw strength from them, he retires to a distance and contemplates. We appeal perhaps more than he to tradition; he appeals more than we to individual conscience. We perhaps run the risk of sacrificing something of the purity of the *idea*, in the pursuit of the means; he runs the risk, without intending it, of deserting his brother-labourers.

Nevertheless, let each follow his own path. There will always be a field for the fraternity of noble spirits, even if they differ in their notion of the present life. Their outward manifestations may vary, but only like the radiations of light upon the earth. The ray assumes different colours, according to the different media through which it passes, according to the surface of the objects upon which it falls; but wherever it falls, it warms and vivifies more or less visibly, and all the beams proceed from the same source. Like the sun, the fountain of terrestrial light, there is a common element in heaven for all human spirits which possess strong, firm and disinterested convictions. In this sanctuary Mr. Carlyle will assuredly meet, in a spirit of esteem and sympathy, all the chosen spirits that adore God and truth, who have learned to suffer without cursing, and to sacrifice themselves without despair. . . .

20. Robert Vaughan, from an unsigned review, *British Quarterly Review*

February 1846, iii, 50–95

Extract from an unsigned review, 'Oliver Cromwell's Letters, etc. by Thomas Carlyle'.

Robert Vaughan (1795–1868), historical and religious writer, Congregationalist divine, was Professor of History at London University and later Professor of Theology and President of Lancashire Independent College. He founded the *British Quarterly Review* after he became dissatisfied with the policies of the *Eclectic Review*. Among Vaughan's many works was a two-volume history, *Protectorate of Oliver Cromwell* (1830), to which he alludes in the last page of his review; and *The History of England Under the House of Stuart* (1840), from which he quotes.

Mr. Carlyle has no wish to be numbered with the Little-Faiths of his generation. Self-distrust is not his besetting infirmity. He believes religiously that the thing he wills to do is the thing he has the power to do. He would not be understood as giving ready harbour room to fear about anything relating to the guidance of his own ways. Nor would he have you suppose that the fears of others on his account are at all a matter in his thoughts. His eyes are open, his path is before him, and no man's foresight can serve him in so good a stead as his own. There is something imposing in a person who takes this attitude, or who even *seems* to take it—provided always that the absence of ability be not such as to make the thing at once ridiculous. Unhappily, in this disjointed world, the self-reliant are not always the self-sustained, the absence of fear is not the same thing with the absence of danger. Hence we must confess, that when we saw it announced that Mr. Carlyle was about to publish a *Life of Cromwell*, or something to that effect, we could not suppress our misgiving. We could imagine, indeed, the wonder, or the contempt with which all such feeling on our part would be regarded. Nevertheless—there it was, a feeling that would obtrude itself.

Hitherto, the works of this distinguished writer, while touching considerably upon history, have been wanting in the calmness and comprehensiveness necessary to bring out the full truthfulness of history. To historical investigation, in its proper sense, Mr. Carlyle has shown himself deeply averse; and his speculations on those great facts of history which are open to every man, have been too much marked by caprice, too much an affair of half-truths, contradictions, and mysticisms, to have warranted large expectations concerning his labours even in that department. The character of Cromwell is the last subject in history for any writer to venture upon who is not a patient and sound man in the walks of historical criticism. So multiplied, and so conflicting are the testimonies relating to the career of this notorious person; so long and so largely has falsehood been mingled with truth in the vast accumulation of documents concerning him; and so complex were the relations of affairs influencing the political casuistry of his times, that your eloquent writer, scorning all obscure labour—your theorist, your one-sided man, must not only be, in this case, an incompetent guide, but a guide who will surely lead you astray. We could not but judge Mr. Carlyle as much too old to *begin* a course of this sort with any great prospect of success. We doubted not, that in his under-tone soliloquizings *about* Cromwell, we should find some things worth looking after; but the praise of historical accuracy, or of complete historical truth, we feared we should not be able to award to him.

In these respects, however, the book which Mr. Carlyle has published is a much better book than we had expected. It is based on an extent of reading and research not unworthy of its subject: and the view which it presents of the character of Cromwell is, we think, on the whole, the most satisfactory in our language. This may seem high praise. But it will not be so regarded by those who know what the state of our literature has been in this particular section of it. The faults of the work before us are as material as its excellences. We meet them in every page, and feel as we proceed, that a Life of Cromwell, which shall be at once truthful and adequate, still remains to be written. Mr. Godwin and Mr. Forster have done good service in this field; but it was not to be expected that the religious character of Cromwell would be appreciated by those gentlemen, however honourable their intentions. Both have shown an undue sympathy with the republican party; have given too ready a credence to the calumnies bruited in that quarter, and in some others; and have failed in those broad views of affairs which were necessary to a complete understanding of their subject. Cromwell was a less faulty, and a far better man than we find in their pages; much such a man, in fact, as Mr. Carlyle has exhibited.

Mr. Carlyle has not explained the principle on which he has endeavoured to separate the thread of truth from fiction in his narrative. But, whatever may have been the process, the conclusions which have followed are in the main sound. Each of the great parties in the later years of Cromwell was bent on playing the tyrant. Such was the spirit, almost equally, of the Royalists, the Presbyterians, and the Republicans. He knew that if there must be arbitrariness, his own would be a much milder yoke than theirs. He determined, accordingly, that the staff of power should remain in his own hands, until hands not less wise and equitable should be found to receive it. But to pursue this course, was to brave the utmost virulence and the utmost calumny of all those disappointed tyrannies. We know the result. History has not another subject making so large a demand on the capacity of the historian to distinguish between rumour and fact—between lies and the truth. Mr. Carlyle gives little credence to the royalist authors who sent forth their lucubrations after the blessed year 1660; nor does he confide in everything said at an earlier period by parties who claim to be honoured as persons governed by strict religious principle, or by a stern Roman virtue. We think he is quite right in being so far suspicious of these people. He has considered their means of knowledge, and their temptations to falsehood, and he has judged of them accordingly.

It is a defect, however, that we have not been informed more distinctly of the grounds of his decision in some cases. But the cause of this deficiency is the cause of defects in this form, and in many more, in all Mr. Carlyle's later productions. We have spoken of him as a gentleman who would fain float on over the sea of literature in the sullen majesty of a Dreadnought. But there is one fear with which this author is beset more than almost any man in the world of letters—the fear of being dull. This is a feeling ever present with him, and to which he does homage with all the obsequiousness of a thorough devotee. The dread of being thought feeble, or commonplace, or not more in earnest than other men, dictates not a little of the eccentricity of his style, and especially the brevity which in general leaves his story not more than half told, and which so often bids you be grateful for hints in place of something more satisfactory. Authors who aim to supply you with the materials of knowledge, with ample means from which to form your own judgment concerning the persons and events of history, are classed with our old friend Dryasdust. 'What!'—we think we hear Mr. Carlyle say—'halt at this point, to show why this piece of stupidity should not be credited here; and at that point, to show why that half-fool, half-knave, should not be credited there! Out upon history so written, fit product for the dog days!' Hence, in history, the labours of our Author have been always a piecemeal business. He has rarely given you anything beyond outline; even that being often left incomplete. Your detention longer in one direction, it is thought, might be fatal to your patience; and your want of information is a small matter, compared with your want of wakefulness. With all his independence, Mr. Carlyle has shown, in this respect, a most praiseworthy consideration of the weakness of our degenerate times. The mischief is, that from this cause, his histories always need to be read along with other histories. They are generally obscure, sometimes wholly unmeaning, if taken alone. What man who has not read the history of the French Revolution elsewhere, could possibly understand the book which Mr. Carlyle has published under that name, and further described as a 'History?' Who among us could tell what to receive and what to reject in the history of modern Europe, if that history had been always written with the contempt of authorities and of completeness observable in that work? In history we want vivacity, but we also want fulness—the whole truth. We want vigour, but we cannot dispense with proofs. The French historians have known how to unite these advantages. But to this object the genius of Mr. Carlyle appears to have been unequal. He has had to make his choice, and, as the result, history in his hands has become too much the art of speechmaking. Men of intelligence read such productions, not with the expectation of being safely instructed on the subject to which they relate, but for the sake of the things which a capricious but clever man may be expected to bring to such a topic.

Nor is it enough that our Author should thus pursue a course of his own. He knows not how to tolerate men who have ever pursued any other. Scarcely a man, it seems, has touched on the story of Cromwell, either in remoter or later times, without writing himself down an ass in so doing. It is something new to find an author of eminence proceeding at this rate through the space of two thick octavo volumes, disposing of one scribe as a 'wooden head,' of another, as a 'pudding head,' of a third as belonging to the 'ape' species, of a fourth as partaking of the 'owl' breed, of others as 'hide-bound pedants,' or as a 'watery' generation—all being somehow below proof, according to Mr. Carlyle's gauge. It must be confessed that the presumption with which weak men have attempted to estimate the character of Cromwell, and the unprincipled malevolence with which bad men have assailed his memory, are a sore trial of one's patience, and may sometimes warrant a little outbreak of indignation. But our philosopher has not known how to distinguish between the weak and the wicked in this case. Such amiable epithets as the above, he has dealt out with nearly equal hand to friend and foe. Mr. Carlyle has the reputation of aiming to be the leader of a literary sect among us; but as we think they are mostly gentlemen whose beards are to come that are likely to be taken by such flowers of rhetoric, the prevalence of a dialect of this sort in such quarters could not, we presume, be regarded by our author as very complimentary. In the hero age—the age of which Mr. Carlyle has now been writing— modesty of speech, and modesty of bearing, especially in the case of ingenuous youth, were accounted as things good and beautiful. We could wish that a little more considerateness in this respect had been brought by our very confident instructor from the past to the present. Our literature should serve a better purpose than the scattering of nicknames. There is ability enough for that elsewhere, and much lower down.

But is it a fact that Mr. Carlyle has brought new light to this old subject—that he has proved himself a discoverer even in this long-explored region? We answer, deliberately and emphatically—no. We have said that we regard the account of Cromwell in these volumes as being, on the whole, the most satisfactory in our language. By this, however, we do not mean to say that there is anything really new in what this book sets forth. It presents the just view of Cromwell in a larger space, and, in some respects, in a more carefully authenticated form than has hitherto been assigned to it. But this is the extent of our commendation.

We have the means of knowing that, until very recently, Mr. Carlyle's acquaintance with this portion of our history was very superficial; and that the reading of some two short years, or so, should have sufficed to raise him greatly above all who have preceded him, and above all who have lived along with him, in this kind of knowledge, does not certainly appear to us as a very probable state of things. It may not be amiss to indicate to our readers the grounds of our distrust in this respect. In the edition of *Hero-Worship* published in 1842, we find the following estimate of the leading puritans of the early years of Charles I.:—

[quotes 'For my own share' to 'gloves on' 'The Hero as King', V, 208–9]

But since this was written, Mr. Carlyle has returned to the study of the 'measured euphuisms, philosophies, parliamentary eloquences, shipmonies,' and other things, which come up in the history of these 'dreadfully dull men;' and in consequence these pieces of 'smooth-shaven respectability,' who some two years ago were 'heavy as lead, barren as brick-clay,' and for whom it was impossible to get up any feeling of reverence, are now spoken of as follows:—

[quotes 'This was the' to 'had to carry' and 'My second advice' to 'Seventeenth Century', *Introduction* VI, 59 and 81–2]

Thus, the men of whom it was said, only so short a time since, that, 'for us there is little or nothing now surviving in them,' Mr. Carlyle has discovered of late to be persons 'who would be worth their weight in diamonds even now,' if we could only achieve so great a miracle as to give existence, in these times, to virtues so 'unattainable—incredible!' From being a dreadfully dull people, 'heavy as lead, barren as brick clay,' they have come to be a people inspired, beyond all example, with a 'heavenly purpose,'—a purpose so profound as to be measureless, so grand as to leave all other possible purposes only as corollaries to it! The truth is, however, that many thousands of reading, thoughtful men have long since seen our parliamentary leaders in the time of Charles I. much as Mr. Carlyle now sees them; but through some strange illusion, it has been concluded that conceptions which are new to our author must of course be new to all the world beside. We think, indeed, that the present tendency of this writer is towards compensating to these men for his past injustice by giving them even higher praise than that to which they are entitled. But with Mr. Carlyle, all moderate people are still very dull.

We shall select one more instance to show that Mr. Carlyle's present knowledge on this subject, is neither so peculiar nor so old as to warrant any great boasting. Our author observes in his *Hero-Worship*, that the 'rub' in the history of Cromwell lies in his dismissal of the Rump Parliament. Men, it is said, who pardon him in almost everything else, cannot pardon him in this matter. Here, if anywhere, we might have supposed Mr. Carlyle would have taken some pains to be up to the level of his subject. In adverting to the explanations attempted on this question, he expresses himself as follows:—

The likeliest is, that this poor parliament still would not, and, indeed, could not dissolve and disperse; that when it came to the point of actually dispersing, they again, for the twelth or twentieth time, adjourned it—and Cromwell's patience failed him. But we will take the favourablest hypothesis ever started by the parliament—the favourablest, though, I believe, it is not the true one. According to this version—at the uttermost crisis, when Cromwell and his officers were met on the one hand, and the fifty or sixty Rump Members on the other, it was suddenly told Cromwell that the Rump, in its despair, *was* answering in a very singular way, and in their splenetic envious despair, to keep out the army at least, these men were hurrying through the house a kind of Reform Bill. Parliament to be chosen by the whole of England, equable electoral division into districts, free suffrage, and the rest of it! A very questionable, or, indeed, for *them*, an unquestionable thing. Reform Bill, free suffrage of Englishmen!

It is clear, from this passage, that in 1842 Mr. Carlyle had not read one of the most accessible and remarkable, and certainly the most valuable of all Cromwell's speeches—the speech which he addressed to the Little Parliament, assembled soon after this time, and in which he gave a full and honest account of the proceedings which had terminated in the dismissal of the Rump Parliament. In that speech, the purport of the 'Reform Bill,' spoken of by Mr. Carlyle, is stated, and sufficient cause is shown for what was done. But Mr. Carlyle has now reprinted this speech, and finds that the explanation there given *is* 'the true one,' and one which furnishes an ample vindication of the conduct of Cromwell in this affair. Thus, light has come in 1845, which, it seems, did not exist in 1842—at least, so far as Mr. Carlyle's knowledge on this subject was concerned. Some seven years since, however, in a history which we presume Mr. Carlyle would regard as belonging to the Dryasdust school of authorship, an account is given of this great 'rub' in the history of Cromwell, derived mainly from the speech adverted to, and which we shall insert in this place.*

* *History of England, under the House of Stuart*, 2 vols. 8vo. Published by the Useful Knowledge Society; vol. ii. pp. 500–502. In this work, more than the usual space is given to the

[Vaughan quotes a three-page extract from his *own* book which was published in 1840.]

This extract supplies what is wanting in Mr. Carlyle's account of this memorable event, as given in his *Hero-Worship*, and is the exact account of the matter given in his present publication.* It would be easy to multiply instances of this sort in relation to the whole chain of occurrences embraced in these volumes, and to show that our author is egregiously mistaken in supposing that he is 'the first actual reader of the speeches of Cromwell for nearly two centuries past,' and that to him has been left the honour of clearing up the obscure in the marvellous history of this hero. We suspect that these speeches had all served the purposes of veracious history before Mr. Carlyle had read one of them; that he is the last, and not the first among his contemporaries who has managed to understand them—though we rejoice to think that, as the fruit of his labour, they will do their office much more effectually in the future than in the past. Our complaint, be it remembered, is not that a man of genius should have bestowed so much attention on this subject without giving to it the attraction of novelty—for, in truth, that was hardly possible; but our regret is, that while this book contains scarcely anything new, it should have been written throughout so as to suggest the contrary of that fact; and that it should not have been deemed enough to assume this tone of superiority without due warrant, but that the names of contempt and scorn should have been cast so freely on nearly all preceding writers. Of the bad taste of all this we have before spoken; and we account the morality of it as not less open to impeachment.

---

history of Cromwell, and it may not be uninteresting to some of our readers to know, that every part of it relating to Cromwell passed under the eye, and obtained the approval, of the late Earl Spencer, while going through the press—a nobleman whose acquaintance with that period of our history is known to have been singularly accurate and comprehensive.

* Mr. Carlyle does not intend that his readers should think thus humbly of his labours on this point; but he must know that this is the fact of the case, inasmuch as the narrative in the above extract is given in the same words, in the introduction to the *Pell Papers*, on the Times of the Protectorate, by the editor of that publication:[1] and that work at least we must suppose Mr. Carlyle to have read, inasmuch as he quotes from it, and has disposed of it with the sort of gratitude, wherewith it has been his pleasure to regard the labours of nearly all his predecessors in this path.

---

[1] The 'Pell Papers' were a series of letters between John Pell and Sir Samuel Morland, Sir William Lockhart, John Thurloe. They made up much of Robert Vaughan's book *The Protectorate of Oliver Cromwell, and the state of Europe during the early part of the reign of Louis XIV . . . with an introduction on the character of Cromwell, and his time.*

In nearly all respects, the estimate of the character of Cromwell published twenty years since by Mr. Macaulay, is fully as independent, honourable, and just, as this now published by Mr. Carlyle. But in one respect we give the precedence greatly to Mr. Carlyle's portraiture. He does justice to the religion of Cromwell. His philosophy, if not always based on the clearest and the most comprehensive logic, is, in this instance, pregnant with candour, and with sound feeling. We may question his maxim—that a truly great man can be neither hypocrite nor liar. But we fully participate in his manly scorn of those narrow-headed and narrow-hearted persons, who can see nothing better than cant, fanaticism, and 'besotted superstition,' in the apparent piety of this great captain. Here the most well-meaning of Cromwell's judges have commonly broken down. They have been able to explain many things which needed explanation; but to suppose that the language in which he expressed himself in respect to his faith and feeling as a Christian, was that of a sincere truth-speaking man, has been their great difficulty. This perplexity, however, will not be greatly felt by men who have hearts as well as heads. Men who have known what that puritanism really is, of which Cromwell was the high-souled embodiment, can believe him to the last, when he tells them of his trust in God as nerving his arm in the day of battle, and of his hope in respect to a future world as being his master hope, even while striving so mightily to give a better adjustment to the affairs of the present. Mr. Carlyle has knowledge enough of the man Cromwell, and of the thing Puritanism, and of the susceptibilities of his own lofty and earnest spirit, to give his hero full credit for integrity in his professed religious feeling. It is this feature of the work before us which is to us its great charm. The man destitute of enthusiasm—the feeling which belongs equally to all the higher forms of genius and religion—can never understand the character of Cromwell. The mind in which the pretended philosophies of our time have dried up the gush and well-spring of emotion—frozen all the natural and bounding sympathies of the soul—will blunder at every step in the career of such a man. His nature was not their nature. But it is ever the tendency of such men to meddle with matters which are too high for them. . . .

We are sorry to say that we think this fault—a fault which bespeaks him poet or artist rather than philosopher—belongs in a marked degree to the genius of Mr. Carlyle. Hence this endless lamentation over modern degeneracy. Hence this prostrate adoration before the real or imaginary greatness of bygone days. He not only does not see piety or virtue in the times in which we live, but would hardly seem to have a wish to see them. He is sure that he doth well to be angry. So thoroughly does he seem to enjoy his grumble, that we can hardly conceive of him as being happy where he could not know the felicity of uttering it. We do not say that there is no sort of ground for the distinction thus made between the former days and our own; but we are well convinced that, in this case, were both equally immediate, both would be in the same degree deplored, and the light and shadow of our poet's dreams would come to an end. Had Mr. Carlyle lived in the seventeenth century in place of the nineteenth, we suspect that the preachings of Cromwell's soldiery would have been as little to his taste then, as is the speech-making which takes place in Exeter Hall now. 'The age of the Puritans,' it is said, 'is not extinct only, and gone away from us, but it is as if fallen beyond the capabilities of Memory herself; it is grown unintelligible, what we may call incredible.' Now this may be true in respect to the great majority of literary people who come much under Mr. Carlyle's observation, and in respect to a large portion of the surface of general society in our age. But the people of England do not consist of literary coteries, nor of mere surface. There may be froth at the top, and sediment at the bottom, and something much better in the middle: and our charge against Mr. Carlyle is, that instead of recognising the Living Puritanism which is in this better element, and doing a bold and large-hearted service in its behalf, he is seen joining with the vulgar pack in putting scorn upon it, and as far as possible in running it down. He does not know—and he does not know, as we fear, because he has hardly a wish to know—that there is at this hour a far greater number of men and women in these nations animated with the true spirit of the religion of such men as Owen and Baxter and Bunyan, than could have been found in this Island in that age of Puritanism with which it is now deemed so becoming to be greatly enamoured. In Great Britain there are, at this moment, some ten thousand pulpits in which the doctrines of our old puritanism, as to the substance of them, are constantly preached; before which multitudes listen to those doctrines who have embraced them with a conviction not less sincere than that of the men whom we see storming the breach or crossing the battle-field at the bidding of Cromwell. These people—myriads, millions of these people, believe in the same God with the puritans of two centuries since, live through the same life of spiritual warfare—warfare against demons without, and not less against a demon within, and are dying every hour full of the same hope of a glorious immortality. It is true, there is a quietism, a decorum—in short, what some men would describe as a tame conventionalism, a soulless formality, about these modern Evangelicals, that may seem to deny the fact of their spiritual relationship to the grave and ardent religionists of the interval from the accession of Charles I. to the Restoration. But the difference is not so much in the men as in the times. Treat these people as the puritans of that age were treated, and you may perhaps learn that the sons are not altogether unworthy of their sires. Place our civil constitution in abeyance, tax men without their consent, imprison them without law, refuse them a jail delivery at pleasure, and fix your lock and chain upon the printing press; silence the ten thousand men who preach Christ's holy gospel to these people, shut up their sanctuaries, summon them to your courts of Star Chamber and High Commission, peel them of their substance, send them to the Fleet, set them in pillories, gather your mobs at Charing Cross to see their ears cut off and their faces branded with hot irons—do all this, ye scorners of modern puritanism, *if you dare*, and then see if Marston Moor and Naseby Fight may not be in a fair way of coming back again! Let the same huge wrong come, and something like the same lion-hearted re-action may follow much sooner than certain loose talkers would feel to be agreeable. But we leave it to our adepts in philosophy—our wizards in their far-reaching views of human nature, to expect that effects should continue when their natural causes have ceased: and to feel surprised that the *men* are not in all respects the same, while the *circumstances* in the two cases have all the world between them!

Something, indeed, of the old tendency towards wrong-doing is still at times manifested—now in favour of some priestly education bill, and now in support of some popish endowment project; and when such signs have been given, these descendants of men who were somewhat notorious for telling their mind to senators in the days of the Long Parliament, have resolved to make themselves heard in their million-voiced petitions at the bar of our legislature. But how have they been greeted, when, roused thus from the quietism which is made their reproach, they have put forth some proofs of that earnestness which in the character of our older puritanism was, as we are told, so wonderfully venerable? All men know that this too has then been made to be their dishonour. In the language of our statists and philosophers this conduct has been denounced as the revival of an ignorant and obsolete bigotry. Their zeal has been a miserable fanaticism. Truly, there are people hard to please—and none more so than the people who belong to the class known in some circles by the name of the 'little vulgar,' that is, the educated would-be philosophical vulgar, a sort of persons who have just light enough to lead them astray, and just wisdom enough to prevent their being honest. Oh! we could lament—lament with a pathos as deep as Mr. Carlyle's, the want among us of that true greatness which fits a man to see events about him as the men of coming centuries will see them! But we must again say, that we find much—very much, in the writings of Mr. Carlyle, unfavourable to such broad, just, and wholesome habits of thought. One-sidedness is his great fault. To the past he gives more than its due, to the present he is wanting in common fairness. In his judgments of individual men, and of generations of men, this weakness is observable. He commonly begins in partial or erroneous calculation, facts being strangely exaggerated or as strangely underrated, and the natural consequences follow. He makes little way towards his object. Calm and sagacious men lose all confidence in his judgment.

In giving expression to these opinions we shall possibly be regarded as unfriendly to the reputation of this writer. But we mean him no wrong. It is from the superficial persons who would raise him to the place of one of his own 'heroes,' and who do their worship to him as thus viewed, that mischief should be apprehended. Men of sense are in danger of withholding from him the honourable testimony to which he is entitled, lest they should seem to be joining in this blind and shallow adoration. It is said that Sir Walter Scott was more vain of his baronetcy, and of his office as sheriff of his county, than of being the author of Waverley. Certain it is, that great men often fall into strange mistakes in judging with regard to the real points of their own greatness. Mr. Carlyle is a passionate Transcendentalist, and has adopted a style of writing monstrously obsolete and uncouth. But his reputation, so far as that is a matter worth possessing, has not become his by reason of these peculiarities, but in defiance of them. These fancies are not his strength, but his weakness. We have many working-day conjurors about us who could manage to invest themselves in the clouds of German metaphysics quite as skilfully as Mr. Carlyle; and there is no half-idiot in the land who might not stalk abroad in the costume of his great-grandfather, with his broad hat and feather, his flat-down collar, his belted vest, his breeches with flounces at the knees, buskin boots, walking sword and all—if to do so would suffice to make people worship as well as stare! But Mr. Carlyle's genius, while disfigured by these mannerisms, is nevertheless sterling. To see the ground on which his solid fame rests, we must look to his various information, to the frequent vigour of his conceptions and discriminations, to the force of his imagination, to the refinement and depth of his feeling, and to the strength of his faith in the reality, the beauty, and the grandeur of being as it exists above the sensual—all of which qualities combined have given him a place, in respect to questions properly literary, in the first rank of living critics. But when Mr. Carlyle comes before us as an oracle, as the Elijah of some new dispensation, as the man sent to show us the true allotment and destiny of our species; and when we are required to sit at his feet, and to believe all this on pain of being numbered with 'owls,' who find their homes in darkness, or with the 'apes' who find their graves on the shores of the Dead Sea, we must confess that this is a kind of discipline against which our old Saxon blood is strongly disposed to rebel. We never feel so prompted to question Mr. Carlyle's pretensions altogether, as when they become thus extravagant. We have all, we suppose, listened to orators whose eloquence has become repellant, just in proportion to the noisy effort made to render it attractive—the one wish of the auditory being that the speaker would cease, or speedily descend to the level of moderation. Too much of this sort is our feeling when Mr. Carlyle talks as though he were the only wise and good man of his generation, soars into his heroics, and surrounds himself with his apocalyptic visions. We confide in him least when he bids us confide in him most. We see him pass out of his depth, and we begin to take care lest an inconvenient fate should be found to be awaiting us both.

But we have occupied much larger space with observations of this nature than we had intended, and we shall now submit to our readers some of the evidence presented in these volumes with regard to the characters of Cromwell as it was known to the men of his own time.

[Vaughan quotes sixteen pages of letters from Carlyle's work and comments on them and then gives his own twelve-page account of Cromwell. His review concludes with these comments:]

If all that Mr. Carlyle has written on Cromwell were taken out of the fragmentary and strange shape into which he has thrown it, and were 'smelted down'—to use a term of his own—into a little smooth, straightforward English, we think it would prove to be nearly such an account as we have now submitted to our readers. But it is due to ourselves to say, that for such views of the character of Cromwell, we owe nothing to the writings of Mr. Carlyle. These views we derived some twenty years since from those sources of information to which Mr.

Carlyle has repaired more recently; and we think we could make it appear that our modern puritans have not now to begin to understand the true character of Cromwell, though it may be quite true, as Mr. Carlyle supposes, that our literati and our dilletanti people, for whom his book is especially intended, have not a little to unlearn on this subject. In such quarters his publication will do eminent service, and in this view we rejoice greatly in its appearance.

21. Henry David Thoreau, from an essay, *Graham's Magazine*

March and April 1847, xxi, 145–52, 238–45

Extract from a signed essay, 'Thomas Carlyle and his Works'.

Thoreau's (1817–62) essay was read by Carlyle and elicited these comments to Emerson in a letter (18 May 1847).

A vigorous Mr Thoreau,—who has formed himself a good deal upon one Emerson, but does not want abundant fire and stamina of his own;—recognises us, and various other things, in a most admiring greathearted manner; for which, as for *part* of the confused voice from the jury-box (not yet summed into a verdict, nor likely to be summed till Doomsday, nor needful to sum) the poor prisoner at the bar may justly express himself thankful!—In plain prose, I like Mr Thoreau very well; and hope yet to hear good and better news of him.—only let him not 'turn to foolishness'; which seems to me to be terribly easy, at present, both in New England and Old!

(*The Correspondence of Emerson and Carlyle*, ed. Joseph Slater [New York, 1964], p. 422.)

. . . When we remember how these volumes came over to us, with their encouragement and provocation from mouth to mouth, and what commotion they created in many private breasts, we wonder that the country did not ring, from shore to shore, from the Atlantic to the Pacific, with its greeting; and the Boons and Crockets of the West make haste to hail him, whose wide humanity embraces them too. Of all that the packets have brought over to us, has there been any richer cargo than this? What else has been English news for so long a season? What else, of late years, has been England to us—to us who read books, we mean? Unless we remembered it as the scene where the age of Wordsworth was spending itself, and a few younger muses were trying their wings, and from time to time, as the residence of Landon; Carlyle alone, since the death of Coleridge, has kept the promise of England. It is the best apology for all the bustle and the sin of commerce, that it has made us acquainted with the thoughts of this man. Commerce would not concern us much if it were not for such results as this. New England owes him a debt which she will be slow to recognize. His earlier essays reached us at a time when Coleridge's were the only recent words which had made any notable impression so far, and they found a field unoccupied by him, before yet any words of moment had been uttered in our midst. He had this advantage, too, in a teacher, that he stood near to his pupils; and he has no doubt afforded reasonable encouragement and sympathy to many an independent but solitary thinker. Through him, as usher, we have been latterly, in a great measure, made acquainted with what philosophy and criticism the nineteenth century had to offer —admitted, so to speak, to the privileges of the century; and what he may yet have to say, is still expected here with more interest than any thing else from that quarter.

It is remarkable, but on the whole, perhaps, not to be lamented, that the world is so unkind to a new book. Any distinguished traveler who comes to our shores, is likely to get more dinners and speeches of welcome than he can well dispose of, but the best books, if noticed at all, meet with coldness and suspicion, or, what is worse, gratuitous, off-hand criticism. It is plain that the reviewers, both here and abroad, do not know how to dispose of this man. They approach him too easily, as if he were one of the men of letters about town, who grace Mr. Somebody's administration, merely; but he already belongs to litera-ture, and depends neither on the favor of reviewers, nor the honesty of booksellers, nor the pleasure of readers for his success. He has more to impart than to receive from his generation. He is another such a strong and finished workman in his craft as Samuel Johnson was, and like him, makes the literary class respectable. As few are yet out of their appren-ticeship, or even if they learn to be able writers, are at the same time able and valuable thinkers. The aged and critical eyes, especially, is in-capacitated to appreciate the works of this author. To such their mean-ing is impalpable and evanescent, and they seem to abound only in obstinate mannerisms, Germanisms, and whimiscal ravings of all kinds, with now and then an unaccountably true and sensible remark. On the strength of this last, Carlyle is admitted to have what is called genius. We hardly know an old man to whom these volumes are not hopelessly sealed. The language, they say, is foolishness and a stumbling-block to them; but to many a clear-headed boy, they are plainest English, and despatched with such hasty relish as his bread and milk. The fathers wonder how it is that the children take to this diet so readily, and digest it with so little difficulty. They shake their heads with mistrust at their free and easy delight, and remark that 'Mr. Carlyle is a very learned man;' for they, too, not to be out of fashion, have got grammar and dictionary, if the truth were known, and with the best faith cudgelled their brains to get a little way into the jungle, and they could not but confess, as often as they found the clue, that it was as intricate as Blackstone to follow, if you read it honestly. But merely reading, even with the best intentions, is not enough, you must almost have written these books yourself. Only he who has had the good fortune to read them in the nick of time, in the most perceptive and recipient season of life, can give any adequate account of them.

Many have tasted of this well with an odd suspicion, as if it were some fountain Arethuse which had flowed under the sea from Germany, as if the materials of his books had lain in some garret there, in danger of being appropriated for waste paper. Over what German ocean, from what Hercynian forest, he has been imported, piece-meal, into England, or whether he has now all arrived, we are not informed. This article is not invoiced in Hamburg, nor in London. Perhaps it was contraband. However, we suspect that this sort of goods cannot be imported in this way. No matter how skillful the stevedore, all things being got into sailing trim, wait for a Sunday, and aft wind, and then weigh anchor, and run up the main-sheet—straightway what of transcendant and permanent value is there resists the aft wind, and will doggedly stay behind that Sunday—it does not travel Sundays; while biscuit and pork make headway, and sailors cry heave-yo! it must part company, if it open a seam. It is not quite safe to send out a venture in this kind, unless yourself go supercargo. Where a man goes, there he is; but the slightest virtue is immovable—it is real estate, not personal; who would keep it, must consent to be bought and sold with it.

However, we need not dwell on this charge of a German extraction, it being generally admitted, by this time, that Carlyle is English, and an inhabitant of London. He has the English for his mother tongue, though with a Scotch accent, or never so many accents, and thoughts also, which are the legitimate growth of native soil, to utter therewith. His style is eminently colloquial—and no wonder it is strange to meet with in a book. It is not literary or classical; it has not the music of poetry, nor the pomp of philosophy, but the rhythms and cadences of conversation endlessly repeated. It resounds with emphatic, natural, lively, stirring tones, muttering, rattling, exploding, like shells and shot, and with like execution. So far as it is a merit in composition, that the written answer to the spoken word, and the spoken word to a fresh and pertinent thought in the mind, as well as to the half thoughts, the tumultuary misgivings and expectancies, this author is, perhaps, not to be matched in literature. In the streets men laugh and cry, but in books, never; they 'whine, put finger i' the eye, and sob' only. One would think that all books of late, had adopted the falling inflexion. 'A mother, if she wishes to sing her child to sleep,' say the musical men, 'will always adopt the falling inflexion.' Would they but choose the rising inflexion, and wake the child up for once.

He is no mystic either, more than Newton or Arkwright, or Davy—and tolerates none. Not one obscure line, or half line, did he ever write. His meaning lies plain as the daylight, and he who runs may read; indeed, only he who runs *can* read, and keep up with the meaning. It has the distinctness of picture to his mind, and he tells us only what he sees printed in largest English type upon the face of things. He utters substantial English thoughts in plainest English dialects; for it must be confessed, he speaks more than one of these. All the shires of England, and all the shires of Europe, are laid under contribution to his genius; for to be English does not mean to be exclusive and narrow, and adapt one's self to the apprehension of his nearest neighbor only. And yet no writer is more thoroughly Saxon. In the translation of those fragments of Saxon poetry, we have met with the same rhythm that occurs so often in his poem on the French Revolution. And if you would know where many of those obnoxious Carlyleisms and Germanisms came from, read the best of Milton's prose, read those speeches of Cromwell which he has brought to light, or go and listen once more to your mother's tongue. So much for his German extraction.

Indeed, for fluency and skill in the use of the English tongue, he is a master unrivaled. His felicity and power of expression surpass even any of his special merits as a historian and critic. Therein his experience has not failed him, but furnished him with such a store of winged, aye, and legged words, as only a London life, perchance, could give account of; we had not understood the wealth of the language before. Nature is ransacked, and all the resorts and purlieus of humanity are taxed, to furnish the fittest symbol for his thought. He does not go to the dictionary, the word-book, but to the word-manufactory itself, and has made endless work for the lexicographers—yes, he has that same English for his mother-tongue, that you have, but with him it is no dumb, muttering, mumbling faculty, concealing the thoughts, but a keen, unwearied, resistless weapon. He has such command of it as neither you nor I have; and it would be well for any who have a lost horse to advertise, or a town-meeting warrant, or a sermon, or a letter to write, to study this universal letter-writer, for he knows more than the grammar or the dictionary.

The style is worth attending to, as one of the most important features of the man which we at this distance can discern. It is for once quite equal to the matter. It can carry all its load, and never breaks down nor staggers. His books are solid and workmanlike, as all that England does; and they are graceful and readable also. They tell of huge labor done, well done, and all the rubbish swept away, like the bright cutlery which glitters in shop-windows, while the coke and ashes, the turnings, filings, dust, and borings, lie far away at Birmingham, unheard of. He is a masterly clerk, scribe, reporter, and writer. He can reduce to writing most things—gestures, winks, nods, significant looks, patois, brogue, accent, pantomime, and how much that had passed for silence before, does he represent by written words. The countryman who puzzled the city lawyer, requiring him to write, among other things, his call to his horses, would hardly have puzzled him; he would have found a word for it, all right and classical, that would have started his team for him. Consider the ceaseless tide of speech forever flowing in countless cellars, garrets, *parlors*; that of the French, says Carlyle, 'only ebbs towards the short hours of night,' and what a drop in the bucket is the printed word. Feeling, thought, speech, writing, and we might add, poetry, inspira-tion—for so the circle is completed; how they gradually dwindle at length, passing through successive colanders, into your history and classics, from the roar of the ocean, the murmur of the forest, to the squeak of a mouse; so much only parsed and spelt out, and punctuated, at last. The few who can talk like a book, they only get reported commonly. But this writer reports a new 'Lieferung.'[1]

One wonders how so much, after all, was expressed in the old way, so much here depends upon the emphasis, tone, pronunciation, style, and spirit of the reading. No writer uses so profusely all the aids to intelligibility which the printer's art affords. You wonder how others had contrived to write so many pages without emphatic or italicised words, they are so expressive, so natural, so indispensable here, as if none had ever used the demonstrative pronouns demonstratively before. In another's sentences the thought, though it may be immortal, is, as it were, embalmed, and does not *strike* you, but here it is so freshly living, even the body of it, not having passed through the ordeal of death, that

[1] Number.

it stirs in the very extremities, and the smallest particles and pronouns are all alive with it. It is not simple dictionary *it*, yours or mine, but IT. The words did not come at the command of grammar, but of a tyrannous, inexorable meaning; not like standing soldiers, by vote of parliament, but any able-bodied countryman pressed into the service, for 'sire, it is not a revolt, it is a revolution.'

We have never heard him speak, but we should say that Carlyle was a rare talker. He has broken the ice, and streams freely forth like a spring torrent. He does not trace back the stream of his thought, silently adventurous, up to its fountain-head, but is borne away with it, as it rushes through his brain like a torrent to overwhelm and fertilize. He holds a talk with you. His audience is such a tumultuous mob of thirty thousand, as assembled at the University of Paris, before printing was invented. Philosophy, on the other hand, does not talk, but write, or, when it comes personally before an audience, lecture or read; and therefore it must be read to-morrow, or a thousand years hence. But the talker must naturally be attended to at once; he does not talk on without an audience; the winds do not long bear the sound of his voice. Think of Carlyle reading his *French Revolution* to any audience. One might say it was never written, but spoken; and thereafter reported and printed, that those not within sound of his voice might know something about it. . . .

Such a style—so diversified and variegated! It is like the face of a country; it is like a New England landscape, with farm-houses and villages, and cultivated spots, and belts of forests and blueberry-swamps round about it, with the fragrance of shad-blossoms and violets on certain winds. And as for the reading of it, it is novel enough to the reader who has used only the diligence, and old-line mail-coach. It is like traveling, sometimes on foot, sometimes in a gig tandem; sometimes in a full coach, over highways, mended and unmended, for which you will prosecute the town; on level roads, through French departments, by Simplon roads over the Alps, and now and then he hauls up for a relay, and yokes in an unbroken colt of a Pegasus for a leader, driving off by cart-paths, and across lots, by corduroy roads and gridiron bridges; and where the bridges are gone, not even a string-piece left, and the reader has to set his breast and swim. You have got an expert driver this time, who has driven ten thousand miles, and was never known to upset; can drive six in hand on the edge of precipice, and touch the leaders anywhere with his snapper.

With wonderful art he grinds into paint for his picture all his moods and experiences, so that all his forces may be brought to the encounter. . . . With his brows knit, his mind made up, his will resolved and resistless, he advances, crashing his way through the host of weak, half-formed, *dilettante* opinions, honest and dishonest ways of thinking, with their standards raised, sentimentalities and conjectures, and tramples them all into dust. See how he prevails; you don't even hear the groans of the wounded and dying. Certainly it is not so well worth the while to look through any man's eyes at history, for the time, as through his; and his way of looking at things is fastest getting adopted by his generation.

It is not in man to determine what his style shall be. He might as well determine what his thoughts shall be. We would not have had him write always as in the chapter on Burns, and the *Life of Schiller*, and elsewhere. No; his thoughts were ever irregular and impetuous. Perhaps as he grows older and writes more he acquires a truer expression; it is in some respects manlier, freer, struggling up to a level with its fountain-head. We think it is the richest prose style we know of. . . .

We believe that Carlyle has, after all, more readers, and is better known to-day for this very originality of style, and that posterity will have reason to thank him for emancipating the language, in some measure, from the fetters which a merely conservative, aimless, and pedantic literary class had imposed upon it, and setting an example of greater freedom and naturalness. No man's thoughts are new, but the style of their expression is the never failing novelty which cheers and refreshes men. If we were to answer the question, whether the mass of men, as we know them, talk as the standard authors and reviewers write, or rather as this man writes, we should say that he alone begins to write their language at all, and that the former is, for the most part, the mere effigies of a language, not the best method of concealing one's thoughts even, but frequently a method of doing without thoughts at all.

In his graphic description of Richter's style, Carlyle describes his own pretty nearly; and no doubt he first got his own tongue loosened at that fountain, and was inspired by it to equal freedom and originality. 'The language,' as he says of Richter, 'groans with indescribable metaphors and allusions to all things, human and divine, flowing onward, not like a river, but like an inundation; circling in complex eddies, chafing and gurgling, now this way, now that;' but in Carlyle, 'the proper current' never 'sinks out of sight amid the boundless uproar.' Again: 'His very language is Titanian—deep, strong, tumultuous, shining with a thousand hues, fused from a thousand elements, and winding in labyrinthic mazes.'

In short, if it is desirable that a man be eloquent, that he talk much, and address himself to his own age mainly, then this is not a bad style of doing it. But if it is desired rather that he pioneer into unexplored regions of thought, and speaks to silent centuries to come, then, indeed, we could wish that he had cultivated the style of Goethe more, that of Richter less; not that Goethe's is the kind of utterance most to be prized by mankind, but it will serve for a model of the best that can be successfully cultivated.

But for style, and fine writing, and Augustan ages—that is but a poor style, and vulgar writing, and a degenerate age, which allows us to remember these things. This man has something to communicate. Carlyle's are not, in the common sense, works of art in their origin and aim; and yet, perhaps, no living English writer evinces an equal literary talent. They are such works of art only as the plough, and corn-mill, and steam-engine—not as pictures and statues. Others speak with greater emphasis to scholars, as such, but none so earnestly and effectually to all who can read. Others give their advice, he gives his sympathy also. It is no small praise that he does not take upon himself the airs, has none of the whims, none of the pride, the nice vulgarities, the starched, impoverished isolation, and cold glitter of the spoiled children of genius. He does not need to husband his pearl, but excels by a greater humanity and sincerity.

He is singularly serious and untrivial. We are every where impressed by the rugged, unwearied, and rich sincerity of the man. We are sure that he never sacrificed one jot of his honest thought to art or whim, but to utter himself in the most direct and effectual way, that is the endeavor. These are merits which will wear well. When time has worn deeper into the substance of these books, this grain will appear. No such sermons have come to us here out of England, in late years, as those of this preacher; sermons to kings, and sermons to peasants, and sermons to all intermediate classes. It is in vain that John Bull, or any of his cousins, turns a deaf ear, and pretends not to hear them, nature will not soon be weary of repeating them. There are words less obviously true, more for the ages to hear, perhaps, but none so impossible for this age not to hear. What a cutting cimiter was that 'past and present,' going through heaps of silken stuffs, and glibly through the necks of men, too, without their knowing it, leaving no trace. He has the earnestness of a prophet. In an age of pedantry and dilettantism, he has no grain of these in his composition. There is no where else, surely, in recent readable English, or other books, such direct and effectual teaching, reproving, encouraging, stimulating, earnestly, vehemently, almost like Mahomet, like Luther; not looking behind him to see how his *Opera Omnia* will look, but forward to other work to be done. His writings are a gospel to the young of this generation; they will hear his manly, brotherly speech with responsive joy, and press forward to older or newer gospels.

We should omit a main attraction in these books, if we said nothing of their humor. Of this indispensable pledge of sanity, without some leaven, of which the abstruse thinker may justly be suspected of mysticism, fanaticism, or insanity, there is a superabundance in Carlyle. Especially the transcendental philosophy needs the leaven of humor to render it light and digestible. In his later and longer works it is an unfailing accompaniment, reverberating through pages and chapters, long sustained without effort. The very punctuation, the italics, the quotation marks, the blank spaces and dashes, and the capitals, each and all are pressed into its service.

Every man, of course, has his fane, from which even the most innocent conscious humor is excluded; but in proportion as the writer's position is high above his fellows, the range of his humor is extended. To the thinker, all the institutions of men, as all imperfection, viewed from the point of equanimity, are legitimate subjects of humor. Whatever is not necessary, no matter how sad or personal, or universal a grievance, is, indeed, a jest more or less sublime.

Carlyle's humor is vigorous and Titanic, and has more sense in it than the sober philosophy of many another. It is not to be disposed of by laughter and smiles merely; it gets to be too serious for that—only they may laugh who are not hit by it. For those who love a merry jest, this is a strange kind of fun—rather too practical joking, if they understand it. The pleasant humor which the public loves, is but the innocent pranks of the ballroom, harmless flow of animal spirits, the light plushy pressure of dandy pumps, in comparison. But when an elephant takes to treading on your corns, why then you are lucky if you sit high, or wear cowhide. His humor is always subordinate to a serious purpose, though often the real charm for the reader, is not so much in the essential progress and final upshot of the chapter, as in this indirect sidelight illustration of every hue. He sketches first with strong, practical English pencil, the essential features in outline, black on white, more faithfully than Dryasdust would have done, telling us wisely whom and what to mark, to save time, and then with brush of camel's hair, or sometimes with more expeditious swab, he lays on the bright and fast colors of his humor everywhere. One piece of solid work, be it known, we have determined to do, about which let there be no jesting, but all things else under the heavens, to the right and left of that, are for the time fair game. To us this humor is not wearisome, as almost every other is. Rabelais, for instance, is intolerable; one chapter is better than a volume—it may be sport to him, but it is death to us. A mere humorist, indeed, is a most unhappy man; and his readers are most unhappy also. . . .

We confess that Carlyle's humor is rich, deep, and variegated, in direct communication with the back bone and risible muscles of the globe—and there is nothing like it; but much as we relish this jovial, this rapid and detergeous way of conveying one's views and impressions, when we would not converse but meditate, we pray for a man's diamond edition of his thought, without the colored illuminations in the margin—the fishes and dragons, and unicorns, the red or the blue ink, but its initial letter in distinct skeleton type, and the whole so clipped and condensed down to the very essence of it, that time will have little to do. We know not but we shall immigrate soon, and would fain take with us all the treasures of the east, and all kinds of *dry*, portable soups, in small tin canisters, which contain whole herds of English beeves, boiled down, will be acceptable.

The difference between this flashing, fitful writing and pure philosophy, is the difference between flame and light. The flame, indeed, yields light, but when we are so near as to observe the flame, we are apt to be incommoded by the heat and smoke. But the sun, that old Platonist, is set so far off in the heavens, that only a genial summer-heat and ineffable day-light can reach us. But many a time, we confess, in wintery weather, we have been glad to forsake the sun-light, and warm us by these Promethean flames.

Carlyle must undoubtedly plead guilty to the charge of mannerism. He not only has his vein, but his peculiar manner of working it. He has a style which can be imitated, and sometimes is an imitator of himself. Every man, though born and bred in the metropolis of the world, will still have some provincialism adhering to him; but in proportion as his aim is simple and earnest, he approaches at once the most ancient and the most modern men. There is no mannerism in the Scriptures. The style of proverbs, and indeed of all *maxims*, whether measured by sentences or by chapters, if they may be said to have any style, is one, and as the expression of one voice, merely an account of the matter by the latest witness. It is one advantage enjoyed by men of science, that they use only formulas which are universal. The common language and the common sense of mankind, it is most uncommon to meet with in the individual. Yet liberty of thought and speech is only liberty to think the universal thought, and speak the universal language of men, instead of being enslaved to a particular mode. Of this universal speech there is very little. It is equable and sure; from a depth within man which is beyond education and prejudice. . . .

Carlyle's works, it is true, have not the stereotyped success which we call classic. They are a rich but inexpensive entertainment, at which we are not concerned lest the host has strained or impoverished himself to feed his guests. It is not the most lasting word, nor the loftiest wisdom, but rather the word which comes last. For his genius it was reserved to give expression to the thoughts which were throbbing in a million breasts. He has plucked the ripest fruit in the public garden; but this fruit already least concerned the tree that bore it, which was rather perfecting the bud at the foot of the leaf stalk. His works are not to be studied, but read with a swift satisfaction. Their flavor and gust is like what poets tell of the froth of wine, which can only be tasted once and hastily. On a review we can never find the pages we had read. The first impression is the truest and the deepest, and there is no reprint, no *double entendre*, so to speak, for the alert reader. Yet they are in some degree true natural products in this respect. All things are but once, and never repeated. The first faint blushes of the morning, gilding the mountain tops, the pale phosphor and saffron-colored clouds do verily transport us to the morning of creation; but what avails it to travel eastward, or look again there an hour hence? We should be as far in the day ourselves, mounting toward our meridian. These works were designed for such complete success that they serve but for a single occasion. It is the luxury of art, when its own instrument is manufactured for each particular and present use. The knife which slices the bread of Jove ceases to be a knife when this service is rendered.

But he is wilfully and pertinaciously unjust, even scurrilous, impolite, ungentlemanly; calls us 'Imbeciles,' 'Dilettants,' 'Philistines,' implying sometimes what would not sound well expressed. If he would adopt the newspaper style, and take back these hard names—but where is the reader who does not derive some benefit from these epithets, applying them to himself? Think not that with each repetition of them there is a fresh overflowing of bile; oh no! Perhaps none at all after the first time, only a faithfulness, the right name being found, to apply it— 'They are the same ones we meant before'—and ofttimes with a genuine sympathy and encouragement expressed. Indeed, there appears in all his writings a hearty and manly sympathy with all misfortune and wretchedness, and not a weak and sniveling one. They who suspect a Mephistophiles, or sneering, satirical devil, under all, have not learned the secret of true humor, which sympathizes with the gods themselves, in view of their grotesque, half-finished creatures.

He is, in fact, the best tempered, and not the least impartial of reviewers. He goes out of his way to do justice to profligates and quacks. There is somewhat even Christian, in the rarest and most peculiar sense, in his universal brotherliness, his simple, child-like endurance, and earnest, honest endeavor, with sympathy for the like. And this fact is not insignificant, that he is almost the only writer of biography, of the lives of men, in modern times. So kind and generous a tribute to the genius of Burns cannot be expected again, and is not needed. We honor him for his noble reverence for Luther, and his patient, almost reverent study of Goethe's genius, anxious that no shadow of his author's meaning escape him for want of trustful attention. There is nowhere else, surely, such determined and generous love of whatever is manly in history. His just appreciation of any, even inferior talent, especially of all sincerity, under whatever guise, and all true men of endeavor, must have impressed every reader. Witness the chapters on Werner, Heyne, even Cagliostro, and others. He is not likely to underrate his man. We are surprised to meet with such a discriminator of kingly qualities in these republican and democratic days, such genuine loyalty all thrown away upon the world.

Carlyle, to adopt his own classification, is himself the hero, as literary man. There is no more notable working-man in England, in Manchester or Birmingham, or the mines round about. We know not how many hours a-day he toils, nor for what wages, exactly, we only know the results for us. We hear through the London fog and smoke the steady systole, diastole, and vibratory hum from, 'Somebody's Works' there; the 'Print Works,' say some; the 'Chemicals,' say others; where something, at any rate, is manufactured which we remember to have seen in the market. This is the place, then. Literature has come to mean to the ears of laboring men, something idle, something cunning and pretty merely, because the nine hundred and ninety-nine really write for fame or for amusement. But as the laborer works, and soberly by the sweat of his brow earns bread for his body, so this man *works* anxiously and *sadly*, to get bread of life, and dispense it. We cannot do better than quote his own estimate of labor from *Sartor Resartus*.

[quotes 'Two men' to 'great darkness', Bk. III, ch. iv, 181–2]

Notwithstanding the very genuine, admirable, and loyal tributes to Burns, Schiller, Goethe, and others, Carlyle is not a critic of poetry. In the book of heroes, Shakspeare, the hero, as poet, comes off rather slimly. His sympathy, as we said, is with the men of endeavor; not using the life got, but still bravely getting their life. 'In fact,' as he says of Cromwell, 'every where we have to notice the decisive, practical *eye* of this man; how he drives toward the practical and practicable; has a genuine insight into what *is* fact.' You must have very stout legs to get noticed at all by him. He is thoroughly English in his love of practical men, and dislike for cant, and ardent enthusiastic heads that are not supported by any legs. He would kindly knock them down that they may regain some vigor by touching their mother earth. We have often wondered how he ever found out Burns, and must still refer a good share of his delight in him to neighborhood and early association. The Lycidas and Comus appearing in *Blackwood's Magazine*, would probably go unread by him, nor lead him to expect a *Paradise Lost*. The condition of England question is a practical one. The condition of England demands a hero, not a poet. Other things demand a poet; the poet answers other demands. Carlyle in London, with this question pressing on him so urgently, sees no occasion for minstrels and rhapsodists there. Kings may have their bards when there are any kings. Homer would *certainly* go a begging there. He lives in Chelsea, not on the plains of Hindostan, nor on the prairies of the West, where settlers are scarce, and a man must at least go *whistling* to himself.

What he says of poetry is rapidly uttered, and suggestive of a thought, rather than the deliberate development of any. He answers your question, What is poetry? by writing a special poem, as that Norse one, for instance, in the *Book of Heroes*, altogether wild and original;— answers your question, What is light? by kindling a blaze which dazzles you, and pales sun and moon, and not as a peasant might, by opening a shutter. And, certainly, you would say that this question never could be answered but by the grandest of poems; yet he has not dull breath and stupidity enough, perhaps, to give the most deliberate and universal answer, such as the fates wring from illiterate and unthinking men. He answers like Thor, with a stroke of his hammer, whose dint makes a valley in the earth's surface.

Carlyle is not a *seer*, but a brave looker-on and *reviewer;* not the most free and catholic observer of men and events, for they are likely to find him preoccupied, but unexpectedly free and catholic when they fall within the focus of his lens. He does not live in the present hour, and read men and books as they occur for his theme, but having chosen this, he directs his studies to this end.

But if he supplies us with arguments and illustrations against himself, we will remember that we may perhaps be convicted of error from the same source—stalking on these lofty reviewer's stilts so far from the green pasturage around. If we look again at his page, we are apt to retract somewhat that we have said. Often a genuine poetic feeling dawns through it, like the texture of the earth seen through the dead grass and leaves in the spring. There is indeed more poetry in this author than criticism on poetry. He often reminds us of the ancient Scald, inspired by the grimmer features of life, dwelling longer on Dante than on Shakspeare. We have not recently met with a more solid and unquestionable piece of poetic work than that episode of 'The Ancient Monk,' in *Past and Present*, at once idyllic, narrative, heroic; a beautiful restoration of a past age. There is nothing like it elsewhere that we know of. *The History of the French Revolution* is a poem, at length got translated into prose; an Iliad, indeed, as he himself has it—'The destructive wrath of Sansculotism: this is what we speak, having unhappily no voice for singing.'

One improvement we could suggest in this last, as indeed in most epics, that he should let in the sun oftener upon his picture. It does not often enough appear, but it is all revolution, the old way of human life turned simply bottom upward, so that when at length we are inadvertently reminded of the 'Brest Shipping,' a St. Domingo colony, and that anybody thinks of owning plantations, and simply turning up the soil there, and that now at length, after some years of this revolution, there is a falling off in the importation of sugar, we feel a queer surprise. Had they not sweetened their water Revolution then? It would be well if there were several chapters headed 'Work for the Mouth'— Revolution-work inclusive, of course—'Altitude of the Sun,' 'State of the Crops and Markets,' 'Meteorological Observations,' 'Attractive Industry,' 'Day Labor,' &c., just to remind the reader that the French peasantry did something beside go without breeches, burn châteaus, get ready knotted cords, and embrace and throttle one another by turns. These things are sometimes hinted at, but they deserve a notice more in proportion to their importance. We want not only a background to the picture, but a ground under the feet also. We remark, too, occasionally, an unphilosophical habit, common enough elsewhere, in Alison's *History of Modern Europe*, for instance, of saying, undoubtedly with effect, that if a straw had not fallen this way or that, why then—but, of course, it is as easy in philosophy to make kingdoms rise and fall as straws. The old adage is as true for our purpose, which says that a miss is as good as a mile. Who shall say how near the man came to being killed who was not killed? If an apple had not fallen then we had never heard of Newton and the law of gravitation; as if they could not have contrived to let fall a pear as well.

The poet is blithe and cheery ever, and as well as nature. Carlyle has not the simple Homeric health of Wordsworth, nor the deliberate philosophic turn of Coleridge, nor the scholastic taste of Landor, but, though sick and under restraint, the constitutional vigor of one of his old Norse heroes, struggling in a lurid light, with Iötuns still, striving to throw the old woman, and 'she was Time'—striving to lift the big cat—and that was 'The Great World-Serpent, which, tail in mouth, girds and keeps up the whole created world.' The smith, though so brawny and tough, I should not call the healthiest man. There is too much shop-work, too great extremes of heat and cold, and incessant ten-pound-ten and thrashing of the anvil, in his life. But the haymaker's is a true sunny perspiration, produced by the extreme of summer heat only, and conversant with the blast of the zephyr, not of the forge-bellows. We know very well the nature of this man's sadness, but we do not know the nature of his gladness. There sits Bull in the court all the year round, with his hoarse bark and discontented growl—not a cross dog, only a canine habit, verging to madness some think—now separated from the shuddering travelers only by the paling, now heard afar in the horizon, even melodious there; baying the moon o' nights, *baying the sun by day*, with his mastiff mouth. He never goes after the cows, nor stretches in the sun, nor plays with the children. Pray give him a longer rope, ye gods, or let him go at large, and never taste raw meat more. . . .

Carlyle speaks of Nature with a certain unconscious pathos for the most part. She is to him a receded but ever memorable splendor, casting still a reflected light over all his scenery. As we read his books here in

New England, where there are potatoes enough, and every man can get his living peacefully and sportively as the birds and bees, and need think no more of that, it seems to us as if by the world he often meant London, at the head of the tide upon the Thames, the sorest place on the face of the earth, the very citadel of conservatism. Possibly a South African village might have furnished a more hopeful, and more exacting audience, or in the silence of the wilderness and the desert, he might have addressed himself more entirely to his true audience posterity.

In his writings, we should say that he, as conspicuously as any, though with little enough expressed or even conscious sympathy, represents the Reformer class, and all the better for not being the acknowledged leader of any. In him the universal plaint is most settled, unappeasable and serious. Until a thousand named and nameless grievances are righted, there will be no repose for him in the lap of nature, or the seclusion of science and literature. By foreseeing it he hastens the crisis in the affairs of England, and is as good as many years added to her history.

As we said, we have no adequate word from him concerning poets—Homer, Shakspeare; nor more, we might add, of Saints—Jesus; nor philosophers—Socrates, Plato; nor mystics—Swedenborg. . . .

To do himself justice, and set some of his readers right, he should give us some transcendent hero at length, to rule his demigods and Titans; develop, perhaps, his reserved and dumb reverence for Christ, not speaking to a London or Church of England audience merely. Let *not* 'sacred silence meditate that sacred matter' forever, but let us have sacred speech and sacred scripture thereon. True reverence is not necessarily dumb, but ofttimes prattling and hilarious as children in the spring. . . .

One more merit in Carlyle, let the subject be what it may, is the freedom of prospect he allows, the entire absence of cant and dogma. He removes many cart-loads of rubbish, and leaves open a broad highway. His writings are all enfenced on the side of the future and the possible. He does not place himself across the passage out of his books, so that none may go freely out, but rather by the entrance, inviting all to come in and go through. No gins, no net-work, no pickets here, to restrain the free thinking reader. In many books called philosophical, we find ourselves running hither and thither, under and through, and sometimes quite unconsciously straddling some imaginary fence-work, which in our clairvoyance we had not noticed, but fortunately, not with such fatal consequences as happen to those birds which fly against a white-washed wall, mistaking it for fluid air. As we proceed the wreck of this dogmatic tissue collects about the organs of our perception, like cobwebs about the muzzles of hunting dogs in dewy mornings. If we look up with such eyes as these authors furnish, we see no heavens, but a low pent-roof of straw or tiles, as if we stood under a shed, with no skylight through which to glimpse the blue.

Carlyle, though he does but inadvertently direct our eyes to the open heavens, nevertheless, lets us wander broadly underneath, and shows them to us reflected in innumerable pools and lakes. We have from him, occasionally, some hints of a possible science of astronomy even, and revelation of heavenly arcana, but nothing definite hitherto.

These volumes contain not the highest, but a very practicable wisdom, which startles and provokes, rather than informs us. Carlyle does not oblige us to think; we have thought enough for him already, but he compels us to act. We accompany him rapidly through an endless gallery of pictures, and glorious reminiscences of experiences unimproved. 'Have you not had Moses and the prophets? Neither will ye be persuaded if one should rise from the dead.' There is no calm philosophy of life here, such as you might put at the end of the Almanac, to hang over the farmer's hearth, how men shall live in these winter, in these summer days. No philosophy, properly speaking, of love, or friendship, or religion, or politics, or education, or nature, or spirit; perhaps a nearer approach to a philosophy of kingship, and of the place of the literary man, than of any thing else. A rare preacher, with prayer, and psalm, and sermon, and benediction, but no contemplation of man's life from serene oriental ground, nor yet from the stirring occidental. No thanksgiving sermon for the holydays, or the Easter vacations, when all men submit to float on the full currents of life. When we see with what spirits, though with little heroism enough, wood-choppers, drovers, and apprentices, take and spend life, playing all day long, sunning themselves, shading themselves, eating, drinking, sleeping, we think that the philosophy of their life written would be such a level natural history as the *Gardener's Calendar*, and the works of the early botanists, inconceivably slow to come to practical conclusions; its premises away off before the first morning light, ere the heather was introduced into the British isles, and no inferences to be drawn during this noon of the day, not till after the remote evening shadows have begun to fall around.

There is no philosophy here for philosophers, only as every man is said to have his philosophy. No system but such as is the man himself; and, indeed, he stands compactly enough. No progress beyond the first assertion and challenge, as it were with trumpet blast. One thing is certain, that we had best be doing something in good earnest, henceforth forever; that's an indispensable philosophy. The before impossible precept, *'know thyself,'* he translates into the partially possible one, *'know what thou canst work at.'* *Sartor Resartus* is, perhaps, the sunniest and most philosophical, as it is the most autobiographical of his works, in which he drew most largely on the experience of his youth. But we miss everywhere a calm depth, like a lake, even stagnant, and must submit to rapidity and whirl, as on skates, with all kinds of skillful and antic motions, sculling, sliding, cutting punch-bowls and rings, forward and backward. The talent is very nearly equal to the genius. Sometimes it would be preferable to wade slowly through a Serbonian bog, and feel the juices of the meadow. We should say that he had not speculated far, but faithfully, living up to it. He lays all the stress still on the most elementary and initiatory maxims, introductory to philosophy. It is the experience of the religionist. He pauses at such a quotation as, 'It is only with renunciation that life, properly speaking, can be said to begin;' or, 'Doubt of any sort cannot be removed except by action;' or, 'Do the duty which lies nearest thee.' The chapters entitled, 'The Everlasting No,' and 'The Everlasting Yea,' contain what you might call the religious experience of his hero. In the latter, he assigns to him these words, brief, but as significant as any we remember in this author:— 'One BIBLE I know, of whose plenary inspiration doubt is not so much as possible; nay, with my own eyes I saw the God's-hand writing it: thereof all other Bibles are but leaves.' This belongs to 'The Everlasting Yea;' yet he lingers unaccountably in 'The Everlasting No,' under the negative pole. 'Truth!' he still cries with Teüfelsdrock, 'though the heavens crush me for following her: no falsehood! though a whole celestial Lubberland were the price of apostacy.' Again, 'Living without God in the world, of God's light I was not utterly bereft; if my as yet sealed eyes, with their unspeakable longing, could nowhere see Him, nevertheless, in my heart He was present, and His heaven-written law still stood legible and sacred there.' Again, 'Ever from that time, [*the era of his Protest,*] the temper of my misery was changed: not fear or whining sorrow was it, but indignation and grim, fire-eyed defiance.' And in the 'Centre of Indifference,' as editor, he observes, that 'it was no longer a quite hopeless unrest,' and then proceeds, not in his best style, 'For the fire-baptized soul, long so scathed and thunder-riven, here feels its own freedom, which feeling is its Baphometic Baptism: the citadel of its whole kingdom it has thus gained by assault, and will keep inexpungable; outward from which the remaining dominions, not, indeed, without hard battling, will doubtless by degrees be conquered and pacificated.'

Beside some philosophers of larger vision, Carlyle stands like an honest, half-despairing boy, grasping at some details only of their world systems. Philosophy, certainly, is some account of truths, the fragments and very insignificant parts of which man will practice in this workshop; truths infinite and in harmony with infinity; in respect to which the very objects and ends of the so-called practical philosopher, will be mere propositions, like the rest. It would be no reproach to a philosopher, that he knew the future better than the past, or even than the present. It is better worth knowing. He will prophecy, tell what is to be, or in other words, what alone is, under appearances, laying little stress on the boiling of the pot, or the Condition of England question. He has no more to do with the condition of England than with her national debt, which a vigorous generation would not inherit. The philosopher's conception of things will, above all, be truer than other men's, and his philosophy will subordinate all the circumstances of life. To live like a philosopher, is to live, not foolishly, like other men, but wisely, and according to universal laws. In this, which was the ancient sense, we think there has been no philosopher in modern times. The wisest and most practical men of recent history, to whom this epithet has been hastily applied, have lived comparatively meagre lives, of conformity and tradition, such as their fathers transmitted to them. But a man may live in what style he can. Between earth and heaven, there is room for all kinds. If he take counsel of fear and prudence, he has already failed. One who believed, by his very constitution, some truth which a few words express, would make a revolution never to be forgotten in this world; for it needs but a fraction of truth to found houses and empires on.

However, such distinctions as poet and philosopher, do not much assist our final estimate of a man; we do not lay much stress on them. 'A man's a man for a' that.' If Carlyle does not take two steps in philosophy, are there any who take three? Philosophy having crept clinging to the rocks, so far, puts out its feelers many ways in vain. It would be hard to surprise him by the relation of any important human experience, but in some nook or corner of his works, you will find that this, too, was sometimes dreamed of in his philosophy.

To sum up our most serious objections, in a few words, we should say that Carlyle indicates a depth,—and we mean not impliedly, but distinctly,—which he neglects to fathom. We want to know more about that which he wants to know as well. If any luminous star, or undissolvable nebula, is visible from his station, which is not visible from ours, the interests of science require that the fact be communicated to us. The universe expects every man to do his duty in his parallel of latitude. We want to hear more of his inmost life; his hymn and prayer, more; his elegy and eulogy, less; that he should speak more from his character, and less from his talent; communicate centrally with his readers, and not by a side; that he should say what he believes, without suspecting that men disbelieve it, out of his never-misunderstood nature. Homer and Shakspeare speak directly and confidently to us. The confidence implied in the unsuspicious tone of the world's worthies, is a great and encouraging fact. Dig up some of the earth you stand on, and show that. If he gave us religiously the meagre results of his experience, his style would be less picturesque and diversified, but more attractive and impressive. His genius can cover all the land with gorgeous palaces, but the reader does not abide in them, but pitches his tent rather in the desert and on the mountain peak.

When we look about for something to quote, as the fairest specimen of the man, we confess that we labor under an unusual difficulty; for his philosophy is so little of the proverbial or sentential kind, and opens so gradually, rising insensibly from the reviewer's level, and developing its thought completely and in detail, that we look in vain for the brilliant passages, for point and antithesis, and must end by quoting his works entire. What in a writer of less breadth would have been the proposition which would have bounded his discourse, his column of victory, his Pillar of Hercules, and *ne plus ultra*, is in Carlyle frequently the same thought unfolded; no Pillar of Hercules, but a considerable prospect, north and south, along the Atlantic coast. There are other pillars of Hercules, like beacons and light-houses, still further in the horizon, toward Atlantis, set up by a few ancient and modern travelers; but, so far as this traveler goes, he clears and colonizes, and all the surplus population of London is bound thither at once. What we would quote is, in fact, his vivacity, and not any particular wisdom or sense, which last is ever synonymous with sentence, [*sententia,*] as in his contemporaries, Coleridge, Landor and Wordsworth.

We have not attempted to discriminate between his works, but have rather regarded them all as one work, as is the man himself. We have not examined so much as remembered them. To do otherwise, would have required a more indifferent, and perhaps even less just review, than the present. The several chapters were thankfully received, as they came out, and now we find it impossible to say which was best; perhaps each was best in its turn. They do not require to be remembered by chapters —that is a merit—but are rather remembered as a well-known strain, reviving from time to time, when it had nearly died away, and always inspiring us to worthier and more persistent endeavors.

In his last work, *The Letters and Speeches of Oliver Cromwell*, Carlyle has added a chapter to the history of England; has actually written a chapter of her history, and, in comparison with this, there seems to be no other,—this, and the thirty thousand or three hundred thousand pamphlets in the British Museum, and that is all. This book is a practical comment on Universal History. What if there were a British Museum in Athens and Babylon, and nameless cities! It throws light on the history of the Iliad and the labors of Pisistratus. History is, then, an account of memorable events that have sometime transpired, and not an incredible and confused fable, quarters for scholars merely, or a gymnasium for poets and orators. We may say that he has dug up a hero, who was buried alive in his battle-field, hauled him out of his cairn, on which every passer had cast a pamphlet. We had heard of their digging up Arthurs before to be sure they were there; and, to be sure they were there, their bones, seven feet of them; but they had to bury them again. Others have helped to make known Shakspeare, Milton, Herbert, to give a name to such treasures as we all possessed; but, in this instance, not only a lost character has been restored to our imaginations, but palpably a living body, as it were, to our senses, to wear and sustain the former. His Cromwell's restoration, if England will read it faithfully, and addressed to New England too. Every reader will make his own application.

To speak deliberately, we think that in this instance, vague rumor and a vague history have for the first time been subjected to a rigid scrutiny, and the wheat, with at least novel fidelity, sifted from the chaff; so that there remain for result,—First, *Letters and Speeches of Oliver Cromwell*, now for the first time read or readable, and well nigh as complete as the fates will permit; secondly, *Deeds*, making an imperfect and fragmentary life, which may, with probability, be fathered upon him; thirdly, this wreck of an ancient picture, the present editor has, to the best of his ability, restored, sedulously scraping away the daubings of successive bunglers, and endeavoring to catch the spirit of the artist himself. Not the worst, nor a barely possible, but for once the most favorable construction has been put upon this evidence of the life of a man, and the result is a picture of the ideal Cromwell, the perfection of the painter's art. Possibly this was the actual man. At any rate, this only can contain the actual hero. We confess that when we read these Letters and Speeches, unquestionably Cromwell's, with open and confident mind, we get glimpses occasionally of a grandeur and heroism, which even this editor has not proclaimed. His 'Speeches' make us forget modern orators, and might go right into the next edition of the Old Testament, without alteration. Cromwell *was* another sort of man than *we* had taken him to be. These Letters and Speeches have supplied the lost key to his character. . . .

And all along, between the Letters and Speeches, as readers well remember, he has ready such a fresh top-of-the-morning salutation as conjures up the spirits of those days, and men go marching over English sward, not wired skeletons, but with firm, elastic muscles, and clang of armor on their thighs, if they wore swords, or the twang of psalms and canticles on their lips. His blunt, 'Who are you?' put to the shadowy ghosts of history, they vanish into deeper obscurity than ever. Vivid phantasmagorian pictures of what is transpiring in England in the meanwhile, there are, not a few, better than if you had been there to see.

All of Carlyle's works might well enough be embraced under the title of one of them, a good specimen brick, *On Heroes, Hero-worship, and the Heroic in History*. Of this department, he is the Chief Professor in the World's University, and even leaves Plutarch behind. Such intimate and living, such loyal and generous sympathy with the heroes of history, not one in one age only, but forty in forty ages, such an unparalleled reviewing and greeting of all past worth, with exceptions, to be sure,—but exceptions were the rule, before,—it was, indeed, to make this the age of review writing, as if now one period of the human story were completing itself, and getting its accounts settled. This soldier has told the stories with new emphasis, and will be a memorable hander-down of fame to posterity. And with what wise discrimination he has selected his men, with reference both to his own genius and to theirs: Mahomet,—Dante,—Cromwell,—Voltaire,—Johnson,—Burns, —Goethe,—Richter,—Schiller,—Mirabeau; could any of these have been spared? These we wanted to hear about. We have not as commonly the cold and refined judgment of the scholar and critic merely, but something more human and affecting. These eulogies have the glow and warmth of friendship. There is sympathy not with mere fames, and formless, incredible things, but with kindred men,—not transiently, but life-long he has walked with them.

The attitude of some, in relation to Carlyle's love of heroes, and men of the sword, reminds us of the procedure at the anti-slavery meetings, when some member, being warmed, begins to speak with more latitude than usual of the Bible or the Church, for a few prudent and devout ones to spring a prayer upon him, as the saying is; that is, propose suddenly to unite in prayer, and so solemnize the minds of the audience, or dismiss them at once; which may oftener be to interrupt a true prayer by most gratuitous profanity. But the spring of this trap, we are glad to learn, has grown somewhat rusty, and is not so sure of late.

No doubt, some of Carlyle's worthies, should they ever return to earth, would find themselves unpleasantly put upon their good behavior, to sustain their characters; but if he can return a man's life more perfect to our hands, than it was left at his death, following out the design of its author, we shall have no great cause to complain. We do not want a Daguerreotype likeness. All biography is the life of Adam,—a much-experienced man,—and time withdraws something partial from the story of every individual, that the historian may supply something general. If these virtues were not in this man, perhaps they are in his biographer,—no fatal mistake. Really, in any other sense, we never do, nor desire to, come at the historical man,—unless we rob his grave, that is the nearest approach. Why did he die, then? *He* is with his bones, surely.

No doubt, Carlyle has a propensity to *exaggerate* the heroic in history, that is, he creates you an ideal hero rather than another thing, he has most of that material. This we allow in all its senses, and in one narrower sense it is not so convenient. Yet what were history if he did not exaggerate it? How comes it that history never has to wait for facts, but for a man to write it? The ages may go on forgetting the facts never so long, he can remember two for every one forgotten. The musty records of history, like the catacombs, contain the perishable remains, but only in the breast of genius are embalmed the souls of heroes. There is very little of what is called criticism here; it is love and reverence, rather, which deal with qualities not relatively, but absolutely great; for whatever is admirable in a man is something infinite, to which we cannot set bounds. These sentiments allow the mortal to die, the immortal and divine to survive. There is something antique, even in his style of treating his subject, reminding us that Heroes and Demi-gods, Fates and Furies, still exist, the common man is nothing to him, but after death the hero is apotheosized and has a place in heaven, as in the religion of the Greeks.

Exaggeration! was ever any virtue attributed to a man without exaggeration? was ever any vice, without infinite exaggeration? Do we not exaggerate ourselves to ourselves, or do we recognize ourselves for the actual men we are? Are we not all great men? Yet what are we actually to speak of? We live by exaggeration, what else is it to anticipate more than we enjoy? The lightning is an exaggeration of the light. Exaggerated history is poetry, and truth referred to a new standard. To a small man every greater is an exaggeration. He who cannot exaggerate is not qualified to utter truth. No truth we think was ever expressed but with this sort of emphasis, so that for the time there seemed to be no other. Moreover, you must speak loud to those who are hard of hearing, and so you acquire a habit of shouting to those who are not. By an immense exaggeration we appreciate our Greek poetry and philosophy, and Egyptian ruins; our Shakspeares and Miltons, our Liberty and Christianity. We give importance to this hour over all other hours. We do not live by justice, but by grace. As the sort of justice which concerns us in our daily intercourse is not that administered by the judge, so the historical justice which we prize is not arrived at by nicely balancing the evidence. In order to appreciate any, even the humblest man, you must first, by some good fortune, have acquired a sentiment of admiration, even of reverence, for him, and there never were such exaggerators as these. Simple admiration for a hero renders a juster verdict than the wisest criticism, which necessarily degrades what is high to its own level. There is no danger in short of saying too much in praise of one man, provided you can say more in praise of a better man. If by exaggeration a man can create for us a hero, where there was nothing but dry bones before, we will thank him, and let Dryasdust administer historical justice. This is where a true history properly begins, when some genius arises, who can turn the dry and musty records into poetry. As we say, looking to the future, that what is best is truest, so, in one sense, we may say looking into the past, for the only past that we are to look at, must also be future to us. The great danger is not of excessive partiality or sympathy with one, but of a shallow justice to many, in which, after all, none gets his deserts. Who has not experienced that praise is truer than naked justice? As if man were to be the judge of his fellows, and should repress his rising sympathy with the prisoner at the bar, considering the many honest men abroad, whom he had never countenanced.

To try him by the German rule of referring an author to his own standard, we will quote the following from Carlyle's remarks on history, and leave the reader to consider how far his practice has been consistent with his theory.

Truly, if History is Philosophy teaching by experience, the writer fitted to compose history, is hitherto an unknown man. The experience itself would require all knowledge to record it, were the All-wisdom needful for such Philosophy as would interpret it, to be had for asking. Better were it that mere earthly historians should lower such pretensions, more suitable for omniscience than for human science; and aiming only at some picture of the things acted, which picture itself, will at best be a poor approximation, leave the inscrutable purport of them an acknowledged secret; or, at most, in reverent Faith, far different from that teaching of Philosophy, pause over the mysterious vestiges of Him, whose path is in the great deep of Time, whom history indeed reveals, but only all History and in Eternity, will clearly reveal.

Who lives in London to tell this generation who have been the great men of our race? We have read that on some exposed place in the city of Geneva, they have fixed a brazen indicater for the use of travelers, with the names of the mountain summits in the horizon marked upon it, 'so that by taking sight across the index you can distinguish them at once. You will not mistake Mont Blanc, if you see him, but until you get accustomed to the panorama, you may easily mistake one of his court for the king.' It stands there a piece of mute brass, that seems nevertheless to know in what vicinity it is: and there perchance it will stand, when the nation that placed it there has passed away, still in sympathy with the mountains, forever discriminating in the desert.

So, we may say, stands this man, pointing as long as he lives, in obedience to some spiritual magnetism, to the summits in the historical horizon, for the guidance of his fellows.

Truly, our greatest blessings are very cheap. To have our sunlight without paying for it, without any duty levied,—to have our poet there in England, to furnish us entertainment, and what is better provocation, from year to year, all our lives long, to make the world seem richer for us, the age more respectable, and life better worth the living,—all without expense of acknowledgment even, but silently accepted out of the east, like morning light as a matter of course.

BOURNEMOUTH COLLEGE
OF TECHNOLOGY

COLLEGE LIBRARY

22. Edgar Allan Poe on Thomas Carlyle

1843, 1846, 1849

Criticisms of Thomas Carlyle by Edgar Allan Poe (1809–49).
The extracts are taken from *The Complete Works of Edgar Allan Poe*,
ed. James A. Harrison (New York, 1902). The first extract is from
an essay on William Ellery Channing, XI, 176–7 and the next two
are from 'Marginalia', XVI, 99–101 and 175.

(*a*)

Mr. Tennyson is quaint only; he is never, as some have supposed him,
obscure—except, indeed, to the uneducated, whom he does not address.
Mr. Carlyle, on the other hand, is obscure only; he is seldom, as some
have imagined him, quaint. So far he is right; for although quaintness,
employed by a man of judgment and genius, may be made auxiliary
to a *poem*, whose true thesis is beauty, and beauty alone, it is grossly,
and even ridiculously, out of place in a work of prose. But in his
obscurity it is scarcely necessary to say that he is wrong. Either a man
intends to be understood, or he does not. If he write a book which he
intends *not* to be understood, we shall be very happy indeed not to
understand it; but if he write a book which he means to be understood,
and, in this book, be at all possible pains to prevent us from understanding it, we can only say he is an ass—and this, to be brief, is our
private opinion of Mr. Carlyle, which we now take the liberty of
making public.

(*b*)

I have not the slightest faith in Carlyle. In ten years—possibly in five—
he will be remembered only as a butt for sarcasm. His linguistic Euphuisms might very well have been taken as prima facie evidence of his
philosophic ones; they were the froth which indicated, first, the shallow-
ness, and secondly, the confusion of the waters. I would blame no man
of sense for leaving the works of Carlyle unread, merely on account of
these Euphuisms; for it might be shown *a priori* that no man capable of
producing a definite impression upon his age or race, could or would

commit himself to such inanities and insanities. The book about 'Hero-Worship'—is it possible that it ever excited a feeling beyond contempt? *No* hero-worshipper can possess anything within himself. That man is no man who stands in awe of his fellow-man. Genius regards genius with respect—with even enthusiastic admiration—but there is nothing of worship in the admiration, for it springs from a thorough cognizance of the one admired—from a perfect *sympathy*, the result of the cogniz-ance; and it is needless to say, that sympathy and worship are antagonis-tic. Your hero-worshippers, for example—what do they know about Shakspeare? They worship him—rant about him—lecture about him—about *him, him*, and nothing else—for no other reason than that he is utterly beyond their comprehension. They have arrived at an idea of his greatness from the pertinacity with which men have called him great. As for their own opinion about him—they really have none at all. In general the very smallest of mankind are the class of men-worshippers. *Not one* out of this class have ever accomplished anything beyond a very contemptible mediocrity.

Carlyle, however, has rendered an important service (to posterity, at least) in pushing rant and cant to that degree of excess which inevit-ably induces reaction. Had he not appeared we might have gone on for yet another century, Emerson-izing in prose, Wordsworth-izing in poetry, and Fourier-izing in philosophy, Wilson-izing in criticism—Hudson-izing and Tom O'Bedlam-izing in everything. The author of the *Sartor Resartus*, however, has overthrown the various arguments of his own order, by a personal *reductio ad absurdum*. Yet an Olympiad, perhaps, and the whole horde will be swept bodily from the memory of man—or be remembered only when we have occasion to talk of such fantastic tricks as, erewhile, were performed by the Abderites.

(c)
The next work of Carlyle will be entitled *Bow-Wow*, and the title-page will have a motto from the opening chapter of the Koran: 'There is *no* error in this Book.'

23. John Stuart Mill's reply to Carlyle, *Examiner*

13 May 1848, 307–8

John Stuart Mill's letter in the *Examiner* was an answer to Carlyle's
'Repeal of the Union', which appeared in the same magazine two
weeks earlier, April 29, signed C.

Mill's letter marks the beginning of the slow erosion of feeling
among intellectuals such as Mill, Arnold, and Clough toward
Carlyle. It was, of course, to culminate in a landslide of hostile
criticism with the publication of *On the Negro Question* (December
1849) and the *Latter-Day Pamphlets* (1850). Of importance, however, is the fact that Mill's disenchantment with Carlyle's Messianism comes a good year and one-half before the usually accepted
date for Carlyle's 'literary madness', the publication of the
Pamphlets. See Introduction, p. 19.

Sir,—In your last week's paper you published a dissertation by a writer
whom, even if you had not named him, it would have been impossible
to mistake, expressive of his judgment on the question of Irish Repeal.
Will you permit one of that writer's earliest admirers to express,
through the same medium, the grounds on which he feels compelled
to declare unqualified dissent from the judgment thus promulgated?

Let me premise that I am not an Irishman, but an Englishman; that
I do not desire Repeal, but, on the contrary, should regard it as a misfortune to all concerned. It is good government that should be agitated
for, not separate government: but separation is better than bad government; and I entirely sympathize in the indignation which an Irishman
is entitled to feel at the reasons given by your correspondent for refusing
it.

The doctrine of your correspondent is (to quote his own words)
that 'the Destinies have laid upon England a heavier, terribler job of
labour than any people has been saddled with in these generations'—

no other than that of 'conquering Anarchy:' that this, which is 'England's work, appointed her by the so-called Destinies and Divine Providence,' cannot go on unless Ireland is either English, or in English hands; and that consequently the repeal of the Union is 'flatly forbidden by the laws of the universe.'

This is a new phasis of the Hebrew prophet of these later days, the Ezekiel of England. The spirit of his prophesying is quite changed. Instead of telling of the sins and errors of England, and warning her of 'wrath to come,' as he has been wont to do, he preaches the divine Messiahship of England, proclaims her the prime minister of Omnipotence on this earth, commissioned to reduce it all (or as much of it as is convenient to herself) into order and harmony, or at all events, under that pretext, into submission, even into 'slavery,' under her own power —will it or will it not.

When an assumption of this sort is coolly made, and the already ample self-conceit of John Bull encouraged to invest itself with the imaginary dignity of an appointed minister of 'the laws of the universe,' the proper answer would seem to be simply to deny the premises. Where is the evidence that England has received any such mandate from the supreme powers? Where are her credentials? By what signs has she shown that the 'conquering of anarchy' is the work specially appointed to her from above?

If the test is to be (and one cannot imagine your correspondent appealing to any other), her having given proof of the *capacity* to do it, it so happens that England is precisely the one country among all others, which has had the opportunity of showing, and has conclusively shown, that she has *not* that capacity. For five centuries, to speak within bounds, has this very corner of earth in question, this Ireland, been given over to her by the 'destinies and divine providences,' as a test of what capacity she has for reducing chaos into order. For five centuries has she had Ireland under her absolute, resistless power, to show what she could do in the way of 'conquering anarchy'—and the result is the most total, disastrous, ignominious failure yet known to history. No other nation ever had such an opportunity for so prolonged a period, and made such a use of it. The Romans were in many respects barbarians, yet the Gauls, within a century after being conquered by them, were a civilized people; and the most recalcitrant of all subjects with whom they had to deal, the people who then, as now, had the strongest natural tendency to anarchy of any in Europe, the Iberian Spaniards, in 150 years after the conquest were perfectly peaceable, and far more civilized than the Romans themselves were when they conquered them. Mahomet, one of your correspondent's heroes, was a savage, and a leader of savages; he lived in one of the worst times of the world's history, yet in a century after his death the most civilized monarchy in the western world, one which kept arts, letters, and commerce alive when they seemed to have perished everywhere else, had been founded at Grenada by the descendants of his wild Arabs. These may be called conquerors of anarchy. But England! and in Ireland! For the first four and a half of her five centuries she had not so much as the wish to do aught but oppress and trample on Ireland for her own supposed benefit. I waive penal laws and all controversial topics, but even in the eighteenth century she purposely and avowedly crushed the nascent manufacturers of Ireland (the hopeful germ of so much that Ireland still needs), lest they should compete with her own. And there was not one of her statesmen who would not have thought it disgracefully unpatriotic to have acted otherwise. This is no peculiar reproach to England; it was the infernal spirit of that time—a time at which England, now the liberator of the negro slave, made wars and treaties for the sake of Assiento contracts for supplying negroes to be worked to death in Spanish America. It is to the honour of England that she was the first to cast off this spirit: and during the present generation, the policy of England towards Ireland has been, in point of intention, as upright and even as generous as was consistent with the inveterate English habit of making the interest of the aristocracy and of the landlords the first consideration. As between the two countries, nothing can now be more disinterested than the policy of England. It is a pity we should be obliged to add, nothing more imbecile; more devoid of plan, or purpose, of ideas, of practical resource. Omitting former times, we had, two years ago, what may prove to have been a last opportunity of regenerating Ireland. A terrible calamity quelled all active opposition to our government, and Ireland was once more a *tabula rasa*, on which we might have inscribed what we pleased. This was an occasion for English politicians to show what they had in them. Here was a field to exercise this divine gift of bringing chaos into order. Whatever ideas they had, they must have then displayed; and it proved that they had none. They spent ten millions in effecting what seemed impossible—in making Ireland worse than before. They demoralized and disorganized what little of rational industry the country contained; and the only permanent thing with which they endowed Ireland, was the only curse which her evil destiny seemed previously to have spared her—a bad poor law.

The eternal laws of justice, which one might have expected that your correspondent at least would have stood champion for, will not permit that a country which has for five hundred years had the power to make what it pleased of another, and has used that power as England has done, and which has no more idea now, than it had 500 years ago, how to make any good use of the power, should now—when its unhappy dependent, weary of such government, declares that it will try what can be done by and for itself—should now say to the dependent, I am appointed to improve and civilize you, and rather than let go my hold of you, I will make you suffer 'a doom that makes me shudder.' *You*, appointed! the dependent country may well retort; then why did you not set about it before? What proof do you give that you mean to attempt it now? And even if you do, has not your capacity, both long since and down to this very hour, been weighed in the balance and found wanting.

There might be somewhat to be said for a pretension of this sort, if made in behalf of England by a Cromwell. If courage and capacity of the highest order, proved through a long period of confusion, in which capacity of every sort rose to the top, had invested some eminent ruler of this island with a temporary dictatorship, thereby enabling him more effectually and speedily to clear away all obstacles to future progress, and erect on the ground thus cleared an enduring edifice of good government, and if every part of his conduct steadily manifested that such was really his purpose, I for one should have nothing to object, if such a ruler claimed it as his duty, and consequently his right, having already Ireland under his power, to do a similar good work for it also; nor is it likely that either the duty or the right would in such case be gainsaid by Ireland itself. But at present the individual in whom England is personified, and who is to regard himself as the chosen instrument of heaven for making Ireland what it ought to be, and is encouraged to carry fire and sword through Ireland, if that assumption should be disputed, is—Lord John Russell!

In regard to the 150,000,000 of subjects whom your correspondent says that the English nation has to care for; it is quite true that in India, having to do, not with 'anarchy' (save in some passing exceptional case, like that of the Sikhs), but with a people inured from numberless generations to submission, the English nation does contrive to govern them some degrees better than they were governed by their tyrannical or incapable native despots. And inasmuch as England was able to do this in spite of Napoleon and of united Europe, she could probably continue to do so in spite of Ireland. As for the remainder of the 150,000,000 (except the comparatively insignificant negro colonies), I am yet to learn that England does any one thing for them which they could not do better for themselves; or that her good government of them consists, when at the best, in anything better than in leaving them alone. With respect to the 'world just now fallen into bottomless anarchy,' and which your correspondent seems to think may expect to be helped out of it by England, is not this the case for saying, 'Physician, heal thyself!' The quellers of anarchy among the English ruling classes will have work enough of that sort to do at home, unless the author of *Past and Present* is a false prophet. With what sort of mental furniture they are fitted out for doing it, we have had some recent specimens in the childish panic of a few days ago, the childish exultation when the panic was over, and that precious proposal from the leaders of all the parties in the state for a 'Public Order Memorial'—a thing to convulse gods and men with 'unextinguishable laughter.' These sages are hardly yet fairly *in* the wood, when they begin to holloa as if they were already out of it.

No, sir: rely on it, that England has no mission, just now, to keep other nations out of anarchy; but on the contrary, will have to learn, from the experience which other nations are now in a way of acquiring, the means by which alone it can henceforth be averted from herself. And your correspondent, of all persons, might have been expected to acknowledge that there is not one of the working men and women now in conference with Louis Blanc at the Luxembourg on the 'organization of labour,' who is not a degree nearer to the overcoming of this difficulty than Lord John Russell or Sir Robert Peel; since those at least know what the problem is, and (however crude and wild their present notions are) place their hopes in attaining a rational and peaceful solution of it, while the Englishmen place theirs in nothing but in crushing it down, and preventing it from being mooted at all. Before I cease to intrude on your space, let me be permitted to express the opinion that Europe, and especially France, which are accused, and by your correspondent, of rushing headlong into anarchy, are in reality affording a proof, and a most precious and salutary one, how utterly repugnant all approach to anarchy is to the present state of the European mind. For six weeks after the revolution there was no police, no organized force, the city guard was annihilated, the troops banished, the Government had no means of making itself obeyed but by argument and persuasion; nothing apparently stood between Paris and anarchy;

yet nothing worse is known to have happened than a few forced illuminations in honour of trees of liberty; and even of common offences, it is said that a smaller number were committed than in ordinary times. Most remarkable is it, that so far from being an anarchical spirit, the spirit which is now abroad is one which demands *too much* government; it is wholly a spirit of association, of organization; even the most extreme anti-property doctrines take the form of Communism, of Fourierism, of some scheme not for emancipating human life from external restraint, but for subjecting it to much more restraint than it has heretofore been subject to, or ever ought to be; and the apostles of those doctrines rely avowedly on moral force and on bringing the rest of mankind to their opinion by experiment and discussion.

I am, sir, your obedient servant,

May 5, 1848   M.

'OCCASIONAL DISCOURSE ON THE NEGRO QUESTION'

1849

24. Introductory paragraph to the full text, *DeBow's Review*

1850, viii, 527

DeBow's Review, begun in 1846, lasted after many suspensions until 1884. The Virginian, James D. B. DeBow, its founder, later took a chair as Professor of Political Economy at the University of New Orleans. His journal furnished economic analyses of the *antebellum* South, and offered a platform for such pro-slavers as George Fitzhugh (No. 30), William Gilmore Simms, William Grayson, and others.

This following paper appeared in a late number of *Fraser's London Magazine*. The style and manner are plainly those of Thomas Carlyle, to whom it is attributed. It is a piece of pungent satire, upon the whole body of pseudo-philanthropists, who, within the last few years, have been a curse to our own country, as well as to England. The West India question is, for the first time, put in its true light before the English people, and it will much surprise us if a reaction, in favor of common sense, is not the result. The reader will not allow the quaint style, and the odd conceits of Mr. Carlyle, to prevent him from giving an attentive perusal to the matter. We are sure that he will agree with us, that the case of Quashee is disposed of with a master hand, and left in its nakedness, without a single prop or support. When British writers can so speak, it is time for Northern fanaticism to pause and reflect.

25. John Greenleaf Whittier on 'Thomas Carlyle on the Slave Question', *Literary Recreations and Miscellanies*

Boston, 1854

Whittier (1807–92), the New England Quaker poet, like Carlyle, was a reformer and a self-educated man. A devoted abolitionist, he became indignant when he read Carlyle's attacks upon the West Indian Negro.

A late number of *Fraser's Magazine* contains an article bearing the unmistakable impress of the Anglo-German peculiarities of Thomas Carlyle, entitled, 'An Occasional Discourse on the Negro Question,' which would be interesting as a literary curiosity were it not in spirit and tendency so unspeakably wicked as to excite in every rightminded reader a feeling of amazement and disgust. With a hard, brutal audacity, a blasphemous irreverence, and a sneering mockery which would do honor to the devil of *Faust*, it takes issue with the moral sense of mankind and the precepts of Christianity. Having ascertained that the exports of sugar and spices from the West Indies have diminished since emancipation,—and that the negroes, having worked, as they believed, quite long enough without wages, now refuse to work for the planters without higher pay than the latter, with the thriftless and evil habits of slavery still clinging to them, can afford to give,—the author considers himself justified in denouncing negro emancipation as one of the 'shams' which he was specially sent into this world to belabor. Had he confined himself to simple abuse and caricature of the self-denying and Christian abolitionists of England—'the broad-brimmed philanthropists of Exeter Hall'—there would have been small occasion for noticing his splenetic and discreditable production. Doubtless there is a cant of philanthropy —the alloy of human frailty and folly—in the most righteous reforms, which is a fair subject for the indignant sarcasm of a professed hater of shows and falsities. Whatever is hollow and hypocritical in politics, morals, or religion, comes very properly within the scope of his mockery, and we bid him God speed in plying his satirical lash upon it.

Impostures and frauds of all kinds deserve nothing better than detection and exposure. Let him blow them up to his heart's content, as Daniel did the image of Bell and the Dragon.

But our author, in this matter of negro slavery, has undertaken to apply his explosive pitch and rosin, not to the affectation of humanity, but to humanity itself. He mocks at pity, scoffs at all who seek to lessen the amount of pain and suffering, sneers at and denies the most sacred rights, and mercilessly consigns an entire class of the children of his Heavenly Father to the doom of compulsory servitude. He vituperates the poor black man with a coarse brutality which would do credit to a Mississippi slave driver, or a renegade Yankee dealer in human cattle on the banks of the Potomac. His rhetoric has a flavor of the slavepen and auction-block—vulgar, unmanly, indecent, a scandalous outrage upon good taste and refined feeling—which at once degrades the author and insults his readers.

He assumes (for he is one of those sublimated philosophers who reject the Baconian system of induction and depend upon intuition without recourse to facts and figures) that the emancipated class in the West India islands are universally idle, improvident, and unfit for freedom; that God created them to be the servants and slaves of their 'born lords,' the white men, and designed them to grow sugar, coffee, and spices for their masters, instead of raising pumpkins and yams for themselves; and that, if they will not do this, 'the beneficent whip' should be again employed to compel them. He adopts, in speaking of the black class, the lowest slang of vulgar prejudice. 'Black Quashee,' sneers the gentlemanly philosopher,—'black Quashee, if he will not help in bringing out the spices, will get himself made a slave again, (which state will be a little less ugly than his present one,) and with beneficent whip, since other methods avail not, will be compelled to work.'

It is difficult to treat sentiments so atrocious and couched in such offensive language with any thing like respect. Common sense and unperverted conscience revolt instinctively against them. The doctrine they inculcate is that which underlies all tyranny and wrong of man towards man. It is that under which 'the creation groaneth and travaileth unto this day.' It is as old as sin; the perpetual argument of strength against weakness, of power against right; that of the Greek philosopher, that the barbarians, being of an inferior race, were born to be slaves to the Greeks; and of the infidel Hobbes, that every man, being by nature at war with every other man, has a perpetual right to reduce him to servitude if he has the power. It is the cardinal doctrine of what John

Quincy Adams has very properly styled 'the Satanic school of philosophy'—the ethics of an old Norse sea robber or an Arab plunderer of caravans. It is as widely removed from the 'sweet humanities' and unselfish benevolence of Christianity as the faith and practice of the East India Thug or the New Zealand cannibal.

Our author does not, however, take us altogether by surprise. He has before given no uncertain intimations of the point towards which his philosophy was tending. In his brilliant essay upon Francia of Paraguay, for instance, we find him entering with manifest satisfaction and admiration into the details of his hero's tyranny. In his *Letters and Speeches of Oliver Cromwell*—in half a dozen pages of savage and almost diabolical sarcasm directed against the growing humanity of the age, the 'rose-pink sentimentalisms,' and squeamishness which shudders at the sight of blood and infliction of pain—he prepares the way for a justification of the massacre of Drogheda. More recently he has intimated that the extermination of the Celtic race is the best way of settling the Irish question; and that the enslavement and forcible transportation of her poor, to labor under armed taskmasters in the colonies, is the only rightful and proper remedy for the political and social evils of England. In the 'Discourse on Negro Slavery' we see this devilish philosophy in full bloom. The gods, he tells us, are with the strong. Might has a divine right to rule—blessed are the crafty of brain and strong of hand! Weakness is crime. '*Væ victis!*' as Brennus said when he threw his sword into the scale—Woe to the conquered! The negro is weaker in intellect than his 'born lord,' the white man, and has no right to choose his own vocation. Let the latter do it for him, and, if need be, return to the 'beneficent whip.' 'On the side of the oppressor there is power;' let him use it without mercy, and hold flesh and blood to the grindstone with unrelenting rigor. Humanity is squeamishness; pity for the suffering, mere 'rose-pink sentimentalism,' maudlin and unmanly. The gods (the old Norse gods doubtless) laugh to scorn alike the complaints of the miserable, and the weak compassions and 'philanthropisms' of those who would relieve them. This is the substance of Thomas Carlyle's advice; this is the matured fruit of his philosophic husbandry—the grand result for which he has been all his life sounding 'unfathomable abysses' or beating about in the thin air of Transcendentalism. Such is the substitute which he offers us for the Sermon on the Mount.

He tells us that the blacks have no right to use the islands of the West Indies for growing pumpkins and garden stuffs for their own use and behoof, because, but for the wisdom and skill of the whites, these islands would have been productive only of 'jungle, savagery, and swamp malaria.' The negro alone could never have improved the islands or civilized himself; and therefore their and his 'born lord,' the white man, has a right to the benefits of his own *betterments* of land and 'two-legged cattle'! 'Black Quashee' has no right to dispose of himself and his labor, because he owes his partial civilization to others! And pray how has it been with the white race, for whom our philosopher claims the divine prerogative of enslaving? Some twenty and odd centuries ago, a pair of half-naked savages, daubed with paint, might have been seen roaming among the hills and woods of the northern part of the British island, subsisting on acorns and the flesh of wild animals, with an occasional relish of the smoked hams and pickled fingers of some unfortunate stranger caught on the wrong side of the Tweed. This interesting couple reared, as they best could, a family of children, who, in turn, became the heads of families; and some time about the beginning of the present century one of their descendants in the borough of Ecclefechan rejoiced over the birth of a man child now somewhat famous as 'Thomas Carlyle, a maker of books.' Does it become such a one to rave against the West India negro's incapacity for self-civilization? Unaided by the arts, sciences, and refinements of the Romans, he might have been, at this very day, squatted on his naked haunches in the woods of Ecclefechan, painting his weather-hardened epidermis in the sun like his Pict ancestors. Where, in fact, can we look for unaided self-improvement and spontaneous internal development, to any considerable extent, on the part of any nation or people? From people to people the original God-given impulse towards civilization and perfection has been transmitted, as from Egypt to Greece, and thence to the Roman world.

But the blacks, we are told, are indolent and insensible to the duty of raising sugar and coffee and spice for the whites, being mainly careful to provide for their own household and till their own gardens for domestic comforts and necessaries. The exports have fallen off somewhat. And what does this prove? Only that the negro is now a consumer of products, of which, under the rule of the whip, he was a producer merely. As to indolence, under the proper stimulus of fair wages we have reason to believe that the charge is not sustained. If unthrifty habits and lack of prudence on the part of the owners of estates, combined with the repeal of duties on foreign sugars by the British government, have placed it out of their power to pay just and reasonable wages for labor, who can blame the blacks if they prefer to cultivate their own garden plots rather than raise sugar and spice for their late masters upon terms little better than those of their old condition, the 'beneficent whip' always excepted? The despatches of the colonial governors agree in admitting that the blacks have had great cause for complaint and dissatisfaction, owing to the delay or non-payment of their wages. Sir C. E. Gray, writing from Jamaica, says that 'in a good many instances the payment of the wages they have earned has been either very irregularly made or not at all, probably on account of the inability of the employers.' He says, moreover,—

'The negroes appear to me to be generally as free from rebellious tendencies or turbulent feelings and malicious thoughts as any race of laborers I ever saw or heard of. My impression is, indeed, that under a system of perfectly fair dealing and of real justice they will come to be an admirable peasantry and yeomanry; ablebodied, industrious, and hard working, frank, and well disposed.'

It must indeed be admitted that, judging by their diminished exports and the growing complaints of the owners of estates, that the condition of the islands, in a financial point of view, is by no means favorable. An immediate cause of this, however, must be found in the unfortunate sugar act of 1846. The more remote, but for the most part powerful, cause of the present depression is to be traced to the vicious and unnatural system of slavery, which has been gradually but surely preparing the way for ruin, bankruptcy, and demoralization. Never yet, by a community or an individual, have the righteous laws of God been violated with impunity. Sooner or later comes the penalty which the infinite Justice has affixed to sin. Partial and temporary evils and inconveniences have undoubtedly resulted from the emancipation of the laborers; and many years must elapse before the relations of the two heretofore antagonistic classes can be perfectly adjusted and their interests brought into entire harmony. But that freedom is not to be held mainly accountable for the depression of the British colonies, is obvious from the fact that Dutch Surinam, where the old system of slavery remains in its original rigor, is in an equally depressed condition. The Paramaribo *Neuws en Advertentie Blad*, quoted in the *Jamaica Gazette*, says, under date of January 2, 1850,

Around us we hear nothing but complaints. People seek and find matter in every thing to picture to themselves the lot of the place in which they live as bitterer than that of any other country. Of a large number of flourishing plantations, few remain that can now be called such. So deteriorated has property become within the last few years, that many of these estates have not been able to defray their weekly expenses. The colony stands on the brink of a yawning abyss, into which it must inevitably plunge unless some new and better system is speedily adopted. It is impossible that our agriculture can any longer proceed on its old footing; our laboring force is dying away, and the social position they held must undergo a revolution.

The paper from which we have quoted, the official journal of the colony, thinks the condition of the emancipated British colonies decidedly preferable to that of Surinam, where the old slave system has continued in force, and insists that the Dutch government must follow the example of Great Britain. The actual condition of the British colonies since emancipation is perfectly well known in Surinam: three of them, Essequibo, Demerara, and Berbice, being its immediate neighbors, whatever evils and inconveniences have resulted from emancipation must be well understood by the Dutch slaveholders; yet we find them looking towards emancipation as the only prospect of remedy for the greater evils of their own system. This fact is of itself a sufficient answer to the assumption of Carlyle and others, that what they call 'the ruin of the colonies' has been produced by the emancipation acts of 1833 and 1838.

We have no fears whatever of the effect of this literary monstrosity which we have been considering upon the British colonies. Quashee, black and ignorant as he may be, will not 'get himself made a slave again.' The mission of the 'beneficent whip' is there pretty well over; and it may now find its place in museums and cabinets of ghastly curiosities, with the racks, pillories, thumbscrews, and branding irons of old days. What we have feared, however, is, that the advocates and defenders of slaveholding in this country might find in this 'Discourse' matter of encouragement, and that our anti-Christian prejudices against the colored man might be strengthened and confirmed by its malignant vituperation and sarcasm. On this point we have sympathized with the forebodings of an eloquent writer in the *London Enquirer*:—

We cannot imagine a more deadly moral poison for the American people than his last composition. Every cruel practice of social exclusion will derive from it new sharpness and venom. The slaveholder, of course, will exult to find himself, not apologized for, but enthusiastically cheered, upheld, and glorified, by a writer of European celebrity. But it is not merely the slave who will feel Mr. Carlyle's hand in the torture of his flesh, the riveting of his fetters, and the denial of light to his mind. The free black will feel him too in the more contemptuous and abhorrent scowl of his brother man, who will easily derive from this unfortunate essay the belief that his inhuman feelings are of divine ordination. It is a true work of the devil, the fostering of a tyrannical prejudice. Far and wide over space, and long into the future, the winged words of evil counsel will go.

In the market-place, in the house, in the theatre, and in the church—by land and by sea, in all the haunts of men—their influence will be felt in a perennial growth of hate and scorn, and suffering and resentment. Amongst the sufferers will be many to whom education has given every refined susceptibility that makes contempt and exclusion bitter. Men and women, faithful and diligent, loving and worthy to be loved, and bearing, it may be, no more than an almost imperceptible trace of African descent, will continue yet longer to be banished from the social meal of the white man, and to be spurned from his presence in the house of God, because a writer of genius has lent the weight of his authority and his fame, if not of his power, to the perpetuation of a prejudice which Christianity was undermining.

A more recent production, *Latter Day Pamphlets*, in which man's capability of self-government is more than doubted, democracy somewhat contemptuously sneered at, and the 'model republic' itself stigmatized as a 'nation of bores,' may have a salutary effect in restraining our admiration and in lessening our respect for the defender and eulogist of slavery. The sweeping impartiality with which in this latter production he applies the principle of our 'peculiar institution' to the laboring poor man, irrespective of color, recognizing as his only inalienable right 'the right of being set to labor' for his 'born lords,' will, we imagine, go far to neutralize the mischief of his 'Discourse upon Negro Slavery.' It is a sad thing to find so much intellectual power as Carlyle really possesses so little under the control of the moral sentiments. In some of his earlier writings—as, for instance, his beautiful tribute to the Corn Law rhymer—we thought we saw evidence of a warm and generous sympathy with the poor and the wronged, a desire to ameliorate human suffering, which would have done credit to the 'philanthropisms of Exeter Hall' and the 'Abolition of Pain Society.' Latterly, however, like Molière's quack, he has 'changed all that;' his heart has got upon the wrong side; or rather, he seems to us very much in the condition of the coal burner in the German tale who had swapped his heart of flesh for a cobble stone.

LATTER-DAY PAMPHLETS

1850

26. Two Parodies of Carlyle, *Punch*

January–June 1850, xviii, 107 and 110

Carlyle's *Latter-Day Pamphlets* called forth two parodies from *Punch*: 'Punch's Police: A Very Melancholy Case' and 'Carlyle Made Easy'. See Introduction, p. 18.

(*a*)

Yesterday a gentleman of the name of THOMAS CARLYLE was brought before Mr. Punch, charged with being unable to take care of his own literary reputation—a very first-rate reputation until a few months past —but now, in consequence of the reckless and alarming conduct of the accused, in a most dangerous condition; indeed, in the opinion of very competent authorities, fast sinking.

The office was crowded by many distinguished persons, all of them manifesting the most tender anxiety towards the accused; who, however, did not seem to feel the seriousness of his situation; but, on the contrary, with folded arms and determined expression of visage, called the worthy magistrate (*Mr. Punch*) a 'windbag,' a 'serf of flunkeydom,' and 'an ape of the Dead Sea.'

JOHN NOKES, a policeman with a literary turn, proved that he had long known the doings of the accused. Witness first became acquainted with him through his *Life of Schiller*, a work done in the very best and decentest manner, in which no offence whatever was committed against the people's English; for he, JOHN NOKES, had no idea that English should be called either 'king's' or 'queen's' but emphatically 'the people's English.' Had since known the accused through *Sartor Resartus*, *The French Revolution*, *Past and Present*, and *Oliver Cromwell*. From time to time, as he went on, witness had marked with considerable anxiety, an

318

increasing wildness, a daring eccentricity of manner in the doings of the accused, frequently observing that he delighted to crack and dislocate the joints of language, and to melt down and alloy sterling English into nothing better than German silver. Nevertheless, witness did not believe the reputation of the accused in any positive danger, until some three or four months back, when he detected him running wildly up and down the pages of *Fraser's Magazine*, pelting all sorts of gibberish at the heads of Jamaica niggars—fantastically reproaching them for being 'up to the ears, content in pumpkins, when they should work for sugar and spices' for their white masters—threatening them with the whip, and, in a word, dealing in language only dear to the heart—witness meant pockets—of Yankee slave-owners and Brazilian planters. Since then, witness had named his suspicions to several most respectable publishers, warning them to have an eye upon the offender.

PETER WILLIAMS, teacher at the Lamb-and-Flag Ragged School, deposed that he had purchased two numbers of a work by the accused, called *Latter-Day Pamphlets*. The first number appeared to him (witness) to develope rabid symptoms,—but in the second, in *Model Prisons*—there was nothing in it, but barking and froth. (Here several passages which created a melancholy sensation in court, many persons sighing deeply, and in more than one instance dropping 'some natural tears.')— Witness did not believe it consistent with public safety that, in his present temper, the accused should be trusted with pen-and-ink. If permitted the use of such dangerous weapons he would—until recovered from his present indisposition—inevitably inflict upon his reputation a mischief from which it could not recover. As it was, witness considered it far from safe.

Mr. Punch asked the accused, if he had anything to say; whereupon accused, with a withering smile, replied—

'Preternatural Eternal Oceans'—'Inhuman Humanitarians'—'Eider-down Philanthropy'—'Wide-reverberating Cant'—'Work Sans Holi-day'—'Three Cheers more, and Eternal, Inimitable, and Antipodean Fraternity'—'Pumpkindom, Flunkeydom, Foolscapdom, and Pen-and-Inkidom!'

Mr. Punch observed, this was a melancholy case. He could not release the accused, unless upon good and sufficient surety. Whereupon two gentlemen—publishers of the first respectability—declared themselves willing to be bound, that accused should not, until in a more healthful frame of mind, be allowed the use of paper and goosequills.

It is believed that if accused again offend, the wholy body of publishers will insist upon his compulsory silence. Let us, however, hope better things.

(b)

Mr. Punch differs very much on many points with MR. THOMAS CARLYLE; nevertheless he recommends everybody to read MR. CARLYLE's *Latter-Day Pamphlets*, because there certainly is much fun in them; for they afford all the amusement that can be derived from the best enigmas. It has, however, struck *Mr. Punch* that for the benefit of the show of comprehension, a CARLYLE made easy, a sort of Delphin CARLYLE, ought to be published, something after the subjoined pattern. *Mr. Punch* is not quite confident that he has rendered MR. CARLYLE in every respect correctly; if he has not, perhaps MR. CARLYLE will point out the mistake—provided that he is perfectly sure that he understands his own meaning. The Author, in Pamphlet No. 1, 'The Present Time,' is describing the 'New Era,' which he supposes to have just commenced:—

THE TEXT

A terrible new country this: no neighbours in it yet that I can see, but irrational flabby monsters (philanthropic and other) of the giant species; hyaenas, laughing *devils*, blue (or perhaps blue and yellow) devils, as ST. GUTHLAC found in Croyland long ago. A huge untrodden, haggard country, the 'chaotic battlefield of Frost and Fire;' a country of savage glaciers, granite mountains, of foul jungles, unhewed forests, quaking bogs; which we shall have our own ados to make arable and habitable, I think!

THE SENSE

This is a novel, alarming, state of things. There are no agents but ourselves at work in it that I can perceive, except irrational, unsound preachers of chimeras (philanthropic and other deceivers) of great note; abusive and satirical journalists, literary wolves that prey on the public morals; probably certain magazines of evil tendency, blue, or perhaps blue and yellow magazines [coloured like the] devils [which] ST. GUTHLAC found in Croyland long ago. An indefinite unexplored dreary state of things, the arena of diametrically opposed principles; an age of frozen charities, stubborn prejudices, filthy mazes of immorality, unreclaimed populations, and social bases threatening

to give way; a state of things
which I think we shall have sufficient work of our own to render
capable of improvement, and
orderly enough for us to exist
under it.

27. William Edmonstoune Aytoun, from an unsigned review, *Blackwood's Edinburgh Magazine*

June 1850, lxvii, 640–58

William Edmonstoune Aytoun (1813–65), Scottish lawyer, satirist, and political writer, is probably best known for his clever *Bon
Gaultier Ballads* on which he collaborated with Sir Theodore
Martin. His burlesque of the Spasmodics, *Firmilian*, published in
Blackwood's, had the effect of dissipating much of the serious attention Alexander Smith, Sidney Dobell, and George Gilfillan had
aroused among readers in the 'fifties. Aytoun contributed many
reviews to *Blackwood's*, some of which were political in nature.

It is nothing unusual, in this wayward world of ours, to find men
denouncing, with apparent sincerity, that very fault which is most
conspicuous in themselves. How often do we detect the most quarrel-
some fellow of our acquaintance, the Hotspur of his immediate circle,
uttering a grave homily against intemperance of speech, and rebuking
for some casual testiness a friend, whose general demeanour and bearing
give token of a lily-liver? What more common than to hear the habitual
drunkard railing at the sin of inebriety, and delivering affecting testimony against the crying iniquity of the ginshop? We have listened to

discourses on the comeliness of honesty, and the degrading tendencies of mammon-worship, from gentlemen who, a few hours before, had given private instructions to their brokers to rig the market, and who looked upon George Hudson as the greatest ornament of the age. Cobden mounts the platform to propose a motion in favour of universal peace and brotherhood, and, by way of argument, suggests the propriety of crumpling up the empire of the Russians, like the sheet of white paper which trembles in his omnipotent hand. He is seconded by a Quaker.

Mr. Thomas Carlyle has, of late years, devoted a good deal of his leisure time to the denunciation of shams. The term, in his mouth, has a most extended significance indeed—he uses it with Catholic application. Loyalty, sovereignty, nobility, the church, the constitution, kings, nobles, priests, the House of Commons, ministers, Courts of Justice, laws, and lawgivers, are all alike, in the eyes of Mr. Carlyle, shams. Nor does he consider the system as of purely modern growth. England, he thinks, has been shamming Isaac for several hundred years. Before the Commonwealth it was overridden by the frightful Incubus of Flunkeyism: since then, it has been suffering under Horsehair and Redtapism, two awful monsters that present themselves to Mr. Carlyle's diseased imagination, chained at the entrances of Westminster Hall and Downing Street. Cromwell, perhaps, was not a sham, for in the burly regicide brewer Mr. Carlyle discerns certain grand inarticulate strivings, which elevate him to the heroic rank. The gentlemen of the present age, however, are all either shams or shamming. The honourable Felix Parvulus, and the right honourable Felicissimus Zero, mounted respectively upon 'desperate Sleswick thunder-horses'—M'Crowdy the political economist —Bobus—Flimnap, Sec. Foreign Department—the Right Honourable Minimus, and various other allegorical personages, intended, we presume, to typify carnal realities, are condemned as Solemn Shams, Supreme Quacks, Phantasm Captains, the Elixir of the Infatuated, and Able-Editor's Nobles.

It is natural to suppose that an individual who habitually deals in such wholesale denunciation, and whose avowed wish is to regenerate and reform society upon some entirely novel principle, must be a man of immense practical ability. The exposer of shams and quackeries should be, in his own person, very far indeed above suspicion of resembling those whom he describes, or tries to describe, in language more or less intelligible. If otherwise, he stands in imminent danger of being treated by the rest of the world as an impertinent and egregious impostor. Now,

Mr. Thomas Carlyle is anything but a man of practical ability. Setting aside his style for the present, let us see whether he has ever, in the course of his life, thrown out a single hint which could be useful to his own generation, or profitable to those who may come after. If he could originate any such hint, he does not possess the power of embodying it in distinct language. He has written a history of the French Revolution, a pamphlet on Chartism, a work on Heroes and Hero-worship, and a sort of political treatise entitled *Past and Present*. Can any living man point to a single practical passage in any of these volumes? If not, what is the real value of Mr. Carlyle's writings? What is Mr. Carlyle himself but a Phantasm of the species which he is pleased to denounce?

We have known, ere now, in England, political writers who, single-handed, have waged war with Ministers, and denounced the methods of government. But they were men of strong masculine understanding, capable of comprehending principles, and of exhibiting them in detail. They never attempted to write upon subjects which they did not understand: consequently, what they did write was well worthy of perusal, more especially as their sentiments were conveyed in clear idiomatic English. Perhaps the most remarkable man of this class was the late William Cobbett. Shrewd and practical, a master of figures, and an utter scorner of generalization, he went at once, in whatever he undertook to the root of the matter, and, right or wrong, demonstrated what he thought to be the evil, and what he conceived to be the remedy. There was no slip-slop, burlesque, or indistinctness about William Cobbett. Mr. Carlyle, on the other hand, can never stir one inch beyond the merest vague generality. If he were a doctor, and you came to him with a cut finger, he would regale you with a lecture on the heroical qualities of Avicenna, or commence proving that Dr. Abernethy was simply a Phantasm-Leech, instead of whipping out his pocket-book, and applying a plaster to the wound. Put him into the House of Commons, and ask him to make a speech on the budget. No baby ever possessed a more indefinite idea of the difference between pounds, shillings and pence. He would go on maundering about Teufelsdrökh, Sauerteig, and Dryasdust, Sir Jabez Windbag, Fire-horses, Marsh-jötuns, and vulturous Choctaws, until he was coughed down as remorselessly as ever was Sir Joshua Walmsley. And yet this is the gentleman who has the temerity to volunteer his services as a public instructor, and who is now issuing a series of monthly tracts, for the purpose of shedding a new light upon the most intricate and knotty points of the general policy of Great Britain!

Something of this kind we have already witnessed in a neighbouring country, but never in the like degree. France has had her Flocons and her Louis Blancs, small, pert, presumptuous animals, chalking out schemes of social regeneration, organized labour, industrial regiments, and the like. We do not intend to insinuate that either of these scribes is entitled to be ranked, for parity of intellect, with Mr. Carlyle, because by doing so we might involve ourselves in a squabble with some of his benighted admirers. But we say, with perfect sincerity, that so far as regards political attainments and information, clear views, and we shall even add common sense (distant as that attribute is from any of the parties above named), MM. Flocon and Blanc are at least as capable guides as Mr. Carlyle can pretend to be. Something tangible there is, however pernicious to society, in the propositions of the former—the latter does not favour us with propositions at all; he contents himself with abusing men and matters in a barbarous, conceited, uncouth, and mystical dialect.

One peculiarity there is about the *Latter-day Pamphlets*, as contra-distinguished from their author's previous incubations, which has amused us not a little. Mr. Carlyle has hitherto been understood to favour the cause of self-styled Liberalism. His mania, or rather his maunderings, on the subject of the Protector gained him the applause of many who are little less than theoretical republicans, and who regard as a glorious deed the regicide of the unfortunate Charles. Moreover, certain passages in his *History of the French Revolution* tended to strengthen this idea; he had a kindly side for Danton, and saw evident marks of heroism in the loathsome miscreant whom, in his usual absurd jargon, he styles 'the pale sea-green Incorruptible,' Robespierre. On this ground his works were received with approbation by a section of the public press; and we used to hear him lauded and commended as a writer of the profoundest stamp, as a deep original thinker, a thorough-paced philanthropist, the champion of genuine greatness, and the unflinching enemy of delusions. Now, however, things are altered. Mr. Carlyle has got a new crotchet into his head, and to the utter discomfiture of his former admirers, he manifests a truculent and ultra-tyrannical spirit, abuses the political economists, wants to have a strong coercive government, indicates a decided leaning to the whip and the musket as effectual modes of reasoning, and, in short, abjures democracy! The sensation caused by this extraordinary change of sentiment has been as great as if Joe Hume had declared himself a spendthrift. Only think of such a document as the following, addressed to the sovereign people!

[quotes 'Speech of the British Prime-Minister' to 'That now is' *The Present Time*, XX, 38–9]

Flat burglary as ever was committed! O villain! thou wilt be condemned into everlasting redemption for this—so say the political Dogberrys to the gentleman whom they used to applaud. We are not surprised at their wrath. It *is* rather hard to be told at this time of day that ballot-boxes and extension of the suffrage are included in Mr. Carlyle's catalogue of Shams, and that Messrs. Thompson, Fox, and Co. must even submit to the charge of talking unveracities and owlism. Surely there is some mistake here. Not a whit of it. Mr. Carlyle is in grim earnest, and lays about him like a man. He has not studied the records of the French Revolution for nothing; and he is not able to discern in the late Continental revolts any ground for general congratulation on the improved prospects of mankind. Such language as the following must sound as a strange rebuke in the ears of divers organs of the public press, who, not long ago, were flinging up their caps in ecstasies at the fall of constitutions, backing up Garibaldi against the Pope, Charles Albert against Radetsky, the Sicilian insurgents against their Sovereign of Naples, Kossuth against the Emperor, Von Gagern against Federalism, Ledru Rollin against Civilisation, and Lamartine against Common-sense.

[quotes 'Certainly it is' to 'to their mind' *The Present Time*, XX, 10]

Sham-kings may and do exist, thinks Mr. Carlyle, but the greatest unveracity of all is this same Democracy, which people were lately so very willing to applaud. It must be admitted that our author is perfectly impartial in the distribution of his strokes. He has no love for Kings, or Metternichs, or Redtape, or any other fiction or figure of speech whereby he typifies existing governments: he disposes of them in a wholesale manner of Impostors and Impostures. But no more does he regard with affection Chartist Parliament, Force of Public Opinion, or 'M'Crowdy the Seraphic Doctor with his last evangel of Political Economy.' M'Culloch is, in his eyes, as odious as the First Lord in Waiting, whoever that functionary may be. Clenching both his fists, he delivers a facer to the Trojan on the right, and to the Tyrian on the left. Big with the conviction that all Governments are wrong, as presently or lately constituted, he can see no merit, but the reverse, in any of the schemes of progress, or reform, or financial change, which have yet been devised. Here follow some of his motions with regard to the most popularly prescribed remedies:—

[quotes 'A divine message' to 'a good deal' *The Present Time*, XX, 17–18]

Now, reader, what do you think of all this? We doubt not you are a good deal puzzled: and an admission to that effect would be no impeachment of your intellect. Well then, let us try to extract from these pamphlets of Mr. Carlyle some tendency, if not distinct meaning, which may at least indicate the current of his hopes and aspirations. Putting foreign governments altogether out of the question, we gather that Mr. Carlyle considers this realm of Britain as most scandalously misgoverned; that he looks upon Downing Street as an absolute sewer; that he decidedly yields to Mr. Hawes in reverence for Lord John Russell; that he regards the Protectionists as humbugs; that he laughs at ballot-boxes, despises extension of the suffrage, and repudiates, as a rule of conduct, the maxim about the markets, which indeed, by this time, stinks in every British nostril as yet unplugged with calico; that he detests the modern brood of political economists with a cordiality which does him credit; and that he is firmly convinced that democracy is a thing for ever impossible. This is a tolerably extensive creed, though as yet entirely a negative one—is there no one point upon which Mr. Carlyle will condescend to be positive?

Yes, one there is; not apparent perhaps to the casual reader, but detectible by him who studies closely those pages of oracular thought—a point very important at the present moment, for this it is—that there is ONE MAN existing in her Majesty's dominions who could put everything to rights, if he were only allowed to do so. Who that man is we may possibly discover hereafter. At present we are hardly entitled to venture beyond the boundaries of dim conjecture. Nor is it very clear in what way the Unknown, or rather the Undeveloped, is to set about his exalted mission. Is he to be minister—or something more? Perhaps Mr. Carlyle did not like to be altogether explicit on such a topic as this; but we may possibly gain a little light from indirect and suggestive passages. Take this for example:

[quotes 'Alas, it is' to 'destruction for him' *The Present Time*, XX, 12–13]

We have been sorely tempted to mark with italics certain portions of the above extract, but on second thoughts we shall leave it intact. After applying ourselves most diligently to the text, with the view of eliciting its meaning, we have arrived at the conclusion, that it is either downright nonsense, or something a great deal worse. Observe what he says. It is to be prayed for by all men that Shams may cease—more especially Sham Kings. But certain solid Englishmen are not prepared for this. They have been 'used to decent forms long since fallen empty of meaning, to plausible modes, solemnities grown ceremonial,—what you in your iconoclast humour call shams.' They thought no harm of them. 'Kings reigned, what they were pleased to call reigning; lawyers pleaded, bishops preached, and honourable members perorated,' &c. And those who differ in their estimate of these things from Mr. Carlyle are 'almost below the level of lowest humanity, and down towards the state of apehood and oxhood:'—and their belief is a 'scandalous blasphemy.' So then, the Monarchy is a sham, and so are the laws, the Church, and the Constitution! They are all lies, and in deliberate long-established lying there can be no help or salvation for the subject! This may not be Mr. Carlyle's meaning, and we are very willing to suppose so: but he has no title to be angry, were we to accept his words according to their evident sense. If men, through conceit or affectation, will write in this absurd and reckless fashion, they must be prepared to stand the consequences. The first impression on the mind of every one who peruses the above passage must be, that the author is opposed to the form of government which is unalterably established in these kingdoms. If this be so, we should like to know in what respect such doctrines differ from the pestilential revolutionary trash which has inundated France and Germany? What kind of overturn does Mr. Carlyle contemplate, for overturn there must be, and that of the most extensive kind, if his views are ever destined to be realised? Is it not, perhaps, as melancholy a spectacle, as may be, to find a man of some genius, and considerable learning, attempting to unsettle the minds of the young and enthusiastic, upon points distinctly identified with all that is great and glorious in our past history; and insinuating doctrines which are all the more dangerous on account of the oblique and uncertain language in which they are conveyed? Fear God and honour the King, are precepts not acknowledged by Mr. Carlyle as the rudiment and foundation of his faith. He does not recognize them as inseparably linked together. He would set up instead some wretched phantom of his own imagination, framed out of the materials which he fondly supposes to be the attributes of the heroic character, and he would exalt that above all other authority, human and divine. He is, if we do not entirely misconstrue the tenor of these pamphlets, possessed at this moment with the notion of the advent of another Cromwell, the sole event which, as he thinks, can save England from being swallowed up by the evils which now beset her. What these evils are, we shall shortly endeavour to ascertain; in the meantime, let us keep our attention fixed on this primary matter of authority.

Cromwellism, then, if we may use the term, is Mr. Carlyle's secret and theory. Cromwellism, is, we know, but another phase for despotism; and we shall not put so harsh a construction on the term as to suppose that it necessarily involves extinguishment of the royal function. The example of Richelieu is sufficient to save us from such a violent interpretation, and therefore we may fairly assume that our author contemplates nothing more than the lodgement of the executive power in the hands of some stern and inexorable minister. To this the whole of his multitudinous political ravings, when melted into intelligible speech, would seem to tend. He has little regard for Kings, despises Lords, contemns Bishops, scouts the House of Commons, sneers at Chartists, repudiates the political economists, spurns the mob, and laughs at the Ten-pounders. There is here a tolerably extensive range of scorn—we doubt whether it could have been equalled by the reflective philosopher of the tub. . . .

Let us now see what sort of government Mr. Carlyle would propose for our adoption, guidance, and regeneration. Some kind of shapes are traceable even in fog-banks, and the analogy encourages us to persevere in our Latter-day researches.

Mr. Carlyle is decidedly of opinion that it is our business to find out the very Noblest possible man to undertake the whole job. What he means by Noblest is explicitly stated. 'It is the Noblest, not the Sham-Noblest; it is God Almighty's Noble, not the Court-Tailor's Noble, nor the Able-Editor's Noble, that must in some approximate degree be raised to the supreme place; he and not a counterfeit—under penalties.' This *Noblest*, it seems, is to have a select series or staff of *Noblers*, to whom shall be confided the divine everlasting duty of directing and controlling the Ignoble. The mysterious process by means of which 'the Noblest' is to be elevated—when he is discovered—is not indicated, but the intervention of ballot-boxes is indignantly disclaimed. 'The Real Captain, unless it be some Captain of mechanical Industry hired by Mammon, where is he in these days? Most likely, in silence, in sad isolation somewhere, in remote obscurity; trying if, in an evil ungoverned time, he cannot at least govern himself.' There are limits to human endurance, and we maintain that we have a right to call upon Mr. Carlyle either to produce this remarkable Captain, or to indicate his whereabouts. He tells us that time is pressing—that we are moving in the midst of goblins, and that everything is going to the mischief for want of this Noblest of his. Well, then, we say, where is this Captain of yours? Let us have a look at him—give us at least a guess as to his outward marks and locality—does he live in Chelsea or Whitehall Gardens; or has he been, since the general emigration of the Stags, trying to govern himself in sad isolation and remote obscurity at Boulogne? If you know anything about him, out with it—if not, why pester the public with these sheets of intolerable twaddle. . . .

Are we to look out for the best poets, and make them Secretaries of State? The best Secretaries of State we have known in our day, were about as poor poets as could be imagined; and we are rather apprehensive that the converse of the proposition might likewise be found to hold good.

How sweet an Ovid was in Melbourne lost!

sighed a Whig critic, commenting with rapture on some of that nobleman's early lucubrations; and yet, after all, we have no reason to think that the roll of British bards has been impoverished by the accidental exclusion. Flesh and blood could not have endured a second tragedy from Lord John Russell, and yet the present Premier, despite of Don Carlos, is thought by some partial friends to cut a tolerably decent figure as a politician. As to that, we shall venture no opinion. Mr. Carlyle, however, is clear for the poets. Listen to his instance.

[quotes 'From the' to 'Reforming Premier' *Downing Street*, XX, 118]

. . . If Burns was alive at the present moment, in the full glory of his intellect and strength, would any sensible constituency think of sending him to Parliament? Of all the trash that Mr. Carlyle has ever written— and there is a good deal of it,—this about Robert Burns, whom he calls the 'new Norse Thor,' not being selected as a statesman, is perhaps the most insufferable. The vocation of a poet is, we presume, to sing; to pour forth his heart in noble, animating, or touching strains; not to discuss questions of policy, or to muddle his brains over Blue Books, or the interminable compilations of Mr. Porter. Not so thinks Carlyle. He would have shut up Burns in Downing Street, debarred him from the indulgence of verse, and clapped him at the head of a Board of Poor-law Commissioners. 'And the meagre Pitt, and his Dundases, and red-tape Phantasms (growing very ghastly now to think of) did not in the least know or understand, the impious god-forgetting mortals, that Heroic intellects, if Heaven were pleased to send such, were the one salvation for the world and for them and all of us.' Mr. Carlyle seems to have most original notions on the subject of nature's gifts. It would be as reasonable to say that, because a nightingale sings more sweetly than its compeers, it ought to be taken to the house and trained as a regular falcon!

We are very far indeed from wishing to maintain that literary men may not be possessed of every quality which is most desirable in a statesman. But instances of this combination are rare, and on the whole we think that our 'Heroic Intellects,' and 'noble young souls,' will acquit themselves most creditably by following out the peculiar bent of their own genius. If they have any political tendency, it will develop itself in due season; but we protest, most strenuously, against a Parliament of men of genius, or a cabinet of literateurs. We have seen quite enough of that in other countries. . . .

In this style Noblest proceeds for a page or two, haranguing the unlucky paupers upon the principle that poverty is crime; taunting them with previous doles of Indian meal and money, and informing them that the Workhouses are thenceforward inexorably shut. Finally, he announces that they are to be embodied into industrial regiments, with proper officers; and marched off

to the Irish Bogs, to the vacant desolations of Connaught now falling into Cannibalism, to mis-tilled Connaught, to ditto Munster, Leinster, Ulster, I will lead you; to the English fox covers, furze-grown Commons, New Forests, Salisbury plains; likewise to the Scotch Hillsides; and bare rushy slopes which as yet feed only sheep.

All these are to be tilled by the slave regiments under the following penalties for recusancy.

Refuse to strike into it; shirk the heavy labour, disobey the rules—I will admonish and endeavour to incite you; if in vain, I will flog you; if still in vain, I will at last shoot you,—and make God's Earth, and the forlorn-hope in God's Battle, free of you. Understand it, I advise you!

O rare Thomas Carlyle. . . .

He would have made a first-rate taskmaster under the old Egyptian economy. He is, with great reason, indignant at the state to which our West Indian Colonies have been reduced by means of Exeter Hall emancipation, and he scouts emancipation itself as a gross delusion of the fiend. It is to be regretted that his views have been so late of ripening. Time was, when a fair and common-sense protest, advanced by a Liberal philosopher, against the absurdity of attempting to change the hue of the Ethiopian by a single momentary scrubbing, might have been of some actual use: now, it is in vain to recommend a protracted application of the tub. The Noblest, when Mr. Carlyle has discovered him and put him forward, will hardly achieve his ends by using the following language, even supposing that he wielded the lightning, and were able to put his threats into execution.

[quotes 'Beautiful Black Peasantry' to 'of late' *Model Prisons*, XX, 66–7]

The meaning of this passage is, that the black population of our colonies ought no longer to be permitted to dwell in perfect idleness in their provision grounds, rearing pumpkins for their own consumption, without regard to the cultivation of the sugar-cane. As we have already remarked, this view is somewhat of the latest; nevertheless truth, like repentance, can never come too late to be received. Divorced from the folly of his speech, Mr. Carlyle's sentiment is sound. Twenty millions of British money, wrung from the hard-taxed labour of our people, were given—for what? Not only to emancipate the Negros, but to place them in such a position that they could effectually control their former masters—our own colonists and countrymen, to whom our faith was solemnly plighted for the maintenance of their privileges and commerce. Let it be granted that slavery was a gross sin, was it incumbent upon us to elevate the emancipated Blacks so high, that they could control the labour market—to give them the status of untaxed yeoman, without any security for the slightest manifestation of their gratitude? It was more than preposterous that those whose freedom was purchased should be placed in a better position, and invested with more immunity from labour and want, than the great bulk of the people who made the sacrifice in order to secure that freedom; and the result has amply demonstrated the gross folly of the scheme. There are thousands, nay millions of men in Britain and Ireland, whose lot, compared with that of the emancipated Blacks of Jamaica, is one of speechless misery—and yet their cry to be relieved from a competition which is crushing them down to the dust, is unheard and uncared for amidst the din of contending politicians, and the perpetual hum of the busy proselytes of Mammon.

Here we cannot forbear from quoting a characteristic passage from Mr. Carlyle's tracts. The idea is not original, but the handling is worthy of Astley's humourist; and we commend it to the special attention of all free-trading philanthropists.

[quotes 'Certainly Emancipation' to 'this hour' *The Present Time*, XX, 25–7]

. . . We must now take our leave of Mr. Carlyle, sincerely regretting that we cannot, with any degree of truth, congratulate him either on the tone or the character of his late lucubrations. These pamphlets, take them altogether, are about the silliest productions of the day; and we could well wish, for his sake, that they had never been compiled. Very few people, we imagine, will be disposed to wait with confidence for the avatar of his Noblest and Noblers, such as he has depicted them. Our faith and hopes lie in a different direction; nor have we any wish to see a Cromwell at the head of affairs, supported by a staff of noble young souls, poetical or otherwise, who require to be bought over for the purpose. Towards the close of his fourth pamphlet, our author lets drop a hint from which we gather that it is not impossible that his Noblest may hereafter appear embodied in the person of Sir Robert Peel. All we shall say on that score is, that Sir Robert has already had sufficient opportunity vouchsafed him to exhibit the extent of his qualifications. It is not likely that the Statesman who, in the eve of life, and enjoying the undiminished confidence of his Sovereign, finds himself in the House of Commons without the semblance of a party to support him, can ever make another desperate rally. It would be difficult to find in the annals of history any instance of a leading politician who has been so often trusted, and impossible to find one who has so often abused that trust. Even Mr. Carlyle cannot deny the Unveracities of which Sir Robert stands convicted; and although he appears to think that lapses from truth are of so common occurrence as to be venial, we beg to assure him that his opinion is not the general one, nor is it altogether creditable to the morality of the man who ventures to express it. We are sorry to observe that, in the conclusion of this latter tract, Mr. Carlyle has condescended to borrow some hints from that most eminent master of modern scurrility, the late Daniel O'Connel. This is, in every respect, to be deplored. Wit is not Mr. Carlyle's forte, and this kind of wit, if wit it be, is, when served up at second hand, both nauseous and revolting. At a calmer moment, and on more mature reflection, we feel convinced that Mr. Carlyle will blush for the terms which he has allowed himself to apply to so eminent a genius as Mr. Disraeli; and that he will in future abstain from testifying his gratitude for a humiliating invitation to dinner in a shape so abject as that of casting personal and low abuse upon the political adversaries of his entertainer.

If Mr. Carlyle feels that his vocation is political—if the true spirit of the prophet is stirring within him—he ought to endeavour in the first place to think clearly, and, in the second, to amend his style. At present his thoughts are anything but clear. The primary duty of an author is to have a distinct understanding of the matter which he proposes to enunciate, for unless he can arrive at that, his words must necessarily be mystical and undefined. If men are to be taught at all, let the teaching be simple, and level to the common capacity; and let the teacher be thoroughly conversant with the whole particulars of the lesson. We have a strong suspicion that Cassandra must have been a prophetess reared in the same school as Mr. Carlyle. Her predictions seem to have been shrouded in such thorough mysticism, that no one gave her credit for inspiration; and in consequence the warnings which might have saved Troy, were spoken to the empty winds. Here, perhaps, we ought to guard ourselves against a similar charge of indistinctness. We by no means intend to certify that Mr. Carlyle is a prophet, or that there is any peculiar Revelation in these *Latter-day Pamphlets* which can avert the fall of Britain, should that sad catastrophe be foredoomed. We simply wish to express our regret that Mr. Carlyle, who may lay claim to the possession of some natural genius and ability, will not allow us the privilege of understanding the true nature of his thoughts, and therefore exposes himself to a suspicion that the indistinctness lies quite as much in the original conception of the ideas, as in the language by means of which they are conveyed. . . .

28. David Masson, an unsigned review, *North British Review*

November 1850, xiv, 1–40

David Masson (1822–1907), Professor at University College, London, then at Edinburgh, was the first editor of *Macmillan's Magazine* and later edited the short-lived, but reputable, *Reader* (1863–6). A voluminous writer, Masson contributed articles to many of the leading periodicals. As scholar, editor, and critic he wrote works on Goldsmith, Drummond of Hawthornden, Luther, Shelley, Wordsworth, and most notably Milton. Masson's friendship with Carlyle is recorded in his autobiographical *Memories of London in the Forties*, ed. Flora Masson (Edinburgh, 1908).

Mr. Carlyle's career presents at least one point of curious contrast with that of most literary men. Most men, in following out their literary tendencies, are observed to begin with the vehement, the intolerant, the aggressive; and to end in the calm, the acquiescent, the otiose. A young man, beginning to employ his pen, usually dashes at once into the midst of affairs; attaches himself to the movement; launches fierce criticisms at existing principalities and powers; denounces, foams, and struggles; and has pleasure only, as we have heard it expressed, in 'always making a row about things.' As he grows older, however, a change slowly creeps over him; he becomes more economic of his energy; the element he lives in becomes more genial to him; and on the whole his tendency is to meddle with the polemical as little as he can, to surround himself with books, pictures, and other amenities, and to seek a placid enjoyment in the cultivation of whatever is beautiful. In the case of Mr. Carlyle, on the other hand, this process seems to have been, in some degree, reversed. He began as the devotee of pure literature; he has ended as the most aggressive man of his age. . . .

[Here follows a brief sketch of Carlyle's development from a critic of 'literature' to one of 'biographic investigation' and finally to one embodying the 'prophetic spirit'.]

He left pure literature and its etiquette behind him, and spoke out as a moral and social reformer, more anxious to rouse than to please, to convey his meaning anyhow than to write charming periods. And this is the character which he has maintained ever since. His *Heroes and Hero-worship*, his *Chartism*, and his *Past and Present*, were but so many addresses or trumpet-blasts to the age, in which marvellous literary tact and ability were compelled into the service of a predominant moral purpose. In his *Oliver Cromwell*, too, though here the artist was abundantly conspicuous, one saw the same supremacy of aim and spirit. And now last of all, as if to present in one series and in a shape expressly adapted for practical application, all his more important criticisms on the existing state of society, he has, after four years of silence and observant bitterness of heart, put forth these *Latter-Day Pamphlets*.

Clearly enough, one would think, the vehemence of a man thus trained and developed into opposition to the reigning influences of his time, ought not to be confounded with that of the juvenile partisan of disaffection and revolution. Of Mr. Carlyle, too, it may indeed be asserted that he is 'always making a row about things;' but in him the spirit of protest and dissatisfaction is not the mere conceit of an unformed nature working itself into connexion with things as they are, it is the deliberate manifestation of a great and powerful mind, that, having tried long and variously to content itself with what society offers to it, still finds that by the very decree of its constitution it cannot be at ease. The duty of every man born into this world is to contribute what is peculiar and specific in him to the general evolution; to find out that portion or that determination of his nature which (no two men being precisely alike) he sees repeated nowhere else, and, in submission to the laws of right and wrong, to diffuse *that* as widely as possible among his neighbours and contemporaries. Here, accordingly, is a man, who, after ample experience of himself and others, finds that what is supreme and ascendant in his nature, is a certain strength of moral displeasure with much that is socially permitted and held in honour; and who discharges his conscience by resolutely expressing it. Whatever presumption, therefore, is to be derived in his favour from all that is otherwise known of him, from the undoubted greatness and clearness of his intellect, from the approved variety and extent of his acquisitions, from the unimpeachable excellence of his private reputation, and from the admitted importance of his past literary services—to the full measure of this presumption ought the public now to listen to him.

A large portion of the public, it would appear, refuse to render him this degree of consideration. For some years, it may have been observed, a reaction has been in process against Mr. Carlyle and his doctrines—a reaction, the elements of which were in existence before, but have only recently come together and assumed something like a declared organization. It is nearly half a generation since Mr. Carlyle became an intellectual power in this country; and certainly rarely, if ever, in the history of literature, has such a phenomenon been witnessed as that of his influence. Throughout the whole atmosphere of this island his spirit has diffused itself, so that there is probably not an educated man under forty years of age, from Caithness to Cornwall, that can honestly say he has not been more or less affected by it. Even in the department of action his existence has been felt. Persons acquainted with the circumstances, and capable of tracing the affiliation, discern evidences of his effects equally in the Irish Rebellion and in the English Catholic movement. And in literature the extent to which he has operated upon society is still more apparent. Not to speak of his express imitators, one can hardly take up a book or a periodical without finding in every page some expression or some mode of thinking that bears the mint-mark of his genius. 'Hero-worship,' 'The Condition-of-England question,' 'Flunkeyism,'—these, and hundreds of other phrases, either first coined by him, or first laid hold of and naturalized by him, are now gladly used by many that upon the whole have no great liking for him, or even hold him in aversion. We have even observed that many of his critics abuse him in language which, when analyzed, is found to consist of a detritus of his own ideas.

But, though his influence has been thus extensive and profound, there have never been wanting men openly antipathetic to it. Even deducting that large class of persons who have joined in attacking him, either from mean envy of his superior reputation, or from a dastardly anxiety to avoid the imputation of having been indebted to him, there would still remain many whose dislike to him was honestly determined by some constitutional peculiarity that made it impossible for them to read him without extreme discomfort. To some men humour is abominable; others detest the very semblance of vehemence; and not a few are qualified to relish truths only when they are presented in abstract form, and in what is called logical coherence. To all such Mr. Carlyle must have been either indifferent or disagreeable; just as there may be men that dislike Cervantes, abhor Dante, and wonder what people find to admire in Richter. On the whole, however, it can have been but a small proportion of the critical antipathy to Mr. Carlyle that was determined by such exceptional causes. . . .

The publication of the *Latter-Day Pamphlets* has brought the controversy to a crisis. Never before, probably, was there a publication so provocative of rage, hatred, and personal malevolence. Whatever amount of antipathy to Mr. Carlyle previously existed throughout the reading community, has been by this concentrated and brought out into explicit manifestation. Simultaneously over the whole kingdom the scattered elements of dislike have mustered themselves; so that nearly the whole force of the critical demonstration that has been made *apropos* of the author's reappearance in the field of literature, has been on the part of the reaction. In all circles, and on the most various occasions, there have been outbreaks of a spirit of resistance to him amounting almost to malignity. Lord John Russell in the House of Commons takes a highly elaborated revenge for certain impolite allusions to him in the *Pamphlets*, by incidentally referring to their author as 'a clever but whimsical writer.' With a similar affectation of condescending unconcern to cover what is in reality the most intense bitterness of feeling, some critics write as if they would have it believed they thought of the author only as a poor driveller that all persons of sense had long ceased to listen to. Others, again, more honestly, assail and vituperate him with the whole force of their undisguised abhorrence. The correspondent of one American newspaper cooly accounts to the Transatlantic public for the 'insane' tone of the *Pamphlets* by the information that 'Thomas is believed to have recently taken to whiskey.' We have ourselves heard him cursed by name in open society; and were it possible to accumulate in some distinct and visible shape all the imprecations and other expressions of rage and ill-will that the pamphlets have elicited, we fancy the display would be something fearful. In short, at the present moment, Mr. Carlyle is unpopular with at least one half of the kingdom.

Now, this is no doubt partly the mere determination upon this new publication of the feelings already existing against the author. All Mr. Carlyle's previous offences, or supposed offences, against the literary canons of taste and opinion, have been here boldly repeated by him; and, as a criminal is visited with severer punishment in proportion to the number of convictions already registered against him, so the critical public has deemed it right to come down, on this occasion, with a heavier exhibition of critical resentment. Accordingly, all the old criticisms upon Mr. Carlyle's manner of writing have been this year abundantly reiterated.—*Punch*, for example, amongst others, takes up the wearisome topic of his style: and, in a mood alarmingly serious for so comic an organ, takes the trouble to read Mr. Carlyle a lecture on style, by showing him one of his own sentences translated into decent English —a sad blunder, as everybody thought at the time, for the shrewd little periodical to have committed, seeing that the 'decent English' occupied in *Punch's* own columns nearly twice the length of the 'piece of jargon' it was meant to supersede.[1] And, along with this renewed outcry against the barbarism of the author's style, have been revived hints of his intellectual indebtedness to those convenient creditors, the dead old gentlemen of Weimar, and revived complaints of his want of practicality and constructive precision.

But there are deeper reasons for the formidable display of animosity with which the *Pamphlets* have been greeted. The *Pamphlets* contain in themselves matter more irritating and blistering than any of the author's previous writings. They come more directly into conflict with prevailing sentiments, parties, and interests; and are, in fact, a more explicit assertion than the author had before made, that he detaches himself from the devotees of pure and pleasurable literature, and regards himself as a social agent or recognized force in the country, charged with a special commission and special responsibilities. He has here, as it were, completed his career of respect for his fellow-men; parted with the last shred of his care for their approbation; reached the pulpit, where it is the condemnation of his own soul if he does not speak out, even if they stone him; and determined with himself that whatever may have been his method hitherto, now it is his function most emphatically to 'make a row about things.' And certainly he has done so. If we may judge of others from ourselves, we should say that there can hardly have been an individual reader of these Pamphlets endowed with the least sensitiveness or the least tendency to try whether the cap that is offered fits him, that has not felt himself aggrieved, wounded, and thrown into a state of dudgeon by much that he there read. We have heard of people rising from their seats and marching out of church, because, either from the extreme searchingness of the sermon, or from the paucity of the audience, they had an uneasy sense that the preacher was getting personal. Something similar, we should think, must have been the effect of certain passages in these Discourses upon the minds of individual readers. At one time, the reader being in a blunt, untender, and self-conceited frame of mind, the effect of some such passage might be 'Psha! mere ethical sound and clamour!' while there would remain, after all, a kind of sullen sense of having been insulted; at another time, the mind being in a better and more docile condition, there would follow, from the

[1] See No. 26.

same passage, all the nervous deliquescence of a conscience touched to its depths, and a paroxysm of self-reproach giving vent to such ejaculations as this—'What a wretch I am; and how much more nobly this man feels than I do!' Precisely so also in those cases where the matter involved might not be pertinent to the character or mental shortcomings of the reader as an individual, but to his social relations and the antecedents of his public career. In these *Pamphlets*, for example, not only is there a blow in the face all round for Democracy, Aristocracy, Monarchy, Political Economy, Protectionism, Mammon-worship, and such other recognized interests and social entities as have already been more or less accustomed to be girded at; but other interests and entities that thought themselves safe and consecrated from attack by the high guardianship of universal opinion, have found themselves ridiculed and made a mock of. The 'Occasional Discourse on the Negro Question,' published by Mr. Carlyle anonymously in *Fraser's Magazine* for December, 1849, was a sort of forewarning to the public of what they were to expect from him should he come forward to treat habitually of such subjects. Even the horror of that paper, however, was outdone by certain of the pamphlets. One remembers yet the simultaneous cry of 'shame' which was elicited by a passage in the first of them, where he spoke of first admonishing, then flogging, and finally shooting paupers if they would not work; and the yet louder cry which greeted him in the second, where he spoke of sweeping criminals into the dust-bin, tumbling them and their concerns over London Bridge, and so getting rid of them.

In considering this extremely unpopular reception which the *Latter-Day Pamphlets* have met with, not in all, certainly, but in many quarters, one thing surely seems pretty clear; to wit—that nobody knew better that the outburst was coming than the author did himself. Whatever unpopularity has been or may yet be the consequence of these Pamphlets, the author has knowingly, resolutely and deliberately braved it. And here lies one of the characteristic differences between his procedure as a social agent by means of the pen, and the procedure of such as are devotees of pure literature. Much as neglected authors and artists console themselves now-a-days, by talking, after Wordsworth, about the necessary unpopularity of all great works, and the propriety of writing or painting only for a few, it is certainly a maxim, approved by the profoundest investigation into human nature, that all works of art ought to desire popularity—*i.e.*, the immediate satisfaction of those that have mastered on each specific occasion the mere essential *technick*; and also, that the greatest works of art do infallibly obtain it. Hence desire to please is so far a fair literary instinct. Watch the author or authoress of a first poem or novel. What eagerness there is to see all the reviews; what fluttering anxiety till the *Athenæum* or other leader among the critical periodicals comes out; what manœuvring, indirectly, to ascertain what *you* in particular think of the book, and what all your friends, and especially *Magnus Apollo*, privately said to you about it! And how many persons are there, that, even after their apprenticeship to literature or to art is over, can honestly say that this feeling has quite left them? Raphael must have liked to hear his pictures praised; nor was the approbation of the German public indifferent even to the octogenarian Goethe. But, though the artist or practitioner of pure literature may so far make a merit of popularity, it is highly different with the moral teacher, or agent of great social changes. Popularity may, indeed, happen to flow from the exertions of such a man; but, to himself, this popularity should exist not as a reward or incentive testifying to the intrinsic fitness or excellence of what he has done; but rather as a means of deciding what proportion of society he has already impregnated, or at least superficially moved in the direction of his own spirit, and how much yet remains to be invaded and brought into subjection. In certain cases, indeed, as where a man charged with a reforming doctrine appears in the midst of a sensual and embruted community, it might even be proper to lay it down as a maxim, that he cannot honestly or efficiently accomplish his office without the production in the first instance, of pain and anger at every step he takes. It was pedantic in Phocion, but by no means a mere antique attempt at a *bon mot*, when, hearing the people cheer him as he spoke, he turned round on the husting to the Greek gentleman that held his hat, and asked whether he had said anything more than usually stupid. When the soldiers of Cortez knocked down the idols of the Mexicans and white-washed the bloody walls of their temples, they did not expect native applause; but had they set up a theatre, and acted Spanish dramas instead, it would have been right for them to look for it. When Mahomet began his reform in Mecca, he did not send out on Saturday morning for the *Mecca Weekly Gazette*, to see whether there was a favourable notice in it of his last blast against unbelief and Polytheism; but we will not say that, so long as he was but a poet, even he may not have been guilty of that pardonable weakness of authorship, in relation, suppose, to some copy of verses on the death of a favourite camel. Now, seeing that it is as a preacher of unpleasant doctrine, on a scale not so large, perhaps, as that of Mahomet, but certainly larger than that of Phocion, that Mr. Carlyle must in his own heart regard himself (whether he is right in the supposition is another question); seeing, in short, that if ever he professed to be a practitioner of pure literature, he has long practically thrown aside that character, or merged it in another,—it ought not, we think, to be a matter of surprise, if he is rather inattentive to contemporary criticism, and if he does not, like the judicious dramatic author after the first performance of a new piece, bow to the popular decision, and hasten to cut out the passages that have been hissed. We should not imagine, for example, that, as he wrote the tract on *Model Prisons*, he expected it would bring him in a great deal of praise; nor, accordingly, should we suppose that he was much disappointed at not getting it. Or, to speak more plainly, there is not, we should infer from all the evidence we can get, a single man connected with the literature of this country, more thoroughly insensible than Mr. Carlyle to the mere titillation of critical opinion. In this respect, we are disposed to believe, he reaches an absolutely heroic standard, the contemplation of which might shame many of us. Much as it might vex some of his critics to be told so, *he*, we verily believe, does not send out for the *Mecca Gazette*, nor care one atom what it says for or against him. Sad, earnest, and great at least in superiority to this littleness, the roar of London notoriety passes, we have been told, totally unheeded around this *tenacem propositi virum*[2] (we leave the *justum* still in dispute) walking in his garden at Chelsea.

And yet, were mere literary reputation his object, he ought in justice to have an accession of it on this occasion. For, though it is chiefly in the *matter* of the pamphlets that their merit or demerit lies, so that, if the public come to a hostile decision with regard to that, they cannot be expected to be very warm in their praises of them with respect to anything else, yet, in point of literary execution, there is certainly much in them, that, with all our previous experience of the author's astonishing powers, might fairly command our highest admiration. One fault may indeed be charged against them, as artistic productions—the perpetual, and often wearisome vehemence, with which they recur to ideas so amply dilated on by the author, as to have become commonplaces to the majority of his readers. But this fault is inherent in the very nature of his enterprise. It is not Mr. Carlyle's aim in these Pamphlets to entertain his readers with a succession of agreeable thoughts and conceptions, each touched off just to that degree of fulness at which it

[2] *justum et tenacem propositi virum.* He who is just and firm in will does not quake before the fury (Horace, *Odes*, III, 3, 1).

can be easily apprehended; it is his aim to insist energetically on certain generalities of doctrine, to compel them into public belief, and to take care that they shall be too effectually taught to be readily forgotten. Hence he necessarily iterates and reiterates; rolls his main notions into view again and again, and, almost of set purpose, conveys them worked up into such profuse heaps of words, that there is induced in the reception of them a sense of surfeit and fatigue. A thing may be intellectually a commonplace, long before it is morally familiar; and as boys used to be taught to remember facts of parochial consequence by receiving beatings contemporaneously with them, so one is none the worse for being belaboured with an important truth through many more sentences, and in much more ponderous language, than might suffice for its mere intellectual conveyance. If, when you have changed your lodging, the postman makes a mistake in the delivery of your letters, it may not be sufficient simply to tell him once more the alteration you wish him to remember; but if you detain him in the street, hold him for ten minutes by the button, and punish him for his mistake by monotonously talking about the matter over and over again, till he actually perspires under your redundancy, you will have a sufficient security in the poor fellow's sensations against any similar blundering in future. And so sometimes with Mr. Carlyle. His pamphlets are, in fact, in many passages, exactly such street lectures to the postman. The reader would fain be off; like the postman he has his letters to deliver along the streets, and his other business to do; and he protests that he perfectly understands what Mr. Carlyle has been good enough to tell him, and that he will not forget it; but all in vain; again and again the information is repeated; the phrases 'justice,' 'the immensities,' 'the eternal fact of things,' are tumbled upon him with a frequency unexampled except in the Koran; and, when at last he is released, it is with a ringing in the ears, a universal sense of stupor, and knees absolutely knocking against each other for faintness. Nay, having laid aside, as Mr. Carlyle seems to have now done, the mere literary or artistic function altogether, the probability is that everything he may hereafter write will, to some degree, have this characteristic. Only, perhaps, in historical composition can we look for farther exhibitions of his genius that shall not be liable to this special criticism—a criticism, however, it should be remembered, true only as regards those that have made themselves familiar with Mr. Carlyle's mode of thinking by previous and intimate acquaintance with him, and probably not true, therefore, with regard to the general public. In historical writing, where, of course, there would be a succession of outwardly-given facts for Mr. Carlyle to pass in review and attend to, this very circumstance would necessarily demand from him an exercise of the purely artistic faculty, sufficiently large to prevent any manifestation of moral vehemence beyond what might be accounted legitimate in pure literature. And remembering what works in this department we have already had from Mr. Carlyle, we should certainly be justified in regretting if, adhering for the future exclusively to the vein he has opened in his *Pamphlets*, he were to refuse to write any more History. What a *History of the Norman Conquest* might he not add to our literature!

But, at the very utmost, the foregoing criticism (and that criticism, we have seen, is rather an appreciation of a necessity of the case than a positive objection) affects but occasional portions of the *Pamphlets*. Even as literary compositions they are, upon the whole, masterly. As our imaginary postman would certainly feel his punishment less if his tormentor, instead of monotonously and dryly droning one thing in his ears for ten minutes, were to diversify and enliven his lecture with anecdotes, corsucations of the fancy, and allusions of thousand-fold significance, and might even at last, in such a case, forget his hurry and almost relish his punishment as a pleasure; so, we should think, must even the most impatient of Mr. Carlyle's readers have felt themselves repaid by the incidental splendours of these *Pamphlets* for any tedium their repetitions of particular thoughts may have caused them. In this special respect our own preference is for the Pamphlets No. III. and No. VIII. of the series, entitled respectively *Downing Street* and *Jesuitism*; but the others, too, have their peculiar beauties. Deep lucid thought, resistless and grotesque humour, high imaginative and pictorial power, richness in anecdote and allusion, sagacious observation, stirring eloquence, extreme felicity of language—all those qualities, in short, that have earned for Mr. Carlyle's previous writings their acknowledged celebrity in our literature, are in these *Pamphlets* freshly approved and illustrated. Let an extract or two suffice by way of remembrance.

[quotes 'Among speculative persons' to 'seen before' *The Present Time*, XX, 26–7; 'Incompetent Duncan M'Pastehorn' to 'is drinking' *Model Prisons*, XX, 67–8; 'Smallest wrens' to 'have known' *Downing Street*, XX, 122; 'For all' to 'for ever' *Hudson's Statue*, XX, 267]

Turning our attention, however, from the literary merits and peculiarities of these *Pamphlets* of Mr. Carlyle to their doctrinal contents let us select for more detailed comment a topic or two out of the vast variety which they present to notice. In doing so, it seems natural rather to omit those topics in the discussion of which it does not appear possible to controvert him, and to select those in connexion with which we really believe that something may be advanced or suggested fairly contradictory of what he has said. Even where one differs most strongly from Mr. Carlyle, and feels almost constrained to fall out with him absolutely and finally as a teacher of what seems to be false, cruel, and mischievous, there is still, we are well aware, one consideration that ought to operate in making one ponder the difference long before expressing it, and in inducing one, if one must express it, to do so as modestly as possible. This is the consideration of Mr. Carlyle's real greatness of intellect, which renders it almost a matter of certainty that you cannot conceive or express any notion in connexion with any of the topics he has formally handled, that he has not himself conceived or expressed before you with far greater clearness and force, and a far more exact appreciation of its real significance and worth. In arguing with such a man— that is, in presenting considerations to his mind that appear to militate against his conclusions—one runs no small risk of committing that unhappy kind of error of which sending coal to Newcastle is a familiar instance. Nevertheless, one must in the end always fall back upon one's own conviction and sentiment; and the throb of the poorest heart, if only it be genuine, or the tear of the meanest eye, if only it drop at the bidding of emotion, is of avail, to an extent not to be arithmetically determined, against the proudest conclusions of the most intellectual of men. Considering what complexities, not only of substance and conformation, but also of quality and disposition, there are in the minds of human beings, one can see that there may be present in the least of existing individuals in a community, some wish, thought, phantasy, or feeling, purely special and idiosyncratic, yet divinely entitled, nay, and in the course of things, destined to modify and even reverse or stultify the generalizations of the greatest. There is a value in the really felt *No* of the poorest of God's creatures; for it may represent some portion of the 'Absolute Fact of Things' not represented in the *Yes* of the most gifted.

On glancing at the *Pamphlets* as a whole, a rough distinction presents itself between such of them as refer to temporary political and social interests, and such of them as more properly relate to the spiritual condition of the individual. In the former class, still proceeding but in a rough way, (for it is one of Mr. Carlyle's characteristics, that he drives the shuttle unceasingly between the spiritual and the social, inextricably involving the Immensities with the Minutiæ, Ego with Everything, and Heaven with Earth), we would, for our part, reckon the five tracts entitled respectively *The Present Time, Model Prisons, Downing Street, The New Downing Street,* and *Parliaments*; in the second class, we would reckon the remaining three, entitled respectively *Stump-Orator, Hudson's Statue,* and *Jesuitism.* We shall select a topic or two for comment, first out of the one class, and then out of the other.

And first, occupying a conspicuous place among Mr. Carlyle's various exhortations on the subject of Social Reform, is his specific recommendation with regard to the immediate treatment of our over-grown pauperism. His counsels and opinions on this matter are most explicitly stated in the conclusion of the first pamphlet, where he intro-duces an imaginary discourse addressed from a conceivable Prime Mini-ster to the entire pauper population of these realms. The most important passages of that discourse are the following:—

[quotes a non-continuous passage from 'Vagrant lackalls' to 'your work' *The Present Time*, XX, 39–46]

Here, certainly, is distinctness and precision enough. What Mr. Car-lyle would do with the pauperism of the country is, according to the foregoing extract, substantially this:—He would abolish the whole sys-tem of our existing Poor-laws, new or old, with their aids and appliances of rates, unions, boards of guardians, and Workhouses; gradually, per-haps, but still thoroughly, he would sweep the country clean of all these things—the accumulated rubbish and solidification of English stupidity, combined with occasional deposits of English sense and ingen-uity, since the days of Elizabeth: then casting loose, for the moment, the three millions of individuals, whose maintenance is at present, at an annual expense of eight or nine millions sterling to the rest of the community, guaranteed upon the said system of institutions, he would permit such of them as chose and were ready to re-enter society on the footing of independent citizens paying their own way; and the rest he would treat really, if not nominally, as serfs of the State, bound to go where the State sent them, and to do the State's bidding, just as soldiers are: and, lastly, as soldiers are submitted to a regular drill and organization, having sergeants, lieutenants, captains, colonels, and gen-erals over them, so would he divide the mass of paupers that would thus be at the public disposal into bands or regiments, each duly officered and appointed, and differing from ordinary regiments only in this, that whereas ordinary regiments are marched from place to place against

345

human foes, these new regiments would be employed in purely industrial or productive services, and chiefly, for the time being at least, in the agricultural labour of reclaiming waste lands at home—one regiment, for example, being sent off under its colonel and his subalterns to the Bog of Allen; a second receiving orders to go to Salisbury Plain and tear a bit of it into fertility; and a third, with some Smith of Deanston at its head, being posted, with similar injunctions, on some lone sheepwalk in Sutherland or Dumfriesshire.

This is a favourite idea of Mr. Carlyle's. He has urged it again and again in his various recent publications, and only repeats it in the pamphlet before us. Nor is the idea peculiar to himself. That the limit of the agricultural resources of this country is by no means yet nearly reached; that not to mention the vast increase of produce that might be extracted by better and more laborious husbandry from the lands already under cultivation, there are thousands of thousands of acres now lying waste in these islands from which rich harvests might be raised, capable of maintaining a large excess of population above what now exists, or is likely soon to exist—is an idea extremely familiar to the popular common sense, and incessantly used by those that appeal to that tribunal. 'I could employ all the unemployed men in Scotland north of the Dee,' said a Chartist speaker, with great effect, once in our hearing. 'Talk of emigration!' is a common saying—'the best and cheapest emigration would be to the waste lands of Ireland, were that but rendered practicable.' In short, to seek to extinguish pauperism by directing pauper labour in considerable masses full against the soil, aye and until the soil take the sustenance of that labour completely on itself, is a notion with which at the present moment the public mind, with the exception perhaps of that small but most impenetrable portion of it wherein the executive lies, is quite surcharged. Moreover, the very form of that notion most congenial to Mr. Carlyle,—that namely, in which the analogy of a military organization is used to suggest and represent the most effective mode of accomplishing the object in view,—is one that has been previously illustrated and recommended times without number. It is essentially, in fact, a conception of modern Socialism. Ever since the time of Fourier, the phrase 'Industrial Armies,' and the whole idea implied in it of the application of the military method of organization, or of something like it, to the general business of production, whether agricultural or manufacturing, have been commonplaces among the more able and thoughtful Socialists; and by Fourier himself, as well as by various of his followers, the idea has been worked out with a degree of detail and specialty foreign to the intellectual habits of Mr. Carlyle.

What is peculiar to Mr. Carlyle, however, in addition to the amazing force and acceptability which his extraordinary union of sagacity with descriptive power enables him to give to this notion, is the element of moral sternness with which,—standing apart herein from the so-called Socialists, as he likes to do from all bodies of men whatever that seek shelter under the umbrella of a dogmatic denomination,—he takes care to invest it. There is no talk with him of that 'attractive labour' or '*travail attrayant*' of which Fourier makes so much; no promises of independence, freedom from restriction, equality, and a voice in the election of office-bearers, such as allure one in Louis Blanc's scheme of the *Ateliers Nationaux*.[3] On the contrary, offering his scheme of Agricultural Regiments only as a scheme for the treatment of that outcast portion of society which has already fallen over into a state of pauperism, (what his opinion may be on the higher question of a reconstruction of all society universally on some such principle of industrial organization, is a matter as yet left obscure,) he carefully abstains from all poetic delineations of its beauty or pleasantness, and insists rather on the fact of its necessity, and the possibility of its severe efficiency. Stepping forward among the 'vagrant Lackalls' not as a kind and smiling philanthropist, telling them that they are his fellows and brethren, and that they have been thrown out of their rights by the mal-arrangements of a false and imperfect civilization, but as a hard and even haughty disciplinarian who views them chiefly as the victims of their own deplorable folly and criminality, interesting only as objects of pity, he does not disguise from them the fact that, in his scheme for their benefit, they are to be accounted, the whole three millions of them, as a class apart and separate, temporarily doomed by the very circumstance of their helplessness, to a position of social inferiority and subjection. They are, he tells them, to be the serfs of the State, bound to comply with such conditions, even of inconvenience and hardship, as the State, in paying and managing them, may find it necessary to impose. Braving the very swordpoints of popular conviction and sentiment, he does not hesitate to call in as applicable to them all those general considerations with respect to the institution of Slavery, with which, by reflecting on the Negro Question, he had already filled his mind; and to pronounce them, in the language, if not of courtesy and custom, yet of fact and reality, bondsmen

---

[3] Social workshops were proposed by Louis Blanc when he was a member of the provisional government in 1848.

347

and slaves. Even the plain speaking of Fletcher of Saltoun, whose views on the subject of pauperism approach nearer those of Mr. Carlyle than perhaps any others that have ever been deliberately published, is but as timidity when compared with some passages in the first of these pamphlets. It is now a hundred and fifty years since that distinguished Scotchman, whose reputation for patriotism and real goodness of heart, as well as for sternness of manner, was probably as great in his day as Mr. Carlyle's is now, wrote a pamphlet in which, as the only effective remedy for the then existing pauperism of his native land, he proposed that the two hundred thousand individuals of which it was composed, should be simultaneously seized and collected; three or four hundred of the worst and least hopeful of them sent by the Scottish government as a present to the Venetians to serve in their galleys against the Turks; and the remainder compulsorily quartered as serfs,—a certain number on each considerable proprietor of the country, who, in return for relieving the State of all anxiety concerning them, should be entitled (subject to certain fundamental restrictions securing to the serfs the advantages of education, and equal safety of life and limb, with all other persons whatever) to the full disposal and usufruct of their services. Even at that time the proposal shocked public opinion; and though Fletcher argued the matter seriously, and addressed himself with all his might to this very objection, 'that he was bringing back slavery into the world,' he probably only escaped the infamy of being reckoned a brute, by undergoing the minor obloquy of being thought a man of crotchets. Yet Mr. Carlyle (whose scheme, however, if examined, would probably turn out to be much less of a return even to formal and reputed slavery than that of Fletcher) is bold enough, in this very different age, and in the face of an Abolition Movement all but universal, to make use of language with respect to three millions of British paupers, whose interest in the property of the country is a vested and traditional right, such as Fletcher did not dare to apply even to the handful of Scottish vagabonds that were the subjects of his problem. There is not a word in Fletcher about the 'beneficent whip;' and he even proposes that it should be enacted that, when his scheme should be carried into effect, the use of the name Slave as applied to the parties concerned, should be strictly forbidden. 'I regard not names,' he said, 'but things; and the misapplication of names has confounded everything.' And here probably Mr. Carlyle would agree with him. Let but his notion of Industrial Regiments of paupers be carried out, and he would probably regard it as a matter of indifference whether they should be called State-serfs, or by some name more flattering and honourable.

There are, of course, two opposite quarters from which Mr. Carlyle's scheme is liable to attack. On the one hand, the Economists, to use a term which has now begun to pass current as distinctive of a certain class of writers, are sure to ply against it all their established maxims and forms of thought. They will say, in the first place, that, by handing over to Government so large a share in the general business of production, as would be involved in the industrial superintendence and maintenance of three millions of paupers, there would be traversed one of the fundamental doctrines of their science—that, namely, which assigns the whole care and direction of national industry to the happy and spontaneous operation throughout the community of the natural law of supply and demand. That the State should constitute itself a master of industry by engaging to find work and wages for any number of individuals whatever, seems to them a ruinous return to ancient ideas of government, and a retrograde step in civilization. The force of this argument, however, which one saw repeated times without number against the so far similar scheme of *Ateliers Nationaux* propounded by Louis Blanc, appears now to be fast waning. For one thing, of whatever avail it is against Mr. Carlyle's scheme, or against that of Louis Blanc as applied to England, of exactly as much avail is it against the existing system of Poor Laws, which it is the design of such schemes to supersede. In the English Poor-Law system, the Government occupies precisely the position of a contractor to the community for the most economical management of the labour of all the national paupers; and what Mr. Carlyle proposes is essentially nothing more than a better mode, as he thinks, for fulfilling the contract. Moreover there has recently sprung up such a force of opinion contradictory of the established maxim of *Laissez-faire*, or at least of this special application of it, and men of so high consideration for talent and character have recently fulminated protests against it, that it begins now to be surmised even among Economists themselves, that the principle of demand and supply, so far from being the last word that science can give respecting the methods of directing labour, will turn out to be but a provisional expression of a convenient truth, and a point of departure for other and larger notions, wherein, not by retrogression, but only by persistent progress, some of the ancient practices of government will again be recognised as legitimate. In short, this particular argument against Mr. Carlyle's scheme is fast getting drowned in an ocean of popular contempt and impatience. More likely to impress people is the argument

349

of its alleged impracticability. Three millions of paupers squatted among the mosses and on the hillsides of the country, armed with spades and pickaxes, accompanied (for surely Mr. Carlyle would be more benevolent in this respect than the Poor-Law Commissioners) with their wives and children, and kept in drill by a hierarchy of semi-military functionaries, receiving their orders from the Secretary of State's office—this is a picture at the contemplation of which the British mind shudders. All the standing armies in the world be nothing to this. If, during the railway mania, there were frequent qualms as to the probable results to society of the accumulation in encampments throughout the country, of such masses of half-heathen navvies, many of them Orsons in physical strength, and all of them fond of fighting; if even now a rumour of the atrocious injustice of the truck-system wafts sometimes into the heart of British civilisation the horrid idea what a fund of lurid fury the iron districts of England and Wales might at any moment vomit forth—in what a state of trepidation, it may be said, should we necessarily live, if we had three millions of fustian-jackets under drill among the hills, ready to rise at an instant, were they enraged, and only a scattered regiment or two of red-coats at command to put them down! Fancy, it may be said, the effect upon one regiment of such State-serfs, of a whipping too severely administered by some unpopular colonel; or the effect upon all the regiments simultaneously of some harsh general order from the Secretary of State. What Sicilian slave-insurrections might we not have? what conquests of our best generals, and of our sturdiest police inspectors, by some band of determined paupers broken loose under the leadership of some Brummagem Spartacus? True, in the case of the army, all these objections have been practically overcome, so that there thousands of men are kept orderly and manageable with ease; but how, it might be asked, in the case of the new army of serfs, should we be able to extemporize such a set of rules and traditions, old as Hengist and the Heptarchy, as that by which the army coheres and has being? And then, in the interim, it might be said, what stupidity, what blundering, what accumulations of abuse worse than were ever presented under the operation of the old poor-law itself? Look, it might be said, to the French Revolution of 1848. There precisely such a scheme as that of Mr. Carlyle was put into temporary practice. When Paris was full of men out of work, a M. Emile Thomas appeared and proposed to brigade them into industrial regiments under the command of students from the Central School of Arts and Sciences, and to employ them on certain public works in and around the city. His plan was eagerly accepted; about a hundred thousand men were actually brigaded; works were devised, and regiments posted at the spots where they were to be executed; and the result was such three months of idleness, singing, buffoonery, and disquietude, as were never before seen in Paris, and as it required a master-stroke of executive audacity to bring to an end. And such, the Economists would probably say, would be the inevitable consequence of any attempt in this country to carry out Mr. Carlyle's scheme.

We cannot say that we wholly agree with them. The Parisian experiment of M. Emile Thomas we hold to have been not a fair trial of the scheme, but a piece of monstrous French bungling and clap-trap, not to be seriously adduced as a precedent at all. And as for the supposed danger of organizing, after the manner proposed by Mr. Carlyle, all the lawless elements now dispersed through the community and weakened by the dispersion—this danger, we conceive, would lie only in the chance that society would maintain a false and unjust relationship to the portion of itself it had thus detached away into the moors and hills; and might even thus, by serving as an indication of something more profoundly wrong than is usually believed in our social arrangements, become a means of enlightening us as to our true path in the future, and of speeding on unknown ulterior developments. As, in the insurrection of Spartacus, there was a motive and a stimulus among the ancient Romans to considerations of policy not likely otherwise to have occurred to them; so the presence among us of three millions of human beings visibly depending on us for guidance and support, and visibly capable of crushing or overpowering us if we do not give it them, may be the very thing necessary to convince us of the wretchedly ephemeral nature of some of our cherished conclusions respecting the constitution of society, and to create the requisite impetus by which we shall be borne along the next, and some golden step it may be, in the historic evolution. We do not, therefore, feel any extreme degree of sympathy with this argument *in terrorem*. More powerful to our mind, from the economic point of view, are those arguments against Mr. Carlyle's scheme, which consist in the general assertion that he has not exhibited its harmony with those specific doctrines of economic science by which its working is intellectually begirt and conditioned. That such a gigantic innovation as Mr. Carlyle proposes on all our established modes of procedure, would necessarily produce a tremor and derangement pervading all British society, is clearly undeniable; and Mr. Carlyle, it may be said, is bound to trace out, as far as may be, beforehand the probable curve and direction of this derangement, as that would be determined by some of the more important of the known laws of Political Economy, and particularly by these three—the Malthusian principle of population; the law that industry is limited by capital; and the law that the rate of increase in agricultural production is one of diminishing proportion to the capital and labour expended in procuring it.

> The waters shall wax, the woods shall wene;
> Hill and moss shall be torn in;
> But the bannock will never be braider

are the words of Thomas the Rhymer; and little as Mr. Carlyle cares for M'Growdy, this remarkable coincidence between that modern gentleman's doctrines and the old saw of the Scottish seer might have deserved to attract his attention. That, if he set himself to it, Mr. Carlyle would be able to fortify his scheme even on the consideration of its economical bearings, is extremely likely. It is not ignorance of Political Economy, (for he has read, he says, 'some barrowfuls' of treatises on that science in his time,) but rather willing contempt for it, that causes him to ignore the necessity of attempting any express conciliation between the scheme he offers and the current maxims of the economists. Still, considering that these maxims, minute and partial as they may appear, really do express certain existing conditions to which every scheme of social reform must submit itself under pain of failure, one cannot but desire such a conciliation, were it but by way of argumentative anticipation; and all the more so that some leading economists of larger and more revolutionary views than their fellows, appear to regard any extensive application of the notion of industrial regiments to the extinction of pauperism as conclusively forbidden by their science, and to incline, on that account, rather to push on the public mind to other means of accomplishing the same end, as, for example, to the scheme of Peasant Proprietorship.

The objections of the Socialists to Mr. Carlyle's scheme would, of course, be radically different from those of the Economists. On the whole, it is true, they would regard it as a step in the right direction. That the State should assume to itself the supreme administration of the business of national production, is the known view of at least one class among the Socialists,—that represented by M. Louis Blanc; and that the State is bound to find work and subsistence for all that cannot otherwise procure it, is a settled tenet in the creed of Socialists of all sects. That a scheme, therefore, of the nature of Mr. Carlyle's should be carried into effect; that on any terms whatever, the State should charge itself with the industrial management of three millions of destitute individuals, would be matter for unmingled satisfaction to the whole Socialist world. But, looking at the scheme as propounded by its author, they would pronounce it a Socialist idea advanced in an aristocratic spirit. Mr. Carlyle, they would say, is a man destitute of the true and characteristic sentiment of Socialism—that sentiment, namely, which delights in contemplating all mankind as equally units in a terrestrial point of view, and of which the French phrases Liberty and Equality are the much-abused expressions; he is a man accustomed rather to that solitary extra-terrestrial point of view, from which the moral inequalities of things are seen more distinctly to come out, and familiarity with which is apt to generate, in a noble man of strict temperament, a spirit of intolerance, despotism, and rigorous compulsion; and hence, while his project for the remedy of pauperism is essentially a coincidence with Socialism, he has put it forth in the language not of a genuine and sentimental equalitarian, but of an old Greek τυραννος,[4] or resolute modern slave-owner, doing the right thing, but kicking you while he does it. But for all this, as we have said, the Socialists would welcome any attempt to put his scheme in force. All that talk about 'the whip' and 'shooting' with it was according to the nature of Mr. Carlyle's genius to clothe the statement of his scheme, would come to nothing, they would say, in the tear and wear of actual experience. Once let the three millions of fustian-jackets be abroad among the morasses and hills, and all the colonels in the world, and all the cobwebs of borrowed military forms that could be invented to back them, would not guarantee society against the vast proletarian influence that would be thus concentrated and made visible;—the peace might indeed be kept and the stipulated work done; but the total effect would be as if society, tired of its slow rate of progress hitherto, had thrown the least timorous and least interested portion of its strength into the advanced guard, and thus shod itself, so to speak, with a democratic ploughshare, fast to cleave the future. Hence it partly is, as we conceive, that of almost all existing political parties, those who like Mr. Carlyle's recent appearances best are the Socialists and extreme Republicans. It is curious enough, too, though readily explicable, that men of the other or aristocratic extreme, with whom also we believe some of Mr. Carlyle's views find favour, are beginning, in like manner, to be popular with the Socialists.

To pass to another topic of the *Pamphlets*: Even more startling than

4 *Tyrannos* (autocratic ruler).

Mr. Carlyle's views regarding the treatment of pauperism, are those he has put forth on the subject of Criminal Reform. To follow him into all the separate particulars of his discussion of this subject—as, for example, into his appreciation of the character and services of Howard, which we believe to be historically just and accurate; or into his defence of Capital Punishments, which appears to us to want something; or into his restatement, against the Simple-prevention School, of the true theory of Punishments in general, which we regard as highly beautiful and philosophical—is at present impossible. We select rather the passage in which he sums up his views as to the general relation in which society ought to try to stand towards the criminal part of it—in other words, his views as to the wisdom of the Criminal Reform movement.

[quotes a non-continuous passage from 'If I had' to 'come from it' *Model Prisons*, XX, 59–61]

Now, it cannot be denied, we think, that there is much in this declaration of the author's sentiments, as true as it is striking. There are few things in the *Pamphlets* more touchingly conclusive than the allusion, so quaint and yet so illustrative of the author's meaning, to the 'poor dark tradeshops with red herrings and tobacco-pipes crossed in the window;' and, as we read, the conviction does flash in upon us, that amid the zeal of our professional philanthropists for this special interest of criminals, the other and larger interest of our poor hard-working myriads of honest people has been wofully neglected. Hints too, we believe, there are in the particular *Pamphlet* under notice, that may be useful in suggesting real improvements in the practical management of our prisons; albeit we cannot but imagine, that in his representation of the comforts of a modern prison-house, with its cocoa, its cleanliness, its chaplain, and its ventilation, Mr. Carlyle has omitted the very element that renders the poor trade-shop with all its discomforts even popularly preferable, namely, the imprisonment.

But, taking the passage as a whole, and trying to extract as fully as possible the general drift of it, namely, that society should dismiss this 'extremely contemptible interest of scoundrels,' tumble it over London Bridge, or summarily get rid of it anyhow; taking, we say, this passage as it stands, there is, we feel bound to admit, no other passage in the whole range of the *Pamphlets* that provoked in us at the first reading, or that does now provoke in us, such a rush of sentimental and deeply-moved negation. 'Wrong, wrong!' we cried, 'by these tears, this nervous tremour, noble man as thou art, thou art here wrong;' and more resolutely and less diffidently than on any other occasion of conscious difference from a great writer, did we openly recognise the difference, and feel willing to stand by it. And we feel so yet. Not that we would care, or that we should be prepared, to construct an argument in favour of the Criminal-Reform Movement upon statistical evidence of what has been accomplished in this way, or upon the *vivâ voce* declarations of good and sensible men largely and even officially connected with prisons, as to the proportion of committed criminals that they personally, judging by their own experience, believe to be absolutely reclaimable. Our recollection of one positive statement of this kind made in our hearing by a prison-governor, leads us to conclude that much might be made of such an argument. Again, there is, we also believe, no small degree of argumentative value in the consideration that a large proportion of the mass of crime is hereditary and transmitted, and therefore less chargeable upon individuals than on society itself. But what we chiefly rest on is feeling, instinct, the inarticulate reason within us; that ultimate faculty of No and Yes, to the foot of whose throne, when the scuffle of all possible articulate controversy is over, every question of this sort must be dragged for decision. And, strictly considered, what is Mr. Carlyle's own deliverance on the point at issue, but the vehement *Egomet dixi*[5] of his peculiar, and, though profound and generous, yet severely constituted nature? That the 'interest of scoundrels' as he calls it, should be tumbled over London Bridge, and so summarily dismissed, is what he feels should be done with 'the interest of scoundrels.' But what if some good man, less great perhaps than he, but more tremulous to certain soft transcendentalisms, some meek-eyed village clergyman, let us say, or some pale and weak-bodied recluse, should feel otherwise; and, after consulting his own heart, should put forth this counter-assertion, that, even though not once in a thousand years should one criminal be reclaimed, yet it is the duty and part of the highest training of every society to persist in the Quixotic effort, and to place the labour of attempting to reabsorb its outcasts foremost among its systematic enterprises? And what if, seeking authority for his own timid feelings against the strength of so unequal an opponent, such a man should venture to call in certain old words once spoken in Judea, and intended to transform the soul of the world, and make it more pitiful for ever? 'They that be whole need not a physician, but they that are sick.' And again, 'I will have mercy and not sacrifice: for I am not come to call the

5 I, myself, have said it.

righteous, but sinners to repentance.' And again, 'How think ye? if a man have an hundred sheep, and one of them be gone astray, doth he not leave the ninety and nine, and goeth into the mountains, and seeketh that which is gone astray?' And again 'Joy shall be in heaven over one sinner that repenteth, more than over ninety and nine just persons, which need no repentance.' All this, of course, Mr. Carlyle is aware of; and takes care to guard himself against. 'Christian Religion!' he says, expressing his disgust at what he thinks the unwarrantable references made in the matter to the authority of the Gospel; 'does the Christian or any religion prescribe love of scoundrels, then? I hope it prescribes a healthy hatred of scoundrels;—otherwise what am I, in heaven's name, to make of it?' Notwithstanding all which, (and there is a truth in this mode of putting the thing, too,) it remains clear to us, that Mr. Carlyle's prescription as to the treatment of the criminal interest, and the prescription of the Christian religion, are not one and the same. Hatred of scoundrels! True! but define your 'scoundrel!' Will the definition, if just, carry in it an approval of your sentence with regard to what is called, in the language customary to this controversy, the criminal portion of society? Ah! far back in the vista of time, may not the reverent fancy still see the face of One who, though he drove money-changers out of the Temple, and rebuked Scribes and Pharisees, yet kept company with publicans and sinners, and told, in gentle parable, how wrong it was in the elder brother to be angry with his father because, instead of dismissing the extremely contemptible interest of the prodigal who had devoured his living with harlots at a distance, he welcomed his return with joy, and regaled him with better entertainment than had ever fallen to the lot of the righteous son who had served faithfully many years, and at no time transgressed? If there was supreme wisdom there, there is vehement error here; for according to no possible interpretation, can such passages as we have quoted from our author be said to be conceived in this spirit.

Speaking scientifically, we should be inclined to say that Mr. Carlyle's peculiar mode of thinking on this subject arises from the dominance in his mind of a very high form of that sentiment by which, in its lowest form, the world at large is accustomed to determine the degree of social consideration that shall be paid to different individuals. Who are the men that get on in the world, that make fortunes, and that rise to place and dignity? They are not the men, generally speaking, of the highest intrinsic merit, either moral or intellectual; they are men, for the most part, of a certain energy of character good solely for this one effect, men of large jaw, and of a narrow and even morose habit of perseverance. Take, reader, any two persons of your own acquaintance, —one that has accomplished, let us say even by the most honourable and legitimate means, a distinct and pronounced success in life, and another that has never got on so far as to have an account with a banker: compare all that you know of the two individuals; think of the entire sensation you have respecting the one when in his presence, as compared with the sensation you have in the same circumstances with respect to the other; calculate, if you can, from this, the sum-total of the really meritorious manifestations both of head and of heart that must have gone forth from the one during his whole life, as compared with the sum-total that must have gone forth from the other; and the chances are that, though you will find certain genuine points of superiority in the richer, you will have to conclude that the other is essentially, and as tried by a spiritual standard, the better, sounder, and more gifted nature. A Goldsmith, we should think, would rank higher, with all his moral defects, than a Benjamin Franklin. Not that there was virtue in the defects of the one, for prudence added to intellect and heart, make the noblest triad; but that there was greater want of virtue in the defects of the other. Now, although Mr. Carlyle is very far from lending his sanction to so coarse a mode of regarding men as that which makes the prudential all in all, and although no man has startled the world more by the audacity with which he has found merit where mankind in general found none, or worse than none; yet we think we per-ceive in him, and especially of late, a tendency to accept as absolute, on the whole, that classification of men which is determined, as we have seen, chiefly by their practical or success-compelling qualities. To say this in the face of his onslaught on Mr. Hudson is somewhat bold; but we think we could prove it. It is the Roman type of mind that Mr. Carlyle prefers, and not the Hellenic. For what is called mere sensibility, the influence of which is invisibly and electrically diffusive, he has but little respect; what he admires is direct energy of character. Hence, as we imagine, somewhat of that tone of severity and reproach with which he thinks it necessary to address his imaginary audience of paupers in the first of these pamphlets. That they *are* paupers, that they have failed to maintain themselves above the level of want, is to him, as indeed it ought legitimately be to all, a *primâ facie* evidence that in some point or other they are weaker than their fellows; but, in attending to this, he seems to forget that, to some extent at least, the worldly struggle in which these men have fared so badly, may not have yet been so organized as to be a fair comparative trial of the whole merits of the competitors. And so, in a certain, though perhaps smaller degree, in the case even of criminals. Can it be said, with any degree of confidence, that the criminals of the world are the worst men in it? May no good qualities of humanity seek a specific refuge even among *them*? Ah! does not Christianity here also help us to a higher speculation? Does it not seem as if its great Founder had intended, by his assiduous presence in the society of sinners, and by his frequent assertions of the superiority of mercy to sacrifice, to indicate a preference for keenness of sensibility over energy of character, and to read the world the permanent lesson that, on this very account, some of the more hopeful elements of our social regeneration are to be found among the outcasts?

To turn to another topic: Not the least interesting of the contents of these *Pamphlets* are the author's expositions of his views regarding the nature, objects, and methods of government. The great end of all government Mr. Carlyle defines, in general terms, to be the conduct of the whole social procedure of a nation in accordance with the permanent laws of the universe. 'To prosper in this world,' he says, 'to gain felicity, victory, and improvement, either for a man or a nation, there is but one thing requisite—that the man or nation can discern what the true regulations of the universe are in regard to him and his pursuit, and can faithfully and steadfastly follow these.' Whatsoever administration, 'were it Russian Autocrat, Chartist Parliament, Grand Lama, Force of Public Opinion, Archbishop of Canterbury, or M'Crowdy, the seraphic doctor, with his last evangel of Political Economy,' can set a nation most surely in the way of these laws, is, by that fact, the best form of government. Something more precise, however, he thinks, it may be possible to determine respecting the mode most likely to attain the great end. If, for example, any means could be devised where by, absolutely, or even approximately, the ablest man in a nation should be raised to the highest official place in it, and surrounded by the men nearest in ability to himself, so as to govern by their aid—this, he thinks, would be as nearly a perfect scheme of national polity as we can hope to live under. For, according to his theory, the ablest man is also necessarily the best man, the most valiant and worthy in all respects, and the truest in his insight into the ways of the universe. Place him, therefore, at the top of a nation, and give him able men as his instruments and subordinates; and, so far as human means can, you guarantee that nation a career of prosperity and rectitude.

Now, though all this is very general, yet, like other generalities, it is a splendid thing to remember, and a thing, nevertheless, very apt to be forgotten. By keeping this ideal scheme of government in mind, one may not indeed be able, thinks Mr. Carlyle, to frame off-hand a set of institutions for its accomplishment, but one will at least have a useful notion of the kind of institutions that will tend that way; and, above all, one will be expert at knowing the kind of institutions that have no such promise in them. For himself, making this critical use of his ideal, he is disposed to protest, it appears, chiefly against one abstraction relative to the art of governing now widely spread throughout the mind of Western Europe—the abstraction, namely, that is couched in the phrase 'Representative System.'

Fairly to get out the collective wishes of a nation with respect to every step of its procedure; fairly to collect the votes of all its component individuals, and accurately to base every act of legislation or administration on the pronounced opinion of the majority, (if indeed some method might not be devised for giving expression in act to the desire of the minority too,) this, for the last century or more, has been the ideal scheme of government painted forth to the eager eyes of nations by our metaphysical politicians. *Vox Populi, vox,* as nearly as possible, *Dei*; perfect, therefore, your system of representation, so as not to leave out of account any particle of opinion lodged anywhere throughout the community, whether in the highest or in the lowest stratum; and by this means alone you will catch the clue of the future. Such is the abstract theory: in practice, of course, there are difficulties in the way. To meet these, it is customary to take up the question in two parts; discussing, first, *the Suffrage,* or that portion of the representative system in which, by the delegation of the right of legislation by the community at large to a limited number of individuals, the first stage in the formularization of its wishes is effected; and, secondly, *the Constitution of Parliaments,* or that other portion of the system, in which, by the adoption of certain modes of procedure among the delegated individuals, the work of formularization is completed. In both these stages of the process, the theory demands the most absolute respect for the representative principle. In the first place, the suffrage should, according to the pure theory, be universal, no man, woman, or child, being excluded; and, in the second place, the constitution of parliaments should be such as, while subjecting them as completely as possible to the flux of opinion out of doors, to secure them perfect independence in deliberation, and the entire control of the executive. This, of course, is only as the matter is represented in theory; for neither in the nature of things is such a thorough scheme of representation possible, nor even in those countries where it has been carried farthest has it attained all the finish that might be practicable. On the whole, the part of the scheme that has been most elaborated in Europe is that referring to the constitution of parliaments. In England and in France, parliaments have now for some time been approximating to the form accounted perfect by the representativists. Hence, in the less advanced countries of Europe, the possession of a parliamentary constitution like that of England was, till lately, regarded as a realization in full of the system of representation. Only in England and France themselves was the other part of the problem, that of the organization of the suffrage, very assiduously worked at. Completing the long effort to bring up the practice to the theory, there arose in each of these countries a Universal Suffrage movement. Recent events have given this movement an *éclat* that a little while ago could hardly have been anticipated; and now it may be said that over all Europe the aspiration of the popular politicians is for a free and exclusively representative parliament, based on universal suffrage. That, and that alone, it is believed, will be the salvation of the nations.

Right into the heart of all this Mr. Carlyle hurls his contradiction. Keeping in view his conclusion as to the end and purpose of government, namely, that nations should be led conformably to the laws of right and justice, he denies, *in toto*, the competence, as regards this end, of the theory of representation. His illustration on this point is very happy.

[quotes 'Your ship' to 'of nature' *The Present Time*, XX, 15–16]

This quarrel with the representative theory of government he carries out in detail. For the suffrage movement, for example, he has no regard whatever, pronouncing it one of the least hopeful speculations in which, at the present day, a man could engage. By no conceivable mode or amount, he thinks, of 'ballot-boxing,' could the only end be served that would entitle that process to any estimation as one of the chief formalities in the business of government,—the discrimination, namely, of the ablest and fittest men from the rest of the community, in order that they might be invested with official rank. To perfect the organization of the suffrage would, therefore, he thinks, be a waste of labour. Again, as regards parliament, his judgment is to the same purpose. A parliament is but a talking-apparatus, and, even were it composed of efficient men, would necessarily, by the very nature of its constitution as a representative body, be less adapted for the true work of government than some other institution easily conceivable. The day of parliaments, he asserts, is all but gone by in England; and already, he thinks, men ought to be beginning to confess as much to themselves, and to be looking forward to the new sort of device, upon which, as he anticipates, the country, if it is to exist in prosperity any longer, must soon come to depend. That device, he believes, will be a reformed Downing-street. Somehow or other, (he is unable to say how; except that he believes the proclamation of the necessity will help to bring about the result, by rousing and setting in motion towards Whitehall the very individuals that are wanted,) the country will have to get together its best intellects; and these, forming themselves into an executive committee, will have to assume the direction of affairs, using such of the old forms of parliamentary procedure as they find convenient, and dispensing with the others. Meanwhile, as a step to this large result, and as a means of bringing it about as gradually, and with as little derangement as possible, he proposes that the present constitution of our parliaments should be at once so far modified as to permit the return to them of a few members who should not be representatives of any constituencies, but direct nominees of the prime minister.

Now, in all this there is much that is deep, and full of wholesome instruction, especially needed at the present hour. To disenchant the popular mind of its illusion as to the absolute sufficiency of a full representative system for the remedy of all social wrongs, and the satisfaction of all social wants, would be a service of the highest importance. Two thousand years ago Socrates made it one of his aims to perform very much the same service for the men of Athens, teaching them, almost in the very words that Mr. Carlyle uses, that right and justice were the ends of all government, and that these ends could no more be accomplished by the hap-hazard association of the citizens, than the business of steering a ship safely could be accomplished by the empiric agreement of the passengers. It is a curious corroboration, also, of the validity of these views of Mr. Carlyle at this particular crisis of the affairs of Europe, that the profoundest speculative politicians of France have of late been pursuing very nearly the same track of thought. Among the best passages in that part of the *Cours de Philosophie Positive* of M. Comte, in which the author contributes his efforts towards the formation of a science of Sociology, are those wherein he criticises the existing maxims of our ordinary liberal politicians, such as that embodied in the phrase 'sovereignty of the people,' and points out how, provisionally useful as these maxims have been, their prolonged existence and reputation tends to keep Europe in a state of anarchy. In the very language of M. Comte, too, diametrically different as his philosophical point of view is from that of Mr. Carlyle, there is an interesting resemblance to the language which Mr. Carlyle employs. Divest Mr. Carlyle's phraseology of its religious spirit, translate his burning 'regulations of the universe,' into the calmer and more algebraic expression, 'positive scientific laws,' and you have exactly what M. Comte has been saying on this subject on the other side of the Channel. Proudhon, too, has been working at the same vein; and among his various intellectual exhibitions during the last year or two, has been as desperate a criticism as we remember ever to have read, on the popular expectation from universal suffrage. In short, here again, we find the most curious coincidence between the conclusions of Mr. Carlyle, and those of the extreme Socialist thinkers.

Practically, however, there is a difference. And, doing our best to find out the precise nature of the difference, we should say that it consists in this, that whereas such French writers as we have named occupy the scientific point of view, and regard the whole subject in the light of that largest and most splendid of scientific generalizations, the idea of evolution; Mr. Carlyle, on the other hand, throws evolution to the winds, and attacks the subject, regardlessly of past or future, by the sheer force of his immediately agitated personality. Hence, however, we cannot but think, that, much as his method enables him to excel in impressiveness, yet, as regards completeness, the others have the advantage of him. Entertaining as low an opinion as Mr. Carlyle of the absolute benefit that would be derived from never so perfect a representative system, and denouncing as distinctly as he does the infatuation of those that build their hopes of social reorganization on universal suffrage, or any such abstraction, MM. Comte and Proudhon would yet, as we believe, allow a certain social value to that direction of political activity for some time to come, and would even, we imagine, consent, with ulterior views, to lend a portion of their personal energy to accelerate the termination of that particular avatar. As many of our best thinkers in this country worked for the repeal of the Corn-Laws, not because they had high expectations of an increase of national prosperity from that measure, but because they wished to get the whole moral hinderance of the subject well out of the way; so there are not a few who believe that, though an extended suffrage will by no means be a panacea, nor even a partial cure for social wrongs, yet, in the inevitable process of evolution, our path lies through a movement in its favour. For one thing, such persons say with a considerable amount of really just irony, there is nothing to be dreaded in universal suffrage, at least in comparison with any existing system according to which the governors of countries are appointed; for another, they believe that there is a benefit in the principle of representation, as applied to government, not yet exhausted, and promised in an extended suffrage—the benefit, namely, of mingling up more thoroughly particulars relative to the proletarian or industrial interests with the general mass of political hubbub and hearsay out of which the genuine germs of government are to be got; and, finally, distinguishing between the permanent methods of government, the sum of which, they would agree with Mr. Carlyle, consists in the appointment of the most competent men in the community to the chief official places, and the variable historic conditions under which at different times these methods must be put in force—they would maintain that the operation of a full representative system is in this age an established *condition* of government, and that the true wisdom would be, not to dash the method in the face of the condition, but to study how, the condition remaining, the method may be carried out. It is a law of the historic evolution, they say, that the number of persons taking ostensible part in the business of governing the world shall increase from age to age; what we should try, therefore, is not to fight against this law, but to put it in harness. But we can pursue the controversialists no farther.

There remains only one other of the topics treated in Mr. Carlyle's *Pamphlets* on which we feel it necessary to say a word. It is the topic formally discussed in the pamphlet entitled *Stump Orator*, but casually adverted to also in other pamphlets of the series—the intrinsic merit, namely, and the present condition of that peculiar mode of human activity called Speech or (more prominently) Literature. The previous topics that we have touched on, may be regarded as of an expressly social character; this topic, however, though it has also a distinct social bearing, is concerned, in the first instance, with considerations that go deep into the nature of the individual. The following sentences contain the kernel of Mr. Carlyle's ideas on the subject:—

[quotes a non-continuous passage from 'It lies deep' to 'the wise man' *Stump Orator*, XX, 172–81]

The observation here presented in its most concentrated shape is developed by Mr. Carlyle, both in that particular pamphlet and in others, into an absolute torrent of invective against certain portions of the procedure of our age. More than half of the various mass of corruption with which our age is labouring may be traced, he seems to think, to this very fact of the undue value assigned in modern times to Speech or Stump-oratory. In the first place, seeing that every new occasion of unnecessary speech compels a new departure from fact and nature, a new thrashing, as it were, of the mere chaff of previous impressions and asseverations,—it has necessarily happened, he thinks, that, in consequence of the inordinate stimulus given during the last century or two to the function of expression, whether oral or written, not only have fallacies and falsehoods been generated during all that while at a rate previously unknown; but, by the incorporation of these fallacies and falsehoods with the hereditary thought of the race, the very faculty of discerning the true from the false has been everywhere sensibly weakened, and the world rendered everywhere less capable of distinguishing the quack from the wise man. Nay more, by the undue determination that has been thus occasioned even of sound and true intellect towards those professions whose business consists chiefly of talk, and especially towards the profession of literature, society, he thinks, has been cheated of the full use and benefit of such intellect; receiving in the shape, as it were, of mere external festooning and adornment, much of that virtue which, under a better economy, might have gone, by means of a natural process of absorption and circulation, to the sustenance of the central vitality, and the improvement of the general health of the body-politic. Thus Burns, instead of helping to govern Great Britain, which was his true function, had to take to writing Scotch songs, pouring his genius as he best could through that gimblet-hole; and Tennyson, a man fit to command an industrial army at the Bog of Allen, has to compose an *In Memoriam*.

Now, here again, great as we consider the service done by Mr. Carlyle in having pressed such reflections on the notice of the public, and fully aware as we are that whatever suggestions may be advanced on the other side must be perfectly familiar to him, we cannot but feel that the effect on the whole is one of exaggeration. To state, in a word, wherein it is that we think the source of this exaggeration lies, we should say that Mr. Carlyle seems throughout this particular discussion to have regarded speech or expression only as a mode of intellectual presentation, whereas it is, in fact, also a mode of intellectual production. 'Considered,' says Mr. Carlyle, 'as the last finish of education, or of human culture, worth, and acquirement, the art of speech is noble, and even divine; it is like the kindling of a Heaven's light to *show* us what a glorious world exists and has perfected itself in a man'. This, it seems to us, is true, but less than the whole truth. The art of speech is noble and divine, not only as being the last finish of human education, but also as being one of the permanent methods of that education; not only as showing what a glorious world may exist in a man, but as conspicuous among the agencies whereby such a world may be created. For, not to concern ourselves with the questions whether men may not, and whether many men do not, think through another symbolic mechanism than that of language, as, for example, by a process of rapid reference to illustrative pictures, diagrams, or models conceived by the mind spontaneously and immediately, and requiring, as it were, to be after-wards interpreted or read off into language—it may certainly be affirmed that men first grasp their thoughts firmly by phrasing them; that even to a man's self his thought does not attain its full value till it has been incorporated in some phrase; that all important human thoughts are connnected with phrases, and nearly all important in-tellectual changes transacted by means of them; and that, as the lost child in the story could trace his way back by the pebbles he had dropped, so every man, in advancing from the first efforts to the full maturity of his intellect, has, in one sense, but marched, as it were, along a succession of phrases. We believe, for example, that Mr. Carlyle's own intellectual route, from its commencement until now, could be traced and historically represented by a series of verbal formulæ. At any one point in that route, we are aware, the phrases accumulated up till then were not all that constituted his being; there was still behind them the strong vital soul that made them, tremulous to its own impulses, reverent under the stars, and melancholy to the moan of the sea; but what we say is, that if at any point in his career he had been struck transcendentally dumb, and denied the power of creating new phrases, then, by the very necessities of the human constitution, according to which, even in poetic minds, the method of intellectual production must be in so far algebraic, he would have sustained an arrest, and been prevented from advancing very much farther. Speech, then, we hold to be the gift of the gods, not for representing noble thought merely, but also for attaining it. Hence, though we see the fine meaning involved in our author's gigantic wish that by some means or other speech could be annihilated over the globe for the space of one whole generation; though we see how, in that case, whirlwinds of verbal nonsense, now loading the intercourse of men, would be blown away, and the general human soul brought back into contact with the hard skeleton of things

—we would yet vote against any proposal to carry the terrible wish into effect, on the score that the dumb interregnum would be positively so much time lost to the intellectual business of our planet. And though all this does not affect the value of Mr. Carlyle's denunciations of Stump-oratory, yet it affects, we think, some of his accompanying asseverations. Even the high social function, for example, which he would still consistently enough reserve for true literature, appears to us far too low. According even to his own views, as it seems to us, it would by no means be necessary to abolish pure literature; to regard the song-writing of a Burns or of a Tennyson as a mere paltry solace in the absence of better work; or to compel such men into more express participation than such devotion to the exquisite would imply, in the ongoings of the social tumult. Much less so, however, according to the view we have attempted to indicate. For if the gift of speech be not independent of the power of thought, but in a manner bound up with it in our present state of being; if this gift be intended not merely as a means of publishing what we have learnt out of Nature, but also as a mechanism whereby we as men may seize upon Nature, and weave forth from her those higher existences called truths, conceptions, imaginations, which it is the part of our race to evolve, and, as it were, introduce into the universe—then we may do more than consent to allow a proportion of our number to devote themselves expressly, under certain laws, to this function of speech; we may encourage them to do so, and honour them, if they do so worthily, as almost the consecrated delegates of our species, the followers of a calling more specifically human than any other.

But Mr. Carlyle's views on this subject, it is easy to see, must be speculatively connected in some profound manner with that peculiar feature in his own development, to which, in the earlier part of this paper, we ventured to direct attention. Having himself begun as a devotee of pure literature, and having in the end forsaken it, or nearly so, to become directly and with all his force a social power in the country, he calls on all others that feel high stirrings within them to begin rather, according to their power and opportunities, with that mode of activity wherein he has in aspiration ended. The whole worth of this advice, given so earnestly by so great a man, it is not for any word of ours to estimate. One remark, however, we may be permitted to offer in conclusion. In the character of every individual of great mark or effect in the world, it may be observed that some particular quality, or combination of qualities, exists in an unprecedented degree; as if

Nature, in every such instance, had purposed to go to her very utter-most in one particular direction. Now, as Nature never repeats herself, she will never again, in developing a man of equal mark, take the same plan as she has taken with Mr. Carlyle. Hence it ought to be the aim of all very daring aspirants among his readers rather to digest and ponder his rich conclusions than implicitly to follow his route.

29. Unsigned review, *Southern Quarterly Review*

July 1850, i, 509

Originally founded and published in New Orleans (1842) by David K. Whitaker, and then later in Charleston (1843), the *Southern Quarterly Review* reflected the thought of the South until the termination of the *Quarterly* in 1857. Like *DeBow's*, the *Southern Quarterly* favoured slavery and printed supporting articles by James D. B. DeBow, William Gilmore Simms (editor from 1849–55), W. J. Grayson, and others.

Here are two very neat editions of Carlyle's *Latter Day Pamphlets*, one of those publications which cannot be dismissed in a single paragraph. We must reserve it for a future moment of greater space and leisure. Carlyle has offended the people of the North, since he has come out, sensibly, philosophically, and like a man, superior to cant and false philanthropy, in favour of negro slavery. They now discover that he is a fool, a twattler, and, like Father Mathew, has lived just a year too long. We perceive but little falling off, in these pamphlets, from the stern, old, prophetic Carlyle whom we have known before. 'He repeats himself!' cry aloud the donkeys of literature; as if they did not repeat themselves, day after day, to the eternal sickening of all good men's stomachs—as if Isaiah, and all the prophets had not need, hourly, to repeat themselves, since the wretched communities to which they addressed entreaty and imprecation, in vain, were also repeating themselves, with increasing vice and venom, with neither remorse nor understanding. But the wonder is, to see so many of our Southern presses —not having read these pamphlets—actually repeating the clamours of their Yankee file-leaders—actually denouncing, in their abominable blindness, one of their best friends and champions. What if Carlyle does sneer at the American people as a race of bores: we need not be solicitous in the defence of the Yankee part of the nation. And, it is this part which has been boring him, and all other English writers, by visit and letter, until the best tempered person in the world might well be angry.

30. George Fitzhugh on Carlyle in *Cannibals All: or Slaves Without Masters*

Richmond, 1857

George Fitzhugh (1806–81), a self-educated Virginian, had no formal education other than a few years in a 'field school'. A descendent of William Fitzhugh who emigrated to Virginia in 1671, George Fitzhugh became one of the great propagandists for the Southern slave interests. Fitzhugh, who was an admitted disciple of Carlyle, had a fierce dislike of *laissez-faire* capitalism, rose-water philanthropy, and opposed the idea of social progress and denounced what Carlyle called the cash-nexus. He has been referred to as the American Carlyle. The following passages are taken from *Cannibals All*—an attack against mammonism, Manchester economics, and the idea of a free society—and draw heavily upon Carlyle's *Latter-Day Pamphlets*, especially *The Present Time*, which suggested the subtitle and provided much of the text.

The neglect of the North to take issue with us, or with the Southern Press, in the new positions which we have assumed, our own observations of the working of Northern society, the alarming increase of Socialism, as evinced by its control of many Northern State Legislatures and its majority in the lower house of Congress, are all new proofs of the truth of our doctrine. The character of that majority in Congress is displayed in full relief, by the single fact, which we saw stated in a Northern Abolition paper, that 'there are a hundred Spiritual Rappers in Congress.' A Northern member of Congress made a similar remark to us a few days since. 'Tis but a copy of the Hiss Legislature of Massachusetts, or the Praise-God-Barebones Parliament of England. Further study, too, of Western European Society, which has been engaged in continual revolution for twenty years, has satisfied us that Free Society every where begets Isms, and that Isms soon beget bloody revolutions. Until our trip to the North, we did not justly appreciate the passage which we are about to quote from Mr. Carlyle's *Latter-Day*

Pamphlets. Now it seems to us as if Boston, New Haven, or Western New York had set for the picture:

To rectify the relation that exists between two men, is there no method, then, but that of ending it? The old relation has become unsuitable, obsolete, perhaps unjust; and the remedy is, abolish it; let there henceforth be no relation at all. From the 'sacrament of marriage' downwards, human beings used to be manifoldly related one to another, and each to all; and there was no relation among human beings, just or unjust, that had not its grievances and its difficulties, its necessities on both sides to bear and forbear. But henceforth, be it known, we have changed all that by favor of Heaven; the 'voluntary principle' has come up, which will itself do the business for us; and now let a new sacrament, that of *Divorce*, which we call emancipation, and spout of on our platforms, be universally the order of the day! Have men considered whither all this is tending, and what it certainly enough betokens? Cut every human relation that has any where grown uneasy sheer asunder; reduce whatsoever was compulsory to voluntary, whatsoever was permanent among us to the condition of the nomadic; in other words, LOOSEN BY ASSIDUOUS WEDGES, in every joint, the whole fabric of social existence, stone from stone, till at last, all lie now quite loose enough, it can, as we already see in most countries, be overset by sudden outburst of revolutionary rage; and lying as mere mountains of anarchic rubbish, solicit you to sing Fraternity, &c. over it, and rejoice in the now remarkable era of human progress we have arrived at. [*The Present Time*, XX, 25.]

Now we plant ourselves on this passage from Carlyle. We say that, as far as it goes, 'tis a faithful picture of the Isms of the North. But the restraints of Law and Public Opinion are less at the North than in Europe. The Isms on each side the Atlantic are equally busy with 'assiduous wedges,' in 'loosening in every joint the whole fabric of social existance'; but whilst they dare invoke Anarchy in Europe, they dare not inaugurate New York Free Love, and Oneida Incest, and Mormon Polygamy. The moral, religious, and social heresies of the North are more monstrous than those of Europe. The pupil has surpassed the master, unaided by the stimulants of poverty, hunger, and nakedness which urge the master forward.

Society need not fail in the Northeast until the whole West is settled, and a refluent population, or excess of immigration, overstocks permanently the labor market on the Atlantic board. Till then, the despotism of skill and capital, in forcing emigration to the West, makes proprietors of those emigrants, benefits them, peoples the West, and by their return trade, enriches the East. The social forms of the North and the South are, for the present, equally promotive of growth and prosperity at home, and equally beneficial to mankind at large, by affording asylums to the oppressed, and by furnishing food and clothing to all. Northern society is a partial failure, but only because it generates Isms which threaten it with overthrow and impede its progress.

Despite of appearing vain and egotistical, we cannot refrain from mentioning another circumstance that encourages us to write. At the very time when we were writing our pamphlet entitled *Slavery Justified*, in which we took ground that Free Society had failed, Mr. Carlyle began to write his *Latter-Day Pamphlets*, whose very title is the assertion of the failure of Free Society. The proof derived from this coincidence becomes the stronger, when it is perceived that an ordinary man on this side the Atlantic discovered and was exposing the same social phenomena that an extraordinary one had discovered and was exposing on the other. The very titles of our works are synonymous—for the 'Latter Day' is the 'Failure of Society.'

Mr. Carlyle, and Miss Fanny Wright (in her *England the Civilizer*) vindicate Slavery by showing that each of its apparent relaxations in England has injured the laboring class. They were fully and ably represented in Parliament by their ancient masters, the Barons. Since the Throne, and the Church, and the Nobility have been stripped of their power, and a House of Commons, representing lands and money, rules despotically, the masses have become outlawed. They labor under all the disadvantages of slavery, and have none of the rights of slaves. This is the true history of the English Constitution, and one which we intend, in the sequel, more fully to expound. This presents another reason why we again appear before the public. Blackstone, which is read by most American gentlemen, teaches a doctrine the exact reverse of this, and that doctrine we shall try to refute.

Returning from the North, we procured in New York a copy of Aristotle's *Politics and Economics*. To our surprise, we found that our theory of the origin of society was identical with his, and that we had employed not only the same illustrations but the very same words. We saw at once that the true vindication of slavery must be founded on his theory of man's social nature, as opposed to Locke's theory of the Social Contract, on which latter Free Society rests for support. 'Tis true we had broached this doctrine; but with the world at large our authority was merely repulsive, whilst the same doctrine, coming from Aristotle, had, besides his name, two thousand years of human approval and concurrence in its favor; for, without that concurrence and approval, his book would have long since perished.

In addition to all this, we think we have discovered that Moses has anticipated the Socialists, and that in prohibiting 'usury of money, and of victuals, and of all things that are lent on usury,' and in denouncing 'increase' he was far wiser than Aristotle, and saw that other capital or property did not 'breed' any more than money, and that its profits were unjust exactions levied from the laboring man. The Socialists proclaim this as a discovery of their own. We think Moses discovered and pro-claimed it more than three thousand years ago—and that it is the only true theory of capital and labor, the only adequate theoretical defence of Slavery—for it proves that the profits which capital exacts from labor makes free laborers slaves, without the rights, privileges, or advantages of domestic slaves, and capitalists their masters, with all the advantages, and none of the burdens and obligations of the ordinary owners of slaves.

The scientific title of this work would be best expressed by the con-ventional French term *'Exploitation.'* We endeavor to translate by the double periphrases of 'Cannibals All; or, Slaves without Masters.'[1]

We have been imprudent enough to write our Introduction first, and may fail to satisfy the expectations which we excite. Our excess of candor must, in that event, in part supply our deficiency of ability.

From Chapter VII 'The World is *Too Little* Governed'

Mobs, secret associations, insurance companies, and social and com-munistic experiments are striking features and characteristics of our day, outside of slave society. They are all attempting to supply the defects of regular governments, which have carried the Let Alone practice so far that one-third of mankind are let alone to indulge in such criminal im-moralities as they please, and another third to starve. Mobs (*vide* California) supply the deficiencies of a defective police, and insurance companies and voluntary unions and associations afford that security and protection which government, under the lead of political economy, has ceased to render. . . .

Mr. Carlyle says,

Among practical men the idea prevails that government can do nothing but 'keep the peace.' They say all higher tasks are unsafe for it, impossible for it, and, in fine, not necessary for it or for us. Truly, it is high time that same beautiful notion of No-Government should take itself away. The world is daily rushing towards wreck whilst it lasts. If your government is to be a constituted anarchy,

---

[1] See *The Present Time*, XX, 42: '. . . or if you prefer the word, or *nomadic, and now even vagrant and vagabond, servants that can find no master on those terms.* . . .'

what issue can it have? Our own interest in such government is, that it would be kind enough to cease and go its way before the inevitable wreck.

The reader will excuse us for so often introducing the thoughts and words of others. We do so not only for the sake of their authority, but because they express our own thoughts better than we can express them ourselves. In truth, we deal out our thoughts, facts, and arguments in that irregular and desultory way in which we acquired them. We are no regular built scholar—have pursued no 'royal road to mathematics,' nor to anything else. We have, by observation and desultory reading, picked up our information by the wayside, and endeavored to arrange, generalize, and digest it for ourselves. To learn 'to forget' is almost the only thing we have labored to learn. We have been so bored through life by friends with dyspeptic memories, who never digest what they read because they never forget it, who retain on their intellectual stomachs in gross, crude, undigested, and unassimilated form every-thing that they read, and retail and repeat it in that undigested form to every good-natured listener; we repeat, that we have been so bored by friends with good memories that we have resolved to endeavor to express what was useful out of facts, and then to throw the facts away. A great memory is a disease of the mind, which we are surprised no medical writer has noticed. The lunatic asylum should make provision for those affected with this disease; for, though less dangerous, they are far more troublesome and annoying than any other class of lunatics. Learning, observation, reading are only useful in the general, as they add to the growth of the mind. Undigested and unforgotten, they can no more have this effect, than undigested food on the stomach of a dyspeptic can add to his physical stature. We thought once this thing was original with us, but find that Say pursued this plan in writing his Political Economy. He first read all the books he could get hold of on this subject, and then took time to forget them, before he began to write.

We will not trouble the reader further, for the present, with our egotisms or our arguments, but refer him to the whole of Carlyle's Latter-Day Pamphlets to prove that 'the world is too little governed,' and, therefore, is going to wreck. We say to the whole of those pamphlets, for that is their one, great leading idea.

From Chapter VIII 'Liberty and Slavery'

It seems to us that the vain attempts to define liberty in theory, or to secure its enjoyment in practice, proceed from the fact that man is naturally a social and gregarious animal, subject, not by contract or agreement, as Locke and his followers assume, but by birth and nature, to those restrictions of liberty which are expedient or necessary to secure the good of the human hive, to which he may belong. There is no such thing as *natural human* liberty, because it is unnatural for man to live alone and without the pale and government of society. Birds and beasts of prey, who are not gregarious, are naturally free. Bees and herds are naturally subjects or slaves of society. Such is the theory of Aristotle, promulged more than two thousand years ago, generally considered true for two thousand years, and destined, we hope, soon again to be accepted as the only true theory of government and society.

Modern social reformers, except Mr. Carlyle, proceeding upon the theory of Locke, which is the opposite of Aristotle, propose to dissolve and disintegrate society, falsely supposing that they thereby follow nature. There is not a human tie that binds man to man that they do not propose to cut 'sheer asunder.' 'Tis true, after their work of destruction is finished, they see the necessity of society; but instead of that natural and historical society, which has usually existed in the world, with its gradations of rank and power, its families, and its slaves, they propose wholly to disregard the natural relations of mankind, and profanely to build up states, like Fourierite Phalansteries, or Mormon and Oneida villages, where religion shall be banished, and in which property, wife and children shall be held somewhat in common. These social establishments, under a self-elected despotism like that of Joe Smith, or Brigham Young, become patriarchal, and succeed so long as such despotism lasts. That is, when the association loses the character intended by its founders, and acquires a despotic head like other family associations, it works well, because it works naturally. But this success can only be temporary; for nothing but the strong rule of a Cromwell or Joe Smith can keep a society together that wants the elements of cohesion in the natural ties that bind man to man; and Cromwells and Joe Smiths are not to be found every day. . . .

LIFE OF JOHN STERLING

1851

31. George Eliot, an unsigned review, *Westminster Review*

January 1852, lxii, 247–9

George Eliot (1819–80), like Carlyle, in her own artistic way was also a prophet and was very much influenced by him. Though Carlyle has almost nothing to say about her novels, she read most of his works and her fondness and admiration for him is documented in her many letters to her friends. In fact when *Adam Bede* was published she sent a copy of the novel to Jane Carlyle, hoping that Carlyle would read it. In a later review (No. 35) she pays tribute to Carlyle's great influence.

As soon as the closing of the Great Exhibition afforded a reasonable hope that there would once more be a reading public, *The Life of Sterling* appeared. A new work by Carlyle must always be among the literary births eagerly chronicled by the journals and greeted by the public. In a book of such parentage we care less about the subject than about its treatment, just as we think the 'Portrait of a Lord' worth studying if it come from the pencil of a Vandyck. The life of John Sterling, however, has intrinsic interest, even if it be viewed simply as the struggle of a restless aspiring soul, yearning to leave a distinct impress of itself on the spiritual development of humanity, with that fell disease which, with a refinement of torture, heightens the susceptibility and activity of the faculties, while it undermines their creative force. Sterling, moreover, was a man thoroughly in earnest, to whom poetry and philosophy were not merely another form of paper currency or a ladder to fame, but an end in themselves—one of those finer spirits with whom, amidst the jar and hubbub of our daily life,

The melodies abide
Of the everlasting chime.

But his intellect was active and rapid, rather than powerful, and in all his writings we feel the want of a stronger electric current to give that vigour of conception and felicity of expression, by which we distinguish the undefinable something called genius; while his moral nature, though refined and elevated, seems to have been subordinate to his intellectual tendencies and social qualities, and to have had itself little determining influence on his life. His career was less exceptional than his character: a youth marked by delicate health and studious tastes, a short-lived and not very successful share in the management of the *Athenæum*, a fever of sympathy with Spanish patriots, arrested before it reached a dangerous crisis by an early love affair ending in marriage, a fifteen months' residence in the West Indies, eight months of curate's duty at Herstmonceux, relinquished on the ground of failing health, and through his remaining years a succession of migrations to the South in search of a friendly climate, with the occasional publication of an 'article,' a tale, or a poem in *Blackwood* or elsewhere,—this, on the prosaic background of an easy competence, was what made up the outer tissue of Sterling's existence. The impression of his intellectual power on his personal friends seems to have been produced chiefly by the eloquence and brilliancy of his conversation; but the mere reader of his works and letters would augur from them neither the wit, nor the *curiosa felicitas* of epithet and imagery, which would rank him with the men whose sayings are thought worthy of perpetuation in books of table-talk and 'ana.' The public, then, since it is content to do without biographies of much more remarkable men, cannot be supposed to have felt any pressing demand even for a single life of Sterling; still less, it might be thought, when so distinguished a writer as Archdeacon Hare had furnished this, could there be any need for another. But, in opposition to the majority of Mr. Carlyle's critics, we agree with him that the first life is properly the justification of the second. Even among the readers personally unacquainted with Sterling, those who sympathised with his ultimate alienation from the Church, rather than with his transient conformity, were likely to be dissatisfied with the entirely apologetic tone of Hare's life, which, indeed, is confessedly an incomplete presentation of Sterling's mental course after his opinions diverged from those of his clerical biographer; while those attached friends (and Sterling possessed the happy magic that secures many such) who knew him best during this latter part of his career, would naturally be pained to have it represented, though only by implication, as a sort of deepening declension ending in a virtual retraction. Of such friends Carlyle was the most eminent, and perhaps the most highly valued, and, as co-trustee with Archdeacon Hare of Sterling's literary character and writings, he felt a kind of responsibility that no mistaken idea of his departed friend should remain before the world without correction. Evidently, however, his *Life of Sterling* was not so much the conscientious discharge of a trust as a labour of love, and to this is owing its strong charm. Carlyle here shows us his 'sunny side.' We no longer see him breathing out threatenings and slaughter as in the *Latter-Day Pamphlets*, but moving among the charities and amenities of life, loving and beloved—a Teufelsdröckh still, but humanized by a Blumine worthy of him. We have often wished that genius would incline itself more frequently to the task of the biographer,—that when some great or good personage dies, instead of the dreary three or five volumed compilations of letter, and diary, and detail, little to the purpose, which two-thirds of the reading public have not the chance, nor the other third the inclination, to read, we could have a real *Life*, setting forth briefly and vividly the man's inward and outward struggles, aims, and achievements, so as to make clear the meaning which his experiences has for his fellows. A few such lives (chiefly, indeed, autobiographies) the world possesses, and they have, perhaps, been more influential on the formation of character than any other kind of reading. But the conditions required for the perfection of life writing,—personal intimacy, a loving and poetic nature which sees the beauty and the depth of familiar things, and the artistic power which seizes characteristic points and renders them with life-like effect,—are seldom found in combination. *The Life of Sterling* is an instance of this rare conjunction. Its comparatively tame scenes and incidents gather picturesqueness and interest under the rich lights of Carlyle's mind. We are told neither too little nor too much; the facts noted, the letters selected, are all such as serve to give the liveliest conception of what Sterling was and what he did; and though the book speaks much of other persons, this collateral matter is all a kind of scene-painting, and is accessory to the main purpose. The portrait of Coleridge, for example, is precisely adapted to bring before us the intellectual region in which Sterling lived for some time before entering the Church. Almost every review has extracted this admirable description, in which genial veneration and compassion struggle with irresistible satire; but the emphasis of quotation cannot be too often given to the following pregnant paragraph:—

The truth is, I now see Coleridge's talk and speculation was the emblem of himself. In it, as in him, a ray of heavenly inspiration struggled, in a tragically ineffectual degree, with the weakness of flesh and blood. He says once, he 'had skirted the howling deserts of infidelity.' This was evident enough; but he had not had the courage, in defiance of pain and terror, to press resolutely across said deserts to the new firm lands of faith beyond; he preferred to create logical *fata-morganas* for himself on this hither side, and laboriously solace himself with these.

The above-mentioned step of Sterling—his entering the Church—is the point on which Carlyle is most decidedly at issue with Archdeacon Hare. The latter holds that had Sterling's health permitted him to remain in the Church, he would have escaped those aberrations from orthodoxy, which, in the clerical view, are to be regarded as the failure and shipwreck of his career, apparently thinking, like that friend of Arnold's who recommended a curacy as the best means of clearing up Trinitarian difficulties, that 'orders' are a sort of spiritual backboard, which, by dint of obliging a man to look as if he were strait, end by making him so. According to Carlyle, on the contrary, the real 'aberration' of Sterling was his choice of the clerical profession, which was simply a mistake as to his true vocation:—

Sterling, (he says), was not intrinsically, nor had ever been in the highest or chief degree, a devotional mind. Of course all excellence in man, and worship as the supreme excellence, was part of the inheritance of this gifted man; but if called to define him, I should say artist, not saint, was the real bent of his being.

Again:—

No man of Sterling's veracity, had he clearly consulted his own heart, or had his own heart been capable of clearly responding, and not been bewildered by transient fantasies and theosophic moonshine, could have undertaken this function. His heart would have answered, 'No, thou canst not. What is incredible to thee, thou shalt not, at thy soul's peril, attempt to believe! Elsewhither for a refuge, or die here. Go to perdition if thou must, but not with a lie in thy mouth; by the eternal Maker, no!'

From the period when Carlyle's own acquaintance with Sterling commenced, the *Life* has a double interest, from the glimpses it gives us of the writer, as well as of his hero. We are made present at their first introduction to each other; we get a lively idea of their colloquies and walks together, and in this easy way, without any heavy disquisition or narrative, we obtain a clear insight into Sterling's character and mental progress. Above all, we are gladdened with a perception of the affinity that exists between noble souls, in spite of diversity in ideas—in what Carlyle calls 'the logical outcome' of the faculties. This *Life of Sterling* is a touching monument of the capability human nature possesses of the highest love, the love of the good and beautiful in character, which is, after all, the essence of piety. The style of the work, too, is for the most part at once pure and rich; there are passages of deep pathos which come upon the reader like a strain of solemn music, and others which show that aptness of epithet, that masterly power of close delineation, in which, perhaps, no writer has excelled Carlyle.

We have said that we think this second *Life of Sterling* justified by the first; but were it not so, the book would justify itself.

32. Francis W. Newman, from an unsigned review, *Prospective Review*

February 1852, viii, 1–15

Francis W. Newman (1805–97), like his older brother, John, attended Oxford, but, unlike him, never made the trip to Rome, remaining, as the *Morning Leader* put it, a 'spiritual radical'. However, his spiritual struggle, his grave doubts about the Thirty-Nine Articles made him an ideal reviewer of Carlyle's *Life of John Sterling* (as well as of Archdeacon Julius Hare's *Sterling's Essays and Tales* [1848], which is also here being reviewed). In 1827, full of missionary zeal, Francis Newman travelled to Baghdad, hoping to convert Islam to Christ. After two years, he returned to marry and to teach classics at Bristol College, later teaching at the Unitarian Manchester New College. In 1846, he beeame Professor of Latin at University College, London, a chair he held until 1863. To some extent his life and works epitomize the crisis of faith many intellectuals faced in the later half of the nineteenth century.

It is not our intention to present our readers with any abstract of the contents of these volumes. Archdeacon Hare's *Life of Sterling* has, we believe, been extensively read; and Mr. Carlyle's is likely to meet a still wider circulation: perhaps, then, we may rather assume that our readers are acquainted with both these works. Indeed, we may congratulate the public on the favourable turn which so powerful a writer as Mr. Carlyle is taking. We would hope that some young David has been exorcizing the evil spirit, and that we shall no longer have to turn away in sorrow from moody querulousness and despairing panegyrics on every form of despotism. Carlyle now shows a sunnier front, and has produced not only an exceedingly agreeable but a truly beautiful book. His portraiture of Coleridge and of Edward Sterling the father, will be to many as interesting as that of John Sterling, especially since the great compactness of the narrative gives the impression of the others more speedily. Although we by no means subscribe to all the sentiments of this pleasant volume, we gratefully acknowledge not only its more genial and sounder morality, but its disposition to speak more distinctly, instead of affecting an oracular and evasive tone, which was very inconsistent with the denunciation of shams and hypocrisy.

It is, however, certainly a curious thing that two lives should thus have professedly been published, of a man whose principal works are scarcely known. Archdeacon Hare has, indeed, re-published Sterling's prose writings, some of them rather juvenile, and such as Sterling himself might have wished to be forgotten: many valuable and interesting extracts from his letters are also given by both his biographers. On the other hand it is to Poetry that Sterling deliberately dedicated his maturest intellect, and it is in his Theological change of mind that the public would feel chief curiosity; yet neither biographer has done what might have been hoped as to the one or the other subject. What would have seemed to us most desirable, is, that the memoir of his life should either have exhibited fully the grounds and process of his theological development, with the results in which he finally rested; or else, that the memoir should have been purely a literary one, and printed uniformly with Sterling's poems, with a common title page for all the little volumes, and an additional similar volume for his last and hitherto unpublished poem, 'Cœur de Lion.' Neither of these courses has been pursued, and his biographers,—*both* with the best intentions,—appear to us *both* to have done him some injustice.

The Archdeacon's reason for writing any memoir at all is not distinctly explained. We know not whether we ought to believe the rumour, that his real object was, to hinder Carlyle from undertaking the task, whom he expected to spoil it by omitting entirely the religious side of Sterling's character. There is plausibility in this. If true, it is singular, that it should so nearly have brought about the thing feared: at least, Carlyle declares that he should *not* have written this life, had it not been already done unsatisfactorily by Hare. Between the two, the reader of both biographies does gain a considerable insight into Sterling's mind, though in neither is there any consecutive attempt to develope the progress of his theological opinions; and indeed it would seem that the authors are alike incapacitated to write on the subject:—Mr. Carlyle, because he despised it, as he pretty plainly tells us; Archdeacon Hare, because he is not only an orthodox believer, but a clergyman. In consequence, so much obscurity is left on the state of Sterling's judgment, that people are enabled to make very erroneous representations. In a recent number of the *Eclectic Review*,—(a publication which deserves honour as remarkably liberal and candid, considering its orthodoxy,)—it is imagined that Sterling was drawn away from Coleridge's philosophy by Carlyle, and, as a result of this, lost his faith in Christianity: moreover, it is added on authority, that at the last, Sterling ceased to be a Carlylist, and died a Christian. It is certainly unfortunate that such topics, if at all dealt with by biographers, should be left in any uncertainty: but the *Eclectic Review* is beyond a doubt in error. Even from Archdeacon Hare it may be clearly enough learnt, that it was from German Theologians that the impulse came to the un-loosening of Sterling's belief in Christianity: and the crisis of his mind seems to have been in reading Ullmann 'On the Sinlessness of Jesus;' (Hare, p. cliii.) of which Sterling writes:—

One of the deepest, bitterest and most lasting disappointments of my life, was, what I think, Ullmann's failure in that Essay. I shall never forget, but, I hope, never again experience, the dismay with which I reviewed his inquiry, and was compelled to say he had not made good his point.

It is, we think, thus quite manifest, that whatever secondary effect Carlyle may have had, the great shock to Sterling's creed came from writers whom Carlyle neglects, and from lines of thought on which Carlyle wholly refused discussion. On the other hand, it is certain that Sterling's attachment to Coleridge's philosophy outlasted his Christian creed; and that to the last, even when he had learned to see Coleridge's personal weaknesses, he felt deeply grateful for the influence which his conversations had exerted. When, indeed, much is made of the statement that Sterling 'died a Christian,' we need to ask what it means. If it means, that he died a believer in the miracles or in the sinlessness or in the authority of Jesus, we can from personal knowledge give it the most pointed and total contradiction.

The conclusion to which he had long come, was, that nothing from *without* can suffice for founding a philosophy *within*; that all science and all duty has its roots in the inner man; that God is not and cannot be revealed to us from without; and that the English idea of 'A Revelation' is essentially a hopeless absurdity. In this conclusion he was so rooted, that he believed the whole structure of his mind would need to be rebuilt before he could doubt of it; and it is most certain that this to the last made it impossible for him to see any 'authority' in the words of Christ or of Isaiah. But it is equally certain, that there was no time at which he did not feel great reverence and admiration for those words. If the fact of his sending for the Bible and reading it in his last days proves him to have been a Christian, then a devout and fervent Christian he always was. In fact, sentiments of his letters quoted in Hare and Carlyle, are not only beautiful and noble, but are in a tone so Christian, that ordinary readers might infer that he believed in miracles,—which is so oddly imagined to be the source of all religious knowledge.

While thus vindicating Sterling's practical religion from the fancy of the evangelical, who supposes him at one time 'an infidel' and at a later time a Christian—totally mistaking him on both occasions, and wrongly supposing there was any change in him;—we yet are disposed to concede much to a remark of Mr. Carlyle on this subject:—

[quotes 'Yet it may' to 'character of him' XI, 265]

Perhaps substantially the same thing may be differently expressed as follows:—'Intellect and admiration of Art, were developed *earlier* in Sterling than Reverence and Awe.' We cannot doubt that his youth was defective in the element of Reverence; hence also his early morality was rather utilitarian than spiritual, and his best qualities, as a young man, those of half-regulated noble impulse. Now we presume that to make the Fakeer and the Fanatic, it is essential that the understanding be *less* developed than the religious element of man; which is the reverse of Sterling's case. But we do not think that the later growths are necessarily superficial, or less pervading to a character. Undoubtedly the great obligation which Sterling felt to Coleridge, turned upon the remedying of his early defect. No topic was more congenial, we have understood, to Coleridge, than to expose the hollowness of the Epicurean *Nil admirari*; and to enforce that Wonder, Admiration and Reverence, are as essential to human perfection as Love; and are alike superior to logic. When Sterling first learnt fundamentally, how vain was all reasoning to implant or to supersede these primitive instincts; when in consequence he more carefully cultivated these instincts, and entered consciously into a religious life;—his intellect was already in the ascendant, and to dark superstition or vain terrors he was inaccessible. But his heart was deep enough for any love, and his power of self-devotion equal to any sacrifice. If his intellect had not rebelled against Biblical Infallibility, we can see nothing to hinder his having advanced into *such* a Church Saint as alone can be admired among Protestants: but it soon appeared to him how little could be done for the religious improvement of England until certain intellectual delusions were swept away: hence his mind was carried into other lines of action as more profitable from him than any direct religious teaching.

It is the closing disaster to Sterling, that the form of mental effort which he especially selected as his own,—namely, Poetry,—has been frowned on by the two friends whom he most trusted, as well as neglected by the public. The reader will say:—'Is it not then the presumption, that the decision is right, and that Sterling's poetry is worthless?'—We do not admit the inference. In the present day, nothing is harder than to gain attention to a small volume of poetry, from an unknown name; and if a man's own biographers assure the public that he has published nothing worth reading, we think he has not fair play, unless indeed nobody at all is to be found of an opposite judgment.

Archdeacon Hare tells us, that 'his poems were mostly rather the imaginative expression of pre-determined moral and philosophical truths, than the spontaneous utterance of a poetical mind;' p. lxxvi.: and thus effectually represses all desire on the reader's part to inquire further. We must complain of this as very hard. . . . Mr. Carlyle by his own account always dissuaded and disparaged Sterling's poetical efforts, for which he makes a partial apology by his present commendation of the very spirited little poem, 'The Election,' which has, indeed, obvious faults in the plan, but is admirable in the execution, and in every page (as we think), except the first, refutes the complaint that there is a lack of spontaneity.

But let us hear Mr. Carlyle's general argument:—

My own advice was, as it had always been, steady against poetry. . . . Had he not already gained superior excellence, in delivering by way of *speech* or prose what thoughts were in him, which is the grand and only intrinsic function of a writing man—? Why *sing* your bits of thoughts, if you *can* contrive to speak them? By your thought, not by your mode of delivering it, you must live or die .

Surely this is an argument against all poetry whatsoever, and almost against prose *style*. As we are not at leisure to enter into that question, it may suffice to say, that Mr. Carlyle totally neutralizes his own authority in the matter, if he presses the argument. But we must add, that Sterling's prose composition was often wordy and ambitious, and far too like his speech,—in which his fluent rapidity and happy selection of words made diffuseness an advantage; but his poetry is terse and chaste. As regards the individual, therefore, we differ from Mr. Carlyle. But he continues:—

Besides, I had to observe, that there was in Sterling intrinsically no depth of *tune*; which surely is the real test of a Poet or Singer, as distinguished from a Speaker. In music proper he had not the slightest ear. All music was mere impertinent noise to him; nothing in it perceptible but the mere march of time. Nor in his way of conception of utterance, in the verses he wrote, was there any contradiction, but a constant confirmation to me, of that fatal prognostic:—as indeed the whole man, in ear and heart and tongue, is one; and he whose soul does not sing, need not try to do it with his throat. *Sterling's verses had a monotonous rub-a-dub, instead of tune*; no trace of music, deeper than that of a well-beaten drum; *to which limited range of excellence the substance also corresponded* being intrinsically always a rhymed, and slightly rhythmical speech, not a song.

We read this with much surprise,—and with no small sympathy with poor Sterling, that he should have such hostile biographers. Assuredly, such a passage from Mr. Carlyle will be accepted by the thousands who read his prose, as finally settling that no one ought to lose time in reading Sterling's poetry. But, as for ourselves, there are many reasons why we cannot receive this dictum. First, we totally deny the metrical theory here propounded. In written poetry, there neither is nor can be, any other metrical melody but that of *time*. The want of an ear for *tune* is no disqualification,—the possession of such an ear is no aid,—to the composing of melodious poetry. It is false, and absurd, to say that poetry ought to be 'a song.' Ancient lyric poetry was sung; so may modern poetry be: but the tune has nothing to do with the intrinsic melody of the verse as written by the poet. Secondly, we are so far from admitting that there is any lack of melody in Sterling's verses, that we should have assented to a critic who commended them for their peculiar melody. Thirdly, we suspect that Mr. Carlyle has given us the clue to his prejudice, by telling us that he did not like Sterling's way of reading out his own verses. . . .

[Newman quotes and defends lines from Sterling's poetry for almost five pages, asking the reader, whether the poetry is mere 'rub-a-dub,' or 'too philosophical'.]

It is not our intention to hold up Sterling as a finished poet; for it seems to us clear that his powers were far greater than his performance. His first volume contains numerous smaller poems, among which the 'Aphrodite' is, perhaps, the most perfect; 'Alfred the Harper' the most spirited; 'Joan of Arc' (with special faults) the most indicative of a rich poetic mind. The 'Election' displayed satirical powers which no one could have suspected from his former writings; his 'Strafford' (which has shared the neglect of most modern tragedies) shows Sterling to be master of a racy Shakspearian dialect, which is amazing to one who comes fresh from his too Latinized prose. But finally, his 'Cœur de

Lion' exhibits a command of various styles, which, we confess (strong as the comparison may be thought), no English poet since Byron appears to us to have attained. Yet Carlyle says that the substance of Sterling's poetry was on a par with the monotony which he could not avoid; and Hare assures us, that it is only philosophy elaborated into the form of poetry. Why, on the contrary, the great fault of his (posthumous and unfinished) poem on Cœur de Lion, is, its purposeless digressions,—its 'overfruitful diffuseness' (to use the phrase of a friendly poet who criticized the MS.)—in consequence of which, the editor of *Frazer's Magazine* refused to continue the printing of it, fearing it would be thought tedious. We do think that it was the part of friendly biographers, to endeavour to gain for Sterling's poetry that moderate degree of attention from the public, which is given to many poetical productions that no one calls first-rate; and although the lamented author has been taken away prematurely, and has by no means produced any complete work fully worthy of his genius, we cannot but believe that the unbiassed public would presently recognise a real poetical genius in him, if only a tranquil reading could be obtained. But, however we may estimate the ability of professional 'tasters' to judge of romances, novels, or books of information, we cannot admit that their decision against poems ought to be final. The poetry which pleases us when we are in one mood, has no charms for us at another time; and we suspect that one who is forced to be a man-of-all-work in literature, is apt to have as little heart for poetry as we understand Mr. Carlyle to profess for himself. But we must in justice to him give his criticism on the first part of 'Cœur de Lion,' in which the reader will be amused with the closing words:—

[quotes 'This time I' to 'try doing it' XI, 250]

We believe, all that Carlyle here praises was burnt by Sterling, who re-wrote nearly all the poem.

Here is a man whom each of his biographers and friends regard as having possessed great abilities;—who spent his strength on two main subjects, on which, at different periods, he desired to appear before the public,—the Theological and the Poetical. His first biographer, in the opinion of his second, damages him theologically;—so, to remedy this, the second damages him poetically; and destroys, perhaps, the last chance of getting a fair reading of his works. No decision of the public against them has been given. They have not been read. If our memory does not deceive us, we heard that *five* copies only were sold of the

'Election', which Mr. Carlyle calls Sterling's best production, and which was highly commended in the *Examiner* newspaper at the time. However, we have said enough on this whole topic.

It would be very imprudent in us to try to mediate between Carlyle and Sterling on questions of philosophy or speculation; but we are a little disposed to complain of the patronizing tone assumed by the former; which is interpreted by not a few readers, as though he claimed Sterling as a young disciple, who, though with many struggles for independence, is at length inevitably dragged in the track of his master. Altogether, we fear the impression is given to the reader, that Sterling was a rather feminine character,—impulsive but unsteady; quick, but superficial; susceptible, ardent, but incapable of permanently resisting in anything the great masculine mind of Thomas Carlyle. We know that it *is* so interpreted. We hardly think Mr. Carlyle meant it, and we believe it to be quite erroneous. Sterling undoubtedly knew how to give full honour to the talents of his friend, and was open to learn from him; but he always preserved his own independence, and he by no means always at length followed Carlyle's judgments. That he wanted steadiness, is a false inference from the changes necessitated by his ill health. Carlyle justly marks it as extraordinary perseverance, that when he had health so feeble, when the friends whose judgment he most esteemed gave so little approbation to his poetry, and the public simply ignored it, he continued to labour at poem after poem, because he had concluded this to be his true vocation. That Sterling was anything but a superficial man; that he penetrated to the fundamental principles of whatever he took in hand, and in comparison despised all secondary questions; is, we think, clear even by the extracts from his letters in the two biographies. But because neither health allowed, nor professional necessity called him, to be elaborately *learned* in anything, the critics, who hate his theological conclusions, assume the right to call him superficial.

Mr. Carlyle comments with due decision on the grand error of Sterling's life,—his having become ordained in the Church of England. When a young man at the usual age passes by routine into this position, without having ever gained independence of judgment, we may often regret it, but can never be surprised. But Sterling was already beyond the crisis at which such a step is ordinary; and in him it was an act so eminently voluntary and personal, that it ought not to have been done without very grave and full deliberation. Sterling himself afterwards compared his state of mind at the time, to that of a nun who takes the veil, in order to get rid of the wicked world. It is certain that he would have justified everything that his friend says against the folly of the proceeding; but we think it does not at all warrant Mr. Carlyle's remark —that 'few gifted living men had less stubbornness of perseverance' than Sterling. This might imply that it would have been admirable to persist in a calling for which (theologically, still more than physically) he soon found himself unsuited. He had too great love of truth to persevere in any form of error. There was, indeed, a fault; *not* that of wanting perseverance, but that of having rushed into action too precipitately, when strong religion was first awakened in him;—a phenomenon, no doubt, common enough. Still, we cannot but wonder that so active a mind seems temporarily to have forgotten the necessity of investigating and establishing the 39 Articles and all that goes along with them, and to have overlooked that they were likely to prove an unbearable yoke.

In conclusion, we strongly recommend any of our readers, who have not yet read Mr. Carlyle's very interesting book, to secure for themselves that pleasure. It has been our business chiefly to find fault; but the book itself will abundantly set that right, and put them in good humour with the author and his subject.

33. John Tulloch, from an unsigned review, *North British Review*

February 1852, xvi, 359–89

John Tulloch (1823–86), Scottish theologian, studied at St Andrews and Edinburgh. Very active in church reform, he was made Moderator of the Assembly of the Church of Scotland, its highest post, in 1878. In his *Movements of Religious Thought in Britain During the Nineteenth Century* (New York, 1885), Tulloch devotes a chapter ('Thomas Carlyle as a Religious Thinker') to Carlyle's revitalizing thought. The extract begins immediately after an extended discussion of the Christian and anti-Christian movements in English literature. See Introduction, p. 19.

It is obvious how complete is the reaction here against the spirit of our eighteenth century Literature. It is no less obvious, we doubt not, to most of our readers, that there is an important element of truth in all that is here said about the divine meaning that lies in every thing and in every man, and of the true dignity of Literature as the interpreter of this meaning. God is everywhere and in all things, and in him alone we live and move and have our being. All in us and around us is holy. The stamp of divinity is on all, and man is verily the true Shekinah, as Chrysostom said of old. All genuine interpretation of man and nature, therefore,—in other words, all genuine forms of Literature, are *religious*. There can never be, as our previous remarks have endeavoured strongly to shew, a disjunction between letters and religion without somewhat fatal injury to both. Where such a disjunction is recognized and defended, Christianity must be dead, and Literature will be dwarfed and feeble and dying.

We acknowledge, therefore, in the warmest manner the earnest efforts of Mr. Carlyle to vindicate the religious character of all true Literature. No one has spoken more noble and touching words on this subject; and it has appeared at times to ourselves strangely repugnant that we should yet be obliged to reckon him very far from a friend to

Christianity. So truly Christian-wise does he often speak, that when we class him, as we have done, at the head of the antichristian section of our Literature, our heart almost misgives us. It is not that we care what any of his worshippers and followers may say to this, but a voice within us bids us tremble lest we do him injustice. The calmer and clearer view of the matter, however, will never allow us any other conclusion. We find as we study him, and the more we study him the more plainly we find, that Literature is not only with him religious but *religion*. It is not only a divine teacher, but *the* Divine Teacher, and the only one left for man in these latter days. Any more special religion than that which is written on the face of nature and in the soul of man, Mr. Carlyle evidently disclaims. He will have no apocalypse save that of which Literature is the acknowledged interpreter. Man, if he will only open his eyes to the beauty which environs him, and listen to the 'still small voice' which speaks from within his own heart, and allow himself to enter into clear and calm communion with the eternal laws of the universe, becomes religious in the highest sense possible for him. And it is just the glory of Literature that it is her peculiar mission to reveal ever more radiantly this beauty, and awaken ever more powerfully this inner voice, and so place man in ever more clearly conscious and calmly intelligent relation to the great laws of his being, and of all being. In characteristic and unmistakable speech, we are told that:

[quotes 'the Maker's Laws' to 'brother, my brother' *Past and Present*, Bk. III, ch. xiv, 229–30]

If any doubt could have remained as to the real meaning of all such utterances, and as to the real significance of the relation which Mr. Carlyle occupies to Christianity, it must at length have been sufficiently removed by the appearance of his *Life of Sterling*, which we have made the occasion of these remarks. To us, we will confess at once, that this book is a very mournful one—the most mournful we have read for many a day. It is not, perhaps, that after all Mr. Carlyle had previously written, we had any right to expect a different book. We now at least clearly enough see that we had no such right. And yet somehow we had expectations regarding it, which, in almost every respect, have been miserably disappointed. We are conscious of admiring Mr. Carlyle in some respects so genuinely, of honouring so heartily the fine and 'rarely bestowed' gift of genius which God has given him; he has withal such a noble insight into Humanity in this nineteenth century, and such a warm and vigorous sympathy with its perplexities, its wrongs, and its miseries, that we looked (the expectation had somehow laid itself so closely to our heart, that we now wonder at ourselves a little) to this book at last for some light to be thrown on the weltering chaos—some breaking of day o'er the confused darkness in which he had hitherto delighted to dwell. The subject was one to encourage us in this expectation: the story of a life which had gone astray amid this same darkness and perplexity in which so many are now wandering—of one who had sought truth with a pure and earnest aim, and yet only found (if, indeed, he had been so far successful) some faint forecasts of it, when he departed to the eternal Silence. Here, if ever, was an opportunity of building on the broken fragments of such a life, some 'sunny dome' of faith and hope for all weary travellers on the same pathway. For any other purpose than this the life was not worth recounting,—certainly not worth again recounting. If Sterling's career was not to teach us in our present imbroglio of faiths and superstitions some lesson of religion, then it had not, that we can see, any lesson at all to teach. It had better, with many others, have remained unwritten; or, at least, enough had been said and written about it. However vain, therefore, we may now see that our expectation was in the matter, we cannot yet think it was altogether unreasonable.

The *significance* which, in almost every quarter had been found to attach to the life of John Sterling, was a religious one. What save this *could* it be? In Literature,—undoubtedly gifted as he was, and full from the beginning of a certain bloom and rich promise, which yet never ripened, and did not seem to be greatly ripening,—he had scarcely achieved for himself a name. He has left behind him nothing that will not soon be forgotten amid the endless article-writing and 'blotting of white paper' in our day. This Carlyle himself sees very well and acknowledges.

Sterling's performance and real or seeming importance in this world, (he says), was actually not of a kind to demand an express Biography, even according to the world's usages. His character was not supremely original; neither was his fate in the world wonderful. What he did was inconsiderable enough; and as to what it lay in him to have done, this was but a problem now beyond possibility of settlement. Why had a Biography been inflicted on this man? why had not No-biography, and the privilege of all the weary, been his lot?

To which emphatic query he strangely enough replies by writing *another* biography of this man, and from what reason? From one just the very opposite of that which, in the feeling of so many, had alone imparted significance and interest to the life of Sterling. Because Archdeacon Hare had viewed the life of his friend mainly in a religious light, and dwelt upon it perhaps somewhat exclusively in this light—for this reason, and to correct the false effects, as he believes, of the picture thus drawn, Mr. Carlyle has re-written his life. He and some correspondent (who seems, in a very marked sense, to be an *alter ego*—a Carlyle the *second*,) do not hesitate, in fact, to express considerable indignation at the misrepresentations in which they conceive the figure of Sterling to stand in the *Memoir* of the Archdeacon. He appears to them to be treated in it merely as a clergyman, in which capacity he only acted for eight months, and the relations of which were, in no degree, the most important of his life.

[quotes 'A pale sickly' to 'appeared in life' XI, 3]

Now while it is no special concern of ours to defend Archdeacon Hare's portrait of his friend, we have no hesitation in saying that he appears to us,—with all the evidence now before us,—to have apprehended and rendered the real meaning of Sterling's life, upon the whole, more truly than Mr. Carlyle. In the present biography we no doubt see Sterling in a more varied and complete light,—generally, indeed, in a quite different light; yet all the obvious efforts of Mr. Carlyle to crush the matter out of sight, fail to convince us that the religious phase of Sterling's career was not, *for others at least*, the most significant and noteworthy through which he passed. If it did not possess all the importance which it assumes in Hare's memoir, it was yet *the* most important feature claiming public attention. It was the point of view especially from which those beyond the mere circle of Sterling's companionship felt that his life had any peculiar interest for them. It very naturally, therefore, assumed the prominence it did in the hands of the Archdeacon, although from the deficiency of his representation in other respects, it now seems to occupy a somewhat too naked and exclusive position. For our own part, however, we feel bound to say that we prefer the portrait of Hare to that of Carlyle. It will not, of course, be supposed for a moment that we intend any comparison between the mere literary merits of the *Memoirs*. The brief sketch of the Archdeacon has, in this respect, no pretensions to rank with the more copious and finished biography before us. But we feel strongly (notwithstanding the somewhat rude bluster we have quoted above), that it is a more loveable and interesting character rises upon us from the faint and rapid outlines of the one than from the more complete picture of the other. We confess, indeed, to no small amount of disenchantment, in reading Carlyle's *Life*. Every touch of the heroic we had hitherto associated with Sterling gradually disappeared. The pure, earnest, struggling aspirant after truth merged into the merely frank, brilliant, somewhat impetuous, and spoiled Dilettante. The halo that had surrounded him, to our vision, was gone. Mr. Carlyle would probably say—so much the better. It was just for this purpose he wrote his book. This was just his aim—to snatch the figure of his friend from the absurd halo of religious interest which had been thrown around it. But we feel satisfied, notwithstanding Mr. Carlyle's asseverations, that such an interest, although not in the measure supposed by some, *did* invest Sterling's life.

If we now pass from these general remarks to some special criticism on the work before us, we feel, first of all, called upon to express our delight with it in a mere literary point of view. We agree with our contemporaries generally in esteeming it, in this respect, one of the best of Mr. Carlyle's books. It has not only here and there touches of exquisite art, but its pervading texture is, to our minds, of a more finely wrought and beautiful character than any of his recent compositions. The style, in its general structure, is the same which, from so many quarters, has provoked assault; but it moves, save at brief intervals, in a clearer, quieter, and more placid flow than usual. If not rising to any of those terrific heights of sublimity, of which it is so capable, crushing and overwhelming the reader with its piled-up and lurid grandeur, and stunning him with the thunder of its march; neither does it ever sink, save in rare instances, into the mere grotesque and fantastic—the mere mimicry of thunder, which not infrequently turns our gravity into a smile in the perusal of Mr. Carlyle's writings. There are, indeed, some scattered passages of a very provocative and impetuous kind, and one or two which, in their ragged and inapposite contrasts, may well call forth a smile; but a character of pathetic softness, of mild and graceful tenderness, is the distinguishing one of the volume. It is impossible to doubt how truly Carlyle loved his friend, or what a deep and pensive fountain of love there is in the man altogether. Down below all his rugged sternness and repulsive bitterness, there is a well of genial and most gentle affection, the stream of which makes glad almost every page of this book. As a work of art, too, as a compact piece of biographic story, in which the principal figure occupies his due prominence, while a group starts into life here and there around him, by a few rapid and picturesque touches, it is very nearly perfect. After we had once begun its perusal, we could not lay it aside nor pause over it. But onward we went, now well-nigh touched to tears, and now, it is true, touched with indignation, at some obvious and gross injustice, but owning every-where the felicitous mastery of the hand that was leading us. A feeling of deep sadness, however, of profound and perplexing sorrow, was *uppermost* with us in its perusal.

In token of the rich literary merit we have ascribed to this volume, we feel bound to present our readers with a few extracts, although most of them, even to those who may not have read the volume, will, we dare say, be familiar from the numerous notices that have appeared of it. They are of that kind, however, which will bear a second reading. Sterling's mother is thus described in the second chapter:—

[quotes 'Mrs. Sterling' to 'his were' XI, 12–13]

We give as a companion picture the following—a very slight thing indeed, but pleasant and attractive:—Charles Barton 'now, in 1829–30, an amiable, cheerful, rather idle young fellow about town;' had been one of Sterling's fellow-students at Cambridge, and, meeting again in London, Sterling became a familiar intimate of his family. The eldest daughter—'a stately, blooming, black-eyed young woman, full of gay softness, of indolent sense and enthusiasm, about Sterling's own age, if not a little older,'—would seem to have especially interested him, as he had undoubtedly found an interest in her eyes. In the meantime there was talk of a Spanish invasion, and of Sterling, now full of enthus-iastic radicalism, joining the invaders.

[quotes 'The ship was' to 'acceptance of it' XI, 72]

It was not till after Sterling had retired from the Church that he made the acquaintance of Carlyle. He had come to London to consult as to the state of his health, which he began to find inadequate for the efficient discharge of his pastoral duties. On this occasion Carlyle first met him at the India House, in company with John Mill.

[quotes 'The sight' to 'than strength' XI, 105–6]

The acquaintance thus begun ripened speedily into a very close and peculiar friendship; and especially when Sterling finally left Herstmonceux, the seat of his brief clerical labours, and took up his abode at Bayswater, the intimacy between him and Carlyle appears to have grown fast, and deepened on the one side into that profound estimation, and on the other into that deep and tender love, which ever afterwards characterized it. Carlyle thus describes the employment and character of his friend at this time:—

[quotes 'Sterling's days' to 'and ingenuous' XI, 126–8]

. . . We had intended to add to these extracts Mr. Carlyle's closing sketch of his friend,—a life-warm and vigorous portrait, very masterly in every literary point of view, but especially interesting as fully expressing that peculiar conception of Sterling's character, which, above all, distinguishes this biography from the previous one by Archdeacon Hare. Some of the foregoing extracts have already, however, pretty clearly indicated this conception; and our space will only permit us to append a few fragments from the concluding chapter in confirmation:—

[quotes non-continuously 'A certain splendour' to 'beautiful for you' XI, 262–7]

It will not be denied that here and elsewhere in the graphic delineation of Mr. Carlyle,—so free and flowing, and yet so nicely and minutely touched,—a very interesting and beautiful character is presented to us. Sterling seems to live before us, and we who never saw him, seem to have known him well,—so bright, and hopeful, and joyful. And there can be no doubt, we infer, that there must have been an element of rare brilliancy and joyousness in him which the sketch of Archdeacon Hare fails to bring out. Yet, as we have said, we cling rather to the portrait drawn by the latter. The Sterling of Hare seems to us, upon the whole, a nobler and worthier character than the Sterling of Carlyle. And not only so, (and this is a consideration in comparison with which every other is of no consequence,) it conscientiously appears to us, that, while the delineation of the Archdeacon must be held somewhat deficient in complete truthfulness, it is yet, upon the whole, the more truthful. It seizes indeed too prominently the earnest, religious aspects of Sterling's character; but Mr. Carlyle has, we think, still more disproportionately undervalued and neglected these. We have sought satisfaction on this point from a renewed converse with the most significant of Sterling's remains; and our conviction decidedly is, that Sterling was far more distinguished by religious earnestness, and even religious sorrowfulness, than Mr. Carlyle would leave us to suppose. An *artist* he no doubt was, with an eye and a heart for the beautiful everywhere, and with that strong repulsion to all that is merely narrow, or exclusive, or gloomy in religion, so characteristic of the artist; but an heroic truth-seeker too, with the most solemn *moral* convictions, and the most ardent and painful longings. And it is *this* side of his character which Mr. Carlyle has just ignored, that to us is the most interesting, and reappears the most frequently throughout his writings. . . .

[Carlyle] has devoted a chapter to Coleridge, presenting a somewhat elaborate delineation of that wonderful man, not unmarked by the masterly strokes which distinguish the other portraits in the volume; but on the whole, a sadly blurred and wretched affair. We have been both amazed and pained at the praise we have seen bestowed on this sketch in some quarters. It is to us the one utterly unworthy feature of the volume—a poor unheroic daub. In the 'old man eloquent,' as he sat on the brow of Highgate Hill discoursing in that indescribable and interminable manner of his, with his ever-recurring *sum-in-jects* and *om-m-jects*, there was no doubt something that could easily be turned into ridicule. There was no doubt in that ever-flowing river of talk many pools of mere darkness. We have Dr. Chalmers' honest and emphatic statement to this effect when he went to visit the Philosopher with his friend Irving who sat so reverently at the Philosopher's feet. But we know also that there was often a divine meaning and beauty in the old man's speech—rich gleams of a far-off sunshine irradiating the soul of the listener. The talk which, day by day, rivetted such a man as Edward Irving, and delighted and *enlightened* we shall say—let Mr. Carlyle say what he likes—John Sterling, could not have been without glorious flashes and even meridian splendours of meaning under all its cloudy phases. Carlyle indeed admits that there were 'glorious islets' ever and anon 'rising out of the haze;' but, generally, according to his representation, it was a very sad and dreary affair this talk. This is decidedly the impression conveyed by his picture. Nay, it appears to us that an ill-concealed air of contemptuous pity breathes throughout it. The aspiring sage of Chelsea had come to the shrine of the expiring sage of Highgate Hill, but it is with no reverence in his heart, and with rather a smile of mockery on his lips. He looks down with some sort of poor compassion on the 'logical fata morganas' with which he sees the other 'labouring to solace himself.' Listen to this account of the Coleridgean remedy for evils in Church and State:—

[quotes 'The remedy' to 'om-m-ject', XI, 59]

There is to us something very intolerable in this tone of Mr. Carlyle,—in continuance of which we have, throughout the volume, more than abundant mention of 'Coleridgean moonshine,' 'Coleridgean legerdemain.' We must say it has kindled our indignation not a little. Where are Mr. Carlyle's remedies for our faithless and aberrant generation, that he feels himself warranted in speaking thus of Coleridge? We can imagine the fine work which some future biographer of another Sterling will in a similar strain make of the Chelsean prescription. Perhaps, too, it may be found when the secrets of another sanctuary are unveiled, that if there was not much 'pious' nor even 'partly courteous snuffle' in the discourse *there*, there was yet in plenty 'a confused unintelligible flood of utterance, threatening to submerge all known land-marks of thought, and drown the world and us'—a vast vituperative commotion which made noise in the ear without bringing much light or life to the heart. But in truth this way of talking about great men is not to our taste at all, and we least of all expected it from such a quarter. We would reverence all spiritual teachers, if we could, and Mr. Carlyle no less in his way. They have all their lesson to teach. Let us learn it if we can. It will never do us any good to laugh at it. The silliest trifler can raise a shout at the most sacred attempt, and mere scorn, Mr. Carlyle should know, is a cheap attribute of fools. Coleridge, no doubt, had his weaknesses. Even *his* great intellect had a halt, as it were, which many weaker and smaller men could see and prate about, as they have already so abundantly done. The treasure here, as everywhere, was in an *earthen* vessel—of glorious framework it is true, yet not without the ineradicable flaw. 'The empyrean element lay smothered under the terrene.' Yea doubtless. But we did not expect Mr. Carlyle to be the man to proclaim this with a jest! There was enough of the *heroic* surely in Coleridge for him and for us to admire for ever, without lifting the veil and pointing to the scars which mark him as our brother in human frailty and sin. The man who has found a hero in Mahomet and Johnson and Burns, might, we think, have trod with a more reverent tenderness round the grave of Coleridge.* Of the substantive value of his contributions to the cause of truth we cannot even for a moment now speak. We *feel*, however, that we hazard no vain conjecture when we express a conviction that future generations will find them upon the whole, perhaps, the worthiest which have descended from our age.

With such views of 'Coleridgean moonshine,' it is not to be wondered at that Mr. Carlyle ceases not throughout the volume to deplore its effect upon Sterling. . . .

Shortly after Sterling quitted the Church, he entered upon that

* We speak sincerely what we think of Mr. Carlyle's personal sketch of Coleridge as a whole. Here and there in it, as well as elsewhere in his essays, he has spoken of him with all the admiration we could wish.

career of theological struggle with which his name has been so associated. Whatever significance may have once attached to that struggle, a wider and more intimate acquaintance with the character of Sterling has pretty well removed. It was indeed, we still think, for others, the most significant phase of his career, but it wanted that breadth of interest and meaning which a deeper, more intense, and on the whole greater character could alone have given it. We now *see* what we had all along felt from a perusal of his writings, that the importance of Sterling as a thinker had been somewhat overrated in his previous biography; or at least, that an exaggerated notion of him in this capacity, founded somehow upon that biography, had arisen. So far we believe Carlyle to be entirely in the right, when he affirms, that 'in spite of his sleepless intellectual vivacity, Sterling was not properly a thinker at all.' He had subtlety, brilliancy, and a certain roundness of intellectual vision which could not yet be called comprehensiveness,—but he wanted depth, penetration, and, above all, calmness and patience. He went at everything—Philosophy, Theology, Poetry, in a certain headlong, dashing manner, which shewed the dexterous *improvvisatore*, (a term by which Mr. Carlyle has more than once characterized him,) rather than the thoughtful worker. 'Overhaste was his continual fault; over-haste and want of the due strength.' His genius flashed and coruscated, playing like sheet-lightning (to adopt Carlyle's comparison) round a subject and irradiating it, rather than 'concentrating itself into a bolt and riving the mountain barriers for us.' Fitted to excel in the fields of pure Literature with his quick, genial grasp, and rich glittering style, (though the glitter is often cold as of polished crystals rather than of living sun-light), and the delicacy and ripe finish of his touch, he was yet greatly deficient in that direct and piercing insight, and that calm laboriousness of inquiry which alone constitute the thinker, and could alone have given the significance claimed for it by some, to the religious crisis which he underwent. That such a *crisis* was deeply experienced by him, however, can admit of no doubt. Tremulously he owned the spiritual agitations of his time. He felt the conflict on all sides of him, and gave himself heartily to it. His undoubtedly valorous spirit bore ever after the dints of a strife which had been no holiday one with him. We would not, for a moment, (as Mr. Carlyle would have us to do,) underrate the potency of the struggle through which he passed. Only, *his* was not the strength to wrestle patiently through it and reach the light of heaven beyond. . . .

Mr. Carlyle, as the reader will have inferred from our previous statements, has dealt in the most scanty and imperfect fashion with this period of Sterling's life. There is indeed in all his talk of his friend, about this time, and of his favourite authors, a tone of insolent pity and injustice that has filled us with feelings of less regard for Mr. Carlyle than we thought we could have ever entertained. 'I remember,' he says, 'he talked often about Tholuck, Schleiermacher, and *others of that stamp*; and looked disappointed, though full of good nature, at my obstinate indifference to them and their affairs. His knowledge of German literature, very slight at this time, limited itself altogether to writers on Church-matters, Evidences, Counter-evidences, Theologies, and rumours of theologies—by the Tholucks, Schleiermachers, Neanders, and I know not whom. Of "the true sovereign souls" of that literature, the Goethes, Richters, Schillers, Lessings, he had as good as no knowledge.' [XI, 125–6]

What strange, hap-hazard, and monstrous talk is this? The Goethes and Lessings exalted to honour, and the Schleiermachers and Neanders trampled under foot! What next? Can Mr. Carlyle fancy he honours his own function as a teacher by such talk . . .?

As we get from Mr. Carlyle no insight into this struggling period of Sterling's life, so we get from him no satisfactory account of its issue. We are indeed told that, by-and-bye, 'Tholuck, Schleiermacher, and the war of articles and rubrics were left in the far distance;' and that 'Literature again began decisively to dawn on him as the goal he ought to aim at.' 'It was years, however, before he got the inky tints of that Coleridgean adventure completely bleached from his mind.' But finally he *did* get emancipated. Of Strauss even, nothing more was heard. 'Strauss had interested him only as a sign of the times, in which sense alone do we find, for a year or two back, any notice of the Church or its affairs by Sterling; and at last even this as good as ceases.' 'Adieu, O Church; thy road is that way, mine is this; in God's name, adieu!' 'What we are going *to*,' says he once, 'is abundantly obscure, but what all men are going *from* is very plain.'

This seems to be the sum of truth, which, according to Carlyle, John Sterling reached,—full of what comfort may be gathered from it by any of our readers. One touching and melancholy corroboration of his statement Mr. Carlyle has furnished in a letter, not just the last one, but nearly so, that he received from Sterling. We give it as about the most deeply pathetic letter we ever read. We cannot even now again read it without a perplexed and swimming feeling as of tears that will not yet flow.

To Thomas Carlyle, Esq., Chelsea, London.

Hillside, Ventnor, August 10, 1844.

MY DEAR CARLYLE,—For the first time for many months it seems possible to send you a few words; merely, however, for Remembrance and Farewell. On higher matters there is nothing to say. I tread the common road into the great darkness, without any thought of fear, and with very much hope. Certainty, indeed, I have none. With regard to you and me, I cannot begin to write; having nothing for it but to keep shut the lid of those secrets with all the iron weights in my power. Towards me it is still more true than towards England, that no man has been and done like you. Heaven bless you! If I can lend a hand when *there*, that will not be wanting. It is all very strange, but not one hundredth part so bad as it seems to the standers by.

Your wife knows my mind towards her and will believe it without asseverations.—Yours to the last,

JOHN STERLING

Sad enough, truly, and dark enough—The beautiful incident in Mr. Hare's memoir comes to shed a gleam of light on this thick darkness; and we rejoice with trembling to think of it. 'As it grew dark he appeared to be seeking for something, and on her (his sister) asking what he wanted, said "only the old Bible which I used so often at Herstmonceux, in the cottages."' Why has Mr. Carlyle not recorded this fact?—*if it be a fact*, which we cannot doubt. Was he ashamed that it should be so said of his friend? Must we blame him for wilful suppression here as we fear elsewhere,—for wilful blindness in overlooking some of the real facts of Sterling's spiritual history which it did not suit him to disclose or at least to dwell upon? With a noble affectionateness Sterling speaks of the good of Carlyle's influence over him. We feel profoundly that we cannot respond to these words of a dying brother.

What precisely Sterling's ultimate views were, it is impossible to say. If uncertainty rested on them before, a deeper uncertainty may be said to rest on them now. That he had not, however, altogether abandoned Christianity, seems undoubted both from his closing interview with his sister, and his own express statement in a letter of farewell to Archdeacon Hare. 'Christianity is a great comfort and blessing to me,' he says, 'although I am quite unable to believe all its original documents.' *What* his *conclusions* were, with our view of his character, is not a matter of special importance to us. While, in the mere fact of the struggle through which he passed, typical of his age, he was yet, as we have endeavoured to explain, not fitted to enter into all the depth of that struggle, and work his way through it into clearness and truth. He was altogether of too light and restless and facile a nature—like his friend Francis Newman, (with his likeness to whom, in some respects, we have been much struck), to mirror in any adequate sense the spiritual progress of our time, and to furnish it with the right solution of its spiritual perplexities.

As for Mr. Carlyle himself,—it is obvious we have no more anything to look for in this way from him, if we ever had. His attitude is now and henceforth plainly and emphatically enough an 'Adieu, O Church.' Whatever spiritual consolation may be possible from Goethe is welcome to the age. Other the biographer of Sterling has not to give. Literature has again in him, through a curious process of religious baptism, culminated in a mere species of philosophic Paganism. We cannot for the life of us make more of Mr. Carlyle's *chief end of man* than this. We have pretty well got rid—thanks to him—of the sceptical Epicureanism of last century; but only, so far as he is concerned, to traverse the more lofty and specious but not less dangerous verge of a stoical Pantheism. There is, we feel assured, a more excellent Way than either. There is a Light of Divine Truth, however dimmed, yet burning in the midst of us. There is a Sun of Christian warmth and vitality still, under whatever obscurities, shining in our poor world, irradiating many a heart, and illuminating many a mind. All has not become mere 'bleared tallow light,' mere 'draggled, dirty farthing candle.' We honestly believe with Coleridge in the inextinguishable power of Christianity, and that there is life in the old Churches yet,—destined to a glorious revival,—let Mr. Carlyle mock as he may. We firmly rejoice with Neander, that Christianity having once entered into the life of Humanity shall go forth, from every temporary lull of its strength, to new conquests over it, and enter into freer and more perfect harmony with it,—till its vitalizing spirit circulates in every vein of the great growth and progress of our race, and effloresces into a richer blossoming of *literary* as of all other excellence.

BOURNEMOUTH COLLEGE
OF TECHNOLOGY

COLLEGE LIBRARY

34. Unsigned review, *Christian Observer and Advocate*

April 1852, lii, 262–76

Conducted by members of the Established Church, the *Observer* was often inclined to expose infidelity and heresy in its pages. See Introduction, p. 20.

Some years ago consternation seized the 'religious world,' as they heard that the literary remains of John Sterling had been edited by a dignitary of the Church, and published with a biographical sketch of the author prefixed, containing, to say the least of it, passages of very questionable orthodoxy. Such was the commotion excited, that good easy men, who had hitherto reposed comfortably in their easy chairs, fondly believing that all around them was as orthodox and decorous as their own creed and practice, began to bestir themselves and enquire, Who is this John Sterling, and what is his biographer? Neither of these questions admitted of a very satisfactory answer. Furthermore, it became known abroad that a certain club existed, bearing the name of this same John Sterling, and Right Reverend Prelates forthwith found themselves eyed askance by their Clergy, and held up to odium in public prints. For some months the compositors must have had considerable practice in filling their sticks with the words Sterling, Hare, Carlyle, Neology, Germanism, Infidel, and so forth. In time, however, the tumult died away. The Sterling club changed its designation, and sunk again into oblivion,—not, however, unshorn of a portion of its Right Reverend honours. Those who had merely echoed the cuckoo cry which they had heard from others, turned to cry down something else, which they probably had never read, and certainly had never considered; for which latter defect, however, the inability of their 'most weak pia mater' must plead their excuse. Clear-minded and right-minded men, who deeply felt the mischief of the lax and unscriptural theology which had given such a baneful tinge to the opinions of Sterling, considered the system itself as infinitely more fraught with evil than the biography which in some measure unveiled its workings. And one consideration there was, which more than anything else contributed to reconcile such men to Mr. Hare, and induce them, if not to pronounce a verdict of acquittal, at least to withdraw the indictment; namely, that, after all, things perhaps were best as they were. There was Scylla and Charybdis. Sterling's life had to be written and his remains published. The only question was, should this task be undertaken by the free-thinking Carlyle, or the Christian, though often mistaken or misled, Archdeacon Hare. Now the fact was, that Sterling was without doubt a man of ill-balanced mind. 'Unstable as water it was not to be expected of him that he should excel.' Whilst he knew that the thing in our land known to many by the name of pitch doth, as ancient writers do report, defile, he has yet to learn that there were pollutions which would still more surely defile and taint the mind. He had not learnt what the humblest student of the Divine records could have told him, that evil communications, whether from books or men, were alike corrupting to the mind. And those doubts and perplexities which thus arose, he did not, as wiser men would have done, ponder in his own bosom; but, with the reckless open-heartedness which so especially marked his character, committed them to paper. At the same time, there was much that was great and noble in him, much that would make one weep that such a heart and such a mind should not have fallen under the influences of better guides than those by whom such irreparable mischief was effected.

It was not to be wondered at, then, that Archdeacon Hare should, as far as possible, have contemplated the character of his friend in this latter light; and that while keenly feeling and sorely mourning over the sad errors of his creed and practice, he should, though integrity obliged him to 'nothing extenuate,' desire still not to 'set down aught in malice.' The Archdeacon, however, seems to have signally failed in his endeavours; for whilst, four years ago, it was, not very ambiguously, hinted that Herstmonceux was the residence of a Venerable infidel, the extreme candour and liberal-mindedness of Mr. Carlyle has been shocked by the bigotry and narrow views displayed in the unhappy biography. In great alarm, therefore, lest the world should suspect that Mr. Carlyle's deceased friend might, after all, be really a believer in the Bible, he has come forward and presented us with a view of Sterling in which the most infidel side of his character is very carefully brought into the light. Certainly Mr. Carlyle has performed his task in an admirable manner, considering the materials with which he had to

CARLYLE

work. He has clearly shewn, that whatever might be the case with
Sterling, he himself has certainly 'his religion to seek,' if we mean by
religion those Divine truths which Mr. Carlyle designates by the
impious name of 'Hebrew old clothes.'

That the present is a religious age, there can be no question; but
whether it is an eminently Christian one, may fairly admit of a doubt.
The powers of evil have changed their tactics. Men no longer in this
present age teach Christianity as if it were 'an agreed point among all
people of discernment' that it is fictitious; they rather extol it, substitut-
ing at the same time a Christianity of their own for the Christianity of
the Bible. . . .

[Several pages are devoted to the history of the ensuing moral and
religious crises taking place in England and to a sketch of Sterling's early
life.]

Mr. Carlyle is perhaps not the only man who finds difficulty in
dissecting and expounding this state of mind, which, under a modified
form, strongly marks many writers and thinkers of the present day.
The solution is to be obtained by considering the matter in a light which
Mr. Carlyle would probably not appreciate, and from a point of view
which would never suggest itself to his mind. The man could not enter
into the horror with which Coleridge said once of himself, that he 'had
skirted the howling deserts of infidelity,' who, enamoured with the
barrenness, regrets simply that Coleridge did no more than skirt them.

We soon find Sterling compelled by the state of his health to leave
England, and, together with his young bride, taking up his abode on a
family estate in the island of St. Vincent. His mind at that period seems
to have assumed a more healthy tone. The military execution of the
Spanish exiles at Malaga, comprising, alas! one young Englishman who
had been persuaded by Sterling to join the enterprise, made a deep
impression upon him. He had himself nearly accompanied Torrijos and
his little band.

From this time he began to think of devoting himself to the ministry
of the Church. A few months' meditation in England and on the
Continent, a conversation with Mr. Hare at Bonn, and a few more
months of reflection, decided him on the course to be taken, and
accordingly we find him established in the curacy of Herstmonceux.

Even Mr. Carlyle cannot quite sneer away the tokens of Christian
feeling which seem at this period to have manifested themselves. He
can only solace himself with laments that 'the bereaved young lady has

taken the veil then,' and impious scoffs at 'Coleridgean moonshine,' 'certain old Jew stars,' and even 'salvation' itself.

It is refreshing to turn to what Mr. Carlyle has so studiously suppressed as unworthy of Sterling, passages where he speaks 'of the benefits of marriage to a man whose heart and principles are scarcely, or very recently, fixed in the line of practical Christianity.'. . .

It is with feelings of unmitigated disgust that we turn to Mr. Carlyle's remarks on this epoch in Sterling's life. We will not pain our readers by transcribing them. A gloom was now to overshadow the rest of poor Sterling's life: he was to be brought within the reach of Mr. Carlyle's personal influence. That Satan has agents striving continually to draw away those of whom it might be hoped that they were beginning to tread the paths of life, can hardly be doubted by those who read that gentleman's own account of his intercourse with Sterling. Our own opinion of Mr. Carlyle was never a very exalted one, but it has been materially modified by the memoir we are now considering. That Mr. Carlyle is possessed of considerable powers, is undoubted; that his clear-sightedness is garbed in most intolerable affectation, is obvious to all; and that his powers are deliberately consecrated to the power of evil is, alas! too plainly manifest to the *Christian Observer*. Even his poor victims could not but feel this occasionally. Sterling could complain 'of Carlyle's utterly condemning our age as void of faith and heroism.' Another, whose fall seems indeed to have been like that of Lucifer, whilst speaking of that 'very great man,' one of the two 'greatly gifted' men 'then living in this England' (F. H. Newman being the other) could yet bitterly exclaim, 'Carlyle! Carlyle only raises questions he cannot answer, and seems best contented if he can make the rest of us as discontented as himself.' Truly Dr. Layard might have found Yezidis without going to Kurdistan to search for them. It is a melancholy thing to reflect that the great and good man to whom we have referred a few pages back should have given his sanction to that which he himself would now probably, if living, be the first to condemn.

We will not sicken our readers by narrating the successive gladiatorial thrusts with which Mr. Carlyle endeavoured to destroy Sterling's weakened religious faith, nor the exultant triumph with which he commemorates each well-planted hit. Sterling might 'look hurt' at the bold attacks on his faith; he might argue for it, he might remonstrate in words which Carlyle 'suppresses;' but, as we should suspect, all in vain. The only excuse for him is that offered by the lord 'of Tamworth tower and town,' for his overthrow by the supposed spectre knight.

In spite, however, of Mr. Carlyle's best endeavours, 'the shadows of the surplice,' 'the sickly shadow of the parish church,' were not so easily or so soon got rid of as he wished. From the time of leaving Herstmonceux, Sterling led an unsettled and an unhappy life. At Bayswater he read theology, chiefly German; occasionally undertook clerical duties; and talked to Carlyle on the worth of Christianity, 'how essential the belief in it' was 'to man,' the danger of Pantheism, and similar matters, which are, by him with whom he held this converse, lightly adverted to with a graceful sneer. . . .

Sterling's life at Clifton passed on in the same unsatisfactory way as heretofore. He was planning another winter at Madeira, but changed his intention, and spent it at Falmouth. For some time his residence seems to have been Clifton and Falmouth alternately with the seasons, till he finally determined to make the latter place his permanent abode.

About this time an incident occurred in which Mr. Carlyle contrives, by a miserable effort, 'out-Heroding' even his usual self in heartlessness, to find a subject for sneers where he ought to have done honour to a striking example of Christian heroism. Surely, 'in higher thoughts, contempt might die.' Two men were engaged in blasting a part of some Cornish mine. By carelessness they had kindled the match whilst they were still below. Both instantly sprang to the basket, and implored the windlass-man immediately to hoist it up, but in vain; their united weight was more than he could raise. One of them instantly quitted the basket, saying to the other, 'Go aloft, Jack; away: in one minute I shall be in heaven.' The explosion almost immediately followed; but by some providential arching of the rocks under which this true hero was buried, he, though almost miraculously, escaped without material injury. The most impressive part of the story is the motive that led to this gallant conduct. The poor miner was a believing humble Christian; and had reason to fear that his comrade was not. He believed that whilst, to him, death would be gain, to his companion it would be loss, and deliberately preferred braving it in its most horrible form, rather than expose his fellow-miner to that death which would be followed by deeper calamity. Mr. Carlyle might have learnt what Christian faith and Christian love really meant from this poor Cornish miner, of whom it could not even be said that he 'knew, and knew no more, his Bible true,' for he could not even read.

During Sterling's abode at Plymouth, and his next continental tour, he seems to have been sinking deeper into the gulf of scepticism. He had now ceased to talk of Strauss, and now took no more notice 'of the

Church or its affairs.' 'What we are going *to*,' he says, 'is abundantly obscure; but what all men are going *from*, is very plain.' Not *all* men, Sterling; not poor Cornish miners.

The lessons of flippancy in the use of Scripture language in which his friend Carlyle had tutored him, had told too powerfully on his mind.

His sneers at Missionaries and their labours were quite in keeping with those opinions he had now imbibed. The man who supposed that the only 'effect produced' upon the poor Blacks, even after what is called their conversion, was to 'adopt pantaloons and abandon polygamy,' might have learned from Mr. Hare that, although the works 'of our generals and statesmen,' 'of our poets and philosophers,' may perish, 'the works which assuredly will live, and be great and glorious, are the works of those poor unregarded men who have gone forth in the spirit of the twelve from Judea, whether to India, to Africa, to Greenland, or to the isles in the Pacific. As their names are written in the Book of Life, so are their works; and it may be that the noblest memorial of England in those days will be the Christian empire of New Zealand.'. . .

It [Carlyle's *Life of Sterling*] is marked by all the worst peculiarities of the author's style of thinking and writing. His faults as a writer—must we not add, as a man?—appear to multiply and aggravate as he proceeds in life. Grey hairs appear to be far from bringing wisdom, or better qualifying him to be, as some were disposed to make him, a guide and oracle of society. The object of this work has in it something almost awfully painful. It is written confessedly to shew that what almost every rational man—though Mr. Carlyle does not—will regard as deep errors of opinion and faults of character in the subject of his memoir, had not been brought to light by Mr. Hare as they ought to be. Sterling, according to the present writer, only deviated occasionally into better things, but was in the main a proud despiser of all established opinion, and a thorough-grained infidel. We are afraid that the biographer has in a measure succeeded in thus lowering the character of Sterling: and that though there was much in him which was calculated to awaken pity, and possibly regard, it is too obvious that there was much also, very much, to lament and condemn.

One remark we may make in conclusion—that the main rock on which Sterling and his present biographer appear to have almost equally split, both as writers and men, is the most egregious *vanity*. More self-sufficient persons it is difficult to conceive. Sterling has gone to give in his great account; and we do not wish to 'make war with the dead.'

Mr. Carlyle still lives to exhibit to the world the most offensive specimen of a man who, without the smallest pretensions to give laws to society either in thinking or acting, nevertheless seats himself, like an Indian despot, on the Musnud, and stretches out his fantastic sceptre, as though all the world were to obey him. Robert Hall, in his celebrated 'Sermon on Atheism,' has taken much pains, and with admirable success, to establish the truth that *vanity* is a *crime*,' and the parent of many crimes. And we need no other proof of his position than the work before us. Mr. Carlyle is so vain of his own opinions, that he spares no opportunity of exhibiting them. And rather than the world should call them in question, he is contented to take hold of the character of a friend, and, as we cannot hesitate to say, to blacken and traduce it, so as to prove him to be his own adherent and disciple. In the prosecution of this bad end, he adopts the most objectionable means. He indulges in the greatest extravagances of writing. He slashes to the right and left at all authors and thinkers but himself. He assails every citadel of established opinion. He treats the Scriptural views of Christianity as a mere chimera. He would leave us with scarcely an article of faith to stand upon. He labours alike to corrupt our taste, temper, and principles: and on the whole, we are free to say, that when lying on the bed of death, and about to give in our account to the Great Father and Judge of all men, there are few works we should regret more to have written than Carlyle's *Life of Sterling*.

35. George Eliot, an unsigned review, *Leader*

27 October 1855, vi, 1034–5

George Eliot is reviewing Thomas Ballantyne's *Passages Selected from the Writings of Thomas Carlyle: With a Biographical Memoir.* For a comment on Eliot see No. 31.

It has been well said that the highest aim in education is analogous to the highest aim in mathematics, namely, to obtain not *results* but *powers*, not particular solutions, but the means by which endless solutions may be wrought. He is the most effective educator who aims less at perfecting specific acquirements than at producing that mental condition which renders acquirements easy, and leads to their useful application; who does not seek to make his pupils moral by enjoining particular courses of action, but by bringing into activity the feelings and sympathies that must issue in noble action. On the same ground it may be said that the most effective writer is not he who announces a particular discovery, who convinces men of a particular conclusion, who demonstrates that this measure is right and that measure wrong; but he who rouses in others the activities that must issue in discovery, who awakes men from their indifference to the right and the wrong, who nerves their energies to seek for the truth and live up to it at whatever cost. The influence of such a writer is dynamic. He does not teach men how to use sword and musket, but he inspires their souls with courage and sends a strong will into their muscles. He does not, perhaps, enrich your stock of data, but he clears away the film from your eyes that you may search for data to some purpose. He does not, perhaps, convince you, but he strikes you, undeceives you, animates you. You are not directly fed by his books, but you are braced as by a walk up to an alpine summit, and yet subdued to calm and reverence as by the sublime things to be seen from that summit.

Such a writer is Thomas Carlyle. It is an idle question to ask whether his books will be read a century hence: if they were all burnt as the grandest of Suttees on his funeral pile, it would be only like cutting down an oak after its acorns have sown a forest. For there is hardly a superior or active mind of this generation that has not been modified by Carlyle's writings; there has hardly been an English book written for the last ten or twelve years that would not have been different if Carlyle had not lived. The character of his influence is best seen in the fact that many of the men who have the least agreement with his opinions are those to whom the reading of *Sartor Resartus* was an epoch in the history of their minds. The extent of his influence may be best seen in the fact that ideas which were startling novelties when he first wrote them are now become common-places. And we think few men will be found to say that this influence on the whole has not been for good. There are plenty who question the justice of Carlyle's estimates of past men and past times, plenty who quarrel with the exaggerations of the *Latter-Day Pamphlets*, and who are as far as possible from looking for an amendment of things from a Carlylian theocracy with the 'greatest man', as a Joshua who is to smite the wicked (and the stupid) till the going down of the sun. But for any large nature, those points of difference are quite incidental. It is not as a theorist, but as a great and beautiful human nature, that Carlyle influences us. You may meet a man whose wisdom seems unimpeachable, since you find him entirely in agreement with yourself; but this oracular man of unexceptionable opinions has a green eye, a wiry hand, and altogether a *Wesen*, or demeanour, that makes the world look blank to you, and whose unexceptionable opinions become a bore; while another man who deals in what you cannot but think 'dangerous paradoxes', warms your heart by the pressure of his hand, and looks out on the world with so clear and loving an eye, that nature seems to reflect the light of his glance upon your own feeling. So it is with Carlyle. When he is saying the very opposite of what we think, he says it so finely, with so hearty conviction—he makes the object about which we differ stand out in such grand relief under the clear light of his strong and honest intellect—he appeals so constantly to our sense of the manly and the truthful—that we are obliged to say 'Hear! hear'! to the writer before we can give the decorous 'Oh! oh'! to his opinions.

Much twaddling criticism has been spent on Carlyle's style. Unquestionably there are some genuine minds, not at all given to twaddle, to whom his style is antipathetic, who find it as unendurable as an English lady finds peppermint. Against antipathies there is no arguing; they are misfortunes. But instinctive repulsion apart, surely there is no one who can read and relish Carlyle without feeling that they could no more wish him to have written in another style than they could wish Gothic architecture not to be Gothic, or Raffaelle not to be Raffaellesque.

It is the fashion to speak of Carlyle almost exclusively as a philosopher; but, to our thinking, he is yet more of an artist than a philosopher. He glances deep down into human nature, and shows the causes of human actions; he seizes grand generalisations, and traces them in the particular with wonderful acumen; and in all this he is a philosopher. But, perhaps, his greatest power lies in concrete presentation. No novelist has made his creations live for us more thoroughly than Carlyle has made Mirabeau and the men of the French Revolution, Cromwell and the Puritans. What humour in his pictures! Yet what depth of appreciation, what reverence for the great and god-like under every sort of earthly mummery!

It is several years now since we read a work of Carlyle's *seriatim*, but this our long-standing impression of him as a writer we find confirmed by looking over Mr. Ballantyne's *Selections*. Such a volume as this is surely a benefit to the public, for alas! Carlyle's works are still dear, and many who would like to have them are obliged to forego the possession of more than a volume or two. Through this good service of Mr. Ballantyne's, however, they may now obtain for a moderate sum a large collection of extracts—if not the best that could have been made, still very precious ones.

To make extracts from a book of extracts may at first seem easy, and to make extracts from a writer so well known may seem superfluous. The *embarras de richesses* and the length of the passages make the first not easy; and as to the second, why, we have reread these passages so often in the volumes, and now again in Mr. Ballantyne's selection, that we cannot suppose any amount of repetition otherwise than agreeable. We will, however, be sparing. Here is

[quotes from 'The Hero as Prophet', 'Oh the whole', to 'question of questions', V, 46–7; 'The Hero as Man of Letters', 'What we call' to 'in this world', V, 180–1; *Past and Present*, 'Gospel of Dilettantism', 'Perhaps few narratives', to 'in our day', X, 152–3]

36. James Martineau, from an unsigned review, *National Review*

October 1856, iii, 449–94

Extract from an unsigned review, 'Personal Influences on Our Present Theology: Newman—Coleridge—Carlyle'.

James Martineau (1805–1900), Unitarian minister, brother of the noted Harriet Martineau, and writer of many philosophical and theological articles, was already a leader in Unitarian circles by the time he published his *Rationale of Religious Enquiry* (1836), a work which widened his reputation as a writer of importance. He contributed to the *London and Westminster Review*, the *London Review*, and was instrumental in founding the distinctive journal, the *Prospective Review* (1845–54), which later became the equally sound *National Review* (1855–64), a journal he edited with the help of such able hands as Walter Bagehot and Richard H. Hutton. See Introduction, p. 7.

Martineau sees three dynamic movements in nineteenth-century theology: Newman at Oxford revitalizing the sagging intellectuality of Christianity against Church Erastianism and the anti-intellectualism of the Dissenters; Coleridge at Highgate—though once at Cambridge—directing his religious efforts against the empirical psychology and utilitarian ethos of the Enlightenment; and Carlyle in the North replenishing the springs of Scottish metaphysics now run dry. The extract begins with Martineau's discussion of Carlyle.

. . . While many still wandered there in hope, there came out of the desert a Scottish *vates*, who had descried an unexhausted spring, and led the way to it by strange paths. Thomas Carlyle gave the first clear expression to the struggling heart of a desolate yet aspiring time, making a clean breast of many stifled unbeliefs and noble hatreds; and if unable to find any certain Saviour for the present, at least preparing some love

412

and reverence to sit, 'clothed and in right mind,' for the Divine welcome, whenever it might come. Is the reader surprised that we keep a niche for the author of *Hero-Worship* in our gallery of *theologians?* Be it so. The officials of St. Stephen's were also surprised at the proposal to put Cromwell's effigy among the statues of the kings. We will only say, that whoever doubts the vast influence of Carlyle's writings on the inmost faith of our generation, or supposes that influence to be wholly disorganising, misinterprets, in our opinion, the symptoms of the time, and is blinded by current phraseology to essential facts. With this conviction, we must treat the *literary* reaction represented by him as the *third* element, completing the modern development.

To these three movements, distinguished by the names of Newman, Coleridge, and Carlyle, must be mainly ascribed the altered spirit, in regard to religion, pervading the young intellect of England. In proceeding to notice them one by one, we must be content with a slight glance at their most salient features. And we must wholly pass by many secondary, though far from unimportant, streams of separate influence which have swelled the confluence of change. The operation of Arnold's life,—of Whately's writings,—of Channing,—of the younger Newman,—of Theodore Parker,—of Emerson,—on the temper and belief of the age, has in each case been considerable. But we limit ourselves to the *prophetæ majores*. Moreover, it is only on the *fresh powers*, cutting into original directions, and making roadways of thought where before was the forest or the flood, that we propose to dwell. Whilst these have been working their way, of course the old tendencies have not quitted the field, or lost their hold. The elder orthodoxies, the elder scepticisms, of established type, are still alive; and now and then, during the last thirty years, have put forth startling reassertions of their vitality. In Comte the physical, in Strauss the historical, negation of theology, may be said not only to reappear, but to culminate. And each of these, again, has its group of related phenomena: the Logic of Mill, the hypothesis of the *Vestiges* (and, we would add, the greater part of the replies), the Psychology of Herbert Spencer, and the propaganda of Secularism, tracing the course of the Positivist tendency; while the freer hand which scriptural criticism every where displays, its more open feeling for the *human* element in the gospel,—qualities, which most conspicuous abroad, are yet familiar to us in Bunsen, Stanley, and Jowett,— indicate a direction from which the *Leben Jesu* has rendered it impossible to recede. These, however, are but the newest steps on beaten tracks of thought. Since the age of Bacon (nay, for that matter, from the days of

Socrates), we have known that to seek only natural law, was the way to find only natural law; and since the time of Semler, there is no excuse for surprise if the critique of Scripture persists in demanding some modification of our faith. To lay down the true bridge from inductive science to the living God,—to settle the relation between the human and the divine factors in the process and monuments of revelation,—these are not new difficulties; nor is it an original device to fall into despair at them, and declare that the problems can be worked only on their finite side. Comte and Strauss, therefore, we disregard, at present, as mere *continuance-phenomena*,—rather clenching the past than opening the future. They do but modify the equilibrium of given conditions: and our purpose is to describe the dynamic elements which have introduced unexpected movement. . . .

[A thirty-page discussion of Newman and Coleridge has been omitted from this review at this point.]

After all, the real force of this school is independent of scientific imperfections. They are *believing men*—afraid of no reality, despairing of no good, and resolute to test their faith by putting it straightway into life. They set to work to realise the kingdom of God in Soho Square and other nameable localities; and in their step towards this end there is as free, confiding, joyful movement, as if with their eyes they expected to see the great salvation. There is more of the future, we suspect, contained in their gospel than in any talking theology whose cry is heard in our streets.

Hence we feel ourselves to be falling *back* a step, when we turn from the preacher of Lincoln's Inn to the prophet of Chelsea. The influence of the latter, vastly the more intense and widespread, appears to us to have reached its natural limit, and taken up the portion of believers allotted to it. As a revolutionary or pentecostal power on the sentiments of Englishmen, it is perhaps nearly spent; and, like the romantic school of Germany, will descend from the high level of a faith to the tranquil honours of literature. So long as Mr. Carlyle spoke with any *hope* to the inward reverence of men, and in giving voice to their spiritual discontents made them feel that they were emerging from mean scepticisms into nobler inspirations, he was a deliverer to captives out of number. But the early voice of hope has become fainter and fainter, first passing into an infinite pathos, and then lost in humorous mocking or immeasurable scorn: and men cannot be permanently held by their antipathies and distrusts, and cease to look for any thing from a rebellion that never ends in peace. He gets us well enough out of Egypt and all its filthy idolatries; but, alas! his Red Sea will not divide, and the promised land is far as ever, and the question presses, whether 'we are to die in the wilderness?' For a just estimate of Mr. Carlyle as an historian and man of letters the time is not yet come. But his specific action on the *religion* of the age (of which alone we speak) already belongs in a great measure to the past, and is little likely to offer new elements for appreciation.

It is difficult now to transfer ourselves back into the age, not yet faded however from living memory, when Boileau and Kames were great canonists in the world of letters, and criticism occupied the mortal form of Dr. Blair. Of what stuff the young souls of that age could be made we cannot imagine, if they really found nutriment in solemn trifles about the unities and proprieties,—the choice of diction,—the length of sentences,—the nature of tropes,—and the rhetorical tempera-ture required for interjection and apostrophes. Mr. Carlyle, among other contemporaries, certainly rose with indignant hunger from such a table of the gods, symmetrically spread with polished covers and nothing under them. In mere analysis of the machinery of expression or even thought, in rules for the manufacture of literary effects, he could find no response to the enthusiasm kindled in him by his favourite authors. The true ambrosia of the inner life was turned into dry ash by the legislators of *belles lettres:* and he was courageous enough to ask for the missing and immortal element. The same external direction had been taken by philosophy, and produced the same consciousness of a miserable void. The searching scepticism of Hume showed the dreary results to which the mere analysis of 'experience' compendiously led. And the devices of utilitarian *cuisine* for putting pleasure into the pot and drawing virtue out betrayed the loss of the very idea of morals. The very things which this desiccating rationalism flung off, were to Mr. Carlyle just the essence and whole worth of the universe: and to show that beauty, truth, and goodness, could not thus be got rid of, while impostors were hired to bear their name; that religion is not hope and fear, or duty prudence, or art a skill to please; that behind the sensible there lies a spiritual, and beneath all relative phenomena an absolute reality,—was evidently, if not his early vow, at least his first inspiration. Surely it was an authentic appointment to a noble work: and on looking back over his quarter-century, no one can deny that it has been manfully achieved.

By what providence Mr. Carlyle learned the German language, in days when the study of it was rare, we cannot tell. But through it he evidently was enabled to 'find his soul;' and gained confidence to proclaim the faith which was stirring from its sleep within, and at once woke up at the sight of its reflected image without. That revolt against rationalism which Dr. Newman apparently *used*, and directed for preconceived ends and in the service of an 'economy,' presents itself in Mr. Carlyle with all its veracious freshness. The same positions that approve themselves to the Oxford Catholic as suitable hypotheses, and to the Highgate philosopher as rational axioms, are seized by the living intuition of the Scottish seer;—that wonder and reverence are the condition of insight and the source of strength;—that faith is prior to knowledge, and deeper too;—that empirical science can but play on the surface of unfathomable mysteries;—that in the order of reality the ideal and invisible is the world's true adamant, and the laws of material appearance only its alluvial growths. In the inmost thought of men there is a thirst to which the springs of nature are a mere mirage, and which presses on to the waters of eternity. Extinguish this thirst by stupefaction of custom,—reduce thought to work *without* wonder,— and several delusions, both doleful and ridiculous, will speedily obtain high commissions in human affairs. The true marvel of Origination being lost, a 'cause-and-effect philosophy' will esteem every thing solved when it has shown how each nine-pin in the universe knocks down the next. The spiritual germ and essence of humanity being forgot or denied, a 'doctrine of circumstances' will discuss the prospect of furnishing to order any required supply of poets, philosophers, or able administrators,—like so many varieties of farm-stock. The idea of a God-given freedom being dismissed with the phantoms of 'the dark ages,' a calculus of 'motives' will be invented for finding the roots of every human problem, and raising any given sentient man to any required moral power. The genuine ground of all communion with the Infinite having sunk away within us, all sorts of logical proofs, and logical disproofs, will quarrel together about primitive certainties that shroud themselves from both. In all these complaints, the substantive concurrence of our author with Mr. Coleridge is conspicuous. And though, in his *Life of Sterling*, the humour has seized him to ridicule the 'windy harangues' and dizzying metaphysics of the Highgate soirées, there was a time when he had no little faith in the same methods as well as large agreement in the same results. In his earlier essays, *he* too expounds the distinction between 'Understanding' and 'Reason,' and sets up the latter as the organ for apprehending the ideal essence, which is the true *real* of things. He speaks with reverential appreciation of Kant's doctrine, both metaphysical and moral; and with hope as well as admiration of the several æsthetic theories developed from similar beginnings. In short, he manifestly put an early trust in the philosophical method to which Coleridge remained faithful to the last. And not less manifestly did he soon break away from this path in despair; and with characteristic vehemence thenceforth inveigh against the propensity to seek it as an illusion of disease. In 1827, he defended the *Kritik der reinen Vernunft* against ignorant objectors, as reputed by competent judges to be 'distinctly the greatest intellectual achievement of the century in which it came to light;' and dwelt with approval on the rule that, in quest of the highest truth, we must look *within*, and thence work outward with the torch we have lit. Yet in 1831 he broached, in his *Characteristics*, his celebrated doctrine of 'Unconsciousness:' which teaches that all self-knowledge is a curse, and introspection a disease; that the true health of a man is to have a soul without being aware of it, —to be disposed of by impulses which he never criticises,—to fling out the products of creative genius without looking at them. In a word, the *reflective* thought on which, in the former year, he had relied for the purest wisdom, had in the latter become the sin and despair of humanity. What can have befallen in the interval? Had the author meanwhile *tried* the metaphysic springs, and after due patience found them, not simply 'saints' wells,' with no healing in them, but poison-fountains, that made the sickly soul yet sicklier? We do not believe it: for there is nowhere any trace that the first clue of entrance into the German philosophy had been followed up; and on the other hand, every indication that Mr. Carlyle's denunciation of metaphysics is the mere judgment of an intuitive genius on methods of reflection, which, however helpful to slower and more formal minds, it is not given him to take. Had he been able to retain and pursue his first hope,—had he taken the severe path of philosophical discipline, and surrendered himself to its promise of deliverance,—we hardly think that we should ever have heard that passionate cry of despair, which proclaims the distinctive glory of man to be his irremediable woe, and asserts that, in finding *himself*, he for ever falls from heaven. The preacher of this doctrine had already started problems within himself, to which no answer (as his own word declares) could be found but by faithful questioning within: and it is a serious thing to go thus far, and yet not abide long enough to hear the reply. But instead of this, he flings away the very problems with a shriek, as the fruit by which paradise is lost; repents of all knowledge of good and evil; claps a bandage round the open eyes of morals, religion, art; and sees no salvation but in spiritual suicide, by plunging into the currents of instinctive nature that sweep us we know not whither. This tragic paradox has, indeed, a generous source, and is even thrown up by a certain wild tumultuous piety. It springs from a deep sense of the hatefulness of self-worship, and the barrenness of mere self-formation. It is a stormy prayer for escape from these; only with face turned, alas! in the wrong direction—*back* towards the west, with its fading visions of Atlantic islands of Unconsciousness, instead of *forwards* to the east, where already the heavens are pale with a light, instead of a darkness, not our own.

Though this despair of the highest objective truth could not fail, in the long-run, to produce pathetic and tempestuous results, yet for a while the mere deliverance from the negations of the empirical schools sufficed for a gospel: and the new sense of divine mystery and meaning, behind all that met the common eye, was little else in effect than a revelation. A certain consecration fell on what had been quite secular before: and with this peculiarity, that its influence spread as an underground beneath the foundations of objects and pursuits previously disconnected, and became a common conductor of fresh reverence into them all. Literature, art, politics, natural knowledge, seemed to sit less apart from religion. Heave off the utilitarian incubus from above, and secret affinities begin to be felt at the roots of their life. When it is no longer 'the sole aim' of poetry 'to please,' of science to 'get fruit' for the storehouses of comfort, of government 'to protect body and goods,' of sculpture and painting to minister to luxury,—they obtain ideal ends, which in essence melt and merge together; and all of them—beauty, truth, and righteousness—culminate in the reality of God. Whatever the theologians may say, the age owes a debt of rare gratitude to the man who, above all others, has awakened this new sense within its soul; has touched with a strange devoutness many a class which book and surplice had ceased to awe; has taken the impertinent self-will out of the movements of pencil, pen, and chisel; and made even Mechanics' Institutions ashamed of their incipient millennium of 'useful knowledge.' The influence of Mr. Carlyle's writings, and especially of his *Sartor Resartus*, has been primarily exerted on classes of men most exposed to temptations of egotism and petulance, and least subjected to any thing above them,—academics, artists, littérateurs, 'strong-minded' women, 'debating' youths, Scotchmen of the phrenological grade, and Irishmen of the Young-Ireland school. In the altered mood of mind which has been induced in these various groups within the last five-and-twenty years we acknowledge a conspicuous good; and could even hear, with more of sadness than of condemnation, the passionate words that once burst from the lips of a believer: 'Carlyle is my religion!'

The *unity*, however, which our prophet's mystic sense discerns among our human 'arts and sciences' is *too* great: and we must reclaim from him a distinction which not even the fusing power of his genius can do more than blur and conceal. Not in the *human and moral* world only, but *quite similarly in the physical*, does he see the expression of the Infinite and Divine. Both are alike symbols of the one spiritual essence, which is hid from the blind, and revealed to the wise, in all. He does not, like Coleridge, separate *nature* and *spirit* into two realms, quite differently related to Him who is the source of both,—the one His moulded fabric, the other His free image,—but treats them indiscriminately as the vehicles of His manifestation, and phenomena through which the Divine force pours. This is not, indeed, done by sinking humanity into a mere object of natural history; rather by raising the objects of natural history up to the spiritual level, adding significance to them, instead of taking it from us. But still, man is not permitted to remain quite *sui generis:* he is simply the *highest* of the countless emblems woven into the universal 'garment of God.' The texture is one and homogeneous throughout:—in one sense all natural, as a determinate product in time; in another, all supernatural, as mysteriously issuing from eternity. The same comprehensive formula, —the appearance of the Infinite in the finite,—serves every where, and equally describes 'the lily of the field' and the Redeemer who interpreted its meaning.

Did we want to turn human life into a mere school of Art, there might be nothing very fatal in the looseness of this doctrine. An impartial conception of some Divine idea in every thing may clear away the film of sense, and open to view the life of much that else were dead. To rend away the veil is the grand condition for enabling the eye to see: whoever does this, may talk as he pleases of the realities behind; they will vindicate themselves. Yet even for truth of *representation*, and infinitely more for faithfulness of character and action, a distinctive reverence for man as *more than natural*, as the abode of God in a sense quite false of clouds and stars, as intrusted with himself that he may surrender to a higher,—is indispensable. For want of this, Mr. Carlyle loses all ground of difference between the *natural* and the *right*,—the out-come of tendency and the free creations of conscience. He is tempted into excessive admiration of mere realising strength, irrespective of any higher test of spiritual worth. Whatever can get upon its feet, and persist in standing on this world, is vindicated in his eyes, and exhibited as a sample of the 'eternal laws:' while that which has nothing to show for itself except that it *ought to be*,—righteousness that knocks in vain at the door of visible 'fact,'—meets with no sympathy from him, and is even jeered for its foolish patience in still sitting on the step with unremitting prayer. True, he does not admit the rights of possession till after a pretty long term, and knows how to treat the 'shams' and upstarts of to-day, the 'flunkey' powers that usurp more venerable place, with withering scorn:—still, however, for a reason which would equally condemn an aspiration transcending human conditions, viz. because they are at variance with the laws of the actual, and are sure to be disowned by the baffling solidity of nature. Against the fickle multitude of momentary facts and popular semblances, he sides with the conservative aristocracy of natural laws; but recognises no divine monarchy with prerogatives over both. The kingdom of heaven and the kingdom of nature being identical, neither transcending the other, but being related only as inner meaning and outward expression, no margin is left for an *ideal* other than the long-run of the *actual*,—for an '*ought*' beyond the '*can*,'—for a will of God surpassing finite conditions. Hence Mr. Carlyle's habit of resolving all ethical evil into 'insincerity' and 'unveracity,'—surely a most inadequate formula for the expression of even commonplace moral judgments. Extend these terms ever so much,—use them to denote *unconscious* as well as *conscious* self-variance, —nay, include in them also defiance of *nature and outward possibility*,— still, what far-fetched circuits must be taken before you can bring under such a definition the sins of envy, covetousness, resentment, and prudent licentiousness! The root of his delusive conception of human goodness lies in the pantheistic assumption, that to fly in the face of natural forces is to withstand the highest that there is; and its fruit, when fully ripe, cannot fail to be an indifference to many a natural sin,—a lowering of the ideal standard of conscience, and a derision of baffled yet trusting righteousness. Every reader of Mr. Carlyle can remember painful instances of entire abdication of all moral judgment on atrocious actions and abandoned men,—a Mirabeau and a September massacre: nay, even ridicule of the whole distinction of moral and immoral applied to actions, as 'the blockhead's distinction;' and many a hint that the difference lies only in the *customariness* (*mores*) of one practice as compared with another. Did it never occur to him to ask whether it is the human usages that make the moral sense, or not rather the moral sense that makes the human usages?

Yet this questionable doctrine, often provoked into expression by some senseless prudery or ungenial rigour, is very far from representing the author's real and deepest mind. Flashes of purer light meet you not rarely, especially in his earlier writings. Who can forget how, in the hour of uttermost desolation, amid the wildest storm of unbelief, the sheet-anchor of the unhappy Teufelsdröckh was the '*infinite nature of Duty;*' and in this form never, in his utmost extremity, did the Divine presence desert him? And are we not told, in many changing tones, that in obedience and reverence alone can any true freedom be found? that we are to recognise God in the *higher* life within us, as opposed to the pleasure-life? that we can find Him only by self-renunciation? In these ingenious days, when no one proposition is so rude as to contradict any other, some disciple of the 'many-sided' poet, or some proficient in the 'dialectic process,' may be able to harmonise such sentiments with the assertion that '*man cannot but obey whatever he ought to obey.*' At present we do not pretend to have reached the 'higher unity' in which appeals to our freedom coalesce with the assertion of universal necessity.

To pull up the fence between 'nature' and 'spirit' within us is to throw the Understanding and the Character into the same field. We are therefore prepared for the celebrated paradox, that intellect and goodness always go together; so that, of mental insight and moral soundness, either may be taken as the measure of the other. If by 'intellect' and 'insight' is meant exclusively what Coleridge calls '*reason,*' this statement not only ceases to be a paradox, but becomes almost a truism: for it is the chief function of this power to make us conscious of moral truth and obligation; and the consciousness fades when faithlessly neglected. But if these terms refer to what Coleridge calls '*understanding,*'—if the possession of this endowment constitutes a claim upon them,—then the doctrine is conspicuously false: for the 'adaptive intelligence,' being an *animal* faculty, is entirely separable from moral conditions; actually exists without them in many tribes of creatures; and in man simply rises to a quickness of generalisation and a skill in the use of means which imply nothing respecting the wise estimate or the faithful pursuit of *ends*. Low passions and selfish impulses are quite capable of enlisting on their behalf all the resources of this mental gift; their partnership with which gives us the idea of a satanic nature. Mr. Carlyle, we believe, means to say, that *this* sort of 'understanding' he will not acknowledge as intellect; it is a mere 'beaver' or 'fox' faculty, not to be noticed among the distinctions of man. Not till you have got beyond mechanical ingenuity and lawyer adroitness do you enter on the proper *human* territory; within which, capacity and character go together. This interpretation, throwing us upon Coleridge's upper region, reduces the maxim to an intelligible truth. But will Mr. Carlyle consent to take it with all its fair consequences? Will he, without flinching, read the truth *both* ways,—inferring *either* term of this constant ratio ('*intellectual*' and '*moral*') from the magnitude of the other? We know that, where he discovers (as in Mirabeau) great force of *mind*, he is ready to plead this in bar of all objections against *character*, and to insist that, in spite of appearances, such brightness of eye *must* carry with it soundness of conscience. But will he turn the problem round, and abide by it still? When he finds, deep hid in the retreats of private life, a goodness eminent and even saintly, a moral clearness and force great in their way as Mirabeau's keen-sightedness, will he accept the sign in evidence of mighty intellect? Will he say that, notwithstanding the meek and homely look, high genius must assuredly be there? We fear not: at least, we remember no instance in which the inference is set with its face this way; whilst it is familiar to all his readers as an excuse for admirations startling to the moral sense. In truth, this maxim, more perhaps than any other indication, expresses the *pagan* character of our author's mind; his alienation from the distinctively Christian type of reverence, rather for the inner sanctities of self-renunciation than for the outward energies of self-assertion. His 'hero-worships' certainly present us with a list far from concurrent with the 'beatitudes:' nor can we fancy that he would listen with much more patience than a Lucian or a Pliny to blessings on the meek and merciful, the pure in heart, the ever-thirsty after righteousness. For him too, as for so many gifted and ungifted men, the force which will not be stopped by any restraint on its way to great achievement,—the genius which claims to be its own law, and will confess nothing diviner than itself,—have an irresistible fascination. His eye, overlooking the landscape of humanity, always runs up to the brilliant peaks of *power*: not, indeed, without a glance of love and pity into many a retreat of quiet goodness that lies safe beneath their shelter; but should the sudden lightning, or the seasonal melting of the world's ice-barriers, bring down a ruin on that green and feeble life, his voice, after one faint cry of pathos, joins in with the thunder and shouts with the triumph of the avalanche. Ever watching the strife of the great *forces* of the universe, he, no doubt, sides on the whole against the Titans with the gods: but if the Titans make a happy fling, and send home a mountain or two to the very beard of Zeus, he gets delighted with the game on any terms and cries, 'Bravo!'

The *Sartor Resartus* finds the manifestation of God in the *entire life* of the universe; in visible nature; in individual man, and especially his *higher* mind; in the march and process of history; and in the organic development of humanity as a whole. The author's tendency, however, has increasingly been to retreat from all other media of Divine expression upon his favourite centre,—the genius and energy of *heroic men*. So much has he gathered-in his lights of interpretation upon this focus, as to incur the charge of setting up the personality of individuals as the single determining agency in the affairs of the world, and forgetting the larger half of the truth, that all persons, taken one by one, are but elements of a great social organism, to whose laws of providential growth they must be held subordinate. History cannot be resolved into a mere series of biographies: nor can the individual be justly estimated in his insulation, and tried by the mere inner law of his own particular nature. It would be a melancholy outlook for the world, if its courses were simply contingent on the genius and life of a few great men, without any security from a general law behind that they should appear at the right time and place, and with the aptitudes for the needful work. And, on the other hand, were the life of nations to be expended in nothing else than the production of its half-dozen heroes; were this splendid but scanty blossoming the great and only real thing it does, there would seem to be a wasteful disproportion between the mighty forest that falls for lumber and the sparse fruit that would lie upon your open hand. There is need, therefore, of some more manifest relation between individual greatness and the collective life of humanity; and to save us from egoism, from fatalism, from arbitrary and capricious morals, we must learn to recognise a divine method of development in both,—*primarily*, in race and nation, and with authority over the *secondary* functions of personal genius.

That Mr. Carlyle's 'hero-worship' requires to be balanced by a supplementary doctrine of society and collective humanity, he would himself perhaps be disposed to allow. But what is this supplement to be? Is it merely to teach that the *individual* is to hold himself at the disposal of *the whole?* to correct his conscience by the general tradition or the permanent voice of humanity; to sink his egoism, to temper it by immersion in the universal element, and become the organ of the progress of the species? Far be it from us to deny that there may be men susceptible of inspiration from such a faith,—capable of dying for such abstractions as a 'law of development,' of being torn limb from limb out of regard for 'the whole.' Still less would we disparage by one word a heroism all the nobler for the faint whispers that suffice to waken it into life. Yet we cannot help feeling that in these impersonal ideas,—of 'collective society,' 'law of the whole,' 'destination of mankind,' &c.— there is a want of natural authority over the conscience, and, missing the conscience, over the personal impulses of individual men. In the mere notions of 'whole and part,' of 'organism and member,' of 'average rule and particular case,' there resides no *moral* element, no *rights over the will:* and if ever they seem to carry such functions, it is only because a deeper feeling lurks behind and lends them in the insignia of a prerogative not their own. In a world of mere 'general laws,' it would ever remain a melancholy thing to see living heroes and saints struck down at the altar of 'historical tendency' by some shadowy dagger of necessity. Love, enthusiasm, devotion, need some concrete and living object; if not to command their allegiance, at least to turn it from sorrow into joy. And you have but to translate your 'progress of the species' into 'Kingdom of Heaven,' and the problem is solved. The ever-living God stands in Person between the 'individual' and the 'whole,'—by His communion mediating between them,—stirring in the conscience of the one, and constituting the tides of advancing good in the other,—and so engaging both in one spiritual life. Surrendering immediately to Him, instead of to the ultimate ratios of the world, faithful men fling themselves into Omnipotent sympathy, and find deliverance and repose. They have a trust that relieves them of every care; and can leave themselves to be applied to the great account and problem of the world by One who is in the midst, and from the first, and at the end, at once. Through Him, therefore, as the common term of all righteousness, must the collective humanity win its due rights and reverence from Each. The private conscience ceases to be private, the public claim to be merely public, when both are to us the instant pleadings of His living authority. In obeying them, we yield neither to a mixed multitude of our own kind, whose average voice is no better than our own, nor even to our mere higher self; but to the august Revealer of whatever is pure and just and true. In enforcing its traditions and inheritance of right, the Nation or Society of men is not proudly riding on its own arbitrary will, but recognizing the trust committed to it and serving as the organism of eternal rectitude.

It is for want of this deliverance from Self at the upper end, that Mr. Carlyle, resolute to break the ignoble bondage on any terms, proposes escape at the lower end; and, preaching up the glories of 'Un-consciousness,' sighs for relapse into the life of blind impulsive tendency. With him, we confess the curse; we groan beneath its misery; but we see from it a double path,—backward into Nature, forward into God —and cannot for an instant doubt that the Self-consciousness which is the beginning of Reason is never to recede, but to rise and free itself in the transfiguration of Faith. Deny and bar out this hope, and who can wonder if the sharpest remedies for man's selfish security are welcomed with a wild joy; if *any* convulsion that shall strip off the green crust of artificial culture and lay bare the primitive rock beneath us, appears as a needful return of the fermenting chaos? How else are the elementary forces of instinctive nature to reassert their rights and *begin again* from their unthinking freshness? In some such feeling as this we find, perhaps, the source, in Mr. Carlyle, of that terrible glee that seems to flame up at the spectacle of revolutionary storms, and to dart with mocking gleams of devilry and tender streaks of humanity over a background of 'divine despair.' Indeed we could not wish for a better illustration of the two paths of escape from Self,—back into Nature, forward into God,—than the contrast of Carlyle and Maurice in the whole colouring and climate of their spirit: the sad, pathetic, scornful humour of the one, capricious with laughter, tears, and anger, and expressive of man-ful pity and endurance, alike removed from fear and hope; and the buoyant, serene, trustful temper of the other, genial even in its indig-nation, and penetrated with the joy of an Infinite Love.

The three schools of doctrine at which we have thus rapidly glanced occupy the most distant points in the English religion of the present age; or, at least, in the new fields of tendency which it has opened. It may seem a vain quest to look for any thing common to the whole. Yet when they are interpreted by their inner spirit, rather than by their out-ward relations, one thought will be found secreted at the heart of all —the perennial Indwelling of God in Man and in the Universe. This is the distinct gain that has been won by the spiritual consciousness of the time; and that already enriches fiction and poetry, art and social morals, not less than direct theology. In the preceding criticisms we have said enough to show that we are not indifferent to the mode and form of doctrine in which this thought is embodied. But however threatening the mists from which it has to clear itself, it is the dawn of a truth,—a blush upon the East,—wakening up trustful hearts to thanksgiving and hope. We know well the anger and antipathy of all the elder parties towards every phase of the new sentiment. We are accustomed to their absurd and heartless attempt to divide all men between the two poles of their logical dilemma,—either absolute Atheism, or else 'our' orthodoxy. But these are only symptoms that the new wine cannot go into the old bottles. They do but betray the inevitable blindness of party-life,—the increasing self-seeking, the loss of genial humility, the conceit of finished wisdom, which mark the decadence of all sects. Precisely in the middle of this pretended alternative of necessity,—far from 'Atheism' on the one hand, and from most 'orthodoxies' on the other,—stand at this moment the vast majority of the most earnest, devout, philosophic Christians of our time; men with trust in a Living Righteousness, which no creed of one age can adequately define for the fresh experiences given to the spirit of another. To them, and not to the noisy devotees and pharisees of party, do we look for the faith of the future.

---

37. George Gilfillan, an unsigned review, *Scottish Review*

January 1859, ix, 36–46

George Gilfillan (1813–78), Scottish Calvinist minister, was also a writer and lecturer. His *Gallery of Literary Portraits* (1845–54) included an essay of excessive praise of *Sartor Resartus* in 1845. However, six years later he attacked Carlyle's *Life of John Sterling* for its irreverent treatment of Christianity (*Eclectic Review*, December 1851, civ). Although Gilfillan appears to have been an acquaintance and early disciple of Carlyle's, his estimate of him changed radically (see Robert A. and Elizabeth S. Watson, *George Gilfillan: Letters and Journals with Memoir* (London, 1892)). Carlyle seemed sceptical of Gilfillan's zealotry. He wrote to Emerson (31 January 1844):

Did you receive a Dumfries Newspaper with a criticism in it? The author is one Gilfillan, a young dissenting minister in Dundee; a person of great talent, ingenuousness, enthusiasm and other virtue; whose position as Preacher of bare old Calvinism under penalty of death, sometimes makes me tremble for him. He has written in that same Newspaper about all the notablest men of his time; Godwin, Corn-Law Elliot and I know not all whom: if he publish the Book, I will take care to send it you. I saw the man for the first time last autumn at Dumfries; as I said, his being a Calvinist Dissenting Minister, economically fixed, and spiritually with such germinations in him, forces me to be very reserved to him (*The Correspondence of Emerson and Carlyle*, ed. Joseph Slater (New York, 1964), 357).

This review has been included in its entirety because it represents so well some of the reponses which are characteristic of the religious press.

Mr Carlyle has many great gifts, but he is sadly deficient in the three Graces. He has little Faith, Hope, or Charity. He believes, apparently, in only a few stray heroes sprinkled throughout ages of dulness and cowardice. He has even less hope than faith, and seems to think that the line of giants has terminated in himself, and that, in the language of the psalm—

> There is not us among
> A prophet more, nor any one
> That knows the time, how long.

His charity to his favourites is indeed unbounded; but on the race in general, especially on the poor 'scoundrels' who have disobeyed the laws, and got into Bridewell, he looks with unmitigated contempt and disgust. He uniformly confounds weakness with guilt, and treats the feeble as if they were the false. In this point, we cannot but contrast his conduct with that of still greater writers. John Bunyan is justly said to have loved best his feeble and gentle characters, such as Little-faith, Mr Fearing, Mr Feeble-mind, Despondency, and Much-afraid. And we fancy that the writers of the Bible, too, loved best such tender, child-like ones as Mephibosheth, Lazarus, Barzillai the Gileadite, and the Beloved Disciple. The inspired writers were, as Bunyan also was, strong and stalwart men; but they had tender affections, too, and these delighted to centre on the lowly, the feeble, and the forgotten. Hence, in the pages of the Scripture are preserved certain names and characters which ordinary chronicles would have passed by as beneath notice. Nay, almost the only instance in which fame—fame universal and undying—is predicted of a human being in Scripture, is in reference to a nameless woman, the woman who anointed Christ's head with precious ointment, and of whom Christ said, 'Verily, I say unto you, wheresoever this gospel shall be preached in the whole world, there shall also this that this woman hath done be told for a memorial of her.' What a strange memorial attached thus to one whose very name is unknown! How many names are constantly seeking fame, but here is fame seeking for a name! And the record thus made in the gospels is quite in keeping with the principle of God, in choosing 'the weak things of the world, and the base things of the world, and the things that are not, to confound the mighty, the honourable, and the things that are.' This is consoling, and is intended so to be to the humble, the feeble, and the poor, and to those whom the brutal and hard-hearted world slumps up as weak characters, silly, well-meaning people; as if all men, the very mightiest, were not weak when compared to God; as if there were any man so strong as to have a right to despise his fellow; as if there were any one so weak as not to be able to do good work, and perhaps work not competent to more powerful men, in behalf of truth and righteousness; and as if the employment of contemptuous language were not calculated to render the feeble still feebler, to drive them to despair or misanthropy, and thus to make the weak wicked. We all remember what the mouse did for the lion in the toils, because the lion had spared him. But, too often, lions of a higher race, by despising meaner creatures, excite their animosity, and have snares woven, instead of broken, by their means. Scripture, so far from encouraging the common spirit of contemning inferior intellects, scarcely ever speaks of diversities of mind at all. When it calls a man a fool, it means a villain; and it says, 'See that ye despise not these little ones; for I say unto you, that in heaven their angels do steadfastly behold the face of my Father which is in heaven'—so that, if they be weak, their celestial guardians are strong, and ever ready to resent affronts to their charge; for is it not written that, 'if any one offend one of these little ones, it were better for him that a millstone were hanged about his neck, and he were cast into the depths of the sea?'

Such is the genius of the Christian religion; but, in the very teeth of this spirit, Carlyle, fiercely, frequently, and ostentatiously, flies. He worships Power, Strength, Valour, and has little pity for weakness. His god, if a god he has at all, is not the Father, is not Love; he is a grim, eyeless, inexorable Fate, the god of Mahomet, not of Jesus Christ. In love and admiration of the magnates, he ignores or tramples on the millions of the race. Although originally himself from the ranks, he has very little sympathy with the common people; and, in this point, is the antithesis to his idol Burns. He will stop by the wayside, and accost a peasant, but does it with the haughty condescension of a feudal chieftain —a Fergus M'Ivor. He haunts the houses of the great, and interests himself in the lords and lordlings, who admire and listen to him with an edifying reciprocity. We can never readily conceive him 'remembering the forgotten,' visiting the fatherless and widows in their affliction, or carrying on any plan of practical philanthropy. At all such things he laughs, and apparently would much rather be an Attila or a Tamerlane, than a Wilberforce or a Howard. He sympathises deeply with these thunderbolts of war, these angels of destruction, and would give worlds to grasp, like Phaethon, the reins of the sun for one day, that he might let loose blazing ruin upon the black races and their white abolition friends. Keats describes Apollo as seated on the ground disconsolate—

Like one who once had wings

Our author may be figured, as a fallen being, with writhing lips, remembering that he once had thunderbolts, or sometimes grimly smiling as he dreams he has them still.

We remember once speaking to a Carlylist, whom we met accidentally, about his hero's unhappiness, to which he promptly and cleverly replied, 'His pangs are those of a birth.' We were struck with the remark, but were tempted to ask what had been the progeny, and to apply to the case the words of the Prophet, 'We have conceived—we have been with child—we have brought forth as it were wind—we have wrought no deliverance on the earth.' So abortive have been the pangs of Sartor's travail. He has undoubtedly startled the minds of thousands, but has satisfied none. Like a fierce flash of lightning he has revealed the darkness of the forest, but he has not guided the wanderer out of its mazes. He has been Prometheus in his sufferings, but not in his deliverance; and the true title of the tragedy of Thomas Carlyle is 'Prometheus Bound, and never to be Un-Bound.' It is lamentable to think how trivial has been the result of all those agonized spasms—all the groans of this giant in torment.

While hinting above at Carlyle's aristocratic leanings, and that he is not without a little of the very 'flunkeyism' which he so unsparingly condemns, we are far from wishing to deny that he is, in the main, a sincere and earnest man. We were very much amused at a story we heard some years ago. A dissenting minister in London, more distinguished by zeal than knowledge, came bustling in one morning to the house of an eminent brother clergyman, and cried out, 'Mr M., have you heard the news? The most extraordinary thing that has occurred in our time, sir, or perhaps since the conversion of St Paul. Thomas Carlyle, I am credibly informed, is under serious impressions; serious impressions, sir.' To which Mr M. coolly replied, that 'he had understood that Carlyle had been under serious impressions all his life long!' The poor man, who had been, we suppose, expecting to hear of Sartor making an open profession of Christianity in a few days, was quite chop-fallen. There can be no doubt that Mr M. was, in a sense, right, and that few men of this age, or of any other, have more resolutely and fervidly sought for religious truth than Carlyle; and from this fact some have entertained the hope that he will still reach it, while others again have come to the conclusion, that since he has failed no one else can succeed, and that there is no such thing to be found in our present state of being. We think, on the other hand, that we see the causes of his failure clearly enough. He wallowed far too much, at one time, in what

he himself called 'the mud' of the French Materialistic writers, such as
Helvetius and Diderot. He was disgusted by the modes of expression
which prevailed in many of our pulpits in his youth, often exceedingly
coarse and crude, especially in reference to future punishments; and
there is a well-known and a perfectly true story about his getting up
into a fearful shriek in Ecclefechan church, while a young probationer
was describing hell, and then rising and rushing out of the meeting.
Rejected, too, and underrated in orthodox Scotland, the first recognition he obtained came from Germany, and especially from Goethe.
He was annoyed at the extravagances of Edward Irving, much as he
admired and loved him; and, on the other hand, he must have regarded
the conduct of some of Irving's opponents as narrow-minded and cruel.
All these circumstances, combined with a certain love of singularity,
and no small intellectual and spiritual pride, tended gradually to wean
him from the faith of his fathers, and the very blamelessness of his
character, as sometimes happens, contributed to deepen the alienation.

But whatever the causes of the result, there can be no doubt of the
deplorable fact. The scepticism of the day is principally sustained,
rendered in a manner respectable, and redeemed from obloquy by the
genius of Carlyle. His power, although, we trust, lessening, is still great
—especially over three classes—litterateurs, the more intelligent of our
working men, and young thoughtful people generally. It is hopeful,
however, to observe that the Carlyle fever is often as short as it is
severe. We know a good many who have emerged from it stronger
than ever; and are even, in some measure, thankful to their terrible
teacher. We know others who, like the lion in Milton's poetic picture of
the Creation, have only half-risen, and are pawing to be more fully
free. There is another class still who are in more danger, that is those
who happen to be on terms of intercourse with the man, and subjected
to the marvellous magic of his conversation. We have often tried to
describe that conversation, but in truth it must be heard, and, especially,
at night. There is a settled melancholy in its tones which harmonizes
with the play of the moonbeams, and with the plaint of the evening
waters. It is like what we might conceive to be the talk of a spirit—we
had almost said of a great lost soul. Ever and anon it is interrupted by
deep sighs, or it dies away in brief but pregnant pauses, or it breaks
out in wild, mystic, unfathomable laughter, which goes, as it were,
away from him half-shuddering in sorrow, and half-rioting in glee.
Then his accent seems a strange but musical rhythm which the woods,
the waters, the winds, and the other nameless and homeless sounds

which traverse the solitudes, have learned from Nature and have taught to him. His eyes and lips move in time to each other, as if performing parts in one wild tune, and, with the melancholy tones of his voice, accords the gloomy grandeur of his imagery. Such is the conversation still sounding on, now by the banks of the Nith, and now by those of the Thames, now awakening the midnight echoes of Sloane Square, and now reverberated from the breezy hills of Malvern, and to which too many of our rising literary men listen as if to the oracle of God. It was the power of this talk which gradually loosened the ties of poor John Sterling to the Church, and to Christianity. He long resisted, but the strong, constant sap at last overthrew the bulwarks, and swept him away. It is this which fascinates many of the leading nobility and the M.P.'s of the land. It is this which wields a deep, and sometimes deadly power, over the intelligent youths or middle-aged litterateurs in London, who are privileged to sit at Sartor's tea table, or to accompany him in his evening walks, and to listen to his eloquent and half-warbled words about the 'Immensities and the Eternities,' the 'Verities' and the 'Silences,' the 'Sincerities of the Past,' and the 'Shams of the Present Day.' Much, indeed, they hear calculated to stir and to solemnize them, but much also to shake their faith in the facts, and still more in the spirit of Christianity; much to darken and distress their minds, and, in some instances, to produce a reaction of profane indifference and sensual infidelity. That this last result is, to an alarming extent, the case among the Carlylists in America, we know upon the best authority. The only man who has been subjected, for years together, to the torrent of the Carlyle talk without injury, and who, while continuing to admire and love the man, has never scrupled to express his difference of opinion, and his sorrow at his misdirected powers and mistaken path, is Thomas Aird, whose Christianity, rooted in the heart, and moral nature, being at once warm and enlightened, orthodox and catholic, has remained high and safe above the reach of the thousand dashing waves, or sullen swells, of his friend's unhappy scepticism.

But it is now time to turn to our author's latest work. It is by many thought his greatest, although we certainly do not coincide with this opinion. Were we to characterise it in a sentence, we might be tempted to call it Carlyle's own caricature of his *History of the French Revolution*. This caricature is elaborate, and done, of course, by a friendly hand; but it is a caricature notwithstanding, and, as usual in such things, the faults are caught more closely than the beauties. The endless repetitions, the flight of nicknames clouding every page, the gross and wilful grammatical freedoms, the glancing plusquam Gibbonic allusions to facts and incidents which the author deems the reader knows, but which are often revealed to him by these side-lights, imperfectly, and for the first time—the subacid stream of contempt and irony, the elaborate search for the picturesque, even in the most out of the way corners, and in defiance of all laws of unity and taste—the preference of bold and brilliant men to the obscurely good and the divinely weak—the exclamations and objurgations, the stifled oaths, half-crushed curses, and all the mad, miserable, yet laughing, rioting talk, as of the Titans in their prison-house of subterranean pain—are to be found in these two volumes of 1858, as well as in the three volumes of the *French Revolution*, published in 1837, although not now producing such a strange and powerful effect. Carlyle is waxing old, (sixty-five, we believe,) and, hence, his original 'fury' no longer 'upholds him' to the full extent. Prometheus is now nodding occasionally on his rock of torment, although the chain be as thick, and the beak of the vulture as keen as ever. Yet the work is far from being unworthy of its author's genius. It discovers an amount of research perfectly marvellous, alike in its extent and its apparent accuracy. It shews in the most vivid, nay, glaring light, the period of history to which it refers, and enables us to realize intensely the characters and incidents of the 18th century. The great objection, indeed, is that he casts a splendid lustre on a number of trifling circumstances, and imbecile or worthless characters. He turns his blazing torch on the haunts of unclean and doleful creatures—on the holes of scorpions, and the damp grassy haunts of toads—as well as on the pastures where oxen fatten, and the lairs where lions repose. Hence, a great portion of both volumes is tedious, not from the defect of power in the writer, but from a want of interest in the subject. Who cares for these miserable 'double marriage' intrigues, or for those carousings of Frederick William with August the Strong? The author himself becomes conscious that he is trying the patience of his reader, and he seeks to arouse attention by doubling the dose of exclamations and minced oaths. He is like a man who, while reading a long tedious law-paper, should interrupt himself, ever and anon, by crying out to the unfortunate listener—'Hearken to this, won't you? Confound you, if you don't! By heavens! have you the impudence to nod at this sentence?' Carlyle tries another dodge still. He divides his dulness into minute portions, his chapters into *chapterlings*, and he spices each of these with a quaint and attractive title. Still, the general effect is weariness. You drag heavily on, although, when he does arrive at a really interesting point of story, you are richly rewarded. Sometimes, too, amidst the flattest of the pages, there occur little pieces of scenic writing which are most beautiful and refreshing. Indeed, all the chapters describing Frederick William's journeys to and from the Reich, consist of description of scenery, and are executed with the hand of a master, although they have little logical connection with the history. Carlyle's mode of describing nature is unique, and in nothing does he discover more genius. He seldom stops to give any elaborate and lengthy picture; but he dashes on the objects he meets in his way such a light as chariot-lamps do while cleaving a dark night—the hills, rocks, woods, and waters appear intensely for a moment, and then vanish, while the chariot moves on with unabated speed. The light, too, is of a sombre and unearthly, as well as a swift-rushing kind; and it falls upon prominent outstanding features, which are not only shewn, but transfigured into poetry.

Whenever, we say, Carlyle in these volumes approaches a worthy theme, either of description, of character-painting, or of historical narrative, he rises to his proper level. Thus he does in his glance at Charles XII.; in his picture of the sufferings of the Crown Prince, and of his noble sister, Wilhelmina; in his account of the Salzburger emigrants, and in the history of the intercourse between Frederick and Voltaire. We would not, indeed, class these passages with the better things in his *French Revolution*, such as the death of Louis XV., the taking of the Bastile, the account of Charlotte Corday, or the deaths of Mirabeau and Danton—they are far inferior to these in condensed power and thrilling interest, but they are, nevertheless, exceedingly graphic and true seeming. Next to such portions of the book which are high wrought and successful in their elaboration, we like the glancing side-lights cast on the myriad characters who cross the stage, whom his one glance sees, and his one beaming or burning word names or nicknames—consigns to everlasting contempt, or elevates to endless honour.

The most important personages in the period he has chosen (Charles the XII. belongs properly to an earlier date) are Frederick William, the Crown Prince, destined to become Frederick the Great, and Voltaire; and to do justice to these he has summoned the whole force of his genius. We think that, in his heart, he admires Frederick William the elder more than his more celebrated son. There is something in the shaggy strength of character, the indomitable will, the bursts of fiery passion, the power of intellect, united to impetuous impulse, the unbending rigour and sternness of disposition, that characterised the older king, which is very attractive to Carlyle; and perhaps it is a 'fellow-feeling' that makes him so 'wondrous kind' to one whom he considers a 'dumb poet.' And thus he pours a requiem over his dust:—

No Baresark of them, nor Odin's self, I think, was a bit of truer human stuff. I confess, his value to me, in these sad times, is rare and great. Considering the usual histrionic, patent-digester, truculent charlatan, (query—Louis Napoleon!) and other species of kings alone attainable for the sunk, flunkey populations of an era given up to Mammon, and the worship of its own belly, what would not such a population give for a Frederick Wilhelm, to guide it on the road BACK from Orcus a little? 'Would give' I have written, but, alas! it ought to have been '*should*' give. What THEY 'would' give is too mournfully plain to me, in spite of ballot boxes—a steady and tremendous truth, from the days of Barabbas, downwards and upwards!

It should be remembered, however, even by an age 'given up to its own belly,' that Frederick Wilhelm was often months, if not years, in which he 'never went to bed sober;' that thus he brought on himself premature old age and death, dying a mere wreck at fifty-two, and was altogether a very fair specimen of his century—a century somewhat more given to belly-worship, if not to Mammon-worship, than even our own.

Of the Crown Prince, afterwards to become Frederick the Great, these volumes contain only the ground-plan and the first story. The public will impatiently expect the far more interesting portions which remain for the coming volumes. We were agreeably disappointed in not finding in Carlyle's account of Frederick, the violent 'hero-worship' we had looked for. Up to the point of his accession to the throne, with which the second volume closes, the view given of the young prince seems exceedingly fair and judicious. His intellect is rated high, although not perhaps so high as his father's, who, with less culture and self-command, had more of a genial and original mind, and who, with less calculation and comprehension, had more 'insights and impulses,' as this biographer would say. Frederick the Great was not strictly an originator, either in war or government; he chiefly distinguished himself by following out and improving his father's ideas. Frederick William organized a magnificent army, which his son turned to use; and all the plans, alike of military discipline and of diplomacy, which raised Prussia for a season to the summit of glory, were devised by the father. In the father, we see inventive genius; in the son, executive talent; in the one, there were turbulent passions, frequently lording it over an iron will; in the other, will generally exerted a supremacy, sometimes, indeed, concealing itself under a profound subtlety which the father's simpler and sublimer soul disdained. The father possessed, not merely fervid passions, but a powerful imagination, being a 'dumb poet;' the son had the capacity of writing clever verse, without a spark of real fire or fancy, and as near Voltaire's style, to use Johnson's words, as Voltaire's valet, who had also been his amanuensis, might have approached. The son knew every bottle of wine, its date and place, in his cellar; the father could drink ten bottles for the son's one. The father's ruling vice, next to severity, was gross and habitual intemperance; the son's, was licentiousness. In religion, the father, although not a Calvinist in the matter of predestination, was a zealous Protestant, and died devout and penitent; the son, was *intus et in cute*, a Philosophe, a Sceptic, if not a Denier. 'Sure, such a pair was never seen,' among the common-place crowd of kings, differing not more from other monarchs in courage, capacity, and energy, than from each other in temperament, and in cast of talent in the points of their strength and weakness; committed against each other for a while in fierce hostility on the one part, and sullen resistance on the other, but ultimately learning mutual love, respect, and admiration.

It is only, after all, the foot of Voltaire which is shown in these volumes. The fuller portraiture is to come afterwards. To say that Carlyle has a love for this gigantic incarnation of the eighteenth century's Doubt is, perhaps, to aver too much; but the view he takes of him is, in our judgment, too calm and favourable. Voltaire was capable, indeed, of noble actions and generous feelings, as his conduct to the Calas family proved; but looking at his history and his writings, as a whole, he was a God-denying scoffer; and his works are repertories of sciolism, heartlessness, licentiousness, and malignity. They are satires on God and man. They fight against the Divine in all its forms, with filthy and unmentionable weapons. It is as the bull-frog of a nation of frogs croaking against the sun; it is a 'gigantic ape toying with the most solemn subjects of human contemplation, as with nut-shells.' His Candide, by far his cleverest production, is one, long, godless grin; and although he is right in his theory that this is not 'the best of all possible worlds,' the spirit in which he defends it is infernal. Beginning to laugh at Leibnitz, he goes on to deride Divinity himself. His only panacea for the ills of the world is a devil's laugh! His 'Philosophical Dictionary' is the greatest misnomer in literature; it ought to be called the *Un*philosophical Dictionary. It is a succession of shallow common-places and sophisms, redeemed from contempt here, because stinged with clever scorn, and there, because tainted with putrid profligacy. His *History of Charles the XII.* is, according to our present author, just a well-written, elegant lie. In his plays, Voltaire is an ape upon the tight-rope. In his *Henriade*—his EPIC (save the mark!)—he is the same creature, doing the sublime, from the top of Notre Dame, mouthing and chattering, gesticulating and making faces. As he fought with coarse weapons, with slime and mud, these should be, and have been, returned upon himself. As he dared to say, in reference to *One* we may not name, 'Ecrasez L'Infame' (Crush the wretch!), let that watchword, snatched from his lips, become that of others, in branding and crushing HIM.

Some of Carlyle's friends have complained that his works have been subjected to the sinister eyes of what are called 'heresy-hunters.' Truly such eyes, of late, have not had to seek very far, or to see very clearly, in order to discover the said contraband article! We rejoice, however, to be able to say that there is very little of it in this, the latest production of his mind. He seems writing under severe restraint; and of irreligious escapades, on the whole, these volumes are guiltless. In one place he avows himself a Predestinarian, or, as he says, one who believes that 'a man is pre-appointed from all eternity either to salvation or the opposite.' This, let it be remembered, is the *only* article of positive faith with which Carlyle has ever favoured the world. He has been writing, if not on, yet about religious themes for some thirty years, and showering down anathemas on all religious parties and persons with the utmost freedom and fury, and yet, not till this year of grace, 1858, has there arrived the first announced article of his creed, and it is one that we must characterize as considerably vague. He says, let us observe, that a man is 'pre-appointed,' but does not say that he is pre-appointed by the will of God. It may be only by the necessity of things, as indeed, if Carlyle still maintains his objections to a 'Personal God,' must be his meaning. It is not the God of 'Calvin' after all he believes in, but in the Pantheistic Whole; the course of which, if such a thing be, is determined by inevitable laws. In a later part of the volume, he speaks of old Frederick William as setting forth to his son the 'horrible results of that Absolute Decree notion which makes God to be the Author of Sin;' but he does not say how far HE coincides with this version of the Crown Prince's belief.

On the whole, the work is an able and worthy contribution to the world's historic literature, although ponderous in size, excessive in price, negative and unsatisfactory in total result, and tediously prolix in many of its details. A clever redacteur might have condensed these two enormous volumes, containing somewhere about 1300 pages, into a moderate octavo of 500. He could have done so on the easy plan of excluding all the oaths, one half of the exclamations, a third of the repetitions, and a fourth of the needless minutiæ, in fact. Were *all* the epithets and outcries, such as 'dilapidated strong,' 'tobacco parliaments,' 'respectable Debourgays,' 'August, the Strong Man of Sin,' &c. &c., to be curtailed, the merit and classical character of the book would doubtless be enhanced, but its personal identity would be destroyed.

We have now (for till this book appeared, Carlyle was rather a poet writing on history, than a historian,) two contending votaries of Clio bidding against each other for popular favour, Macaulay, and the author of *Frederick the Great*. We do not think either of them answers to the ideal of a great historian. Both aim more at effect than at truth—although Macaulay seeks it by style, antithesis, and gossip—Carlyle, by oddity, recklessness, and wilful disregard of all rhetorical rules. Both have succeeded in rescuing history from its 'old almanac' form, and have made it in general entertaining and instructive—but neither has attained those wide views, those thorough sympathies, those religious feelings, and that *Shaksperean* simplicity and strength of style (we use the above epithet advisedly, remembering how Marlborough declared Shakspere's plays to be the best, nay the only history of England he ever read) which should distinguish the historian whom our wondrous mother-age requires and expects. Shade of Tacitus, when shall another such as thou appear, with thy consummate sagacity, thy Dantesque touch, now of gloomy strength, and now of simple beauty; thy condensation of style, and thy sincerity and righteous wrath of spirit! Yet, in thee too, we desiderate some elements of the ideal historian, and it would require the addition of the enlightened religious fervour of an Arnold, and the easy-flowing graces and munificent eloquence of a Livy, to entitle even a soul like thine to be the painter and poet in historic prose of such a strange transition period as the present!

38. Herman Merivale, from an unsigned review, *Quarterly Review*

July 1865, cxviii, 225–54

For a comment on Herman Merivale, see No. 8.

We left Mr. Carlyle, several years ago, at the end of the two preliminary volumes of his great and laborious work, the crowning effort of a life of unremitted literary industry. In his third, he carries his hero on to the outbreak of the Seven Years' War, the most prominent period in his biography and in the history of the eighteenth century; down to the French Revolution; the war which established his place among the eight or ten chief military captains of mankind, and which, at the same time, elevated a new power to rank among the first-rate monarchies of Europe. In the two last volumes, now before us, he recounts, in very minute detail, the intricate events of that contest, and, as it certainly appears to us, with disproportionately small development, the internal history of Prussia, and the particulars of his hero's life, down to his decease. All the reading world has had before its eyes these remarkable volumes: all that can be said of their inordinate tendency to hero-worship; the intolerant dictation to the reader of all that he is to think and feel, under pain of heresy; the familiar and characteristic extravagances of style and dictation; has been urged already by a thousand ready pens. And almost as ample testimony has been borne by critics to the power and picturesqueness of the narrative; the thousand touches of humor and pathos by which the writer's lessons, if too didactically enforced, are illustrated and accompanied; the genuine sense of what is right in human action and lofty in human character which underlies his overstrained idolatry. After all that can be objected, and after all deduction on the score of the injury which the writer has inflicted upon himself, greater than any his critics could have occasioned him, by the choice of a subject so unpromising for one of his peculiar temperament, and by his manner of dealing with it in extreme and yet unequal copiousness of detail, always lengthiest, as it seems to us, where the matter

439

is least attractive, it will remain in truth a great work, and a substantial contribution at once to accurate history and to high literature. For our own part, sincerely attached as we are to our profound Master of Paradoxes, we cannot but be enchanted to welcome him on his liberation from this self-imposed labour: to think of him as once more at liberty to astonish and amuse us with the wayward flights of his fancy, as well as instruct us with the hard, strong sense which redeems so many of his vagaries: no longer labouring away at that most hopeless of all his chimeras, the endeavour to make a perfect hero, without fear or reproach, of one who commonly passes for the most unloveable, if not absolutely odious, of all the really great men recorded in history; a task under which he has for these five years reminded us of nothing so much as of a set of busy children, in a winter garden, endeavouring, with vast activity and perseverance, to build up a Man of Snow. We feel ourselves well able to combine the sentiment of thankfulness for what we have got, with that of sympathetic relief at seeing the labourer himself quit of the mighty burden which he has laid down at our feet.

The fifth volume opens with the second campaign in chronological order, but which in substance may be almost called the opening one of the Seven Years' War—that of 1757. Excited by Frederic's audacious occupation of Saxony, the three great allies, France, Russia, and Austria, have resolved on his speedy extinction, or reduction to the limits of the 'March of Brandenburg.' They have dragged into the quarrel that anomalous body the Holy Roman Empire (which Mr. Carlyle, after his fashion, will persist in calling the Reich, though he might quite as gracefully style France 'the Royaume'), and even the misgoverned and decayed state of Sweden, in virtue of its old claims on Pomerania: as to which last addition to the alliance Mr. Carlyle remarks, with truth, that its chief value was, that it served for an answer to the plausible representation that Catholic states were coalescing against a Protestant sovereign. In point of fact, it may be said at the outset, that questions of religion were soon felt by all parties—except a few of our determined English Protestants—to have no more to do with the Seven Years' War than they had afterwards with those of Napoleon. Frederic has only England at his side; and England, as yet, has little more than an army of observation, on the Rhine, under the Duke of Cumberland. Four invading masses—Russia from north-east, Sweden north-west, France and the 'Reich' south-west, Austria south-east, are collecting at once on the frontiers of his disjointed States. All the on-lookers, with one judgment, seem to have made up their mind that they will remain on the defensive, and make Saxony his battle-field; that is, suffer himself to be gradually squeezed into collapse by the folds of the 'boa-constrictor,' to use an illustration which recent American campaigns have made famous. But 'it is by no means Frederic's intention that Saxony itself shall need to be invaded. Frederic's habit is—as his enemies might by this time be beginning to learn—not that of standing on the defensive, but that of going on it, as the preferable method, wherever possible.' Accordingly, in April of this year, Frederic dashes with upwards of 150,000 men out of Saxony into Bohemia—*why* Saxony and Bohemia, while Silesia is sometimes 'Schlesien,' Lusatia and Pomerania always 'Lausitz' and 'Pommern,' we can on no principle, whether of philology or euphony, conjecture—and lays siege to 'Prag.' The siege is admirably described; the description of the country in which the leading events take place, as fine and accurate a piece of picturesque writing as we have met with. The siege—more properly a series of attacks on a hostile army intrenched within lines comprehending a city—proves a failure. 'Prag cannot be got at once.' And hereby comes a complication, which produces, to us, Englishmen, one of the most interesting portions of Mr. Carlyle's work. England, hitherto loyally, if not very energetically, engaged in support of Prussia, begins to waver, under the doubtful aspect of affairs in Bohemia, and the extremely unstable character of her own statesmen.

It is in this crisis (if we may anticipate the complete development of events by a few months) that Pitt steps forward as the founder of England's European greatness, but as the very saviour of Prussia. We are so much more accustomed to dwell on him in the first character than the last—the cause of Prussia, for various reasons intelligible to most, though ignored by Mr. Carlyle, not having been one of abiding popularity—that it is as it were a new lesson to us, and a very valuable one, to have it pointed out how entirely, next to his own good sword, Frederic owed his political salvation to Pitt's personal character and resolution. The union of France and Austria had long been the contingency against which thoughtful English statesmanship had most sedulously sought to guard. The contingency had now taken place. Pitt had that true political insight which revealed to him alone, perhaps, of his contemporaries, the importance to Britain of the erection of a new, independent military power in Northern Europe, sufficient with our aid to counterbalance France and Austria both. To this object he devoted, without hesitation, all the energy of his will: for this purpose he inflamed the spirit of England to the highest pitch of hardihood and resolution.

That he has become thereby a prime favourite with Mr. Carlyle—'an authentically royal style of man,' 'not born King; alas, no, not officially so, only naturally so: has his kingdom to seek: the conquering of Silesia, the conquering of Pelham Parliaments,'—it is easy to anticipate. But allowing at once for extravagances of diction, and also for the kind of collateral bias which thus helps to direct his judgment, Pitt has seldom been more thoroughly appreciated, or more worthily celebrated, than by the author of these volumes. But we have not space to bring this subject fairly before the reader. We will content ourselves, on English affairs, with a singular bit of by-praise not at all undeserved, in our opinion, but which shows how far the force of the *lues biographica*—the passion of a biographer for his hero—can overcome even the most congenital antipathies. Mr. Carlyle—of all conceivable people—actually bestows a *coup de chapeau* on Horace Walpole! The common tie of connexion being the love of Pitt, whom Mr. Carlyle loves as the supporter of Frederic, while Walpole praised him, in truth, because he superseded the Pelhams, who had risen on the fall of Sir Robert:

[quotes 'Walpole's *George the Second*' to 'an editor' XVII, 158]

Of the results of Pitt's final accession to power in 1757 on Frederic's destinies—the extinction of 'Newcastleisms and impious poltrooneries' at home, the punctual payment abroad of subsidies which under the reign of Newcastle had been promised and not paid at all, the generous vigour with which the whole weight of France was at once removed from the mass which lay on Frederic, and that country forced to employ nearly all her means in fighting England alone, in America and in Germany, Mr. Carlyle has of course much to say; and according to our impression it has never been so well said before. Unfortunately these, like all the really valuable parts of the work, are reduced to so disjointed a state from his singular method of composition or rather decomposition of his subject into minute fractions—they are only to be disinterred with such an infinity of trouble from under the dead weight of tons of battles and sieges, that very few readers of the ordinary class will derive from them so much instruction as they might on one of the most interesting and glorious passages in our domestic history.

Prag, as we have seen, 'cannot be got at once:' Daun is moving from eastward to relieve it: Frederic raises the siege and advances against Daun: and in the battle of Kolin (June 1757) receives his first defeat —a pretty decided one. Invincible up to that point, he could scarcely believe in its reality. According to one account, Frederic stood his ground till nearly left alone:—

In his rear, man after man fell away, till Lieutenant-Colonel Grant (not 'Le Grand,' as some call him, and indeed there is an accent of Scotch in him still audible to us here) had to remark, 'Your Majesty and I cannot take the battery ourselves!' Upon which Friedrich turned round, and, seeing nobody, looked at the enemy through his glass, and slowly rode away—on a different errand.

Happily for the hero, Daun, completely victorious, 'would not let the sun go down upon his wrath,' stood all night under arms, and next day 'returned to his camp again, as if he had been afraid the king would come back!' Except the raising of the siege of 'Prag,' things remained as before.

The battle of Kolin is well described; and not quite at such tedious length as is the case—to our own apprehension—with too many of the feats of arms recorded in these pages. It is a point on which we distrust our own judgment, having no vocation for battle-descriptions: which are, on the contrary, evidently labours of love to our author, who has devoted much toil and travel to the patient inspection of field after field of the great war. But our own general criticism would be this: his accounts are, we presume, careful: they are certainly, if not clear from perspicuity of style on the first glance, reducible at least to clearness with the aid of thought and of maps: they are vigorous in parts: but they do not amount to battle-painting: they do not bring the scene either before the eyes of the fancy or within the grasp of the intellect, as compositions by really great masters in that line, and especially professional masters, sometimes do. But we readily leave the question to be solved for themselves by readers (of whom there are very many) who will take greater interest in this special branch than we do.

For the first time—a thing so often afterwards repeated—the beaten Frederic, hemmed in by Austria, France, the Empire, was spared simply by the inconceivable hesitation of his antagonists, whom it is difficult to suspect of having been in earnest. He remains posted the rest of the summer, as if in defiance, at Leitmeritz—halfway between Prag and Dresden—until the gaps in his legions are filled again, and the momentary shock to his invincibility repaired. Undoubtedly this was one of the most depressing periods of his life: for although even more pressing evils beset him later in his career, he had by that time trained himself to meet them with a sterner cynicism. While at Leitmeritz, too, he lost his mother, to whom he was attached with an affection cemented by the years of common misery they had undergone under the sway of her husband:—

[quotes 'At Leitmeritz' to 'joyful fact' XVII, 195]

That an observer of human nature at once so acute and profound as Mr. Carlyle should put up with such commonplace as this, when the defence of a favourite is concerned, only adds one more proof of the lowering effect of hero-worship on the intellect. Because Frederic was (as almost all men of genius are) of a very refined, excitable temper of mind, and easily moved even to tears, therefore the supposition that he could be 'cruel and unfeeling' can be the result only of 'furious stupidity'! We beg Mr. Carlyle's pardon. Of the blackest monsters whom the annals of criminal justice have made immortal, rather a large proportion have been very sentimental persons, whose tears have been ready on the slightest provocation. We will not enter into controversy with him on the inner depths of his favourite's moral character, as to which we entertain very different notions from himself. We will say but this—that if those who have judged of him the worst—who have esteemed him unfeeling, selfish, cold, false, bad-hearted, to an extent rarely equalled among distinguished men—if these are to be esteemed as refuted merely by showing that Frederic shut himself up and cried on losing the battle of Kolin and his mother, a great many characters at present labouring under general disapproval will have to be rehabilitated on the same principle.

After this melancholy halt at Leitmeritz, finding himself still unmolested from the Austrian side, Frederic moves westward into Thuringia against the French and the 'Reich's Armée.' 'This forlorn march of Friedrich's—one of the forlornest a son of Adam ever had' Mr. Carlyle calls it: somewhat to our surprise. We should deem of it rather as an adventure entered on in the rapture of consummate daring and consummate skill. Frederic had fully 'discounted' the worst that could happen; and we imagine that his assumed airs of intended suicide, and the poetical moans addressed at this period to his sister and others,

> Ainsi mon seul asile et mon unique sort,
> Se trouve, chère sœur, dans les bras de la Mort,[1]

(Macaulay, it will be remembered, represents him as 'going about with a bottle of poison in one pocket and a quire of bad verses in another') were, in 1757 (whatever his feelings in later and darker periods of his

[1] Therefore, dear sister, my only refuge, my destiny, is in the arms of death.

career) no more than half ironical fanfaronades, carelessly thrown out by the strong swimmer exulting in the immediate prospect of his conflict with the waves. However this may be, he came up at last with his new enemies (October, 1757) in the valley of the Saale which, even more than the plains round Brussels, seems to have been chosen by Fate for the scene of the great and decisive battle of modern nations; and then and there administered to them, at Rossbach—22,000 against 60,000—one of the most complete, decisive, ignominious thrashings ever bestowed in fair field by men on men: loss of the vanquished 8000, of the victors hardly 500. It was Shakspeare's Agincourt over again, with the additional interest of the victor repelling, instead of conducting, an overbearing invasion. And all the circumstances were so combined by Fate as if to enhance the triumph and point the humiliation; the utter and inevitable destruction from which it rescued the King—his eagle swoop, with Seidlitz's invincible cavalry, just on the weak point of the enemy—the inconceivable fatuity, presumption, stupidity of the unlucky allies—the very 'insouciance' of the French themselves, who seemed rather to enjoy their own defeat as a remarkable joke, and alleviated the smart of their mortification by lampoons on their officers, of a vastly superior class to the coarse and pointless epigrams with which the victorious king himself pursued their flight. 'Almost never, not even at Cressy or Poitiers, was an army better beaten; and truly, never did any one better deserve it, so far as the chief parties went.' And the universal German shout of exultation thereupon arose, not from the Prussian side only, but from every circle of the ancient empire, rejoicing in its own nominal defeat.

The joy of poor Teutschland at large; and how all Germans, Prussian and Anti-Prussian alike, flung up their caps with unanimous *lebe hoch* at the news of Rossbach, has been often remarked, and is indeed still almost touching to see. The perhaps bravest nation in the world, though the least braggart, so long insulted, snubbed, and trampled on, by a luckier, not a braver!

After the battle of Rossbach the French disappear, to be brought into contact with Frederic no more, and only to wage war against him collaterally on the Rhine; the 'Reich's armée,' army of the Circles, vanishes; 'Armée des Cercles et des Tonneliers,' of hoops and coopers, Frederic had called it, in a joke which he considered so good that he now and then repeated it; but surely his very shade must be weary by this time of the biographer's endless iteration of it! But the great result of the day was what is above indicated. German Unity, still in infancy, had died at Lützen. It revived at Rossbach; and struggles slowly towards substantial existence ever since. To us the battle is typified by a favourite old print, representing a story which is in all the anecdote books—we are sorry, by the way, to see Mr. Carlyle treat this source of intelligence so contemptuously as he does. A Prussian hussar is chasing a Frenchman; an Austrian turns to defend his alley, 'Bruder Deutscher,' says the Prussian, 'lass mir diesen Franzosen!' 'Nimm ihn!'[2]

Frederic's only use for a triumph over one enemy is to take breath for a moment, and push against another. . . . His over-mastering severity towards those of his generals who had committed errors, or had merely been unsuccessful—one of his worst faults of heart and character in common opinion, whatever its success as matter of policy —we are told to view only as affording an illustration of the heroic.

[quotes 'About Friedrich's severity' to 'his captains' XVIII, 117–18]

So in the more important case of Fink, the unfortunate leader at Maxen, who got a year's imprisonment at Spandau.

No ray of pity visible for him, then or afterward, in the royal mind. . . . And truly it would have been more beautiful to everybody, for the moment, to have made matters soft to poor Finck; had Friedrich ever gone on that score with his generals and delegates: which, though the reverse of a cruel man, he never did.

We will only contrast Macaulay's remarks on the conduct generally exhibited in like cases by Napoleon, though not so universally as Macaulay would imply.

Bonaparte knew mankind well; and as he acted towards his surgeon at the time of the birth of the King of Rome (according to a well-known anecdote), he acted towards his officers. No sovereign was ever so indulgent to mere errors of judgment; and it is certain that no sovereign ever had in his service so many military men fit for the highest commands.

If both systems succeeded in practice—and it would certainly seem that they did—the reason is probably to be sought, not in the respective characters of the 'kings of men' themselves (to which Mr. Carlyle habitually attributes everything), but in those of the materials with which these leaders had to deal. Braver men than the soldiers of Frederic, or those of Napoleon, never 'flung themselves rejoicingly on death,' under the eye and at the command of an idolised leader. But agreeing in this essential feature, they differed in almost everything

2 'Brother German,' 'Leave me this Frenchman!' 'Take him.'

besides. The Germans had been made what they were under a training, for many generations past, of coarse and brutal severity—hardened in the very fire of adversity. The disgraced general took his censure and imprisonment, just as the soldier-culprit, fresh from confronting an odds of five against one before an Austrian battery, submitted to be thrashed by his corporal's cane, or torn to pieces by the rods of his comrades; as allotted portions of that heritage of misery which he and his fathers before him had endured from time whereof the memory of man ran not to the contrary. But the sufferings which he bore with simple, hard resignation—sometimes with a touching religious heroism —under one of the hateful drill sovereigns of the ordinary German breed, became as it were glorified in his eyes, when inflicted as part of the discipline which created Frederic's unrivalled army. Unrivalled, assuredly, in all history; for these men, in their simple Platt-Deutsch valour, as Mr. Carlyle is fond of terming it, were in the habit of encountering, not now and then, but day after day, double, threefold, and fourfold odds as a mere matter of course, without hope of advancement in an army officered by nobles, or of personal glory where the work was too stern and overwhelming for decorations, honourable mentions, and the like, and where the highest honour a veteran could attain was some rough coarse notice from the royal soldier, who well knew the effect which he, and he alone, could thus produce.* Frenchmen are of a different mould. They used to put up very uneasily with the Prussian discipline even before the Revolution, after it not at all: and if Napoleon would have found it impossible to drive his troops into action by the corporal's cane or flat of the sabre, so, and for the same reason, he would have found it a very barren experiment habitually to scold, censure, degrade, or imprison French generals, guilty of ill success, in the manner which Frederic seems to have found both pleasant and profitable. . . .

[There follows an account of the Seven Years' War.]

The Seven Years' War had left Prussia apparently prostrated: her population, it is said, diminished by an eighth; her feeble commerce all but annihilated; not a province which had not been trampled under the feet of armed legions, extorting the very utmost of her substance by

* See among other and like instances the favourite old Prussian soldiers' military ballad:—
Fridericus Rex, unser König and Herr,
Der rief seine Soldaten allesammt ins Gewehr, &c.
Ihr verfluchten Kerls, sprach seine Majestat.
(You cursed rascals, said His Majesty, &c. &c.)

military requisition; scarcely a town which had not been reduced to buy itself off from the invader by incurring a load of debt; not to mention the unavoidable, but most severe, exactions by which the government itself contrived to maintain its all but desperate existence. That Prussia recovered herself from this collapse in three or four years at the utmost is well known: that the King, at the end of these exhausting campaigns, found himself in the possession of a full if not overflowing treasury: that he devoted its contents to a well-considered, most economical, but thoroughly well-apportioned series of contributions to the distresses of those parts of the country which had suffered the most, is well known also. But the details of this most singular and perhaps unexampled piece of Royal economy, which sets Frederic as absolutely at the head of administrators as his campaigns did at the head of captains, are almost unapproachable to ordinary readers. Not that they are wanting; but they are only to be collected with infinite pains and labour from a mass of original and most intractable materials. A worthier task for one whose purpose, like Mr. Carlyle's, was the apotheosis of Frederic, cannot assuredly be imagined. Unfortunately, as we have already observed, the bent of Mr. Carlyle's genius does not tend that way. He lets the great occasion pass by him with no attempt whatever to improve it, except by a few of the wildest possible sparrings at the ancient object of his antipathy, the 'Dismal Science,' which assuredly is very innocent of all concern in the matter.

[quotes 'Friedrich begins' to 'at this day' XIX, 10]

The Dismal Science, according to ordinary popular views of it, consists of two parts: first, a body of scientific deductions, which it is given to nobody to understand who will not take the trouble to master them, but on the mind of him who has once so mastered them, neither Carlylesque nor Ruskinesque eloquence can make the slightest impression; and, secondly, the application of certain principles in matters of finance to the art of government, as to which opinions may vary and do vary, although those of the Carlyle and Ruskin order (if to be termed opinions at all) are likely to prove very misleading. It seems that Frederic—though by what miracles of economy and self-denial he effected it remains, as we say, unexplained—contrived, at the beginning of every year of war, to have funds in hand to meet the estimate for that year. At the Peace of Hubertsburg, accordingly, he had, we are told, twenty-five million of thalers in his treasury, or enough for the consumption of three or four years of peace. The course which sound financial principle, special reasons apart, would have indicated, would have been to remit his subjects' taxation to that amount, and allow the twenty-five millions to 'fructify' in their pockets. Nature would then, to use Mr. Carlyle's simile, which is certainly more in the vein of Ruskin than Ricardo, have 'clothed the ruins with lichen' in her own good time: in plainer English, capital would have found its way to render productive the districts which had suffered most by the war, because in those districts there would probably have been found (without returning security) the most effective demand for it. Frederic, therefore, by spending this money according to his own notion of what was most required, may have been only interfering with, and retarding the wholesome sanative process of nature. So apparently thought Mirabeau (the father, in his *Monarchie Prussienne*[3]), and so have thought many others. Nevertheless, it is certain that there are considerations on the other side fairly to be taken into the account. One of these is the propensity to hoard money, universal in times of insecurity and terror, such as were likely, in a backward country like Prussia, long to outlast the immediate pressure of an exhausting war. Much of the twenty-five millions, had Frederic left it to the taxpayers, would probably have found its way into mere dead accumulations of treasure, to the evident damage of the body politic. Other reasons might be given in his favour without any disloyalty to the 'Dismal Science,' for which we have not space here; and, on the whole, there is no heresy in believing that Frederic, with his stern economy and genius for stewardship, may have done more good in these exceptional circumstances with his subjects' money than his subjects would themselves have done with it.

The topic, however, is one which opens a much wider field of thought, and one to which economical writers, so far as we have remarked, have not yet devoted the attention which it deserves. How far is the principal of mutual insurance between members of the same body politic likely to extend itself with advancing civilisation? There is no reason, in theory, why it should not do so, until every loss sustained by an individual were made to fall on the general fund. But, stopping short of such far-reaching speculations, it is certain that the measure and manner in which national relief, in case of local catastrophes, or supposed local wants, may be afforded with advantage by contributions from the State at large, has never been made, as it ought to have been, the subject of definite political investigation. This is one of the directions in which absolute sovereigns, especially Oriental sovereigns,

[3] *De la monarchie prussienne sous Frédéric le Grand* (1788).

have loved to exercise their capricious benevolence, if that can be called so which is exercised at the expense of others. Remissions of taxation and conscription to provinces thought deserving of relief—which, of course, only means supporting them at the expense of other provinces —these are among the commonest features of Eastern sovereignty in its milder moods, and have constantly called forth the praises of the ignorant, as if they were real acts of generosity. So, when the rulers of Russia and of Prussia spent large sums in reclaiming wastes and planting colonies, they were only carrying into execution the oldfashioned Oriental pattern of paternal government, sometimes, it may well be, with advantage, more often, probably, to the general loss. This principle, or rather occasional usage, of compulsory insurance, if it may be so termed, has always been less practised in the Western States of Europe, a circumstance which may arise from their early Roman education in some of the more important elements of self-government. In our own country, it has been chiefly confined to occasional Parliamentary grants in aid of local distress, generally (and rightly) bestowed with grudging, often degenerating into mere jobs in the administration. But on some great occasions—the Irish distress of 1847, the Lancashire distress of 1863—the principle of insurance has been carried out in a still more irregular, though perhaps more efficacious, way, through voluntary contributions on a scale befitting national efforts. The problem, which may possibly be one day elaborated by the best heads devoted to the Dismal Science, is that of satisfying the social need of mutual assurance against local calamity by some approach to general arrangement, and not leaving it either to the caprices of a monarch, even though accidentally a 'hero,' or to those of an impulsive public.

The next crisis of importance in the reign of Frederic is that of the first partition of Poland in 1772. As to Mr. Carlyle's singular views on this subject, much might be said. Though history is the most irrefragable of moral teachers, it by no means follows, in our opinion, that it is the duty of every historian to improve her texts by getting up into the pulpit on all occasions and preaching for himself. It is too common a belief among this class of writers, that they are bound to let no great action or event pass by them without calling the attention of their public to its various moral phases, and apportioning praise and blame in their own scales. This we hold to be a misapprehension, and we know full well that its consequences are too often exceedingly wearisome, and very useless. We should, for our own parts, be perfectly well pleased to dispense with any fresh repetition of what Mr. Carlyle calls the 'shrieks, the foam-lipped curses of mistaken mankind' over such events as the partition of Poland, in the pages of modern historians, and content ourselves with the calm verdict of one who should simply say, without mouthing or emphasis, 'Thus did Frederic, and Catherine, and Joseph, and thus suffered the Poles.' But, it is quite unnecessary to say, such passionless exposition must not be sought for from Mr. Carlyle. It would be to require of him a self-discipline absolutely contradictory to the laws of his nature. And, more than this, it would take 'half his worth away.' His peculiar charm lies in that hearty resolution not only to lead, but to drive if needful, the reader along with him—to cram him with doctrine without stint or reticence—to compel him to enter, and not leave go of him until the very last rinsings of Mr. Carlyle's own judgment and feelings have been thoroughly infused into him. Our author's vocation is to 'teach the nations how to live,' not by merely laying examples before them, still less by gentle persuasion, but by laying down the only true faith on pain, as we said, of intellectual damnation. He must preach, or hold his tongue altogether. Such being the conditions of his literary existence, nothing could be more unfortunate than that he should be forced by his position to handle such a subject as the Partition of Poland; and to make his views on it fit in, by every conceivable Procrustean process, with those which impel him to canonise one of the arch-robbers, his hero. The result is to our mind a strangely disjointed, and very inconsistent, series of half vaunts and half apologies. . . .

[There follows an analysis of the 'Partition of Poland'.]

Frederic reigned thirteen years longer, after the first partition of Poland. It was a period of comparatively small interest as regards foreign affairs: or rather the interests which then came to the surface, very important at the time, have not proved of permanent consequence. The Prussian War of 1778, popularly termed the Kartoffel-Krieg or Potato-War, from a general feeling of impatience at the series of small manœuvrings and skirmishes about convoys of which it was chiefly made up: the 'Fürsten-Bund,' or league of sovereign princes of the German Empire against the ambitious tendencies of Joseph the Second towards 'unification:' soon became historically obsolete, when in a very few years more the Empire itself had become a thing of the past. 'To the present class of readers,' says Mr. Carlyle, 'Fürstenbund has become nothing:' and he says it somewhat regretfully: for he has been pointing out, and with admirable force and perspicacity, how great a feat of statesmanship 'Fürstenbund' really was. The whole course of German politics in the year 1777–1785 contains a fine though forgotten lesson of kingly contrivance. If the headstrong encroachments of Joseph had not been met by so profound a combination of sagacity with courage as none but Frederic could show, the Kaiser would most assuredly then and there have restored the Empire to something like a reality, a body of vassals under one Imperial head. Not less admirable was the skill which, with so far inferior means, could enter on war with Austria on terms of equality and almost superiority: and this singular self-abnegation, which could make the first soldier of his, if not of any day, deliberately decline to risk the chances of that war, brave the somewhat contemptuous judgment of the world and the impatience of his own troops and subjects, and hold in his hand 200,000 men and a thousand cannon, motionless, a whole summer through, until the object for which seas of blood might perhaps have been shed in vain, was effected at no cost at all, and Germany built firmly up into a solid confederacy, defying, for the time and for the rest of Frederic's life, all that Austrian ambition and perseverance might effect. These seem to us triumphs almost as great as those of the Seven Years' War itself; and their true import and bearing cannot be more ably pointed out than they are by Mr. Carlyle, though always in his cynical way:—

The Prussian army was full of ardour, never abler 'for fight' (insists Schmettau,) which indeed seems to have been the fact on every small occasion: 'but fatally forbidden to try!' Not so fatally, perhaps had Schmettau looked beyond his epaulettes: was not the thing, by that slow method, got done? By the swifter method, awakening a new Seven Years business, how infinitely costlier might it have been!

. . . We should have had some satisfaction, even in the less ambitious occupation of tracing the growth of Berlin from insignificance to splendour on its Sahara-like site—of Silesia from a dismal region of feudal decay and obstruction to one of the wealthiest provinces, both in agricultural and commercial prosperity, which Europe has to show. Unfortunately, we must say it, Mr. Carlyle leaves us entirely without help on these and similar questions. Whether he is really so gluttonous an amateur of military details as to think that every forgotten skirmish in the Bohemian mountains requires to be embalmed in long pages, while the various stages of social progress and civil administration are below the notice of the historian of a hero: or whether, as we are rather inclined to conjecture, he has become in the sixth volume thoroughly tired of his work: the fact is at all events so: and it is precisely our admiration of Mr. Carlyle, our sense of his singular originality of judgment on human affairs, and of the power which he possesses beyond almost all men of projecting himself into the past as he describes it, which causes us to regret it the more deeply.

Mr. Carlyle, however, as himself would say, can only do his work in his own appointed fashion; and, in this fashion, he beckons his disciples onward to partake in the last scene of all—the exit of his hero. 'His death,' we are told, 'seems very stern and lonely; a man of such affectionate feelings, too; a man with more sensibility than other men! But so had his whole life been, stern and lonely.' Who made it so? He had indeed outlived his companions of early life—we cannot call them his friends—but to most men, of even ordinary 'sensibility,' there arises a second crop in old age of younger lives, in which they take an interest often far exceeding that with which they watched the fortunes of their contemporaries. To Frederic this most interesting chapter of human existence was all but absolutely sealed. He had cared little for those who had grown by his side; he cared less (*pace* Mr. Carlyle and his one or two stories about great nephews) for those who were to come after him. His affectionate relations with one or two female members of his family, of which Mr. Carlyle makes the most, were almost entirely confined to correspondence—for their society he never seems to have wished. With his brothers, especially the generous Prince Henry, he appears to have been, particularly towards the end of his life, on terms of systematic coldness. Of his relations with his wife, in the latter part of his reign, Mr. Carlyle, his admirer, shall himself speak:—

When the King, after the Seven Years' War, now and then, in Carnival season, dined with the Queen in her apartments, he usually said not a word to her. He merely, on entering, on sitting down at table and leaving it, made the customary bows, and sat opposite to her. Once (in the Seventies) the Queen was ill of gout: table was in her apartments. . . . On this occasion the King stepped up to the Queen, and inquired about her health! The circumstance occasioned among the company present, and all over the town as the news spread, great wonder and sympathy! This is probably the last time he ever spoke to her.

In this frame of mind, more and more solitary and saturnine, he made himself ready, in his stern way, to confront the last enemy:—

[quotes 'He well knew' to 'with doing that' XIX, 290–1]

Thus far, at all events, we agree with Mr. Carlyle: that there is something of the awful in the contemplation of the last years of this strange great man's life and activity. Without love in this world, without hope in the next; inexpressibly weary of life, and having long outlived its illusions: without interests, without objects, without companions; we find him still living and working on, still straining every nerve in the performance, even to the uttermost farthing, of his rigid, self-imposed debt of duty, labouring like the journeyman whose task-work has to be done ere the night approaches, though others, for whom he cares not an atom, are to reap whatever of benefit may result from it: a spectacle perhaps without example in the history of sovereigns, and one which disposes us to part with Frederic on terms of more heartfelt, though still distant, reverence, than all Mr. Carlyle's vehement demands on our admiration could possibly extort from us.

Differing, as we must do, widely from him in our estimate of his hero's character, and in our estimate, also, of the historical interest and importance of a vast proportion of the heavy details which he has dragged so painfully to light, we cannot nevertheless lay down his book without regret at parting with an animated and interesting companion, or without increased respect for the extraordinary power which he has lavished on what seems to us so intractable a subject. As a writer, Mr. Carlyle's fame is established: criticism has done its worst on him: imitation and flattery have done their worst also: in this character 'nothing can touch him farther,' and we certainly shall not profane the great work before us by the slight handling of an ordinary review. Enough to say, that, after forming the literary taste of England and America to an extent which no contemporary (unless, possibly, one of a very different class, Macaulay) has approached, he has become, while yet alive and at work among us, something of a classic. His peculiar style and mannerism seem already things of the past to this generation. Imitators of Carlyle abounded not many years ago, and a serious infliction they became. They are already comparatively rare. It is something strange to see the great Master himself stepping forward, after years of silence, and occupying again the same field which his very followers had deserted; to trace, in his own pages, the very same strange but impressive diction, the same *tours de force* of style, and the same settled eccentricities of thought, not softened in the least degree by age or disuse, which we had already begun to regard as antiquated in those who took them up at second hand. It is like the return of the magician, in Goethe's ballad, to the house which he had abandoned to the experiments of his foolish and conceited apprentices, and his calm resumption of authority over the spirits which others might call, but he alone could control when called:—

Denn, als Geister,
Ruft euch nur, zu seinem Zweeke,
Ernst hervor der alte Meister.[4]

[4]As a spirit,
When he wills, only your master
Calls you; then it is time to hear.'
From Goethe's 'Der Zauberlehrling' ('The Sorcerer's Apprentice').

OBITUARIES AND 'REMINISCENCES'

1881

---

39. Walt Whitman on Carlyle, (*a*) *Critic* and (*b*) *Specimen Days*

(*a*) 12 February 1881
(*b*) New York, 1914

Obituary, 'Death of Thomas Carlyle', the *Critic*, 12 February 1881, and 'Later Thoughts and Jottings: Carlyle from American Points of View', from *Specimen Days* in *Complete Prose Works, Walt Whitman* (New York, 1914).

> Walt Whitman (1819–92) knew Carlyle's work well, having reviewed *On Heroes, Sartor Resartus, The French Revolution,* and *Past and Present* in the 1840s. Having once attacked Carlyle's 'Shooting Niagara' as 'comic-painful hullabaloo and vituperative cat-squalling', he later came to regard him with affection—as we can see from the following essays. Carlyle's earliest judgments of Whitman were likewise harsh (as if the 'town bull had learned to hold a pen'), but he changed his opinion of the American after he read *Democratic Vistas*.

(*a*)
And so the flame of the lamp, after long wasting and flickering, has gone out entirely.

As a representative author, a literary figure, no man else will bequeath to the future more significant hints of our stormy era, its fierce paradoxes, its din, and its struggling parturition periods, than Carlyle. He belongs to our own branch of the stock too; neither Latin nor Greek, but altogether Gothic. Rugged, mountainous, volcanic, he was himself more a French Revolution than any of his volumes.

456

In some respects, so far in the Nineteenth Century, the best equipt, keenest mind, even from the college point of view, of all Britain; only he had an ailing body. Dyspepsia is to be traced in every page, and now and then fills the page. One may include among the lessons of his life— even though that life stretched to amazing length—how behind the tally of genius and morals stands the stomach, and gives a sort of casting vote.

Two conflicting agonistic elements seem to have contended in the man, sometimes pulling him different ways, like wild horses. He was a cautious, conservative Scotchman, fully aware what a fœtid gas-bag much of modern radicalism is; but then his great heart demanded re-form, demanded change—an always sympathetic, always human heart —often terribly at odds with his scornful brain.

No author ever put so much wailing and despair into his books, sometimes palpable, oftener latent. He reminds me of that passage in Young's poems where as Death presses closer and closer for his prey the Soul rushes hither and thither, appealing, shrieking, berating, to escape the general doom.

Of short-comings, even positive blur-spots, from an American point of view, he had serious share; but this is no time for specifying them. When we think how great changes never go by jumps in any depart-ment of our universe, but that long preparations, processes, awakenings, are indispensable, Carlyle was the most serviceable democrat of the age.

How he splashes like leviathan in the seas of modern literature and politics! Doubtless, respecting the latter, one needs first to realize, from actual observation, the squalor, vice and doggedness ingrained in the bulk-population of the British Islands, with the red tape, the fatuity, the flunkeyism everywhere, to understand the last meaning in his pages.

Accordingly, though he was no chartist or radical, I consider Carlyle's by far the most indignant comment or protest anent the fruits of Feudalism to-day in Great Britain—the increasing poverty and degradation of the homeless, landless twenty millions, while a few thousands, or rather a few hundreds, possess the entire soil, the money, and the fat berths. Trade and shipping, and clubs and culture, and prestige, and guns, and a fine select class of gentry and aristocracy, with every modern improvement, cannot begin to salve or defend such stupendous hoggishness.

For the last three years we in America have had transmitted glimpses of Carlyle's prostration and bodily decay—pictures of a thin-bodied, lonesome, wifeless, childless, very old man, lying on a sofa, kept out of

457

bed by indomitable will, but, of late, never well enough to take the open air. News of this sort was brought us last fall by the sick man's neighbor, Moncure Conway; and I have noted it from time to time in brief descriptions in the papers. A week ago I read such an item just before I started out for my customary evening stroll between eight and nine.

In the fine cold night, unusually clear, (Feb: 5, '81,) as I walked some open grounds adjacent, the condition of Carlyle, and his approaching—perhaps even then actual—death, filled me with thoughts, eluding statement, and curiously blending with the scene. The planet Venus, an hour high in the west, with all her volume and lustre recovered, (she has been shorn and languid for nearly a year,) including an additional sentiment I never noticed before—not merely voluptuous, Paphian, steeping, fascinating—now with calm, commanding, dazzling serious-ness and hauteur—the Milo Venus now. Upward to the zenith, Jupiter, Saturn, and the Moon past her quarter, trailing in procession, with the Pleiades following, and the constellation Taurus, and red Aldebaran. Not a cloud in heaven. Orion strode through the south-east, with his glittering belt—and a trifle below hung the sun of the night, Sirius. Every star dilated, more vitreous, nearer than usual. Not as in some clear nights when the larger stars entirely outshine the rest. Every little star or cluster just as distinctly visible, and just as nigh. Berenice's Hair showing every gem, and new ones. To the north-east and north the Sickle, the Goat and Kids, Cassiopea, Castor and Pollux, and the two Dippers.

While through the whole of this silent indescribable show, enclosing and bathing my whole receptivity, ran the thought of Carlyle dying. (To soothe and spiritualize and, as far as may be, solve the mysteries of death and genius, consider them under the stars at midnight.)

And now that he has gone hence can it be that Thomas Carlyle, soon to chemically dissolve in ashes and by winds, remains an identity still? In ways perhaps eluding all the statements, lore and speculations of ten thousand years—eluding all possible statements to mortal sense—does he yet exist, a definite, vital being, a spirit, an individual—perhaps now wafted in space among those stellar systems, which, suggestive and limitless as they are, merely edge more limitless, far more suggestive systems?

I have no doubt of it. In silence, of a fine night, such questions are answered to the soul, the best answers that can be given. With me too, when depressed by some specially sad event, or tearing problem, I wait till I go out under the stars for the last voiceless satisfaction.

(b)

There is surely at present an inexplicable *rapport* (all the more piquant from its contradictoriness) between that deceas'd author and our United States of America—no matter whether it lasts or not.* As we Westerners assume definite shape, and result in formations and fruitage unknown before, it is curious with what a new sense our eyes turn to representative outgrowths of crises and personages in the Old World. Beyond question, since Carlyle's death, and the publication of Froude's memoirs, not only the interest in his books, but every personal bit regarding the famous Scotchman—his dyspepsia, his buffetings, his parentage, his paragon of a wife, his career in Edinburgh, in the lonesome nest on Craigenputtock moor, and then so many years in London—is probably wider and livelier to-day in this country than in his own land. Whether I succeed or no, I, too, reaching across the Atlantic and taking the man's dark fortune-telling of humanity and politics, would offset it all, (such is the fancy that comes to me,) by a far more profound horoscope-casting of those themes—G. F. Hegel's.†

First, about a chance, a never-fulfill'd vacuity of this pale cast of thought—this British Hamlet from Cheyne row, more puzzling than the Danish one, with his contrivances for settling the broken and spavin'd joints of the world's government, especially its democratic dislocation. Carlyle's grim fate was cast to live and dwell in, and largely embody, the parturition agony and qualms of the old order, amid crowded accumulations of ghastly morbidity, giving birth to the new. But conceive of him (or his parents before him) coming to America,

* It will be difficult for the future—judging by his books, personal dis-sympathies, &c.,—to account for the deep hold this author has taken on the present age, and the way he has color'd its method and thought. I am certainly at a loss to account for it all as affecting myself. But there could be no view, or even partial picture, of the middle and latter part of our Nineteenth century, that did not markedly include Thomas Carlyle. In his case (as so many others, literary productions, works of art, personal identities, events,) there has been an impalpable something more effective than the palpable. Then I find no better text, (it is always important to have a definite, special, even oppositional, living man to start from,) for sending out certain speculations and comparisons for home use. Let us see what they amount to—those reactionary doctrines, fears, scornful analyses of democracy—even from the most erudite and sincere mind of Europe.

† Not the least mentionable part of the case, (a streak, it may be, of that humor with which history and fate love to contrast their gravity,) is that although neither of my great authorities during their lives consider'd the United States worthy of serious mention, all the principal works of both might not inappropriately be this day collected and bound up under the conspicuous title: *Speculations for the use of North America, and Democracy there, with the relations of the same to Metaphysics, including Lessons and Warnings (encouragements too, and of the vastest,) from the Old World to the New.*

recuperated by the cheering realities and activity of our people and country—growing up and delving face-to-face resolutely among us here, especially at the West—inhaling and exhaling our limitless air and eligibilities—devoting his mind to the theories and developments of this Republic amid its practical facts as exemplified in Kansas, Missouri, Illinois, Tennessee, or Louisiana. I say *facts*, and face-to-face confrontings—so different from books, and all those quiddities and mere reports in the libraries, upon which the man (it was wittily said of him at the age of thirty, that there was no one in Scotland who had glean'd so much and seen so little,) almost wholly fed, and which even his sturdy and vital mind but reflected at best.

Something of the sort narrowly escaped happening. In 1835, after more than a dozen years of trial and non-success, the author of *Sartor Resartus* removing to London, very poor, a confirmed hypochondriac, *Sartor* universally scoffed at, no literary prospects ahead, deliberately settled on one last casting throw of the literary dice—resolv'd to compose and launch forth a book on the subject of *The French Revolution*—and if that won no higher guerdon or prize than hitherto, to sternly abandon the trade of author forever, and emigrate for good to America. But the venture turn'd out a lucky one, and there was no emigration.

Carlyle's work in the sphere of literature as he commenced and carried it out, is the same in one or two leading respects that Immanuel Kant's was in speculative philosophy. But the Scotchman had none of the stomachic phlegm and never-perturb'd placidity of the Königsberg sage, and did not, like the latter, understand his own limits, and stop when he got to the end of them. He clears away jungle and poison-vines and underbrush—at any rate hacks valiantly at them, smiting hip and thigh. Kant did the like in his sphere, and it was all he profess'd to do; his labors have left the ground fully prepared ever since—and greater service was probably never perform'd by mortal man. But the pang and hiatus of Carlyle seem to me to consist in the evidence everywhere that amid a whirl of fog and fury and cross-purposes, he firmly believ'd he had a clue to the medication of the world's ills, and that his bounden mission was to exploit it.★

There were two anchors, or sheet-anchors, for steadying, as a last

★ I hope I shall not myself fall into the error I charge upon him, of prescribing a specific for indispensable evils. My utmost pretension is probably but to offset that old claim of the exclusively curative power of first-class individual men, as leaders and rulers, by the claims, and general movement and result, of ideas. Something of the latter kind seems to me the distinctive theory of America, of democracy, and of the modern—or rather, I should say, it *is* democracy, and *is* the modern.

resort, the Carlylean ship. One will be specified presently. The other, perhaps the main, was only to be found in some mark'd form of personal force, an extreme degree of competent urge and will, a man or men 'born to command.' Probably there ran through every vein and current of the Scotchman's blood something that warm'd up to this kind of trait and character above aught else in the world, and which makes him in my opinion the chief celebrater and promulger of it in literature— more than Plutarch, more than Shakspere. The great masses of humanity stand for nothing—at least nothing but nebulous raw material; only the big planets and shining suns for him. To ideas almost invariably languid or cold, a number-one forceful personality was sure to rouse his eulogistic passion and savage joy. In such case, even the standard of duty hereinafter rais'd, was to be instantly lower'd and vail'd. All that is comprehended under the terms republicanism and democracy were distasteful to him from the first, and as he grew older they became hateful and contemptible. For an undoubtedly candid and penetrating faculty such as his, the bearings he persistently ignored were marvellous. For instance, the promise, nay certainty of the democratic principle, to each and every State of the current world, not so much of helping it to perfect legislators and executives, but as the only effectual method for surely, however slowly, training people on a large scale toward voluntarily ruling and managing themselves (the ultimate aim of political and all other development)—to gradually reduce the fact of *governing* to its minimum, and to subject all its staffs and their doings to the telescopes and microscopes of committees and parties—and greatest of all, to afford (not stagnation and obedient content, which went well enough with the feudalism and ecclesiasticism of the antique and medieval world, but) a vast and sane and recurrent ebb and tide action for those floods of the great deep that have henceforth palpably burst forever their old bounds—seem never to have enter'd Carlyle's thought. It was splendid how he refus'd any compromise to the last. He was curiously antique. In that harsh, picturesque, most potent voice and figure, one seems to be carried back from the present of the British islands more than two thousand years, to the range between Jerusalem and Tarsus. His fullest best biographer justly says of him:

He was a teacher and a prophet, in the Jewish sense of the word. The prophecies of Isaiah and Jeremiah have become a part of the permanent spiritual inheritance of mankind, because events proved that they had interpreted correctly the sign of their own times, and their prophecies were fulfill'd. Carlyle, like them, believ'd that he had a special message to deliver to the present age. Whether he was correct in that belief, and whether his message was a true message, remains to be seen. He has told us that our most cherish'd ideas of political liberty, with their kindred corollaries, are mere illusions, and that the progress which has seem'd to go along with them is a progress towards anarchy and social dissolution. If he was wrong, he has misused his powers. The principles of his teachings are false. He has offer'd himself as a guide upon a road of which he had no knowledge; and his own desire for himself would be the speediest oblivion both of his person and his works. If, on the other hand, he has been right; if, like his great predecessors, he has read truly the tendencies of this modern age of ours, and his teaching is authenticated by facts, then Carlyle, too, will take his place among the inspired seers.

To which I add an amendment that under no circumstances, and no matter how completely time and events disprove his lurid vaticinations, should the English-speaking world forget this man, nor fail to hold in honor his unsurpass'd conscience, his unique method, and his honest fame. Never were convictions more earnest and genuine. Never was there less of a flunkey or temporizer. Never had political progressivism a foe it could more heartily respect.

The second main point of Carlyle's utterance was the idea of *duty being done*. (It is simply a new codicil—if it be particularly new, which is by no means certain—on the time-honor'd bequest of dynasticism, the mould-eaten rules of legitimacy and kings.) He seems to have been impatient sometimes to madness when reminded by persons who thought at least as deeply as himself, that this formula, though precious, is rather a vague one, and that there are many other considerations to a philosophical estimate of each and every department either in general history or individual affairs.

Altogether, I don't know anything more amazing than these persistent strides and throbbings so far through our Nineteenth century of perhaps its biggest, sharpest, and most erudite brain, in defiance and discontent with everything; contemptuously ignoring, (either from constitutional inaptitude, ignorance itself, or more likely because he demanded a definite cure-all here and now,) the only solace and solvent to be had.

There is, apart from mere intellect, in the make-up of every superior human identity, (in its moral completeness, considered as *ensemble*, not for that moral alone, but for the whole being, including physique,) a wondrous something that realizes without argument, frequently without what is called education, (though I think it the goal and apex of all education deserving the name)—an intuition of the absolute balance, in time and space, of the whole of this multifarious, mad chaos of fraud, frivolity, hoggishness—this revel of fools, and incredible make-believe and general unsettledness, we call *the world;* a soul-sight of that divine clue and unseen thread which holds the whole congeries of things, all history and time, and all events, however trivial, however momentous, like a leash'd dog in the hand of the hunter. Such soul-sight and root-centre for the mind—mere optimism explains only the surface or fringe of it—Carlyle was mostly, perhaps entirely without. He seems instead to have been haunted in the play of his mental action by a spectre, never entirely laid from first to last, (Greek scholars, I believe, find the same mocking and fantastic apparition attending Aristophanes, his comedies,)—the spectre of world-destruction.

How largest triumph or failure in human life, in war or peace, may depend on some little hidden centrality, hardly more than a drop of blood, a pulse-beat, or a breath of air! It is certain that all these weighty matters, democracy in America, Carlyleism, and the temperament for deepest political or literary exploration, turn on a simple point in speculative philosophy.

The most profound theme that can occupy the mind of man—the problem on whose solution science, art, the bases and pursuits of nations, and everything else, including intelligent human happiness, (here to-day, 1882, New York, Texas, California, the same as all times, all lands,) subtly and finally resting, depends for competent outset and argument, is doubtless involved in the query: What is the fusing explanation and tie—what the relation between the (radical, democratic) Me, the human identity of understanding, emotions, spirit, &c., on the one side, of and with the (conservative) Not Me, the whole of the material objective universe and laws, with what is behind them in time and space, on the other side? Immanuel Kant, though he explain'd or partially explain'd, as may be said, the laws of the human understanding, left this question an open one. Schelling's answer, or suggestion of answer, is (and very valuable and important as far as it goes,) that the same general and particular intelligence, passion, even the standards of right and wrong, which exist in a conscious and formulated state in man, exist in an unconscious state, or in perceptible analogies, throughout the entire universe of external Nature, in all its objects large or small, and all its movements and processes—thus making the impalpable human mind, and concrete nature, notwithstanding their duality and separation, convertible, and in centrality and essence one. But G. F. Hegel's fuller statement of the matter probably remains the last best word that has been said upon it, up to date. Substantially adopting the scheme just epitomized, he so carries it out and fortifies it and merges everything in it, with certain serious gaps now for the first time fill'd, that it becomes a coherent metaphysical system, and substantial answer (as far as there can be any answer) to the foregoing question—a system which, while I distinctly admit that the brain of the future may add to, revise, and even entirely reconstruct, at any rate beams forth to-day, in its entirety, illuminating the thought of the universe, and satisfying the mystery thereof to the human mind, with a more consoling scientific assurance than any yet.

According to Hegel the whole earth, (an old nucleus-thought, as in the Vedas, and no doubt before, but never hitherto brought so absolutely to the front, fully surcharged with modern scientism and facts, and made the sole entrance to each and all,) with its infinite variety, the past, the surroundings of to-day, or what may happen in the future, the contrarieties of material with spiritual, and of natural with artificial, are all, to the eye of the *ensemblist*, but necessary sides and unfoldings, different steps or links, in the endless process of Creative thought, which, amid numberless apparent failures and contradictions, is held together by central and never-broken unity—not contradictions or failures at all, but radiations of one consistent and eternal purpose; the whole mass of everything steadily, unerringly tending and flowing toward the permanent *utile* and *morale*, as rivers to oceans. As life is the whole law and incessant effort of the visible universe, and death only the other or invisible side of the same, so the *utile*, so truth, so health are the continuous-immutable laws of the moral universe, and vice and disease, with all their perturbations, are but transient, even if ever so prevalent expressions.

To politics throughout, Hegel applies the like catholic standard and faith. Not any one party, or any one form of government, is absolutely and exclusively true. Truth consists in the just relations of objects to each other. A majority or democracy may rule as outrageously and do as great harm as an oligarchy or despotism—though far less likely to do so. But the great evil is either a violation of the relations just referr'd to, or of the moral law. The specious, the unjust, the cruel, and what is called the unnatural, though not only permitted but in a certain sense, (like shade to light,) inevitable in the divine scheme, are by the whole constitution of that scheme, partial, inconsistent, temporary, and though having ever so great an ostensible majority, are certainly destin'd to failures, after causing great suffering.

Theology, Hegel translates into science.* All apparent contradictions in the statement of the Deific nature by different ages, nations, churches, points of view, are but fractional and imperfect expressions of one essential unity, from which they all proceed—crude endeavors or distorted parts, to be regarded both as distinct and united. In short (to put it in our own form, or summing up,) that thinker or analyzer or overlooker who by an inscrutable combination of train'd wisdom and natural intuition most fully accepts in perfect faith the moral unity and sanity of the creative scheme, in history, science, and all life and time, present and future, is both the truest cosmical devotee or religioso, and the profoundest philosopher. While he who, by the spell of himself and his circumstance, sees darkness and despair in the sum of the workings of God's providence, and who, in that, denies or prevaricates, is, no matter how much piety plays on his lips, the most radical sinner and infidel.

I am the more assured in recounting Hegel a little freely here,† not only for offsetting the Carlylean letter and spirit—cutting it out all and several from the very roots, and below the roots—but to counterpoise, since the late death and deserv'd apotheosis of Darwin, the tenets of the revolutionists. Unspeakably precious as those are to biology, and henceforth indispensable to a right aim and estimate in study, they neither comprise or explain everything—and the last word or whisper still remains to be breathed, after the utmost of those claims, floating high and forever above them all, and above technical metaphysics. While the contributions which German Kant and Fichte and Schelling and Hegel have bequeath'd to humanity—and which English Darwin has also in his field—are indispensable to the erudition of America's future, I should say that in all of them, and the best of them, when compared with the lightning flashes and flights of the old prophets and *exaltés*, the spiritual poets and poetry of all lands, (as in the Hebrew Bible,) there seems to be, nay certainly is, something lacking—something cold, a failure to satisfy the deepest emotions of the soul—a want of living glow,

---

* I am much indebted to J. Gostick's abstract.

† I have deliberately repeated it all, not only in offset to Carlyle's ever-lurking pessimism and world-decadence, but as presenting the most thoroughly *American points of view* I know. In my opinion the above formulas of Hegel are an essential and crowning justification of New World democracy in the creative realms of time and space. There is that about them which only the vastness, the multiplicity and the vitality of America would seem able to comprehend, to give scope and illustration to, or to be fit for, or even originate. It is strange to me that they were born in Germany, or in the old world at all. While a Carlyle, I should say, is quite the legitimate European product to be expected.

fondness, warmth, which the old *exaltés* and poets supply, and which the keenest modern philosophers so far do not.

Upon the whole, and for our purposes, this man's name certainly belongs on the list with the just-specified, first-class moral physicians of our current era—and with Emerson and two or three others—though his prescription is drastic, and perhaps destructive, while theirs is assimilating, normal and tonic. Feudal at the core, and mental offspring and radiation of feudalism as are his books, they afford ever-valuable lessons and affinities to democratic America. Nations or individuals, we surely learn deepest from unlikeness, from a sincere opponent, from the light thrown even scornfully on dangerous spots and liabilities. (Michel Angelo invoked heaven's special protection against his friends and affectionate flatterers; palpable foes he could manage for himself.) In many particulars Carlyle was indeed, as Froude terms him, one of those far-off Hebraic utterers, a new Micah or Habbakuk. His words at times bubble forth with abysmic inspiration. Always precious, such men; as precious now as any time. His rude, rasping, taunting, contradictory tones—what ones are more wanted amid the supple, polish'd, money-worshipping, Jesus-and-Judas-equalizing, suffrage-sovereignty echoes of current America? He has lit up our Nineteenth century with the light of a powerful, penetrating, and perfectly honest intellect of the first class, turn'd on British and European politics, social life, literature, and representative personages—thoroughly dissatisfied with all, and mercilessly exposing the illness of all. But while he announces the malady, and scolds and raves about it, he himself, born and bred in the same atmosphere, is a mark'd illustration of it.

40. Unsigned obituary, *Saturday Review*

12 February 1881, 199–200

Founded in 1855, this liberal but critical review became one of the most important weeklies of the nineteenth century. Begun after Carlyle's career had passed its zenith, the *Saturday* did manage to notice Carlyle's later publications, namely *Frederick the Great*, 'Shooting Niagara', and re-issues of old works. Often opposed to Carlyle's over-emphasis of the hero, the *Saturday* nevertheless began to recognize his qualities as an artist. In the first thirteen years most of the reviews of Carlyle were done by Fitzjames Stephen or G. S. Venables, both of whom were friends and frequent visitors of Carlyle.

The death of Mr. Carlyle will have caused, notwithstanding his advanced age, a widespread feeling of regret. Not only his friends, but those who knew him only by his writings, found themselves connected with him by a kind of personal association. Other men of genius put the best of themselves into their works, which thenceforth possess a detached and independent existence. Carlyle, though he was, in the opinion of many capable judges, the greatest writer of his time, always seemed to be a living teacher, or, as he has often been called, a prophet. His revelations were, like the chapters of the Koran, occasional and fragmentary, always characteristic and essentially consistent, but containing no body of systematic doctrine. He has inspired and modified the mode of thought rather than the opinions of one or two generations; but the imitators of his mannerism are not to be counted among his genuine disciples. More than one thoughtful essayist has within the last few days attempted, with more or less success, to define his theological and ethical convictions. They undoubtedly derived their form, and in some degree their substance, from the Calvinistic belief of his early youth; but it was not his habit or the tendency of his intellect to embody his creed in formal propositions. Though his conception of the moral order of the world may be called dynamic, unfriendly critics who accused him of deifying force were wholly mistaken. He was never tired of asserting the right of a hero to compel the obedience of ordinary men, but always on the condition that he was a hero, and not a vulgar despot. His own judgment in the selection of heroes was not infallible, but it excluded mere tyrants and usurpers. His contempt for the claim of license to do wrong blinded him in some degree to the advantages of liberty. His ruling principle is perhaps best expressed in the old formula τὸ κράτος τῷ κρείττονι,[1] a phrase which cannot be at the same time literally and adequately translated into English, because the Greek word means at the same time better and stronger. Carlyle entertained little respect for the first Napoleon, who was the most perfect modern representative of material force. Napoleon III. in the height of his prosperity and power always appeared to Carlyle a vulgar charlatan. His admiration for Cromwell and, in a less degree, for Frederick the Great was but incidentally connected with a disposition to glorify success. In his estimation a martyr might be the equal of the best of conquerors. One of the most eloquent passages in his works is the imaginary description of the canonization of Edmund, the East Anglian King and martyr.

In this manner did the men of the Eastern Counties take up the slain body of their Edmund, where it lay cast forth in the village of Hoxne; seek out the severed head and reverently reunite the same. They embalmed him with myrrh and sweet spices, with love, pity, and all high and awful thoughts; consecrating him with a very storm of melodious, adoring admiration, and sun-dried showers of tears; joyfully, yet with awe (as all deep joy has something of the awful in it), commemorating his noble deeds and godlike walk and conversation while on Earth. Till, at length, the very Pope and Cardinals at Rome were forced to hear of it; and they, summing up as correctly as they well could, with *Advocatus Diaboli* pleadings and other forms of process, the general verdict of mankind, declared that he had in very fact led a hero's life in this world; and, being now gone, was gone, as they conceived, to God above and reaping his reward there. Such, they said, was the best judgment they could form of the case, and truly not a bad judgment.[2]

The apotheosis of the semi-mythical St. Edmund may be set off against some capricious eulogies of such despots as Frederick William I. and the Dictator Francia; and it may be admitted that Carlyle was not always superior to the temptation of paradox. His political sympathies

[1] Plato, *Republic*, Bk. I, 'The power to the stronger'.
[2] *Past and Present*, Bk. II, ch. iii, 55-6.

became less and less revolutionary as he grew older. In *Sartor Resartus* there is a strong tendency to Communism, and in *Chartism* he still regards universal suffrage as a right, if not as an expedient arrangement. In later years he utterly distrusted the judgment of the multitude, which, in his opinion, needed guidance and discipline much more than political power. His estimate of men was often extraordinarily sagacious, though the severity of his judgment was not unfrequently qualified by the influence of social relations. His dislike of Sir Robert Peel, whom he had ungraciously ridiculed as Sir Jabesh Windbag, was exchanged for sincere respect and esteem when he made his acquaintance in a house where they both were frequent guests. His feelings towards other statesmen of his time may probably have been affected by similar circumstances, for he was the most genial, though not the most tolerant, of men.

There are still many persons, not without literary cultivation, to whom Carlyle's manner is distasteful; and it may be admitted that he would in many cases have done better in adopting a pedestrian and ordinary style; but the habit of regarding all things from his own special point of view had become inveterate, and his language accurately represented his imagination and his humour. The Lowland Scotch, which was his mother-tongue, was the basis of his well-known diction. He borrowed some of his peculiarities from German, though the influence on his method of Jean Paul Richter, who was himself through one or two descents a follower of Sterne, has sometimes been exaggerated. Of Carlyle, if not of other writers, the saying is true, that the style is the man. That it was perfectly natural was sufficiently proved by the fact that he spoke exactly as he wrote, though, if possible, with more uniform brilliancy and force. Those who had the good fortune to be admitted to his society are almost unanimous in their opinion that his powers of conversation, or rather of familiar speech, were in their experience unequalled; yet it is intelligible that Luttrell, a witty diner-out of a past generation, should have been unable to appreciate Carlyle's originality. If he sometimes engrossed a large share of attention, the freshness of his fancy and the flow of his humour were alike inexhaustible. His imagination was so plastic that he could scarcely describe the commonest object without notice of some characteristic feature or picturesque peculiarity. It is to be hoped that some of his friends have preserved reminiscences of his descriptive or epigrammatic language; but it would be impossible to reproduce his spontaneous abundance of illustration. He denounced one of his friends who, with a purpose as humorous as his own, challenged him by affecting a tone of moral indifference, as fit to be President of the Heaven and Hell Amalgamation Society. He assured a member of Parliament who, with a similar object, excused a vote on the pretence of deferring to the wish of his constituents, that at the day of judgment the excuse would not serve. 'It will be you that will be damned, and not your constituents.' He once interrupted a eulogy which he considered excessive on an eminent economist, for whom he had nevertheless a sincere regard, by declaring that he was 'an inspired bagman who believed in a calico millennium'; but isolated fragments of talk accidentally retained in the memory are little better than fragmentary specimens of some great work of architecture. In conversation, as in literary composition, he sometimes caused an irritation which was scarcely justifiable by steadily declining controversy. His hearers or readers were welcome to learn what he had to tell them; but he neither answered objections nor engaged in discussion. Those who differed from him were at liberty to hold their own opinions, but not to extract from him reasons which were inseparably connected with his feelings and his character. It would have required some obtuseness of perception not to recognize in personal intercourse his intellectual and moral elevation. His friends would sometimes have gladly received an interpretation of the meaning of the oracle; but they were compelled to be content with the responses. They could always count in turn on his ready appreciation of their thoughts, and on his hearty laughter.

Carlyle's rank as a moral teacher and a humorist has sometimes interfered with the recognition of his laborious study of historical facts. His minute industry is most remarkably exhibited in the *Memoirs of Cromwell* and in the *Life of Frederick the Great*. The plan of the *Life of Cromwell* was borrowed from Mr. Spedding, though the *Life of Bacon* was published at a later period. The scheme is exhaustive, but it has a tendency to be tedious; and, as a rule, the historian ought not to submit the raw material of his studies to the reader. The Remains of Cromwell are, fortunately, limited in bulk, and they receive a meaning and a kind of unity from Carlyle's suggestive comments. Even the chaotic, but not frivolous, speeches of the Protector are strangely illuminated by occasional interpolations, such as 'Hear, hear, your Highness.' It is true that the biographer is not exempt from an idolatry which suggests and justifies a certain scepticism in accepting his conclusions; but no other historian has made the character of Cromwell so consistent and so intelligible. For his later hero Carlyle's sympathy was far less perfect, and the history of Frederick's early years is told in unnecessary detail, while the twenty years during which he survived the Seven Years' War are slurred over in a few pages; but the history of Prussia in the first volume is an admirable specimen of concise narrative; and scarcely any writer has described battles so intelligibly, though Carlyle was otherwise unacquainted with military affairs. He has scarcely communicated to his English readers his own qualified admiration for his hero; but it must be remembered that all patriotic Germans feel an enthusiasm for Frederick and even a certain gratitude to his unattractive father.

The merits of Carlyle's prose epic on the French Revolution are of a different and of a higher order. The only copy of the first volume of the book was destroyed by an accident, and Carlyle always believed that the version which he was compelled to substitute was inferior to the original; but it is difficult to believe that the brilliant and pathetic narrative which remains could have been surpassed. There are fuller accounts of the Revolution, but many students remember the principal events most vividly by reference to the history which made them more interesting than scenes in a romance. His half-serious excuse for the people which always found itself baffled on the verge of an expected Paradise is perhaps the best apology for the crimes and follies of the Revolution. His admiration for Mirabeau is more justifiable than his characteristic tenderness for Danton. The chief author of the massacres of September was perhaps to be preferred to his successful rival; but the narrow pedantry of Robespierre, which excited the contemptuous aversion of Carlyle, was a venial aggravation of the guilt of the most murderous of tyrants. The *History of the French Revolution* first made Carlyle popular, and perhaps taught him his true vocation; but before and after its publication he exercised a wide influence by his contributions to literary criticism. His 'Essay on Voltaire' displayed a remarkable power of appreciating both the merits and defects of the most typical of Frenchmen. The review of Croker's edition of Boswell has finally exploded the shallow prejudices against Johnson and his biographer which culminated about the same time in Macaulay's shallow and paradoxical criticism. The study of German literature in England has been more effectually promoted by Carlyle's early writings than by any other single cause. His devotion to the person and genius of Goethe is difficult to reconcile with his later predilections, for he was in after life not an enthusiastic admirer of poetry, or of literary eminence; and Goethe's sublime indifference to national interests and to other disturbing elements might have been thought uncongenial to the temperament of his devoted admirer. The impression produced by the great German writer was as permanent as it was profound. Long after he had entered on other fields of intellectual activity, Carlyle retained his original reverence for his master. Some correspondence had passed between them; but Goethe received coldly the overtures of his young admirer, who would willingly have made a pilgrimage to Weimar. No modern English writer is now so well known in Germany, which Carlyle always seemed to regard as a second mother country. Foreigners are probably less sensitive than English readers to the peculiarities of style. On the other hand, they are more likely to overlook or misinterpret his incessant employment of humour. In common with some other authors, he received general recognition in America earlier than in England; and his only successful imitator is a popular American essayist. In other copies his manner, denuded of his humorous imagination, becomes tedious and distasteful. It would be idle in a limited space to attempt even imperfectly to analyse Carlyle's peculiar and original powers. He had happily time and opportunity to indulge his genius to the full. His simple habits enabled him to choose for himself in dignified seclusion the subjects of his indefatigable literary labours. Whatever is incomplete in his works corresponds to the instinctive or deliberate limitations which he imposed on himself. It may be repeated that Carlyle was not a philosopher, but a prophet.

41. Edward Dowden, obituary, *Academy*

12 February 1881, 117–18

Edward Dowden (1843–1913), educated at Queen's College, Cork, and Trinity College, Dublin, was one of a company of important literary critics of the late nineteenth century. He is perhaps best remembered for his work on Shakespeare, in particular *Shakespeare: His Mind and His Art* (1875). His most ambitious work was the *Life of Shelley* (1886). The complete obituary is included. See Introduction, p. 22.

The old, inevitable commonplace of death repeats itself; another voice silent for ever; another face veiled by the shadow. That a man of fourscore and six years should prove mortal does not carry surprise to any heart. Yet the event, always uniform in certain superficial incidents, varies to the spiritual eyes as much as sunsets vary in their fiery intensities, or solemn splendours, or calm acquiescence of decline. Had we among us one of such visionary faculty as William Blake in his lucid moods, a veritable seer, to represent the reality of what has happened he would show us no poor worn-out body on its bier, but a dead prophet whose venerable form is still instinct with miraculous power— a prophet who was also a pilgrim, his pilgrim staff now laid along, having ended his wayfaring and finished his course; nor should we be unaware of spiritual presences at the head and feet, sorrowing, yet fervently aspiring.

Carlyle's prime influence was a religious one; he was a preacher before he was a critic or an historian. James Carlyle, one of 'the fighting masons of Ecclefechan,' not only could lay the stones straight and firm, but, as a member of the Relief Church, had doubtless a Scottish clearness and vigour in matters of the faith, and, we are informed, loved to read old books which told of Reformation times and the deeds of the Covenanters. It was intended that Thomas, his eldest son, should be a minister of the Church. A brilliant French critic has called Carlyle a Puritan, and Carlyle himself described Puritanism as 'the last of our

Heroisms.' His heritage of faith was indeed transformed, but it was never cast away. To view life, at times sadly, at times sternly, and always seriously, is the Puritan habit, and it was Carlyle's, only relieved by the sudden tenderness of his heart, and by his humour as an artist, often almost Aristophanic, before which the whole world would appear in a moment as a huge farce-tragedy. To bear about with us an abiding sense of the infinite issues of human existence is a part of Puritanism. Poor, indeed, is this little life of man for pleasure or for pride; yet of measureless worth, since heaven and hell environ it. Each deed, each moment is related to Eternity. God and the devil, one at odds with the other, are not names, but terrible realities; righteousness and sin stand apart from one another by the whole diameter. On whose side does each of us find himself? The many are foolish, slumbering and sleeping, hearing no cry in the night. The wise are few, ever ready, with the loins girt and the lamp lit.

But Puritanism, in its desire to fortify the moral will, contracts the sensibilities, impoverishes the affections, averts its gaze from half of nature and of human life. How is one of stormy sensibility, to whom all of life is dear, an artist and a poet, a lover of beauty, a lover of strength even when ill-regulated, full of tenderness, pity, wrath; full also, in this new century, of new aspiring thoughts and impulses of revolt—how is such an one to be a Puritan? By his twenty-first year it had become clear to Carlyle that if he were to be a preacher he must preach another gospel than that of the Presbyterian Kirk. And in due time the authentic voice, calling him to be 'a writer of books,' grew audible. He must preach, if at all, through literature.

A broad way in literature for men of passionate temper had been opened by Byron. His victories had followed one another so brilliantly, so rapidly, that only one other career seemed like his—that of Napoleon. He had revolted against a society of decencies and respectability, of social hypocrisies, and moral cant; and with that revolt Carlyle sympathised. He had known the fever of a deep unrest; he had been miserable among negations and extinct faiths; with such unrest, such misery, Carlyle was not unacquainted. In Byron he recognized a certain desperate sincerity, underlying all superficial insincerities. Yet for one who had learnt that 'man's chief end is to glorify God,' who had heard of obedience to a divine will, of service to a divine King, Byron's egoistic revolt, though of service as a protest against the false, seemed to go but a little way towards attaining the liberty of true spiritual manhood. Is no better way possible? Is a religious freedom unattainable? Is it possible to be 'a clear and universal man,' and at the same time a man of faith? Carlyle, like Teufelsdröckh, closed his Byron; like Teufelsdröckh, he opened his Goethe. And in Goethe he found his own problem and the problem of his time solved. 'The question,' he writes in his essay on Goethe's works, 'Can man still live in devoutness, yet without blindness or contraction; in unconquerable steadfastness for the right, yet without tumultuous exasperation against the wrong; an antique worthy, yet with the expansion and increased endowment of a modern? is no longer a question, but has become a certainty and ocularly visible fact.'

Puritanism had said 'Live resolutely for God in what is good,' but Puritanism had narrowed the meaning of the word 'good' as Carlyle henceforth could not narrow it; Puritanism had renounced the experiment of entering the kingdom of heaven otherwise than maimed and blind. Goethe said, 'Live resolutely a complete human life, in what is good and true, in the whole of things'—*Im Ganzen, Guten, Wahren resolut zu leben.* So the seriousness which is at the heart of Puritanism might grow large, and free, and beautiful. What Carlyle wrote of Goethe was not the mere expression of a literary judgment; he wrote with the sense that it was Goethe who had made it possible for him to live. He did not approach Goethe, like poor Sterling, with questions as to his classification—Was Goethe a Pagan, or a Christian? a Pantheist, or perchance a 'Pot-theist'? He found, or thought he found, in Goethe a complete, heroic, modern man. 'Carlyle breakfasted with me,' wrote Crabb Robinson in 1832,

and I had an interesting morning with him. . . . His voice and manner, and even the style of his conversation, are those of a religious zealot, and he keeps up that character in his declamations against the anti-religious. And yet, if not the god of his idolatry, at least he has a priest and prophet of his church in Goethe, of whose profound wisdom he speaks like an enthusiast. *But for him, Carlyle says, he should not now be alive. He owes everything to him*!

Those were happy days in the moorland solitude of Craigenputtoch, when, having conquered the egoistic despair of youth, and found in renunciation and a wise limited activity his 'Everlasting Yea,' Carlyle moved with a free, courageous step through untrodden regions of literature, and was for a time a prophet of joy and hope. He talked to De Quincey of founding a 'Misanthropic Society,' its members uniting to 'hurl forth their defiance, pity, expostulation over the whole universe, civil, literary, and religious.' But in truth he was no Timon; around him was the solitude which nourished his soul—

a solitude altogether Druidical—grim hills tenanted chiefly by wild grouse, tarns and brooks that have soaked and slumbered unmolested since the deluge of Noah, and nothing to disturb you with speech, except Arcturus and Orion, and the Spirit of Nature, in the heaven and in the earth, as it manifests itself in anger or love, and utters its inexplicable tidings, unheard by the mortal ear.

But, adds this misanthrope, 'the misery is the almost total want of colonists.' Yet, when he returned to his fireside, there was sufficient human society in the wife, whose 'soft invincibility, capacity of discernment, and noble loyalty of heart' were to stand him in stead during forty years; in her, and in that pile upon his library table, eyed with the pride of a young literary athlete—'such a quantity of German periodicals and mystic speculation, embosomed in plain Scottish *Peat-moor*, being nowhere else that I know of to be met with.'

In full manhood, and with none of the edges of his individuality worn away, Carlyle removed in 1834 from the solitude with society of Craigenputtoch to the society with deeper solitude of London. His experiment of public lectures, though deeply interesting to those who were present (and they, if few—sometimes one hundred—were a fit audience), could not please himself. One constitutionally shy and nervous finds his bodily presence a slight but difficult barrier between his spirit and the spirits on which his influence should play; moreover, from the time a course was announced till it was finished, we are told, Carlyle scarcely slept. The American Ticknor, who found the lecture impressive and picturesque, saw before him 'rather a small, spare, ugly Scotchman, with a strong accent.' And even his warm-hearted friend Harriet Martineau, to whom Carlyle's rugged face appeared always 'steeped in genius,' had her courage dashed by the lecturer's evident anxiety and distress: 'Yellow as a guinea, with downcast eyes, broken speech at the beginning, and fingers which nervously picked at the desk before him, he could not for a moment be supposed to enjoy his own effort.' After the fourth annual experiment it became clear that thenceforward Thomas Carlyle was to be, if anything, what he names himself in his Petition on the Copyright Bill, 'a writer of books.'

In temperament Carlyle differed widely from his master, Goethe. When he came from his Northern solitude to London his age was the same as that of Goethe in the year of his return from Italy to Weimar. In solitude or congenial society, freed from the multifarious cares of a great public servant, delivering his heart from the exaltation of an ideal passion which could not transform itself into duty and happiness nor into creative activity, surrounded by the marble aristocracy of antique art, Goethe in Rome attained a serenity of vision and a comprehensive definiteness of purpose which some have described as resulting in a *refroidissement* of his genius. Carlyle, combative as a son of one of 'the fighting masons of Ecclefechan' must needs be, with stormy sensitiveness pained by all the griefs and wrongs and follies of the time, lost such serenity as had been his in his moorland home, saw in tempestuous vision the old Puritan conflict between the powers of hell and heaven renewing itself in our modern world, and could not choose but show forth his vision, announce the woes that were coming on the earth, and declare, to those who had ears to hear, the all-but impossible way of salvation for society. 'The savageness which has come to be a main characteristic of this singular man is, in my opinion,' wrote Harriet Martineau, 'a mere expression of his intolerable sympathy with the suffering.' Goethe's wide and luminous view is, like that of Shakspere in his last period, a gazing down upon human life from some clear outpost on the heights. Carlyle, with marred visage and rent prophetic robe, is hurtled hither and thither in the tumult of the throng. It is for his fellows that he enters the tumult; for his own part, could he but stand alone, his feet are established on a rock.

From the prophets we do not get the *axiomata media* of wise living, individual or social. They tell of righteousness, mercy, and judgment to come. Others of trained intelligence must apply their doctrine to life. Carlyle helped to make us feel that the issues of our time for evil or for good are momentous; that the chasm between truth and falsehood, between right and wrong, is sheer and of infinite depth; that all things do not of necessity tend from bad to good; that, on the contrary, bad often grows to worse; that a nation, by faithlessness and folly, may indeed go straight to the devil; that each bit of needful work done soundly, honestly, contributes to avert that catastrophe. This was an awakening piece of nineteenth-century prophecy. But how to find the truth? how to distinguish, in the complex material of life, between good and evil? how to attain the right? Worship of heroes (sometimes of questionable heroism), government by the Best (but where to find them?), drilling of Democracy (which will surely drill itself in the only effectual ways)—these suggestions did not greatly serve to make our path clear. The patient intellect of man had pursued other methods leading to other results. These were indignantly exploded by our trans-cendental prophet as the manufacture of logic-mills, fragments of the Dismal Science, leavings of the Pig Philosophy, wisdom of National Palaver, and such like. Happily, it was among the elemental forces of individual character that Carlyle wrought with chief power; his influence, therefore, without losing its virtue, could submit to manifold transformations. Many a democrat will acknowledge Carlyle's influence as having inspired his conduct with faithfulness and courage. Many a Utilitarian will confess that the reviler of the Pig Philosophy has been his chief spiritual master.

Carlyle's transcendentalism was part of the spirit of his time, part of the reaction moral, intellectual, and imaginative against the eighteenth century. The Carlylean transcendentalism derived its unique character from the Scottish Peat-moor, 'Druidical Solitude,' 'speech only of Arcturus, Orion, and the Spirit of Nature'—from these mingling with influences from that pile of 'German periodicals and mystic speculation' upon his library table. He needed a vast background, Immensities, Eternities, through which might wander 'the passion-winged ministers of thought,' Wonder, and Awe, and Adoration. But in the foreground of clear perception and sane activity, all was limited, definite, concrete. From Goethe he had learnt, what, indeed, his own shrewd Scottish head could well confirm, that to drift nowhither in the Inane is not the highest destiny of a human creature; that, on the contrary, all true expansion comes through limitation, all true freedom through obedience. Hence the rule, 'Do the work that lies nearest to your hand;' hence the preciousness of any fragment of living reality, any atom of significant fact. If Carlyle was a mystic, he was a mystic in the service of what is real and positive. Still the little illuminated spot on which men toil and strive, and love and sorrow, was environed, for Carlyle's imagination, by the Immensities; the day, so bright and dear, wherein men serve or sin, was born from a deep Eternity which swiftly calls it back, engulphs it. From which contrast between the great and the little, the transitory and the eternal, spring many sudden surprises of humour and of pathos, which at length cease to surprise, and grow but too familiar to the reader of Carlyle.

To History, the region of positive, concrete fact, his mind gravitated. As a critic of literature he had done signal service by showing that a passionate sympathy is often needful to attain the ends of justice. The essays on Burns and Johnson are illuminated by fine intelligence, yet less by intelligence than by pity, reverence, and love. While scornfully intolerant of dilettantism and 'the poor Fine Arts,' founded on unveracity, Carlyle had done much to introduce into England the Continental feeling for art and the artist as important factors in human society; but the art of which he spoke must be one founded on true insight into man's life and genuine belief; the artist must possess something more than manipulative dexterity; he must be in some measure a *vates*, whose conscious activity has, underlying it, a deep, unconscious energy. As a literary critic, Carlyle was sometimes perverse; he missed proportions; now and again he would resolutely invert things, and hold them up to mockery, in grotesque disarray. A certain leaven of Puritanism made him impatient of some harmless wiles and graceful pastimes of 'the poor Fine Arts.'

A poet of our century, who was also one of its most admirable prose writers, has told in verse the reproof which he received as rhymer from 'Clio, the strong-eyed Muse.' History pleased Carlyle, for its matter is robust, and yet it may be steeped in sentiment. What he could not endure was to attenuate history to a theory, or to relegate its living, breathing actors to a classification. He would fain lift up a piece of the past whole and unbroken, as a fragment of veritable human experience, with its deep inarticulate suggestions to the conscience and the will. Nothing should be lost, except what is unvital, mere wrappage and encumbrance of history. Working as an artist, with an idea of the whole, and a genius for distinguishing essentials from non-essentials in the myriad of details, the historian must attempt the almost impossible feat of rivalling reality, of presenting things in succession so that they may live in the imagination as simultaneous, since once they were so in fact; of presenting a *series* so that it may be recognized as a *group*. Much that is characteristic in Carlyle's work as historian has its origin in the marvellously quick and keen glance of his eye, his power of reading off some minute visible incident into its invisible meaning, and thus interpreting character by picturesque signs and symbols, together with the studiously elaborated style which quickens and exalts the reader's sensitiveness almost to the point of disease, playing upon every nerve-centre with snapping sparks of a new kind of electricity, until he tingles between pleasure and pain. The strain in Carlyle's writing is caused by his desperate resolve to produce in narrative, which, as he says, is *linear*, the effect of action, which is *solid*.

It is not in acted as it is in written History: actual events are nowise so simply related to each other as parent and offspring are; every single event is the off-spring not of one but of all other events, prior or contemporaneous, and will in its turn combine with all others to give birth to new: it is an ever-living, ever-working Chaos of Being, wherein shape after shape bodies itself forth from innumerable elements.

In other writers we may read more correctly the causes and the effects of the French Revolution. If we would enter the suck of the maëlstrom and explore its green-glimmering terror we must accompany Carlyle.

From the work which endures our thoughts return to the man whom we have lost. To the spiritual eye a prophet and a pilgrim; but perhaps, more than all else, a soldier—the last in our time of the Ironsides. His heart, a well-spring of living tenderness; his pity, fine and piercing; his laughter, sudden and deep, at times even stupendous. Yet his best praise is that of a plain and faithful soldier in the warfare of man's life, and more particularly of life in this our century. We would turn away to our own toil and strife with a courageous thought, as he would bid us were it possible, and it cannot be better uttered than in words of his:

He that has an eye and a heart can even now say, Why should I falter? Light has come into the world; to such as love Light, and as Light must be loved, with a boundless all-doing, all-enduring love. For the rest, let that vain struggle to read the mystery of the Infinite cease to harass us. It is a mystery which, through all ages, we shall only read here a line of, there another line of. Do we not already know that the name of the Infinite is GOOD, is GOD? Here on earth we are as Soldiers, fighting in a foreign land; that understand not the plan of the campaign, and have no need to understand it; seeing well what is at our hand to be done. Let us do it like Soldiers, with submission, with courage, with a heroic joy. 'Whatsoever thy hand findeth to do, do it with all thy might.' Behind us, behind each one of us, lie Six Thousand Years of human effort, human conquest; before us is the boundless Time, with its as yet uncreated and unconquered Continents and Eldorados, which we, even we, have to conquer, to create; and from the bosom of Eternity there shine for us celestial guiding stars.

42. Leslie Stephen, an unsigned obituary, *Cornhill Magazine*

March 1881, xliii, 349–58

Leslie Stephen (1832–1904), philosopher, man of letters, moun-
taineer, and first editor of the *DNB*, was educated at Eton and
Cambridge. A prolific writer, Stephen contributed many articles
to the *Saturday Review*, *Pall Mall Gazette*, and *Cornhill* of which
he became editor and remained in that post for more than eleven
years. His ambitious *History of English Thought in the Eighteenth
Century* appeared in 1876. Although his interests were primarily
philosophic, his contributions to biography and literary history are
outstanding. For the 'English Men of Letters' series, he wrote
books on Johnson, Pope, Swift, George Eliot, and Hobbes. This
obituary by one of Carlyle's friends is printed in full. See Introduction, p. 22.

I do not propose at the present time to attempt anything like a critical
estimate of the great man who has just passed from our midst. Better
occasions may offer themselves for saying what has to be said in that
direction. For the present it would seem that there is little need of
speech. Much has been written, and not a little admirably written, in
commemoration of the teacher and the message which he delivered to
mankind; as also there has not been wanting the usual snarl of the
cynic irritated by a chorus of eulogy. Even the feeblest of critics could
scarcely fail to catch some of the characteristic features of one of the
most vigorous and strongly-marked types that ever appeared in our
literature. The strongest amongst them would find it hard to exhaust
the full significance of so remarkable a phenomenon. Despair of saying
anything not palpably inadequate or anything not already said by many
writers might suggest the propriety of silence, were it not that in any
review which claims a literary character it might seem unbecoming not
to make some passing act of homage to one who was yesterday our foremost man of letters. To do justice to such a theme we ought to have
been touched by the mantle of the prophet himself. We should have

been masters of the spell wrought by his unique faculty of humorous imagination. When Mr. Carlyle spoke, as he has spoken in so many familiar passages, of the death of a personal friend, or of one of those heroes whom he loved with personal affection, he could thrill us with a pathos peculiar to himself; for no one could adopt more naturally or interpret more forcibly the mood of lofty Stoicism, dominating without deadening the most tender yearning; or enable us at once to recognise the surpassing value of a genuine hero and to feel how dreamlike and transitory all human life appears in presence of the eternal and infinite, and how paltry a thing, in the moments when such glimpses are vouch-safed to us, is the most towering of human ambitions. To express adequately these solemn emotions is the prerogative of men endowed with the true poetic gift. It will be enough for a prosaic critic to recall briefly some of the plain and tangible grounds which justify the pride of his fellow-countrymen—especially of those who follow his calling—in Mr. Carlyle's reputation.

One remark indeed, suggests itself to every one. Carlyle's life would serve for a better comment than even his writings upon his title, 'the hero as man of letters.' And it is in that capacity that I shall venture to consider him very briefly without attempting to examine the special significance or permanent value of his writings. Carlyle, as we all know, indulged in much eloquent declamation upon the merits of silence as compared with speech. Like many other men of literary eminence, he seemed rather to enjoy the depreciation of his own peculiar function. As Scott considered that a mere story-teller or compounder of rhymes was but a poor creature compared with one who played his part on the stage of active life, Carlyle delighted to exalt the merits of the rugged, silent, inarticulate heroes, who used a rougher weapon than the pen, and conquered some fragment of tangible order from the primeval chaos. He idolised Cromwell all the more because the tangle of half intelligible and wholly ungrammatical sentences which the rough-hewn Puritan dashed down upon paper recall the struggles of some huge monster splashing through thick and thin regardless of anything but the shortest road to his end. If Frederick condescended to play at writing verses with Voltaire, it was the pardonable condescension of a great man who could not really for a single instant put the smartest of writers on a level with a genuine king of men. Heartily as Carlyle loved certain great literary teachers, more or less congenial to his own temperament, he always places them on a level distinctly beneath that of statesman or soldier; and as his utterances of this kind often took the form of an unqualified exaltation of silence, it was natural that to some of us he should appear to be guilty of a certain inconsistency. If action were so superior to speech, why not choose the better part himself? Was it not rather extravagant—even for a professed humourist—to pour forth such a torrent of words in order to demonstrate the inutility of words? If he believed in his own doctrine, should he not have preferred to carry a musket or to wield a spade rather than to wear out so vast a quantity of pens and paper? Contempt for literature, though rarely avowed, is one of the commonest sentiments of practical men; but is it not a suicidal creed for a man of letters?

To this, I imagine, Carlyle could have given a very sufficient answer. For, in the first place, he made no special claim upon the respect of mankind in virtue of his office. This task lay in his way to do, and it was not for him to decide whether the task was humble or exalted. Should a man be borne in a station of life, from which the best available outlook was the career of a successful scavenger, let him do his scavenging with a will, as heartily and effectually as possible. In that ideal state of the world when each man will have that to do which he can do most perfectly, the parts will be differently distributed. But in the distracted welter, as Carlyle would have called it, of modern social arrangements, each of us is stuck down at random in his separate niche, and must be content to snatch at such waifs and strays of work as happen to be floated nearest to him by the eddies of the perplexed whirlpool of life. Carlyle at another period might have been a Knox heading a great spiritual movement, or at least a Cameronian preacher stimulating the faith of his brethren under the fire of persecution. Under actual circumstances, no precise post in the army of active workers was open to him; and he was forced to throw in his lot with the loose bands of literary skirmishers each of whom has to fight for his own hand, and to strike in here and there without concert or combination. The duty might not be a very exalted one; but it was that which lay nearest at hand. Had he pleased, however, he might have adopted a stronger line of defence. In truth, it would be interpreting a humourist too strictly if we mistook his intense jets of scorn or exhortation for the measured language of prosaic admonition. He did not really mean to assert that silence was better than speech, absolutely and unconditionally; for that would be something very like nonsense; nor, again, to declare that the influence which reaches us through the spoken word is essentially inferior to that which breathes from the accomplished deed. For there are words which are among the best of deeds; as there are certainly

483

deeds which ought properly to be classified amongst the emptiest of words. The fribbler and busybody is certainly not the more tolerable because he does not exhale in mere talk but is absorbed in a round of petty activity which hinders what it seems to help, or in painfully building up structures which crumble before they are finished. And, as clearly, we must reckon as amongst the most potent of rulers, the men who have spoken a word in season and welded together the vague, unguided aspirations of mankind into a force capable of overthrowing empires and reconstructing societies. The sentiment which really animated Carlyle—to which he gave at times grotesque or extravagant expressions, was simply the expression of a nature marked, perhaps, by some Puritanical narrowness, but glowing with genuine zeal and animated by the deepest possible sense of the solemnity and seriousness of life. The qualities which he admired with his whole soul were force of will, intensity of purpose, exclusive devotion to some worthy end. What he hated from the bottom of his heart were any practices tending to dissipate the energy which might have accomplished great things or to allow it to expend itself upon unreal objects. We may remember, to quote one amongst a thousand instances, his references to that remarkable religious reformer, Ram Dass, who declared himself to have fire enough in his belly to burn up the sins of the whole world. A man, according to his view, is valuable in proportion as he has a share of that sacred fire. We are tempted unfortunately to use it up merely for cooking purposes, or to turn it to account for idle pyrotechnical displays. He is the greatest who uses the fire for its legitimate purposes and in whom it burns with the whitest and most concentrated heat. Perhaps in enforcing this doctrine from every possible point of view, Carlyle may have shown some want of appreciation for certain harmless and agreeable modes of dissipating energy. The Puritan in grain—and certainly the name applies to no one if not to Carlyle—finds a difficulty in coming to an understanding with the lover of a wider culture. But, in any case, it is not really a question between the means of speech and of action, but between those who have and those who have not an overpowering sense of the paramount importance of the ends to be obtained.

Now it may be fairly said that Carlyle's words have in this sense the quality of deeds. Intensity is the cardinal virtue of his style. The one essential thing with him is to make a deep impression; he must strike at the heart of the hearers and grasp at once the central truth to be inculcated; he cares less than nothing for the rules of art so long as he can gain his end; and will snatch at any weapons in his power, whether he

is to be grotesque or sublime, tender or cynical in expression, or to produce an effect not capable of being tabulated under any critical category.
The blemishes as well as the surpassing merits of his writings spring
equally from a characteristic which naturally makes him unintelligible
and at times offensive to men of different temperaments. Now whatever the literary consequences, the man's own personality derived from
it a singular impressiveness. Great men are sometimes disappointing;
but no one could possibly be disappointed who made a pilgrimage to
the little house in Chelsea. It is a feeble expression of the truth to say that
the talk resembled the writing; it seemed more frequently to be the
quintessence of this writing. Ever afterwards, if you took up *Sartor
Resartus* or the *French Revolution*, you seemed to have learnt the inevitable cadence of the sentences; you heard the solemn passages rolled
out in the strong current of broad Scotch, and the grotesque phrases
recalled the sudden flash of the deep-set eyes and the huge explosions of
tremendous laughter full of intense enjoyment, and yet dashed with an
undertone of melancholy; or you saw the bent frame in its queer old
dressing-gown, taking the pipe from its lips and rapping out some
thundering denunciation of modern idols with more than Johnsonian
vigour. You came to understand how the oddities which strike some
hasty readers as savouring of affectation really expressed the inmost
nature of the man; and that the strange light cast upon the world
represented the way in which objects spontaneously presented themselves to his singularly constituted imagination. Instead of fancying that
he had gradually learnt a queer dialect in order to impress his readers,
you came to perceive that the true process was one of gradually learning
to trust his natural voice where he had at first thought it necessary to
array himself more or less in the conventional costume of ordinary
mortals. Briefly it became manifest that the contortions of the Sibyl (to
quote Burke's phrase about Johnson) was the effect of a genuine
inspiration, and the very reverse of external oddities adopted of *malice
prepense*.

The character had thus a power quite independent of the special
doctrines asserted. One proof of Carlyle's extraordinary power was the
influence which he exercised upon men who differed from him
diametrically upon speculative questions. Nobody, for example,
represented the very antithesis to his doctrines more distinctly than
J. S. Mill. Benthamism and the whole philosophy in which Mill
believed were among the favourite objects of Carlyle's denunciation.
Yet Mill admits in his Autobiography that he did not feel himself

competent to judge Carlyle; that he read the *Sartor Resartus* 'with enthusiastic admiration and the keenest delight,' and felt towards the author as the reasoner who 'hobbles' along by proof should feel to the poetic seer who perceives by intuition. And many, I believe, of Mill's disciples would be found to owe even more to the stimulus received from their dogmatic opponent than to the direct teaching of their more congenial master. Nobody, indeed, could have gone to Carlyle in order to discuss the evidence of some disputed theory, to balance conflicting considerations, or clear up a point which required dispassionate examination and delicate reasoning. Disciple or antagonist, you had to sit at his feet, to refrain from anything bordering remotely upon argument, and simply to submit to the influence of a nature of extraordinary power and profound convictions. From such a man perhaps more is to be learnt by those who differ than by those who humbly follow. It is rarely good for any man to be fairly overpowered and swept away in the current of another man's thoughts, however lofty their import; and it was as well to have some independent source of mental influence before taking a strong dose of philosophy according to Carlyle. And perhaps, if I may say so, it was by comparing the man with his ardent disciples that one first became sensible of his true magnitude; for almost in proportion to the greatness of the teacher himself was the danger to his humble followers. His head was strong enough to bear a doctrine which seemed to have an intoxicating influence upon those who received it at secondhand. His own writing has merits almost unapproachable in their peculiar character; but Carlylese in the mouths of imitators is amongst the most pestilent jargons by which modern English literature has been disfigured—and that is certainly to say a good deal.

It is unfortunately a common experience to feel that one would be, say, a Radical, were it not for the Radicals. The tail of a party—and the tails of parties are apt to be the largest part of them—is very frequently the strongest argument against the head. It is perhaps a still more melancholy experience that the leaders frequently become the victims of the disciples whom they raise up. The subtle flattery of admiration, the temptation to sustain authority by exaggerating the doctrine which has made a success, is often enough to turn a strong head. And it is one of Carlyle's titles to honour, that he never degenerated into the vulgar president of a mutual admiration society. He had too much self-respect, and was made of materials too sturdy and well-seasoned, to fall into such an error. He had been brought up in too stern a school. For years he had preached to deaf ears, and had been regarded by respectable editors of the Jeffrey variety as the kind of person of whom something might possibly be made, if he could only be induced to run quietly in the traces. There is no appearance that such treatment inflicted lasting wounds upon his vanity, or induced him to swerve an inch from his line of objectionable eccentricity, or to attempt to gain a hearing by any condescension to the tastes of the average reader. He was content to do the best work he could according to his own notions of what was right, and to leave it to win its way gradually to the place, whatever it might be, which it deserved. He was as independent in life as in thought. There is something in its way sublime about Carlyle's dogmatism; the absolute confidence with which he holds to his creed, and explains all dissent from it by the simple, and certainly in some sense well-founded, consideration of the general stupidity of mankind. It is of course easy to condemn the harshness of many of his judgments; and to hold that he was really showing his own blindness in his sweeping censures of whole schools of philosophers and politicians. But given the conviction, of which I do not here discuss the justification, he acted in the spirit of his creed. It was not, it seems, till he published the *Cromwell*—that is, till he was about fifty—that he gained anything to be called popularity. It would indeed be a libel upon our fathers not to admit that most competent judges had discovered the merits of *Sartor Resartus* or the *French Revolution*. Yet on the whole he was clearly one of the writers whose fame ripens slowly, and ripens all the more surely when he is strong enough to stick to his true vocation in spite of an absence of recognition. A man possessed of Carlyle's amazing power of vivid portraiture had many temptations to cover slightness of work by that sham picturesque with which superficial imitators have made us too familiar. But no one denies that, whatever the accuracy of the colouring in his historical studies, they at least imply the most thoroughgoing and conscientious labour. If Dryasdust does not invest Cromwell or Frederick with the same brilliant lights as Carlyle, he admits fully that Carlyle has not scamped the part of the work upon which the Dryasdust most prides himself. At worst, he can only complain that the poetical creator is rather ungrateful in his way of speaking of the labours by which he has profited. If the *French Revolution* is not in this respect the equal of the later works (in some other qualities it is their superior), it is only, I imagine, because the materials which would be required by a modern historian were not accessible near fifty years ago. It is, indeed, a subsidiary pleasure, in reading all Carlyle's writings, to feel that the artist is always backed up by the conscientious workman. If some of the early articles touch upon subjects fully studied, he has at least done thoroughly whatever he professes to have done; and even in reading later studies upon the same subjects, it is generally manifest that Carlyle's errors are never those of the indolent or superficial scribbler.

The quality manifested is the absolute self-respect and independence of a man who scorns to owe success to anything but the intrinsic merit of good work, or to measure success by the instantaneous harvest of flattery and admiration. No one could stand more firmly upon his own legs, or be more superior, not only to the vulgar forms of temptation, but to those which sometimes assail the loftiest minds. He gave what was in him to give, and spared no pains to give it in the most effective shape; but he never stooped to court the applause of the unintelligent and unsympathetic. If there was ever a risk of such condescension, it was perhaps at the period when he took to writing pamphlets upon questions of the day. There seemed to be a possibility of his descending from his lofty position to join in the inferior squabbles of politicians and journalists. There is certainly some admirable writing in those pamphlets; but they touch upon the topics in which his real power deserted him and gave some opportunity to the cavillers. The common criticism that he pointed out defects without suggesting remedies, had then a certain plausibility; for it is certainly natural to challenge a critic of any particular line of policy to name the policy which would meet his approval. If you attack protection you must advocate free trade, and general denunciation upsets its own aim. Happily Carlyle did not wander long in this region; and returned to the strong ground of those general moral principles which are independent of the particular issues of every-day politics. The reproach, indeed, followed him beyond its appropriate sphere. Some writers complain that Carlyle did not advance any new doctrine, or succeed in persuading the world of its truth. His life failed, it is suggested, in so far as he did not make any large body of converts with an accepted code of belief. But here, as it seems to me, the criticism becomes irrelevant. No one will dispute that Carlyle taught a strongly marked and highly characteristic creed, though one not easily packed into a definite set of logical formulæ. If there was no particular novelty in his theories, that was his very contention. His aim was to utter the truths which had been the strength and the animating principles of great and good men in all ages. He was not to move us, like a scientific discoverer, by proclaiming novelties, but to utter his protest in behalf of the permanent truths, obscured in the struggle between conflicting dogmas and drowned in the anarchical shrieks of contending parties. He succeeded in so far as he impressed the emotions and the imagination of his fellows, not in so far as he made known to them any new doctrine. Nor was his life to be called a failure, judged by his own standard, because he failed to produce any tangible result. Rightly or wrongly, Carlyle was no worshipper of progress, nor, indeed, a believer in its existence. The fact that an opinion did not make its way in the world was not even a presumption against its truth and importance in a world daily growing more and more chaotic, plunging wildly over Niagaras, falling more hopelessly under the dominion of shams and pursuing wilder phantasms into more boundless regions of distracted bewilderment. His duty was accomplished when he had liberated his own soul; when he had spoken so much truth as it was given to him to perceive, and left it to work as it might in the general play of incalculable forces. Here is truth: make what you can of it; if you can translate it into action, so much the better; if it only serves to animate a few faithful Abdiels, struggling with little hope and even less success against the manifold perplexities of a collapsing order, it has at least been so far useful. The sower must be content when he has cast the seed; he must leave it to the Power which rules the universe to decide whether it shall bear fruit a thousandfold, or be choked amongst the tares which are sprouting up in every direction with a growth of unparalleled luxuriance. He has played his part; and the only pay which he desires or deserves is the consciousness of having played it manfully.

That, as I conceive, would be Carlyle's attitude of mind. It is one which is rare and difficult to sustain amongst professed teachers of men. The keen sensibility which makes a man alive to the miseries of the race and anxious to rouse them from their slumbers, is apt to be a dangerous endowment; and only the strongest can bear the responsibility of such endowments unharmed. The dangers which beset such men are familiar enough, and may take many shapes of more or less vulgar temptation. The sense of power over the sympathies of your fellows may generate a morbid vanity. People take so much interest in your heart that you are tempted to invite the world at large to be spectators of its most secret emotions, to make a show of your agonies, and to attitudinise as a sentimental sufferer in presence of admiring multitudes. You are anxious to do good by your preachings; you welcome proselytes to your teaching gladly, because they are proselytes to the truth; and so you surround yourself with the most demoralising of all audiences—a crowd of submissive admirers who do their best to applaud your worst weaknesses and lead you on in the attempt to outrival yourself by caricaturing your own extravagances. You fancy yourself to be an oracle, and descend to be a mere popular preacher, accepting the vulgarest applause, and courting it by the most facile achievements. You think yourself infallible, and begin to resent every opposition as the proof of a corrupt antipathy. You grow irritable because the world is not converted out of hand, and fritter away your powers on petty controversies which serve only to show that a man may make himself ridiculous in spite of high purposes and great abilities. The type is familiar, and it is needless to quote instances. The reformers of mankind are too often martyrs not only in the sense of suffering at the hands of antagonists, but in the sense of sacrificing much of the purity and loftiness of their own natures in the trial to which they all are exposed. Perhaps we owe them some gratitude even for that kind of sacrifice; and certainly we must admit that we owe a great debt to many men who, like Rousseau, for example, have been led into countless weaknesses, and even moral errors, under temptations to which they have been rendered liable by a superabundance of genuine sensibility. Men of coarser fibre would have committed fewer errors and been useless to their fellows.

Happily we have no such delicate problems of casuistry in the case of Carlyle. Some people would have been more attracted to him had he not been armed with this grand stoical independence. They feel that there is something harsh about him. They utterly fail to perceive his intense tenderness of feeling, because they cannot understand the self-restraint which forbade him to wear his heart upon his sleeve. They see indifference to suffering in his profound conviction of the impotence of spasmodic attempts at its relief; and fancy that he was cynical when, in fact, he was only condemning that incontinence of sentiment which cannot bear to recognise the inexorable barriers of human fate. They cannot understand that a man can really be content to give the most concentrated expression to a melancholy view of human life without fidgeting over the schemes of practical reform. There seems to be a kind of antithesis between the apparent pride of a self-contained independence and the ardent sympathies of genuine benevolence. I do not think, indeed, that any one can really love Carlyle's books without becoming sensible of the emotional depth which underlies his reserve and his superficial harshness; nor is it possible to read the *Life of Sterling*—the most purely charming of his writings—without understanding the invincible charm of the man to a fine and affectionate nature. But upon these points we shall be better qualified to speak when we have the biography, which, if one may prophesy in such matters, bids fair to be one of the most delightful of books. For the present, it is enough to say that, whatever else may be said, Carlyle remains the noblest man of letters of his generation; the man who devoted himself with the greatest persistency to bringing out the very best that was in him; who least allowed himself to be diverted from the highest aims; and who knew how to confer a new dignity upon a character not always—if the truth must be spoken—very remarkable for dignity. He showed his eccentricity—as a critic naïvely tells us—by declining the mystic letters G.C.B. But he missed none of the dignity which comes from the unfeigned respect borne by all honest men to a character of absolute independence, the most unspotted honour in every relation of life, and the exclusive devotion of a long life to the high calling imposed by his genius.

What Carlyle's opinion may have been of the state of English literature during his generation it is perhaps better only guessing. Undoubtedly he must have held that it shared in that general decay which, according to him, is a symptom of a state of spiritual and social anarchy. I do not speak, of course, of that kind of printed matter which is held for the moment to be a part of literature, though it should rather be called a quasi-literary manufacture. Grub Street is always with us, and perhaps at the present time it is in a rather more blatant and exuberant condition than usual. But Carlyle would have had a good many hard things to say about writers of high pretensions, and about some in whom one could wish that he should have been more ready to recognise genuine fellow-workers instead of setting them down as mouthpieces of the general babbles of futile jargonings. According to him, most of us would do better to hold our tongues or to seek for some honest mode of living which would not involve any swelling of the distracting chorus of advice bestowed by 'able editors' upon a bewildered public. A very infinitesimal fraction of modern literature would pass this severe censor as deserving to escape the waste-paper basket. But one must not interpret a humourist too rigidly; and we may follow, so far as we may, Carlyle's example without troubling ourselves too much about his rather sweeping dogmas. That little house in Chelsea will long be surrounded with ennobling associations for the humbler brethren of the craft. For near fifty years it was the scene of the laborious industry of the greatest imaginative writer of the day, and the goal of pilgrimages from which no one ever returned without one great reward—the sense, that is, of having been in contact with a man who, whatever his weaknesses or his oddities, was utterly incapable of condescending to unworthy acts or words, or of touching upon any subject without instinctively dwelling upon its deepest moral significance. If his views of facts might be wrong or distorted and his teaching grotesque in form, it could never be flippant or commonplace, or imply any cynical indifference to the deepest interests of humanity. The hero in literature is the man who is invariably and unflinchingly true to himself; who works to his end undistracted by abuse or flattery, or the temptations of cheap success; whose struggles are not marked by any conspicuous catastrophes or demands for splendid self-sacrifices; who has to plod on a steady dull round of monotonous labour, under continual temptation to diverge into easier roads, and with the consciousness that his work may meet with little acceptance, or with a kind of acceptance which is even more irritating than neglect; and who must therefore place his reward chiefly in the work itself. Such heroism requires no small endowment of high moral qualities; and they have seldom or never been embodied more fully than in this sturdy, indomitable Scotchman, whose genius seemed to be the natural outcome of the concentrated essence of the strong virtues of his race.

43. Richard Holt Hutton, an essay, *Good Words*

April 1881, xxii, 282-8

Richard Holt Hutton (1826–97), theologian, literary critic, and journalist, was joint editor with Meredith Townsend of the influential periodical, the *Spectator*. A biographer, Hutton wrote lives of Scott and Newman and many perceptive and pointed articles for the *Spectator* (later collected as *Criticisms on Contemporary Thoughts and Thinkers* (London, 1894).

The common figment that we have lost a great writer for the first time, when first there ceases to be any place on the earth where his living body can be found, is perhaps more obviously a figment in the case of Thomas Carlyle than in that of any author of this century. For many years back it had been tolerably certain that Carlyle would add nothing more to that body of unique imaginative work which constitutes his real contribution to the life of man, except whatever of reminiscences and correspondence might be forthcoming at his death. And we now know not only that this has added, and will add, much very rich material to our knowledge of him, but also that what it adds will be exactly of the kind most fitted to increase the due appreciation of his great genius, and temper the undiscriminating idolatry of his special adorers. An author is best known, known in the best manner, when the largest number of those who are accessible to his influence first realise most clearly what he was as a whole; and it is certain that a much larger number of people will recognise more clearly what Carlyle was as a whole, during the next ten years, than have ever realised it up to the present moment.

Carlyle seems to me to have had the temperament and the powers of a great artist, with what was in effect a single inspiration for his art, and that one which required so great a revolution in the use of his appropriate artistic materials, that the first impression he produced on ordinary minds was that of bewilderment and even confusion. This subject—

493

almost his only subject—whether he wrote history or biography or the sort of musings which contained his conceptions of life, was always the dim struggle of man's nature with the passions, doubts, and confusions by which it is surrounded, with special regard to the grip of the infinite spiritual cravings, whether good or evil, upon it. He was always trying to paint the light shining in darkness and the darkness comprehending it not, and therefore it was that he strove so hard to invent a new sort of style which should express not simply the amount of human knowledge, but also, so far as possible, the much vaster amount of human ignorance against which that knowledge sparkled in mere radiant points breaking the gloom. Every one knows what Carlylese means, and every apt literary man can manufacture a little tolerably good Carlylese at will. But very few of us reflect what it was in Carlyle which generated the style, and what the style, in spite of its artificiality, has done for us. Indeed I doubt if Carlyle himself knew. In these reminiscences he admits its flavour of affectation with a comment which seems to me to show less self-knowledge than usual. Of his friend Irving's early style, as an imitation of the Miltonic or old English Puritan style, he says,—

At this time, and for years afterwards, there was something of preconceived intention visible in it, in fact of real affectation, as there could not well help being. To his example also I suppose I owe something of my own poor affectations in that matter which are now more or less visible to me, much repented of, or not.

I suspect of the two alternatives suggested in this amusing little bit of characteristic mystification, the 'not' should be taken as the truth. Carlyle could not repent of his affectation, for it was in some sense of the very essence of his art. Some critics have attempted to account for the difference in style between his early reviews in the *Edinburgh* and his later productions by the corrections of Jeffrey. But Jeffrey did not correct Carlyle's *Life of Schiller*, and if any one who possesses the volume containing both the life of Schiller and the life of Sterling will compare the one with the other, he will see at once that, between the two, Carlyle had deliberately developed a new organon for his own characteristic genius, and that so far from losing, his genius gained enormously by the process. And I say this not without fully recognising that simplicity is after all the highest of all qualities of style, and that no one can pretend to find simplicity in Carlyle's mature style. But after all the purpose of style is to express thought, and if the central and pervading thought of all which you wish to express, and must express if

494

you are to attain the real object of your life, is inconsistent with simplicity, let simplicity go to the wall, and let us have the real drift. And this seems to me to be exactly Carlyle's case. It would have been impossible to express adequately in such English as was the English of his *Life of Schiller*, the class of convictions which had most deeply engraved themselves on his own mind. That class of convictions was, to state it shortly, the result of his belief—a one-sided belief no doubt, but full of significance—that human language, and especially our glib cultivated use of it, had done as much or more to conceal from men how little they do know, and how ill they grasp even that which they partly know, as to define and preserve for them the little that they have actually puzzled-out of the riddle of life. In the very opening of the *Heroes and Hero Worship*, Carlyle says:—

Hardened round us, encasing wholly every notion we form, is a wrappage of traditions, hearsays, mere *words*. We call that fire of the black thunder-cloud 'electricity,' and lecture learnedly about it, and grind the like of it out of glass and silk. But what is it? What made it? Whence comes it? Whither goes it? Science has done much for us, but it is a poor science that would hide from us that great deep sacred infinitude of Nescience whither we can never penetrate, on which all science swims as a mere superficial film. This world, after all our science and sciences, is still a miracle; wonderful, inscrutable, *magical*, and more, to whosoever will think of it.

That passage reminds one of the best of the many amusing travesties of Mr. Carlyle's style, a travestie which may be found in Marmaduke Savage's *Falcon Family*, where one of the 'Young Ireland' party praises another for having 'a deep no-meaning in the great fiery heart of him.' But in Mr. Carlyle's mind this conviction of the immeasurable ignorance (or 'nescience,' as he preferred to call it in antithesis to science), which underlies all our knowledge, was not in the least a 'deep no-meaning' but a constant conviction, which it took a great genius like his to interpret to all who were capable of learning from him. I can speak for myself at least, that to me it has been the great use of Carlyle's peculiar *chiaro-oscuro* style, so to turn language inside out, as it were, for us, that we realise its inadequacy, and its tendency to blind and mislead us, as we could never have realised it by any limpid style at all. To expose the pretensions of human speech, to show us that it seems much clearer than it is, to warn us habitually that 'it swims as a mere superficial film' on a wide unplumbed sea of undiscovered reality, is a function hardly to be discharged at all by plain and limpid speech. Genuine Carlylese—which, of course, in its turn is in great danger of becoming

495

a deceptive mask, and often does become so in Carlyle's own writings, so that you begin to think that all careful observation, sound reasoning, and precise thinking is useless, and that a true man would keep his intellect foaming and gasping, as it were, in one eternal epileptic fit of wonder—is intended to keep constantly before us the relative proportions between the immensity on every subject which we fail to apprehend, and the few well-defined focal spots of light that we can clearly discern and take in. Nothing is so well adapted as Carlyle's style to teach one that the truest language on the deepest subjects is thrown out, as it were, with more or less happy effect, at great realities far above our analysis or grasp, and not a triumphant formula which contains the whole secret of our existence.

Let me contrast a passage concerning Schiller in the *Life of Schiller*, and one concerning Coleridge in the *Life of Sterling*, relating to very nearly the same subject, the one in ordinary English, the other in developed Carlylese, and no one, I think, will doubt which of the two expresses the central thought with the more power. 'Schiller,' says Carlyle,—

Does not distort his character or genius into shapes which he thinks more becoming than their natural one; he does not bring out principles which are not his, or harbour beloved persuasions which he half or wholly knows to be false. He did not often speak of wholesome prejudices; he did not 'embrace the Roman Catholic religion because it was the grandest and most comfortable.' Truth with Schiller, or what seemed such, was an indispensable requisite; if he but suspected an opinion to be false, however dear it may have been, he seems to have examined it with rigid scrutiny, and, if he found it guilty, to have plucked it out and resolutely cast it forth. The sacrifice might cause him pain, permanent pain; but danger, he imagined, it could hardly cause him. It is irksome and dangerous to tread in the dark; but better so than with an *ignis-fatuus* to guide us. Considering the warmth of his sensibilities, Schiller's merit on this point is greater than it at first might appear.

And now let me take the opposite judgment passed upon Coleridge in the *Life of Sterling*:—

[quotes 'The truth is' to 'very lamentable manner' XI, 60–2]

I think Carlyle was driving by implication at something which seems to me quite false in the latter passage, and possibly even in the former also. But no one can doubt, I think, which of these two styles conveys the more vividly the idea common to both—that it is very easy and very fatal to deceive ourselves into thinking or believing what we only wish to believe, and that a mind which cannot distinguish firmly between the two, loses all sense of the distinction between words and things. And how much more powerfully is the thought expressed in the strange idiom of the later style. The fundamental difference between the two styles is that while the former aims, like most good styles, at what Carlyle wants to say expressly, the latter is, in addition, lavish of suggestions which come in aid of his express meaning, by bringing out in the background the general chaos of vague indeterminate agencies which bewilder the believing nature, and render a definite creed difficult. Take the very characteristic Carlylese phrase 'in a tragically ineffectual degree,' and note the result of grafting the stronger thought of tragedy on the weaker one of ineffectuality,—how it dashes in a dark background to the spectacle of human helplessness, and suggests, what Carlyle wanted to suggest, how the powers above are dooming to disappointment the man who fortifies himself in any self-willed pet theory of his own. So, too, the expressions 'logical fatamorganas,' 'tremulous, pious sensibility,' 'a ray of empyrean embedded in such weak laxity of character,' 'spectral Puseyisms,' 'monstrous illusory hybrids,' 'ecclesiastical chimæras,'—all produce their intended *daunting* effect on the imagination, suggesting how much vagueness, darkness, and ignorance Carlyle apprehended behind these attempted philosophical 'views' of the great *à priori* thinker. Observe, too, the constant use of the plurals—'indolences and esuriences,' 'god-like radiances and brilliancies,' which just suggest to the mind in how very many different forms the same qualities may be manifested. And finally observe the discouraging effect of the touch which contrasts the conventionality of caste-costume, 'our poor Wigs and Church tippets,' with the 'Eternal Powers that live for ever'—a touch that says to us in effect, 'Your conventions mystify you, take you in, make you believe in an authority which the Eternal Powers never gave.' And all this is conveyed in such little space, by the mere suggestion of contrasts. The secret of Carlyle's style is a great crowding-in of contrasted ideas and colours,—indeed, such a crowding in, that for any purpose but his, it would be wholly false art. But his purpose being to impress upon us with all the force that was in him, that the universe presents to us only a few focal points of light which may be clearly discerned against vast and almost illimitable tracts of mystery,—that human language and custom mislead us miserably as to what these points of light are,—and that much of the light, all indeed which he himself does not recognise, comes from putrefying and phosphorescent *ignes fatui*, which will only betray us to our doom,—the later style is infinitely more effective than the first. He does contrive to paint the incapacity of the mind to grasp truth, its wonderful capacity to miss it, the enormous chances against hitting the mark precisely in the higher regions of belief, with a wonderful effect which his earlier style gave little promise of. It seems to me a style invented for the purpose of convincing those whom it charmed, that moral truth can only be discerned by a sort of brilliant imaginative tact and audacity in discriminating the various stars sprinkled in a dark vault of mystery, and then walking boldly by the doubtful light they give;—that very much cannot be believed except by self-deceivers or fools;—but that wonder is of the essence of all right-mindedness;—that the enigmatic character of life is good for us, so long as we are stern and almost hard in acting upon the little truth we can know;—but that any sort of clear solution of the enigma must be false,—and that any attempt to mitigate the sternness of life must be ascribed to radical weakness and the smooth self-delusions to which the weak are liable.

In speaking of his style, I have already suggested by implication a good deal of the drift of Carlyle's faith. What he loves to delineate is the man who can discern and grope his way honestly by a little light struggling through a world of darkness—the man whose gloom is deep, but whose lucidity of vision, so far as it goes, is keen—the man who is half hypochondriac, half devotee, but wholly indomitable, like Mahomet, Cromwell, Johnson. Thus he says of Cromwell:—

And withal this hypochondria, what was it but the very greatness of the man, the depth and tenderness of his ideal affections; the quantity of *sympathy* he had with things? The quantity of insight he could yet get into the heart of things; the mastery he could get over things; this was his hypochondria. The man's misery, as men's misery always does, came of his greatness. Samuel Johnson is that kind of man. Sorrow-stricken, half-distracted, the wide element of mournful *black* enveloping him—wide as the world. It is the character of a prophetic man; a man with his whole soul *seeing* and struggling to see.

In his life of *Frederick the Great*, writing on Voltaire, Carlyle describes the same sort of character as the ideal Teutonic character, a type which recommended itself to Voltaire because it was the reverse of his own.

A rugged, surly kind of fellow, much-enduring, not intrinsically bad; splenetic without complaint; standing oddly inexpugnable in that natural stoicism of his; taciturn, yet with strange flashes of speech in him now and then—something which goes beyond laughter and articulate logic, and is the taciturn elixir of these two—what they call 'humour' in their dialect.

Every hero he had was great in proportion as he displayed at once this profound impression of the darkness and difficulty of life, and this vehement dictatorial mode of acting on the glimpses or visions he had by way of showing valour in defiance of the darkness. Carlyle's characteristic delight in Odin and the Scandinavian mythology is a mere reflection of this strong appreciation of the religion of the volcano, the thunder-cloud, and the lightning-flash, mingled with a certain grim enjoyment of the spectacle of the inadequacy of human struggle. If Carlyle loved also to describe keen, clear wits like Jeffrey and Voltaire —if he revelled, too, in the picture of thin, acrid natures like Robespierre's, it was as foils to his favourite portraits of grim, vehement, dictatorial earnestness. As his style is *chiaro-oscuro*, so his favourite figures and characters are *chiaro-oscuro* also. Carlyle did not love too much light;—did not believe in it even as the gift of God. Mankind to him were 'mostly fools.' To make the best of a bad business was the highest achievement of the best men. He had a great belief in the sternness of purpose behind creation, but little belief in the love there. In his reminiscences he describes the attitude of Irving's schoolmaster, 'old Adam Hope,' towards his average scholars as being summed up thus:— 'Nothing good to be expected from you, or from those you come of, ye little whelps, but we must get from you the best you have, and not complain of anything.' And so far as I understand his religion, that is very much how Carlyle represents to himself the attitude of the Eternal mind towards us all. He tells us candidly in his account of Irving, that he had confessed to Irving that he did not think as Irving did of the Christian religion, and that it was vain for him to expect he ever should or could. And, indeed, no one who knows Carlyle's writings needed the avowal. Carlyle had a real belief in the Everlasting mind behind nature and history; but he had not only no belief in anything like a true revelation, he had, I think, almost a positive repulsion, if not scorn, for the idea, as if an undue and 'rose-water' attempt to alleviate the burden of the universe by self-deception, were involved in it. When, for instance, his coarse favourite, Friedrich Wilhelm, dies—the king, I mean, who assaulted his own daughter in his rage, struck her violently, and would have kicked her—Carlyle delights to tell you that he slept 'with the primeval sons of Thor,' and to comment on his death thus:

No Beresark of them, nor Odin's self, was a bit of truer human stuff; I confess his value to me in these sad times is rare and great. Considering the usual Histrionic Papin's Digester, Truculent Charlatan, and other species of kings, alone obtainable for the sunk flunkey populations of an era given up to Mammon and the worship of its own belly, what would not such a population give for a Friedrich Wilhelm, to guide it on the road *back* from Orcus a little? 'Would give,' I have written; but alas, it ought to have been '*should* give.' What *they* 'would' give is too mournfully plain to me, in spite of ballot-boxes, a steady and tremendous truth, from the days of Barabbas downwards and upwards.

If this be not meant as a hint that, for Carlyle, such a hero as Friedrich Wilhelm was rather the king to be desired than He for whom Barabbas was really substituted—and this, perhaps, is an overstrained interpretation—it certainly does suggest that Carlyle's mind habitually adhered by preference to the Scandinavian type of violent smoke-and-flame hero, even at those times when the lessons of his childhood carried him back to the divine figure of the crucified Christ.

I do not think that any portion of Carlyle's works contains clear traces of the sort of grounds on which he came to reject the Christian revelation. Probably his correspondence when it appears may clear up this point. But I should judge that at the root of it was a certain contempt for the raw material of human nature, as inconsistent with the Christian view, and an especial contempt for the particular effect produced upon that raw material by what he understood to be the most common result of conversion. Dyspepsia may have had something to do with his preference for a decidedly dyspeptic type of religion—dyspepsia itself, and the imaginative mould into which dyspepsia cast his vivid thoughts. Certainly he always represents the higher fortitude as a sort of 'obstinacy,' rather than as a pious submission to the Divine will, and conceives the matter as if God were trying what stuff we are of by first setting us tasks, and then besetting us with difficulties in performing them. Thus, speaking of his own dyspepsia in these *Reminiscences*, he does not in the least mince his language about it, though it would seem that at bottom he does regard it as something which it tasks his 'faith' to bear.

The accursed hag, Dyspepsia, had got me bitted and bridled, and was ever striving to make my waking living day a thing of ghastly nightmares. I resisted what I could; never did yield or surrender to her; but she kept my heart right heavy, my battle being sore and hopeless. One could not call it hope, but only desperate obstinacy, refusing to flinch, that animated me. 'Obstinacy as *of ten mules*' I have sometimes called it since; but, in candid truth, there was something worthily human in it, too; and I have had, through life, among my manifold unspeakable blessings, no other real bower-anchor to ride by in the rough seas. Human 'obstinacy' grounded in real faith and insight, is good, and the best.

Of the existence of something hard,—something of the genuine task-master—in the mind of the Creator, something requiring obstinacy, and not mere submission, to satisfy its requirements, Carlyle had a deep conviction. I think his view of Christianity—reverently as he always or almost always spoke of the person of Christ—was as of a religion that had something too much of love in it, something slightly mawkish, and that if he could but have believed the old Calvinism, its inexorable decrees would in many respects have seemed to him more like the ground-system of creation than the gospel either of Chalmers or of Irving. His love of despots who had any ray of honesty or insight in them, his profound belief that mankind should try and get such despots to order their doings for them, his strange hankerings after the institution of slavery as the only reasonable way in which the lower races of men might serve their apprenticeship to the higher races—all seems to me a sort of reflection of the Calvinistic doctrine that life is a subordination to a hard taskmaster, directly or by deputy, and that so far from grumbling over its severities, we must just grimly set to work and be thankful it is not worse than it is. 'Fancy thou deservest to be hanged (as is most likely),' he says in *Sartor Resartus*, 'thou wilt feel it happiness to be only shot; fancy thou deservest to be hanged in a hair halter, it will be a luxury to die in hemp.' That seems to me to represent Carlyle's real conviction. He could not believe that God does, as a matter of fact, care very much for the likes of us; or even is bound to care. His imagination failed to realise the need or reality of Divine love. 'Upwards of five hundred thousand two-legged animals without feathers lie around us, in horizontal position, their heads all in nightcaps, and full of the foolishest dreams,' he wrote, in describing a city at midnight. And you could easily see that his whole view of life was accommodated to that conception. And the Creator, in Carlyle's view, takes I think very much the same account of these 'two-legged animals with heads full of the foolishest dreams,' as Adam Hope did of his stupid scholars; not much is to be expected of us or got out of us, but God will get out of us the best he can, and 'not complain of anything.' Even the best of our race show that they are the best by estimating their own deserts at the very lowest, by saying 'we are unprofitable servants.' As for the common sort they deserve not so much Divine love and salvation, as to be driven out of 'the dog-hutch' of their own self-love into the pitiless storm. Such seems to me to be the general drift of Carlyle's religion. He has had his incredulity as to the Christian miracles, historical evidence, and the rest; but his chief doubt has been as to the stuff of which mankind

BOURNEMOUTH COLLEGE
OF TECHNOLOGY

COLLEGE LIBRARY

is made—on which his verdict seems to me to be this—'not of the kind worth saving or to be saved, after Christ's fashion, at all, but to be bettered, if at all, after some other and much ruder fashion, the "beneficent whip" being, perhaps, the chief instrumentality.'

Carlyle has exerted, I think, a very potent influence on the political history of our day,—more, however, through the power of his imaginative picture of the turbulent fermentations and molten fury of popular democracy, than by his attempt to persuade the peoples to give up 'palavers,' 'ballottings,' &c., and to let wise men guide them and rule them. Such books as his *Chartism, Past and Present, Latter Day Pamphlets,* in spite of all their humour and all their various truth of insight,—which was not small—did little if anything to influence the popular mind. And as to his apologies for slavery, and his vehement attacks on 'Black Quashee,' they were so utterly inconsistent with the drift of the known facts of the case, and contained practical advice so malign in its tendency, not only to the slaves but to the slave-owners, that I think they altogether failed, in this country at least, of political effect. But his wonderful and unique picture of a democracy stirred to its depths, in *The French Revolution,* produced a profound impression of warning, and partly even of terror, on those who could understand it; and through them the impression spread to many, so that the dangers of democracy have been more fully appreciated ever since, and will be the better understood for all time to come in consequence of Carlyle's marvellous picture. On those who, like myself, read it in their youth, no book probably ever produced so vivid and startling an impression. One reads in the *Reminiscences* how deeply Carlyle himself was excited by the composition of it, nay one sees how exactly he found in it the concentration of his general view of human life—the alloy only left out.

The thorough possession it had taken of me, (he says) dwelling in me day and night, keeping me in constant fellowship with such a 'flamy cut-throat scene of things,' infernal and celestial, both in one, with no fixed prospect but that of writing it, though I should die, had held me in a fever blaze for three years long; and now the blaze had ceased, problem *taliter qualiter* was actually done, and my humour and way of thought about all things was of an altogether ghastly, dim-smouldering, and as if preternatural sort.

The book itself corresponds with this description of Carlyle's mood in writing it. The mawkish sentimentalisms of the earlier stage of the French Revolution,—the fierce and bloody passions of its later stage,—the miseries of the famished French people—the conventionalities of the effete aristocracy—the unreal platitudes of political philosophers—the deep envies and mutual suspicions of the different candidates for popular confidence, are painted in that book with such wonderfully living force as render it to me no little marvel that almost all the leading events in it were well over before Thomas Carlyle was born. That any statesman who has read that book should ever be able to rid himself of the feeling that popular passion is a sort of volcano on the slopes of which we all live, and which may some day break up even the crust of English phlegm by a shock of earthquake, seems to me impossible. No doubt Carlyle never makes sufficient account of the hard baked clay of the Teutonic races, and sifts away not a little of the slow customary dulness, even of Celtic or Franko-Celtic peasant life. He puts too much of his own fire into the interpretation of even these lurid phenomena. Still the picture is, in its essence, as true as it is imposing and appalling; and, doubtless, it has had as much effect in preaching the inevitable advance of democracy, and teaching that it is as righteous as it is inevitable that the future should be moulded so as to secure the good of the multitude rather than so as to secure the uplifting of a select few on the shoulders of the multitude, as it has had in pointing out the difficulties which stand in the way of the self-government of the ignorant by the ignorant, and in disheartening triumphant makers of paper constitutions. *The French Revolution* is, perhaps, the book of the century—a book which could hardly have been written except by a man in a fever—a fever such as the advance of democracy would naturally produce in a mind at once full of popular sympathies, and of the deepest scorn for popular ignorance and superstition.

In origin a peasant, who originated a new sort of culture and created a most artificial style full at once of affectation and of genuine power; in faith a mystic, who rejected Christianity while clinging ardently to the symbolic style of Christian teaching; in politics a pioneer of democracy, who wanted to persuade the people to trust themselves to the almost despotic guidance of Lord-protectors whom he could not tell them how to find; in literature a rugged sort of poet, who could not endure the chains of rhythm, and even jeered at rhyme,—Carlyle certainly stands out a paradoxical sort of figure, solitary, proud, defiant, vivid. The *Reminiscences* will do, I think, at least as much to immortalise his faults as to show the penetrating brilliance of his keen literary glance; at least as much to diminish the fascination of his spiritual example as to increase the fascination of his genius. But after all, no literary man in the nineteenth century is likely to stand out more distinct, both for flaws and genius, to the centuries which will follow.

44. Andrew Lang, a review, 'Mr. Carlyle's Reminiscences', Fraser's Magazine

April 1881, n.s. xxiii, 515–28

Andrew Lang (1844–1912) was educated at St. Andrews and at Oxford. His tremendous industry touched upon many subjects: folklore, myth, ballad-origins, history, and the classics. One of his best known works, *Myth, Ritual, and Religion* (1887), is an investigation into totemism. With S. H. Butcher, he translated the *Odyssey* (1879) and with Ernest Meyers and Walter Leaf, the *Iliad* (1883). Lang's amazing versatility made him one of the greatest bookmen of his day. See Introduction, p. 21.

Though Mr. Carlyle was for some time anxious that his biography should never be written, he was one who owed the world a biography. No writer had insisted so much as he on the value of a true record of a great man's thoughts, words, and deeds. No writer ever did so much to make the illustrious dead immortal in their habit as they had lived. His own career was that of a hero, in his sense of the term, of a leader and guide. For his complete biography we have still to wait, but his *Reminiscences*, edited by Mr. Froude, already suffice to make the contrasts of his nature and of his teaching intelligible. It is as an explanation of his work that we intend to review them. In these volumes we, who did not know him, hear him talk in unbroken, pathetic, and humorous converse between himself and the world, the dead and the past. Here is explained the secret of the affection and the contempt (*un amour rentré*) which he entertained for man. In studying these soliloquies on the people whom he had known and loved, or seen through (as he believed) and despised, we come to perceive how he could so greatly desire certain ends, and so heartily detest certain means to these ends. Like his own Teufelsdröckh, he proposes the toast, *Die Sache der Armen in Gottes und Teufels Namen*—'the cause of the poor in Heaven's name and Hell's'—and then pours out his contempt on everyone who practically

tries to aid the cause of the poor, on all 'philanthropists' from Wilberforce to the Kyrle Society. He speaks—no one with a more certain
voice—about the awfulness and 'earnestness' of human life, and then,
the leaven of the Covenant and the Cameronians working in him, he
finds 'all human work transitory, small in itself, contemptible'—in
short, 'filthy rags.' He falls down at the feet of conquerors and warriors,
he deifies force and fighting; but the same man, at school and always,
'succeeds ill in battle, and fain would have avoided it,' 'in the war element had little but sorrow,' and 'wept often,' he says in *Sartor Resartus*,
'indeed to such a degree that he was nicknamed *Der Weinende*, the
Tearful.' Like his favourite Ram Dass, the Indian mystagogue, Mr.
Carlyle's heart had 'fire in it to burn up all the sins in the world,' nor
was he ill pleased if the sinners, too, got slightly toasted in the process. . . .

He was on the side of the poor, and, when there were risings and
repressions in the west of Scotland, when the middle classes were being
drilled and armed in Edinburgh, the doubt in his mind was, 'on which
side' he should carry a musket. With all his inherited sympathies thus
engaged, his almost fanatical love of order enlisted him for anyone who
would introduce 'a whiff of grapeshot' among the people when the
people grew riotous and anarchic. Thus it was never easy to class Mr.
Carlyle with politicians. Indeed, his politics were as remote as possible
from practice. It was a matter of the victory of one or the other sympathy. He might be of the party of the poor and the oppressed (as long
as the poor and oppressed were not black or Irish), or he might be on
the side of Cromwell, or not opposed to the first Bonaparte. Democracy
he naturally detested, as far as democracy was inconsistent with the
absolute power of the best men. But, on the other hand, his stoicism,
his fatalism (if we may use the word), compelled him at times to see in
democracy the inevitable, a thing against which protest was no more
effectual than against death. The people who felt with him about the
poor were less quick than himself to recognise the necessary limitations
of human endeavours, were more hopeful of scaling the 'un-o'erleaped
mountains of necessity.' Therefore, in his stoicism he despised them and
their schemes almost as heartily as he scorned persons who were quite
careless, sportsmen and dandies, and æsthetic upholsterers. It was not
easy to be in harmony with Mr. Carlyle. A certain bitterness remained
in him, a deposit, perhaps, of many centuries of hereditary poverty and
ill-rewarded toil. . . .

Many pages are occupied with the story of Edward Irving, and of
that singular friendship between Mr. Carlyle and the popular preacher.

This chapter scarcely enables us to understand Irving. He was brilliant, ambitious, and religious, with no doubtful sincerity, but we still fail to understand how he was sympathetic to Mr. Carlyle, and how, being a sane and educated man, he lapsed into the ignorant absurdities of the 'tongues,' and was sucked into the 'foul gulfs of London pulpit popularities.' Irving's history is an unexplained tragedy, something like Mr. Browning's 'Paracelsus.' He was too honest a man to be a successful charlatan, and yet we see, from a dozen touches in this sketch, that the nature of the charlatan was not wholly foreign to him. To his example, perhaps, we owe Mr. Carlyle's literary manner. That manner a descreet but dry French critic has lately spoken of as 'the style of a mystagogue.' It is very difficult for our generation, which has become so accustomed to Mr. Carlyle's voice, to judge as to its chance of permanence, as to its possible power of reaching and touching future generations. If foreigners, as is sometimes said, represent posterity, and if M. Scherer represents foreigners, then the odds are that, in the twentieth century, Mr. Carlyle's books will find but few students. His own theory of style is thus expressed in the *Reminiscences*: 'The ultimate rule is: learn so far as possible to be intelligent and transparent—no notice taken of your style, but solely of what you express by it.' But was Mr. Carlyle intelligible and transparent? 'The chaotic nature of these paper-bags aggravates our obscurity,' he says, as editor of 'Teufelsdröckh.' Some of Mr. Carlyle's books, *Frederick* especially, are not badly described as 'chaotic paper-bags;' not so much books, as the raw material of books. As to his expression, it is like that of a man accustomed to the company of 'solitude and the night,' and much given to soliloquy and a kind of short-hand thought. His constant exclamations, his nicknames—'apes,' 'dead dogs,' 'windbags,' 'niggers,' and all the rest of them—are the language of a man talking angrily and vehemently to himself. Because he had so much worth hearing to say, because he looked about him with eyes absolutely clear and honest, because, like his namesake of Ercildoune, 'True Thomas,' he had the tongue that could not lie, the world was compelled to listen to him. His utterances about the sorrows and confusions of his own time are often not much more articulate than the voice in which the spirits of dead New Zealanders speak through their *tohunga*, 'like the sighing sound of the wind in an empty vessel.' His *Latter-day Pamphlets* are the lamentations of a hopeless Jeremiah. Yet it was in this wise, apparently, that Mr. Carlyle found it easiest to be 'intelligent and transparent.' 'His own poor affectations,' he says, 'he caught more or less from Irving. He affected the Miltonic or old English

Puritan style, and strove visibly to imitate it more and more till almost the end of his career, when indeed it had become his own, and even the language he used in utmost heat of business for expressing his meaning. At this time (1816) and for years afterwards, there was something of preconceived intention visible in it, in fact of real affectation, as there could not well help being.' Perhaps, with the necessary changes, these words explain that much debated matter, Mr. Carlyle's own style. 'Puritan' it is, but rather in the manner of an emphatic Nithsdale than of a scholarly old English Puritan. It is crossed by poetry, by true eloquence and passion, and broken up by a habit of soliloquy, and of the petulant tossing about of nicknames. The style had to be tolerated, because, in private life, or in addressing the public, it was the style of the oracle.

The education which the world was giving Mr. Carlyle was a very hard one. It took the shape of poverty, disease, and doubt. Teaching small boys and girls became intolerable to him. He looked wistfully towards literature; his knowledge of German and French enabled him to make small sums by translating. In these evil years his father stood by him bravely. 'When I had peremptorily ceased from being a school-master, though he inwardly disapproved of the step as imprudent, and saw me in successive summers lingering beside him in sickliness of body and mind, without outlook towards any good, he had the forbearance to say, at worst, nothing, never once to whisper discontent with me.' The pilgrim was a captive in the castles of Giants Dyspepsia and Doubt. From the former he never escaped, nor could the temporary disuse of tobacco, a life in the noiseless country, and riding exercise amounting to 30,000 miles, during the composition of *Frederick*, shake off the fiend that sat *post equitem*. Mr. Carlyle returns to the topic again and again. Probably he thought too much about his own inside, and was more or less hypochondriac. But his lifelong sufferings have left their mark on the work of his life, and many a hard word and bitter judgment of his contemporaries may be attributed, not so much to himself, as to his *lutin*, his evil familiar spirit, dyspepsia. Every one over eighteen, who reads at all, has passed through his course of Mr. Carlyle, and has been obliged to see the world, for a season, draped in mourning. Many a bad quarter of an hour he has given all of us. Let younger people, who have these *Reminiscences* to explain things, take heart. Cakes and ale have not ceased to exist because Mr. Carlyle was dyspeptic. The sun is not abolished, nor has life at all left off being worth living, because Mr. Carlyle was put on a regimen of oatmeal porridge, and wrote books when perhaps he would have been better employed in playing golf. There is a time for *Latter-day Pamphlets* and a time for Rabelais. Pantagruel will see Teufelsdröckh out, and the curé of Meudon was a wiser man than the recluse of Craigenputtoch. It is positively a comfort, in its way, to read Mr. Carlyle's ferocious judgments of men we know to have been kind, humorous, and wise. If he maligns *them*, the world too may be less black than he paints it. He runs amuck among friends and indifferent people with his swashing blow, or kicks them out with a word of contemptuous praise. About some of the kindest and most blameless people, still surviving, Mr. Carlyle wrote, in his moody old age, words which we are sure he never meant to be published. Charles Lamb is the greatest sufferer. Mill fares but badly, Coleridge still worse, and De Quincey's unkind review of Schiller is amply avenged by this blow of the dead hand: 'He was a pretty little creature, full of wiredrawn ingenuities, bankrupt enthusiasms, bankrupt pride, with the finest silver-toned low voice, and most elaborate gently-winding courtesies and ingenuities in conversation.' All these men, Coleridge, Lamb, De Quincey, were more heavily handicapped by health and constitution than Mr. Carlyle himself, and they had not his strength to bear the burden. He judged men hardly, and the world harshly; neither they nor it deserve his petulant contempt, nor need we take to shrieking and lamenting, because Mr. Gladstone is not Ireton, 'nor inspired young Goschen,' Cromwell. The constitution of things is averse to the secular triumph of Puritanism, other ways of conceiving of life must have their innings, and, whatever the piece that is mounted on the world's boards, it is not so bad as to deserve the ceaseless hoots and cat-calls of Mr. Carlyle.

His dyspepsia has wronged him, and his age, and many of his contemporaries, but it has not been a wasted force. His pessimism, though exaggerated, was almost necessary, as a check to the washy optimism of thirty years ago. That was the time when war was abolished, when a gratifying diminution of crime was anxiously expected, when education was to make all the world moral, when commerce was to render it comfortable exceedingly, when Free Trade and political economy, and the sweet influences of the suffrage were received as literally a kind of gospel. The thirty years have passed, the millennium is no nearer, war is not extinct, and the time is strewn with the wrecks of opinions exploded and renounced. Mr. Carlyle helped to destroy them. On the granite of his scepticism the tides of sentiment broke, and disappeared in foam. . . .

Mr. Carlyle was believed, by young men in spiritual trouble, to have found something out, so to speak; to have private information about the secret of the painful earth. Many men in our time, in all times, have this mysterious reputation. They are known to have wandered in the wilderness, and to have come out, on the other side, into a promised land of content. What message did they hear from Sinai? People still in the wilderness want to know, and Mr. Carlyle was accustomed to the visits of earnest young inquirers. He was almost always kind and friendly to young men; he took great trouble to give them helpful advice; his character and presence strengthened and encouraged them. . . .

His real literary genius consisted in a kind of retrospective second sight. Though so often called a 'prophet,' it was the past rather than the future that he was skilled to discern. His industry and accuracy were great and laborious. A student who has worked at the history of the French Revolution, with the aid of all the new documents, informs me that he only once found Mr. Carlyle in an error—a mistake about the number of a certain French regiment. But no industry, nothing but native genius could have enabled him to see the past as he did, to behold the actors as they lived and suffered, to make all the crowded scene visible to every spectator, and construct the whole into a prose epic, full of humour, full of tragedy, as true, though not as musical, as the *Iliad*. The *French Revolution* appears to me to be by far the greatest of Mr. Carlyle's books. It was written in the maturity of his strength. He was unspoiled by that position of a 'Master' which his disciples thrust on him. He was not yet the slave of his own mannerisms. His heart was still pitiful over a poor poet like Camille Desmoulins. Force, the force of Mirabeau and Danton, attracted and allured, but had not dominated his genius. He had not, in the excess of his careful industry, lost the sense of literary proportion. He knew how good his own book was. Mr. Thackeray, after writing the last scene between Becky, Rawdon Crawley, and Lord Steyne, slapped his hand on the table and said, 'By George, that's genius.' And Mr. Carlyle said, when he had written his last paragraph, 'What they will do with this book none knows; but they have not had, for a two hundred years, any book that came more truly from a man's very heart, and so let them trample it under foot and hoof, as they see best.' Some booby in the 'Athenæum' did 'trample;' but better judges, Thackeray and Southey, were full of praise. It seems extraordinary that the *French Revolution* did not at once establish Mr. Carlyle's popular fame and lighten the burden of his poverty. But he had to wait till *Cromwell* brought him popularity, and not till the sudden revival of public interest in his writings, in 1866, did much money reward his labours. He never cared for money, and in 1866 Mrs. Carlyle died, and everything became indifferent to an old and life-weary man. Who would be great at such a price? Who would buy so much misery with so much labour? His toils were no pleasure, but an agony, to Mr. Carlyle. He grew more and more gloomy, or so at least he represents his life, and so it appeared to him in mournful memories after his wife left him lonely and uncomforted. Most men like their work. In his Mr. Carlyle seems to have found the curse imposed on Adam. He says that the study of Cromwell and the events of 1848 made him the lover of dictators that he became. The same tendency was visible in his biography of Dr. Francia, written in 1843. He cultivated contempt of the kindly race of men 'most of them fools.' One might answer ('I speak as a fool') that it is better to be of the majority, to make a thousand blunders, to aim at little and fail in that, and to take pleasure withal in the world, in life, in friendship, than to be wise and disdainful, successful and sullen, with a heart full of misery, scorn, despair, of old rancours against the errors of friends. We many millions of fools have taken Mr. Carlyle's railings in very good part, and kissed the hand that smote us. No one persecuted this Jeremiah. He admits that he had not, properly speaking, an enemy. But his was not the true wisdom. He was the Alceste of our age, with

> Those fine curses which he spoke,
> The old Timon, with his noble heart,
> That, strongly loathing, greatly broke.

He strongly loved as well as loathed: every page of these sad papers bears too clear evidence of the height and depth of his affection. Had he not been thus pitiful and tender, in spite of his scorn, he would not have been the great humourist he was, greater than Swift, and only not so great as Shakespeare and Molière.

We do not follow Mr. Carlyle's story to the end, being anxious to see his genius in the making, rather than to examine his private life after character and genius are made and have taken their ply. It is not the place, at the end of a review, to ask what Mr. Carlyle did for England and the world. Every reader of his books may ask himself, What have I learned from Carlyle? They say that he was only a negative teacher. He showed no way of lifting the yoke from the neck of the poor, and the men who fancied they had remedies he hindered. His real message was the lesson of the necessity of work, of endurance of toil, of contempt of pleasure. We have not learned his lesson; we continue to erect Tay bridges and to send armies into the field without tent-pegs. There never was a prophet yet that saved a people. Jeremiah, Isaiah, Ezekiel, were all failures, voices that, as far as practical effect went, might as well have cried aloud in the wilderness. Only here and there a disciple follows in the path indicated by the master. A few souls are saved, to put it in the Scriptural language which Mr. Carlyle preferred to use, and this is as great success as ever rewarded any prophet.

It is easy for the ideal whippersnapper to see Mr. Carlyle's faults and limitations. Forms of beauty, forms of truth that were not in his line, he merely kicked aside. He despised the 'haggard' poetry of Shelley, as much as the 'stupid' speculations of Mr. Darwin. The dullest of us can sneer at this want of 'catholicity.' The object of Mr. Carlyle was to bid men keep their powder dry and not waste their fire. He had no sympathy with vague pyrotechnic exhibitions. It would be a howling wilderness of a world if we were all Carlyles. Some of his followers do appear to be the most forcible-feeble people extant; literary creatures who have painfully acquired the bitterness of Calvinism without its belief. The figure of the master remains the grandest of his time; he had the clearest eyes, and the tongue incapable of aught but truth, and his very sadness was not all his own, but the melancholy of a man who bore painfully the burden of the sorrows of the race. He did not cast it off, as some do, when his private troubles were over for a season. He did not carry it with the languid and conscious elegance of Chateaubriand. Indeed, his virtues and his foibles all came from this, that he could take no repose, that, as Jeffrey complained, he was too 'dreadfully in earnest.'

Since Mr. Carlyle's death, and especially since the publication of his *Reminiscences*, a hundred judgments and criticisms of the man and of his work have been pronounced. Probably the most remarkable, the most worthy of attention, are the memorial sermon preached by his friend and neighbour, Mr. Blunt, of Chelsea, and the essay in the *Revue des Deux Mondes* (March 1) by M. Valbert. Between these two opinions all are included. Mr. Blunt sees in Mr. Carlyle only that nobility of soul, that deep, undying sense of man's misery and of man's duty, which he shared with prophets like Sakya Muni. It was this that made him unhappy, and too little sympathetic with the lighter joys of the world. In Mr. Blunt's public farewell to an old friend and an old neighbour, there is, naturally, no remark on the indiscriminate censoriousness of Mr. Carlyle. That quality is painfully revealed in the *Reminiscences*, and may most charitably be regarded as the expression of the hurt sensitiveness of an artist. For this was Mr. Carlyle's misfortune, to combine the nature of an artist, of a poet, with the ethical character of a peasant-Puritan. These contradictions within him could never be reconciled, this strife inevitably deepened the pain which life inflicted on his soul. In M. Valbert's essay we see how the artistic aspect of Mr. Carlyle's nature and genius appears, to a French critic, to be the most essential and important one. Mr. Carlyle was not a reasoner, not a philosopher, not an historian, M. Valbert declares, but a poet, a bird that could sing, and persisted in refraining from singing. He reached his ideas by intuition, not by argument, and he condemned, without a hearing, the reasoned philosophy of evolution, which won the ear of the world. That philosophy, of course, does not absolutely contradict Mr. Carlyle's favourite theory of the influence of heroes. Evolution is a system of action and reaction, of general influences that produce the individual and his environment, of the individual who helps to raise and develop the general type. But Mr. Carlyle absolutely declined even to examine the new hypothesis. 'With regard to Man, his origin and destiny, he held a high and lofty faith,' says Mr. Blunt; 'and I have heard him say, when some were canvassing the new theories of man's descent from the animal world, that "if indeed it were true, it was nothing to be proud of, but rather a humiliating discovery, and the least said about it the better."' But truths have to be faced, whether they are humiliating or the reverse, and Mr. Carlyle's own teacher, Goethe, would have been the last man to acquiesce in this obscurantism.

It is not easy, it is not possible, to say the last word about Mr. Carlyle. Posterity will regard him with deep sympathy and reverence, as one of the greatest of literary forces; thwarted, like Byron, by selfwill; torn, like Swift, by *sæva indignatio*,[1] and all his life vexed, almost physically, by a fierce hunger and thirst after righteousness.

[1] Cruel indignation.

45. Dean Arthur Penrhyn Stanley, a funeral sermon on Carlyle's death

London, 1881

From *Sermons on Special Occasions*, 255–63. Preached in Westminster Abbey.

Dean Stanley (1815–81) was a close friend of Carlyle for many years. Educated at Rugby, where he was deeply influenced by Thomas Arnold, then later at Balliol, he was appointed Professor of Ecclesiastical History at Christ Church in 1856. In 1864, he became Dean of Westminster, a position he held until his death, not long after that of Carlyle. Among his many works, his *Life and Correspondence of Thomas Arnold* (1844) is most notable. Froude tells us that Dean Stanley tried to persuade him to have Carlyle buried in Westminster Abbey, but that Carlyle had anticipated such a move and had objected for many reasons and was buried where he was born, in Ecclefechan among his kinsmen.

The kingdom of heaven is likened unto a man which sowed good seed in his field.— Matthew xiii. 24.

The Gospel of this day starts with a comparison of the kingdom of heaven to a sower. It is the same as that with which the more celebrated parable begins, 'A sower went forth to sow.' They both fix our minds on the manner in which God's kingdom—the kingdom of truth, beauty, and goodness—is carried on in the world. The kingdom of all that is good is fostered, not so much by direct and immediate plantation, or grafting, or building, or formation of any kind; but rather by the sowing of good seed, which in time shall grow up and furnish a rich harvest.

It is so with regard to the truths of the Bible. They are sown in the world; the good which grows up after them is never in outward form like the truth which came from the actual source. Institutions spring up. They may derive their vitality from the 'corns of wheat which fall into the ground and die;'* but they cannot be the very thing itself. There is not a single form or a single doctrine of Christendom of which the outward shape is not different in some way from the principle of life which gave it birth.

There is only one instance in the whole Bible of a ready-made scholastic doctrine, and that has been long known to be spurious. It is not the verse of the three witnesses, but the parable of the Good Shepherd, the poetry of the Prodigal Son, the pathetic story of the Crucifixion that have been the true seeds of the Christian life. In this way it is that the Divine origin of these truths proves itself. The bright and tender words can never grow old, because they are not flowers cut and dried, but seeds and roots, which are capable of bearing a thousand applications.

Again, this is the ground of our looking forward with a hope which nothing can extinguish towards the transformation, the renewal of the human life, for a moment perishing, to re-appear, we trust, in some future world instinct with the capacities for good or evil with which it was endowed or which it has acquired in the world that now is. 'The seminal form within the deeps of that little chaos sleeps,' which will, we trust, in the Almighty Providence of God, restore that chaos of decayed and broken powers into conditions more elevated than now we can dream of.

Again, characters appear in the world which have a vivifying and regenerating effect, not so much for the sake of what they teach us, as for the sake of showing us how to think and how to act. What Socrates taught concerning man and the universe has long since passed away; but what he taught of the method and process of pursuing truth—the inquiry, the cross-examination, the sifting of what we do know from what we do not know—this is the foundation, the good seed, of European philosophy for all time. What St. Paul taught concerning circumcision and election or grace is among the things hard to be understood, which the unlearned and the unstable may wrest to their own destruction, or which, having served their generation, may be laid asleep; but what he taught of the mode and manner of arriving at Divine truth, when he showed how 'the letter killeth and the spirit maketh alive;' when he sets forth how charity is the bond of all perfectness; when he showed how all men are acceptable to God by fulfilling, each in his vocation, whether Jew or Gentile, whether slave or free, the commandments of God—when he said these things he laid the true foundation of Christian

* John xii. 24.

faith; he planted in the heart of man the seed, the good seed, of Christian liberty and Christian duty, to bear fruit again and again amidst the many relapses and eclipses of Christendom. When Luther dinned into the ears of his generation the formulas of transubstantiation and of justification by faith only, this was doomed to perish and 'wax old as doth a garment;' but his acts, his utterances of indignant conscience, and of farsighted genius, became the seed of the Reformation, the hope of the world. When John Wesley rang the changes on the well-known formula of assurance, it was the word of the ordinary preacher; but his whole career of fifty years of testifying for holiness and preaching against vice—that was the seed of more than Methodism; it was the seed of the revival of English religious zeal. Such seeds, such principles, such infusions, not of a mechanical system, but of a new light in the world, are not of every-day occurrence; they are the work of a few, of a gifted few; and it is therefore so much the more to be observed when any one who has had it in his power to scatter such seeds right and left passes away, leaving us to ask what we have gained, what we can assimilate of the peculiar nourishment which his life and teaching may have left for our advantage. Few will doubt that such a one was he who yesterday was taken from us. It may be that he will not be laid, as might have been expected, amongst the poets and scholars and sages whose dust rests within this Abbey; it may be that he was drawn by an irresistible longing towards the native hills of his own Dumfriesshire, and that there, beside the bones of his kindred, beside his father and his mother, and with the silent ministrations of the Church of Scotland, to which he still clung amidst all the vicissitudes of his long existence, will repose all that is earthly of Thomas Carlyle. But he belonged to a wider sphere than Scotland; for though by nationality a Scotchman, he yet was loved and honoured wherever the British nation extends, wherever the English language is spoken. Suffer me, then, to say a few words on the good seed which he has sown in our hearts.

In his teaching, as in all things human, there were no doubt tares, or what some would account tares, which must be left to after times to adjust as best they can with the pure wheat which is gathered into the garner of God. There were imitations, parasitic exaggerations, of the genuine growth, which sometimes almost choked the original seed and disfigured its usefulness and its value; but of this we do not speak here. Gather them up into bundles and burn them. We speak only of him and of his best self. Nor would we now discourse at length on those brilliant gifts which gave such a charm to his writings and such an unexampled splendour to his conversation. All the world knows how the words and the deeds of former times became in his hands, as Luther describes the Apostle's language, 'not dead things, but living creatures with hands and feet.' Every detail was presented before us, penetrated through and through with the fire of poetic imagination, which was the more powerful because it derived its warmth from facts gathered together by the most untiring industry. Who can ever, from this time forward, picture the death of Louis XV., or the flight of the king and queen, without remembering the thrill of emotion with which, through the *History of the French Revolution*, they became acquainted with them for the first time? Who can wander amongst the ruins of St. Edmund's at Bury without feeling that they are haunted in every corner by the life-like figure of the Abbot Samson, as he is drawn from the musty chronicle of Jocelyn? Who can read the letters and the speeches of Cromwell, now made almost intelligible to modern ears, without gratitude to the unwearied zeal which gathered together from every corner those relics of departed greatness? What German can fail to acknowledge that not even in that much-enduring, all-exhausting country of research and labour—not even there has there been raised such a monument to Frederick the Second, called the Great, as by the simple Scotchman who, for the sake of describing what he considered the last hero-king, almost made himself for the time a soldier and a statesman?

But on these and many like topics this is not the time or place to speak. It is for us to ask, as I have said, what was the good seed which he sowed in the field of our hearts, and in what respects we shall be, or ought to be, the better for the sower having lived and died among us.

It was customary for those who honoured him to speak of him as a 'prophet.' And if we take the word in its largest sense he truly deserved the name. He was a prophet, and felt himself to be a prophet, in the midst of an untoward generation; his prophet's mantle was his rough Scotch dialect, and his own peculiar diction, and his own secluded manner of life. He was a prophet most of all in the emphatic utterance of truths which no one else, or hardly any one else, ventured to deliver, and which he felt to be a message of good to a world sorely in need of them. He stood almost alone among the men of his time in opposing a stern, inflexible, resistance, to the whole drift and pressure of modern days towards exalting popular opinion and popular movements as oracles to be valued above the judgment of the few, above the judgment of the wise, the strong, and the good. Statesmen, men of letters, preachers, have all bowed their heads under the yoke of this, as they believed, irresistible domination, under the impression that the first duty of the chiefest man is not to lead but to be led, the necessary condition of success to ascertain which way the current flows, and to swim with it as far as it will bear us. To his mind all this proved an insane delusion. That expression of his which has become, like many of his expressions, almost proverbial in the minds of those who like them least, will express the attitude of his mind—his answer to the question, 'What are the people of England?' 'Thirty millions—mostly fools.' The whole framework and fabric of his mind was built up on the belief that there are not many wise, not many noble minds, not many destined by the Supreme Ruler of the universe to rule their fellows; that few are chosen, that 'strait is the gate and narrow is the way, and few there be that find it.' But when the few appear, when the great and good present themselves, it is the duty and the wisdom of the multitude to seek their guidance. A Luther, a Cromwell, a Goethe, were to him the born kings of men. This was his doctrine of the work of heroes; this, right or wrong, was the mission of his life. It is, all things considered, a fact much to be meditated upon; it is, all things considered, a seed which is worthy of our cultivation.

There is another feeling of the age to which he also stood resolutely opposed, or, rather, a feeling of the age which was resolutely opposed to him—the tendency to divide men into two hostile camps, parted from each other by watchwords and flags, and banners and tokens which we commonly designate by the name of party. He disparaged, perchance unduly, the usefulness, the necessity, of party organisation or party spirit as a part of the secondary machinery by which the great affairs of the world are carried on; but he was a signal example of a man who not only could be measured by no party standard, but absolutely disregarded it. He never, during the whole course of his long life, took an active part—never, I believe, even voted—in those elections which, to most of us, are the very breath of our nostrils. For its own sake he cherished whatever was worth preserving; for its own sake he hailed whatever improvement was worth effecting. He cared not under what name or by what man the preservation or the improvement was achieved. This, too, is an ideal which few can attain, which still fewer attempt; but it is something to have had one man who was possessed by it as a vital and saving truth. And such a man was the Prophet of Chelsea. But there was that in him which, in spite of his own contemptuous description of the people, in spite of his scorn for the struggles of party, endeared him in no common degree even to those who most disagreed with him, even to the humblest classes of our great community. He was an eminent instance of how a man can trample on the most cherished idols of the market-place if yet he shows that he has in his heart of hearts the joys, the sorrows, the needs of his toiling, suffering fellow-creatures. In this way they insensibly felt drawn towards that tender, fervid nature which was weak when they were weak, which burned with indignation when they suffered wrong. They felt that if he despised them it was in love; if he refused to follow their bidding it was because he believed that their bidding was an illusion.

And for that independence of party of which I spoke, there was also the countervailing fact that no man could for a moment dream that it arose from indifference to his country. He was no monk; he was no hermit dwelling apart from the passions which sway the destinies of a great nation. There is no man living to whom the thrift, the industry, the valour of his countrymen was so deeply precious. There is no man living to whom, had it been possible for him to have been aroused from the torpor of approaching death, the news would have been more welcome that the Parliament of England had been in the past week saved from becoming a byeword and reproach and shame amongst the nations of the earth. And all this arose out of a frame of mind which others have shared with him, but which, perhaps, few have been able to share to the same extent. The earnestness—the very word is almost his own—the earnestness, the seriousness with which he approached the great problems of all human life have made us feel them also. The tides of fashion have swept over the minds of many who once were swayed by his peculiar tones; but there must be many a young man whose first feelings of generosity and public spirit were roused within him by the cry as if from the very depths of the heart, 'Where now are your Hengists and your Horsas? Where are those leaders who should be leading their people to useful employments, to distant countries—where are they? Preserving their game!' Before his withering indignation all false pretensions, all excuses for worthless idleness and selfish luxury fell away. The word which he invented to describe them has sunk perhaps into cant and hollowness; but it had a truth when first he uttered it. Those falsities were shams, and they who practised them were guilty of the sin which the Bible, in scathing terms, calls hypocrisy.

And whence came this earnestness? Deep down in the bottom of his soul it sprang from his firm conviction that there was a higher, a better world than that visible to our outward senses. All who acted on this conviction—whether called saints in the middle ages, or Puritans in the seventeenth century, or what you like in our own day—he revered them, with all their eccentricities, as bright and burning examples of those who 'sacrificed their lives to their higher natures, their worser to their better parts.' In addressing the students at Edinburgh he bade them remember that the deep recognition of the eternal justice of heaven, and the unfailing punishment of crimes against the law of God, is at the origin and foundation of all the histories of nations. No nation which did not contemplate this wonderful universe with an awe-stricken and reverential belief that there was a great unknown, omni-potent, all-wise, and all-just Being superintending all men and all interests in it—no nation ever came to very much, nor did any man either, who forgot that. If a man forgot that, he forgot the most im-portant part of his mission in the world. So he spoke, and the ground of his hope for Europe—of his hope, we may say, against hope—was that, after all, in any commonwealth where the Christian religion exists, nay, in any commonwealth where it has once existed, public and private virtue, the basis of all good, never can become extinct, but in every new age, and even after the deepest decline, there is a chance, and, in the course of ages, the certainty, of renovation. The Divine depths of sorrow, the sanctity of sorrow, the life and death of the Divine man— these were to him Christianity. We stand, as it were, beside him whilst the grave has not yet closed over those flashing eyes, over those granite features, over that weird form on which we have so often looked, whilst the silence of death has fallen on that house which was once so frequented and so honoured. We call up memories which occurred to ourselves. One such, in the far past, may perchance come with peculiar force to those whose work is appointed in this place. Many years ago, whilst I belonged to another cathedral, I met him in St. James's Park, and walked with him to his own house. It was during the Crimean War; and after hearing him denounce with his vigorous and perhaps exaggerated earnestness the chaos and confusion into which our Ad-ministration had fallen, and the doubt and distrust which pervaded all classes at the time, I ventured to ask him, 'What, under the circum-stances, is your advice to a Canon of an English Cathedral?' He grimly laughed at my question. He paused for a moment and then answered in homely and well-known words; but which were, as it happened, especially fitted to situations like that in which he was asked to give his counsel—'Whatsoever thy hand findeth to do, do it with all thy might.' That is no doubt the lesson he leaves to each one of us in this place, and also to this weary world—the world of which he felt the weariness as age and infirmity grew upon him; the lesson which, in his more active days, he practised to the very letter. He is at rest; he is at rest; delivered from that burden of the flesh against which he chafed and fretted! He is at rest! In his own words, 'Babylon, with its deafening inanity, rages on, innocuous and unheeded, to the dim forever.' From the 'silence of the eternities' of which he so often spoke, there still sound, and will long sound, the tones of that marvellous voice.

Let us take one tender expression written three or four years ago, one plaintive yet manful thought which has never yet reached the public eye.

Three nights ago, stepping out after midnight, and looking up at the stars which were clear and numerous, it struck me with a strange, new kind of feeling—Hah! in a little while I shall have seen you also for the last time. God Almighty's own theatre of immensity—the infinite made palpable and visible to me—that also will be closed—flung to in my face—and I shall never behold that either any more. The thought of *this* eternal deprivation (even of *this*, though this is such a nothing in comparison) was sad and painful to me. And then a second feeling rose upon me, What if Omnipotence that has developed in me these pieties, these reverences, and infinite affections, should actually have said, Yes, poor mortal, such as you who have gone so far *shall* be permitted to go farther? Hope, despair not!—God's will. God's will; not ours if it is unwise.[1]

God's will, not ours, be done. Yes, God's will be done for us and for him. The Lord gave and the Lord taketh away.

[1] Froude gave this passage from Carlyle's last journal to Stanley. See J. A. Froude, *Thomas Carlyle: A History of His Life in London* (London, 1884), II, 470-1.

BOURNEMOUTH COLLEGE
OF TECHNOLOGY

COLLEGE LIBRARY

Bibliography

This select bibliography is of works dealing with Carlyle's reception and reputation.

BEVINGTON, MERLE MOWBRAY, 'The Saturday Review': 1855–1868: Representative Educated Opinion in Victorian England, New York, 1941: Carlyle was in general favourably received in this weekly.

EVERETT, EDWIN MALLARD, The Party of Humanity: 'The Fortnightly Review' and its Contributors, 1865–1874, Chapel Hill, 1939: this liberal weekly was generally hostile to Carlyle.

JUMP, J.D., 'Weekly Reviewing in the Eighteen-Fifties', Review of English Studies (January 1948), xxiv (see below).

—, 'Weekly Reviewing in the Eighteen-Sixties', Review of English Studies (July 1952), N.S. iii: contains a survey of Carlyle's reception in the powerful weeklies: Athenaeum, Saturday Review, Spectator.

MARCHAND, LESLIE A., 'The Athenaeum': A Mirror of Victorian Culture, Chapel Hill, 1941: assesses Carlyle's reception in this important weekly.

MOTT, FRANK LUTHER, 'Carlyle's American Public', Philological Quarterly (July 1925), iv: dates Carlyle's popularity in America with the publication of Sartor Resartus.

NEFF, EMERY, Carlyle, New York, 1932: discusses the reception in the press of Carlyle's major works.

SEIGEL, JULES PAUL, 'Thomas Carlyle and the Periodical Press: A Study in Attitudes', Unpublished dissertation, University of Maryland, 1965: surveys political and religious attitudes of the press toward Carlyle.

TAYLOR, ALAN C., Carlyle et la pensée latine, Paris, 1937: discusses Carlyle's reception and influence in France, Italy, Spain, and other 'Latin' countries.

WIDGER, HOWARD D., 'Thomas Carlyle in America: His Reputation and Influence', Unpublished dissertation, University of Illinois, 1940: a collection of countless references in letters and reviews to Carlyle, but with little analysis.

Select Index

In preference to a straightforward alphabetical listing of contents I have grouped the index references as follows: I Periodicals and journals from which material has been quoted or to which reference has been made. II Critics and reviewers. III References to the works of Thomas Carlyle which prompted significant comment.

I

II

III

BOURNEMOUTH COLLEGE
OF TECHNOLOGY

COLLEGE LIBRARY

THE CRITICAL HERITAGE SERIES

GENERAL EDITOR: B. C. SOUTHAM

Volumes published and forthcoming

YEOVIL COLLEGE
LIBRARY